Sexual Harassment and Retaliation
A Practical Handbook for Plaintiff and Defense

Sexual Harassment and Retaliation
A Practical Handbook for Plaintiff and Defense

ROXELLA T. CAVAZOS AND
SANDRA R. McCANDLESS, EDITORS

AMERICAN BAR ASSOCIATION
Defending Liberty
Pursuing Justice

TORT TRIAL
& INSURANCE
PRACTICE

Cover design by Tahiti Spears/ABA Design

23 22 21 20 19   5 4 3 2 1

ISBN: 978-1-64105-301-3
e-ISBN: 978-1-64105-302-0

Library of Congress Cataloging-in-Publication Data

Names: Cavazos, Roxella T., editor. | McCandless, Sandra R., editor.
Title: Sexual harassment and retaliation : a practical handbook for plaintiff
   and defense / Roxella T. Cavazos, co-editor and Sandra R. McCandless,
   co-editor.
Description: Chicago, Illinois : American Bar Association, 2019.
Identifiers: LCCN 2019010132 (print) | LCCN 2019016143 (ebook) | ISBN
   9781641053020 (ebook) | ISBN 9781641053013 (pbk.)
Subjects: LCSH: Sexual harassment—Law and legislation—United States. |
   Sexual harassment—Law and legislation—United States—Trial practice.
Classification: LCC KF3467 (ebook) | LCC KF3467 .S49 2019 (print) | DDC
   344.7301/4133—dc23
LC record available at https://lccn.loc.gov/2019010132

Discounts are available for books ordered in bulk. Special consideration is given to state bars, CLE programs, and other bar-related organizations. Inquire at Book Publishing, ABA Publishing, American Bar Association, 321 N. Clark Street, Chicago, Illinois 60654-7598.

www.ShopABA.org

Contents

CHAPTER 3
Investigating, Preparing, and Responding to the Administrative Charge and Court Complaint: Plaintiff's Perspective   47

CHAPTER 4
Responding to the Charge and the Complaint   75

CHAPTER 5
Employment Practices Liability Insurance   85

CHAPTER 6
Representing and Defending the Alleged Harasser   93

CHAPTER 7
Arbitration Issues and Considerations   117

CHAPTER 8
Multi-Plaintiff Litigation and Class Actions: Plaintiff's Perspective · 135

CHAPTER 9
Multi-Plaintiff Litigation and Class Actions: A Defense Perspective · 153

CHAPTER 10

Discovery and Deposing the Plaintiff and Plaintiff's Witnesses: Defense Perspective   197

CHAPTER 11

Discovery and Deposing the Alleged Harasser and Defense Witnesses: The Plaintiff's Perspective   213

CHAPTER 12
Motion for Summary Judgment: Defense Perspective

233

CHAPTER 13
Opposing Motions for Summary Judgment: Plaintiff's Perspective

257

CHAPTER 14
Work, Sex, and the Morning News: An Updated Look at Discovering Juror Attitudes in Sexual Harassment Cases

275

CHAPTER 15
Voir Dire and Plaintiff's Opening Statement: Plaintiff's Perspective   299

CHAPTER 16
Voir Dire and Opening Statement: Defense Perspective   327

CHAPTER 17
Evidentiary Issues in Workplace Harassment and Retaliation Litigation   345

CHAPTER 21
Damage Issues and Mitigation 451

CHAPTER 22
Using Psychiatric and Psychological Experts at Trial: Defense Perspective 479

CHAPTER 23
Closing Argument and Jury Instructions: Plaintiff's Perspective   511

CHAPTER 24
Closing Argument and Jury Instructions: Defense Perspective   **541**

Preface

We are pleased to bring you this book in the "MeToo" era with the contributions of seasoned employment law practitioners from across the country. This book is a best practices guide for attorneys who litigate cases on behalf of plaintiff/employees and defendant/employers. While Title VII of the Civil Rights Act of 1964 prohibits workplace discrimination against individuals in several protected classes, this book focuses only on gender harassment and retaliation. But many, if not most, of the techniques addressed in this book can be applied to cases involving alleged discrimination on the basis of other protected classes.

In a way, this book has been a work in progress since the American Bar Association published *Litigating the Sexual Harassment Case* to guide practitioners after sexual harassment litigation increased in the 1990s as a result of highly publicized allegations of sexual harassment against a U.S. Supreme Court nominee and the sitting President. In 2000 the American Bar Association published the second edition of *Litigating the Sexual Harassment Case*.

In 2010, the ABA published *Litigating the Workplace Harassment Case*, recognizing that the courts had expanded the concept of harassment to include protected criteria other than sex but still focusing in the book on sexual harassment, which is a form of discrimination on the basis of sex. Since 2010, retaliation claims have increased, expanding claims of harassment on the basis of sex, beyond sexual conduct or language, and making them more difficult to defend on an overall basis.

This book provides best practices for attorneys to apply to claims alleging harassment on the basis of all aspects of sex discrimination. Chapter 1 provides the platform to asses and handle gender harassment and retaliation cases by discussing the elements which have to be proven and should be kept in mind throughout the litigation of a claim, including planning and defending depositions. Chapter 2 assists the practitioner in investigating allegations before and after they become internal or administrative claims. Chapter 2 also assist the practitioner in examining the relevant policies which may become defenses or liabilities to overcome. Chapters 5 on Employment Practices Liability Insurance reminds the practitioner to consider insurance coverage from the beginning of the claim. Chapter 7 on Arbitration educates the practitioner on arbitration, including that arbitration must be timely asserted or can always be pursued by agreement in lieu of court litigation. The remaining chapters guide the practitioner through the process of litigation and trial, including assessment of damages and use of experts and trial consultants.

Although this book focuses on gender harassment and retaliation under Title VII, which is of national applicability, practitioners are cautioned to not overlook the applicable state anti-discrimination statutes and common law which may provide more favorable venues and remedies for claimants, as is the case in California.

We consider our work on this book as a contribution to the profession and a partnership of two seasoned employment law practitioners who have been ABA, TIPS, and LEL colleagues and collaborators for over 25 years. We hope this book empowers you in your employment law practice and sparks passion for the practical application of the law.

Roxella T. Cavazos, Co-Editor
Sandra R. McCandless, Co-Editor

About the Authors

Chapter 1

VICTORIA M. PHIPPS is a shareholder in the Littler Mendelson Houston office. She is Board Certified in Labor and Employment law by the Texas Board of Legal Specialization and represents employers in all aspects of labor and employment law in a variety of industries, including oil and gas, healthcare, retail, and higher education. Vickie has significant litigation experience that includes successfully defending employers in jury trials in federal and state courts and conducting arbitrations for public and private employers. She also has particular experience with developing legally compliant leaves of absence policies and procedures, conducting workplace investigations and employment practices audits, First Amendment rights of public employees, and advising employers with regard to reasonable accommodations under the Americans With Disabilities Act.

Vickie has written several articles on preventing workplace discrimination and is a frequent speaker at the University of Texas Labor and Employment Law Conference.

Chapter 2

MARGARET J. GROVER has been guiding employers and employees through the legal thicket that is California based employment law since the mid-1980s. She also an experienced mediator, who enjoys resolving litigated cases and workplace disputes. Maggie has 15 years of dispute resolution experience and enjoys finding creative solutions to workplace disputes. In addition to dispute resolution, her other areas of emphasis include employment litigation, crafting personnel policies and procedures, consulting with human resources professionals consultant, conducting in investigations, and providing workplace training on a variety of topics. Maggie also speaks frequently on employment-related issues for a variety of business and professional organizations. She practices with the California-based law firm of Wendel, Rosen, Black & Dean, LLP, where she heads the Employment Practices Group.

Chapter 3

MICHELLE A. REINGLASS is the principal in the ADR Office of Michelle A. Reinglass in Orange County, California. She is a full-time mediator following a 30-year litigation career, handling all aspects of employment, business, insurance and personal injury cases. Michelle is a member of ABOTA, a fellow of the College of Labor and Employment Lawyers, and a Distinguished Fellow of the International Academy of Mediators (IAM). She is a past President of the Orange County Bar Association (OCBA), past Chair of the California Employment Lawyers Association (CELA), and past Chair and lawyer representative (two terms) of the Central District Delegation to the Ninth Circuit Judicial Conference. Michelle is the recipient of many honors including "Top Gun Trial Lawyer of the Year" in Orange County. She has also been recognized as one of The Daily Journal "Top 100 Most Influential Lawyers in California," "Top Female Litigators," "Top Labor and Employment Lawyers," as well as one of "California's Top 50 Neutrals." She has been named as one of California's "Super Lawyers" every year since 2004 and was inducted into the Western State University College of Law Hall of Fame.

RACHEL GOLDSTEIN is a contract attorney in Orange County, California, who has been practicing primarily employment law for most of her 19 plus years in practice. She has worked with several attorneys and law firms in Orange County and Los Angeles throughout her legal career. Rachel assists with discovery matters, law and motion, and with preparation through trial on both state and federal court cases. Rachel is a member of the California State Bar and the Orange County Bar Association. She is also a member of the Orange County Bar Association's Community Outreach Committee. Rachel received her Juris Doctor degree cum laude from Chapman University School of Law. She also holds Master's degrees from Harvard University and Loyola Marymount University and a Bachelor of Arts degree from the University of California at Berkeley.

Chapter 4

MATTHEW B. SCHIFF leads the Labor and Employment group at Sugar Felsenthal Grais & Helsinger LLP in Chicago. Matt represents management in defense of claims of discrimination, retaliation, harassment, workers' compensation and employment torts. He counsels employees and executives in transition in all aspects of employment and labor relations. He served as editor of "Litigating the Sexual Harassment Case" and its Edition 2000 published by the ABA. Matt is an experienced litigator who has tried many cases in court and at arbitration and argued appeals. He also counsels and litigates wage and hour disputes and assists his clients in protecting their trade secrets and enforcing non-compete and non-solicitation agreements. Matt assists clients in developing employee handbooks and contracts. He negotiates collective bargaining agreements and helps clients with contract administration.

KATHRYN ("KATIE") NADRO is an associate with the law firm of Sugar Felsenthal Grais & Helsinger LLP in Chicago. She advises clients on a diverse array of business matters, including commercial and business disputes, employment issues, and data security and privacy compliance including policy drafting and compliance with state, federal, and international law. Katie has broad experience as in-house and outside counsel in representing companies and individuals in contract, non-compete, discrimination, harassment, fiduciary duty, and trade secret litigation in state and federal court. Katie assists clients in navigating employment issues, ranging from employee handbooks and FMLA policies to litigating discrimination and harassment claims, to meet business needs and objectives. Katie works with individuals and businesses of all sizes to craft successful resolutions tailored to each individual matter.

Chapter 5

ELLIS B. MUROV is a general partner of the firm of Deutsch Kerrigan in New Orleans, where he has twice served on the firm's management committee. Mr. Murov represents employers in all aspects of labor and employment law. He has arbitrated employment-related disputes for the American Arbitration Association and is a certified mediator. He is a member of the ABA Labor and Employment Section and a prior chair of the Employer-Employee Relations committee of the ABA Tort, Trial and Insurance Practice (TIPS) Section. He is a contributing author to several ABA/TIPS books for employment practitioners. Ellis graduated *summa cum laude* from Tulane University in 1979. While at Tulane, he was a member of the Tulane Law Review and Order of the Coif.

ANDREW J. BAER is an attorney at Deutsch Kerrigan, L.L.P. in New Orleans, Louisiana. He is a member of the firm's Labor and Employment department, assisting employers in the defense of discrimination, harassment, retaliation, and other employment related claims. Additionally, Andrew assists employers in drafting employee handbooks, employment policies, and conducting investigations of workplace complaints. Andrew obtained his law degree from Louisiana State University.

Chapter 6*

PETER BENNETT is the managing partner of The Bennett Law Firm with offices in Portland, Maine and Boston, Massachusetts. He advises employers throughout the northeast in all aspects of labor and employment law, with particular emphasis in representing management in collective bargaining negotiations and related traditional labor law matters. Peter also represents clients in state and federal courts as well as before various administrative bodies and in arbitration. He serves as Treasurer and Trustee of The National Judicial College, board member of the Appellate Judges Education Institute, member of the American Bar Association Standing Committee on the Federal Judiciary, immediate past Chair of the ABA Standing Committee on Judicial Independence, past Chair of the ABA Tort Trial and Insurance Practice Section, and past President of the Boston University School of Law Alumni Association. Peter is a Fellow of the College of Labor and Employment Lawyers. Peter appears annually in *Best Lawyers in America*, *Chambers USA*, and *New England Super Lawyers* and has received numerous awards including "Top 100 Most Powerful Employment Attorneys in the Nation."

Peter received his B.A., *cum laude*, from Harvard University and his J.D., *cum laude* and his M.B.A. from Boston University School of Law and Graduate School of Management.

TIMOTHY H. POWELL is an associate at The Bennett Law Firm with offices in Portland, Maine and Boston, Massachusetts. He advises employers on a broad range of labor and employment matters, including issues of hiring, discipline, and discharge; discrimination and retaliation; leaves and accommodations; wage and hour; non-competition agreements; employee handbooks; employment contracts; and severance agreements. He represents clients in proceedings before state and federal courts and administrative agencies, including state human rights commissions, the Equal Employment Opportunity Commission, the Occupational Safety and Health Administration, the Department of Labor, and the National Labor Relations Board. Prior to joining The Bennett Law Firm, Tim was an associate at the Massachusetts law firm Bowditch & Dewey, LLP, practicing labor, employment, and higher education law. Tim has published several articles with national and regional media outlets on current topics in employment law, including workplace bullying, age discrimination, sexual harassment, and non-competition agreements. Tim holds a B.A., *cum laude*, in Economics from Colgate University and a J.D., *cum laude*, from Boston University School of Law, where he served as Note Editor for the Boston University Law Review.

Chapter 7

DEBORAH S. WEISER is Of Counsel in the Employment Law practice of Paul Hastings and is based in the firm's Los Angeles office. She works exclusively in the representation of private and public employers in all aspects of employment law, including discrimination, fair pay and wage and hour class actions. She regularly partners with in-house counsel and Human Resources professionals on significant employment issues, including advising and managing wage-and-hour pay practice audits, restructuring compensation systems and practices, and implementing and enforcing employment arbitration agreements. Deborah has extensive experience in arbitrations, including motions to compel arbitration. She is the author of a chapter on Arbitration of Employment Disputes, published in California Employment Law by Matthew Bender. Deborah received her JD degree (*summa cum laude*) from Loyola Law School, Los Angeles and her BA from University of California at San Diego (*cum laude*).

Chapter 8*

MAUREEN S. BINETTI is a partner with the Woodbridge, New Jersey law firm of Wilentz, Goldman & Spitzer, P.A., one of the largest firms in New Jersey, and the only large firm in New Jersey which regularly handles employment matters on behalf of employees. Certified by the New Jersey Supreme Court as a Civil Trial Attorney, Maureen has extensive experience in all aspects of employment law, particularly the litigation of sexual harassment claims and wage and hour class actions. She often serves as an independent investigator of internal employee complaints and a state-approved mediator of employment claims. Maureen is a Fellow of the College of Labor And

Employment Lawyers and a member of the New Jersey Chapter of the National Academy of Distinguished Neutrals. She has been selected for inclusion in *The Best Lawyers in America*® in the practice areas of Employment Law from 2007–2017 and in New Jersey *Super Lawyers*® since 2005. She currently serves as Co-Chair of the ABA Section's Trial Advocacy/Moot Court Competition Committee and on the Executive Committee of the NJSBA Section. Maureen is a 1982 graduate of Rutgers Law and has been with the Wilentz firm since that time.

ASHLEY E. MORIN is an associate at the law firm of Wilentz, Goldman & Spitzer, P.A. She is a member of the firm's Employment Law Department and regularly represents both employers and employees. Prior to joining the firm, Ashley worked as a law clerk for the Honorable David F. Bauman in the Superior Court of New Jersey, Monmouth Vicinage. Ashley graduated *summa cum laude* from Rutgers University and *cum laude* from Rutgers Law School—Newark.

Chapter 9*

KENNETH M. WILLNER is vice chair of the Paul Hastings Employment Law Department and is based in the firm's Washington, D.C. office. He is a recognized leader of the management bar in the fields of employment discrimination class actions, employment testing and validation, pay equity, wage/hour collective actions, statistics, disability discrimination; protection of employer intellectual property; and drug and alcohol testing. Ken represents employers in employment law and litigation in federal and state courts and before the Equal Employment Opportunity Commission and Office of Federal Contract Compliance Programs. He also has extensive experience with discrimination litigation; sexual harassment claims; affirmative action; compliance reviews; labor relations; unfair labor practice charges; executive contract negotiations; and non-competition covenants. Ken is a Fellow of the College of Labor and Employment Lawyers, and he is recognized as a preeminent practitioner of labor and employment law by *Chambers* and *Partners; Best Lawyers in America*; *The Legal 500*; and Washington, D.C. *Super Lawyers*. He is a graduate of the University of Virginia School of Law (J.D., 1987; Order of the Coif; *Virginia Law Review*) and the University of Virginia, B.A., 1984; with Distinction). He is widely published in the field of employment law.

Chapter 10

SANDRA R. MCCANDLESS is a Partner in the San Francisco office of the global law firm Dentons. She represents employers in employment litigation, arbitration, and mediation and counsels employers in all aspects of their employment practices. Sandra is also an Arbitrator on the American Arbitration Association Employment Panel and an Early Neutral Evaluator for the United States District Court for the Northern District of California. Sandra is listed in Best Lawyers, Employment Law—Management and Chambers USA: America's Leading Lawyers for Business, Labor & Employment in California and is an elected Member of the College of Labor and Employment and a member of the American Employment Law Council and National Financial Industry Employment Law Council. Sandra has served the American Bar Association in many roles, including member of the Board of Governors, Chair of the Finance Committee, and Chair of the Tort Trial and Insurance Practice Section (TIPS). Currently, she serves as a Commissioner of the ABA Commission on Women, a California State Bar Delegate to the ABA House of Delegates, and on the Council of the Section of International Law. Sandra graduated from Harvard College with honors and obtained her law degree from the Georgetown University Law Center.

Chapter 11

CYNTHIA N. SASS has been specializing in employment law for over 27 years. Her five-attorney law firm in Tampa, Florida exclusively practices labor and employment law, primarily representing employees from both the private and public sectors. Nationally, her practice has been recognized as a leader in the field of labor and employment. Cynthia's recent accolades include being named by Florida Super Lawyers as one of the Top 50 Women Lawyers in Florida, being named by Best Lawyers as the 2017 Lawyer of the Year in Employment Law for Individuals in Tampa, and her firm's selection by U.S. News and World Report as a Best Law Firm in Employment Law for Individuals. She is a fellow of The College of Labor and Employment Lawyers which is a non-profit professional association composed of the leading Labor and Employment lawyers nationwide. She holds various leadership positions with the American Bar Association, The Florida Bar and the Hillsborough County Bar Association. Cynthia frequently speaks on a variety of employment law topics.

Chapter 12

ZASCHA BLANCO ABBOTT is Counsel with Liebler Gonzalez & Portuondo in Miami, Florida. She focuses her practice on the representation of public and private employers in labor and employment matters. Her experience includes defending employers in a variety of employment-related lawsuits, such as discrimination, hostile work environment, breach of contract, constitutional violations, Florida Whistleblower statute, wage and hour, and Title VII and workers compensation retaliation claims. Zasha also practices in the area of labor law, including preparing collective bargaining proposals and agreements as well as providing employers with guidance on labor issues. She provides employers with training on discrimination and harassment free workplace and conducts employment-related audits. Zascha also represents employers in U.S. Department of Labor investigations and before administrative agencies such as the Equal Employment Opportunity Commission. Prior to joining her current firm, Zasha practiced with Sioli Alexander Pino and a national law firm, exclusively representing employers in their labor and employment matters. She also served as an Assistant City Attorney for the City of Miami, Office of the City Attorney, in the labor and employment division, representing the City's departments in labor and employment matters.

Chapter 13

WILLIAM C. JHAVERI-WEEKS is the principal of Jhaveri-Weeks Law in San Francisco, California where he handles employment matters for employees and offers general litigation services to organizations and individuals. He was previously a partner at Goldstein, Borgen, Dardarian & Ho, in Oakland, California, where he brought class and collective actions primarily in the area of employment law. Before that, he was an associate at Debevoise & Plimpton LLP in New York and a law clerk for a federal appellate judge in the Sixth Circuit. Mr. Jhaveri-Weeks speaks and writes frequently on developing issues in litigation, particularly in the areas of employment law and class actions. He graduated from Yale College and New York University School of Law.

SHAJUTI T. HOSSAIN is a fellow at Public Advocates, a legal non-profit in San Francisco, California. She was a 2018 summer associate at Goldstein, Borgen, Dardarian & Ho in Oakland, California, and the Lawyers' Committee for Civil Rights Under Law in Washington, DC. Shajuti received her J.D. and undergraduate degrees from Duke University.

Chapter 14

SUSAN G. FILLICHIO is a Vice President and trial consultant with DecisionQuest, a national trial consulting firm. She leads the research consulting team at DecisionQuest in Los Angeles and specializes in trial strategy development, behavioral research and jury analysis. Susan assists counsel in developing case themes and strategies designed to effectively communicate clients' messages to jurors, judges and arbitrators and assist counsel during mediation and settlement negotiations. She specializes in preparing witnesses, including CEOs and high profile individuals, for depositions and testifying at trial. Susan has been nominated for *The Los Angeles Business Journal's* Women Making a Difference awards, as a Rising Star. Prior to joining DecisionQuest, she was a partner with Morgan Lewis & Bockius LLP, Los Angeles, where she held a managing position in the Labor & Employment Practice Group. She also completed internships with the Senate Labor Subcommittee (under Chairman Don Nickles, OK), for Representative Arlan Stangland (MN), and with the American Bar Association. Susan is proficient in French and a regular presenter of programs on trial strategies. Susan earned her law degree from De Paul College of Law, J.D. and a bachelor's degree in English and Political science from Indiana University Bloomington.

STEVEN J. SON is a senior consultant with DecisionQuest, a national trial consulting firm. He has been the lead researcher on hundreds of mock trials, mock arbitrations, and focus groups as well as the lead on designing, implementing, and analying juror surveys (juror profiling studies, juror and community attitude surveys, change of venue and online studies) and conducting post-trial interviews, shadow juries and trial monitoring. Through those processes, he has worked extensively with scientific and economic expert witnesses and those whose first language is not English. Steven has assisted counsel in developing voir dire strategies in hundreds of cases and has specifically executed those strategies in the courtroom in nearly 100 trials. He has worked in venues across the U.S., U.S. Territories, and Canada on cases involving many areas of law, including contracts, employment law, and class actions. Prior to joining DecisionQuest, Steven's academic research was directed at the qualitative analysis of attorney conducted voir dire, especially in capital cases. Steven earned a Ph.D. in Interdisciplinary Social Psychology from the University of Nevada, Reno, an M.S. degree in Experimental Psychology from Indiana State University, and a B.S. degree in Psychology from the University of Illinois, Champaign-Urbana.

THI QUANG is a research associate with DecisionQuest, a national trial consulting firm. She oversees the training and management of research analysts both in the Los Angeles office and across the country and has been integral in establishing the social media practice across all DecisionQuest offices. Thi conducts and moderates jury research exercises and analyzes both quantitative and qualitative data collected from focus groups, strategic theme development, and arbitration studies. Thi has almost two decades of experience in the litigation consulting field working in state and federal venues across the country. She has worked on thousands of cases in a variety of litigation, including employment disputes, and been involved in conducting hundreds of shadow juries. Thi has assisted on hundreds of jury selections through analysis of supplemental questionnaires and extensive social media research efforts. She has interviewed thousands of jurors in post-trial juror interviews and has engaged in online survey analysis, phone survey analysis, and assisting with change of venue surveys. Thi earned two bachelor's degrees from the University of California, San Diego, one with a major in psychology and another with a major in economics.

Chapter 15*

MARIAN H. BIRGE is a shareholder at Garcia & Birge, APC. She is a civil litigator, a trained mediator and an experienced appellate lawyer, with a practice focusing in the areas of employment law, civil rights, wrongful termination, employment torts, and business disputes. In addition to representing plaintiffs and defendants in litigation and mediations, Marian has been a volunteer mediator with the San Diego County Small Claims Courts and an instructor with the People's Law School. She has served as Vice President of the Board of Directors for the North San Diego County Bar Association (2015–2017) and as an Adjunct Professor of Law at Thomas Jefferson School of Law, San Diego, CA. Marian received her Juris Doctor degree from Thomas Jefferson School of Law, formerly Western State University College of Law, in San Diego, California and her mediation training at the National Conflict Resolution Center in San Diego.

Chapter 16

NADIA P. BERMUDEZ is a shareholder with the law firm of Klinedinst, PC in San Diego California where she focuses on employment litigation and counseling and general business litigation. Nadia has tried employment cases involving sexual harassment, discrimination, wage and hour, wrongful termination, defamation, trade secrets, and a wide range of other matters. She advises public and private employers on all aspects the employment relationship, best practices, policies, and human resources issues and conducts training on sexual harassment prevention and other employment topics. Nadia has been recognized in San Diego Super Lawyers®, named a Top Attorney in Labor and Employment by the San Diego Daily Transcript, and voted Best of the Bar by San Diego Business Journal. Nadia also was chosen as a Top Attorney Under 40 by the Hispanic National Bar Association and awarded the Service Award for Diversity by the San Diego County Bar Association. She has held leadership roles with the American Bar Association, Hispanic National Bar Association, and San Diego County Bar Association. Nadia received her law degree from Stanford University School of Law and her undergraduate degree (*cum laude* and Phi Beta Kappa) from the University of California, Irvine.

GREG A. GARBACZ is a shareholder and Chief Strategy Officer with the law firm of Klinedinst, PC in San Diego California. He is an experienced litigator and trial attorney, having handled complex litigation and trials in state and federal courts, involving employment disputes, wage and hour class actions, real estate/housing discrimination, product liability, professional/director & officer liability, and fraud/business tort cases. Greg also represents clients in contractual arbitration and mediations and counsels on executive/ employment contracts, employment issues, litigation avoidance techniques, contract/ dispute negotiation, misappropriation claims, unfair business practices, confidentiality and non-compete agreements, and trade secrets disputes. An AV-rated attorney since 1997, Greg is regularly featured in Southern California Super Lawyers® and other publications that identify the best lawyers in Southern California. He regularly takes on pro bono employment and housing cases for the San Diego Volunteer Lawyer Program and serves as chair of the Housing Discrimination Defense and Civil Rights group and co-chair of the Business and Commercial Litigation group. Greg graduated from Washington & Lee University School of Law where he was a member of its Law Review. He earned his Bachelor of Arts degree from Lafayette College in Easton, Pennsylvania.

PATRICK J. GOODE II is an associate attorney with the law firm of Klinedinst in San Diego, California. He represents entities and individuals in employment, business, and commercial litigation and provides counseling regarding employment issues. Prior to joining Klinedinst, Patrick started his legal career representing and advising corporations and individuals in labor and employment matters, contract disputes, and entity formation and dissolution issues. He also advised public entities in labor and employment matters, including collective bargaining agreements. Patrick earned his law degree from Florida Coastal School of Law where he graduated magna cum laude and received certificates in business law and legal research, writing, and drafting. While in law school, Patrick served on the Editorial Board of the Florida Coastal Law Review as the Research and Writing Editor and was honored to be selected Law Review Member of the Year by his peers. He also participated as a brief writer on the Florida Coastal Moot Court Honor Board, which was ranked number one nationally among all law schools. Patrick obtained his undergraduate degree from the University of Central Florida, where he majored in Business Administration.

Chapter 17

HARRIET E. COOPERMAN is a partner and former chair of Saul Ewing LLP's Labor and Employment Group, where she focuses her practice on representing businesses, educational institutions, and non-profit organizations in all aspects of labor and employment law and litigation. Harriet is Vice Chair of the Maryland State Higher Education Labor Relations Board of Maryland and served on the Board since 2001. Harriet is a Fellow of the American College of Trial Lawyers and College of Labor and Employment Lawyers. She has been named as one the Nation's Most Powerful Employment Attorneys-Top 100 by Lawdragon, *Human Resources Executive* each year since 2010, named to *The Best Lawyers in America* list in the areas of Labor and Employment Law and Litigation and as one of "America's Leading Lawyers in Employment Law" by *Chambers USA*. She is a former Chairperson of the Section on Labor and Employment Law of the Maryland State Bar Association and the Employer-Employee Relations Committee of the Tort and Insurance Practice Section, American Bar Association. Harriet received her B.S. degree from Cornell University, School of Industrial and Labor Relations, and her law degree from the University of Maryland School of Law.

GILLIAN A. COOPER is an associate in Saul Ewing LLP's Labor and Employment Group, representing businesses in employment law and litigation. Gillian has litigated cases involving federal and state statutory employment discrimination, leave issues, wage and hour and wage payment claims, and contract and common law disputes. She regularly counsels employers in a wide range of employment matters and provides proactive training for managers and employees. In 2017, Gillian was named a "Rising Star" by New Jersey Super Lawyers. She received her B.A. degree from Rutgers University and her J.D. degree from Rutgers Law School.

Chapter 18

WAYNE E. PINKSTONE is a partner with Fox Rothschild LLP in Princeton, New Jersey, whose practice centers on employment litigation and counseling. His clients include employers in the health care, manufacturing, service, retail, technology and financial services industries. Wayne defends employers in the federal and state courts and before administrative agencies in claims involving sexual harassment, discrimination, wrongful discharge, whistleblowers, occupational health and safety, restrictive covenants, and wage and hour collective actions. He conducts in-house training sessions on topics such as leave and disability, hiring practices, harassment prevention and supervisory skills and practices. Wayne speaks frequently on such topics as the interplay between the ADA and FMLA, workplace harassment, FLSA compliance and internal investigations. He serves as a volunteer attorney for the Support Center for Child Advocates and is admitted to practice in New Jersey and Pennsylvania. Wayne received his bachelor's degree from Rutgers University and his law degree from Widener University School of Law.

Chapter 19

JOSEPH Y. AHMAD is a founding partner in the Houston law firm of Ahmad, Zavitsanos, Anaipakos, Alavi & Mensing P.C. and Board Certified in Labor and Employment Law by the Texas Board of Legal Specialization. He represents executives in employment-related litigation, including trade secret and non-compete cases and other clients in other high-profile employment-related litigation, including discrimination, harassment, retaliation, and traditional labor disputes. Having tried more than 50 employment cases and argued more than a dozen cases on appeal, Joseph was elected to the American Board of Trial Advocates. He has been named one of the "Best Lawyers in America," "2015 Lawyer of the Year" in the Employment Individual category for the Houston area, and one of the leading Employment & Labor Law attorneys in "Chambers USA: America's Leading Lawyers for Business." Joseph is repeatedly recognized in *Texas Super Lawyers*, *Texas Super Lawyers Top 100 in Houston*, and *Texas Super Lawyers Top 100 in Texas*. He comments on employment law issues for *The Wall Street Journal*, *The New York Times*, and *Houston Chronicle*. He maintains a blog, Legal Issues in the Executive Suite, to discuss covenants not to compete, executive compensation, and other matters of importance to executives.

Chapter 20

ROBERT B. FITZPATRICK is the principal in the law firm of Robert B. Fitzpatrick, PLLC in Washington, D.C. and has practiced law for over 40 years. He represents employees in the private and public sector in employment law and employee benefits litigation and non-litigation matters. He negotiates separation, settlement agreements, and employment contracts on behalf of employees, including executives. He has represented attorneys in workplace disputes, such as transitioning to a competing law firm and discrimination and retaliation. Robert has been named to the *Washington, D.C. Super Lawyers* list and has been listed in The Best Lawyers in America for two decades. He is a Fellow of the College of Labor and Employment Lawyers and admitted to practice in Washington, D.C. Maryland, and Virginia. Robert received his undergraduate degree from George Washington University and his Juris Doctor degree with honors from the George Washington University Law Center.

Chapter 21

AMY S. WILSON is a member in the Indianapolis, Indiana, office of Frost Brown Todd LLC and practices in the firm's Labor and Employment Practice Group. She concentrates her practice in employment litigation and employer counseling. Amy represents employers in single plaintiff and class and collective action litigation matters under Title VII, the ADEA, the ADAAA, the FMLA, the FLSA, covenants not to compete, wage claims, and various other federal and state law claims. In addition, Amy counsels employers on all aspects of the employer-employee relationship, provides management and employee training, and drafts agreements, policies, and procedures. Amy also speaks frequently on employment law topics for a variety of business and professional organizations. She is the editor and one of the authors of "The Practitioner's Guide to Defense of EPL Claims," published in 2018 by the American Bar Association and its Trial, Tort and Insurance Practice Section. Amy received her JD degree, summa cum laude, from the Indiana University Robert H. McKinney School of Law and a BA from Hanover College.

Chapter 22

HOLLY M. ROBBINS is a shareholder at Littler Mendelson, an international employment law firm, and practices at the firm's Minneapolis, Minnesota office. Holly represents employers in all stages of litigation, from administrative proceedings, to discovery and motion practice, to jury and court trials and administrative evidentiary hearings, to appeals, in state and federal courts and administrative agencies. She has defended employers against lawsuits involving discrimination, harassment, whistleblowing, contracts, torts, and other employment-related issues. Holly has experience litigating against and negotiating with the Equal Employment Opportunity Commission and trying cases before the Office of Administrative Law Judges at the Department of Labor. Holly also advises employers on employment-related issues, including successful strategies for reductions-in-force, disciplinary actions and terminations, policies and procedures, accommodations, leaves, investigations, employee and management training, and other workplace actions. She is a frequent speaker on employment law topics and represents employers in industries such as hospitality, retail, transportation, health care, manufacturing, finance, and technology. Holly received her undergraduate degree from Haverford College and graduated with honors from the George Washington University National Law Center.

SUSIE P. WINE is a research attorney with Littler Mendelson, an international employment law firm, and is assigned to the Knowledge Management department in the Minneapolis, Minnesota office. She conducts research and analysis of employment laws and assists with drafting and editing firm publications. She is a contributor to Littler GPS®, for which she provides analysis of recently enacted statutes and regulations and assists with 50-state surveys covering various labor and employment law topics. Prior to joining Littler, Susie was a labor and employment associate at a national firm and worked on a variety of single plaintiff and class action defense cases. Susie received a Bachelor of Science degree from the University of Notre Dame, a Master of Education degree from the University of Missouri, and a J.D. degree (*magna cum laude*) from the University of Notre Dame.

CECILIA B. WAGNER is a research attorney with Littler Mendelson, an international employment law firm, and is assigned to the Knowledge Management department in the Kansas City, Missouri office. She monitors legislative and regulatory developments and conducts research in all areas of labor and employment law. Cecilia is also a contributor to Littler GPS®, for which she provides analysis of recently enacted statutes and regulations and assists with 50-state surveys covering various labor and employment law topics. Prior to joining Littler, Cecilia was an attorney advisor at federal and District of Columbia agencies which handle administrative appeals. She also served as a judicial law clerk in Maryland. Cecilia received her bachelor's degree (*cum laude*) from Colgate University and her law degree with honors from The George Washington University School of Law.

Chapter 23

LYNNE BERNABEI is a founding partner of the law firm of Bernabei & Kabat, PLLC in Washington, D.C. She represents individuals and high level federal employees in employment discrimination, civil rights, and whistleblower cases across the country, including whistleblowers in the financial services, defense, health care, and nuclear industries as well as. Lynne serves on the editorial board of the *Labor Law Journal* and teaches continuing legal education to the American Bar Association and other legal groups. She has been selected as a member of the College of Labor and Employment Lawyers and is an arbitrator on the National Roster of the American Arbitration Association ("AAA"). Lynne has been recognized among The Best Lawyers In America since 2006 and in *SuperLawyers* since 2007. She has been named one of Best Attorneys in Washington, D.C. by Washingtonian Magazine and a top 12 Leading Labor & Employment Litigator in Washington, D.C. by Legal Times Magazine. Lynne has appeared on "Sixty Minutes" and other broadcasts and been quoted by New York Times, Washington Post, Wall Street Journal, and National Law Journal. She received a B.A. degree from Harvard University and a J.D. degree from Harvard Law School.

ALAN R. KABAT is a name partner in the law firm of Bernabei & Kabat, PLLC in Washington, D.C. Alan has handled employment and other litigation matters for twenty years, with an emphasis on representing employees in discrimination and retaliation cases, along with defamation claims. He also has researched and drafted amicus briefs for non-profit organizations at the US Supreme Court and the lower appellate courts. Alan has co-authored numerous articles, including "The Effect of Unemployment and Workers' Compensation Agency Decisions on Employment Discrimination Litigation" in the Journal of Employment Discrimination Law and "Seven Questions for Sarbanes-Oxley Whistleblowers to Ask," in the The Practical Lawyer for the American Bar Association. He is the author of "How (Not) to Litigate A Sexual Harassment Class Action," published in The Labor Lawyer for the ABA Labor and Employment Section. Alan presents continuing legal education programs, covering a wide range of issues in employment law. He received his B.S. degree from the University of Washington and his J.D. degree from Georgetown University.

DEVIN WRIGLEY is an associate with the law firm of Bernabei & Kabat, PLLC in Washington, D.C. She represents employees in matters involving discrimination, retaliation, sexual harassment, and other employment-related claims. Devin joined Bernabei & Kabat as a Legal Fellow in September 2016, and became an Associate at the firm in March 2017. Devin graduated with Honors from the George Washington University Law School, where she served as an Articles Editor on the Federal Communications Law Journal. In her last year of law school, Devin served as a Student Attorney in GW's Public Justice Advocacy Clinic, where she represented low-income clients on employment, disability, and civil rights claims in federal and administrative courts. During law school, Devin also interned with the Department of Education, Office of Hearings and Appeals, the Voice on the Net Coalition, the Recording Industry Association of America, and the United States Copyright Office. She earned her B.A. summa cum laude and Phi Beta Kappa from Clemson University's Honors College.

Chapter 24

ROXELLA T. CAVAZOS is board certified in labor and employment law by the Texas Board of Legal Specialization. She currently practices her specialty in San Antonio, Texas as Associate General Counsel with the Alamo Community College District, which includes five independently accredited junior colleges. Before joining the College District, Roxella was in private practice for 25 years in Houston, Texas, representing private and public sector employers in Texas and other states in litigation, arbitrations, and administrative claims and counseling domestic and international employers on legal compliance and every aspect of the employer-employee relationship, including due diligence in acquisitions of union and non-union companies. Her administrative practice has extended from state agencies to the Equal Employment Opportunity Commission and National Labor Relations Board. She has served in ABA leadership positions and authored chapters for ABA books, including *Employee Benefits Law*, published by the ABA Labor and Employment Section, and *The Practitioner's Guide to Defense of EPL Claims*, published by the ABA Tort, Trial and Insurance Practice Section. Roxella received her undergraduate degree from The University of Texas at Austin, a master's degree from the University of Houston-Clear Lake, and her J.D. degree from the University of Houston Law Center.

---

* The contributions of the following contributors to *Litigating the Workplace Harassment Case* (ABA Publishing, 2010) are acknowledged:

Chapter 6: Luis Antonio Cabassa authored the original chapter in the 2010 book, and the chapter was updated in 2019 by the current authors, Peter Bennett and Timothy H. Powell.

Chapter 8: Christopher W. Hager and Gregory B. Noble assisted Maureen S. Binetti, lead author, with the similar chapter in 2010, and that chapter was updated for 2019 by the current authors, Maureen S. Binetti and Ashley E. Morin.

Chapter 9: Andrew B. Rogers assisted Kenneth M. Willner, lead author, with the similar chapter in 2010, and that chapter was updated for 2019 by Kenneth M. Willner.

Chapter 15: Sylvia Garcia co-authored the chapter in the 2010 book, and the chapter was updated for 2019 by her law partner and co-author, Marian H. Birge.

CHAPTER 1

Gender Harassment and Retaliation

Victoria M. Phipps

Statutory protection for employees who believe they have been sexually harassed or retaliated against for reporting sexual harassment in the workplace has been expanding since the enactment of Title VII of the Civil Rights Act of 1964 (Title VII) and the 1998 landmark US Supreme Court cases of *Burlington Industries, Inc. v. Ellerth*[1] and *Faragher v. City of Boca Raton*.[2] This chapter discusses the basic elements of bringing forth sexual harassment and retaliation claims and the defenses available to employers.

I. TITLE VII OF THE CIVIL RIGHTS ACT OF 1964

A. Basic Legal Analysis Under Title VII

Title VII protects employees from workplace discrimination based on certain protected characteristics, including sex and gender, and from retaliation for reporting claims of harassment or discrimination.[3] Title VII covers any employer having more than fifteen employees during any twenty-week period in the current or preceding year.[4]

Under Title VII, discrimination claims may be based on allegations of disparate treatment or disparate impact discrimination.[5] Disparate treatment refers to instances where the employer intentionally treats the employee differently based on a protected characteristic, including race, sex, national origin, color, or religion. In contrast, disparate impact claims involve allegations that the employer engaged in a certain practice or implemented policies that had the effect or impact of subjecting employees to discrimination, even if the intent to discriminate is not present.[6] This chapter will focus on the elements of claims related to disparate treatment discrimination or harassment.

---

1. 524 U.S. 742 (1998).
2. 524 U.S. 775 (1998).
3. 42 U.S.C. § 2000e-2(a)(1) (1994).
4. 42 U.S.C. § 2000e-2(b)(1994).
5. *See* Munoz v. Orr, 200 F.3d 291, 299 (5th Cir. 2000) (1994).
6. *See* 42 U.S.C. § 2000e-2(k) (1994).

In very few cases, employees have direct evidence of discrimination, such as where the employer admits to discriminating on the basis of a protected qualification. Direct evidence of discrimination is "evidence, which if believed, proves the fact of discriminatory animus without inference or presumption."[7] If an inference is required for the evidence to be probative as to an employer's discriminatory animus, the evidence is circumstantial, not direct. However, cases of direct evidence discrimination are rare.[8]

Most cases rely upon circumstantial evidence. In cases where the plaintiffs are relying on circumstantial evidence, federal courts, since 1973, have used the three-stage analysis established in *McDonnell Douglas Corp. v. Green* to decide intentional employment discrimination cases.[9] Under the *McDonnell Douglas* burden-shifting framework, plaintiffs may present a *prima facie* case of disparate treatment by showing these basic elements:

- The plaintiff is a member of a protected class under Title VII (race, color, sex, religion, and national origin).
- The plaintiff is qualified for the position and applied for the position in question.
- The plaintiff was rejected despite his qualifications and the employer continued to seek applications from persons with the same qualifications as the plaintiff.

If the plaintiff establishes this *prima facie* case, which creates the presumption that the employer has unlawfully discriminated, the burden of production next shifts to the defendant employer to articulate a legitimate, nondiscriminatory reason for the employment action.[10] The plaintiff must then demonstrate that the employer's reason was a pretext for discrimination.

However, the Court in *McDonnell Douglas* noted that the elements of a *prima facie* proof will vary depending on different factual situations.[11] The *McDonnell Douglas* framework was intended to create a sensible, orderly way to evaluate the evidence in light of common experience as it bears on the critical question of discrimination."[12] This has resulted in some federal circuit courts requiring an alternative fourth prong necessary to prove a *prima facie* case of discrimination, to wit, whether "nonmembers of the protected class were treated more favorably."[13] In *Taylor v. Virginia Union University,* the Fourth Circuit stated that in order to state a Title VII *prima facie* case of

---

7. Sandstad v. C.B. Richard Ellis, 309 F.3d 893, 897 (5th Cir. 2002), *cert. denied* 539 U.S. 926, 123 S. Ct. 2572 (2003).

8. *See* Scott v. Univ. of Miss., 148 F.3d 493, 504 (5th Cir. 1998).

9. 411 U.S. 792 (1973).

10. Reeves v. Sanderson Plumbing Products, Inc., 530 U.S. 133, 142 (2000); quoting St. Mary's Honor Center v. Hicks, 509 U.S. 502, 506 (1993); Texas Dept. of Community Affairs v. Burdine, 450 U.S. 248, 254 (1981).

11. 411 U.S. at 802 n.13; *see also* Governors v. Athens, 460 U.S. 711, 715 (1983) (the *prima facie* case was "never intended to be rigid, mechanized or ritualistic"); Furnco Construction Corp. v. Waters, 438 U.S. 567, 577 (1978) (the *prima facie* case test of *McDonnell Douglas* "was not intended to be an inflexible rule.").

12. 438 U.S. at 577.

13. *See* Goosby v. Johnson & Johnson, Medical, Inc., 228 F.3d 313, 318, 319 (3rd Cir. 2000).

disparate discipline, a sex discrimination plaintiff must show that "she suffered more severe discipline for her misconduct as compared to those employees outside the protected class."[14]

Similar to the Fourth Circuit, the Fifth Circuit has required that, absent direct evidence, a plaintiff must point to a similarly situated employee as part of his *prima facie* case.[15] The Fifth Circuit has required that to be similarly situated, "those employees' circumstances, including their misconduct, must have been 'nearly identical' to support a plaintiff's burden of proof in disparate treatment cases."[16]

In some circuits, even if a plaintiff has established a *prima facie* case and presented evidence that a defendant's legitimate, nondiscriminatory justification for its actions was a pretext, a defendant can still be entitled to summary judgment when "no rational fact finder could conclude that the action was discriminatory."[17] If the employee chooses the mixed-motive alternative and proves that discrimination was a motivating factor, the burden shifts back to the employer to prove that it would have made the same decision despite the discriminatory animus.[18] If the defendant meets its burden of demonstrating that it would have made the same decision regardless of any retaliatory motive, then it is entitled to summary judgment.[19]

B. Gender Discrimination and Sexual Harassment Under Title VII

1. Types of Harassment

In the past, two types of sexual harassment claims were recognized: *quid pro quo* and hostile environment. Generally, *quid pro quo* harassment was found in situations that involved harassment based on gender, whereas hostile work environment harassment applied to all types of unlawful harassment.[20] The traditional meaning of harassment changed somewhat in the Supreme Court decisions in *Burlington Industries v. Ellerth*[21] and *Faragher v. City of Boca Raton*.[22] In this set of cases, the Supreme Court modified the meaning of harassment to include:

    a. tangible employment action, and
    b. hostile work environment.

---

14. 193 F.3d 219 (4th Cir. 1999), *cert. denied.*

15. *See generally* Rutherford v. Harris County, 197 F.3d 173, 183–84 (5th Cir. 1999); Urbano v. Cont'l Airlines, Inc., 138 F.3d 204, 206 (5th Cir. 1998) (*cert. denied*); Rohde v. K.O. Steel Castings, Inc., 649 F.2d 317, 322 (5th Cir. 1981); Williams v. Trader Publ'g Co., 218 F.3d 481, 484 (5th Cir. 2000).

16. *See* Javier Perez v. Texas Department of Criminal Justice, 395 F.3d 213 (5th Cir. 2004); *see also* Little v. Republic Ref. Co., 924 F.2d 93, 97 (5th Cir. 1991); Smith v. Wal-Mart Stores, 891 F.2d 1177, 1180 (5th Cir.1990) (*per curiam*); Wyvill v. United Cos. Life Ins. Co., 212 F.3d 296 (5th Cir. 2000); Mayberry v. Vought Aircraft Co., 55 F.3d 1086 (5th Cir. 1995).

17. *See Reeves*, 530 U.S. at 148.

18. Richardson v. Monitronics, 434 F.3d 327, 333 (5th Cir. 2005).

19. *Id.*

20. *See* Tang v. Citizens Bank, 821 F.3d 206 (1st. Cir. 2016).

21. 524 U.S. 742 (1998).

22. 524 U.S. 775 (1998).

2. What Is a Tangible Employment Action?

A tangible employment action is a significant change in employment status, such as firing, failing to hire, failing to promote, reassignment with significantly different responsibilities or a significant change in benefits.[23] A tangible employment action is based on a threat of a job detriment or a promise of a job benefit in exchange for sexual favors which, if refused, results in an adverse employment action, such as termination, denial of a raise, etc. As discussed in further detail as follows, employers are strictly liable for conduct by supervisors that constitutes a tangible employment action.

3. Hostile Work Environment

Hostile environment harassment is harassment that creates adverse working conditions, but does not result in a tangible employment action. This type of harassment is not limited to gender, but may also be used to prove harassment based on other protected classifications, such as race, national origin, religion, age, disability, and color. Examples of hostile work environment harassment include unwelcome jokes of a sexual nature, graffiti, comments, stories, photographs, gestures, emails, or any conduct based on gender that interferes with the employee's work performance.

In order to prove a *prima facie* case of coworker hostile work environment exists, a plaintiff must prove that:

1. she belongs to a protected class;
2. she was subject to unwelcome sexual harassment;
3. the harassment was based on sex;
4. the harassment affected a term, condition, or privilege of employment; and
5. the employer knew or should have known of the harassment and failed to take prompt remedial action.[24]

Threats of job loss or promises of job-related advantages/benefits that do not result in tangible employment action are suitable claims for hostile environment harassment, if the threats or promises create an intimidating, hostile, or offensive work environment.[25] Examples of behaviors that may create a hostile work environment include:

- unwanted sexual advances;
- offering employment benefits for sexual favors;
- leering, making sexual gestures, displaying derogatory pictures, emails, cartoons, or drawings;
- sexually derogatory comments, epithets, slurs, or jokes;
- verbal abuse, degrading words to describe men or women;

---

23. *See Ellerth*, 524 U.S. at 761.

24. Harvill v. Westward L.L.C., 433 F.3d 428 (5th Cir. 2005); DeAngelis v. El Paso Mun. Police Officers Ass'n, 51 F.3d 591, 593 (5th Cir. 1995); Jones v. Flagship Int'l, 793 F.2d 714, 719 (5th Cir. 1986).

25. *See* Meritor Savings Bank FSB v. Vinson, 477 U.S. 57 (1986).

- touching, assault, impeding, or blocking movements; and
- retaliating against an employee for complaining of sexual harassment.

C. Employer Liability for Unlawful Harassment by Managers and Supervisors

Employers are strictly liable under Title VII for any sexual harassment by a supervisor that results in a tangible employment action. The elements of a *prima facie* case of tangible employment action harassment are:

1. the plaintiff is a member of a protected group;
2. the plaintiff was subjected to unwelcome sexual advances or requests for sexual favors;
3. the harassment was sexually motivated;
4. the employee's reaction to the supervisor's advances affected a tangible aspect of the employment; and
5. a basis for employer liability has been established.[26]

If the harassment does not result in a tangible job detriment, the Supreme Court has held that the employer may still be liable for a hostile work environment by supervisors.[27] However, an employer may avoid liability for a hostile environment created by managers and supervisors under two conditions:

a. if the employer used reasonable care to prevent and correct any harassment, including implementing a sexual harassment policy and training employees on the complaint procedures; and
b. if the employee unreasonably failed to make a complaint under the policy or to avoid harm otherwise.[28]

Having a sexual harassment policy will not be enough, by itself, to avoid liability using the affirmative defenses provided in *Ellerth* and *Faragher*. If the employer does not comply with the policy or promptly address the alleged behavior, some courts have found that the affirmative defenses were not available to the employer.[29] In *Homesley v. Freightliner*

---

26. Tang v. Citizens Bank, N.A., 821 F.3d 206, 215 (1st Cir. 2016); Cook v. Life Credit Union, 138 F.Supp.3d 981, 991 (M.D. Tenn. 2015); Byrd v. Wis. Dep't of Veterans Affairs, 98 F.Supp.3d 972, 980 (W.D. Wis. 2015); *see also* Puleo v. Texana MHMR Ctr., 187 F. Supp.3d 769, 780 (S.D. Tex. 2016) (internal punctuation marks omitted) (noting that the ultimate question for a *quid pro quo* claim is "whether the tangible employment action suffered by the employee resulted from her acceptance or rejection of her supervisor's alleged sexual harassment").

27. *Id.*

28. Pullen v. Caddo Parish Sch. Bd., 830 F.3d 205, 209–10 (5th Cir. 2016); Jones v. Se. Pa. Transp. Auth., 796 F.3d 323, 328 (3rd Cir. 2015).

29. *See* Homesley v. Freightliner Corp., 61 F. App'x 105 (4th Cir. 2003) (employer was not entitled to an affirmative defense in a sexual harassment case in part because the company did not comply with its harassment policy and did not act promptly to address the alleged harassment).

Corp., the supervisor told the plaintiff, who complained of sexual harassment, that she should have asked her husband to "whip the alleged harasser's butt" as a remedy for the harassment.[30] The employer's failure to promptly investigate and resolve the complaint prevented it from being able to rely on the *Ellerth* and *Faragher* affirmative defenses. The court also held that the plaintiff reasonably tried to take advantage of corrective measures offered by the employer, because she promptly complained about the behavior.[31]

1. Who Is a Supervisor?

Employers may be strictly liable for the harassing conduct by supervisors, thus it is important to understand the definition of the term "supervisor" in a Title VII claim for sexual harassment. In *Vance v. Ball State University*,[32] the Supreme Court held that an employee is a supervisor for purposes of vicarious liability under Title VII if he is empowered by the employer to take tangible employment action against the complaining employee.[33] In *Vance*, the court held that the alleged harasser, who considered himself a coworker of the plaintiff, was not actually her supervisor because he could not promote, fire, hire, transfer, or discipline the plaintiff.[34]

2. Who Is the Employer's Proxy?

If the alleged harasser is the employer's proxy, that is, stands in the place of the employer, the employer may be automatically vicariously liable for the proxy's harassing conduct. In *Ackel v. National Communications*,[35] the Fifth Circuit held that the president of the company, who sat on its board of directors and owned 2 percent of the company stock stood in proxy for the employer. The employer could not use the *Ellerth/Faragher* affirmative defenses to liability because the alleged harasser was high enough in management to be regarded as speaking and acting for the company.[36]

D. Employer Liability for Acts of Coworkers

An employer is liable for a hostile work environment created by a coworker of the complaining party if the employer knew or should have known of the harassment and failed to take prompt remedial action.[37] In *Star v. West*, the court ruled that a medical center was not liable for the conduct of the male coworker of a female plaintiff, because the

---

30. *Id.* at 108.

31. *Id. See also* O'Rourke v. City of Providence, 235 F.3d 713 (1st Cir. 2001) (female firefighter's case of sex harassment against her supervisors and coworkers was allowed to proceed because the employer allegedly made no effort to stop the harassing conduct).

32. 133 S. Ct, 2434, 2439 (2013).

33. *Id.*

34. *Id.* at 2443.

35. 339 F.3d 376 (5th Cir. 2003).

36. *See also* Townsend v. Benjamin Enterprises, 679 F.3d 41 (2d Cir. 2012), where the court affirmed that the alleged harasser, who worked as the employer, was the alter ego to the employer.

37. *See* Star v. West, 237 F.3d 1036 (9th Cir. 2001).

employer investigated the complaints and immediately transferred the alleged harasser to another shift and warned him to stay away from the plaintiff. After the company took this action, the harassing conduct stopped. The Court held that the employer's prompt response halted the harassment and was adequate to eliminate liability.[38]

1. Liability for Acts of Nonemployees

Under Title VII, an employer is liable for the harassment of a nonemployee if it was negligent, either in discovering the harassment, or remedying the harassment.[39] The employee must prove that the employer failed to provide a reasonable method for reporting the complaint, or that it knew, or should have known, about the harassment, yet failed to take appropriate remedial action.[40] In assessing whether the employer took appropriate remedial action, the court looks to whether the response was immediate or timely and appropriate in light of the circumstances. In *Summa v. Hofstra*, after a female team manager complained of harassing conduct on the part of the football team, the school instructed the players to remove objectionable social media postings, remove R-rated movies and eject an offending player within 48 hours after the plaintiff complained.[41]

E. Personal Liability for Harassment

Courts have generally ruled that managers and supervisors may not be found personally liable for sexual harassment under Title VII.[42]

F. Defenses to Hostile Work Environment Claims

Employers have defenses to hostile environment sexual harassment claims where:

1. the conduct was not unwelcome,
2. the conduct was not based on the sex or gender of the victim,
3. the conduct was not offensive to a reasonable person or to the alleged victim,
4. the alleged victim failed to exhaust the remedies offered by the employer, and
5. the employer exercised reasonable care to prevent and correct the alleged harassment and the employee unreasonably failed to take advantage of the company's reporting procedures.

---

38. *See also* Muhammed v. Caterpillar, 767 F.3d 694 (7th Cir. 2014); Foster v. University of Maryland, 787 F.3d 243 (4th Cir. 2015).

39. *See* Nischan v. Stratosphere Quality, LLC, 865 F.3d 922, 931 (7th Cir. 2017); Freeman v. Dal-Tile Corp., 750 F.3d 413, 423–24 (4th Cir. 2014); Turnbull v. Topeka State Hospital, 255 F.3d 1238, 1244 (10th Cir. 2001).

40. *See* Summa v. Hofstra University, 708 F.3d 115 (2nd Cir. 2013).

41. *Id.*

42. *See* Fantini v. Salem State College, 557 F.3d 22, 30–31 (1st Cir. 2009); Grant v. Lone Star College, 21 F.3d 649 (5th Cir. 1994); Sheridan v. E.I. du Pont de Nemours & Co., 100 F.3d 1061, 1077–78 (3rd Cir. 1996).

If the alleged harasser is a supervisor, and the supervisor's actions did not result in a "tangible employment action" against the employee, employers may assert the *Ellerth/Faragher* defenses, which require the employer to prove by a preponderance of the evidence:

a. that the employer exercised reasonable care to prevent and correct promptly any sexually harassing behavior, and
b. that the plaintiff employee unreasonably failed to take advantage of any preventive or corrective opportunities provided by the employer or to avoid harm otherwise.[43]

1. Conduct Not Unwelcome

Flirting at work among coworkers can create confusion when one of the flirting employees claims he or she was harassed by the other. Accordingly, courts have held that a necessary element to proving a sexual hostile environment claim is that the conduct is unwelcome.[44] Where there is evidence that the alleged victim welcomed the conduct by not complaining about the conduct, appearing to enjoy spending time with the alleged harasser, or is seen flirting with the alleged harasser, employers may rely upon the *Ellerth/Faragher* defense.[45] The courts look at the totality of the circumstances, including the alleged victim's behavior and relationship with the alleged harasser, for proof that he or she perceived the conduct as unwelcome.[46]

2. Conduct Not Offensive to a Reasonable Person

In order to prove a sexually hostile working environment, an employee must show that he or she found the alleged harasser's conduct offensive and that a reasonable person in the employee's position would have found the conduct offensive.[47] Title VII does not prohibit all verbal or physical harassment in the workplace; it is directed only at "discriminat[ion] . . . because of sex."[48] Workplace harassment, even harassment between men and women, is not automatically deemed discrimination based on sex

---

43. *Faragher*, 524 U.S. at 807; *see also* Lauderdale v. Texas Dep't of Criminal Justice, Institutional Div., 512 F.3d 157, 164 (5th Cir. 2007).

44. *See* Stephens v. Rheem Manufacturing, 220 F.3d 882 (8th Cir. 2000); Blake v. MJ Optical, Inc., 2017 U.S. App. LEXIS 16742 (8th Cir. 2017).

45. *Id.*

46. *Id.*

47. *See* Harris v. Forklift Systems, 510 U.S. 17 (1993); the court held that: "(1) to be actionable under Title VII as 'abusive work environment' harassment, the conduct need not seriously affect an employee's psychological well-being or lead the employee to suffer injury; (2) the Meritor standard requires an objectively hostile or abusive environment as well as the victim's subjective perception that the environment is abusive; and (3) whether an environment is sufficiently hostile or abusive to be actionable requires consideration of all the circumstances, not any one factor."

48. Oncale v. Sundowner Offshore Servs., Inc., 523 U.S. 75, 80, 118 S. Ct. 998, 1002 (1998) (emphasis added).

merely because the words used have sexual content or connotations.[49] Courts consider the totality of circumstances, including the frequency of the offensive conduct, its pervasiveness and severity, any physical threats or violence, or humiliating as opposed to being a mere offensive utterance.[50] Courts also look at whether there is evidence that the conduct unreasonably interfered with the employee's work performance.[51]

In *Gupta v. Florida Board of Regents*,[52] a female professor claimed she was sexually harassed by a department chairman who she claimed leered at her body, took her to lunch frequently, took her and another couple to dinner, told her she was attractive, and called her at home late at night. The Eleventh Circuit court found that this conduct did not constitute sexual harassment from an objective perspective because an employer cannot guarantee that supervisors will not look at other employees or call subordinates attractive.[53]

Also in *Cram v. Lamson & Sessions Co.*, a supervisor who had previously made polite romantic overtures to an employee got into an off-duty altercation with that employee and her date at a bar.[54] Following the altercation, the supervisor told the employee that "you know I'll get you for this."[55] The court rejected Title VII employer liability, noting that the altercation at the bar was "not in any way work-related."[56]

3. Severe or Pervasive Conduct

For sexual harassment to be actionable, it must be sufficiently severe or pervasive "to alter the conditions of [the victim's] employment and create an abusive working environment."[57] In determining whether an environment is "hostile" or "abusive" within the meaning of Title VII, courts look at the totality of the circumstances including "the frequency of the discriminatory conduct; its severity; whether it is physically threatening or humiliating, or a mere offensive utterance; and whether it unreasonably interferes with an employee's work performance."[58] Courts also consider whether the complained of conduct undermines the plaintiff's workplace competence.[59]

---

49. *Id.*

50. *Id.*

51. *Id. See* 864 F.3d 541, 549 (7th Cir. 2017).

52. 212 F3d. 571 (11th Cir. 2000).

53. *Id.*

54. 49 F.3d 466, 470–71 (8th Cir. 1995).

55. *Id.* at 471.

56. *Id.* at 475; *see also* Fontenot v. Buus, 370 F. Supp.2d 512 (W.D. La. 2004) (finding no hostile work environment where most of harassing conduct took place outside the workplace); Carter v. Caring for the Homeless of Peekskill, Inc., 821 F. Supp. 225, 228 (S.D.N.Y. 1993) (incidents occurring off work premises and not related to employment did not constitute sexual harassment).

57. Meritor Sav. Bank, FSB v. Vinson, 477 U.S. 57, 67, 106 S. Ct. 2399, 91 L.Ed.2d 49 (1986).

58. Harris v. Forklift, 510 U.S. 17, 23 (1993).

59. Hockman v. Westward Commc'ns, 407 F.3d 317, 326 (5th Cir. 2004) (citing Butler v. Ysleta Indep. Sch. Dist., 161 F.3d 263, 270 (5th Cir. 1998)). "To be actionable, the challenged conduct must be both objectively offensive, meaning that a reasonable person would find it hostile and abusive, and subjectively offensive, meaning that the victim perceived it to be so." Shepherd v. Comptroller of Pub. Accounts, 168 F.3d 871, 874 (5th Cir. 1999).

Plaintiffs do not have to prove that a specific number of harassing incidents occurred in order to meet the severe and pervasive threshold. The Supreme Court has stated that even isolated incidents, if egregious, can alter the terms and conditions of employment. Courts have often recognized that "even one act of harassment will suffice [to create a hostile work environment] if it is egregious."[60] However, incidents must be severe. It is important to remember that "Title VII, is not a 'general civility code,' and 'simple teasing, offhand comments, and isolated incidents (unless extremely serious)' will not amount to discriminatory changes in the 'terms and conditions of employment.'"[61]

4. Conduct Not Based on Gender

Some alleged harassers treat everyone, both male and female employees, equally harshly. Some courts have found that the "equal opportunity offender" cannot be liable for offensive sexual conduct if he treats men and women the same. For example, in *Reine v. Honeywell International Inc.*,[62] the Fifth Circuit found that when the conduct is equally harsh toward men and women, there is no hostile work environment based on sex.[63] However, not all courts agree with the *Reine* decision. In *McGinest v. GTE Service Corp.*,[64] the Ninth Circuit held that a harasser's abuse of women and men did not provide an excuse of defense to a harassment claim. Accordingly, because the "equal opportunity harasser" defense is not accepted by all courts, employers should not rely upon this defense when reviewing how to respond to complaints about such a harasser.

5. Employee Failed to Take Advantage of Internal Administrative Remedies

One element of the *Ellerth/Faragher* defense is that the employee unreasonably failed to take advantage of any preventive or corrective opportunities provided by the employer. Courts will consider the way in which the employer publicized its anti-harassment complaint procedure, the number of avenues the employee had to complain, and the effectiveness of the company's response to employees who used the complaint procedure.[65] This is true, even when the employee complains of the sexual harassment to the person who is harassing her. Whether a plaintiff's complaints to the harasser constitute reasonable use of an employer's sexual harassment policy is to be determined by the

---

60. Lockard v. Pizza Hut, Inc., 162 F.3d 1062, 1072 (10th Cir. 1998) (holding that a single incident of physically threatening and humiliating conduct can be sufficient to create a hostile work environment for a sexual harassment claim); Tomka v. Seiler Corp., 66 F.3d 1295, 1305 (2d Cir. 1995), abrogated on other grounds.

61. *Faragher*, 524 U.S. at 788, 118 S. Ct. 2275; *see also* Worth v. Tyler, 276 F.3d 249, 268 (7th Cir. 2001).

62. 362 F. App'x 395, 398 (5th Cir. 2010).

63. *Id. See also* Bagley v. Regis Corp., 2004 WL 2826810 at *3 (N.D. Tex. Dec. 7, 2004) ("Atchison's alleged discussions of homosexuality and male genitalia, which he directed toward men and women, and which were not motivated by plaintiff's gender, cannot have attributed to the alleged hostile work environment.").

64. 360 F.3d 1103 (9th Cir. 2004).

65. *See* Leopold v. Baccarat, Inc, 239 F.3d 243, 244 (2nd Cir. 2001); *see also* Madray v. Publix Supermarkets, 208 F.3d 1290 (11th Cir. 2000).

specific facts and circumstances of each case.[66] In *Gorzynski v. JetBlue Airways*, the Second Circuit held that the employer was not entitled to summary judgment using the *Ellerth/Farragher* defense, because a fact issue existed as to whether it was unreasonable for *Gorzynski* to have complained of sexual harassment to her supervisor, who was also the harasser, rather than pursing alternative options listed in her employee manual.[67]

In contrast, in *Wyatt v. Hunt Plywood Co.*,[68] the plaintiff reported her supervisor's harassment to his supervisor, who dealt ineffectively with the harassment and subsequently began harassing the plaintiff himself. The Fifth Circuit held that it was unreasonable for the plaintiff not to report the harassment to another person listed in the defendant's reporting policy once her initial complaint was obviously ineffective. The Supreme Court has held that once an employee knows his initial complaint is ineffective, it is unreasonable for him not to file a second complaint, so long as the employer has provided multiple avenues for such a complaint."[69]

G. Types of Claims

1. Same-Sex Stereotyping as Harassment

Where the alleged harasser is the same sex as the alleged victim, or the harasser discriminates because the victim does not conform to expectations of how he/she should act, courts have held that employees may still bring claims of sexual harassment or discrimination under Title VII. In *Price Waterhouse v. Hopkins*,[70] the Supreme Court recognized that employment discrimination based on sex stereotypes (e.g., assumptions and/or expectations about how persons of a certain sex should dress, behave, etc.), is unlawful sex discrimination under Title VII. In *Price Waterhouse*, the employer denied the plaintiff a promotion, in part, because other partners at the firm felt that she did not talk, dress, or act as feminine as the firm thought a woman should act.[71] The Court found that this constituted evidence of sex discrimination as "[i]n the . . . context of sex stereotyping, an employer who acts on the basis of a belief that a woman cannot be aggressive, or that she must not be, has acted on the basis of gender."[72] This reasoning was repeated in *Oncale v. Sundowner Offshore Servs.*[73] In *Oncale*, the Supreme Court held that same-sex harassment is sex discrimination under Title VII, where the sex

---

66. Gorzynski v. JetBlue Airways Corp., 596 F.3d 93, 96 (2d Cir. 2010).

67. *Id.*

68. 297 F.3d 405, 412 (5th Cir. 2002).

69. *Faragher*, 524 U.S. at 807. *See also* Lauderdale v. Texas Dep't of Criminal Justice, Institutional Div., 512 F.3d 157, 165 (5th Cir. 2007).

70. 490 U.S. 228 (1989).

71. *Id.* at 230–31, 235.

72. *Id.* at 250. The Court further explained that Title VII's "because of sex" provision strikes at the "entire spectrum of disparate treatment of men and women resulting from sex stereotypes." *Id.* (quoting City of Los Angeles Dep't of Water & Power v. Manhart, 435 U.S. 702, 707 n. 13 (1978)).

73. 523 U.S. 75 (1998).

discrimination is based on sexual stereotyping.[74] In *Oncale,* the plaintiff was a male employee who was physically assaulted and threatened with rape because he did not appear sufficiently masculine to his male coworkers.[75]

In an effort to provide additional guidance, the *Oncale* decision limited liability to cases involving same-sex conduct, which a reasonable person in the plaintiff's position would find severely hostile or abusive. The Court re-emphasized that Title VII is an employment discrimination statute, not a remedy for every unfortunate act occurring in the workplace. To be actionable, the harassment must not only be "severely hostile or abusive" conduct, but must also be "because of" the victim's sex, meaning gender.[76]

2. Sexual Orientation Harassment

Most recently, the Seventh Circuit became the only federal appellate court to rule that discrimination based on sexual orientation is a form of sex discrimination and thus prohibited by Title VII.[77] Until the court ruling in *Hively v. Ivy Tech. Comm. College,* appellate courts had not ruled that discrimination, based solely on sexual orientation, was actionable under Title VII. A plaintiff could survive summary judgment if he claimed he was discriminated against because he was seen as "feminine," but could not typically claim discrimination for being or being perceived to be gay, lesbian, or bisexual. However, the circuit courts are now split on this topic.

In March 2017, the Eleventh Circuit dismissed a similar lawsuit and held that Title VII does not protect against sexual orientation discrimination.[78] The court rejected the argument that sexual orientation discrimination is another form of gender stereotyping. Thus, outside of the Seventh Circuit, the most likely successful elements of a sexual discrimination claim for employees who believe they have been discriminated against because of their sexual orientation, is to allege that the employer treated the employee differently because they did not conform to gender stereotypes.[79]

---

74. *Id.* at 79–80.

75. *Id.*

76. *Id.*

77. Hively v. Ivy Tech Community College of Indiana, 853 F.3d 339 (7th Cir. 2017).

78. *See* Evans v. Georgia Regional Hospital, 850 F.3d 1240 (11th Cir. 2017); *see also* Zarda v. Altitude Express, 855 F.3d 76 (2nd Cir. 2017) (court permitted same sex orientation claim under New York Statute, but dismissed claims under Title VII).

79. Several states have enacted statutes that protect employees based on their sexual orientation:
   - California: Cal. Gov't Code § 12940(a) (2018) prohibits discrimination because of sexual orientation.
   - Colorado: Colo. Rev. Stat. § 24-34-402 (2016) prohibits employment discrimination on the basis of sexual orientation. Colo. Rev. Stat. § 2-4-401(13.5) (2016) defines sexual orientation to include "a person's orientation toward heterosexuality, homosexuality, bisexuality, or transgender status or another person's perception thereof."
   - Connecticut: Conn. Gen. Stat. § 46a-81c (2012) prohibits employment discrimination on the basis of "the individual's sexual orientation."
   - Delaware: 19 Del. C. §711(a) (2016) prohibits employment discrimination on the basis of "sexual orientation."
   - District of Columbia: D.C. Code § 2-1402.11 (2017) prohibits employment discrimination on the basis of "sexual orientation."

3. Gender Identity Claims

The Equal Employment Opportunity Commission (EEOC) has taken the position that Title VII's meaning of a person's "sex" includes a person's biological sex as well as pregnancy, sexual orientation, gender identity, and gender-based stereotypes, perceptions, or comfort level.[80] The EEOC Fact Sheet expressly states the following actions violate Title VII:

- "Denying an employee equal access to a common restroom corresponding to the employee's gender identity is sex discrimination.
- An employer cannot condition this right on the employee undergoing or providing proof of surgery or any other medical procedure.
- An employer cannot avoid the requirement to provide equal access to a common restroom by restricting a transgender employee to a single-user restroom instead (though the employer can make a single-user restroom available to all employees who might choose to use it)."

- Hawaii: Haw. Rev. Stat. § 378-2 (2013) prohibits employment discrimination on the basis of "sexual orientation."
- Illinois: 775 Ill. Cons. Stat. 5/1-103(Q), 5/2-102 (2015) prohibit employment discrimination on the basis of "sexual orientation," which 775 Ill. Cons. Stat. 5/1-103(O-1) defines as "actual or perceived heterosexuality, homosexuality, bisexuality, or gender-related identity, whether or not traditionally associated with the person's designated sex at birth."
- Iowa: Iowa Code § 216.6(1)(a) (2016) prohibits employment discrimination on the basis of "sexual orientation."
- Kansas: Only potential state-wide protection is for hiring of Kansas Department of Motor Vehicles employees. Kan. Admin. Reg. § 92-52-15 (2008).
- Maine: 5 Me. Rev. Stat. § 4572 (2005) prohibits employment discrimination on the basis of "sexual orientation," which 5 Me. Rev. Stat. § 4553(9-C) (2005) defines as "a person's actual or perceived heterosexuality, bisexuality, homosexuality or gender identity or expression."
- Maryland: Md. Code Ann., State Gov't § 20-606(a) (2009) prohibits employment discrimination on the basis of "sexual orientation."
- Massachusetts: Mass. Gen. Laws. ch. 151B § 4(1) (2016) prohibits employment discrimination because of "sexual orientation."
- Minnesota: Minn. Stat. § 363A.08 (2014) prohibits employment discrimination on the basis of "sexual orientation."
- Montana: Mont. Admin. R. 2.21.4005 (2016) prohibits employment discrimination by government agencies (but not private employers) on the basis of "sexual orientation."
- Nevada: Nev. Rev. Stat. § 613.330 (2017) prohibits employment discrimination on the basis of sexual orientation.
- New Hampshire: N.H. Rev. Stat. Ann. § 354-A:7 (2015) prohibits employment discrimination on the basis of sexual orientation.
- New Jersey: N.J. Stat. Ann. § 10:5-12 (2013) prohibits employment discrimination on the basis of "affectional or sexual orientation."

80. The U.S. Congress specifically included "pregnancy" in Title VII's definition of "sex" with the passage of the Pregnancy Discrimination Act of 1972. Congress has not passed any legislation to include sexual orientation or gender identity into Title VII's definition of sex.

The EEOC has been involved in several cases in its efforts to expand the scope of Title VII to include discrimination based on gender identity and transgender status:

- *EEOC v. Lakeland Eye Clinic, P.A.* (M.D. Fla., filed Sept. 25, 2014). EEOC alleged in the now settled lawsuit that the employer discriminated based on sex in violation of Title VII by firing an employee because she is transgender, transitioning from male to female, and/or not conforming to the employer's gender-based expectations, preferences, or stereotypes.
- *Lewis v. Highpoint Reg'l Health Sys.*, 2015 WL 221615 (E.D.N.C. Jan. 15, 2015). In that case, the EEOC filed a brief in support of the transgender female employee who brought the lawsuit arguing that failing to hire an individual because she is transgender violates Title VII.
- *Lusardi v. McHugh*, EEOC Appeal No. 0120133395 (April 1, 2015). The EEOC ruled that denying employees use of a restroom, consistent with their gender identity and subjecting them to intentional use of the wrong gender pronouns, constitutes discrimination because of sex, and thus violates Title VII. The EEOC specifically analyzed the bathroom issue and the accommodation of allowing the transitioning employee to use a unisex restroom. They found that because the decision to use a different restroom than the gender the employee identifies with is based on gender identity, it is a violation of Title VII, even if the employee consents to the accommodation.[81]

Despite the EEOC's position as stated in its Fact Sheet, there is no federal statute, including Title VII, which explicitly prohibits discrimination in the workplace against individuals based on sexual orientation or gender identity. In fact, nearly every year since 1994, Congress has failed to enact a proposed Employment Non-Discrimination Act (ENDA), which would make it illegal for employers with fifteen or more full-time workers to refuse to hire, terminate, or otherwise discriminate against any individual on the basis of his or her actual or perceived sexual orientation or gender identity. Prior to 2017, various federal agencies, during the Obama administration, issued regulations that required federal contractors and/or employers to provide equal treatment to transgender employees with regard to bathroom privileges.[82]

---

81. Further, the EEOC ruled that discrimination based on sexual orientation is also sex discrimination under Title VII. Complainant v. Foxx, EEOC, Appeal No. 0120133080 (July 16, 2015).

82. OSHA Guidance: On June 1, 2015, OSHA published its Guide to Restroom Access for Transgender Workers. "The core principle is that all employees, including transgender employees, should have access to restrooms that correspond to their gender identity," said Assistant Secretary of Labor for Occupational Safety and Health Dr. David Michaels. "OSHA's goal is to assure that employers provide a safe and healthful working environment for all employees." *See* https://www.osha.gov/newsrelease/trade-20150601.html; *see also* Exhibit A: OSHA Guide to Restroom Access for Transgender Workers.

OFCCP: On December 3, 2014, the OFCCP issued final rules implementing Executive Order 13672, which prohibits government contractors from discriminating in employment on the basis of gender identity. In its FAQ Guidance on the issue of restroom use, the OFCCP states:

On February 22, 2017, the US Department of Justice and the US Department of Education issued a "Dear Colleague" letter withdrawing the prior statements of policy and guidance issued by the Department of Education on January 7, 2015, and the Departments of Justice and Education on May 13, 2016. In the February 22, 2017, letter, the Office of Civil Rights division of both departments stated that the previous guidance to schools regarding access to restrooms for transgender students was being withdrawn. Also, the Department of Justice filed an *amicus curiae* brief in 2017, arguing that Title VII does not reach sexual orientation discrimination.[83] At this time, in most federal circuit courts, claims under Title VII arguing gender identity or transgender discrimination are not likely to be successful unless the plaintiff also alleges gender stereotyping discrimination.

4. Retaliation

Title VII prohibits employers from retaliating against employees who have either (1) opposed any practice made an unlawful employment practice under Title VII, or (2) filed a charge, testified, assisted, or participated in any manner in an investigation, proceeding, or hearing "under this subchapter."[84] These provisions, respectively, are commonly known as the "opposition" and the "participation" clauses of the statute. In order to establish a *prima facie* case of retaliation, under the opposition or participation provisions, a plaintiff must show the following: that he (1) engaged in an activity protected by Title VII, (2) the employer knew of the employee's engagement in protected activity, (3) the employer took adverse action against the plaintiff after he or she engaged in protected activity, (4) and a causal connection existed between the protected activity engaged in by the employee and the adverse action taken by the employer.[85]

5. Protected Activity

Many federal courts have held that an employee engages in the most basic form of protected activity when she tells her harasser that he must stop harassing her.[86]

Title VII does not spell out each act that might constitute "engaging in protected activity." There is little dispute that filing discrimination charges with administrative agencies, participating in investigations, and filing internal company complaints in compliance with company procedures constitutes engaging in protected activity. However, there is still some confusion regarding the scope of other types of conduct

---

"Under the Final Rule, contractors must ensure that their restroom access policies and procedures do not discriminate based on the sexual orientation or gender identity of an applicant or employee. In keeping with the federal government's existing legal position on this issue, contractors must allow employees and applicants to use restrooms consistent with their gender identity." http://www.dol.gov/ofccp/lgbt/lgbt_faqs.html#Q35

83. 548 U.S. 53 (2006).

84. 42 U.S.C. 2000e-3(a) (1994).

85. *See* St. Mary's Honor Ctr. V. Hicks, 509 U.S. 502, 515–17(1993), EEOC v. New Breed Logistics, 783 F.3d 1057(6th Cir. 2015); Adams v. Groesbeck I.S.D., 475 F.3d 688, 691 (5th Cir. 2007).

86. *See* Ogden v. Wax Works, Inc., 214 F.3d 999, 1007 (8th Cir. 2000), Reed v. Cracker Barrel Old Country Store, Inc, 133 F. Supp. 2d 1055 (M.D. Tenn. 2000).

which could constitute engaging in protected activity. The US Supreme Court provided guidance in *Crawford v. Metropolitan Government of Nashville & Davidson County.*[87] In *Crawford*, the court recognized that "the term 'oppose' is not defined by the statute. Thus, the court relied upon its ordinary meaning: 'to resist or antagonize . . . , to contend against, to confront, resist, withstand . . . .'"[88] Accordingly, in many cases, employee complaints to management and less formal protests of discriminatory conduct constitutes engaging in protected activity. However, the Fifth Circuit stands slightly apart on this issue by concluding that communication directly and solely to a harassing supervisor may not constitute protected activity. In *Frank v. Harris County*, the Fifth Circuit held that the plaintiff provided no authority for the proposition that a single express rejection to a harassing supervisor constitutes engaging in protected activity as a matter of law.[89]

6. Materially Adverse Action

In *Burlington Northern and Santa Fe v. White*, the US Supreme Court defined a materially adverse employment action for purposes of a Title VII retaliation claims to be any conduct that "well might have dissuaded a reasonable worker from making or supporting a charge of discrimination.[90] Loss of pay or benefits, termination, and demotion clearly constitute materially adverse actions.[91] However, under *Burlington Northern & Santa Fe Railway Co. v. White*, an action constitutes an adverse employment action only if it is "materially adverse," meaning that it would "dissuade[] a reasonable worker from making or supporting a charge of discrimination."[92] Courts have often noted that Title VII "does not set forth a general civility code for the American workplace."[93] Thus, not every disagreeable workplace action constitutes retaliation; rather, retaliation must produce "an injury or harm."[94] At least one circuit court, the Seventh Circuit

---

87. 555 U.S. 271 (2009).

88. *Id.*

89. 118 Fed. Appx.799, 804 (5th Cir. 2004).

90. 548 U.S. 53, 68 (2006).

91. *See* Howington v. Quality Restaurant Concepts, 298 Fed. Appx, 436, 442 (6th Cir. 2008). Courts have also held that the adverse action requirement was satisfied when an employee was forced to use a grievance procedure to get overtime work assignments that were routinely awarded to others, Fonseca v. Sysco Food Servs. of Ariz., Inc., 374 F.3d 840, 848 (9th Cir. 2004), when an employee was assigned more hazardous work than her co-workers, *Davis*, 520 F.3d at 1089–90, and when an employee was laterally transferred or received undeserved poor performance ratings, Yartzoff v. Thomas, 809 F.3d 1371, 1376 (9th Cir. 1987).

92. 548 U.S. 53, 68 (2006).

93. *Id.*

94. *Id.* at 67. *See, e.g.,* Whittaker v. N. Ill. Univ. (7th Cir. 2005) 424 F.3d 640, 644, 647–48 (Although the plaintiff's receipt of a negative evaluation, receipt of a written warning for absenteeism and placement on "proof status" were "putatively disciplinary measures," none "resulted in tangible job consequences and therefore [were] not adverse employment actions actionable under Title VII."); Longstreet v. Ill. Dep't of Corrections (7th Cir. 2002) 276 F.3d 379, 384 (the plaintiff's "negative performance evaluations and being required to substantiate that her absences from work were illness-related . . . did not result in tangible job consequences and therefore are not adverse employment actions actionable under Title VII"); Oest v. Ill. Dep't of Corrections (7th Cir. 2001) 240 F.3d 605, 613 (holding that neither "unfavorable performance evaluations" nor "oral or written reprimands" constitute adverse employment actions).

Court of Appeals, has divided adverse actions into categories. In *Herrnreiter v. Chicago Housing Authority,* the court noted that materially adverse employment actions can be categorized into three groups of cases involving: (1) the employee's current wealth such as compensation, fringe benefits, and financial terms of employment including termination; (2) the employee's career prospects thus impacting the employee's future wealth; and (3) changes to the employee's work conditions including subjecting her to "humiliating, degrading, unsafe, unhealthful, or otherwise significant negative alteration in [her] work place environment."[95]

7. Causal Connection

To establish a causal connection between the protected activity and the adverse action, a plaintiff must demonstrate that a retaliatory motive played a part in the adverse employment action.[96] Adverse conduct that occurred before the employee engaged in protected activity cannot be retaliation under Title VII.[97] In the Fifth Circuit, the plaintiff must also demonstrate that the employer had actual decision-making knowledge that the plaintiff had engaged in a protected activity.[98]

The plaintiff bears the burden of proving that the employer took the adverse action *because of* the plaintiff's protected activity.[99] In other words, the plaintiff must provide evidence that "but for" the protected activity, the adverse employment action would not have occurred.[100] This requires a showing of retaliatory animus. Some courts have also held that a plaintiff can show indirectly that retaliatory animus caused the adverse employment action by showing that the protected activity was closely followed by an adverse employment action.[101] However, temporal proximity alone is generally not sufficient to establish causation without other compelling evidence.[102] In cases where temporal proximity is sufficient to establish a *prima facie* case of causality, the temporal proximity must be very close. Courts have held that three months or more distance between the protected activity and the adverse action is insufficient to infer causation.[103]

---

95. Herrnreiter v. Chicago Hous. Auth., 315 F.3d 742, 744–45 (7th Cir. 2002).

96. *See* Cifra v. G.E. Co, 252 F.3d 205, 216 (2d Cir. 2001).

97. Gentile v. Potter, 509 F.Supp.2d 221, 239 (E.D.N.Y.2007); Clark County Sch. Dist. V. Breeden, 532 U.S. 269 (2001).

98. *See* Corley v. Jackson Police Dept., 639 F.2d 1296, 1300 n.6 (5th Cir. 1981) (constructive notice does not suffice).

99. *See* Hicks v. Baines, 593 F.3d 159 (2d Cir. 2010).

100. *See* Mota v. U.T. Houston Health Science Center, 261 F.3d 512, 519 (5th Cir. 2001); *see also* EEOC v. Ford Motor Co., No. 12–2484, 2015 WL 1600305 at *14 (6th Cir. 2015); Ward v. Jewell, 772 F.3d 1199, 1203 (10th Cir. 2014); Beard v. AAA of Mich., 593 F. App'x 447, 451 (6th Cir. 2014); Smith v. City of Fort Pierce, Fla., 565 F. App'x 774, 778–79 (11th Cir. 2014) (*per curiam*).

101. *See* Clark v. New York State Elec & Gas Corp., 67 F.Supp.2d 63 (N.D. N.Y. 1999) aff'd 216 F.3d 1071 (2d Cir. 2000).

102. *See, e.g.,* Vereecke v. Huron Valley Sch. Dist., 609 F.3d 392, 401 (6th Cir. 2010), Clark County School District v. Breeden, 532 U.S. 268, 273–74 (2001).

103. O'Neal v. Ferguson Constr. Co., 237 F.3d 1248, 1253 (10th Cir. 2001). *See, e.g.,* Richmond v. ONEOK, Inc., 120 F.3d 205, 209 (10th Cir. 1997) (three-month period insufficient); Hughes v. Derwinski, 967 F.2d 1168, 1174–75 (7th Cir. 1992) (four-month period insufficient); Mesnick v. General Elec. Co., 950 F.2d 816,

8. Employer's Burden

After the employee has provided sufficient evidence to demonstrate causation, the burden then shifts to the employer to show that its purportedly retaliatory action was in fact the result of a legitimate nonretaliatory reason.[104] If the employer makes this showing, the burden shifts back to the plaintiff to rebut the employer's evidence by demonstrating that the employer's purported nonretaliatory reasons "were not its true reasons, but were a pretext for discrimination."[105]

In *University of Texas Southwestern Medical Center v. Nassar*,[106] the Supreme Court gave further guidance on what Title VII retaliation plaintiffs must show to survive a motion for summary judgment. In *Nassar*, the Court held that a successful retaliation plaintiff must prove that *retaliatory animus* was a "but-for" cause of the challenged adverse employment action, eliminating mixed-motive liability under the "lessened" motivating factor test. However, the *Nassar* Court was silent as to the application of "but-for" causation in *McDonnell Douglas* pretext cases. Other courts have held, either expressly or implicitly, that *Nassar* did not alter the elements of a *prima facie* case.[107]

A plaintiff who establishes a *prima facie* case of retaliation bears the "ultimate burden of persuading the court that [she] has been the victim of intentional [retaliation]."[108] In order to carry this burden, a plaintiff must establish "both that the [employer's] reason was false and that [retaliation] was the real reason for the challenged conduct."[109] The employee must show that "the employer's reason is actually a pretext for retaliation," which the employee accomplishes by showing that the adverse action would not have occurred "but for" the employer's retaliatory motive . . . ."[110]

---

828 (1st Cir. 1991) (where some problems predated protected activity, nine-month period insufficient); Bishop v. Bell Atl. Corp., 299 F.3d 53, 60 (1st Cir. 2002) (finding one-year gap between protected activity and adverse employment action insufficient*)*; Feist v. La. Dept. of Justice, Office of the Attorney Gen., 730 F.3d 450, 454 (5th Cir. 2013).

104. McDonnell Douglas Corp. v. Green, 411 U.S. 792, 802 (1973); Raggs v. Miss. Power & Light Co., 278 F.3d 463 468 (5th Cir. 2002).

105. Reeves v. Sanderson Plumbing Prods., Inc., 530 U.S. 133, 143 (2000); *see also* Merritt v. Old Dominion Freight Line, Inc., 601 F.3d 289, 295 (4th Cir. 2010). *See also* Tex. Dep't of Cmty. Affairs v. Burdine, 450 U.S. 248, 256 (1981); Clark v. Huntsville City Bd. of Education, 717 F.2d 525, 527 (11th Cir. 1983).

106. 133 S. Ct. 2517 (2013). Many believe *Nassar* significantly altered the causation standard for claims based on direct evidence of retaliatory animus by rejecting the "mixed motive" theory of liability for retaliation claims. *Cf.* Harris v. Powhatan Cnty. Sch. Bd., 543 F. App'x 343, 346 (4th Cir. 2013) (noting that the Supreme Court in Gross v. FBL Fin. Serv. Inc., 557 U.S. 167 (2009), an analogous case upon which the *Nassar* court relied heavily.

107. *See* Montell v. Diversified Clinical Servs., Inc., 757 F.3d 497, 507 (6th Cir. 2014); Butterworth v. Lab. Corp. of Am. Holdings, 581 F. App'x 813, 817 (11th Cir. 2014) (*per curiam*).

108. *Hill*, 354 F.3d at 285 (quoting Tex. Dep't of Cmty. Affairs v. Burdine, 450 U.S. 248, 256 (1981)); *see also Merritt*, 601 F.3d at 294–95 (identifying the "ultimate question" in any Title VII case under either framework as "discrimination *vel non*" (quoting U.S. Postal Serv. Bd. of Governors v. Aikens, 460 U.S. 711, 714 (1983))).

109. Jiminez v. Mary Washington Coll., 57 F.3d 369, 378 (4th Cir. 1995) (quoting St. Mary's Honor Ctr. v. Hicks, 509 U.S. 502, 515 (1993)).

110. *Hague*, 560 F. App'x at 336 ("An employee establishes pretext by showing that the adverse action would not have occurred 'but for' the employer's retaliatory reason for the action.") (citing *Nassar*,

9. Co-Worker Retaliation

Retaliatory conduct by coworkers may include subjecting the victim to demeaning comments, or ridiculing them for reporting sexual harassment.[111] The Sixth Circuit Court of Appeals determined that an employer should be liable for a coworker's retaliatory acts if: (1) the coworker's retaliatory conduct is sufficiently severe to discourage a reasonable worker from making or supporting a charge of discrimination, (2) the employee's management has actual or constructive knowledge of the retaliatory behavior, and (3) supervisors or members of management have condoned, tolerated, or encouraged the acts of retaliation by inadequately responding to the employee's complaints.[112] An inadequate response on the part of the employer manifests indifference or unreasonableness under these circumstances.[113]

---

133 S. Ct. at 2533–34); *see also* Scrivener v. Socorro Ind. Sch. Dist., 169 F.3d 969, 972 (5th Cir. 1999) ("To carry her ultimate Title VII burden, an employee must also show that her employer would not have taken the adverse employment action 'but for' the employee's participation in the protected activity.").

111. *See* Moore v. City of Philadelphia, 461 F.3d 331, 341 (3rd Cir. 2006).

112. *See* Hawkins v. Anheuser-Busch, 517 F3d. 321 (6th Cir. 2008). (The plaintiff's co-worker set fire to the plaintiff's car and threatened her life after she made a complaint of sexual harassment against him.).

113. *Id.*, 517 F.3d at 347.

CHAPTER 2

Workplace Harassment: Policies and Investigations

Margaret J. Grover

I. WORKPLACE HARASSMENT PREVENTION POLICIES

An effective workplace harassment prevention policy is key to preventing sexual harassment as well as other forms of discrimination and harassment in the workplace. It also may be valuable in defending any claim of sexual harassment. Federal and state legislators and regulators have long recognized the importance of antiharassment policies. In 1980, the US Equal Employment Opportunity Commission (EEOC), the agency charged with the enforcement of Title VII of the Civil Rights Act of 1964 (Title VII),[1] adopted regulations advising employers to "take all steps necessary to prevent sexual harassment from occurring, such as . . . informing employees of their right to raise and how to raise the issue of harassment."[2] The current regulations provide: "An employer should take all steps necessary to prevent [sexual] harassment from occurring, such as affirmatively raising the subject, expressing strong disapproval, developing appropriate sanctions, informing employees of their right to raise and how to raise the issue of harassment under Title VII, and developing methods to sensitize all concerned."[3]

The US Supreme Court's analysis of an employer's liability for sexual harassment examined the employer's prevention efforts, including the adoption and dissemination of the sexual harassment policy. In June 1998, the US Supreme Court issued two landmark decisions that clarified the standards governing employer liability under Title VII: *Faragher v. City of Boca Raton*[4] and *Burlington Industries v. Ellerth*.[5] These cases analyzed the conditions under which an employer would be liable for sexual harassment by supervisory employees. If harassment results in a "tangible job action," such as termination, demotion, denial of promotion, or denial of benefits, an employer cannot avoid liability. The Court, however, established a two-prong defense available to

---

1. 42 U.S.C. §§ 2000e–2000e-17 (1991).
2. 29 C.F.R. § 1604.11(f) (1997).
3. 29 C.F.R. § 1604.11(f) (1999).
4. Faragher v. City of Boca Raton, 524 U.S. 775 (1998).
5. Burlington Indus., Inc. v. Ellerth, 524 U.S. 742 (1998).

employers when no "tangible job action" has occurred. The employer can avoid liability by proving that (1) it took reasonable steps to prevent and stop harassment, and (2) the employee failed to take reasonable steps to avoid the harassment.

In 2016, the EEOC published the *Select Task Force on the Study of Harassment in the Workplace, Report of Co-Chairs Chai R. Feldblum & Victoria A. Lipnic.* This report contained specific recommendations regarding the elements of a harassment prevention policy. It also provided guidance on best employer practices for preventing workplace harassment, including the following:

- Employers should adopt and maintain a comprehensive antiharassment policy (which prohibits harassment based on any protected characteristic and which includes social media considerations) and should establish procedures consistent with the principles discussed in this report.
- Employers should ensure that the antiharassment policy, and in particular details about how to complain of harassment and how to report observed harassment, are communicated frequently to employees, in various forms and methods.
- Employers should offer reporting procedures that are multifaceted, offering a range of methods, multiple points of contact, and geographic and organizational diversity where possible for an employee to report harassment.
- Employers should be alert to any possibility of retaliation against an employee who reports harassment and should take steps to ensure that such retaliation does not occur.
- Employers should periodically "test" their reporting system to determine how well the system is working.
- Employers should devote sufficient resources so that workplace investigations are prompt, objective, and thorough. Investigations should be kept as confidential as possible, recognizing that complete confidentiality or anonymity will not always be attainable.
- Employers should ensure that where harassment is found to have occurred, discipline is prompt and proportionate to the behavior(s) at issue and the severity of the infraction. Employers should ensure that discipline is consistent, and does not give (or create the appearance of) undue favor to any particular employee.
- In unionized workplaces, the labor union should ensure that its own policy and reporting system meet the principles outlined in this section.

The first prong of what is commonly called "the *Faragher/Ellerth* defense" highlights the importance of a clear and effective workplace harassment policy. (*See* "Model Workplace Harassment Prevention Policy," pp. 24–26.) The policy should not be limited to a written employee manual or handbook. Rather, the employer should develop a multifaceted approach to its antiharassment efforts. In addition to the written policy, the employer should take steps to disseminate written materials; list appropriate avenues for bringing complaints; specify procedures for investigating complaints; take prompt, effective remedial action, if required; and ensure an overall corporate culture that understands harassment is unlawful and will not be tolerated.

The written policy should contain a clear definition of sexual harassment as well as other forms of prohibited harassment in the workplace.[6] The description can be enhanced by providing specific examples of verbal and nonverbal conduct that may result in harassment. The policy should state that if an employee believes he or she is being harassed, the employee is encouraged to tell the harasser to stop. Because harassment often involves an abuse of power, the policy should recognize that the victim may be reluctant to speak with the person who is making her or him uncomfortable. The policy should also explain how to bring forward a complaint of harassment. Where possible, three or more individuals should be identified by name and position as persons who can receive complaints of harassment. The identified individuals to whom a complaint may be brought should include both men and women, as employees may be reluctant to discuss matters of a sexual nature with a member of the opposite sex. The policy should also specifically state that the employee may, but has no obligation to, advise his or her supervisor before bringing forward the harassment complaint. The ability to avoid advising the immediate supervisor is critical when the supervisor is the source of the problem.

For employers who provide internet and email access, the workplace harassment policy should include prohibitions for harassment via electronic communications (for example, sending emails containing unwelcome, offensive comments or sexually explicit photographs downloaded from the internet). The employer should also have a computer use policy stating that the computer network, internet access, and email are company property, and are to be used only for company purposes. The policy should explain that computers and electronic communications are not to be used to access or disseminate offensive materials and may be monitored at any time.

The policy should also address harassment using electronic media that is not provided by the employer. Because electronic forms of communications evolve rapidly, the employer should include broad language, with some specific examples of prohibited conduct, such as harassment through a social media site such as Facebook, Twitter, or Snapchat; sending harassing, intimidating, or inappropriate text messages; sending explicit or offensive photos or videos through electronic media; and harassing an employee by following her or him on social media, blogs, or other websites, which is often termed "cyberstalking."

The workplace harassment policy should advise employees that the company does not tolerate harassment, will investigate all complaints of harassment, and will take prompt, effective, remedial action if it discovers harassment. Finally, the policy should contain a section prohibiting retaliation to ensure that complaining parties, witnesses,

---

6. Employers may also want to have the policy apply to all forms of unlawful harassment. Separate examples of harassment on the basis of race, religion, disability, age, or classes protected under state law will be helpful in fleshing out the employer's antiharassment policies, encouraging complaints of unlawful behavior so that they can be resolved, and defending any litigation that arises alleging other types of unlawful harassment.

and potential witnesses understand that bringing a complaint of harassment or participating in an investigation will not have any negative effect on their job. From 1997 through 2016, the number of new retaliation cases filed with the EEOC has increased almost every year.[7] In 1997, only 22.6 percent of the claims filed included retaliation, while in 2016, retaliation was an element in 45.9 percent of the cases filed. The workplace harassment policy should be periodically reviewed to ensure that it complies with all applicable laws and regulations.

Once the employer has established a written workplace harassment policy, the policy must be disseminated. It should be contained in the employee handbook and posted on employee bulletin boards. The policy should also be distributed to each employee and the employee should sign and date an acknowledgment of receipt of the policy. The acknowledgment should be maintained in the employee's personnel file.

Ideally, all employees should participate in harassment prevention training so they understand the type of behavior prohibited and how to lodge a complaint under the antiharassment policy. Antiharassment training should be an element of any managerial or supervisory training program and should be periodically repeated and updated.

II. MODEL WORKPLACE HARASSMENT PREVENTION POLICY

[Employer's name] prohibits sexual harassment as well as harassment and discrimination based on race, color, religion, national origin, age, gender, sexual orientation, gender identity, disability, or other status legally protected by federal or state law. Such harassment is unlawful and will not be tolerated. Harassment includes verbal, physical, and visual conduct, as well as conduct through electronic communications, if the submission to the conduct is made an explicit or implicit condition of employment or where the submission to or rejection of any harassment is used as the basis for an employment decision or the harassment interferes with an employee's work performance or creates an intimidating, hostile, or offensive work environment.

A. Sexual Harassment Defined

Applicable state and federal laws define sexual harassment as unwanted sexual advances, requests for sexual favors, or visual, verbal, or physical conduct of a sexual nature when (1) submission to the conduct is made a term or condition of employment, (2) submission to or rejection of the conduct is used as a basis for employment decisions affecting the individual, or (3) the conduct has the purpose or effect of unreasonably interfering with the employee's work performance or creating an intimidating, hostile, or offensive working environment. This definition includes many forms of offensive

---

7. *See* EEOC CHARGE STATISTICS FY 1997 THROUGH FY 2016, *available at* http://eeoc.gov/eeoc/statistics/enforcement/charges.cfm (last visited January 15, 2018).

behavior. The following is a partial list containing examples of inappropriate and unacceptable behavior:

- Unwanted sexual advances
- Offering employment benefits in exchange for sexual favors
- Making or threatening reprisals after a negative response to sexual advances
- Visual conduct, such as leering, making sexual gestures, or displaying sexually suggestive objects, pictures, cartoons, or posters
- Verbal conduct, such as making or using derogatory comments, epithets, slurs, sexually explicit jokes, or comments about any employee's body or dress
- Verbal sexual advances or propositions
- Verbal abuse of a sexual nature, graphic verbal commentary about an individual's body, sexually degrading words to describe an individual, or suggestive or obscene letters, notes, or invitations
- Physical conduct such as touching, assault, or impeding or blocking movements
- Harassment by electronic communication, including texts, sexting, email, blogs, and social media, such as Facebook, Instagram, Snapchat, or Twitter
- Retaliation for reporting harassment or threatening to report harassment

It is unlawful for males to sexually harass females or other males, and for females to sexually harass males or other females. Sexual harassment on the job is unlawful whether it involves co-worker harassment, harassment by a supervisor, or by persons doing business with or for [employer's name]. [Employer's name] prohibits sexual harassment in any area of its facilities and during meetings and business-related gatherings.

B. [Employer's name]'s Complaint Procedure

If you believe you have been harassed on the job, or if you are aware of the possible harassment of others, you should ask the harasser to stop the conduct or you should provide a written or verbal complaint as soon as possible to your supervisor, or to [name and position of two or three individuals, preferably both male and female in human resources or management]. Your complaint should be as detailed as possible, including the names of individuals involved, the names of any witnesses, direct quotations when language is relevant, and any documentary evidence (for example, notes, pictures, or cartoons). You may initiate your complaint in person or by telephone, voicemail, email, letter, or memorandum.

All incidents of prohibited harassment that are reported will be investigated promptly. The investigation will be completed and a determination regarding the reported harassment will be made and communicated to the employee who complained and to the accused harasser(s).

If [employer's name] determines that prohibited harassment has occurred, [employer's name] will take effective remedial action fitting to the events. Appropriate action will also be taken to deter any future harassment. If a complaint of prohibited harassment is substantiated, appropriate disciplinary action, up to and including discharge, will be taken. The employee who complained will be advised whether [employer's name] has substantiated the complaint and taken remedial measures. The employee who complained will not, however, be advised of the nature of any remedial measures taken.

C. Liability for Harassment

Any employee of [employer's name], whether a co-worker or supervisor, who is found to have engaged in prohibited harassment or retaliation is subject to disciplinary action, up to and including discharge from employment. [Employer's name] does not consider conduct in violation of this policy to be within the course and scope of employment or the direct consequence of the discharge of one's duties.

D. Retaliation Prohibited

[Employer's name] encourages all employees to report immediately any incidents of discrimination, harassment, or other unlawful conduct in the workplace so that complaints can be quickly and fairly resolved. [Employer's name] will not retaliate against any employee for making or filing a complaint, or for offering evidence, statements, or testimony in support of any complaint. In addition, [employer's name] will not knowingly tolerate or permit retaliation by supervisors, managers, employees, or co-workers.

All incidents of prohibited retaliation that are reported will be investigated. [Employer's name] will immediately undertake or direct an effective, thorough, and objective investigation of the retaliation allegations. The investigation will be completed and a determination regarding the reported retaliation will be made and communicated to the employee who complained and to the accused retaliator(s).

If [employer's name] determines that prohibited retaliation has occurred, [employer's name] will take effective remedial action commensurate with the circumstances. Appropriate action will also be taken to deter any future retaliation. If a complaint of prohibited retaliation is substantiated, appropriate disciplinary action, up to and including discharge, will be taken.

The employee who complained will be advised whether [employer's name] has substantiated the complaint and taken remedial measures. The employee who complained will not, however, be advised of the nature of any remedial measures taken.

For more information, contact any human resources manager with [employer's name].

III. INVESTIGATING ALLEGATIONS OF HARASSMENT

Investigations are also an important element in establishing the defense available under *Faragher*[8] and *Ellerth*.[9] The first prong of this defense is for the employer to establish that it took reasonable steps to prevent and stop harassment. "The most significant

---

8. *Faragher*, 524 U.S. 775 (1998).

9. *Ellerth*, 524 U.S. 742 (1998).

immediate measure an employer can take in response to a complaint of harassment is to launch a prompt investigation to determine whether the complaint is justified. An investigation is a key step in the employer's response and can itself be a powerful factor in deterring future harassment."[10]

In addition, federal law and the laws of several states and units of local government require the employer to investigate all complaints of sexual harassment or other prohibited harassment in the workplace.[11] The duty to investigate arises from the employer's obligation to exercise reasonable care to prevent and correct promptly unlawful harassment.[12] Thus, an employer's duty to investigate arises even when the complaining party expressly states that she or he does not want the allegations investigated. In addition, the employer should not wait for a complaint. The obligation to investigate will arise whenever the employer observes acts or statements that suggest prohibited activity.

The investigation results and the information obtained and considered by the employer may be admissible evidence in subsequent litigation. If the employer is relying on the investigation to establish its affirmative defense, the plaintiff may be entitled to discovery regarding the investigation. Therefore, both plaintiffs and defendants have an interest in the scope and fairness of the investigation.

A step-by-step approach will enhance the likelihood that the employer's determination will be based upon all the evidence. It will also provide all interested parties with the ability to present their perspectives. The following steps will enhance the employer's ability to plan and carry out an effective, impartial investigation: (1) select the appropriate investigator(s), (2) review and analyze the available documents and other tangible evidence, (3) conduct interviews, (4) synthesize information and reach conclusions, (5) document results, and (6) determine what, if any, action is necessary or appropriate.

Before beginning the investigation, the employer should consider whether any steps are necessary to prevent additional incidents during the course of the investigation. Employers may place the complaining party on administrative leave with pay, pending the outcome of the investigation. Another means of ameliorating potential harm is to separate the accused and accuser by relocating the alleged harasser. The employer must carefully avoid any action that could be viewed as retaliatory toward the complaining party.

A. Selecting the Investigative Team

Selecting the appropriate investigator or investigative team is key to an effective, appropriate investigation. No one person will be effective in all types of investigations. The investigator's background and training should be appropriate to the issues presented by the complaint. Other factors that should be considered in selecting an investigator

---

10. Swenson v. Potter, 271 F.3d 1184, 1193 (9th Cir. 2000).

11. *See* EEOC, Policy Guidance on Current Issues on Sexual Harassment (Mar. 19, 1990), *available at* http://www.eeoc.gov/policy/docs/currentissues.html (last visited January 15, 2018).

12. *See* Farley v. Am. Cast Iron Pipe Co., 115 F.3d 1548, 1553–54 (11th Cir. 1997).

are the relative authority of the person bringing the complaint and the person against whom the complaint is brought; the sex of the complaining party; the potential impact of the alleged acts on the business; potential public relations issues; the person's ability to get the witnesses to provide complete and accurate responses; and perceptions of bias. Investigators can come from within the employer organization, such as a human resources representative, a member of management, or in-house legal department. Outside legal counsel or consultants may be very effective in conducting investigations, particularly when the alleged wrongdoer or witnesses are members of senior management.[13]

1. Investigator's Training and Qualifications

The investigator's understanding of sexual harassment law and prevention techniques is fundamental to conducting an effective investigation of sexual harassment complaints. In addition, the investigator must have outstanding interview skills, including active listening and the ability to help witnesses focus. The investigator should also have empathy, patience, and persistence.

In addition to gathering the information, the investigator will need to prepare recommendations and be able to support them. To analyze effectively the information gathered and report on it, the investigator must have good perception and the ability to think critically.

Credibility is also a significant characteristic of a good investigator. The person should be neutral, fair, thorough, and objective. Finally, the investigator should be familiar with the employer's policies, procedures, history, and culture.

---

13. An April 1999 opinion letter from the Federal Trade Commission (FTC) concluded that an outside consultant or lawyer's investigation of sexual harassment allegations constitutes a "consumer report" under the Fair Credit Reporting Act (FCRA), 15 U.S.C. §§ 1681–81x (1970). The FCRA does not apply to investigations that an employer conducts itself through its own personnel. However, if a law firm or other outside consultant conducts a workplace investigation, it must comply with the FCRA's requirements. The employer or the investigator is required to (1) give the employee notice of the investigation; (2) obtain the employee's consent to the investigation; and (3) give the employee a copy of the investigation report if the employer intends to use the report to make an adverse employment decision about the employee.

In an August 1999 opinion letter, the FTC clarified its earlier opinion and offered suggestions on how employers could comply with the FCRA when using outside firms to investigate harassment claims. According to the FTC, the FCRA does not apply if the employer uses a third party that does not "regularly engage" in preparing investigative reports and thus does not fall under the FCRA definition of "consumer reporting agency."

The FTC also offered several suggestions for complying with the FCRA's requirements if outside investigation agencies are used. First, the FTC opined that an employer can routinely obtain an employee's consent "at the start of employment, thereby relieving the employer of the awkward prospect of having to ask a suspected wrongdoer for permission to allow a third party to provide an investigative (or other) consumer report to the employer." The FTC also suggested that an employer can comply with the FCRA requirements without alerting a suspected wrongdoer by asking "all current employees to sign a consent form, and provide them any required notice, at the same time." Finally, the FTC noted that an investigative agency may minimize the risks associated with disclosing the report to the individual under investigation "by not naming parties that provide negative information regarding the employee."

Even when a single person has all the qualities needed to complete the investigation, it may be helpful to include a second investigator. The second person can corroborate information gathered during the investigation. A second person familiar with the allegations and evidence will be useful in determining whether all evidence has been considered and all witnesses have been interviewed. In addition, a team member can "test" the conclusions to be sure that the results are fair and based upon objective evidence. It is often a good strategy to have the second person act strictly as a note taker during the interviews.

2. Use of Outside Consultants as Investigators

Some employers rely on professional investigators to conduct investigations. Bringing in an outsider may enhance the appearance of neutrality, particularly when the alleged harasser is a member of senior management. However, professionals are costly and may be difficult to locate and retain when the employer needs to conduct a prompt investigation. Moreover, although a consultant may have particular information about the subject of the investigation, as well as the skills necessary to conduct an appropriate investigation, he or she will not be familiar with the employer, the corporate culture, and the parties' relationships.

3. Use of Lawyers as Investigators

Lawyers are often selected as investigators because the employer anticipates that it may want to protect the investigation results. In evaluating whether a lawyer is necessary or appropriate, the employer should be aware that the attorney-client privilege may not apply if the lawyer's report contains primarily business-related advice, rather than legal advice.[14]

To avoid the risk of being unable to represent the employer in any subsequent litigation, the employer's regular employment counsel should not conduct an investigation. A lawyer with a long-standing relationship with the corporate employer may be perceived as lacking the necessary impartiality, particularly if the alleged harasser is a member of management or human resources. In addition, before agreeing to undertake an investigation, lawyers should consider the potential risk to the client relationship, either as the result of litigation attacking the investigation results or the client failing to follow the lawyer investigator's recommendation.

Frequently, the ability to claim privilege for a workplace investigation provides only a limited benefit. If the employer asserts that it conducted an adequate investigation, the attorney-client privilege will probably be waived.[15] Summaries that reflect the attorney's opinion may be protected under the attorney work-product doctrine.[16] Before asserting

---

14. *See* W. Freedman, Internal Company Investigations and the Employment Relationship 85 (Quorum Books 1994). *But see* United States v. Adlman, 134 F.3d 1194 (2d Cir. 1998) (holding that privilege applies to business-related advice).

15. *See* Harding v. Dana Transp., Inc., 914 F. Supp. 1084, 1096 (D.N.J. 1996).

16. Brownell v. Roadway Package Sys., Inc., 185 F.R.D. 19, 26 (N.D.N.Y. 1999).

any privilege, the employer should determine whether the investigation is an essential part of the employer's proof of its affirmative defense.

B. Identifying, Gathering, and Preserving Evidence

Tangible evidence must be identified, located, and preserved appropriately. In many cases, documents are the primary form of evidence. Electronically stored data is becoming increasingly important. For example, sexual harassment investigators will want to review email messages between the complaining party and the alleged harasser. Other nondocumentary evidence that should be considered may include voicemail messages, telephone use records, records of access to the workplace, computer use records, photographs, and security videotapes. Attendance records and time cards should be reviewed to verify claims that certain individuals were present during alleged events or conversations.

The originals of all relevant, or potentially relevant, evidence should be maintained in a secure location. When the interviewer uses documents or other evidence during investigations, it is best to present only a copy. If the employer has nondocumentary evidence, it is a good idea to print out, transcribe, or otherwise convert the evidence to documentary form to enable the investigator to review it easily and to have an alternate means of recording the information. Given the pace of technological development, stored electronic data may not be easily accessible after relatively short periods of time. Examples of perishable evidence include surveillance-camera tapes that are recorded over and production records that are routinely destroyed.

Before beginning the interviews, tangible evidence should be gathered to the greatest extent possible. The evidence can provide valuable guidance in framing the investigation. It may also be useful for refreshing a witness's memory. The investigator should not assume that all evidence has been gathered before beginning interviews and should continue to seek out relevant documents and other tangible evidence throughout the investigation.

C. Interviewing Witnesses

1. Preliminary Considerations

Interviews should be conducted in a quiet, private room. At the outset of the interview, the investigator should explain the company's policy prohibiting the conduct. In addition, the investigator should explain that the company encourages employees to come forward with complaints to help the company provide a workplace free of unlawful harassment and discrimination. Before beginning the interview the investigator should stress the need for the witness to be candid and to provide complete, accurate responses. The interviewer should also explain that the employer has a policy prohibiting retaliation against any employee who brings a complaint or participates in an investigation. This explanation can be emphasized by instructing the witness about the company's complaint procedures if the witness believes retaliation has occurred because of participation in the investigation.

The interviewer should explain the purpose of the investigation in general terms, taking care not to divulge significant details. Undue disclosure will undermine the neutrality of the investigation by suggesting the responses. In addition, needless disclosure of the charges could subject the employer and the investigator to liability for defamation or invasion of privacy. Other information that the investigator should provide before asking questions includes an explanation that the company has an obligation to investigate the allegations, confirmation that the interview is only one step in the investigation, and assurances that the company will not make a determination until all relevant evidence has been gathered and all witnesses interviewed. An explanation of the investigation procedure is also helpful, particularly when meeting with the complaining party or the alleged harasser.

2. Order of Interviews

Generally, the complaining party should be interviewed first, followed by the witnesses identified by the complaining party or in the documentary evidence. Once the interviewer has a complete understanding of the allegations, the alleged harasser can be interviewed. The alleged harasser may also identify witnesses who should be interviewed. The investigator should ask each witness whether he or she is aware of anyone else who may have information.

After completing the initial round of interviews, in most cases, the investigator should re-interview the complaining party to obtain his or her reaction to the evidence gathered thus far and the alleged harasser's perceptions. The re-interview may also help explain apparent inconsistencies between the complaining party's story and the versions presented by other witnesses. At this point, the interviewer should use the additional knowledge gained while interviewing other witnesses to probe the complaining party's recollection and evaluate the complaint for consistency. The complaining party's recitation of events made during the follow-up interview should be compared to the complaining party's original description and examined in light of the information provided by witnesses.

A final interview with the alleged harasser should close out the information-gathering phase of the investigation. During this final meeting, the alleged harasser should be fully apprised of the charges and given an opportunity to explain. The alleged harasser should be provided a reasonable opportunity to present a defense to the charges. As with the complaining party, the alleged harasser's repeated description of events should be compared with the original description and evaluated for consistency with the descriptions provided by witnesses.

3. Maintaining Impartiality

The interviewer must remain impartial until all the facts are gathered. Maintaining the appearance of neutrality is just as important as actual impartiality. Questions asked during interviews should not be accusatory or conclusory. The investigator must understand that the complaining party and the alleged harasser have a right to a prompt, thorough, and impartial investigation.

4. Confidentiality

The investigator should refrain from unnecessary disclosure of information gained during the investigation. However, each witness should be advised that the information is not confidential. The interviewer may have to disclose statements made by the complaining party to question other witnesses or to advise the alleged harasser of the charges. In addition, the final report may reveal specific information gained during the interview process.

The interviewer should determine whether it is appropriate to caution each witness not to discuss the interview with anyone else. The EEOC has long recommended that the investigator take steps to assure that the employer will protect the confidentiality of harassment complaints to the extent possible.[17] Gossip between witnesses can impair the integrity of the investigation, making it very difficult to evaluate credibility and reach a fair conclusion.

However, Section 7 of the National Labor Relations Act guarantees employees have a right to engage in "concerted activities for the purpose of collective bargaining or other mutual aid or protection."[18] "[T]he Act 'protects employees' rights to discuss organization and the terms and conditions of their employment, to criticize or complain about their employer or their conditions of employment, and to enlist the assistance of others in addressing employment matters.' Under 'settled Board precedent,' the right to discuss the terms and conditions of employment encompasses the 'right to discuss discipline or disciplinary investigations with fellow employees.[19]'"

According to the National Labor Relations Board (NLRB), employers may tell employees not to discuss an ongoing investigation only when the employer has a "legitimate and substantial business justification" for requesting confidentiality that outweighs the employees' Section 7 rights. In any dispute regarding whether a confidentiality instruction was appropriate, the employer will be required to demonstrate objectively reasonable grounds for believing that confidentiality is necessary. A general concern regarding threats to the integrity of an investigation will not be sufficient. However, other factors may be, including: need to protect witnesses; danger that evidence will be destroyed; danger that testimony will be fabricated; or there is a need to prevent a cover-up.[20] Before giving a confidentiality instruction, the investigator and employer should balance the need for confidentiality and limit the witnesses' ability to discuss the matter only when there is an objective reason for doing so.

5. Noncooperation

Any individual who refuses to cooperate with the investigation should be informed that the investigation will proceed with or without that individual's participation. The complaining party or the alleged harasser should also be informed that the interview

---

17. *See* Best Practices for Employers and Human Resources/EEO Professionals, https://www.eeoc.gov/eeoc/initiatives/e-race/bestpractices-employers.cfm (last visited January 15, 2018).

18. 29 U.S.C. § 157 (1947).

19. Banner Health System v. National Labor Relations Board, 851 F.3d 35, 40 (D.C. Cir. 2017).

20. *Banner Health System*, 362 NLRB No. 137 (June 26, 2015).

is the opportunity to tell his or her side of the story and to refute any allegations that have been made. The individual's refusal to participate will be noted in the investigation report and conclusions may be made based on that individual's noncooperation. The investigator should also state that a decision will be made based on all available evidence and appropriate action will be taken.

6. Questioning Style

A written list of questions the investigator plans to ask should be prepared in advance for each witness to ensure that each interview is complete. In the information gathering stage of the interview, the investigator should ask open-ended, nonleading questions. Use of active listening skills, such as repeating or rephrasing the witness's answer in the next question, will help ensure that the interviewer correctly understands the witness.

The interviewer should keep the discussion focused, rather than permitting witnesses to discuss all problems they have observed. This requires persistent pursuit of specific, accurate, and complete information.

If the witness appears uncomfortable with a particular question or line of questioning, the investigator may wish to return to it later in the interview. Often, the second series of questions will elicit new information or additional detail. The investigator should be attuned to hints or contradictions by the witness and ask follow-up questions.

7. Sample Interview Questions for the Complaining Party

The following outline is skeletal, not exhaustive. It should be tailored to fit the particular facts and needs of the situation. Tangible evidence can be beneficial in framing interview questions.

1. Who are you complaining about?
2. Does that individual supervise you or have any control over your work?
3. Did you experience inappropriate conduct more than once?
4. For each incident of inappropriate conduct:
   - What specific acts or statements are the basis of this incident?
   - When did the incident take place?
   - Where did the incident take place?
   - What happened just before the incident?
   - How did you react?
   - How did the incident end?
   - How did you feel about the incident?
   - Do you have any tangible evidence related to the incident?
   - Were there any witnesses to the incident? If so, who?
   - Did you tell anyone about the incident when it occurred? If so, who?
5. Do you know whether anyone else has observed similar incidents? If so, who?
6. Do you know of any motive for the alleged acts?
7. How do you feel about the situation now?
8. What action would you like to see taken? (Be careful not to say anything that could be perceived as a promise that any particular action will be taken.)

9. Why did you not complain about the incident when it happened or soon after it happened? (This is a question to ask if there was any delay in bringing the complaint.)

8. Sample Interview Questions for Witnesses
   1. Have you observed any inappropriate sex-based behavior in the workplace?
   2. Have you observed any conflicts between the complaining party and the alleged harasser?
   3. If so, for each incident, provide specific details:
      - What happened?
      - When did the incident take place?
      - Where did the incident take place?
      - Who were the participants?
      - What was said during the incident?
      - Did the complaining party react to the incident? If so, what was said or done?
      - Did anyone else say or do anything during the incident?
      - Do you have any tangible evidence related to the incident?
      - Were there any witnesses to the incident? If so, who?
      - Did you tell anyone about the incident?
   4. Do you know whether anyone else has observed similar incidents? If so, who?
   5. Do you know of any motive for the alleged acts?

9. Sample Interview Questions for the Alleged Harasser
   1. Were you in the vicinity of the incident on the date of the alleged harassment?
   2. Did you observe any inappropriate behavior?
   3. If so, what did you see?
   4. Did you participate in the alleged events?
   5. If so, what was your role?
   6. Was anyone else present?
   7. What is your working relationship with the complaining party?
   8. Are the allegations described by the complaining party true? (For each incident described by the complaining party, advise the accused of the specific allegations.)
   9. If the accused denies the incident, ask:
      - Do you recall where you were or what you were doing at the time of the alleged incident?
      - Were there any witnesses to your activities?
      - Is there any tangible evidence that would support your statement?
      - Do you know of any reason that someone might want to accuse you of these acts?
   10. If the accused admits the incident, or part of the incident, ask:
       - What happened?
       - When did the incident take place?
       - Where did the incident take place?

- Who were the participants?
- What was said during the incident?
- Did the complaining party react to the incident? If so, what was said or done?
- Did anyone else say or do anything during the incident?
- Do you have any tangible evidence related to the incident?
- Were there any witnesses to the incident? If so, who?
- Did you tell anyone about the incident?

11. Have you previously been accused of discrimination or harassment? If so, was any investigation conducted? What were the findings?
12. Have you ever been counseled or disciplined for discrimination, harassment, or related acts?

10. Witness Statements

At the conclusion of the interview, the investigator should prepare a written statement to be signed by the witness. A statement should also be taken from the alleged harasser. The investigator should ask each witness to review the statement, make any necessary corrections, add any additional facts that would be relevant, and sign the statement. Many investigators ask the witness to make handwritten corrections on the face of the statement to demonstrate that the statement was in fact reviewed by the witness.

D. Documentation and Decision-Making

Once all of the evidence has been gathered, the employer should begin the process of sifting and evaluating evidence. It will usually be necessary to assess the witnesses' credibility. In making this assessment, the investigator should examine the details of the statements provided.

- Were the witnesses' statements internally consistent?
- Were the statements consistent with the observations provided by others?
- Were the statements consistent with the tangible evidence?

The investigator should also consider whether the witness had any reason to be less than truthful. The witness's nonverbal communications, such as unwillingness to maintain eye contact or sitting with tightly crossed arms during the interview, may also provide insight to credibility. However, unless the investigator knows the witness, nonverbal cues may merely be the witness's normal appearance or indicators of discomfort with the situation. Thus, they should not be given undue importance.

Typically, the investigator will wish to prepare a written report detailing the findings and recommendations of the investigation. Although the written report may be used to cross-examine the investigator in any subsequent litigation, it will also be extremely useful in refreshing the investigator's recollection of the investigation and conclusions. The investigator must take care to provide adequate objective evidentiary support for each conclusion contained in the written report. Having a draft of the report reviewed by counsel or a human resources professional who did not participate in the investigation can help ensure that the report is objective and neutral and that it contains adequate evidentiary support.

If the investigation concludes that the complaint has merit, the employer must then decide what discipline is appropriate. Factors contributing to this determination may include the nature of the offense, the severity of the offense, whether the employee has engaged in prior inappropriate conduct, and whether there are any mitigating factors, issues of credibility, or public and employee relations' issues.

E. Communicating Investigation Results

In general, the employer should disseminate the investigation results only to those with a "need to know." The nature of the allegations and the number of people who participated in the investigation will help identify those people with a need to know. Because the employer has a duty to prevent harassment, the employer may have a legitimate business reason for disclosing the investigation results to a broader group, such as the entire work unit.

Although the specific discipline imposed should not be disclosed, the employer should advise the complaining party, and perhaps the work unit, that the employer has taken steps to prevent any recurrence of the offending behavior. Disclosure of the investigation results provides an excellent opportunity to reinforce the employer's anti-harassment and antidiscrimination policies. Care should be taken to avoid defamation or emotional distress torts.

F. Potential Liability Issues

When a complaint is made, the employer may be exposed to liability for its actions or its inactions. The employer has a duty to investigate sexual harassment complaints and to take prompt and effective remedial action if the complaint has merit. The employer also owes certain duties to the witnesses and the alleged harasser. The following discussion highlights some of the more typical employer liability issues arising from or relating to investigations.

1. Invasion of Privacy

Many state constitutions provide public employees or all citizens with privacy protections. In addition, some state constitutions apply to government and private sector employees.[21]

a. Searches and Seizures

Employees who have been subjected to investigations or searches have recovered for invasion of privacy under both constitutional and common law theories of invasion of privacy. The Fourth Amendment to the US Constitution prohibits unreasonable

---

21. *See, e.g.*, Hill v. NCAA, 865 P.2d 633 (Cal. 1994); Ill. Const. art. 1, § 6 (provides right to privacy for all Illinois citizens).

searches and seizures only when they are undertaken by government agencies or officials or under color of law.[22] Thus, employer searches do not violate the Fourth Amendment unless the employer is a public entity or acts in concert with the police or other government representatives.

i. Desks, Offices, and Lockers

Courts have sustained tort claims against private employers for conducting searches. For instance, a court in Texas awarded an employee damages when an employer searched her purse that was in the locker assigned to her.[23]

Employee search cases essentially balance two issues: (1) the reasonableness of the employee's expectation of privacy in the area searched and (2) the reasonableness of the search, including the employer's legitimate reason for the search. Courts recognize that employees may have a reasonable expectation of privacy in their lockers and desks. However, office policies, practices, and procedures can limit the employee's expectation of privacy. In *O'Connor v. Ortega*,[24] a case arising under the Fourth Amendment, the US Supreme Court held that a doctor had a reasonable expectation of privacy in his office because he had occupied his office for seventeen years, he did not share his desk, and the hospital had no policy notifying employees not to put personal papers in their desks. The Court stated that the expectation of privacy could be diminished by "actual office practices and procedures, or by legitimate regulation."[25]

In *Chicago Fire Fighters Local 2 v. City of Chicago*, the court said that unannounced locker searches by the fire department did not invade firefighters' privacy because they had constructive knowledge of department regulations, which provided for locker searches to enforce rules against drug and alcohol possession.[26] Similarly, in *Johnson v. C & L, Inc.*,[27] the court dismissed an employee's claim for invasion of privacy based on the employer's inspection of her desk because the employee did not have a reasonable expectation of privacy in an office desk owned by the employer and under the employer's control. Many employers distribute policies stating that desks, lockers, and computers are company property subject to search at any time. The policy can be reinforced by prohibiting locks except for those issued by the employer.

ii. Electronic Mail

The primary statute governing retrieval of electronic mail is the federal Electronic Communications Privacy Act of 1986 (ECPA), an amendment to Title III of the Omnibus Crime Control and Safe Streets Act of 1968.[28] The ECPA prohibits unauthorized

---

22. Burdeau v. McDowell, 256 U.S. 465, 475 (1921).

23. K-Mart Corp. v. Trotti, 677 S.W.2d 632 (Tex. Ct. App. 1984), *writ refused*, 686 S.W.2d 593 (1985).

24. O'Connor v. Ortega, 480 U.S. 709 (1987).

25. *Id.* at 717 (1987).

26. Chicago Fire Fighters Local 2 v. Chicago, 717 F. Supp. 1314 (N.D. Ill. 1989).

27. Johnson v. C & L, Inc., 1996 WL 308282, No. 95C6381 (N.D. Ill. June 6, 1996).

28. 18 U.S.C. §§ 2510–22 (2008).

interception, retrieval, or dissemination of email.[29] In the case of email interceptions, employers have three exemptions to justify their monitoring.

First, email communications can be intercepted when one party consents.[30] This consent can be express or implied.[31]

Second, the "business extension" or "ordinary course of business" exemption also applies to email interception. This exemption permits interception only of business-content communications. Because employers review personal email messages for reasons other than to determine whether the message is business or personal, this exemption would probably not provide protection.

Third, the statute authorizes the provider of the communications service to monitor communications in the normal course of business and while engaged in any activity that is necessary to render the service or protect the service provider's rights or property.[32] In addition, service providers have a broad exemption permitting essentially unlimited access to stored communications.[33] Under the provider exemption, an employer is free to review communications sent and stored on its own system.[34] Email messages sent through an outside service provider, however, would not necessarily fall within this exemption. Employers should notify employees that the email system is company property and can be monitored by the employer at any time. Many employers limit computer use to business purposes and prohibit private communications. This policy forecloses an expectation of privacy.

iii. Telephonic Communications and Voicemail

Employers monitor employee telephone calls to evaluate the quality of service, to determine whether the employee is making inappropriate use of the telephone through excessive personal phone calls or dissemination of proprietary information, and to determine whether the employee is involved in criminal activity.

Various state courts have found that surreptitious tape recording by one party to a conversation is sufficient to state a claim for common law invasion of privacy.[35] A specific and communicated office practice of monitoring employee telephone calls may diminish an employee's reasonable expectation of privacy.[36] However, even when the employer adopts and publicizes a policy of monitoring certain telephone calls, any

---

29. 18 U.S.C. § 2511 (2008) (interception during transmission); 18 U.S.C. § 2701 (2002) (access to stored electronic communications).

30. 18 U.S.C. § 2511(2)(d) (2011) (consent to interception); 18 U.S.C. § 2702(b)(3) (2015) (consent to access to stored communications).

31. *See, e.g.*, Griggs-Ryan v. Smith, 904 F.2d 112, 116 (1st Cir. 1991).

32. 18 U.S.C. § 2511(2) (2011).

33. 18 U.S.C. § 2701(c)(1) (2015).

34. Fraser v. Nationwide Mut. Ins. Co., 352 F.3d 107, 114–15 (3d Cir. 2003); Bohach v. Reno, 932 F. Supp. 1232 (D. Nev. 1996).

35. *See, e.g.*, Sistok v. Nw. Tel. Sys., Inc., 615 P.2d 176, 182 (Mont. 1980), and cases cited therein.

36. United States v. McIntyre, 582 F.2d 1221, 1224 (9th Cir. 1978).

monitoring should be carefully limited to those communications specified under the policy.

The ECPA, which governs telephone monitoring, prohibits unauthorized interception or retrieval of any wire, oral, or electronic communication. It also prohibits disclosure and use of information obtained from an unauthorized interception.[37] Interception or disclosure of electronic communications can constitute a criminal offense punishable by fine, imprisonment, or both.[38] It can also result in civil liability, including both actual and punitive damages.[39]

Employers often rely upon two exemptions to the ECPA in monitoring employees: the employees' consent and the "business extension" or "ordinary course of business" exemptions. Interception of a telephone call does not violate the ECPA when one party consents, as long as the interception is not for the purpose of committing a criminal or tortious act.[40] Consent may be express or implied. "[C]onsent inheres where a person's behavior manifests acquiescence or a comparable voluntary diminution of his or her otherwise protected rights."[41] The business extension exclusion to the ECPA exempts interceptions made by telephone equipment "furnished to the subscriber or user by [a communications carrier] in the ordinary course of its business and being used by the subscriber or user in the ordinary course of its business."[42] This exception requires that the employer (1) use equipment provided by the communications carrier, and (2) conduct the monitoring as part of its ordinary course of business.

iv. Surveillance Cameras and Videotape

Closed-circuit cameras may provide helpful evidence in a workplace investigation. Even hidden cameras do not invade the employees' privacy when the employer's purpose is lawful and the camera is located in a nonprivate area, where there is a diminished expectation of privacy.[43] However, when a camera is located in an area where the employee has a right to expect privacy, such as a bathroom or dressing room, the employee can state a claim for invasion of privacy even if he or she was not viewed performing a private act.[44] The NLRB has held that the use of hidden cameras in the workplace is a mandatory issue of bargaining.[45]

---

37. 18 U.S.C. § 2511 (2011).

38. 18 U.S.C. § 2511(4) (2011).

39. 18 U.S.C. § 2520 (2002).

40. 18 U.S.C. § 2511(2)(d) (2011).

41. Griggs-Ryan v. Smith, 904 F.2d 112, 116 (1st Cir. 1991).

42. 18 U.S.C. § 2510(5) (2010).

43. Sacramento County Deputy Sheriffs Ass'n v. County of Sacramento, 51 Cal. App. 4th 1468, 1487, 59 Cal. Rptr. 2d 834, 846–47 (1997).

44. Doe v. B.P.S. Guard Servs., Inc., 945 F.2d 1422, 1427 (8th Cir. 1991).

45. Colgate-Palmolive Co. & Local 15, Int'l Chem. Workers Union AFL-CIO, 323 NLRB 515, 155 L.R.R.M. (BNA) 1034 (1997).

v. Medical Condition

Employees may have a right of privacy regarding their medical condition. Although this right can be waived, an employer who exceeds the scope of an authorization or who uses medical information in a manner other than permitted by the authorization may be liable for invasion of privacy.[46]

vi. Medical Records

In some situations, employees have a right of privacy in connection with their medical condition and medical records. For example, the Health Insurance Portability and Accountability Act (HIPAA) privacy rules regulate the use and disclosure of any information about health status, provision of health care, or payment for health care that can be linked to an individual. Employers who are self-insured for group medical coverage or who administer benefits internally may be covered under the HIPAA privacy rules.[47]

vii. Drug and Alcohol Testing

Privacy rights may also be implicated by drug and alcohol testing. Under the Fourth Amendment, government employees have a reasonable expectation of privacy in both the act of urination and the information contained in the sample. However, in evaluating the use of a drug test, courts balance the employee's right of privacy against the government's interest in conducting the search. Testing has been accepted when employees are in safety-sensitive positions or in industries that are heavily regulated due to safety concerns.[48] A similar balancing analysis is used under state constitutions, which may provide protections for both private and public sector employees.[49]

b. Confidentiality

In some states, an employee might sue for invasion of privacy if the investigator publicizes certain information about an individual's private affairs that would be highly offensive to a reasonable person and not of legitimate concern to the public. In *Miller v. Motorola*,[50] the plaintiff, a 23-year employee, consulted with the company nurse about obtaining a leave of absence to have a mastectomy. She was told that her consultations would be confidential. Plaintiff returned to work and learned that her co-workers knew of her surgery. She filed a lawsuit claiming she suffered emotional distress for "public

---

46. *See* Fletcher v. Price Chopper Foods of Trumann, Inc., 220 F.3d 871 (8th Cir. 2000).

47. 45 C.F.R. §§ 164.500–34 (2000).

48. *See, e.g.,* Nat'l Treasury Employees Union v. Von Raab, 489 U.S. 656 (1989); Skinner v. Ry. Labor Execs. Ass'n, 489 U.S. 602 (1989).

49. *See, e.g.,* Loder v. Glendale, 927 P.2d 1200 (Cal. 1997) (upholding pre-employment testing of all applicants for city jobs under both federal and state constitutions and rejecting pre-promotional testing for current city employees on the basis of the employer's lowered interest in testing a current employee), *cert. denied*, 522 U.S. 807 (1997); *see also* Congreso de Uniones Industriales v. Bacardi Corp., 961 F. Supp. 338 (D.P.R. 1997) (upholding a reasonable suspicion-based drug and alcohol testing policy); Hennessey v. Coastal Eagle Point Oil Co., 609 A.2d 11 (N.J. 1992) (mandatory random drug testing may be an invasion of privacy).

50. Miller v. Motorola, 560 N.E.2d 900 (Ill. App. 1990).

disclosure of private facts." A motion to dismiss the suit was denied, thereby recognizing this privacy tort.

2. Defamation

Defamation is another claim often raised by employees who are the subject of workplace investigations. To establish defamation, the employee must demonstrate that the employer made a false, unprivileged statement that injured the employee.[51] The employer may be protected by a qualified privilege if it made the statement without malice, if it held a good faith belief that the statement was true, if the statement was made for a legitimate business purpose, and if the statement was published only to those individuals who had a need to know. This qualified privilege should protect statements made by the investigators if the employer has a good faith belief that an employee has engaged in inappropriate behavior and limits disclosure to those persons who are potential witnesses or in the employee's chain of command. The privilege is lost if the investigation is tainted by malice.[52]

3. Intentional Infliction of Emotional Distress

Employees may seek to recover for inappropriate investigations under a theory of intentional infliction of emotional distress. The elements of intentional infliction generally include reckless or intentional conduct by the defendant that was intended to and did cause the plaintiff to suffer severe emotional distress. The defendant's conduct must be so extreme or outrageous as to arouse resentment in the average member of the community and lead him to exclaim, "Outrageous!"[53]

4. False Arrest or Imprisonment

Inappropriate tactics during a workplace search or investigation may expose employers to claims for false arrest or imprisonment. In one case, an employee was "grabbed" and searched by a guard after being observed with his pockets bulging leaving an area where theft was a major problem. The employee had no company property in his possession and he successfully sued the company for slander, assault, false imprisonment, and punitive damages.[54] In another case, the court concluded that an employee had stated a claim for false imprisonment when, during the course of investigating employee theft, the employee was taken into a windowless interrogation room, where managers and security agents accused her of stealing, threatened to have her arrested and charged with a crime unless she confessed, and falsely stated that witnesses to the incident were waiting in the next room.[55]

---

51. W. PROSSER & W. KEETON, PROSSER AND KEETON ON THE LAW OF TORTS 773–78 (5th ed. 1984).

52. Gibson v. Philip Morris, Inc., 685 N.E.2d 638 (Ill. Ct. App. 1997).

53. RESTATEMENT (SECOND) OF TORTS § 46 & cmt. d (1965).

54. Gen. Motors Corp. v. Piskor, 340 A.2d 767 (Md. Ct. Spec. App. 1975), *aff'd in part and rev'd in part*, 352 A.2d 810 (Ct. App. 1976), *overruled as to standard for punitive damages in* Le Marc's Mgmt. Co. v. Valentin, 709 A.2d 1222, 1225–26 (Ct. App. Md. 1998).

55. Fermino v. Fedco, Inc., 872 P.2d 559 (Cal. 1994).

Simply requiring the employee to sit for an interview upon pain of losing her job is not false imprisonment and is a normal part of the employment relationship. However, "when an employer forcibly and criminally deprives an employee of her liberty, even as a means to otherwise legitimate ends, it steps outside its 'proper role,' whether it uses assault and battery to enforce that false imprisonment, or employs some other coercive stratagem."[56]

5. Assault and Battery

Be aware that employees may use allegations of assault and battery to counteract the results of an investigation. An assault may occur if the interviewer creates a reasonable fear in the employee that the investigator is going to touch the employee in a harmful or offensive way. No actual touching is necessary for an assault. A battery is an intentional harmful or offensive touching. If the interviewer intentionally touches the employee or any part of the employee's person (such as a purse), a battery may have occurred. There need not be any actual physical harm to the employee. Battery claims are often associated with drug and alcohol testing.

6. Improper Use of Polygraphs

The Employee Polygraph Protection Act of 1988 (EPPA)[57] regulates the use of mechanical or electrical polygraph tests. Under the EPPA, an employer may not discipline, discharge, or discriminate against any employee or applicant (1) for refusing to take a polygraph test, (2) based on the results of a polygraph test, or (3) for taking any actions to preserve employee rights under the EPPA. However, one exception to the EPPA authorizes an employer to test employees who are suspects of an "ongoing investigation." This exception is available only in carefully circumscribed situations:

1. The employer is engaged in an ongoing investigation involving economic loss or injury to its business.
2. The suspected employee had access to the property at issue.
3. The employer has a reasonable suspicion that the employee was involved in the incident.
4. Before the test, the employer must give the employee a statement that thoroughly explains the incident or activity that triggered the investigation and the basis for testing the employee.
5. The employer must retain a copy of all such statements for a minimum of three years.

Various state statutes also regulate or prohibit polygraph testing. For example, California prohibits employers from compelling applicants or employees to take a polygraph

---

56. *Id.* at 571 (Cal. 1994).

57. 29 U.S.C. §§ 2001–09 (1988).

test as a condition of employment or continued employment.[58] Before electing to use a polygraph as part of a workplace investigation, the employer should consult with counsel to determine whether, and under what circumstances, a polygraph test is appropriate.

7. Adequacy of Investigations

To date, few judicial decisions discuss the scope or adequacy of a sexual harassment investigation. The articulated concerns, however, appear to be fairness, notice to the accused employee, and an opportunity to respond.

In a case dealing with free speech rights of public employees, the US Supreme Court described the standards by which an employer's investigation will be judged, stating:

> We think employer decision making will not be unduly burdened by having courts look to the facts as the employer reasonably found them to be. It may be unreasonable, for example, for the employer to come to a conclusion based on no evidence at all. Likewise, it may be unreasonable for an employer to act based on extremely weak evidence when strong evidence is clearly available—if, for instance, an employee is accused of writing an improper letter to the editor, and instead of just reading the letter, the employer decides what it said based on unreliable hearsay.
>
> If an employment action is based on what an employee supposedly said, and a reasonable supervisor would recognize that there is a substantial likelihood that what was actually said was protected, the manager must tread with a certain amount of care. This need not be the care with which trials, with their rules of evidence and procedure, are conducted. It should, however, be the care that a reasonable manager would use before making an employment decision—discharge, suspension, reprimand, or whatever else—of the sort involved in the particular case.[59]

In a significant decision regarding the need for adequate investigations, *Cotran v. Rollins Hudig Hall International*, the California Supreme Court declined to provide specific investigative standards, but stated that, at minimum, an investigation must include "notice of the claimed misconduct and a chance for the employee to respond."[60] Similar standards were articulated in *Baldwin v. Sisters of Providence* in Washington.[61]

In *Cotran*, the court concluded that the employer's investigation of a sexual harassment charge was adequate. In that case, the employer had received complaints of sexual harassment. The employer interviewed the charging parties, then advised the alleged harasser of the allegations and explained that an investigation would be made. During

---

58. Cal. Lab. Code § 432.2 (1981).

59. Waters v. Churchill, 511 U.S. 661, 677–78 (1994).

60. Cotran v. Rollins Hudig Hall Int'l, Inc., 948 P.2d 412, 422 (Cal. 1997).

61. Baldwin v. Sisters of Providence in Wash., 769 P.2d 298, 303 (Wash. 1989).

the investigation, the alleged harasser was suspended from work. Over a two-week period, the investigator interviewed twenty-one people who had worked with the alleged harasser, including five individuals the alleged harasser had identified as potential witnesses. In reaching a conclusion, the investigator articulated objective grounds for finding the complaints to be credible, including testimony of past obscene telephone calls, confirmation that plaintiff had telephoned both complaining parties at home, and the fact that no one interviewed had said it was "impossible" to believe the alleged harasser had committed the alleged sexual harassment.

Conducting an investigation will not necessarily insulate an employer who ultimately makes an erroneous decision. In *Southern Co. v. Hamburg*,[62] for example, the plaintiff recovered under a breach-of-contract claim because he was able to prove that he had not engaged in the wrongdoing alleged. In an appropriate circumstance, however, conducting an investigation may at least insulate an employer from a finding that the employer acted in bad faith when it erroneously, but in good faith, terminated an employee under a for-cause provision.

One example of an improper investigation is *Carr v. Allison Gas Turbine Division, General Motors Corp.*[63] In *Carr*, the female plaintiff was a tinsmith in an overwhelmingly male-dominated position. She complained several times to her immediate supervisor about alleged harassment over a four-year period. The employer arranged several meetings between plaintiff and the alleged harassers. At one meeting, the plaintiff and one of her harassers were asked to apologize to each other. No other investigation was made. No disciplinary action was taken against any of the plaintiff's co-workers. The harassment continued. The court found that the employer's response to the plaintiff's complaint was negligent.

Other decisions examining the adequacy of workplace investigations include the following:

- *Fuller v. Oakland*,[64] which held that the City of Oakland Police Department's handling of a sexual harassment complaint was not adequate. The police department closed its investigation and concluded that the complaint was "unfounded" even though the investigators had failed to interview numerous witnesses and had not promptly interviewed the alleged harasser. In addition, none of the documentary evidence indicated that the complaining party had been untruthful. Finally, the investigator failed to give sufficient weight to evidence that tended to corroborate the complaint.
- *Kestenbaum v. Pennzoil Co.*,[65] in which the New Mexico Supreme Court affirmed a judgment of $1 million in favor of an employee who was found to be

---

62. S. Co. v. Hamburg, 470 S.E.2d 467 (Ga. Ct. App. 1996).

63. Carr v. Allison Gas Turbine Division, General Motors Corp., 32 F.3d 1007 (7th Cir. 1994).

64. Fuller v. Oakland, 47 F.3d 1522 (9th Cir. 1995).

65. Kestenbaum v. Pennzoil Co., 766 P.2d 280 (N.M. 1988), *cert. denied*, 490 U.S. 1109 (1989).

wrongfully terminated on the basis of false sexual harassment charges that had been summarily and ineffectively investigated.

- *Silva v. Lucky Stores, Inc.,*[66] in which the court concluded that a sexual harassment investigation was appropriate based on the following factors: The employer had a written policy that described how to investigate allegations of harassment; the employer had promptly assigned a neutral human resources representative to conduct the investigation; the investigation began on the day of the alleged incident and lasted for one month; the investigator interviewed fifteen employees and recorded interview notes; the witnesses were allowed to clarify their statements or explain information that tended to undermine their credibility; and the alleged harasser was interviewed three times and provided an opportunity to comment on the information gathered during the investigation.[67]

8. Retaliation[68]

An employee who is terminated, demoted, or suffers an adverse employment action even a year or so after complaining about discrimination or harassment or after participating in an investigation may claim that the action was taken in retaliation for his or her prior activity. Even former employees can sue for retaliation.[69]

---

66. Silva v. Lucky Stores, Inc., 65 Cal. App. 4th 256, 76 Cal. Rptr. 2d 382 (Cal. App. 1998).

67. *But see* Kariotis v. Navistar Int'l Transp'n Co., 131 F.3d 672 (7th Cir. 1997) (disability discrimination case in which the court severely criticized the company's investigation; however, the plaintiff could not prevail on discrimination claim because the employer "honestly believed" that she had committed disability fraud).

68. *See* general discussion regarding retaliation in Chapter 1.

69. Robinson v. Shell Oil Co., 519 U.S. 337 (1997).

Investigating, Preparing, and Responding to the Administrative Charge and Court Complaint: Plaintiff's Perspective

Michelle A. Reinglass and Rachel Goldstein

I. INTAKE AND SCREENING

The prospective client sounded credible on the phone and in her intake-questionnaire responses. She had complained to her employer about her supervisor's sexual advances and graphic sexual language, and then she lost her job. She presented well at the initial "live" interview and repeated the same graphic sexual comments and advances, and you signed her up as a client. Months later, however, during depositions, in document productions, or worse, at trial, you learned that your client did not report the sexual harassment until years after it occurred, at a time when she was experiencing some disciplinary action.

Furthermore, it is discovered that after the alleged harassment took place, she brought to the office a calendar in which she posed provocatively in a revealing bathing suit, and showed the calendar to the alleged harasser. Evidence also came out that this client talked often with that same alleged harasser and co-workers about her breast augmentation, offered to show the scar, and flirted with several people in the office. You are caught off guard and angry at your client for failing to tell you this potentially damaging information, and you are now worried about your case. However, this might have been prevented if some simple steps had been taken at the start of the case and prior to filing the complaint.

Chapter 4 outlines an employer's defenses. However, a plaintiff's counsel should be thinking about those defenses early in the case, before meeting the defense counsel. Waiting until after the complaint has been filed and answered to learn the defendant's positions may be too late to salvage the case or rehabilitate the plaintiff. Of course, it is expected that the plaintiff side will learn a few surprises during depositions or the discovery process. But a plaintiff's counsel will be well served to learn as much as possible about the client and case before filing the complaint.

The time to fully analyze a plaintiff's claims and the defendant's positions is before retention as counsel, and certainly before filing the complaint. This applies to all employment cases, and particularly to sexual harassment cases and discrimination cases. Sexual harassment cases tend to be very emotional on both sides, and filing such a case will just about ensure that the plaintiff will be closely examined and vetted, "googled," researched, scrutinized, investigated, and maybe even psychologically profiled, by the defense. His or her claims will be dissected and peeled back; both the plaintiff and the plaintiff's case will be put under a microscope and skewered. The prospective client or plaintiff must be told in advance that this will occur, and that there will likely be serious consequences in the case for not being fully honest with his or her counsel. It is important for the lawyer to ask questions about the client's interactions with other employees and with the alleged harasser, as well as about the prospective client's background and activities, including social media.

Everyone enters adulthood with some type of emotional baggage. In many cases that "baggage" or history will be found by the other side during litigation. Jurors know and expect this and generally do not hold it against a plaintiff. However, untruthful statements, conduct that contradicts the allegations being asserted, or conduct that belies the plaintiff's claim of being offended, or experiencing emotions, may erase any empathy or sympathy the jury was feeling for the plaintiff. Learning all the information that can hurt a harassment victim's case is something the plaintiff's lawyer has the power to control, because the plaintiff's lawyer controls the filing time for the complaint. (That is, unless the plaintiff comes to the attorney at the last minute before the statute of limitations expires, which, as discussed later in this chapter, is cause to be very wary).

A. Preliminary Screening

By necessity, the initial intake process is time-consuming. It starts with the preliminary screening. Prospective clients typically call or email requesting representation. What they often really want is for the lawyer to immediately take their call and give them immediate advice. There are pitfalls in doing so that are too lengthy for this chapter. Bear in mind that if inclined to take those calls, often these prospective clients are emotional and angry, and are not in a frame of mind to listen, nor to take, any advice given. They are even less inclined at that moment to undergo any form of screening process and are often seeking someone to vent to. A busy lawyer taking such calls will quickly realize that doing so may accomplish nothing more than consuming time.

Assuming the lawyer does preliminary screenings before providing counsel, the process will generally involve having an administrative assistant or paralegal handle the call or email and obtain further information. The intake person should understand that the prospective client will attempt to obtain legal advice from this person and that it is never legal, proper, or appropriate for the intake person to give legal advice. Even if the intake person is a lawyer, there is simply insufficient time in a brief telephone conversation to learn enough information to give legal advice without that lawyer putting himself or herself in jeopardy. Thus, in every preliminary screening, it should be made clear that no advice can be given at this early stage; rather, additional information will be needed to determine whether this is a case that the attorney may be able to consider.

It is essential that the intake person ask a number of questions of prospective clients. This should start with a telephone conversation asking prospective clients for their name, contact information, and how they got the attorney's name or were referred to this attorney. The prospective clients should be asked to fully identify their employer, provide the inclusive dates of employment (including whether they are still employed), the inclusive dates of the harassment or other adverse action(s), whether there was any retaliation, their positions held, the name and position of the alleged harasser, whether the prospective clients complained about the harassment to anyone, and if so, to whom, when, what was done and what the outcome was.

Some practitioners, in addition to or in lieu of the initial intake telephone call, send out a written questionnaire to prospective clients. This is fine as far as a mechanism to get basic dates and information. However, for workplace harassment victims, it is probably not the most effective means of identifying the specific acts of harassment, which may more likely be obtained in the initial conversation and particularly during the actual attorney consultation. Providing a written recitation of the events at this early stage may be more than prospective clients can handle, and may heighten their emotional or psychological pain.

However, it is still essential at some point, before retaining the client, to have her or him prepare a written chronology of events forming the workplace harassment or retaliation and have done, preferably by the time of the initial consultation. The lawyer must also keep in mind that any challenges the prospective client may have in compiling a complete and accurate chronological list of the acts and events may be the effects of depression or other emotional tolls suffered from the harassment. It may also be that the prospective client has had limited education or has language difficulties. These are among the many things that the lawyer will need to watch for and assess during the initial interview.

This initial screening process will enable the lawyer to assess any conflicts of interest, or incidents that extend beyond the statute of limitations, as well as any matters where the "harassment" has no connection with sex, gender, or other protected category, although this latter issue is often one requiring the length of time afforded during an in-person consultation rather than a quick recitation or listing of events. Often, prospective clients are unfamiliar with legal jargon, or that there is a distinction between general "harassment" and protected harassment. That may be more conducive to a discussion during the consultation.

B. Initial Interview

At the initial interview, further information needs to be obtained, and hard questions may need to be asked. It should be kept in mind that the prospective client may be a genuine victim of sexual or other harassment, may be fragile or an "eggshell plaintiff," and thus may have difficulty trusting someone who is essentially cross-examining and questioning veracity. This can be ameliorated by carefully explaining to the prospective client what could lie ahead if this exercise is not done and that this process, done in the friendly environment of the plaintiff lawyer's office, may pale in contrast with what the defense will do, and the plaintiff will need to be able to withstand that type of scrutiny. Every lawyer at some point is faced with the balancing act of weighing efforts not to scare a victim of harassment or sexual assault away from litigation against finding out sufficient information and giving enough warnings to avoid preventable surprises.

1. Documents to Obtain

Part of the investigative aspect of the initial interview is finding out what documents exist and obtaining those documents. The following are some of the more critical documents to request in a sexual harassment case:

- Documentation or evidence of the acts of harassment, such as a card, note, text message, or email from the harasser, photos, social media posts, and so on
- Written memorialization of the acts of harassment by the prospective client, such as a contemporaneous writing, or an email detailing the acts of harassment or other written complaints made about the harassment, plus any witness statements.
- Any complaints made by the prospective client, whether to the company, a supervisor, human resources, management, a complaint hotline, and so on.
- Any charges of discrimination that were filed either internally or with a state agency (e.g., Department of Fair Employment and Housing or DFEH or the Equal Employment Opportunity Commission or EEOC), as well as right-to-sue letters; complaints about labor violations filed with the Department of Labor (which may contain other information).
- Calendars, organizers, journals, diaries, or memos, including notes made pertaining to the harassment (paper and electronic).
- Employee handbooks or written policies and procedures that govern harassment, retaliation, and discrimination, and that explain how to make complaints to the company. If there is a complaint mechanism offered by the company, also ascertain if the prospective client submitted any complaints.
- Personnel records and files of the prospective client. The prospective client should request a copy of his or her personnel file, and make an appointment to review it as well.[1]
- Any written employment agreements or agreements governing the prospective client's employment.
- Any arbitration or other alternative dispute resolution agreements.

---

1. In California, for example, employees are entitled to review and receive a copy (at the employee's copy expense) of their own entire personnel file within 30 days of a written request and to receive a copy of all documents signed by the employee upon request. See CAL. LAB. CODE §§ 432, 1198.5. Employees are also entitled to inspect or copy payroll records regarding them within twenty-one days of an oral or written request. CAL. LAB. CODE §226(b).

- List of witnesses, including their addresses and all telephone numbers (home, cell, and work, unless it is with the same employer); their employment status with the employer and their titles and positions; and a brief description of the information that each witness may have or be able to provide.
- Any other relevant documents that the prospective client may have.

The initial interview is also the lawyer's opportunity to assess the prospective client. At this interview, the prospective client should be instructed to label any further documentation that she prepares for the lawyer or the case (e.g., written chronology, witness list) as privileged and confidential so that such items are segregated from any others that might be discoverable during litigation. Make sure that such documents are in fact maintained in a segregated subfile clearly marked "Privileged and Confidential," so that down the road, when a paralegal or other person is reviewing documents to produce, there is no chance that the documents that were intended to be attorney-client or work-product privileged make their way into any document production.

2. Who Should Be or Should Not Be Present

Often, prospective clients will bring someone to the initial consultation for moral support. Seeing a lawyer is usually a difficult first step toward dealing with sexual or other harassment at work, so a prospective client may bring a spouse, family member, or good friend. The prospective client should be strongly discouraged from having that person in the meeting room, for a number of reasons. (An exception may be made if the prospective client needs a translator.)

First, there is the attorney-client privilege. Having another person in the room could result in a waiver of the privilege. Even if there is another applicable privilege, such as a spouse or marital privilege prohibiting one spouse from divulging communications with the plaintiff, there is a second valid reason to keep that person out of the initial consultation: The spouse may be a critical witness to the client's emotional distress, and when called to give testimony at deposition or trial, there is a risk that person will be asked questions that could compel divulging confidential information.

A third reason why prospective clients should meet alone with the attorney is that clients need to be able to stand on their own feet during deposition and at trial, without help from a spouse or supportive friend. It is too tempting for a supporter to step in and "help" with the recitation of the facts or events when the prospective client stumbles. Sometimes, plaintiffs feel forced or pressured by a loving and otherwise well-meaning spouse to pursue legal action, yet they are not themselves committed to doing so. Having a third person in the room with the prospective client makes it more difficult for the client to be honest with the lawyer.

Additionally, the initial consultation will help the lawyer to get a true feel about the prospective client, and perhaps may be the last truly objective occasion to do so. There is only one occasion to have a first impression about the person who may end up your client. The lawyer needs to be aware of any nagging feelings or concerns about someone, which could include some red flags indicating the prospective client is not being truthful, or that there is something else going on driving the client to take this action.

If a third person is constantly interjecting, protecting the client, filling in deficiencies in memory or gaps in the story, it becomes more difficult to assess whether this is a good prospective plaintiff. Unfortunately, it is easy to become enamored with what sound like good facts, and if the lawyer proceeds with the case, it will be easier to justify or explain away those nagging feelings in the pursuit of the case and justice, and it will be more difficult to have that hard talk with the client about problems in the case as they develop—and they will appear, sometimes too late to take control or reverse them.

3. Interview Topics

The initial client interview serves numerous purposes, including learning the facts and story of the case, assessing the strength of the case and liability against the employer, and determining the prospective client's damages and mitigation efforts. The initial interview is also an important place to set ground rules of the relationship between the lawyer and client and evaluate compatibility. Additionally, this meeting provides a means to assess the prospective client's commitment to the case and how cooperative he or she will be throughout the litigation, as well as what kind of witness he or she will make.

The prospective client should be told of the importance of his or her active participation in the case, as well as the fact that information will be received from the other side and the client's prompt input on that information will be needed.

Critical information to gather at the initial interview includes the following:

1. The employer's full name, including any parent and subsidiary companies. Ask the client which company or companies were believed to be the employer. Ask for paycheck stubs and W-2 forms. A client's pay stubs may provide further verification of who the employer is, and will establish the prospective client's pay to verify loss of wages. Naming the wrong employer can lead to empty discovery responses, law and motion, and possible dismissal of the case.
2. The prospective client's full employment history, including start date, ending date, promotions, disciplinary action, and dates of the harassment. This information may become relevant because of the tendency of jurors (and some judges) to believe that an employee who endures harassment for an extended period of time, or makes no effort to find another job, was not that offended or bothered by the conduct.
3. Information about the harasser, including titles and positions held and extent of authority or supervisory responsibility, particularly over the prospective client; other employees he or she supervised and their genders; and any other instances of harassment by this individual, or other potential victims of the harassment.
4. A verbal recitation of the acts of harassment. It is important to pin the prospective client down on what incidents occurred, as these will be requested at their deposition as well.
5. Dates and descriptions of complaints made by the client and to whom they were made. What was the recipient's position and title, and why did the client select

that person to tell? What was that person's response to the complaint? Was any action taken after the complaint was made, and if so, what, by whom, and when?

6. If no complaints were ever made, find out the reason. For example, was the alleged harasser a senior executive or owner? Is there evidence of futility or retaliation toward others who did make complaints? Did someone intimidate the client from making a complaint? Was there a cultural or language barrier to making such a complaint?

7. Any performance problems or personnel issues on the part of, or disciplinary actions taken against, the prospective client. This is an important area to probe for as much detail as possible, including dates, type, number of incidents or warnings, and proximity in time to the making of a complaint of harassment by this prospective client.

8. Any known disciplinary problems on the part of the alleged harasser, including any disciplinary action against the alleged harasser arising out of the client's complaint.

9. Any other sexual harassment that occurred in the workplace (to assess the existence of a hostile work environment), and whether there are witnesses to or recipients of such harassment.

10. The prospective client's duties and responsibilities at the company.

11. Any training given by the company to employees and managers on sexual harassment.

12. If the prospective client is no longer employed at the defendant company, was it a voluntary, involuntary, or forced (e.g., constructive) termination? Also, what were the reasons for the termination?

13. Whether the employer conducted any investigation into the workplace harassment allegations. The employer is required to take all steps necessary to prevent harassment, which includes promptly investigating any and all complaints about sexual harassment. It is important to find out if the prospective employee was interviewed, and if so by whom. Was it an inside employee of the company, such as someone from human resources, a manager, or was it an outside, neutral investigator? Gather as much information about the company's questions and the prospective client's answers. Find out if the investigator took notes during the interview, or if the interview was recorded through any type of recording device or by a court reporter. Ask if the investigator came back to the employee to ask further questions or to get her response to comments made by the alleged harasser or other witnesses. Find out if the prospective client was told the outcome of the investigation, or of any action taken against the alleged harasser. If the employee was given any report or knows a report was made, it is essential to get a copy.

14. Damage mitigation efforts made by the prospective client. This is important as failure to mitigate is a potential affirmative defense the employer may use to minimize or eliminate recovery of damages. Ask for copies of any job applications submitted, letters written, or other correspondence written to

or from the prospective employer, as well as any job offers. If there was no, or minimal, mitigation effort made, find out the reason. Was the employee under a doctor's care, or on disability or other medical leave that prevented working? All such subjects need exploration.

15. Emotional distress symptoms, and any treatment for them, including from a general practitioner, psychologist, or psychiatrist; and any counseling received, whether from someone in the mental health field, a pastoral counselor, a spouse or family member, a close friend, or someone else. If no treatment or counseling was received but the client suffers from emotional distress, get an explanation why no action was taken to receive treatment.

16. Economic damages, including lost income and benefits, and any consequential or residual damages resulting from the harassment.

17. Evaluate potential affirmative defenses that may be raised. Some of the more common ones include:

    a. *Failure to complain when a complaint mechanism was in place limits damages.*[2] Preparing for this defense requires exploring the complaints made, any futility to making them, and actions or inactions by the employer.

    b. *Statute of limitations.* Administrative charge deadlines for filing with the EEOC (federal claims) are 300 days or 180 days after unlawful employment practice; state agency (e.g., California's Department of Fair Employment and Housing) deadlines are one year after last adverse employment practice. Shorter periods (e.g., six months) apply to government tort claims when filing against a public entity. Limitations periods for common law tort and statutory claims usually range from one to two years. Consider equitable tolling or continuing violation theories as offsets to limitations defenses.

    c. *Individual liability.* Although the majority of courts following *Miller v. Maxwell's International*[3] have held that supervisors are not individually liable under Title VII, individual liability for sexual harassment or retaliation may be available under state law.[4]

    d. *Isolated or trivial incidents (also called "stray remarks"); conduct not severe or pervasive.* Preparing for this defense requires exploration of other incidents or comments, as well as the level of offensiveness, as even one comment or action, if severe, may be enough to overcome summary judgment or to prevail at trial. The standard for determining whether conduct is severe varies between jurisdictions. For example, in the Seventh Circuit, the standard is "severe *and* pervasive." However, in the Ninth Circuit, and in

---

2. *See, e.g.*, Burlington Indus., Inc. v. Ellerth, 524 U.S. 742 (1998) (Title VII case); Faragher v. City of Boca Raton, 524 U.S. 775 (1998) (same); State Dept. of Health Services v. Superior Court (McGinnis), 31 Cal. 4th 1026 (Cal. Ct. App. 2003); California Fair Employment and Housing Act, CAL. GOV'T CODE §§ 12940–52.

3. 991 F.2d 583 (9th Cir. 1993), *cert. denied sub nom.* Miller v. LaRosa, 510 U.S. 1109 (1994).

4. For example, individual liability is available under California laws for sexual harassment and retaliation, CAL. GOV'T CODE §§ 12940(j)(3),12940(h), but not for discrimination, CAL. GOV'T CODE § 12940 (a).

California state courts, the standard is "severe *or* pervasive," evaluated under the "reasonable woman" standard espoused in *Ellison v. Brady* (Ninth Circuit)[5] and *Harris v. Forklift* (US Supreme Court).[6]

Some courts hold that in order for conduct to be deemed "severe," it would need to involve physical contact, propositioning, or threats (*Haberman v. Cengage Learning, Inc.*).[7]

If it is one isolated incident, it is necessary to explore the severity of the action, or why it was so upsetting to the prospective client. Perhaps there is evidence that the plaintiff's known "eggshell" fragilities were exploited by the alleged harasser. Otherwise, plaintiff faces the risk that the incident complained about will be deemed as "occasional, isolated, sporadic, or trivial," which has been found to be nonactionable (*Hughes v. Pair*[8] and *Haberman v. Cengage Learning Inc.*). In *Haberman v. Cengage,* the plaintiff sued her employer and two former supervisors for a number of claims, including sexual harassment based on several alleged comments made by supervisors over a three-year period. The comments were on their face offensive and referenced her appearance ("So pretty," "drop-dead gorgeous," a co-worker having "the hots" for her), and asking for referrals to friends for sex. Summary judgment was granted for the employer, and upheld in both cases, holding the conduct involved sporadic, isolated comments spread apart by long gaps of time.

e. *Failure to exhaust administrative remedies.* To prepare for this defense, obtain copies of any charges of discrimination filed by the prospective client, and review to ensure the proper defendants were named and the correct boxes were checked. Substantial compliance may suffice. California law, for example, requires the plaintiff to serve the charge of discrimination and right-to-sue letter upon the employer, but failure to do so is generally deemed not jurisdictional.

f. *Conduct was wanted or not offensive.* Preparing for this defense generally requires evaluating the prospective client's conduct, behavior, and response to the harassment: whether he or she acted flirtatiously or suggestively, or initiated or invited sexual contact or conduct. Sometimes an employee will go along with the comments and not voice opposition for fear of jeopardizing his or her job. The employer has the burden to prove this defense, which can be overcome, thus this provides a factual area that warrants exploration during the initial consultation.

---

5. Ellison v. Brady 924 F.2d 872 (9th Cir. 1991).

6. Harris v. Forklift Systems Inc. 510 U.S. 17 (1993).

7. Haberman v. Cengage Learning Inc. 180 Cal. App. 4th 365 (2009); Hughes v. Pair, 49 Cal. 4th 1035 (2009). But also see Zetwick v. County of Yolo 850 F.3d 436 (2017), holding that hostile conduct including over 100 unwelcome hugs and a kiss on her lips, etc., spanning twelve years was sufficiently severe. (The court used incorrect legal standards, including severe and pervasive).

8. *Id.*

g. *Third-party harassment, defense that it is not actionable against employer*: Exceptions can occur, such as in the recent case of *M.F. vs. Pac. Pearl Hotel Mgmt LLC*.[9] The Court of Appeal reversed the trial court's dismissal of the plaintiff's claims of sexual harassment and sexual assault (rape) by a nonemployee, an intoxicated trespasser. The court noted defendant's prior knowledge of the trespasser's harassment of its employees, including one who was aggressively propositioned, before plaintiff was attacked. The court also cited defendant's lack of communication and failure to check on housekeeping staff in support of its holding that the employer was responsible.

18. Find out if the plaintiff has been involved in any other litigation, whether workers' compensation, divorce, small claims, civil action, or a criminal case. Also, find out if any unemployment claim was filed. Records of these other cases should be obtained, and they should be discussed early on with the prospective client, as the employer will certainly learn about them and they will become fodder for the employer to try to tear apart the plaintiff's claims. (Criminal records should be more closely evaluated.) State unemployment claims departments do not maintain their records for very long, so it is important to get these records as soon as possible, as they may contain statements given by the employer's representations about the reasons for terminating or taking adverse action against the plaintiff, or about an investigation or the harassment allegations. The employee's own statements of reasons for termination contained in a filing for unemployment records will be scrutinized for consistency or inconsistency with the claims now being made for the civil lawsuit. If any appeal was taken from an unemployment claims decision, there was probably a hearing, and transcripts of the testimony should be obtained as well.

19. Find out if the plaintiff has seen other lawyers or been represented by other lawyers in connection with the current claims. If so, it is important to learn why. Multiple lawyers may signal that the plaintiff is unable to be pleased, or is a problem client who was fired by other lawyers. You may need to obtain that other lawyer's records as well, and will want to find out if there is any lien being imposed by prior lawyers against any settlement or proceeds generated in this case.

20. Special care must be given to a prospective client who has experienced a sexual assault or rape, especially if the client has not received any or adequate counseling. Some victims of sexual harassment are unable to contain their emotions, and are constantly teary every time they think of or talk about the events. Others may have experienced significant damage but are unable to express themselves emotionally. These prospective clients may take more patience to get their story; they may need more than one consultation to provide information or to process the challenges of pursuing action. It may be necessary

---

9. M.F. v. Pac. Pearl Hotel Mgmt LLC, 16 Cal. App. 5th 693 (2017).

to refer the prospective client to a medical or psychological professional for the prospective client's health. However, it can be discovered that the attorney made the referral, which may raise an argument by the defense that the lawyer was trying to increase the client's damages. This should not be a deterrent to sending the client to professionals for treatment where needed. Further evaluation may be needed before deciding to undertake representation of the prospective client. No retention should take place until the lawyer has satisfied himself or herself of the merit in such representation, after conducting an adequate pre-litigation investigation and evaluation of the available evidence.

21. Evaluate any potential claims of retaliation. As noted earlier, inquiry must be made about any complaints made by the prospective client. Questioning should continue to ascertain if there have been any adverse employment actions taken, which might be considered retaliatory for making a complaint, or objecting to perceived illegal conduct. California practitioners should take note of two recent cases, *Landig v. CooperSurgical, Inc., et al.*[10] and *Husman v. Toyota Motor Credit Corp.*[11] In *Landig*, the Central District Court had granted summary judgment as to some of the Fair Employment and Housing Act (FEHA) related claims, but allowed the claim of retaliation to stand. The Court stated: "[T]o establish a prima facie case of retaliation under the FEHA, a plaintiff must show (1) he or she engaged in a 'protected activity,' (2) the employer subjected the employee to an adverse employment action, and (3) a causal link existed between the protected activity and the employer's action." *Yanowitz v. L'Oreal USA, Inc.*[12] Lawyers would be served well to review the extensive discussion in *Yanowitz* about adverse employment actions among other things. From there, it is important to elicit information from the prospective client relating to any claim of retaliation. Pay close attention to evidence supporting causal connection between the protected activity (e.g., complaint or objection) and the adverse employment action (e.g., termination).

    In *Husman*, the Court made the opposite holding, reversing summary judgment on his discrimination claim based on sex or gender stereotyping, but affirmed summary judgment as to his retaliation (and related common law tort) claims, ruling that generalized comments about more work being needed toward creating lesbian, gay, bisexual, and transgender diversity, were insufficient to constitute "criticism or opposition salient to an act reasonably believed to be prohibited by FEHA."

---

10. Landig v. CooperSurgical, Inc., et al., Case No. 2:16-cv-07144-CAS(KSx), 2017 WL 5633036, *1, *19–21 (C.D. Cal. November 20, 2017).

11. Husman v. Toyota Motor Credit Corp. 12 Cal. App. 5th at 1188–89.

12. Yanowitz v. L'Oreal USA, Inc., 36 Cal. 4th at 1042.

II. PRE-LITIGATION INVESTIGATION AND EVALUATION

A. Review All Relevant Documents

After asking for and receiving the documents identified already, it is important to thoroughly review them. This duty to investigate will continue past even retention of the attorney for further legal services, but at least initially the following must be examined and analyzed:

1. Documentation or Evidence of the Acts of Harassment

Defendants readily request production of any documentary evidence of the harassment. This evidence can include any emails, memos, cards, or text messages sent by the alleged harasser containing sexual content, requests for dates, comments about an employee's body, and so on. Absent something generated by the alleged harasser, defendants look to any documentation of the harassment maintained or generated by the plaintiff. These may be in journals, diaries, calendars, or organizers, or other notes kept on a daily basis by the plaintiff. They may exist in written chronologies that the plaintiff kept on her or his computer, or a running list maintained somewhere. They may be handwritten, typed, or prepared electronically; hence all possible sources need to be reviewed.

Having such documentation can be a double-edged sword—on the one hand, it is beneficial as it contemporaneously documents the acts of harassment, which certainly can help bolster and support the plaintiff's testimony about the incidents one or two years later. However, an employer may also characterize such documentation as evidence that the employee was trying to manipulate or set up the alleged harasser. The plaintiff's lawyer will need to be prepared for any such defense arguments. Further preparation will be needed with regard to the anticipated later production of such documents.

Typically, these same items, including the plaintiff's daily calendar, journals, diary, or other recorded notes contain not just events involving the defendant or alleged harasser but also private and personal information about the plaintiff, such as doctor appointments, notes about relationship or marital difficulties, finances, and third parties' private information.

Steps will need to be taken to protect or redact such private information, but the prospective client will need to be informed that the information contained therein may need to be disclosed during litigation, and that not all judges will be sensitive to the plaintiff's or third-party privacy interests that you will be seeking to protect.

2. Complaints About the Discrimination and/or Retaliation

Whether the employee made a complaint about the harassment is usually a hotly litigated issue, particularly in sexual harassment cases. If the alleged harasser is a supervisor, it is generally not required that the employee complain about the conduct for there to be liability. However, if the harassment was by co-workers or nonsupervisory employees, the plaintiff has the burden of proving that the employer was on notice of or aware of the harassment, or reasonably should have been aware of such conduct (e.g. because it was so frequent, obvious or blatant, or well-known throughout the department or company). One way of ensuring notice to the employer is through the employee's complaint to someone in management or human resources, or another responsible upper-level individual.

The employer will argue that the absence of a complaint is indication that the harassment did not occur, or that the employee was not offended, or, depending on the circumstances, that the company is not liable. Furthermore, as discussed already, the employer may make the argument that it had viable policies in place outlining steps that should have been, but were not, taken by the plaintiff, including reporting the harassment. Had such a complaint been made, the employer would have been able to investigate and potentially resolve or stop the harassment. The employer would thus be using the absence of or failure to make a complaint, in support of its *Ellerth/Faragher* defense.[13] As stated herein, that may bar or reduce damages, but is not a complete bar to the case.

If the plaintiff did make a complaint, it provides possible grounds for other potential legal claims, such as the employer's failure to take all reasonable and necessary steps to stop the harassment, or retaliation due to the reporting, as noted earlier. It is important to probe with the plaintiff any and all responses, if any, by the employer, to the complaint, as well as documentation of such responses, or investigations, conducted by the employer.

3. Administrative Charges of Discrimination

It is critical to find out if the employee filed a prior administrative charge of discrimination, whether within the company or with an outside agency such as the EEOC or the state's administrative agency vested with responsibility for these complaints. First, filing of an administrative charge is a mandatory prerequisite to the filing of a civil complaint. If one was not filed, the lawyer will need to prepare one for the prospective client. If one has been filed, the lawyer needs to carefully examine it to ensure that the proper employer and parties are named, all of the correct boxes were checked, and dates and events are correctly stated. Missing a box, such as for retaliation, may lead to the plaintiff's loss of that claim. Citing a wrong date may lead to unnecessary arguments of missing the statute of limitations that the plaintiff will have to fight throughout the litigation.

A right-to-sue letter is also required before proceeding with a civil lawsuit. If that has already been obtained before consulting with the lawyer, then it is important to make sure that the time to file the lawsuit has not already elapsed, thereby triggering a statute of limitations defense.

Even if the administrative charge was not filed, the employee may still pursue common law tort claims and obtain most of the same remedies. The employee may lose those remedies or damages that are solely afforded by statute, such as recovery of attorney's fees, but may still pursue the claim and seek all economic and noneconomic

---

13. Ellerth/Faragher defense, *supra* note 2.

damages incurred. The lawyer evaluating a prospective client's claims must be aware of what remedies are available and viable before proceeding with the case.

4. Employee Handbooks and Company Policies and Procedures

Counsel must review the employer's policies governing workplace harassment, and other relevant policies such as retaliation, investigations of complaints, discrimination, and making complaints. These must be read not only for their content and what is required of the employee and employer, but also to evaluate whether these policies meet certain minimum criteria. A good resource is the local EEOC guidelines,[14] which will outline such minimum criteria governing the company's internal policies. At a minimum, the following assessments should be made:

- whether the policy contains an adequate definition of sexual harassment and illustrative examples of the different types of harassment, such as making unwanted sexual advances; unwanted touching; making offensive comments of a sexual nature; derogatory comments, epithets, jokes, or slurs; displaying graphic drawings, posters, cartoons, and so on that are sexually suggestive; leering or staring in a provocative manner; or using sexually degrading words;
- whether the policy contains a complaint procedure, and if so, if that procedure identifies alternative individuals to whom the employee may report the complaint other than the alleged harasser;
- whether the policy identifies the investigation process;
- whether the policies and procedures governing sexual harassment and the making of complaints about harassment are distributed to all employees, or how the employee learned about them; and
- whether the policies provide adequate protections for the employee including with regard to her or his privacy and confidentiality other than as needed for purposes of conducting the investigation and addressing the harassment, and with regard to protecting the employee against retaliation.

Upon reviewing the applicable policies, counsel should evaluate the employer's and employee's compliance with the policies, and if the employee did not make any complaint to the employer, counsel should learn the reason.

5. Personnel Files and Documents

As stated already, employees are entitled by law to see their entire personnel file, and to be given copies of everything that they signed. If the plaintiff has not already done so, it is prudent to advise him or her to make an appointment to view the file, and to take along paper and pen, and perhaps a camera in case there are documents that the employee has never seen before. The employee should be instructed to write down everything that exists in the file, and in the order as reflected, and include dates and

---

14. EEOC Guidelines on Sexual Harassment, 29 C.F.R. § 1604 (1980).

descriptions of each item. The employee should write in these notes the date of this inspection. The employee should take particular note of anything reflecting the complaint of harassment, as well as any personnel issues or disciplinary action involving or taken against the employee.

The employee should also be instructed to ask the employer for a copy of the entire personnel file. Some employers will as a matter of course provide employees with a full copy of their file. Other employers will only provide what is required of them by law. The employee should be further instructed that if the employer refuses either to allow inspection or to provide any copies, that the employee should inform them of their obligations under the particular state statute.[15]

After the employee reviews the personnel file, counsel should review those records and notes carefully. Counsel will want to review any relevant documents to the claims, or any adverse action taken against the employee; counsel should fully assess plaintiff's documented employment history from the file, including the initial employment application. This document often provides fodder for claims by the employer of "after acquired evidence" as the application form is scoured to find any errors or misstatements. It is prudent to review that application with the employee, particularly paying attention to education and past employment history to verify accuracy, or understand anything that is not accurate. It is also important to review with the employee any personnel or disciplinary action that was taken against the employee and why.

The employee's personnel records from the early inspection can also be used to compare to a later production of the personnel file during the course of litigation, to see if any documents were removed, withheld, added, or created following the initial inspection. It is important to determine if the client signed any type of employment agreement, and if so, evaluate the terms for company compliance or breaches. Always ask the employee to inform the lawyer of anything missing from their personnel file, such as letters of commendations or performance reviews, as well as documents never before seen, such as counseling or disciplinary memos.

Review of the company's policies, and the personnel file, will usually reveal as well if there is an arbitration agreement, which may bar the employee from filing a claim in court. In such event, the lawyer should carefully analyze the policies or agreement compelling arbitration to ensure that they are compliant with state and federal law and that they provide the employee with the requisite fairness and due process as mandated by law, or whether there are grounds to set aside the arbitration requirement and proceed in court.

6. Prior Complaints or Litigation

Counsel should ascertain and discuss with the prospective client whether the client has made any other complaints of sexual or any form of harassment, discrimination, or retaliation, either at this employer or previously. Also, counsel should find out if there has been any prior litigation of any type filed by the prospective client. This includes

---

15. *E.g.*, Cal. Lab. Code § 432 (copies of signed documents), § 1198.5 (full inspection right).

bankruptcy, divorce, evictions, small claims, and workers' compensation. Those types of cases provide great fodder of personal information, even prior depositions taken, that the employer may not otherwise obtain during normal discovery. The defense will explore this information at deposition in the current matter, and may have already ascertained such information from their own research and investigation.

There are many tools available online and elsewhere to find out about other lawsuits, and networking within the industry may turn up prior complaints of a similar nature made by the plaintiff with other employers. Defendants may use such information to accuse the plaintiff of being a chronic complainer or of having a pattern and practice of bringing unfounded complaints to avoid being terminated or disciplined. It is important to find out this information in advance and discuss it with the prospective client to evaluate what weight or effect it has on the case, and work out how to address it when it arises during litigation or negotiations.

7. Union Grievances

If the prospective client is a member of a union, it is important to find out early about any grievances that were filed and if so, whether any are related to the claims of sexual harassment. If the employee utilized grievance mechanisms to register other complaints but made no complaint about the harassment, the employer will try to use it against the employee, so counsel must be prepared to address the issue. The lawyer should get a copy of any applicable collective bargaining agreements to determine if any of the claims being brought may be preempted or if there are any administrative filing prerequisites.

8. Unemployment, Disability, and Workers' Compensation Claims

It is important to find out if the employee has filed any claims for benefits in another forum such as unemployment, disability, or workers' compensation. If so, counsel needs to quickly take steps to obtain any files and records generated, exhibits used in hearings, depositions taken (e.g., for workers' compensation), or testimony given, particularly of the plaintiff or defendant. This is to ascertain if there is any damaging testimony or evidence given by the plaintiff that may jeopardize or be inconsistent with the harassment claims, as well as to obtain any recorded testimony and statements from the employer. Workers' compensation files often include the plaintiff's medical or psychological records, and it is crucial to obtain these records early, rather than later after the plaintiff's deposition in the civil case.

9. Medical and Psychological Records

Counsel should have the prospective client sign authorization forms to enable the attorney to obtain full medical and psychological files and records from treating doctors and medical facilities, and should evaluate those records early on. The records should be carefully and thoroughly reviewed and evaluated as to any recording of the sexual harassment (or lack of any such documentation), as well as past medical and psychological history, which will be a gold mine of information for the defense in any sexual harassment or other employment-related case. It is not uncommon for an employee to forget having taken an antidepressant several years earlier, or having seen a psychologist for some other purpose, such as marital counseling. Counsel will need to go over the information with the client, both to be prepared to handle an issue before it arises and to consider whether it affects counsel's decision to take the case.

Moreover, it is prudent to be prepared in advance for the eventual and ubiquitous subpoena from the defense seeking any and all medical records going back nearly to birth. Having advance knowledge of private and confidential information that is not relevant to the current action, such as a prior treatment of herpes (a common term cited in medical records for a host of conditions), birth control pills, gynecological records, and mammograms will help counsel be prepared to meet and confer about producing redacted records to the employer, and know what battles need to be fought in court.

Defendants will probe as far and wide as possible. It is incumbent on the plaintiff's counsel to take all possible steps to protect the client's privacy. Defendants often seek information about the plaintiff's sexual life (barred in most if not all states by statute) and issues such as alcohol and substance abuse, domestic violence, or other forms of victimization. These issues, for the most part, are completely irrelevant, and disclosure would constitute an unlawful violation of the employee's constitutionally protected right of privacy.

Such privacy rights also need to be explained to the prospective client to start the training process for depositions, to avoid inadvertent blurting out of information to which defense is not entitled. Extra precautions need to be taken to protect these fundamental rights and prevent their disclosure beyond the scope of permissible discovery.

10. Statute of Limitations, Tolling, and Continuing Violations

You may have a perfect case but it will not go anywhere if it is stale and too late, and worse, you may put yourself at risk of legal malpractice by taking on a case close to or after the running of a statute of limitations. Particularly in cases where there has been no adverse action for a while, but where there seems to be a lot of continuous activity, it is important to obtain all available documents that will help to evaluate the timeliness of the claims and if there is any potential challenge based on the statute of limitations, and if so, whether it is overcome by a tolling agreement or by a pattern of continuing violations that will extend any filing deadlines.

Caution signs should be flashing if you see that the last event happened two years ago, or that multiple attorneys preceded you. There may be valid reasons and still time to bring an action for this prospective client, but foremost, lawyers must protect themselves. If you are in trial, or swamped with preexisting work and deadlines, and the prospective client appears to have a statute or deadline quickly approaching, then it is unwise for the busy lawyer to take on such a case, as it carries with it a risk of missing a deadline. There is too little room for error or missing an obscure deadline, such as with university cases having their own internal administrative remedies, public entity cases that involve the earlier filing of government claims, or, as occurs in some cases, an arbitration agreement that requires preliminary steps before filing the action. Do your homework, take heed, and exercise caution.

B. Witness Interviews

Sexual harassment claims are by their nature credibility contests. They pit one employee making an accusation against another employee denying the accusation. Counsel cannot just rely on the prospective client's recounting of the events; it is also important where possible to interview potential witnesses to the events. Once they have been interviewed, it is helpful to pin down as many early declarations as possible.

When employers are made aware of the possible litigation with the plaintiff, they often issue an edict to their employees right away instructing them not to have any contact with the plaintiff or plaintiff's counsel. Despite potentially constituting an improper restriction on the co-worker's constitutionally protected rights of free speech and association, such an edict may and generally does intimidate and instill fear in the other employees about cooperating or answering questions. That is another reason why early witness contacts are important.

Thus, as noted earlier, it is helpful for the prospective client to compile and provide counsel with a list of potential witnesses, along with all contact information. Counsel should decide whether to do the interviewing, or to hire a private investigator to locate and interview prospective witnesses. It may smooth the path toward communication with the witnesses to have the prospective client speak to some or all of the witnesses, if nothing more than to let them know counsel's name and to ask their permission to pass along their contact information.

This can avoid the situation where the employee witness is willing to speak to the plaintiff's counsel, but does not recognize the name and thus does not take the call. However, all clients and prospective clients must be cautioned to keep their communication with witnesses to an absolute minimum, to avoid discussing the case or facts with them, and to understand their role is to help the lawyer find and communicate with the witnesses.

Once there has been communication, it is advisable to prepare a sworn declaration or affidavit for cooperative witnesses. Even some seemingly uncooperative witnesses will still sign a declaration. This will be helpful for mediation and summary judgment motions, as well as to lock in testimony.

Caution needs to be exercised with regard to potential witnesses who are part of the employer's "control group." These include employees whose statements, actions, or inactions could be imputed to the employer or whose actions or inactions could bind the employer for liability toward the plaintiff.[16] Plaintiff's counsel may contact former employees, and current employees as long as they are not a part of the employer's control group. Also, the attorney is prohibited from communicating with any witness whom the lawyer knows to be represented by counsel. Thus, if the employer's counsel has put plaintiff's counsel on notice that he or she also represents certain employees, then such witnesses cannot be contacted directly by the plaintiff's counsel.

---

16. *See, e.g.*, CAL. RULES OF PROF'L RESPONSIBILITY R. 2–100.

C. Evaluation of Company's Financial Status and Insurance

In evaluating a prospective client's claims, it is equally important to assess the financial viability of the prospective defendant. The client may have great claims, but if the lawyer is going to be chasing down any verdict or payment, that fact should be known upfront if possible. Also, if the prospective client has such information, counsel should find out all that is possible in advance about the company's insurance coverage. This will become important both in the event the company experiences financial difficulty and in understanding the impact on any litigation. Even if the prospective client has no information about the company's insurance coverage, this is important information to obtain during litigation, as it will affect the company's defense handling, settlement prospects, who runs the litigation (e.g., insurer or employer), as well as financial standing. Thus, ask the prospective client if he or she is aware of any employment policy liability insurance; commercial general liability policy; directors, officers, and entity liability coverage; errors and omissions; or workers' compensation and employer's liability package policies. If the client does not have this information, it is important to seek full insurance coverage discovery from the employer once in litigation, and the employer is required to produce such information.

Investigation into a company's financial condition should start with the prospective client. Find out if the prospective client has any information or documents about the company's financial status and standing. If documents are turned over that are confidential, you should find out how the prospective client obtained them and assess whether they should be returned to the company. Counsel should be making such inquiries for the client's protection as well as for counsel's protection once the possession of these records becomes known.

There is usually a gold mine of information on the internet and through businesses that rate a company's credit, such as Dun & Bradstreet. Other sources such as Securities and Exchange Commission (SEC) filings and filings from state corporate divisions will also reflect how a company is doing and whether some imminent bankruptcy or other financial downfall is on the horizon. If the company is publicly traded, its annual and quarterly SEC reports are usually available, although there may be a modest cost charged to retrieve them. There are services that regularly research and report on companies' financial status. For public entity employers, it may be possible to make Freedom of Information Act requests for information. The goal is to ensure that it will be worth all the work and cost involved in litigating a harassment claim.

D. Evaluation of Plaintiff's Potential Legal Claims and Any Defenses

It is incumbent upon counsel to be or become familiar with all of the potential laws governing the potential client's claims, and the available claims. Some states have statutes that are similar to federal statutes, but are better for employees. For example, it is generally believed that the California FEHA is a better vehicle for a plaintiff's sexual harassment claim than Title VII of the Civil Rights Act of 1964 (Title VII).[17] Under Title VII, there is no individual liability of the harasser, whereas under the FEHA, the harasser may be individually named as a defendant. Title VII includes damages caps on compensatory and punitive damages, of between $50,000 and $300,000 depending on the size of the employer.[18]

The standards for liability as identified through case law are more favorable to employees using California's state statutes rather than Title VII. In some other states the employee has to proceed under Title VII. Counsel should compare any existing state statutes to the federal ones and proceed under whichever statute provides the client with the best remedies. Of relevance to that decision is whether it is better to proceed in state court or federal court. Asserting a claim under Title VII or any other federal statute will trigger the potential for removal to federal court.

A plaintiff in a sexual harassment case may also have claims for common law torts, such as invasion of privacy, false imprisonment, defamation, wrongful termination in violation of public policy,[19] sexual assault, and sexual battery. California statutes provide protection to employees for gender violence and sexual battery.[20] In addition, it is important to pay attention to any potential claims of retaliation. Although a plaintiff may be subjected to risk of losing in the "he said/she said" battle in sexual harassment litigation, the plaintiff does not necessarily need to prove the merit of an underlying complaint to support a retaliation claim. Plaintiff's burden in a retaliation case is to prove that there was a reasonable basis for believing in the legitimacy or merit of that claim, along with proximity in time or a nexus between that protected activity and the ultimate adverse employment action.

During the initial analysis of the case, it is good practice to read and be familiar with all jury instructions potentially governing the claims. It is also important, as mentioned earlier, to thoroughly evaluate all of the potential defenses raised or that may be raised.

As stated earlier, it is also important to step into the shoes of the defendant and try to anticipate the defenses that will be raised, and how to respond to or handle them.

E. Evaluation of Plaintiff's Damages

Many a bleeding heart lawyer has taken a case because the client was wronged, or the employer committed wrongdoing, only to end up with a very low settlement or verdict. The reason is often simply that the client's damages are low. Just because a prospective client has low damages is not a reason in and of itself to reject the case. However, a lawyer should do a cost/benefit analysis before plunging into representation of a prospective client.

---

17. 42 U.S.C. §§ 2000e–2000e-17.

18. *Id.* at § 1981A(b)(3).

19. *E.g.*, Rojo v. Kliger, 52 Cal. 3d 65, 276 Cal. Rptr. 130 (1990); Cal. Const. art. 1, § 8.

20. Cal. Civ. Code §§ 51.7, 51.9, 52.1, 52.4.

If there is a statutory claim, such as Title VII on the federal side, or a state statute such as the California FEHA, often there is an attorney's fee provision in the statute, meaning that if the claim is good, you may recover all or most of your fees at trial. There are still costs associated with each case, such as filing fees, depositions, expert witness fees, treating doctors, costs of graphics, and jury and reporter fees at trial.

In a case where there is a substantial risk of losing the case, the plaintiff will not only have incurred her or his own costs but may be assessed the defense costs. Absent a showing of a frivolous filing, there is limited risk of an award of attorney's fees against a plaintiff.[21] Nonetheless, any risk should be explained to the prospective client before filing or taking legal action. Such explanation should be documented for the file. A better action might be memorializing such risks in a follow-up letter to the client.

1. Economic Damages

Evaluation of what a prevailing plaintiff may recover generally includes all lost earnings, including lost salary and benefits, such as insurance and stock options. If plaintiff is a low-wage earner, or becomes re-employed at comparable pay fairly quickly, that may present an impediment to winning sizeable economic damages.

However, earning potential is also a factor. If the plaintiff was on an upwardly moving career track, the mere fact that she or he obtained comparable employment does not mean that she or he has the same opportunities for growth.

Sometimes it is necessary to retain an economist or vocational expert to assess the full extent of the plaintiff's economic losses. Both past and future economic losses should be calculated and evaluated. It is important to obtain all earnings statements from the prospective client in order to make these calculations.

2. Noneconomic Damages

More commonly the bulk of a plaintiff's damages in a sexual harassment suit are noneconomic, such as for emotional distress. To evaluate this type of damage, it is important at the initial consultation and during the early stages of investigation to thoroughly assess the prospective client's emotional state and damage, including evaluation of any treatment received from medical and psychological providers, any prescription medications prescribed due to the harassment, physical distress caused by the harassment, and any other resultant harm suffered.

It generally helps if the client has sought or obtained a form of counseling from someone regarding the sexual harassment. It becomes problematic when the client has a hefty medical history, but no mention anywhere of the sexual harassment. Probing the reason for such omission with the client is also an important component in the case evaluation process.

Find out if the client has sought counseling elsewhere, and why she or he has not obtained professional psychological counseling if it appears that such was needed. Sometimes one's culture makes it difficult to obtain counseling, particularly with men,

---

21. *See, e.g.*, Christiansburg Garment Co. v. EEOC, 434 U.S. 412 (1978).

or persons from a culture that discourages discussing personal feelings and emotions. Find out what outlet has been used to survive. For example, does the prospective client talk to her or his spouse about the experiences? A pastor or other representative of a religion? A trusted family member or close friend who gives comfort? Does this person act out his or her depression in compulsive behavior, or angry outbursts? It may be necessary in these cases to retain a psychiatric expert to conduct evaluations and testing on your client and to be able to explain to the jury why the plaintiff was unable to talk about these issues.

It should be considered that any claim for emotional distress carries with it the potential for the employer to seek a defense mental exam. A motion for such an exam will be denied if the plaintiff is only seeking "garden variety" emotional distress from the harassment, or if the distress is not ongoing and/or no treatment was obtained. Consideration must be given to whether the particular conduct is of the sort that would reasonably cause someone to suffer emotional distress. For example, a jury may not be persuaded that a couple of bad jokes caused severe emotional distress warranting treatment, whereas a physical touching may more readily be understood to cause significant emotional distress to the plaintiff.

Although jurors tend to expect that a plaintiff suffering from emotional distress will have sought some sort of medical or psychological treatment, testimony from a plaintiff's spouse, family members, long-term associates, colleagues, and friends may be equally credible and compelling to support the plaintiff's emotional distress claim.

It is important to explore what the prospective client's life was like before the harassment versus afterward. Find out what types of activities were engaged in and how often, and whether they have been curtailed or stopped. What amount of sleep did the plaintiff get in the past versus now? What sports and athletic events did the plaintiff engage in then versus now? Have contacts with friends or family changed, and how? Have social outings and interactions diminished? Talk to these witnesses about what the plaintiff was like before the harassment, and what changes they have noticed.

3. Mitigation

Plaintiff's mitigation efforts must be explored early on as well. It is good practice to ask the prospective client to continue looking for employment on a regular, ongoing basis, compile all job search documents and to keep copies of every ad responded to (whether in print or via online job banks), any letters sent to prospective employers, resumes submitted, emails or other communications with prospective employers or with networking resources for potential jobs, and notes of follow-up calls. The prospective client should be asked to turn over, or at least show, documentation of the ongoing job search and told to keep it in one spot, such as a "job search" notebook or folder. Find out if the prospective client signed up or worked with a recruiting or search company.

4. Punitive Damages

Assess the punitive damage potential. How did you feel toward the harasser and employer when you first heard the facts? These are important gut feelings to contemplate in the intake notes. A small damage case may still rile a jury to award large punitive damages. If this is a punitive damages case, keep that fact in mind during discovery, as there are generally statutes prohibiting discovery into a company's financial status until after either a finding at trial that punitive damages are to be assessed or on a pretrial motion presenting evidence of the likelihood of a finding of punitive damages.

Finally, you are ready to decide about representing this prospective client.

III. RETAINER AGREEMENTS

Once the decision is made to take the case and represent the client, it is essential to enter into a client retainer agreement. The attorney should make a decision as to the type of fee agreement he or she is willing to enter into, whether hourly, pure contingency, or a hybrid of both. With the exception of very high-wage-earner clients, most plaintiffs in harassment cases are unable to afford the high costs associated with the heavy litigation that occurs in such cases. Thus, most practitioners take these cases on a contingent-fee basis. Many will require the plaintiff to pay costs, although some will advance the costs. No matter what arrangement is made, the agreement must be in writing.[22] Any important term that is not covered in the written agreement between lawyer and client puts the lawyer at risk of not being paid at least some portion of costs or fees incurred. Even something as seemingly small as an obligation to pay for copy costs should be included in the retainer agreement to avoid any confusion or misunderstanding.

Go over the agreement in detail with the client, and have it signed by both client and lawyer. A good practice is to have the client initial each separate page and particular clauses.

It is often advisable in fact-intensive and witness-controlled sexual harassment cases to handle the representation of the client in stages. First, prepare a pre-litigation, negotiation-only retainer agreement. During the course of negotiations, even if the case does not settle, at least further information will be obtained, including the employer's counter-positions, further information about its investigation, and findings during the investigation into the plaintiff's sexual harassment claims. Make sure the pre-litigation agreement clearly spells out that it covers only pre-litigation negotiations, and that it does not cover litigation if the case fails to settle.

After doing an investigation, and having the client sign a retainer agreement, then it is time to draft up a demand letter and initiate negotiations with the employer. Use the negotiation process to conduct further investigation, and then discuss with the client the additional information gleaned. If additional facts were learned that cause concern, they should be discussed with the client at that time.

If the lawyer decides after this process not to take the case further, or that it is not worth litigating, it is imperative to so inform the client of this decision, as well as to advise of any time limits. They should be told and encouraged to seek other legal advice

---

22. *See, e.g.*, Cal. Bus. & Prof. Code § 6147 (requiring all contingent fee retainer agreements to be in writing).

if they still want to pursue their potential claims. The decision not to represent the client further should then be memorialized in writing.

If, on the other hand, the lawyer decides he or she is interested in proceeding further, then the next step is to discuss litigation, as well as the possibility of settlement, with the client. Here it is important to discuss in detail what the client may expect going through this process, cautioning that it will not be easy, explaining about discovery, depositions, and the need for a substantial amount of preparation time for the plaintiff; that the plaintiff will be heavily involved in the litigation; and it will often become difficult or demoralizing for the plaintiff. Another written retainer agreement will be prepared, this one for litigation only. It should clearly spell out the scope of the representation, that it is for the litigation only, and not for appeals or other matters. It too should be discussed in detail with the client, and both lawyer and client should sign the agreement.

Clients should always be told of the confidentiality of all communications, that they are not to discuss these communications with their spouse or any other person. Why? Because it is possible their family members, spouse, and friends may become witnesses in the case. In that event, their depositions may be taken. Whether they are giving testimony at deposition or at trial, they will undoubtedly be asked about any conversations or communications they had with the plaintiff about the case, which may delve into conversations with the plaintiff's attorney. Hence, caution to the client about talking with anyone about the case is important.

IV. FILING THE SEXUAL HARASSMENT CLAIM

A. Filing the Charge

A mandatory prerequisite to filing a civil suit for sexual harassment under either the federal or state anti-harassment statutes is to exhaust administrative remedies. This is satisfied by filing an administrative charge of discrimination with the governmental agency. For a federal claim under Title VII, the employee must file the charge of discrimination with the EEOC. Counsel should ascertain whether their state laws contain a similar provision governing exhaustion of administrative remedies prior to filing a civil suit for sexual harassment.

The administrative agency may draft the administrative charge of harassment, discrimination or retaliation, but it may be more prudent for the plaintiff's counsel to draft it. This will ensure that the proper form boxes are checked, that the correct employer (or individual alleged harasser) names are listed, and that all rights are preserved. If the employee has already filed with the state or federal agency before coming to see the lawyer, then it is important for the lawyer to carefully review what was filed, to make sure it is correct. If any errors or omissions are noted, then an amended or supplemental charge must be promptly filed.

The employee will have the right either to request an immediate right-to-sue letter or to have the employee's claim investigated. It is often the case that these investigations take a long time, and more often than not, particularly in "he said-she said" types of sexual harassment claims, the agency will render a finding that it was unable to substantiate the claims. Thus, except in very strong cases or cases with enough plaintiffs and/or witnesses to support the claims, it may be a better course of action to ask for an immediate right-to-sue letter. This will then enable the expedient filing of a civil suit in state or federal court.

It is important not only to ensure that the box for "sexual harassment" or another prohibited form of "harassment" is checked, but also, if there is a claim for retaliation, that that separate box is also checked. There may be other claims as well, including discrimination on the basis of sex or other protected categories. It is important to make sure that all relevant boxes are checked on the form to avoid the plaintiff losing the right to pursue such claim.

Technical defects in these forms may result in dismissal of statutory claims filed by the plaintiff. Thus, counsel should remain very involved in every step of the process, if possible. In Title VII claims, if conduct does not fall within the 300 days prior to the filing of the charge of discrimination, or 180 days in a nondeferral jurisdiction, the statute of limitations may be applied to defeat the claims. In that instance, counsel should evaluate whether there are continuing violations, and if there are, they should be pled in the administrative charge.

Finally, other potential pre-litigation filings need to be born in mind. For example, if the actions involve a public entity, there may by a need to file a government tort claim (likely covered in other portions of this book, and reading of the statutes of the particular state is essential). Additionally, cases against universities and hospitals, there may be additional administrative pre-filing requirements. A lawyer needs to make themselves aware of the possibility of a company or entity's pre-filing ADR (Alternative Dispute Resolution) requirements, such as participating in a mediation before filing a complaint.

B. Drafting the Civil Complaint

There are time limits within which a civil complaint must be filed. In Title VII claims, generally the complaint must be filed within 90 days after issuance of the right-to-sue letter issued by the EEOC. State claims have different time limits and vary from state to state. In California, the plaintiff has one year from the issuance of the right-to-sue letter to file a civil suit in state court. Counsel should check their state statutes to ensure that any complaint is timely filed after issuance of the right-to-sue letter.

The complaint should include a theme and sufficient facts to adequately tell the story of what occurred, as well as plead any continuing violations to head off a statute of limitations defense. Counsel should factor into the drafting such issues as removal to federal court, which will occur if federal claims are pled. If there is a better state claim and the federal claim is not necessary or is duplicative, and if the plaintiff has a better shot in state rather than federal court, then perhaps only the state claims should be pled.

If any federal claims are pled, or if there is diversity jurisdiction between the parties, there is a chance of removal to federal court. Counsel and the client need to evaluate which forum is best for the plaintiff. If the basis for removal is diversity jurisdiction, and state court is preferred over federal court for the case, then an evaluation should be made as to whether there is a good faith basis to name other defendants who may defeat diversity, such as an individual harasser.

Consideration should be given to whether certain claims will trigger insurance. This is particularly important if the employer has any financial instability. The complaint should include every remedy and every form of relief available. This should include not only economic damages (including past and future lost earnings) and noneconomic damages (including emotional distress damages) but also prejudgment interest, punitive damages, consequential damages, and attorney's fees and costs.

If injunctive relief is applicable and being sought, that should be separately pled. Injunctive relief should be sought particularly where the plaintiff remains employed by the defendant employer. For example, injunctive relief may be appropriate to prohibit the employer from engaging in further unlawful acts of sexual harassment or retaliation. If the plaintiff is no longer employed, counsel may consider seeking reinstatement of the plaintiff to her or his former position.

Consideration should be given not only to forum, but also to venue if, for example, the employer has multiple locations or has local sites and a headquarters in a different location. Factors to consider in deciding whether to file in state or federal court include

- the applicable burden of proof under each legal theory;
- the availability of emotional distress damages, punitive damages, and attorney's fees;
- the right to a jury trial;
- the requirement of a unanimous verdict in federal court, versus less than unanimous in most state courts;
- the community from which the potential jurors are selected;
- the trial judges available;
- the availability of a change of venue;
- procedural differences, including the code of civil procedure and local rules of court;
- counsel's familiarity and experience with the court system; and
- the risk of removal to federal court based on diversity of citizenship, or pleading federal claims.

If counsel has a choice of venue, then careful consideration should be given to the differences in jury and judge pools, and evaluated in relation to the plaintiff, plaintiff's gender, race, profession, income, and other such factors.

If the case may be removed to federal court, because of the strict time lines for filing a jury demand, it is advisable to always include in the complaint a separate Demand for Jury Trial, stated both in the caption and at the end of the complaint. This has been deemed in many, if not all, jurisdictions to satisfy the federal requirement for asserting a demand for jury trial and will avoid an inadvertent waiver of that right.

Finally, it is advisable to always consider settlement opportunities before filing. Most cases are ultimately resolved by settlement at some point. An early filed (or pre-litigation) case, has an upside to settlement in that damages and attorneys' fees are lower, and there may be more of a chance to obtain a reasonable resolution without spending all the time and money on litigation. The downside is not knowing all that a plaintiff might feel is needed for settlement talks, or the parties may not feel they are ready, emotionally, to put the case behind them, or they want a "pound of flesh." Consider picking up the phone and calling a general counsel if there is one, or someone in the law department.

Alternately a letter (often referred to as "demand letter") can be sent to the head of the company, advising of the wrongs inflicted on the plaintiff, and inquiring if there is an interest in pursuing an early resolution before embarking on litigation. If the case is already in litigation, ask the court if it conducts a mandatory settlement conference which is overseen by the judge, or a volunteer lawyer. It is incumbent on the lawyer to bear in mind the toll that litigation can take on a client, and that early resolution may be in the client's best interest. Some cases need to be litigated. Some parties need litigation to commence before they can be open to resolution. Either way, if the steps set forth here have been followed, then everyone is ready to proceed.

V. RECENT RELATED LEGISLATION

A. California Legislation (Harassment/Discrimination)

SEXUAL HARASSMENT AND TRAINING: SB 1300, signed into law by California Governor Jerry Brown in September 2018, lowers the standard of proof on a sexual harassment claim and the employee's risk on an unsuccessful claim, among other provisions. SB 1343 was also signed into law by Governor Brown in September 2018. This expands the scope of required sexual harassment training by employers.

GENDER IDENTITY HARASSMENT AND TRAINING: SB 396 was signed into law by Governor Brown in October 2017. This statute expands the scope of mandatory sexual harassment training to supervisory employees; to include gender identity, gender expression, and sexual orientation; and to post related posters in accessible, prominent locations in the workplace.

CONFIDENTIALITY (in sexual harassment claims): SB 820, SB 954, and AB 3109, in various ways, impact confidentiality in settlement of sexual harassment and assault cases. There are other newly passed bills that generally extend protection for victims in sexual harassment cases. These include AB 2338, which requires talent agencies to provide training materials on sexual harassment to clients; AB 2779, which broadens the definition of privileged publication under California Civil Code Section 47 to include sexual harassment complaints; and SB 224, which expands the list of business relationships that can give rise to a sexual harassment lawsuit. These bills are set to become effective in January 2019.

B. Federal Legislation

Confidentiality/Tax Status in Sexual Harassment cases: Presumably arising out of the "Me Too" movement, § 13307 of the Tax Cuts and Jobs Act states that no tax deduction is allowed for any settlement or payment related to sexual harassment or sexual abuse, if the settlement or payment is subject to a nondisclosure agreement. It also prohibits taking tax deductions for attorneys' fees related to confidential sexual harassment settlements or payments. It is predicted that this may have an effect on the settlements, possibly the valuation of settlements, and pleadings of claims in employment cases. All lawyers on both the plaintiff and defense sides need to be aware of this newly enacted law and the impacts it will have on their cases and settlements. Thus far, such cases are being handled in myriad ways. Therefore, it is important for all counsel to think through and discuss these issues with their client, and opposing counsel, in advance of a mediation or settlement conference.

CHAPTER 4

Responding to the Charge and the Complaint

Matthew B. Schiff and Kathryn Nadro

Defending your first sexual harassment case can be daunting—the drama among the participants may cause excessive stress for your client and witnesses, the factual elements of the claims may be complex and extensive, and the administrative process may be entirely new and unfamiliar. Further, discrimination law under Title VII of the Civil Rights Act of 1964 (Title VII) is a constantly evolving topic as the Equal Employment Opportunity Commission (EEOC) and the courts have added different interpretive glosses to the statutory text.[1]

This chapter will provide guidance on two related topics: responding to a sexual harassment administrative charge and responding to a sexual harassment complaint filed in court. How the employer responds to the charge of discrimination frequently shapes its defenses to the administrative charge and eventually the lawsuit. Although this chapter will mainly discuss procedure and case law related to claims under Title VII[2], attorneys should be aware that many sexual harassment cases are brought under state or local law.[3] Some state statutes, including those in California and Hawaii, are more protective of complainants than federal law. Many state statutes, for example, may not have damages caps as Title VII does.[4] Knowing the key differences between your state and local law and Title VII is critical in forming the defense strategy for your client.

---

1. For example, several circuit courts of appeal have held that discrimination based on sexual orientation or transgender status qualifies as sex discrimination. *See, e.g.,* E.E.O.C. v. R.G & G.R. Harris Funeral Homes, Inc., 884 F.3d 560 (6th Cir. 2018) (Title VII prohibits discrimination based on transgender identity as unlawful sex discrimination); Zarda v. Altitude Express, Inc., 883 F.3d 100 (2d Cir. 2018) (*en banc*) (employee entitled to bring Title VII claim for discrimination based on sexual orientation); Hively v. Ivy Tech Community College of Indiana, 853 F.3d 339 (7th Cir. 2017) (*en banc*) (Title VII prohibits discrimination based on sexual orientation).

2. 42 U.S.C. §§ 2000e–2000e-15 (West, WestlawNext through P.L. 115–223).

3. *See, e.g.,* Illinois Human Rights Act, 775 Ill. Comp. Stat. 5/1-101 through 10/104 (West, WestlawNext through P.A. 100–1114, of the 2018 Reg. Sess.) and Chicago, Illinois Municipal Code §§ 2-160-010 through 2-160-120.

4. *See* 42 U.S.C. § 1981a(b)(3) (West, WestlawNext through P.L. 115–223).

I. RESPONDING TO THE ADMINISTRATIVE CHARGE

Before a charging party may take her case to federal court under Title VII, she[5] must first exhaust her administrative remedies. Typically, the charging party will file a charge of discrimination with the EEOC and/or with an appropriate state fair employment practices agency. Failure to file a charge with the EEOC will bar the charging party from pursuing her case in federal court.

A. Evaluating the Charge

Once the charge has been filed, the employer (known as Respondent at the administrative level) will be sent a copy of the charge along with procedural information from the EEOC. At that time, the employer will come to you, the litigator who will handle the case, to conduct an initial review of the charge and either perform or supervise the subsequent investigation.

The defense attorney's first order of business should be to identify any weaknesses and potential defenses on the face of the charge itself. These weaknesses may include whether the right entity is named as the defendant employer or whether the charge was filed within the proper limitation period. In states where a state or local agency also enforces a prohibition against the same type of employment discrimination (deferral states), a charging party may file a charge for events that occurred in the 300 days prior to the filing date.[6] Otherwise, the charging party must file within 180 days of the unlawful discrimination. Events that occurred prior to that date are time-barred and the employer's response to the charge should make note of that defense.

The employer must also have 15 or more employees working for 20 or more weeks to be considered an "employer" under Title VII.[7] If the company does not employ enough employees, this should be brought to the investigator's attention immediately. Some state and local fair employment practices statutes have jurisdiction over smaller employers, so the defense attorney should be mindful of the varying laws the client's employer may be subject to.[8]

Additionally, the attorney should determine whether the charging party has alleged any facts that invoke the continuing violation doctrine or has only alleged discrete acts of unlawful discrimination. The continuing violation doctrine provides that when a plaintiff alleges a hostile work environment claim, "as long as the employee files her complaint while at least one act which comprises the hostile work environment claim

---

5. Although the authors on occasion use feminine pronouns to refer to the hypothetical charging party or plaintiff, sexual harassment claims are by no means filed solely by women against men. *See* "Charges Alleging Sex-Based Harassment FY 2010-FY2017," Equal Employment Opportunity Commission, https://www.eeoc.gov/eeoc/statistics/enforcement/sexual_harassment_new.cfm.

6. 42 U.S.C. § 2000e-5(e)(1) (West, WestlawNext through P.L. 115–223).

7. 42 U.S.C. § 2000e (West, WestlawNext through P.L. 115–223).

8. *See, e.g.,* Illinois Human Rights Act, 775 Ill. Comp. Stat. 5/2-101(B)(1)(b) (an "employer" for sexual harassment complaints is any company employing one or more employees).

is still timely, 'the entire time period of the hostile environment may be considered by a court for the purpose of determining liability.'"[9] The Supreme Court in *Morgan* distinguished discrete acts that form the basis for traditional discrimination claims from continuing conduct that forms the basis of hostile work environment claims. Only hostile workplace claims are subject to the continuing violation doctrine. This should indicate to the defense attorney that there is a way to attack the charge. If the plaintiff has alleged only one specific discrete act of unlawful discrimination, for example, then a charge alleging a hostile work environment may be very weak as the factual allegations do not suggest a continuing course of discriminatory conduct.

Finally, the defense attorney must evaluate the scope of the charge to determine which protected classes and wrongful actions are implicated in the charge. The facts alleged in the charge itself will indicate the scope of the EEOC's investigation, potentially the employer's investigation, and the possible future lawsuit filed by the plaintiff. The charge contains boxes that the charging party must check to indicate which protected class is implicated in the charge or upon which basis the charge is brought. If the charging party fails to check the appropriate boxes, her claim may be significantly narrowed. For example, if the charging party fails to check the box for "sex" and in her narrative statement alleges retaliation based upon a prior complaint of sex discrimination, only the retaliation claim may be viable.[10] The attorney should also carefully examine all the allegations to which the employer must respond, as well as any details described in the employee's narrative. These allegations will be the starting point for the internal investigation into the charge.

B. Conduct the Investigation and Draft the Position Statement

After reviewing the administrative charge, the defense attorney's next objective is to learn as much as possible about the facts and circumstances of the case. The attorney should speak to the appropriate point of contact with the employer to gather information about the charging party, the events and circumstances implicated in the charge's allegations, and the factual bases for the charging party's claims. It is often helpful to make a personal visit to the worksite to conduct the investigation. Identifying and interviewing witnesses with personal knowledge of the events is critical. Do not make the mistake of relying solely on a secondhand account from upper management. Early interviews of critical witnesses may prevent loss of key evidence due to memory lapse, employee turnover, or even worse, spoliation.

In addition to witness interviews, you will need to gather pertinent documents. It is critical to issue a litigation hold letter to the company to ensure compliance with the duty to preserve evidence. The litigation hold letter and any follow-up guidance should

---

9. Heath v. Bd. of Supervisors for S. Univ. & Agric. & Mech. Coll., 850 F.3d 731, 736 (5th Cir. 2017), *as revised* (Mar. 13, 2017), quoting National R.R. Passenger Corp. v. Morgan, 536 U.S. 101, 117, 122 S. Ct. 2061, 153 L.Ed.2d 106 (2002).

10. *See, e.g.,* Richter v. Advance Auto Parts, Inc., 686 F.3d 847, 852 (8th Cir. 2012) ("[r]etaliation claims are not reasonably related to discrimination claims").

include specific instructions regarding electronic data (e.g., advise the client to turn off all auto-archive or auto-delete functions for relevant custodians for the duration of the case). The defense attorney should also inquire into personal devices such as cell phones, which may have relevant text messages or voicemails that must also be preserved and collected.

The first documents to gather are typically the employee's personnel file, the employee handbook, and any documents regarding the employee's performance, attendance, or disciplinary actions. You should also gather parallel information on any similarly situated employees to bolster the defense of nondiscrimination. In gathering the documents, ensure you have all documentation of any adverse employment actions, whether implicated in the charge or not. These will include demotions, salary reductions, and terminations, but may also include seemingly minor incidents such as oral and written warnings or a change of workstation. Finally, collect any applicable policies from the employer that were not in the employee handbook, such as the nondiscrimination and anti-harassment policy, anti-retaliation policy, acceptable use policy for computers or other employer technology, or leave of absence policy.

Witness interviews should be conducted after an initial review of the documents. Your interview list should include all individuals mentioned in the charge, decision-makers, and supervisors of the charging party, as well as anyone having relevant information. This may include coworkers, contractors, or vendors. Conducting witness interviews early in the process will lock in testimony and preserve evidence in the event the witnesses are later unavailable.

Although a full discussion of retaliation is outside the scope of this chapter, during the internal investigation into the complaint or charge of sexual harassment or discrimination, the employer's attorney should make it very clear that any adverse employment actions taken against the charging party may be considered retaliation for engaging in protected activity. A weak sexual harassment case may be converted into a compelling retaliation case under Title VII if any of the employer's supervisors take actions against the charging party or against witnesses supporting the charging party that may be considered retaliation. Emphasizing this point during interviews may prevent that bad outcome.

C. Participate in the EEOC Process

Upon receiving the charge, the employer's attorney should consider whether mediation at the EEOC is a worthwhile route to resolving the dispute. The EEOC asks both the employee and employer whether they are interested in voluntary mediation. If either party refuses to mediate, the charge is referred to an investigator. If the parties agree to mediate, the EEOC will refer the charge to an internal mediator. If mediation fails, then the charge is referred back to an investigator. The mediation itself is free and can potentially resolve disputes faster than proceeding through the charge process.

If mediation is not pursued, the employer must submit a position statement that responds to the charge. The position statement should identify, explain, and expose the weaknesses in the charge. It should also highlight information from the employer's internal investigation that refutes or undermines allegations in the charge. This often includes attached documents such as employee demographic charts, information from personnel files of similarly situated employees, and policies from the employer. The position statement's function is to illustrate why no discriminatory, harassing, or retaliatory actions occurred and give the investigator a reason to recommend a "no cause" finding. When drafting the position statement, the attorney should also be sure to gather any specific information and documents requested by the EEOC to provide along with the position statement itself. In many cases, the investigator will perform an on-site visit to the employer's worksite to conduct employee interviews. Although the defense attorney may be present for any interviews with management personnel of the employer, the EEOC investigator is permitted to interview nonmanagement personnel without the employer's attorney or other representative present.[11]

The employer's attorney should be diligent and thorough in conducting or overseeing the internal investigation and providing responses to the EEOC's requests for information. Although this process may be time-consuming, a proper response to the EEOC is more likely to generate a finding of no cause and increase the likelihood of resolving the dispute favorably to the employer prior to any litigation being filed.

After submitting the position statement and supplying the requested information to the EEOC (a process that can occasionally go through several rounds of additional information requests), the investigator will ultimately make a recommendation to the EEOC of a finding of "cause" or "no cause" with respect to the charge of discrimination. If the EEOC determines that there is no reasonable cause to believe unlawful discrimination occurred, then the charging party will receive a Notice of Right to Sue, which informs the charging party of her right to file a complaint in federal court within 90 days of receipt of the notice. The employer is also given a copy of the right to sue letter.

If, however, the EEOC determines that there is reasonable cause to believe unlawful discrimination occurred, then the employer and charging party will receive a Letter of Determination, which states that discrimination occurred and invites the parties to join the agency in the conciliation process. This is an informal process wherein the EEOC and charging party work with the employer to reach a confidential settlement before a lawsuit is filed. The EEOC is required to engage in conciliation in good faith. Defense counsel should document all negotiations in the conciliation process. The Supreme Court in *Mach Mining, LLC v. E.E.O.C.* held that a court may review the EEOC's efforts at conciliation to determine whether the process had been undertaken in a good faith effort to resolve the dispute prior to filing suit.[12] If conciliation fails, then the EEOC can choose to file a lawsuit on the charging party's behalf or the charging party will be given a right to sue letter.

Although beyond the scope of this chapter, from the employer's standpoint, an individual lawsuit filed by the charging party is nearly always preferable to a lawsuit filed by the EEOC, which typically occurs in a higher profile case in which the EEOC wants

---

11. *See* "What You Can Expect After a Charge is Filed," Equal Employment Opportunity Commission," https://www.eeoc.gov/employers/process.cfm (April 17, 2018).

12. 135 S. Ct. 1645 (2015).

to make an example. An EEOC lawsuit will generally be accompanied by significantly more publicity, experience, resources, and manpower than an individual lawsuit. Many of these suits are multi-plaintiff or class action lawsuits alleging a pattern or practice of discrimination. Sexual harassment suits may be brought by the EEOC on behalf of a group of aggrieved persons without certifying the case as a class action and complying with Fed. R. Civ. P. 23.[13]

II. RESPONDING TO THE COMPLAINT

A. Evaluate the Complaint for Potential Defenses

Once the EEOC or appropriate state agency has issued a Notice of Right to Sue to the charging party, he or she has 90 days in which to file a lawsuit in court. Although plaintiffs may file their lawsuits in state court, particularly where state law is more plaintiff-friendly than federal law, the typical sexual harassment case is filed in federal court.

Upon service of the complaint, the employer's attorney should examine the face of the complaint for defenses. The first consideration is once again timeliness—has the plaintiff filed the complaint within the 90-day period after receiving the Notice of Right to Sue? Title VII plaintiffs must file their lawsuits within 90 days of receiving a Notice of Right to Sue from the EEOC.[14] The "mailbox rule" creates a legal presumption that an addressee receives a letter within five days of the letter having been placed in the mail properly stamped.[15]

The defense attorney should also evaluate whether there are any improper defendant, co-employer, or joint employer issues. An improper defendant may, for example, be an individual supervisor in addition to the company. Under Title VII, individual supervisors cannot be sued for discrimination.[16] By contrast, individual supervisors may be named under certain state fair employment practices statutes.[17] A savvy plaintiff may file suit in state court under state law and join as a defendant an individual supervisor to defeat an employer's removal motion by destroying diversity jurisdiction. In assessing the complaint, the defense attorney should evaluate whether removal may be an option and whether the joinder of any individual supervisors in state court could be fraudulent.[18] An extraordinarily weak cause of action brought against an individual

---

13. E.E.O.C. v. Pitre, Inc., 908 F. Supp. 1165, 1173 (D. N. Mex. 2012).

14. 42 U.S.C. § 2000e-5(f)(1) (West, WestlawNext through P.L. 115–223); Madden v. Value Place Prop. Mgmt., LLC, No. 1:12CV21, 2012 WL 3960416, at *2 (N.D. Ind. Sept. 7, 2012).

15. *Id.* at *3.

16. Discriminatory acts of supervisors may be imputed to the employer under vicarious liability in some circumstances—*see* Vance v. Ball State Univ., 570 U.S. 421 (2013).

17. *See, e.g.,* Asplund v. iPCS Wireless, Inc., 602 F. Supp. 2d 1005, 1010 (N.D. Iowa 2008) (noting that Iowa's fair employment practices law allows for employment discrimination claims against "persons" whereas Title VII permits claims only against "employer[s]").

18. *See, e.g.,* Saginaw Housing Com'n v. Bannum, Inc., 576 F.3d 620, 624 (6th Cir. 2009) ("Fraudulent joinder occurs when the non-removing party joins a party against whom there is no colorable cause of action.").

supervisor under state law may indicate fraudulent joinder and could preserve the employer's ability to remove the case.

Another issue to assess is whether there is a potential joint employer who may also be a proper defendant. Joint employer issues may arise when workers are employed by temporary staffing agencies but are staffed to specific worksites where both companies "share or co-determine those matters governing the essential terms and conditions of employment."[19]

B. Consider Whether a Motion to Dismiss Is Appropriate

The employer's attorney may determine that a motion to dismiss the complaint is appropriate. Motions to dismiss based upon Fed. R. Civ. P. 12(b) are potentially useful, particularly for failures in the pleading, which cannot be cured. Such a motion for failure to exhaust administrative remedies, for example, may be dispositive of the entire dispute if the last event in question occurred prior to 300 days before the filing of the charge.

Similarly, if the complaint alleges facts or legal theories that are not found within the scope of the charge, or reasonably related to those in the charge, it may be dismissed. Claims not included in the EEOC charge may only be pursued in federal court if they are "reasonably related" to the claim filed with the EEOC. A claim is "considered reasonably related if the conduct complained of would fall within the scope of the EEOC investigation which can reasonably be expected to grow out of the charge that was made."[20] State tort claims such as battery, defamation, and invasion of privacy may be added under supplemental jurisdiction without exhausting administrative remedies.[21]

Although motions to dismiss based on a failure to state a claim may be successful, the defense attorney should bear in mind that if a complaint is dismissed, the court will often allow the plaintiff to replead and the process may be repeated. If this seems likely, it may be more efficient and cost-effective for the defendant employer to simply answer the complaint and assert affirmative defenses.

C. Removal

In the event the plaintiff has filed her lawsuit in state court, the defendant has the option to remove the case to federal court if (1) the plaintiff has alleged federal causes of action, such as under Title VII (granting the federal court federal question jurisdiction under 28 U.S.C. § 1331) or (2) if there is diversity jurisdiction under 28 U.S.C. § 1332. Diversity

---

19. Butler v. Drive Auto. Indus. of Am., Inc., 793 F.3d 404, 408 (4th Cir. 2015), quoting Bristol v. Bd. of Cnty. Comm'rs, 312 F.3d 1213, 1218 (10th Cir. 2002) (*en banc*).

20. Gomez v. New York City Police Dep't, 191 F. Supp. 3d 293, 299 (S.D.N.Y. 2016) (claim of sexual harassment dismissed as EEOC charge only alleged failure to accommodate a disability and wrongful termination on the basis of disability, not sexual harassment).

21. *See, e.g.,* Young v. Howard Indus., 2013 WL 6095472 (S.D. Miss. November 20, 2013) (dismissing Title VII claim for failure to exhaust administrative remedies but permitting state law intentional infliction of emotional distress claim to proceed).

jurisdiction is less common in employment cases, as the plaintiff-employee is typically a citizen of the same state as the defendant employer and claimed damages do not always exceed the jurisdictional threshold. Under 28 U.S.C. § 1446(b)(1), the defendant has 30 days from receipt of the complaint to file a notice of removal. Receipt of a courtesy copy starts the clock on removal.[22]

The state law causes of action asserted by the plaintiff may be litigated under the supplemental jurisdiction of the federal court. In the event only state law claims have been asserted, a defense that asserts federal question jurisdiction is not sufficient to remove the case to federal court. "Federal jurisdiction cannot be predicated on an actual or anticipated defense: 'It is not enough that the plaintiff alleges some anticipated defense to his cause of action and asserts that the defense is invalidated by some provision of [federal law].'"[23] Additionally, if the federal court dismisses the federal claim, the case may be remanded to state court to litigate the state law causes of action.

D. Drafting the Answer and Affirmative Defenses

As an initial matter, an attorney who has been intimately involved in the employer's investigation and administrative process prior to the lawsuit has a significant advantage over an attorney brought in only when a lawsuit is filed. The former has the advantage of having either participated in or closely supervised the investigation, including witness interviews, document gathering, and drafting the position statement. The attorney may even have discussed the case details with the EEOC investigator, which may give insight into the how the case is viewed at the EEOC in the event that the agency participates in the lawsuit.

However, frequently an employer will not retain an attorney until a lawsuit is filed, preferring to handle the internal investigation and administrative process with either a human resources professional or other management personnel. In this situation, the attorney must first evaluate the investigation and position statement drafted by the employer and identify any potential minefields created by that process. If the defense attorney is new to the case, then he or she must become familiar with the facts behind the complaint in order to draft the answer. The attorney must also interview a representative of the employer most familiar with the facts and circumstances alleged in the complaint to determine whether to properly admit or deny each of the complaint's allegations.

In federal court, the defendant employer typically must answer the complaint within 21 days of service, unless service was waived or some other extension has been granted.[24] Always be sure to check the court's local rules for any changes to the time to respond to a complaint. The answer filed by the employer in court must admit, deny, or

---

22. *See* 28 U.S.C. § 1446(b)(1) (West, WestlawNext through P.L. 115–223) (time period to file removal motion begins when the defendant receives the complaint "through service or otherwise").

23. Vaden v. Discover Bank, 556 U.S. 49, 60, 129 S. Ct. 1262, 1272 (2009).

24. *See* Fed. R. Civ. P. 12(a)(1).

affirm a lack of knowledge sufficient to admit or deny in response to every allegation in the complaint under Fed. R. Civ. P. 8(b). The answer should also include any affirmative defense that may be viable. A failure to assert such a defense in the answer will result in waiver of that defense. Some of the most common affirmative defenses in sexual harassment cases are as follows:

- Statute of limitations bars all or part of the claims (including claims arising more than 300 days before the filing of the charge; the complaint was not filed within 90 days of the issuance of the Notice of Right to Sue).
- Failure to exhaust administrative remedies.
- Claims are barred that are beyond the scope of the charge filed in the administrative agency.
- Claims against defendants not named in the administrative agency charge are barred.
- Claims are barred because the plaintiff had not suffered any adverse action related to those claims.
- Claims are barred in whole or in part as a result of the plaintiff's own acts or omissions being the proximate cause of any damages sustained.
- Claims of lost wages are barred as the plaintiff has not suffered lost wages.
- Failure to mitigate damages.
- Damages for mental anguish or emotional distress, if any, resulted in whole or in part from acts or events that are unrelated to the defendant's conduct or actions.
- The employer acted reasonably in preventing and responding to claims of harassment, and the charging party acted unreasonably in not utilizing the internal complaint procedure (the *Faragher-Ellerth* defense).

III. CONCLUSION

Preparing and executing a defense to a sexual harassment charge and/or complaint requires a thorough understanding of the facts and law of the case. This chapter has given a high-level overview of how to approach an internal investigation and some initial attacks to be made upon a complaint filed in court. However, each sexual harassment case is a fact-intensive inquiry that will require careful witness interviews, discussions with decision-makers, and negotiations with the EEOC and plaintiff's counsel. A successful defense attorney will engage in the investigation process with equal vigor and attention to detail as the potential litigation process. Careful investigation and responses to charges may result in early and cost-effective conclusion of meritless claims.

CHAPTER 5

Employment Practices Liability Insurance

Ellis B. Murov and Andrew J. Baer

I. BACKGROUND

Employment practices liability (EPL) insurance originated in the late 1980s.[1] The earliest policies provided coverage only for the costs of defense for a limited time period while subject to a monetary limit of liability.[2]

With the enactment of the Civil Rights Act of 1991,[3] which, for the first time, authorized recovery of compensatory and punitive damages up to $300,000 for violations of Title VII of the Civil Rights Act of 1964 (Title VII), demand for EPL coverage increased.[4] Title VII plaintiffs could still recover back pay, reinstatement, or front pay.[5]

Then, the Clarence Thomas nomination hearings caused the nation to focus on sexual harassment in the workplace. The "hearings, coupled with the newly implanted teeth of available damages for these claims, caused the number of Charges of Discrimination involving sexual harassment filed before the Equal Employment Opportunity Commission (EEOC) to soar beginning in 1992."[6]

---

1. Ellis B. Murov, The Practitioner's Guide to Defense of EPL Claims 1 (ABA 2005) [hereinafter Practitioner's Guide].

2. *Id.*

3. *See* 42 U.S.C. § 1981a.

4. 42 U.S.C. §§ 2000e–2000e-17 (1991).

5. Reinstatement is still the preferred remedy. *See* Weaver v. Amoco Prod. Co., 66 F.3d 85, 88 (5th Cir. 1995). *See also* Kurcia v. Se. Ark. Cmty. Action Corp., 284 F.3d 948 (8th Cir. 2002) (front pay is permissible only where reinstatement is not feasible).

6. Joseph P. Monteleone, *Employment Practices Liability Insurance*, in Practitioner's Guide, *supra* note 1, at 2. (At the time of writing his chapter, Mr. Monteleone was vice president and claims counsel for The Hartford, Hartford Financial Products, New York.) In fact, there were 63,898 and 73,302 charges filed with the EEOC in 1991 and 1992, respectively. There were 82,792 filed in 2007.

II. COVERAGE

The typical EPL policy expressly covers sexual harassment claims, as well as wrongful terminations, including constructive and retaliatory discharge claims. The insurer will, under most policies and subject to policy limits, fund settlements as well as judgments, including amounts for back and front pay, pre- and post-judgment interest, attorney's fees, costs of court, and defense expenses. Punitive damages are discussed in § IV.B.

Moreover, many policies provide third-party coverage, that is, coverage for claims of discrimination, including harassment, brought by a company's vendors or customers or employees of those customers or vendors.[7]

Finally, employers, as well as their directors, officers, and employees, are normally covered under EPL policies.

III. EPL POLICIES ARE CLAIMS-MADE POLICIES

A. Typical Language

EPL policies are claims-made policies. Accordingly, coverage is typically triggered when an insurer is notified of a claim, as opposed to when an event-triggering decision is made or occurs.

Moreover, the claim itself must also be reported to the insurer within a certain time period. Some policies call for the insured to notify the carrier as soon as practical. Other policies require notification to occur during the policy period.

B. Claims-Made Policies Are Enforceable

Claims-made policies "are neither ambiguous, unconscionable, nor violative of public policy."[8]

Notice provisions in claims-made policies serve a different purpose from those in occurrence policies.[9] For occurrence policies, notice provisions "are included to help the insurer investigate, settle, and defend claims; they do not define coverage and should be 'liberally and practically construed.'"[10]

---

7. Practitioner's Guide, *supra* note 1, at 2–3.

8. FDIC v. Barham, 794 F. Supp. 187 (W.D. La. 1991) (citing Hunter v. Office of Health Servs. & Envtl. Quality Dep't of Health & Human Res., 385 So. 2d 928 (La. App. 2 Cir. 1980)), *aff'd*, 995 F.2d 600 (5th Cir. 1993).

9. Am. Cas. Co. of Reading, Pa. v. Continsio, 17 F.3d 62, 68 (3d Cir. 1994).

10. *Id.*

Claims-made policies, by contrast, are strictly construed.[11] The event invoking coverage is the transmittal of notice of the claim to the insurance carrier.[12] Extending the notice period, thus, constitutes "an unbargained-for expansion of coverage, gratis, resulting in the insurance company's exposure to a risk substantially broader than that expressly insured against in the policy."[13]

The strict notice requirements in claims-made policies ensure that exposure ends at a fixed point in time. These policies are, accordingly, less expensive, since the underwriter is better able to calculate risks.[14]

C. Insurers Generally Do Not Need to Show Prejudice in Order to Enforce Claims-Made Policies

Some courts have held that an insurer can deny coverage for late reporting under such language only if it can establish that it was prejudiced by the insured's late reporting of the claim. That is often difficult to do, as the test is generally whether the insurer would have done anything differently had it received notice of the claim in what would be held to be a timely fashion.[15] These cases, however, do not appear to have been addressing a claim under a claims-made policy.

Rather, courts hold that an insurer need not show actual prejudice to avoid coverage on a claims-made policy where an insured gives late notice.[16]

---

11. *Barham*, 995 F.2d at 604 n.9.

12. *Am. Cas. Co. of Reading, Pa.*, 17 F.3d at 68 (citing Zuckerman v. Nat'l Union Fire Ins. Co., 495 A.2d 395, 406 (1985)).

13. *Id.*

14. *Id.* Stated differently, the notice requirements of claims-made policies "allow the insurer to close its books" on a policy at its expiration and therefore "attain a level of predictability unattainable under standard occurrence policies." *Id.* at (citing Resolution Trust Corp. v. Ayo, 31 F.3d 285, 289 (5th Cir. 1994)).

15. *See, e.g.,* Guardian Trust Co. v. Am. States Ins. Co., 1996 WL 509638 (D. Kan. 1996) (finding that the insurer must show it would have handled the claim differently if it had timely notice *and* the different handling would have reduced the loss exposure).

16. *Barham*, 794 F. Supp. at 193–94 (citing Driskill v. El Jamie Marine, Inc., No. 87-4136, 1988 WL 93606 (E.D. La. 1988)). *See also* MGIC Indem. Corp. v. Cent. Bank of Monroe, La., 838 F.2d 1382 (5th Cir. 1988) (concluding the insured's failure to give notice of a claim when required to do so as a condition precedent to coverage, regardless of whether the insurer shows actual prejudice, may bar recovery for such claims); Matador Petroleum Corp. v. St. Paul Surplus Lines Ins. Co., 174 F.3d 653, 569 (5th Cir. 1999) (stating the notice provision in a claims-made policy is an element of the covered risk, and to require an insurer to prove prejudice from untimely notice could result in an unbargained-for expansion of coverage); Burns v. Int'l Ins. Co., 929 F. 2d 1422 (9th Cir. 1991); Am. Home Assur. Co. v. Int'l Ins. Co., 684 N.E.2d 14 (N.Y. App. 1997); E. Tex. Med. Ctr. Reg'l Healthcare Sys. v. Lexington Ins. Co., 2007 WL 2048660, at *8 (E.D. Tex. 2007) (holding that under Fifth Circuit law governing claims-made policies, an insured is not required to show prejudice for untimely notice).

D. Litigation Regarding "as Soon as Practical" Clauses

Some policies contain "as soon as practicable" clauses. These provisions, however, do not act as an indefinite extension of the notice of claims provisions.[17] Rather, notice must be given as soon as practicable, and delays of even fifty-four days and longer have been held to be unreasonable.[18]

E. Threats and Extended Coverage

Some policies require claims to be first made and reported during the policy period. "Taken to a black letter interpretation, this would require an insured to report a claim first made in the waning hours of the last day of the policy period to the insurer before the clock literally struck midnight on that day. Once common, these strict

---

17. *Barham*, 794 F. Supp. at 194, *aff'd*, 995 F.2d 600 (5th Cir. 1993); Murray v. City of Bunkie, 96–297 (La. App. 3 Cir. 11/6/96). In *Barham*, the court considered an insured's argument that an "as soon as practicable" clause in a claims-made policy allowed the insured to provide notice of a claim after the expiration of the policy period, as long as the notice was given "as soon as practicable." *Barham*, 794 F. Supp. at 194. The court rejected the insured's argument, finding such an interpretation "would render the carefully worded notice requirements moot and would produce absurd results." *Id.*

18. McPherson v. St. Paul Fire & Marine Ins. Co., 350 F.2d 563, 567–68 (C.A. Tex. 1965) (holding that notice sent to insurer fifty-four days after petition was filed did not constitute notice "as soon as practicable"); Pine Oak Builders, Inc. v. Great Am. Lloyds Ins. Co., 2006 WL 1892669, at *7 (Tex. App.–Houston [14th Dist.] 2006) (claims-made policies are less expensive than occurrence-based policies because they cover only injuries or damages that come to the attention of the insured and are made known to the insurer during the policy period); Precis, Inc. v. Fed. Ins. Co., 2005 WL 1639319 (N.D. Tex. 2005) ("as a matter of law, the delay of over nine months" from insured's receipt of notice of the claim until the insured notified the insurer that a claim was being made "was not 'as soon as practicable' and did not trigger coverage under the policy."); E. Tex. Med. Ctr. Reg'l Healthcare Sys., 2007 WL 2048660 ("[t]o require coverage under a claims-made policy where the insurer is not notified of a lawsuit until over seven months after the policy expires would unquestionably expand the risks covered and undermine or destroy the benefits of the claims-made coverage."); Am. Ctr. for Int'l Labor Solidarity v. Fed. Ins. Co, 518 F. Supp. 2d 163 (D.D.C. 2007) (notice to the insurer provided over seventeen months after the insured received notice of the claim was not notice "as soon as practicable").

In *American Center*, plaintiff was seeking to recover monies incurred in defense and settlement of an employment discrimination suit. The court granted the insurer's motion for summary judgment and denied plaintiff's cross-motion for summary judgment because of the following:

1. The employment practices liability policy therein was a claims-made policy.
2. Plaintiff received an EEOC charge filed by an employee on August 9, 2002. Plaintiff received a second EEOC charge on November 14, 2002.
3. Rather than reporting the charge to Federal, its insurer, plaintiff defended the charge.
4. The EEOC dismissed the charge and issued a right-to-sue letter on September 16, 2003.
5. The employee sued on December 12, 2003, making allegations similar to those contained in the charge of discrimination.
6. Plaintiff notified Federal of the pending lawsuit on January 20, 2004.
7. The court held that the charge was a claim, and the court sustained Federal's denial of coverage based on the failure to report a claim as soon as practical.

American Center, 518 F. Supp. 2d at 163.

and narrow provisions are much less prevalent in EPL and other claims-made policy forms today."[19]

To deal with claims-made and reported policies, as well as problems arising out of an insured's becoming aware of a claim at the very end of a policy period and not immediately notifying the insurer, some policies contain an "extended reporting period." Insurers, of course, require payment of an additional premium and require the company to exercise the extended reporting period option within, say, thirty days.

IV. EXCLUSIONS
A. General

EPL policies generally cover bodily injury, property damage, and personal injury claims. However, carriers either expressly or by practice do not apply the exclusion where the damage arises out of, for example, sexual battery or harassment. However, "[i]n cases where there are allegations of rape or physical assault, there may result an allocation between covered and noncovered aspects of the claim, such that the EPL insurer may be unwilling to fund the entire amount of any judgment or settlement, if not also to seek an allocation of defense expenses."[20]

B. Punitive Damages

As a result of the Civil Rights Act of 1991, Title VII plaintiffs can recover punitive damages by demonstrating that the employer acted "with malice or with reckless indifference to the federally protected rights of an aggrieved individual."[21] In interpreting this language, the US Supreme Court in *Kolstad v. American Dental Association*[22] potentially limited the availability of punitive damages for violation of Title VII. The Court stated:

> An employer may not be vicariously liable for the discriminatory employment decisions of managerial agents where these decisions are contrary to the employer's good-faith efforts to comply with Title VII.[23]

Insurers historically did not cover punitive damages and states did not allow companies to insure against such claims.[24] Now, most carriers provide coverage to the extent allowed by the states. As a result, thirty-six states permit recovery where employers

---

19. Practitioner's Guide, *supra* note 1, at 4.
20. *Id.* at 11.
21. 42 U.S.C. § 1981a(b)(1) (1991).
22. 527 U.S. 526 (1999).
23. *Id.* at 545.
24. *E.g.*, Nw. Nat'l Cas. Co. v. McNulty, 307 F.3d 432 (5th Cir. 1962).

have been found to be vicariously liable; twenty-five states permit same even if punitive damages are directly assessed against the employer.[25]

C. FLSA Claims

EPL policies typically preclude coverage for claims made under the Fair Labor Standards Act (FLSA). As wage and hour claims are on the rise, this exclusion can be extremely problematic for employers.

EPL policies typically include an exclusion for "alleged violations of the Fair Labor Standards Act . . . or any similar federal, state, or local statute." If the policy does not contain an exclusion, some insurers argue that the wage and hour claim does not constitute a "loss" under the policy.

EPL policies providing coverage for FLSA claims typically only provide coverage for the defense, not indemnity. As such, the employer would still be uninsured with respect to paying any assessed damages.

V. APPLICATIONS

Although placing a discussion of applications after punitive damages might seem odd, in fact, there is connexity. Some policy applications require the company to disclose the existence of internal policies or procedures for addressing, for example, sexual harassment claims, because the absence of such a policy has been held to evince reckless indifference.[26]

However, employers generally have not been able to show good faith compliance efforts by virtue of employee handbook provisions alone. Employers generally must train employees on its policies and make a good faith effort to enforce those policies.[27]

---

25. RICHARD L. BLATT, ROBERT W. HAMMESFAHR & LORI S. NUGENT, PUNITIVE DAMAGES: A STATE-BY-STATE GUIDE TO LAW AND PRACTICE § 4.6 (Thomson West, 2007); *Liability Insurance Coverage as Extending to Liability for Punitive or Exemplary Damages*, 16 ALR 4th 11 (1982).

26. Harris v. L&L Wings, Inc., 132 F.3d 978, 982 (4th Cir. 1997).

27. *E.g.*, Romano v. U-Haul Int'l, 233 F.3d 655, 670 (1st Cir. 2000); EEOC v. Wal-Mart Stores, Inc., 187 F.3d 1241, 1248 (10th Cir. 1999). *But see* Barrett v. Applied Radiant Energy Corp., 240 F.3d 262, 266 (4th Cir. 2001) (citing Lissau v. S. Food Servs., Inc., 159 F.3d 177 (4th Cir. 1998)).

    The court in McInnis v. Fairfield Cmtys., Inc., 458 F.3d 1129, 1138 (10th Cir. 2006), stated:

    To avail itself of *Kolstad*'s good-faith-compliance standard, an employer must at least 1) "adopt anti-discrimination policies; 2) make a good faith effort to educate its employees about these policies and the statutory prohibitions; and 3) make good faith efforts to *enforce* an anti-discrimination policy." *Cadena v. Pacesetter Corp.*, 224 F.3d 1203, 1210 (10th Cir. 2000) (quotations omitted) (emphasis in original). "While there is some debate regarding whether Fairfield demonstrated good-faith efforts to educate its employees about its specific policies, we need not address that issue because the jury could have reasonably concluded that Fairfield failed to enforce, or make good-faith efforts to enforce, any anti-discrimination policies it adopted. We have previously explained that, even if an employer adduces evidence showing it maintains on paper a strong non-discrimination policy and makes good faith efforts to educate its employees about that policy and Title VII, a plaintiff may still recover punitive damages if she demonstrates the employer failed to adequately address Title VII violations of which it was aware." 224 F.3d at 1210.

VI. IMMIGRATION STATUS: CUTTING-EDGE COVERAGE ISSUES

Federal law prohibits employers from hiring illegal immigrants.[28] Employers, however, continue to do so. Sooner or later an illegal immigrant will bring a sexual harassment claim, thereby triggering a coverage issue.

For example, the EPL policy is triggered by a charge by an employee for sexual harassment. At issue is whether an illegal immigrant is an employee.

Some policies define "employee." Others reference "employee" and define other terms, but no policies of which this author is aware define the term "employee" with reference to immigration status. Thus, the policy provisions would not appear to bar coverage.

Title VII and state laws patterned thereafter define "employee" as an "individual employed by an employer."[29] The FLSA contains an almost identical definition of employee.[30] An examination of FLSA jurisprudence shows that an employee's immigration status has no effect on the employee's ability to receive earned wages pursuant to the FLSA.[31]

The National Labor Relations Act[32] broadly defines "employee" to include "any employee."[33] Yet the US Supreme Court in *Hoffman Plastics Compounds v. NLRB*[34] held that the National Labor Relations Board could not impose a back pay penalty in favor of an undocumented alien where said award was based on hours that would have been worked but for illegal discrimination.[35] It is not too great a stretch to predict that one or more states will hold that it is against public policy to insure against the claim of an illegal alien for sexual harassment, though none have yet gone that far,[36] and, in fact, California has clearly gone in the opposite direction.[37]

---

28. *See* Immigration Reform & Control Act of 1986, 8 U.S.C. § 1324a.

29. 42 U.S.C. § 2000e(f). *See, e.g.,* La. Rev. Stat. § 23:302(1).

30. 29 U.S.C. § 203(e)(1).

31. Sure Tan, Inc. v. NLRB, 467 F.2d 883 (1984); Patel v. Quality Inn S., 846 F.2d 700 (11th Cir. 1988); Zavala v. Wal-Mart Stores, Inc., 393 F. Supp. 2d 295, 322 (D.N.J. 2006). *See also* Flores v. Limehouse, 2006 WL 1328762 (D.S.C. 2006) (rejecting defendants' motion for summary judgment, which was based on plaintiff's presentation of forged documents and essentially certifying a class of undocumented aliens who had not been paid in accordance with FLSA based on *Sure Tan* and *Patel* particularly where a contrary decision would provide employers with incentives to violate the FLSA).

32. 29 U.S.C. § 151–59.

33. *Id.* at § 152.

34. 122 S. Ct. 1275, 1284–85 (2002).

35. One could read *Hoffman Plastics* as precluding, in effect, a full back pay remedy, but that is hardly the only reading. One could also read it as suggesting that illegal aliens have no rights to authorized remedies, because they have no right to be working.

36. *Cf.* Legal Arizona Workers Act, Ariz. Rev. Stat. Ann. § 23–212 (imposing civil as well as criminal penalties and fines against employers who hire undocumented aliens).

37. Cal. Gov't Code § 7285(b) makes a person's immigration status irrelevant to the issue of liability and discovery in employment-related matters. Inquiries into a person's immigration status are impermissible except where the inquirer clearly and convincingly establishes that the questions are necessary in order to comply with federal immigration laws.

Likewise, New York has not felt compelled to follow *Hoffman*. In *Madeira v. Affordable Housing Foundation, Inc.*,[38] the district court stated:

New York's public policy does not bar compensation in the form of back pay for undocumented workers who are injured in the manner of the instant plaintiff.... Plaintiff's counsel argued to the jury that plaintiff hoped to remain in the United States (and was working on obtaining his documentation), but also told the jury that even if plaintiff were to be deported, he would be unable to work in Brazil. The jury was not required to specify where plaintiff would have earned money in the future, and clearly reached a verdict that he would have been able to earn some money somewhere, be it in the United States or elsewhere, were it not for his accident. The jury's determination will not be set aside.[39]

---

38. 315 F. Supp. 2d 504 (S.D.N.Y. 2004).

39. *Id.* at 507–08.

CHAPTER 6

Representing and Defending the Alleged Harasser

Peter Bennett and Timothy H. Powell

I. INTRODUCTION: THE LAWYER'S CHALLENGE

Lawyers representing an alleged harasser in the workplace face unique challenges. In many instances, the lawyer represents the interests of both the employer and the alleged harasser. In other situations, the lawyer represents only the individual alleged harasser. In the course of defense, the lawyer must be careful to understand who his or her client is. Prior to entering an appearance, the lawyer should assess and minimize potential conflicts of interest, evaluate potential privilege issues, and consider the best strategy and timing for successfully resolving the case on the client's behalf. In addition, preventing discovery abuses regarding the client's own sexual and personal background and providing a "unified front" with the employer's defense are matters that must be considered as the case progresses.

II. INITIAL CONSIDERATIONS WHEN REPRESENTING THE ALLEGED HARASSER

A. Determining Whether Joint Representation Is Appropriate

Rarely will a harassment plaintiff sue only the alleged harasser. As a result, a lawyer's first contact regarding possible representation of an alleged harasser usually comes from the alleged harasser's employer who often seeks joint representation of both the individual defendant and the employer. ABA Model Rule of Professional Conduct ("Model Rule") 1.13 allows a lawyer representing an organization to represent any director, officer, employee, member, shareholder, or other constituent of the organization, subject to the provisions of Model Rule 1.7. At the inception of the relationship, the lawyer should make clear who he or she represents and that there can be joint representation only if allowed under the jurisdiction's rules of professional conduct after an initial investigation to determine whether it is appropriate.

In assessing the appropriateness of joint representation, the lawyer should consider whether there exists a "significant risk" that representation of either the employer or the employee would be "materially limited" by the lawyer's responsibility to the other, as set forth in Model Rule 1.7(a). Only where the lawyer perceives no such significant risk should he or she consider representing both the employer and individual defendants.

The practical reasons for joint representation are rather obvious: lower attorney's fees and costs to the employer while simultaneously coordinating a united front to both plaintiff and fact finder as well as facilitating common access to all facts.

The initial appeal of joint representation must be weighed, however, against potential problems and negative consequences. One disadvantage, for example, is the possible shadow of guilt by association that may be cast upon either the employer (for allowing the alleged conduct to occur) or the individual (who may be blamed because the employer did not conduct a thorough and effective investigation that would have revealed his innocence). If the jury believes that one party, but not the other, is responsible for the harassment, it may still punish the other party. The consequences could be devastating for the individual defendant, who is less likely to have insurance coverage or resources to cover a large award.

The lawyer must also consider that the alleged harasser may conceal facts he or she does not want revealed and that may impact the employer's defense. In those instances, the lawyer cannot jointly defend both and depending on what the lawyer has learned, he or she may require withdrawal from representing both parties.

B. Employer's Vicarious Liability and Affirmative Defenses

Under the US Supreme Court's decisions in the companion cases *Burlington Indus., Inc. v. Ellerth*[1] and *Faragher v. City of Boca Raton*,[2] when a supervisor's sexual harassment culminates in a tangible employment action, such as dismissal or reassignment, the employer will be held vicariously, and strictly, liable. Thus, issues of joint representation will be easier to resolve where an employee alleges a tangible employment action resulting from a supervisor's sexual harassment, as both the employer's and supervisor's interests will be aligned in defending the employment action taken by the supervisor.

In contrast, the wisdom of joint representation must be carefully considered in cases where no tangible employment action is alleged. The legal standard applied to such claims under Title VII will vary depending on whether the alleged harasser is considered a "supervisor" or merely a co-worker of the employee being harassed. If the alleged harasser is a co-worker, the employer will only be liable for the harassing conduct if the plaintiff can show that the employer was negligent in either discovering or remedying the offending conduct.[3] If the harasser is a supervisor, however, the standard for employer liability changes significantly. Even where a supervisor did not cause a tangible employment action, the employer will be held vicariously liable for the harassment unless it can establish, as an affirmative defense, that it immediately undertook

---

1. 524 U.S. 742 (1998).

2. 524 U.S. 775 (1998).

3. 29 C.F.R. § 1604.11(d).

an investigation that was followed by appropriate remedial and disciplinary action. As established in *Ellerth* and *Faragher*, an employer will have an affirmative defense to vicarious liability for a sexual harassment claim against a supervisor only if it can demonstrate that (1) the employer exercised reasonable care to prevent and promptly correct harassment, and (2) the employee unreasonably failed to take advantage of any preventive or corrective opportunities provided by the employer.[4] Importantly, an employer may be "insulated from liability under Title VII" for a hostile environment sexual harassment claim when the employer adopts an anti-discrimination policy that is "comprehensive, well-known to employees, vigorously enforced, and provides alternative avenues of redress."[5]

Thus, the determination of vicarious liability often focuses on whether the offending employee was considered to be a "supervisor." In *Vance v. Ball State Univ.,*[6] the US Supreme Court, resolving a split among the circuits that developed post-*Ellerth* and *Faragher*, attempted to determine the appropriate definition of supervisor and clarify employer liability for supervisor harassment under Title VII. Under *Vance*, "an employer may be vicariously liable for an employee's unlawful harassment only when the employer has empowered that employee to take tangible employment actions against the victim, *i.e.*, to effect a significant change in employment status, such as hiring, firing, failing to promote, reassignment with significantly different responsibilities, or a decision causing a significant change in benefits."

Whether the alleged harasser is a supervisor or a co-worker, the prudent attorney should evaluate the likelihood of the employer's vicarious liability and the availability of any affirmative defense under these standards based on the employer's knowledge of, and response to, the alleged harassing conduct. The employer's potential for liability and any potential conflicts with the alleged harasser's own defense should be considered carefully in deciding whether to move forward with joint representation.

The attorney will also want to consider the availability of an indemnity claim against the individual defendant in the event of vicarious liability. Employers in jurisdictions where courts have allowed indemnity claims against employees for actions giving rise to harassment claims will generally be forced to retain separate counsel for the individual defendant or to require that individual to retain his or her own lawyer.[7]

---

4. *See, e.g.*, Faragher, 524 U.S. 775 (in accordance with *Ellerth*); Minix v. Jeld-Wen, Inc., 237 Fed. Appx. 578 (2007) (holding that the employer lacked actual notice as well as constructive notice of supervisor's sexual harassment, and the employer successfully established defense to vicarious liability); Sconce v. Tandy Corp., 9 F. Supp. 2d 773, 778 (W.D. Ky. 1998) (summary judgment granted in favor of employer because employer conducted immediate investigation upon learning of alleged harassment and reprimanded supervisor).

5. Farley v. Am. Cast Iron Pipe Co., 115 F.3d 1548, 1554 (11th Cir. 1997).

6. 570 U.S. 421 (2013).

7. *Compare* Gilmore v. List & Clark Constr. Co., 866 F. Supp. 1310 (D. Kan. 1994) (employer cannot proceed against supervisor for indemnity), *and* Nw. Airlines, Inc. v. Transp. Workers Union, 451 U.S. 77 (1981) (no right to indemnity or contribution under Title VII), *with* Biggs v. Surrey Broad. Co., 811 P.2d 111 (Okla. Ct. App. 1991) (employer that settled sexual harassment suit may have right to sue alleged harasser for indemnification).

The same result may be required in situations where the "corporate" employer is a municipality that may defend on the theory that the individual was not acting in his or her "official capacity."[8]

One of the most troublesome difficulties with joint representation is the potential conflict of interest that could arise if the defense of the case is based on a total denial by the alleged harasser. During discovery or trial, information may become available that suggests that some or all of the alleged conduct actually occurred, potentially leading to a conflict of interest between the employer and the alleged harasser. Thus, the prudent practitioner will need to immediately meet with the employer and the alleged harasser to gather facts surrounding the allegations of the plaintiff's lawsuit and determine whether joint representation of both parties is appropriate or even possible. If joint representation is pursued, joint clients must be advised of the potential for losing the attorney–client privilege as between themselves, and the possibility that independent representation may later be needed if a conflict develops.

C. Individual Liability of the Alleged Harasser

Title VII of the Civil Rights Act of 1964 (Title VII) does not impose personal liability on supervisors. Harassment lawsuits, however, often add state law claims, and the alleged harasser is potentially liable for his or her conduct under the legal theories of assault, battery, intentional infliction of emotional distress, and invasion of privacy. In addition, some state anti-discrimination statutes allow for individual liability or claims for aiding and abetting.

The prudent practitioner should consider the jurisdiction where the lawsuit is filed and any recent developments in case law because an alleged harasser may still face individual liability for harassment under state law. For example, the New Hampshire Supreme Court recently addressed the issue of individual liability for workplace harassment. In *U.S. Equal Employment Opportunity Comm'n v. Fred Fuller Oil Co., Inc.*,[9] the court established that individual employees can be held personally liable for aiding and abetting workplace discrimination or engaging in retaliatory conduct under New Hampshire's Law Against Discrimination. More specifically, the *Fred Fuller* decision permits a plaintiff employee to sue the employer and bring individual claims under New Hampshire law for discrimination, harassment, and or retaliation against the alleged harasser and those in the workplace who allegedly aided, abetted, or assisted the alleged harasser. For New Hampshire as well as some other states, this means that owners, supervisors, and human resource professionals can face individual claims.

---

8. *See, e.g.*, Johnson v. Bd. of County Comm'rs for the County of Fremont, 85 F.3d 489, 493–94 (10th Cir. 1996) (noting potential conflict for attorney representing government official sued in official capacity); Tout v. County of Erie, 2 F. Supp. 2d 320 (W.D.N.Y. 1998) (noting that a municipality may avoid liability by showing official did not act within scope of his or her duties).

9. 134 A.3d 17 (N.H. 2016).

III. ETHICAL ISSUES AND RULES WHEN REPRESENTING THE ALLEGED HARASSER

Joint representation of the individual defendant (employee/alleged harasser) and the corporate defendant (employer) is permissible under Model Rule 1.13, subject to the provisions of Model Rule 1.7. The following are recommendations and considerations for addressing the ethical issues that arise under joint representation of the alleged harasser and the employer.

A. The Joint Representation Agreement

A joint representation agreement and a prospective waiver of conflict should be obtained from both potential clients and consideration should be given to potential conflicts that may arise and how they will be handled. A sample of such a document is shown at the end of this chapter in Appendix 6A. This agreement should include language stating that the individual defendant consents to the representation being provided, and paid for, by the employer in compliance with Model Rule 1.8(f). The individual defendant must understand his or her right to retain separate counsel and should be instructed to consult with independent counsel prior to executing the joint representation agreement. In most situations, this document will be written so that the lawyer may continue to represent the employer defendant if a conflict or potential conflict exists and continued representation of one of the two parties remains possible.

The Joint Representation Agreement is based on the "joint defense privilege" or "common interest privilege," which permits a client to disclose information to her attorney in the presence of joint parties and counsel without waiving the attorney-client privilege and is intended to preclude joint parties and their attorneys from disclosing confidential information learned as a consequence of the joint defense without permission.[10] Importantly, joint representation of the parties allows the lawyer to develop a coordinated strategy.

B. Addressing Conflict of Interest Issues During Joint Representation

A lawyer's worst nightmare in joint representation is to obtain an admission from the individual client that the alleged harassing conduct actually occurred. Verification from independent witnesses might have the same effect. At that point, the lawyer has a responsibility to inform the employer client, who is then faced with the difficult decision of whether (and when) to discipline the offending employee.

A conflict of interest exists at this point in the litigation, as representation of one client is materially limited by the lawyer's responsibilities to the other client. While Model Rule 1.7 allows for continued representation under these circumstances with

---

10. *See* United States v. Schwimmer, 892 F.2d 237 (2d Cir. 1989).

the informed, written consent of each client, it would be unwise for an employer to consent to such a situation due to the necessity to take appropriate disciplinary action in a timely manner in order to preserve a defense to an alleged harassment claim.[11]

Courts have addressed the joint representation conflict issue in various ways. For example, in *Klemm v. Superior Court of Fresno County*,[12] the appellate court in a mandamus proceeding directed the trial court to reconsider a lawyer's motion to be allowed to represent both parties to a marriage dissolution with the consent of the parties. The court noted that under such circumstances "if the conflict is merely potential, there being no existing dispute or contest between the parties represented as to any point in litigation, then with full disclosure to and informed consent of both clients there may be dual representation at a hearing or trial."[13] The court went on to note that the key factor in determining whether joint representation is appropriate is whether the conflict of interest is potential or actual.[14]

In contrast, *O'Reilly v. Executone of Albany, Inc.*[15] involved a law firm that was representing both a corporate employer and two of its employees. The court noted that the law firm was seeking to withdraw from representation of the individual defendants due to a conflict of interest. Ultimately, the court held that the law firm could not represent both the corporate employer and the employee since the law firm might defend on grounds that the corporate employer was not responsible for any misconduct by the employee because it had no knowledge of the improper actions.[16]

Obtaining a joint representation agreement at the beginning of representation helps avoid potential privilege and conflict problems.[17] In a situation where the individual defendant later confesses to improper behavior, a lawyer who has not entered a joint defense agreement would ordinarily be prohibited from telling the employer of the confession and offending conduct, likely resulting in withdrawal from representation of both clients.[18] By obtaining the consent of both parties at an early stage of the litigation to a joint defense agreement that allows for the sharing of joint defense materials and information, the lawyer fulfills the duty to give full disclosure to the clients. A well-drafted joint defense agreement will also help to ensure continued representation on behalf of the corporate client in the event that a conflict emerges, a fact that is often of utmost concern to both the lawyer and a long-standing corporate client.[19]

---

11. *See* Section II.B., *supra*; *Ellerth*, 524 U.S. at 765.

12. 75 Cal. App. 3d 893, 900 (1977).

13. *Id.* at 899.

14. *Accord* Butler v. Nat'l Urban League, Inc., No. 96 CIV3880, 1997 WL 538824 (S.D.N.Y. Sept. 2, 1997).

15. 522 N.Y.S.2d 724 (1987).

16. *Id.*

17. *See* Appendix 6A, Sample Joint Representation Agreement and Appendix 6B, Sample Engagement Letter.

18. *See* ABA Informal Op. 1476 (1981), at 10–13.

19. *See, e.g.*, Feng v. Sandrik, 636 F. Supp. 77 (N.D. Ill. 1986) (denying motion to disqualify counsel where defendant established it had long-standing policy of indemnifying employees when sued for actions made within scope and course of employment and all defendants consented in advance, and in writing, to joint representation).

However, no advance waiver of potential conflicts is ironclad. It is virtually impossible to disclose all potential consequences before withdrawal may become necessary. As a result, any lawyer who agrees to represent both the employer and individual defendants in an employment lawsuit should be aware of the possibility that total withdrawal may be required at some point. The clients should be informed of this possibility at the inception of the relationship. The lawyer should also recognize the potential for court-ordered withdrawal on behalf of both parties. In short, the prudent practitioner must carefully evaluate the costs and benefits of joint representation.

C. Settlement Discussions

Another possibility for conflict could arise during settlement discussions. Although both parties may agree on the facts and defenses to a lawsuit, they may have different expectations or needs with regard to resolving the lawsuit. For example, if an employer has been sued for harassment allegedly caused by a supervisor, the plaintiff may offer to settle the case for $35,000. The employer may not wish to pay this amount in settlement, perhaps because there is no proof of economic damage and emotional distress damages are questionable. However, the supervisor may believe that the matter should be settled immediately and may wish to avoid further embarrassment in the remaining litigation. The supervisor may be more concerned about the potential for punitive damages with regard to various state law tort claims made solely against him. Thus, even if both parties deny that improper conduct occurred, the individual defendant may desire settlement while the employer is reluctant to set a precedent by "caving in" to the demands of a questionable plaintiff. A good plaintiff's lawyer will not always separate out the settlement demand by the defendant, creating a conflict between the best interests of the individual and employer defendants.[20]

In a situation involving an employment practices liability insurance policy, an individual defendant may be more inclined to settle a case, thereby reducing any personal exposure. However, the employer defendant may be more interested in pushing the matter toward trial and ultimate exoneration. The employer may be trying to discourage suits from other employees, who may see settlement as evidence of weakness. Similarly, the employer may not wish to settle due to questions involving underwriting or retention issues.

A possible conflict of interest with regard to resolution of the case could also occur in a situation involving a Federal Rule of Civil Procedure 68 offer of judgment. Offers of judgment are used in employment cases because they may represent an ability to cut off the accrual of plaintiff's attorney's fees. If an offer of judgment is made, however, the clients need to be prepared to have the offer accepted, thereby resulting in an actual

---

20. *See, e.g.*, Fiandaca v. Cunningham, 827 F.2d 825, 829–31 (1st Cir. 1987) (counsel should have been disqualified after settlement offer proposed that would benefit some clients but not others). *Accord* Conigliaro v. Horace Mann Sch., No. 95 CIV. 3555, 1997 WL 189058 (S.D.N.Y. Apr. 17, 1997) (where law firm's partner was also individual defendant who may be witness, attorney's joint role as defendant/ counselor caused conflict where role as defendant could affect settlement status).

judgment taken against them. Depending on the circumstances of the particular case, either the employer defendant or the individual defendant may be more willing than the other to bear the risk of a possible adverse judgment to either resolve the case or to push along settlement negotiations. Each of these settlement situations must be dealt with on a case-by-case basis and the individual circumstances of the various defendants must be weighed carefully before joint representation is agreed upon by the defendants.

D. In-House Counsel

In-house counsel have additional concerns regarding joint representation issues. According to Model Rule 1.13(a), an attorney employed by a company "represents the organization acting through its duly authorized constituents." The in-house lawyer's primary duty is to the corporation. If the lawyer is representing a management employee, particularly a high-level one, a question exists as to whether the best interests of the company would be served by continued representation by the same lawyer. Indeed, if the in-house lawyer has already represented to the high-level employee that he or she will provide representation and facts are later learned that suggest the employee violated company policy, then the in-house lawyer may be excluded from further representation of the company and outside counsel will need to be retained to represent both parties. Practically speaking, the in-house lawyer may lose the trust or confidence of the former client or other high-ranking officials at the company. The ethical basis of this decision is identical to that discussed earlier regarding outside counsel representing both the employee and the employer. As a result, any lawyer representing a corporation, whether in-house or outside counsel, must carefully weigh the costs and benefits of joint representation.

IV. ATTORNEY-CLIENT PRIVILEGE ISSUES IN JOINT REPRESENTATION

Not surprisingly, a lawyer representing more than one client in a harassment case will likely face various issues surrounding attorney-client privilege and work-product privilege. Many of these issues can be resolved, as discussed earlier, through the use of a joint representation agreement. Nevertheless, a lawyer taking on multiple representation duties should be aware of potential privilege minefields to ensure that the joint representation arrangement does not explode.

Conflict in joint representation scenarios can arise when one defendant (or an independent witness) reveals facts inconsistent with the position taken by the other defendant. For example, assume the alleged harasser reveals to the lawyer, in a privileged communication, that the harasser has engaged in an improper sexual relationship with a subordinate employee, but not with the plaintiff. Because the attorney-client privilege belongs to the client, the lawyer is prohibited from revealing this information to the employer without the consent of the individual defendant.[21] The lawyer's duty to the employer, however, requires revealing the information so that the employer can undertake the necessary investigation and, if required, impose disciplinary action that may adversely affect the lawyer's individual client. The lawyer's duty to exercise independent judgment may require the lawyer to advise one or both clients not to waive the privilege.[22]

A joint representation agreement can help avoid this quandary by having the parties agree that any communications made by one client may be shared with the other. If no such agreement exists, then the attorney-client privilege will likely require the lawyer to withdraw from further representation of both clients at some point. The privilege may be maintained if both the individual and employer defendants retain separate counsel, although the original lawyer may later be placed in the unhappy situation of being called as a witness in a subsequent lawsuit by the employer against the employee.

Entering into a joint representation agreement, as advised earlier, can help maintain the privilege. Although entry of a joint representation agreement is not a prerequisite to application of the joint defense privilege, it helps to establish the privilege. The elements of a joint defense privilege are similar throughout the US Circuit Courts of Appeal. A party asserting the privilege must show "[1] the communications were made in the course of a joint defense effort, [2] the statements were designed to further the effort and [3] the privilege has not been waived."[23]

The criminal cases *United States v. Melvin*[24] and *United States v. Weissman*[25] provide insight as to the role of the joint defense privilege when the parties to a common defense have entered into a joint representation agreement. In *Melvin*, the court observed that "there is a respectable body of law from other courts to the effect that attorney-client privilege applies to confidential communications among attorneys and their clients for purposes of a common defense" as long as "the disclosures [were] made in circumstances which indicate that they were made in confidence."[26]

The court in *Weissman* expounded on the *Melvin* decision, essentially providing a "mini-treatise" on the joint defense privilege. The court discussed the varying degrees of protection that the US Circuit Courts of Appeal have given to joint defense agreements. Virtually all of the circuit courts have at least recognized that where parties actually engage in a common defense of a lawsuit, any communications made toward that common defense will maintain their attorney-client and work-product protection.

---

21. Relatedly, Model Rule 1.6 governs the confidentiality of information in an attorney-client relationship and requires that a "lawyer shall not reveal information relating to the representation of a client unless the client gives informed consent, the disclosure is impliedly authorized in order to carry out the representation or the disclosure is permitted by paragraph (b)."

22. *See* MODEL RULES OF PROF'L CONDUCT R. 1.7.

23. Haines v. Liggett Group, Inc., 975 F.2d 81, 94 (3d Cir. 1992).

24. 650 F.2d 641 (5th Cir. 1981).

25. No. S194CR760, 1996 WL 737042 (S.D.N.Y. Dec. 26, 1996).

26. *Melvin*, 650 F.2d at 654–46.

As a result, entry of a joint defense agreement places both lawyers and their respective clients on notice of the possibility of conflicts. It further protects the lawyers' ability to continue representation of a party if a conflict later develops. Finally, it provides a fundamental basis for ensuring that attorney-client privilege issues are preserved throughout the course of representation.

V. PROTECTING THE ALLEGED HARASSER FROM DISCOVERY ABUSES

Although a plaintiff who has filed a sexual harassment case will likely be advised by counsel that his or her own sexual history will be the subject of inquiry during discovery, most individual defendants in sexual harassment cases do not realize that intimate aspects of their lives may become matters of public record. It is not at all unusual, however, for a zealous plaintiff's counsel to conduct in-depth discovery regarding the sexual history of a defendant, especially in situations alleging quid pro quo harassment or where there are rumors that the individual defendant previously engaged in relationships (either consensual or not) in the office and even outside of the office.

The most frequently contested discovery issues in harassment suits include the following: discovery of plaintiff's psychological and medical condition; discovery of prior conduct of both plaintiff and the alleged harasser (including sexual history); discovery of other incidents of harassment; and employer's investigation of same. While discovery into these matters may be pursued by a zealous plaintiff's lawyer eager for any advantage for her client, there are limits to the scope and purposes of such inquiry.[27] For example, Model Rule 4.4 states that "[i]n representing a client, a lawyer shall not use means that have no substantial purpose other than to embarrass, delay, or burden a third person, or use methods of obtaining evidence that violate the legal rights of such a person."

The Federal Rules of Civil Procedure (FRCP) provide similar warnings regarding discovery abuses: FRCP 30(d)(3) states that a deposition should not be conducted "in such a manner as unreasonably to annoy, embarrass or oppress the deponent or party."[28] In some circumstances, the directive in Federal Rule of Civil Procedure 26

---

27. *See* Comments to Model Rule 1.3 ("A lawyer should act with commitment and dedication to the interests of the client and with zeal in advocacy upon the client's behalf. However, a lawyer is not bound to press for every advantage that might be realized for a client. A lawyer has professional discretion in determining the means by which a matter should be pursued.").

28. FED. R. EVID. 412 provides some protection from sexual history inquiry to a plaintiff who alleges that she is the victim of sexual harassment. The language of the Rule, however, applies only to "alleged victims" and does not mention defendants or third parties. *See, e.g.,* Stalnaker v. K-Mart Corp., 95-2444-GTV, 1996 WL 427762 (D. Kan. July 25, 1996) (Rule 412 bars introduction of evidence relating to sexual activities of nonparties); Biggs v. Nicewonger Co., 897 F. Supp. 483, 484 (D. Or. 1995) (court prohibits evidence of sexual behavior of co-employees unless plaintiff introduces evidence that defendant previously sexually harassed the co-employee). *But see* Burger v. Litton Indus., 91 CIV. 0918, 1995 WL 476712 (S.D.N.Y. Aug. 10, 1995) (noting that Advisory Committee believed that language of Rule 412 applied to both parties and nonparties). *See* discussion of Rule 412 in Chapter 16.

regarding discovery only as to matters "reasonably calculated to lead to the discovery of admissible evidence" may provide fodder for a protective order.

In most situations, however, merely mentioning to opposing counsel that the FRCP prohibit the type of inquiry sought will be insufficient to stop questioning. Similarly, many lawyers are hesitant to threaten reports of violations of the Model Rules of Professional Conduct. Most courts have been more willing to protect the reputation of an alleged victim than that of the alleged harasser.

A. Federal Rule of Evidence 415

With the advent of Federal Rule of Evidence (FRE) 415 in 1995, plaintiffs' counsel added yet another weapon to its arsenal of attack against individual defendants. FRE 415 provides that in cases involving damages based "on a party's alleged commission of conduct constituting an offense of sexual assault or child molestation," evidence of the party's commission of another offense of sexual assault or child molestation is admissible and may be considered pursuant to FRE 413 and 414.[29] FRE 415 is especially troublesome to individual defendants and alleged harassers because the rule changes the long-standing presumption against "propensity" evidence and allows such evidence in certain circumstances. Although the rule does not, on its face, apply directly to employment cases, several courts have considered the relevancy of the rule to sexual harassment claims.

For example, in *Frank v. County of Hudson*,[30] the plaintiffs sued their employer, alleging that they had been sexually harassed by their supervisor. Plaintiffs' counsel obtained a statement from the supervisor's stepdaughter (which was not shown to opposing counsel or to plaintiffs) stating that the supervisor had sexually abused the stepdaughter for ten years. The supervisor filed a protective order seeking to exclude the evidence. The trial court found that the evidence constituted evidence of "sexual abuse" as contemplated by Rule 415, but determined that its probative value was substantially outweighed by unfair prejudice to the defendant under FRE 403.

The *Frank* decision demonstrated the court's application, for the first time, of FRE 415 in the context of an employment case. In subsequent case law, some courts have held that Rule 415 evidence can be admitted to show that an alleged harasser has a "propensity" to commit illegal acts.[31] In some instances, however, the courts have taken

---

29. The rules provide that if a party intends to offer Rule 415 evidence, it must disclose the evidence to the party against whom it will be offered (including statements of witnesses or a summary of the substance of the testimony) at least fifteen days before the date of a hearing set specially for the purpose of considering the evidence.

30. 924 F. Supp. 620 (D.N.J. 1996).

31. *See, e.g.,* Jones v. Clinton, 993 F. Supp. 1217 (E.D. Ark. 1998) (noting, in dicta, that if president's relationship with Monica Lewinsky was not consensual, it would be appropriate Rule 415 evidence in a case brought by Paula Jones); Sanders v. Baucum, 929 F. Supp. 1028 (N.D. Tex. 1996) (testimony regarding nonparty parishioners' alleged relationships with minister who was subject of sexual assault case was properly admitted as Rule 415 evidence).

a more tempered view, finding that the alleged harasser should not be branded merely because of former allegations of abuse.[32]

B. Character or Habit Evidence

In another attempt to discredit either the employer or individual defendant, the plaintiff's counsel will often attempt to prove that harassment (or other forms of discrimination) has occurred by relying on evidence of the defendant's "character" or "habit." The admissibility of this evidence is generally governed by FRE 404 (character) and 406 (habit).

1. Character Evidence: FRE 404 and Relevant Case Law

FRE 404(b) provides: "[e]vidence of other crimes, wrongs or acts" is generally inadmissible "to prove the character of a person in order to show action in conformity therewith." However, under FRE 403(b), such evidence may be admissible to show "proof of motive, opportunity, intent, preparation, plan, knowledge, identity, or absence of mistake or accident." As a result, a number of courts have allowed evidence of prior acts of alleged discrimination on the grounds that it is the only evidence available to establish the motive or intent of the alleged harasser.

For example, the plaintiff in *Garvey v. Dickinson College*[33] alleged that she was sexually harassed by David Peck, an associate professor who was plaintiff's immediate supervisor. Defendants filed a motion in limine seeking to exclude evidence of Peck's alleged sexual harassment of other employees. The court denied the motion, noting that intent is an element of a sexual harassment case and that "[s]tate of mind can be proven through circumstantial evidence such as evidence of past conduct or prior incidents."[34] Evidence of the individual defendant's alleged harassment of others was found to be "clearly relevant" because it tended to show his attitude toward women and his treatment of them in the workplace. In so holding, the court relied heavily on Rule 404, reasoning that in an employment discrimination case, evidence that the defendant has made disparaging remarks about the class of persons to which plaintiff belongs may be introduced to show that the defendant harbors prejudice toward that group. Such evidence is often the only proof of the defendant's state of mind, and if it

---

32. *See, e.g.*, Cleveland v. KFC Nat'l Mgmt. Co., 948 F. Supp. 62 (N.D. Ga. 1996) (evidence of prior sexual misconduct perpetrated by former manager was Rule 415 evidence that would generally be admissible, but only after engaging in a Rule 403 analysis as to both the probative value of the information and whether the conduct itself corroborated plaintiff's story); Shea v. Galaxie Lumber & Constr. Co., Ltd., No. 94 C 906, 1996 WL 111890 (ND. Ill. Mar. 12, 1996) (excluding evidence of harassment cases previously filed against corporation where it is unclear whether the prior harassment alleged actually constituted "sexual assault").

33. 763 F. Supp. 799 (MD. Pa. 1991).

34. *Id.* at 801.

were excluded, the plaintiff would have no means of proving that the defendant acted with discriminatory intent.[35]

The court did, however, limit the evidence to those incidents that were close in time to the allegations made by the plaintiff and to those incidents involving members of the department where she worked.[36]

The court reached a similar result in *Webb v. Hyman* and determined that evidence of other sexual discrimination and harassment was admissible because it helped to establish both intent and a "contemporaneous hostile environment."[37] Plaintiff proffered the testimony of co-employees regarding other sexual discrimination and harassment allegedly perpetrated by defendant "within the past few years."[38] In considering posttrial motions, the court held that the evidence was properly admitted because it helped to establish both intent and a "contemporaneous hostile environment."[39] The court also rejected the defendant's argument that the events in the complaint were too remote in time to be relevant to the issues raised in the lawsuit.

Furthermore, in *Alaniz v. Zamora-Quezada*,[40] evidence of a supervisor's sexual harassment of other employees was deemed admissible to show the employer's knowledge and failure to act upon complaints by other employees.

Several other decisions reflect the courts' willingness to admit evidence of the alleged harasser's character or reputation. In *Heyne v. Caruso*,[41] testimony by other female employees that the defendant sexually harassed them was found to be admissible to prove motive in a sexual harassment lawsuit. Similarly, in *Phillips v. Smalley Maintenance Services, Inc.*,[42] the testimony of another former female employee regarding alleged sexual harassment was admissible pursuant to Rule 404, but the court "took care to preface the testimony with an instruction that the testimony was relevant only to . . . [the] reasons for terminating [plaintiff] and therefore went to motive and intent of defendant."[43]

Some courts have held, however, that FRE 404 prohibits the introduction of character evidence. The plaintiff in *Schweitzer-Reschke v. Avnet, Inc.*[44] filed suit alleging that

---

35. *Id.*

36. *Id.* at 802.

37. 861 F. Supp. 1094 (D.D.C. 1994).

38. *Id.* at 1111.

39. *Id.*

40. 591 F.3d 761, 775–76 (5th Cir. 2009).

41. 69 F.3d 1475, 1480–81 (9th Cir. 1995).

42. 711 F.2d 1524, 1532 (11th Cir. 1983).

43. *See also* EEOC v. Nat'l Cleaning Contractors, Inc., No. 90 CIV 6398, 1996 WL 278078 (S.D.N.Y. May 23, 1996) (Rule 404(b) prohibits the use of other incidents of sexual harassment to prove propensity but does not prohibit introduction of the evidence to show motive or intent); Stair v. Lehigh Valley Carpenters Local Union No. 600, 813 F. Supp. 1116, 1120 (E.D. Pa. 1993) (court allows testimony of co-employees' allegations of harassment by another supervisor on grounds that it could help establish motive or intent under Rule 404); Allen v. Park-Ohio Indus., Inc. No. C-87-730, 1992 WL 309899 (N.D. Ohio July 23, 1992) (testimony by other employees regarding the circumstances of their discharge may be relevant as evidence of motive and intent).

44. 881 F. Supp. 530 (D. Kan. 1995).

she had been sexually harassed. In an attempt to avoid summary judgment, the plaintiff filed an affidavit stating that the alleged harasser was "known as" or "had the reputation of being a male chauvinist."[45] The court distinguished the type of evidence relied on by the plaintiff in this case from evidence of specific acts of discrimination, noting that only the latter type of evidence is contemplated by Rule 404(b).[46]

Similarly, in *McCue v. State of Kansas, Department of Human Resources*,[47] the appellate court held that the trial court erred in admitting evidence that a supervisor assigned work in a sexually discriminatory manner two years after the plaintiff's termination. The court found that the evidence was offered to show that the supervisor "had the character of one who sexually discriminates" in violation of FRE 404(b).

2. Evidence of Habit: FRE 406 and Relevant Case Law

In addition to FRE 404, plaintiffs in harassment litigation may rely on evidence of the alleged harasser's "habit," pursuant to FRE 406. Rule 406 provides that "evidence of the habit of a person . . . is relevant to prove that the conduct of the person . . . on a particular occasion was in conformity with the practice." Defendant in *Priest v. Rotary*[48] sought information about the plaintiff's past intimate relationships in an effort to show that she had a habit of living with men for economic gain. The court rejected the defendant's argument, concluding that it was merely a "thinly disguised attempt to seek character evidence."[49]

On the other hand, in *Scott v. American Broadcasting Co.*,[50] the court held that a plaintiff improperly sought to introduce FRE 406 evidence of the company's "policy" of engaging in discrimination. According to the appellate court, evidence of the company's "policy" of engaging in discrimination was correctly excluded since it was based merely on a subjective perception by the plaintiff and was insufficient to show any routine practice of discrimination. The court's analysis in *Scott* should be considered in situations involving corporate defendants who allegedly have "policies" of harassing or engaging in discrimination of individuals. In such a case, counsel for defendant will need to argue that the Rule 406 argument is improper insofar as it is designed primarily to deal with policies and procedures, rather than intentions of a particular individual.[51]

A lawyer representing an alleged harasser will need to be aware of all of these evidentiary issues long before motions in limine are filed. By anticipating the various avenues

---

45. *Id.* at 532.

46. *Id.* at 533. *See also* Tomson v. Stephan, 705 F. Supp. 530, 536 (D. Kan. 1989) (court prohibits introduction of evidence that defendant made sexual advances to waitress at topless bar on grounds that plaintiff could not establish what motive or intent the evidence was designed to establish and on grounds that waitress was never employee of defendant).

47. 165 F.3d 784, 790 (10th Cir. 1999).

48. 98 F.R.D. 755, 758 (N.D. Cal. 1993).

49. *Id.* at 759. *See also* Sanchez v. Zabihi, 166 F.R.D. 500 (D.N.M. 1996).

50. 878 F.2d 386 (9th Cir. 1989).

51. *See, e.g.*, Garvey v. Dickinson Coll., 763 F. Supp. 799 (MD. Pa. 1991) (noting that Rule 406 is designed to deal with policies and routine procedures).

of discovery likely to be sought by plaintiffs, the defense lawyer can better prepare his or her client and take preemptive action to exclude discovery on issues that may be potentially embarrassing and extremely prejudicial. If the issues are dealt with at the discovery stage, it is far less likely that the evidence will be admitted at the time of trial.

3. Dealing with Expert Testimony on Key Elements of a Harassment Case

The use of expert or opinion testimony in workplace harassment cases has become a much-debated issue. Expert witnesses may be human resources or employment practices professionals, sociologists, psychologists, or medical physicians. The relevant rules regarding witness testimony are as follows: FRE 701 (rule for lay opinion); FRE 702 (basic standards for expert testimony); and FRE 403 (reasons for which testimony may be excluded). In a harassment case, an expert witness may be designated to opine on any of the following potential subjects: the plaintiff's psychological and mental condition; perceptions and behavior of the reasonable woman or victim; and adequacy (or inadequacy) of the employer's anti-harassment policies, procedures, and investigations. For example, in *Kimzey v. Wal-Mart Stores, Inc.*,[52] the plaintiff's expert testified about the employer's open-door policy encouraging employees to report harassment. The expert witness explained that, to implement this policy in a company the size of Wal-Mart, a manager who becomes aware of a problem with an employee should investigate, interview other employees, and prepare a written report. The plaintiff's supervisor then testified that he had received no training on the policy and there was no evidence introduced by defendant to indicate that training was, in fact, in place to implement Wal-Mart's policy.[53]

VI. PRESENTING A UNIFIED FRONT AT TRIAL

A lawyer representing the alleged harasser at the trial of a harassment lawsuit must take great care to ensure that the client is presented in the best light possible. The mere fact that a plaintiff has made certain unsavory allegations about the individual defendant will cause at least some doubt in the minds of most jurors. The best defense to these allegations will often be the firm support of the corporate employer, which often leads to the perception that the allegations are meritless.

Obviously, in those cases where the employer and the employee have agreed to joint representation and the defense is a total denial of the plaintiff's allegations, it is easier to present a united front at trial. However, in situations where the corporate employer is represented by a separate lawyer, the two lawyers should work as closely as possible to ensure that the defenses are consistent. In addition, the lawyer representing the individual defendant must start swaying the jury from the time the first voir dire question is asked.

---

52. 107 F.3d 568, 571 (8th Cir. 1997).

53. *Id.* at 571.

Although it will sometimes be possible for the two lawyers to work together, in other instances the interests of the two parties may be adverse. *Bonner v. Guccione* illustrates this situation.[54] Shortly before the trial in *Bonner*, the plaintiff filed a motion pointing out a conflict of interest between the two defendants who were represented by the same law firm. The plaintiff did not seek to disqualify the law firm from representing both the employer and two of the individual partners of the partnership. She did, however, seek assurance that none of the defendants would later be able to raise a conflict argument in the event she obtained verdicts against one, the other, or both. As a result, she sought waivers signed by the various parties. The court granted the plaintiff's motion, in part, noting that each of the individual defendants had an interest in any verdict assessed against the other individual defendant. It was possible that counsel for the defendants would make contradictory arguments to advance their respective interests. Specifically, it may be in the best interest of the alleged harasser to argue that his other partner encouraged improper behavior, but it would be in the best interest of the second partner to argue that appropriate rules were set up seeking to prevent the inappropriate behavior.

Often, an employer and alleged harasser are represented by two separate lawyers. When separate counsel is retained, the corporation will likely allege that while the harassment may have occurred, it took immediate action to remedy the situation and it had a solid policy in place. Once the corporation puts forth this argument, it is difficult for the alleged harasser to appear to be in unity with the interest of his co-defendant. To the extent that the employer and individual defendants can work together in presenting a unified defense (for example, showing the co-defendant's knowledge of the harassment policy and training received regarding that policy), the chances of an adverse verdict against the individual defendant may decrease somewhat.

In summary, while joint representation will often work to the advantage of both the corporate employer and the alleged harasser, the lawyer representing the alleged harasser must be mindful of all possible conflicts, which will not always be apparent at the onset of litigation. As a result, the lawyer representing the alleged harasser must carefully evaluate and reevaluate the facts of his or her case to ensure that the client receives the best possible representation and ultimate result.

---

54. No. 94 Civ. 7735, 1997 WL 91070 (S.D.N.Y. Mar. 3, 1997).

Appendix 6A

Sample Joint Representation Agreement

Scope of Agreement. This Joint Representation Agreement (hereinafter referred to as the "Agreement") is entered into on or about _____, 2017, by and between COMPANY X ("Company") and JOHN DOE ("John Doe" and, collectively with Company, the "Parties"), and shall apply to the investigation and defense of the claims asserted in *Jane Doe v. Company X and John Doe.*

The Parties and their respective counsel believe that the sharing of information protected from discovery by the attorney work-product doctrine and/or the attorney-client privilege will facilitate their joint defense and the Parties wish to maximize the exchange of information between themselves and their respective counsel and their employees, officers, experts, consultants, and agents. The undersigned therefore agree on the following.

1. *Common Interest and Applicability of Joint Defense Doctrine.* The Parties have entered into a business relationship that appears to be the subject of the Litigation and therefore have interests in common in the preparing for and responding to the Plaintiff's allegations and requests for information, and in Company and John Doe sharing certain information, including without limitation, documents, work product, conversations, mental impressions of counsel, legal and factual analysis, interview reports, expert reports, proposed court filings, and oral or written information, including the confidences of the Parties (collectively, the "Defense Materials"), which have and will continue to serve the common interests of the Parties and facilitate the rendition of professional legal services to the Parties. The Defense Materials are privileged from disclosure to third parties as a result of the attorney-client privilege, the work-product privilege, the joint defense or common-interest privilege, and other applicable privileges, rights, or rules. The Parties and their counsel have disclosed and exchanged, and have agreed to disclose and exchange, Defense Materials between and among themselves, their employees, officers, consultants, experts, and agents to further the Parties' common interests. Such exchanges or disclosures have been made and will be made for the sake of securing, advancing, or supplying legal representation to the Parties.

2. ***Access to Defense Materials.*** Only employees, officers, consultants, experts, agents, and counsel of the Parties will be privy to Defense Materials under this Agreement. The Parties shall direct their respective employees, officers, consultants, experts, agents, and counsel involved in their common defense to honor the terms of this Agreement and each of the Parties agrees (a) to maintain as confidential the Defense Materials obtained under the terms of this Agreement, and (b) to be responsible for any breach of the terms hereunder by their representatives.

3. ***No Obligation to Share.*** Counsel and the Parties believe that the sharing and disclosure of the Defense Materials is essential to the effective representation of the Parties by their respective counsel. However, this Agreement does not obligate the Parties and their counsel to share Defense Materials.

4. ***Communications Do Not Waive Privileges and Rights.*** The Parties and their counsel agree that the exchanges and disclosures of the Defense Materials referred to in this Agreement are not intended to diminish in any way the confidentiality of such Defense Materials. It was and is their further understanding that any exchange of Defense Materials is not intended to and will not be deemed to constitute a waiver of the attorney-client privilege, the work-product privilege, or any other available privilege or right.

5. ***Agreement Not to Disclose to Third Parties and Scope of Use.*** Counsel and the Parties have agreed that neither counsel nor the Parties will disclose Defense Materials received from each other or obtained through their joint efforts, or the contents thereof, to anyone except each other, their counsel, employees, consultants, officers, experts, or agents without first obtaining consent in the following manner: (a) for Defense Materials received from each other, the advance written consent of counsel for the Party or the Party who produced such Defense Materials; and (b) for Defense Materials obtained through combined efforts, the advance written consent of counsel for each party or each of the parties. Defense Materials are to be used solely by counsel and the parties and their employees, officers, consultants, experts, and agents in the preparation of defenses to the respective claims or claims against the parties. the parties and their counsel agree that Defense Materials and the contents thereof will not be used at any time against any other party, even if such party develops adverse interests. The parties agree that should any of their respective employees, officers, consultants, experts, or agents testify in trial or discovery proceedings against any other party, said testimony will not utilize Defense Materials or the contents thereof. The parties agree that, should they or any of their respective employees, officers, consultants, experts, or agents testify in trial or discovery proceedings, counsel for the nontestifying parties will not be disqualified from cross-examining the testifying party, employee(s), officer(s), consultant(s), expert(s), or agent(s) for any reason arising out of the existence of this agreement, including the grounds that such counsel are privy to Defense Materials pursuant to this Agreement. Defense Materials or the contents thereof, however, will not be used in any way in connection with any

such cross-examination. These limitations are not intended to and do not waive a party's right to assert claims against any other party and do not prohibit the use for cross-examination or otherwise of public information or information or materials that are independently developed from sources other than the Defense Materials and obtained solely as a result of the Party's separate and independent efforts.

6. ***Disclosures by Court Order.*** A Party receiving Defense Materials covered by this agreement may disclose the Defense Materials if required by an order from a court of competent jurisdiction. Counsel and the parties have agreed that if they receive any order, summons, subpoena, or similar process, or request to produce information or materials that include Defense Materials under this Agreement, they will (a) assert all applicable privileges and rights with regard to Defense Materials, in the absence of written waivers or consent pursuant to the procedures set forth elsewhere in this agreement; and (b) immediately notify all other parties of the order or request, supply all other parties with copies of the order, summons, subpoena, or similar process or request, and provide not less than five (5) days' notice before production, in order to permit other parties and their counsel to intervene. If five days' notice cannot be provided, because of the return date of the process or the order, the counsel or party upon whom the order or request is made agrees to bring a motion to stay the proceedings in order to allow provision of five days' notice to other counsel and parties.

7. ***Each Party Understands It Is Represented by Its Own Counsel Only.*** Each party, by signing this agreement, verifies that the party understands and acknowledges that they are represented exclusively by their own counsel in this matter and that while counsel representing other parties to this agreement have a duty to preserve the confidences disclosed to them pursuant to this agreement, each counsel will not be acting as counsel for any other party. In other words, each party understands and agrees that this agreement itself does not and will not create any attorney-client relationship with counsel for any other party. The fact that any counsel has entered into this agreement shall not preclude the counsel who represents a party to this agreement from representing that party adverse to the other parties to this agreement.

8. ***Waiver of Possible Conflicts.*** Except as provided in paragraph 5 herein, the Parties and their employees, officers, consultants, experts, and agents agree (a) that they waive any and all objections that may arise by reason of their access to or their receipt of Defense Materials and the contents thereof and (b) that no counsel, employee, officer, consultant, expert, or agent shall be disqualified by reason of their access to or their receipt of Defense Materials and the contents thereof.

9. ***Right to Terminate Participation; Termination Is Prospective Only.*** Any Party and its counsel may withdraw from this agreement upon giving twenty (20) days' prior written notice to all other parties to this agreement and their counsel, in which case this agreement shall no longer be operative as to the withdrawing party and their counsel but shall continue to protect all Defense

Materials and the contents thereof disclosed to or by the withdrawing party or its employees, officers, consultants, experts, or agents prior to the party or counsel's notification of withdrawal. Upon demand, a withdrawing party and its counsel and its employees, officers, consultants, experts, and agents shall immediately return all written Defense Materials and all copies and summaries thereof to the party or counsel from whom the Defense Materials were received, or for Defense Materials obtained through combined efforts, to one of the remaining parties to the agreement with notification to the other parties to the agreement. Any such withdrawal shall not constitute a waiver of the attorney-client privilege, the attorney work-product doctrine, or any other applicable privilege or right with respect to the Defense Materials and the contents thereof.

10. ***No Claim of Conflicts by Remaining Counsel.*** Any Party that terminates and withdraws from this agreement shall not claim or assert that counsel representing other parties have a conflict of interest in their continued representation of said other parties, nor shall any such party object to the continued representation of said other parties by their counsel in connection with this matter or any related proceedings. Nothing contained in this agreement shall be used by any of the parties as a basis for seeking to disqualify any counsel from representing a current or future client in connection with this matter or any other related proceeding, and no counsel who has entered this agreement shall be prevented from examining or cross-examining any party who testifies at any proceeding because of such counsel's participation in this agreement.

11. ***Confidentiality of Joint Defense Agreement Itself.*** Absent an order of a court, counsel and the Parties agree not to reveal the terms of this Agreement. Any dispute or disagreement arising out of or because of the existence of this Agreement shall be resolved in appropriate *in camera* proceedings.

12. ***Informed Consent.*** By executing this agreement, the undersigned attorneys acknowledge that they have conferred with their respective client-party and the parties agree to be bound by the terms of this agreement.

13. ***Modification of Agreement—Addition of New Parties.*** Additional parties and their counsel may join in this agreement with the prior written consent of each party or party's respective counsel. The Parties and their counsel understand and agree that Defense Materials and the contents thereof will not be shared with or provided to new parties and their counsel unless and until all parties to this agreement and such new parties and their counsel have executed an addendum to this agreement. Written consent in the addendum may be provided by counterparts.

14. ***Substitution of Parties or Counsel.*** The parties and their counsel understand and agree that Defense Materials and the contents thereof will not be shared with substitute or associated counsel who may appear on behalf of any party unless and until such counsel and all parties and their counsel have executed an addendum to this agreement, which may be done in counterparts. This

agreement shall not be subject to abrogation by any heir, assign, or other successor in interest to any party or their counsel. Nor shall such heir, assign, or successor in interest waive any applicable privilege or doctrine with regard to Defense Material and the contents thereof.

15. ***Enforcement of Agreement.*** The parties and their counsel understand and agree that specific performance or injunctive relief is an appropriate remedy to compel compliance with the provisions of this agreement.

16. ***Sole Nature, Execution, and Modification of Agreement.*** This agreement constitutes the sole and complete agreement between and among the parties and memorializes the earlier oral agreement entered into by the undersigned counsel and parties. Any modification of this agreement shall be effective only if such modification is in writing and signed by all parties or their counsel.

17. ***Neutral Construction.*** The undersigned acknowledge and agree that the drafting of this agreement has been a joint effort by the undersigned and that the agreement shall not be deemed prepared or drafted by any one of the parties or counsel.

18. ***Designation of Joint Defense Material.*** Any party or its counsel, employees, officers, consultants, experts, or agents who transmit or prepare Defense Material shall mark the Defense Material with a legend or label as "Joint Defense Privilege." The absence of such legend on any materials or documents exchanged by the parties or their counsel or their employees, officers, consultants, experts, or agents shall not be construed as an indication that such materials are not subject to this agreement.

19. ***Severability.*** If any provision of this Agreement is determined to be invalid or unenforceable, the remaining provisions shall continue to be fully operative to the extent permissible.

20. ***Modifications to This Agreement.*** Any change to this agreement, including this paragraph, must be in writing and signed by all parties and their counsel.

So agreed, as evidenced by the signatures of each Party and each counsel below.

COMPANY X   Joe Anylawyer, Esq.

By: _____   Counsel for Company X

Title: _____   _____

JOHN DOE   Bob Anylawyer, Esq.

By: _____   Counsel for JOHN DOE

Title: _____   By:_____

Sample Engagement Letter

Re: Jane Doe v. Company X and John Doe

Dear Mr. Doe:

This letter will confirm the terms upon which we will act as your legal counsel in connection with the lawsuit filed by Jane Doe against Company X and yourself.

We will provide you with all legal services necessary to defend your interest in the case. Our representation will involve a complete defense on all procedural and substantive grounds, and will cover all incidents of litigation, including motions, pretrial proceedings, discovery, hearings, and, if necessary, trial and appeals. It will not, however, include any counterclaims or "offensive" legal action that you may wish to pursue against Jane Doe, so if you desire to bring such claims, please consult other counsel as soon as possible so that you do not miss any deadlines for initiating suit.

We will be representing Company X in addition to you in this action. In a situation like this, involving multiple parties, there is a possibility that the individual parties' interests may conflict. Even when all parties' interests initially are compatible, a conflict can develop later as the lawsuit progresses. Based on our review of the allegations made in the complaint in this action, and on our preliminary investigation to date of the facts, we do not perceive a conflict between your interest and the interest of Company X in this lawsuit. We will inform both you and Company X immediately should a conflict appear. In such an event, we would have to withdraw from representing you, and you strongly would be advised to obtain substitute counsel.

You also should be aware that all information that is disclosed or discovered in the course of our defense may be disclosed to Company X. If you know of any information regarding this lawsuit that you believe should be kept confidential, you should consult with an independent attorney. If any such information ever comes to your attention, you should advise us in writing of that fact, without disclosing the information, so that we can determine whether it is appropriate for us to continue representing you.

If these terms meet with your approval, please date and sign the enclosed copy of this letter where indicated and return it to this office.

If you have any questions regarding any of these arrangements, please do not hesitate to call me.

Very truly yours,

Attorney

ACCEPTED AND AGREED TO on this day of _____, 2018.

BY: _____

John Doe

CHAPTER 7

Arbitration Issues and Considerations

Deborah S. Weiser

Although this book focuses on litigating harassment and retaliation claims in court, these claims may be litigated in an arbitration forum pursuant to a binding and enforceable arbitration agreement. Following is a summary of the law on the enforceability of employment arbitration agreements and related issues.

I. THE PREEMPTIVE FORCE OF THE FEDERAL ARBITRATION ACT

The Federal Arbitration Act (FAA)[1] provides that a "written provision in . . . a contract evidencing a transaction involving commerce to settle by arbitration a controversy thereafter arising out of such contract or transaction, or the refusal to perform the whole or any part thereof, shall be valid, irrevocable, and enforceable, save upon such grounds as exist at law or in equity for the revocation of any contract."[2]

The US Supreme Court has held that the FAA is a "congressional declaration of a liberal federal policy favoring arbitration agreements, notwithstanding any state substantive or procedural policies to the contrary. The effect of [the Act] is to create a body of federal substantive law of arbitrability, applicable to any arbitration agreement within the coverage of the Act. . . . [The Act] establishes that, as a matter of federal law, any doubts concerning the scope of arbitrable issues should be resolved in favor of arbitration."[3] The Court has further held that by enacting the FAA, "Congress declared a national policy favoring arbitration and withdrew the power of the states to require a judicial forum for the resolution of claims which the contracting parties agreed to

---

1. 9 U.S.C. § 1 *et seq* (1947).
2. *See* 9 U.S.C. § 2 (1947).
3. Moses H. Cone Hosp. v. Mercury Constr. (1983) 460 U.S. 1, 24–25, 103 S. Ct. 927, 74 L. Ed. 2d 765.

resolve by arbitration."[4] Further, when parties agree to arbitrate all disputes arising under their contract, questions concerning the validity of the entire contract are to be resolved by the arbitrator in the first instance, not by a federal or state court.[5]

Where the FAA applies, it preempts state laws. When parties agree to arbitrate all questions arising under a contract, state laws lodging primary jurisdiction in another forum, whether judicial or administrative, are superseded by the FAA.[6] The contract need not mention interstate commerce. An employment contract involves commerce under the FAA simply if the transaction, in fact, involves interstate commerce, regardless of the parties' subjective intent when they signed the agreement.[7]

In *Circuit City Stores, Inc. v. Adams*,[8] the US Supreme Court reversed the Ninth Circuit's holding[9] that the FAA does not apply to labor or employment contracts. The employee in *Circuit City* had completed a required employment application that contained a dispute resolution agreement requiring employees to submit all claims and disputes to binding arbitration. The employee later sued the employer in state court for sexual harassment, retaliation, constructive discharge, and intentional infliction of emotional distress under California's antidiscrimination laws and sexual orientation discrimination. The employer petitioned in federal district court to stay the state court proceedings and compel arbitration. The district court granted the employer's petition, but the Ninth Circuit reversed on the ground that the FAA did not apply. The US Supreme Court reversed the Ninth Circuit, and held that the FAA applies to labor and employment contracts and excludes from its coverage only contracts of employment of transportation workers.[10]

The FAA exempts from its coverage "contracts of employment of seamen, railroad employees, or any other class of workers engaged in foreign or interstate commerce."[11]

---

4. Preston v. Ferrer (2008) 552 U.S. 346, 128 S. Ct. 978, 981, 169 L. Ed. 2d 917; Southland Corp. v. Keating (1984) 465 U.S. 1, 10–11, 104 S. Ct. 852, 79 L. Ed. 2d 1; *see also* Gilmer v. Interstate/Johnson Lane Corp. (1991) 500 U.S. 20, 26–33, 111 S. Ct. 1647, 114 L. Ed. 2d 26 (Age Discrimination in Employment Act action subject to compulsory arbitration under FAA).

5. Buckeye Check Cashing, Inc. v. Cardegna (2006) 546 U.S. 440, 126 S. Ct. 1204, 163 L. Ed. 2d 1038 (2006).

6. Perry v. Thomas (1987) 482 U.S. 483, 490–491, 107 S. Ct. 2520, 96 L. Ed. 2d 426 (FAA preempted California state law providing that employees must bring civil action to collect unpaid wages notwithstanding any private agreement to arbitrate).

7. Allied-Bruce Terminix Companies, Inc. v. Dobson (1995) 513 U.S. 265, 277, 115 S. Ct. 834, 130 L. Ed. 2d 753.

8. Circuit City Stores, Inc. v. Adams (2001) 532 U.S. 105, 121 S. Ct. 1302, 149 L. Ed. 2d 234.

9. *See* Circuit City Stores, Inc. v. Adams (9th Cir. 1999) 194 F.3d 1070.

10. Circuit City Stores, Inc. v. Adams (2001) 532 U.S. 105, 113, 121 S. Ct. 1302, 149 L. Ed. 2d 234. *See also* Circuit City Stores, Inc. v. Najd (9th Cir. 2002) 294 F.3d 1104, 1106–7 (Supreme Court decision in *Adams* directly forecloses argument that FAA exempts all employment contracts from FAA coverage; Adams held exemption only applies to employment contracts of transportation workers).

11. 9 U.S.C. § 1. *See* Circuit City Stores, Inc. v. Adams (2001) 532 U.S. 105, 109, 121 S. Ct. 1302, 149 L. Ed. 2d 234.

The provision exempting "any other class of workers engaged in foreign or interstate commerce" has been defined to mean "transportation workers."[12] Truck drivers who cross interstate lines usually are considered transportation workers.[13]

Arbitration contracts are enforceable under state law, and parties are free to enter into contracts providing for arbitration under state law rather than the FAA.[14] Although the FAA preempts state laws that require a judicial forum for the resolution of claims the contracting parties agree to resolve by arbitration, the FAA does not prevent the enforcement of agreements to arbitrate under different rules than those set forth in the FAA itself.[15] When the parties have agreed to abide by state rules of arbitration, enforcing those rules according to the terms of the agreement is fully consistent with the goals of the FAA, even if the result is that arbitration is stayed when the FAA would otherwise permit it to go forward.[16] Thus, parties are free to contract around the FAA by incorporating state arbitration rules into their agreements.[17] To do so, however, there must be clear and unmistakable evidence that the parties agreed to apply nonfederal arbitrability law.[18]

II. INDIVIDUAL ARBITRATION AGREEMENTS

A. Statutory Employment Claims

In *Gilmer v. Interstate/Johnson Lane Corp.*,[19] the US Supreme Court held that arbitration agreements generally do not conflict with or hinder the purposes and policies of equal employment opportunity laws.[20] In *Gilmer*, the Court held that an age discrimination

---

12. Circuit City Stores, Inc. v. Adams (2001) 532 U.S. 105, 121, 121 S. Ct. 1302, 149 L. Ed. 2d 234.

13. Harden v. Roadway Package Systems, Inc. (9th Cir. 2001) 249 F.3d 1137, 1140 (FAA is inapplicable to drivers engaged in interstate commerce).

14. Volt Information Sciences, Inc. v. Bd. of Trustees of the Leland Stanford Junior Univ. (1989) 489 U.S. 468, 478–79, 109 S. Ct. 1248, 103 L. Ed. 2d 488.

15. *Id* (internal citations omitted).

16. *Id.*

17. *See* Wolsey Ltd. v. Foodmaker, Inc. (9th Cir. 1998) 144 F.3d 1205, 1209, quoting Volt Information Sciences, Inc. v. Bd. of Trustees of the Leland Stanford Junior Univ. (1989) 489 U.S. 468, 479, 109 S. Ct. 1248, 103 L. Ed. 2d 488.

18. Brennan v. Opus Bank (9th Cir. 2015) 796 F.3d 1125, 1129 (federal law governed arbitrability question by default because arbitration agreement was covered by FAA, where parties had not clearly and unmistakably designated that nonfederal arbitrability law applied, and where employment agreement containing arbitration agreement did not clearly and unmistakably indicate that California's law of arbitrability should apply as it stated only that "any controversy of claim . . . shall be settled by binding arbitration.").

19. Gilmer v. Interstate/Johnson Lane Corp. (1991) 500 U.S. 20, 111 S. Ct. 1647, 114 L. Ed. 2d 26 (ADEA).

20. *See, e.g.,* Gilmer v. Interstate/Johnson Lane Corp. (1991) 500 U.S. 20, 27–32, 111 S. Ct. 1647, 114 L. Ed. 2d 26 (ADEA).

action under the Age Discrimination in Employment Act (ADEA)[21] was subject to compulsory arbitration pursuant to an arbitration agreement contained in a securities registration application. The Court declared that compulsory arbitration of ADEA claims is not inconsistent with the ADEA's statutory framework and underlying purposes.[22]

Plaintiffs thereafter contested the arbitrability of Title VII claims, asserting that the Civil Rights Act of 1991 (CRA), which grants a jury-trial right for Title VII claims, impliedly exempted discrimination claims from FAA coverage. That theory originally prevailed in *Duffield v. Robertson Stephens & Co.*[23] Relying on legislative history, the *Duffield* court held that Congress intended to prohibit in the 1991 Act mandatory requirements under which prospective employees agree as a condition of employment to surrender their rights to litigate future Title VII claims in a judicial forum.[24] Although the 1991 Act contained language encouraging the alternative resolution of disputes "where appropriate" and to "the extent authorized by law," the *Duffield* court said that this was limited to situations in which (1) arbitration furthers the purpose and objective of the CRA—by affording victims of discrimination an opportunity to present their claims in an alternative forum, a forum they find desirable—not by forcing an unwanted forum on them; and (2) the parties knowingly and voluntarily elect to use those methods.[25] Predispute agreements, according to the *Duffield* court, do not meet that test. The *Duffield* court held, however, that the plaintiff was still required to arbitrate breach of contract, deceit, and intentional infliction of emotional distress claims, which do not arise under the discrimination laws.[26]

In *Equal Employment Opportunity Commission v. Luce, Forward, Hamilton & Scripps,*[27] the Ninth Circuit, *en banc*, held that the circuit had erred in *Duffield* in concluding that the CRA precludes mandatory arbitration of Title VII claims. The court acknowledged that after the US Supreme Court's decision in *Gilmer,*[28] the decision in *Duffield* stood alone and all of the other circuits had concluded that Title VII does not

---

21. 29 U.S.C. § 621 *et seq.*

22. Gilmer v. Interstate/Johnson Lane Corp. (1991) 500 U.S. 20, 27–9, 111 S. Ct. 1647, 114 L. Ed. 2d 26.

23. Duffield v. Robertson Stephens & Co. (9th Cir. 1998) 144 F.3d 1182, 1203, overruled by EEOC v. Luce, Forward, Hamilton & Scripps (9th Cir. 2003) 345 F.3d 742 (*en banc*).

24. *Id.* at 1189–1199 (because every securities industry employer requires employees to sign Form U-4, the form is especially violative of Congress' limitations), overruled by EEOC v. Luce, Forward, Hamilton & Scripps (9th Cir. 2003) 345 F.3d 742 (*en banc*).

25. *Id.* at 1191–7 (court did not reach issues such as whether agreement to arbitrate was knowing, whether arbitration process is adequate to vindicate Title VII rights, and whether Form U-4 is unconscionable), overruled by EEOC v. Luce, Forward, Hamilton & Scripps (9th Cir. 2003) 345 F.3d 742 (*en banc*). *Compare* Rosenberg v. Merrill Lynch, Pierce, Fenner & Smith, Inc. (D. Mass. 1998) 995 F. Supp. 190, 203 (1991 Act precludes compulsory arbitration of Title VII claims under Form U-4) with *Johnson v. Hubbard Broadcasting, Inc.* (D. Minn. 1996) 940 F. Supp. 1447, 1457–1458 (reaching opposite conclusion despite noting indications to contrary in Act's legislative history).

26. *Id.* at 1203, overruled by EEOC v. Luce, Forward, Hamilton & Scripps (9th Cir. 2003) 345 F.3d 742 (*en banc*).

27. EEOC v. Luce, Forward, Hamilton & Scripps (9th Cir. 2003) 345 F.3d 742, 746–53.

28. Gilmer v. Interstate/Johnson Lane Corp. (1991) 500 U.S. 20, 111 S. Ct. 1647, 114 L. Ed. 2d 26.

bar compulsory arbitration agreements.[29] The court also held that a right to jury trial does not preclude compulsory arbitration of Title VII claims.[30]

B. Enforceability of Individual Arbitration Agreements

Under the FAA, arbitration clauses in contracts are valid, irrevocable, and enforceable, except upon grounds existing at law or in equity for the revocation of any contract, such as fraud, duress, or unconscionability.[31] Contract-based challenges are governed by applicable state law.[32] Under the FAA, a state cannot apply to an arbitration agreement any rule to invalidate a contract that is different from or more rigorous than that applied to other contracts.[33]

1. Whether Contract Is Formed

Although the FAA requires a written agreement to arbitrate,[34] there is no requirement that it be signed by the parties. Employee handbooks and other unilaterally

---

29. *See, e.g.,* Rosenberg v. Merrill Lynch, Pierce, Fenner & Smith, Inc. (1st Cir. 1999) 170 F.3d 1, 10–11; Desiderio v. National Ass'n of Securities Dealers, Inc. (2d Cir. 1999) 191 F.3d 198, 205; Seus v. John Nuveen & Co., Inc. (3d Cir. 1998) 146 F.3d 175, 183; Hooters of America, Inc. v. Phillips (4th Cir. 1999) 173 F.3d 933, 937; Mouton v. Metropolitan Life Ins. Co. (5th Cir. 1998) 147 F.3d 453, 455; Alford v. Dean Witter Reynolds, Inc. (5th Cir. 1991) 939 F.2d 229, 229–30; Koveleskie v. SBC Capital Markets, Inc. (7th Cir. 1999) 167 F.3d 361, 365; Patterson v. Tenet Healthcare, Inc. (8th Cir. 1997) 113 F.3d 832, 837; Todd-Watkins v. Continental Airlines, Inc. (9th Cir. Feb. 1, 1999, No. 97-55832) 1999 U.S. App. LEXIS 2627 *2, n.1; Metz v. Merrill Lynch, Pierce, Fenner & Smith, Inc. (10th Cir. 1994) 39 F.3d 1482, 1487; Weeks v. Harden Mfg. Corp. (11th Cir. 2002) 291 F.3d 1307, 1315–6; Bender v. A.G. Edwards & Sons, Inc. (11th Cir. 1992) 971 F.2d 698, 699 (*per curiam*); Borg-Warner Protective Services Corp. v. EEOC (D.C. Cir. 2001) 245 F.3d 831, 835. *See also* Farac v. Permanente Med. Group (N.D. Cal. 2002) 186 F. Supp. 2d 1042, 1045.

30. EEOC v. Luce, Forward, Hamilton & Scripps (9th Cir. 2003) 345 F.3d 742, 750. *See also* Desiderio v. National Ass'n of Securities Dealers, Inc. (2d Cir. 1999) 191 F.3d 198, 205; Rosenberg v. Merrill Lynch, Pierce, Fenner & Smith, Inc. (1st Cir. 1999) 170 F.3d 1, 11.

31. 9 U.S.C. § 2 (1947).

32. Cox v. Ocean View Hotel Corp. (9th Cir. 2008) 533 F.3d 1114, 1121.

33. Perry v. Thomas (1987) 482 U.S. 483, 492 n.9, 107 S. Ct. 2520, 96 L. Ed. 2d 426; *First Options of Chicago, Inc. v. Kaplan* (1995) 514 U.S. 938, 944, 115 S. Ct. 1920, 131 L. Ed. 2d 985 (when deciding whether parties agreed to arbitrate dispute, courts generally should apply ordinary state law principles).

34. A "written provision" to arbitrate shall be valid, irrevocable, and enforceable. 9 U.S.C. § 2. The Ninth Circuit has held that such an agreement exists so long as its execution was a condition precedent to an individual's receiving employment, even if the underlying employment agreement disclaims an intention to alter the employee's at-will status. Circuit City Stores v. Adams, 194 F.3d 1070, 81 FEP 720 (9th Cir. 1999), *rev'd on other grounds*, 532 U.S. 105, 121 S. Ct. 1302, 149 L. Ed. 2d 234 (2001); Circuit City Stores v. Ahmed, 195 F.3d 1131 (9th Cir. 1999). *See also* Baptist Health Sys., Inc. v. Mack, 860 So. 2d 1265, 2003 Ala. LEXIS 114 (Ala. Apr. 18, 2003) (signing acknowledgment that dispute resolution program governs continuing employment sufficient to warrant compelling arbitration of retaliatory discharge claim); Johnson v. Long John Silver's Restaurants, 414 F.3d 583 (6th Cir. 2005) (relying upon implied in fact contract theory, thus avoiding the need to actually find that the employee signed the agreement).

Although the FAA requires the arbitration agreement to be in writing, it has also been held that it does not require the agreement to be signed by the employee. Caley v. Gulfstream Aerospace Corp., 428 F.3d 1359 (11th Cir. 2005).

promulgated documents may be a valid source of the "agreement" that arbitration will be the exclusive forum for disputes arising from employment, including termination.

After *Gilmer*, some courts have found these unilaterally published arbitration statements to be enforceable. Thus, such clauses have been enforced when they were contained in employee handbooks[35] and in employment applications.[36] In the view of some courts, a contractual agreement to arbitrate disputes can exist separate and apart from any other enforceable contract rights.

2. Inadequate Consideration

Plaintiff attempts to avoid arbitration on the ground that the promise was not supported by consideration have been largely unsuccessful. Some courts have held that the employer's promise to submit the dispute to arbitration and refrain from insisting upon a judicial determination of the claim was, in fact, sufficient consideration for the employee's promise.[37] At least one court has held that the consideration inquiry is confined solely to the agreement to arbitrate. Thus, in one case, an employee who agreed to submit employment-related claims to arbitration was also subject to a nonbinding internal dispute resolution program that could be unilaterally terminated by the employer. The court held that the claimed illusory nature of the internal dispute resolution program was irrelevant to determining whether the arbitration agreement

---

35. *See, e.g.,* Mago v. Shearson Lehman Hutton, Inc., 956 F.2d 932 (9th Cir. 1991) (arbitration clause incorporated into application was signed by employee at time of application); Lang v. Burlington N. R.R. Co., 835 F. Supp. 1104 (D. Minn. 1993); Painewebber v. Agron, 49 F.3d 347 (8th Cir. 1995); Bakri v. Continental Airlines, Inc., 1992 U.S. Dist. LEXIS 22162 (C.D. Cal. Sept. 25, 1992); Kinnebrew v. Gulf Ins. Co., 67 Fair Empl. Prac. Cas. 189 (N.D. Tex. 1994). *Compare* Hergenreder v. Bickford Senior Living Group, *LLC*, 656 F.3d 411 (6th Cir. 2011) (where handbook did not mention arbitration and referred only to another document that was not given to the employee, describing the employer promulgated plan, the court held that there was neither an offer nor acceptance of the arbitration provision).

36. Brown v. KFC Nat'l Mgmt. Co., 82 Haw. 226, 921 P.2d 146, 12 I.E.R. Cas. (BNA) 1021 (Haw. 1996). Another court concluded that a minor plaintiff, who executed the employment application containing the arbitration provision, could not disaffirm the contract under state law. Sheller v. Frank's Nursery & Crafts, Inc., 957 F. Supp. 150, 73 FEP 870 (N.D. Ill. 1997). In one instance, the employee executed an employment application with a merger clause and a separate arbitration agreement. The US Court of Appeals for the First Circuit rejected the employee's claim that the merger clause in the application rendered the arbitration agreement unenforceable, reasoning that they were separate and independently executed agreements. Pelletier v. Yellow Transp., Inc., 549 F.3d 578 (1st Cir. 2008).

37. *See* Circuit City Stores v. Najd, 294 F.3d 1104 (9th Cir. 2002); Johnson v. Circuit City Stores, Inc., 148 F.3d 373, 77 FEP 139 (4th Cir. 1998) (employer's agreement to be bound by arbitration sufficient consideration for requiring applicants to enter into such agreements as a condition prerequisite to having application for employment considered); Michalski v. Circuit City Stores, 177 F.3d 634, 79 FEP 1160 (7th Cir. 1999) (same); Bauer v. Morton's of Chicago, 82 FEP 286 (N.D. Ill. 2000) (same, even when claim asserted that it constituted a unilateral change in plaintiff's terms and conditions of employment); Moorning-Brown v. Bear, Stearns & Co., 81 Fair Empl. Prac. Cas. 1488 (S.D.N.Y. 2000); Labor Ready Central III L.P. v. Gonzalez, 64 S.W.3d 519, 2001 Tex. App. LEXIS 7995, 87 FEP 612 (Tex. Ct. App. 2001); O'Neil v. Hilton Head Hosp., 115 F.3d 272 (4th Cir. 1997).

was supported by consideration.[38] Other courts have held that the promise of continued employment was sufficient consideration for the employee's agreement to submit disputes to arbitration.[39]

3. Unconscionability

Most cases finding unconscionability involve one or more of the following factors: (1) promulgated rules provide or allow for a biased process or arbitration panel; (2) lack of mutuality; (3) limitations to the relief the employee can seek in court; (4) shifting arbitration costs to the employee; and (5) restricted discovery.

a. Fairness of the Arbitral Administration and Process

Enforceability of private arbitration clauses often turns on the overall fairness of the process, particularly whether the employer is provided an unfair advantage or undue control over the arbitration procedure. If too much control over the procedure is deemed to be exercised by the employer, courts often find such agreements to be substantively unconscionable.[40] In *Hooters of America, Inc. v. Phillips*,[41] the employer-promulgated arbitration rules effectively gave the employer full control over the composition of the arbitration panel, reserved to the employer the right to discovery, to expand the scope of the arbitration, and to seek judicial review of awards, while simultaneously denying those rights to employees. The Fourth Circuit held that the rules were so one-sided that it effectively breached the contractual obligation to have disputes resolved by a bona fide third-party neutral. The court thus concluded that by creating "a sham system, unworthy even of the name of arbitration," the employer failed to perform its duty of assuring that disputes were resolved by an impartial third party.[42]

---

38. Hill v. Peoplesoft, USA, Inc., 412 F.3d 540, 2005 U.S. App. LEXIS 11959 (4th Cir. 2005). *See also* Soto-Fonalledas v. Ritz-Carlton San Juan Hotel Spa & Casino, 640 F.3d 471 (1st Cir. 2011) (employer's agreement to waive certain defenses in exchange for employee's agreement to submit disputes to arbitration was bilateral promise providing consideration for employee's promise, as was the mutual obligation of the parties to submit all of their claims to the arbitration process).

39. Davis v. Nordstrom, Inc., 755 F.3d 1089 (9th Cir. 2014); Hardin v. First Cash Financial Services, 465 F.3d 470 (10th Cir. 2006); Marino v. Dillard's Inc., 413 F.3d 530 (5th Cir. 2005).

40. *See, e.g.*, Kristian v. Comcast Corp., 446 F.3d 25 (1st Cir. 2006); Kinney v. United Healthcare, 70 Cal. App. 4th 1322, 83 Cal. Rptr. 2d 348 (1999).

41. 173 F.3d 933, 79 FEP 629 (4th Cir. 1999).

42. *See also* Floss v. Ryan's Family Steak Houses, Inc., 211 F.3d 306 (6th Cir. 2001) (finding agreement unenforceable where employer had "unfettered discretion in choosing the nature of [the arbitral forum]" and could alter the applicable rules and procedures without notice to or consent from employees); Walker v. Ryan's Family Steak Houses, 400 F.3d 370, 385–386 (6th Cir. 2005) (holding arbitration agreements unenforceable under the FAA due to state-law contract defenses and under the FAA because they did not allow for effective vindication of federal claims; "The Arbitration Agreements and related rules and procedures at issue in this case demonstrate that EDSI's arbitral forum is not neutral and, therefore, the agreements are unenforceable.").

b. Mutuality

The validity of an agreement that does not operate equally against both employers and employees is dependent on state law. In *Armendariz v. Foundation Health Psychcare Services, Inc.*,[43] the California Supreme Court held that employment arbitration agreements that are not bilateral and reciprocal will be denied enforcement on the grounds of unconscionability. In *Armendariz*, the applicable agreement required the employee to submit all disputes to arbitration, while not precluding the employer from litigating claims it may have against the employee in court. The court held that the lack of mutuality inherent in that agreement rendered the agreement unconscionable and, therefore, unenforceable against plaintiff.[44] In *Ferguson v. Countrywide Credit Indus.*,[45] the Ninth Circuit applied California state law in finding an arbitration agreement unfairly one-sided and, therefore, substantively unconscionable because it compelled arbitration of the claims the employees were most likely to bring against the employer, yet exempted those the employer was most likely to bring against employees. Notably, the Fifth Circuit found the same agreement enforceable due to differences in Texas state law.[46]

c. Limitations on Relief

Arbitration agreements that fail to give arbitrators the authority to provide remedies coextensive with those provided by statute are often found invalid. In some cases, the claims for punitive damages or other remedies limited by the arbitration agreement, but which would be available at law, has been severed and considered post-arbitration by the court.[47] Some courts have severed out the remedial limitations and then ordered the case to arbitration.[48] Other courts have suggested that such restrictions upon the arbitrator's remedial authority rendered the underlying agreement to arbitrate unconscionable or unenforceable.[49]

---

43. 24 Cal. 4th 83, 99 Cal. Rptr. 2d 745, 6 P.3d 669, 83 FEP 1172 (Cal. 2000).

44. Armendariz v. Foundation Health Psychcare Services, Inc., 24 Cal. 4th 83, 99 Cal. Rptr. 2d 745, 6 P.3d 669, 83 FEP 1172 (Cal. 2000).

45. 298 F.3d 778 (9th Cir. 2002).

46. Carter v. Countrywide Credit Indus., 362 F.3d 294, 301 fn. 5 (5th Cir. 2004) ("Given this dramatic difference between the two states' laws, *Ferguson* is hardly persuasive in applying Texas law.").

47. *See, e.g.*, Mulder v. Donaldson, Lufkin & Jenrette, 623 N.Y.S.2d 560, 1995 N.Y. App. Div. LEXIS 2528 (App. Div. 1995) (plaintiffs may seek punitive damages in court after recovering compensatory damages in arbitration); Willoughby Roofing & Supply Co. v. Kajima Int'l, Inc., 598 F. Supp. 353 (N.D. Ala. 1984) (plaintiff may bring action based on breach of contract and other claims not within the scope of claims or remedies permitted by arbitration agreement).

48. Booker v. Robert Half Int'l, Inc., 413 F.3d 77 (D.C. Cir. 2005); Hadnot v. Bay Ltd., 344 F.3d 474 (5th Cir. 2003); Gannon v. Circuit City Stores, Inc., 262 F.3d 677, 86 FEP 755 (8th Cir. 2001); Armendariz v. Foundation Health Psychcare Services, Inc., 24 Cal. 4th 83, 99 Cal. Rptr. 2d 745, 6 P.3d 669, 83 FEP 1172 (Cal. 2000); Shubin v. William Lyon Homes Inc., 84 Cal. App. 4th 1041, 101 Cal. Rptr. 2d 390 (Cal. App. 4th 2000); Wright v. Circuit City Stores, 82 F. Supp. 2d 1279, 83 FEP 877 (N.D. Ala. 2000).

49. McCaskill v. SCI Management Corp., 285 F.3d 623, 88 FEP 705, revised, 298 F.3d 677 (7th Cir. 2002) (holding that arbitration agreement requiring each party to bear its own attorneys' fees rendered agreement unenforceable because the award of attorneys' fees to the prevailing party was deemed integral to the purposes of Title VII); Cole v. Burns Int'l Sec. Servs., 105 F.3d 1465, 72 FEP 1775 (D.C. Cir. 1997)

d. Cost Allocation

In *Cole v. Burns International Security Services*,[50] the court held that when an employer imposes mandatory arbitration as a condition of employment, the agreement or process cannot require the employee to bear expenses beyond those the employee would incur to litigate the statutory claims in court.[51] The District of Columbia Circuit has been joined by the US Courts of Appeals for the Ninth,[52] Tenth,[53] and Eleventh Circuits.[54] At the state level, California similarly follows *Cole*'s reasoning.[55]

In *Williams v. Cigna Financial Advisors, Inc.*,[56] the Fifth Circuit rejected the plaintiff's argument that the requirement that, as the nonprevailing party, he pay half the costs of arbitration was contrary to public policy. The court rejected that claim, reasoning that *Gilmer* would require such a finding only if the fee allocation provision "prevented him from having a full opportunity to vindicate his claims effectively or prevented the arbitration proceedings from affording him an adequate substitute for a federal judicial forum."

In *Green Tree Financial Corp. v. Randolph*,[57] the US Supreme Court held that silence in an arbitration agreement regarding arbitration costs was insufficient to render the agreement unenforceable because the risk that the weaker party would be saddled with prohibitive costs was too speculative. The Court found that when a party seeks

---

(dictum); Hooters of Am., Inc. v. Phillips, 39 F. Supp. 2d 582, 76 FEP 1757 (D.S.C. 1998), aff'd, 173 F.3d 933 (4th Cir. 1999); Johnson v. Hubbard Broad., Inc., 940 F. Supp. 1447, 73 Fair Empl. Prac. Cas. 8 (D. Minn. 1997); McCoy v. Superior Court of Orange County, 87 Cal. App. 4th 354, 104 Cal. Rptr. 2d 504, 17 IER Cases 417 (Cal. App. 4th 2001); Stirlen v. Supercuts, Inc., 51 Cal. App. 4th 1519, 60 Cal. Rptr. 2d 138, 12 IER Cases 1127 (Cal. Ct. App. 1997); Trumbull v. Century Mktg. Corp., 12 F. Supp. 2d 683, 77 FEP 571 (N.D. Ohio 1998) (arbitration provision precluding award of the remedies provided by applicable statutes renders the arbitration forum inappropriate for the resolution of those claims); DeGaetano v. Smith Barney, 983 F. Supp. 459, 75 FEP 579 (S.D.N.Y. 1997) (arbitration agreement prohibiting award of attorney's fees to party prevailing on Title VII claim is void as against public policy; discussion suggesting that other limitations on legal remedies would be similarly void); Derrickson v. Circuit City Stores, 84 F. Supp. 2d 679 (D. Md. 1999); Pricewaterhouse Coopers v. Rutlen, 83 FEP 235 (S.D.N.Y. 2000) (policy permitting arbitration to award only "direct damages" is not equivalent to statutory remedies).

50. 105 F.3d 1465, 323 U.S. App. D.C. 133, 72 FEP 1775 (D.C. Cir. 1997).

51. Cole, 105 F.3d at 1484.

52. Ferguson v. Countrywide Credit Indus., 298 F.3d 778 (9th Cir. 2002) (agreement required employee to pay $125 filing fee, the employer pay for the first hearing day, and all other arbitration costs to be shared equally by the employee and employer).

53. Shankle v. B-G Maintenance Management, 163 F.3d 1230 (10th Cir. 1999) (provision in an arbitration agreement requiring the employee to pay one half of the arbitrator's fee).

54. Paladino v. Avnet Computer Techs., Inc., 134 F.3d 1054, 76 FEP 1315 (11th Cir. 1998) (arbitration agreement required the claimant to pay a filing fee of $2,000, far in excess of applicable court filing fees).

55. Armendariz v. Foundation Health Psychcare Services, Inc., 24 Cal. 4th 83, 110–1, 99 Cal. Rptr. 2d 745, 6 P.3d 669, 83 FEP 1172 (Cal. 2000) ("we conclude that when an employer imposes mandatory arbitration as a condition of employment, the arbitration agreement or arbitration process cannot generally require the employee to bear any *type* of expense that the employee would not be required to bear if he or she were free to bring the action in court").

56. 197 F.3d 752, 81 FEP 747 (5th Cir. 1999).

57. Green Tree Financial Corp.-Alabama v. Randolph (2000) 531 U.S. 79, 121 S. Ct. 513, 148 L. Ed. 2d 373.

to invalidate an arbitration agreement on the ground that arbitration would be prohibitively expensive, that party bears the burden of showing the likelihood of incurring such costs.[58] Although *Green Tree* did not elaborate on the kinds of cost-sharing arrangements that would be unenforceable, dicta in that case and several federal cases interpreting it suggest that federal law requires only that employers not impose "prohibitively expensive" arbitration costs on the employee.[59]

e. Discovery Limitations

In *Gilmer,* the Supreme Court noted that discovery procedures that are not as extensive as in federal courts are a trade for the "simplicity, informality and expedition of arbitration."[60] In *Hooters of America, Inc. v. Phillips,*[61] however, the court found unconscionable, as a matter of state law, an arbitration agreement that severely limited the plaintiff's discovery opportunities by limiting the plaintiff to the taking of one deposition, by requiring the plaintiff to provide the employer with a witness list, and by subjecting the plaintiff's witnesses to sequestration without imposing similar limitations and obligations upon the employer. Those factors, among many other considerations, resulted in the district court's refusing to order the plaintiff's Title VII claim to arbitration. In *Sanchez v. Carmax Auto Superstores Cal., LLC,*[62] a California court held an arbitration agreement was not substantively unconscionable where it limited each party to twenty interrogatories and three depositions, but allowed the arbitrator to allow additional discovery on the request of any party and a showing of "substantial need," because the employee made no showing of how the limitation would prevent him from vindicating his rights.

---

58. Green Tree Financial Corp.-Alabama v. Randolph (2000) 531 U.S. 79, 91–92, 121 S. Ct. 513, 148 L. Ed. 2d 373.

59. *See* Circuit City Stores v. Adams (9th Cir. 2002) 279 F.3d 889; Ball v. SFX Broadcasting, Inc. (N.D.N.Y. 2001) 165 F. Supp. 2d 230, 239 (all holding that "prohibitively expensive" standard in *Green Tree* does not affect validity of categorical position that employer should pay the costs of mandatory employment arbitration of statutory claims). *See* Blair v. Scott Specialty Gases (3d Cir. 2002) 283 F.3d 595, 609; Nelson v. Insignia/Esg, Inc. (D.D.C. 2002) 215 F. Supp. 2d 143; Bradford v. Rockwell Semiconductor Systems, Inc. (4th Cir. 2001) 238 F.3d 549 (all holding that *Green Tree* requires case-by-case analysis based on such factors as employee's ability to pay arbitration fees and differential between projected arbitration and litigation fees). *See* Mildworm v. Ashcroft (E.D.N.Y. 2002) 200 F. Supp. 2d 171; Boyd v. Town of Hayneville (M.D. Ala. 2001) 144 F. Supp. 2d 1272 (holding that information presented by employee before arbitration was too speculative to warrant invalidation of arbitration agreement, while retaining jurisdiction to reconsider cost issue after arbitration).

60. *Gilmer,* 500 U.S. at 31.

61. 39 F. Supp. 2d 582, 76 FEP 1757 (D.S.C. 1998*), aff'd on other grounds,* 173 F.3d 933, 79 FEP 629 (4th Cir. 1999).

62. Sanchez v. Carmax Auto Superstores Cal., LLC (2014) 224 Cal. App. 4th 398, 404–406, 168 Cal. Rptr. 3d 473. *See also* Poublon v. C.H. Robinson (9th Cir. 2017) 846 F.3d 1251, 1269–70 (no unconscionability where employee could obtain all "relevant documents," request her personnel records, and take three depositions; and where employee could obtain additional discovery merely by showing good cause, including demonstrated need for discovery "sufficient to adequately arbitrate" her claim).

C. Class Arbitration and Class Action Waivers

1. Where Agreement Contains Explicit Class Action Waiver: *Concepcion*

Arbitration agreements often include clauses providing that claims subject to mandatory arbitration cannot be arbitrated on a class or collective basis. Prior to 2011, there was considerable disagreement regarding the enforceability of such agreements. For example, in California, "class action waivers" generally were held to be unenforceable after decisions by the California Supreme Court holding them unenforceable in a consumer case[63] and an employment case.[64]

In *AT&T Mobility LLC v. Concepcion*, a consumer class action, the US Supreme Court held that courts cannot refuse to enforce an arbitration agreement because it does not permit the class-based arbitration of claims.[65] The Supreme Court found that the FAA preempted the California rule regarding unconscionability, which was an obstacle to the national policy favoring arbitration. Arbitration, the Court observed, is attractive because it tends to be relatively cheap, expeditious, and free of the cumbersome formalities and technicalities of court litigation. By its very nature, the Court reasoned, a class case is none of those things. A primary concern in the administration of class litigation procedures is fairness to absent parties. The procedures that must be followed to ensure that those absent parties are treated fairly are antithetical to the things that make arbitration worthwhile. If the state can require that parties permit class arbitrations, it would sacrifice the informality and speed that are the principal advantages of that type of dispute resolution, and would pressure defendants into settling even frivolous claims because of the higher stakes involved.

After *Concepcion*, courts found state rules similar to those in California (precluding consumer and employment class actions) preempted by the FAA.[66] *Concepcion* was a consumer class action, but it has been applied to invalidate all state rules that interfered with the enforcement of arbitration agreements.

---

63. Discover Bank v. Superior Court (2005) 36 Cal. 4th 148, 30 Cal Rptr. 3d 76, 113 P.3d 1100.

64. Gentry v. Superior Court (2007) 42 Cal. 4th 443, 64 Cal. Rptr. 3d 773, 165 P.3d 556.

65. AT&T Mobility LLC v. Concepcion (2011) 563 U.S. 333, 131 S. Ct. 1740, 179 L. Ed. 2d 742.

66. *See* Litman v. Cellco P'ship (3d Cir. 2011) 655 F.3d 225, 230–231 (under *Concepcion*, the FAA preempted a New Jersey rule invalidating adhesive consumer contracts with class waivers); King v. Advance Am. (E.D. Pa. Aug. 31, 2011, No. 07-3142) 2011 U.S. Dist. LEXIS 98630, at *16 (same; a similar Pennsylvania rule for consumer contracts with class waivers); Clerk v. Cash Cent. of Utah, LLC (E.D. Pa. Aug. 24, 2011, No. 09-4964) 2011 U.S. Dist. LEXIS 95494, at *10 (same); Alfeche v. Cash Am. Int'l, Inc. (E.D. Pa. Aug. 12, 2011, NO. 09-0953) 2011 U.S. Dist. LEXIS 90085, at *17 (same); Cruz v. Cingular Wireless, LLC (11th Cir. 2011) 648 F.3d 1205, 1213–4 ("[T]o the extent that Florida law would . . . invalidate the class waiver simply because the claims are of small value, the potential claims are numerous, and many consumers might not know about or pursue their potential claims absent class procedures, such a state policy stands as an obstacle to the FAA's objective of enforcing arbitration agreements according to their terms, and is preempted."); Webster v. Freedom Debt Relief, LLC (N.D. Ohio July 13, 2011, No. 1:10-cv-1587) 2011 U.S. Dist. LEXIS 85843, at *20 ("In the wake of *Concepcion*, any public policy in favor of class action for consumers in the [Ohio Consumer Sales Practices Act] is clearly super[s]eded by the FAA as it is an obstacle to the accomplishment of the purposes and objectives of Congress."); Green v. SuperShuttle Int'l, Inc. (8th Cir. 2011) 653 F.3d 766, 769 (*Concepcion* foreclosed plaintiff's argument that Minnesota law rendered a class waiver unenforceable).

Shortly after the Supreme Court decided *Concepcion*, the National Labor Relations Board (NLRB) embraced a narrow interpretation of it and held that a class action waiver was unenforceable under the National Labor Relations Act (NLRA).[67] The NLRB held that an agreement proscribing class and representative actions violated the NLRA, which gives employees the right to engage in concerted activities for the purpose of collective bargaining or other mutual aid or protection.[68] According to the Board, its conclusion did not conflict with the FAA because the right to engage in collective legal action is the core substantive right protected by the NLRA on which the NLRA and federal labor policy rest.[69] The NLRB further concluded that its decision did not implicate either *Concepcion* or *Stolt-Nielsen*,[70] because neither involved the waiver of rights protected by the NLRA or employment agreements.[71] The Board also distinguished *Concepcion* on the grounds that it involved a conflict between the FAA and state law, not the potential conflict of two federal statutes.[72] The Board emphasized that it did not require class arbitration to protect employees' rights under the NLRA. Instead, it held only that employers could not compel employees to waive their NLRA right to collectively pursue litigation of employment claims in all forums, arbitral and judicial.[73] The Fifth Circuit refused to enforce the portion of the NLRB's opinion holding that the NLRA generally prohibits contracts that compel employees to waive their right to participate in class proceedings to resolve wage claims.[74] It affirmed the board's determination that the arbitration agreement violated the NLRA insofar as it contained language that would lead employees to reasonably believe they were prohibited from filing unfair labor practice charges with the board.

Thereafter, a split developed among the Circuit Courts of Appeal regarding the issue of whether the NLRA permits collective action waivers in arbitration agreements, with the Second,[75] Fifth,[76] and Eighth[77] Circuits not enforcing the NLRB's opinion holding that the NLRA generally prohibits contracts that compel employees to waive their right to participate in class proceedings to resolve wage claims. The Sixth,[78] Seventh,[79] and

---

67. *D.R. Horton, Inc.*, 2012 NLRB LEXIS 11, 357 NLRB No. 184, 192 L.R.R.M. 1137.

68. *Id.* at *6, quoting 29 U.S.C. § 157.

69. *Id.* at *43.

70. Stolt-Nielsen S.A. v. AnimalFeeds International Corp. (2010) 559 U.S. 662, 130 S. Ct. 1758, 176 L. Ed. 2d 605.

71. *Id.* at *54.

72. *Id.*

73. *Id.* at *58.

74. D.R. Horton, Inc. v. NLRB (5th Cir. 2013) 737 F.3d 344.

75. Sutherland v. Ernst & Young LLP, 726 F.3d 290 (2d Cir. 2013) (*per curiam*).

76. D.R. Horton, Inc. v. NLRB (5th Cir. 2013) 737 F.3d 344; National Labor Relations Board v. Murphy Oil USA, Inc., 808 F.3d 1013 (5th Cir. 2015).

77. Owen v. Bristol Care, Inc., 702 F.3d 1050, 1055 (8th Cir. 2013); Cellular Sales of Missouri, LLC v. NLRB, 824 F.3d 772, 776 (8th Cir. 2016).

78. NLRB v. Alternative Entertainment Inc., 858 F.3d 393 (6th Cir. 2017).

79. Epic Systems Corporation v. Lewis, 823 F.3d 1147 (7th Cir. 2016).

Ninth Circuits[80] held the opposite. However, the Ninth Circuit held that where an arbitration agreement containing a class and collective action waivers is not a condition of employment, NLRA is not violated.[81]

The issue was finally decided by the US Supreme Court in *Epic Systems Corp. v. Lewis*,[82] holding that the FAA protects and enforces arbitration agreements that require individualized proceedings, notwithstanding the NLRA's protection for employee "concerted activity." First, the Court rejected reliance on the FAA's savings clause, which preserves generally applicable defenses to contract formation. That clause covers defenses like fraud, duress, or unconscionability, not "defenses that target arbitration either by name or by more subtle methods, such as 'interfer[ing] with the fundamental attributes of arbitration.'"[83] Second, the Court held that the NLRA, which entitles workers to engage in concerted activity for the purpose of collective bargaining or other mutual aid or protection, does not override the FAA. Section 7's catch-all term— "other concerted activities for the purpose of . . . other mutual aid or protection"— covers only similar activities that fall within the ambit of traditional labor law, and class litigation is far afield from those.[84] Third, the Court declined to defer to the NLRB's holding in *D.R. Horton*,[85] that the NLRA prohibits individualized arbitration agreements. However, in *D.R. Horton,* the NLRB sought not only to interpret the NLRA, but also the FAA, which it does not have the power to interpret, let alone administer.[86] In sum, the majority thought that "[t]he policy may be debatable but the law is clear." In the FAA, "Congress has instructed that arbitration agreements . . . must be enforced as written."[87]

2. Where Agreement Is Silent Regarding Class Arbitration

Many arbitration agreements are simply silent on the issue of class arbitration. In *Stolt-Nielsen S.A. v. AnimalFeeds International Corp.*,[88] the Court held that, where an agreement is governed by the FAA, parties cannot be compelled to a classwide arbitration unless it is determined that the parties agreed to submit their disputes to class arbitration. The Court reasoned that "the FAA imposes certain rules of fundamental

---

80. Morris v. Ernst & Young LLP, 834 F.3d 975 (9th Cir. 2016).

81. Johnmohammadi v. Bloomingdale's, Inc. (9th Cir. 2014) 755 F.3d 1072, 1073–77 (finding no basis for concluding that the employer interfered with or restrained her in the exercise of her right to file a class action, because she could have opted out of the arbitration agreement).

82. Epic Systems Corporation v. Lewis, — S. Ct. —, 2018 WL 2292444, 211 L.R.R.M. (BNA) 3061, 27 Wage & Hour Cas.2d (BNA) 1197 (May 21, 2018).

83. Epic Systems Corporation v. Lewis, — S. Ct. —, 2018 WL 2292444, at *6, 211 L.R.R.M. (BNA) 3061, 27 Wage & Hour Cas.2d (BNA) 1197 (May 21, 2018) (citations omitted).

84. *Id.* at 9.

85. *D.R. Horton, Inc.,* 2012 NLRB LEXIS 11, *54, 357 NLRB No. 184, 192 L.R.R.M. 1137.

86. Epic Systems Corporation v. Lewis, — S.Ct. —, 2018 WL 2292444, at *8, 14, 211 L.R.R.M. (BNA) 3061, 27 Wage & Hour Cas.2d (BNA) 1197 (May 21, 2018).

87. *Id.* at 17.

88. Stolt-Nielsen S.A. v. AnimalFeeds International Corp. (2010) 559 U.S. 662, 130 S. Ct. 1758, 176 L. Ed. 2d 605.

importance" concerning the construction of arbitration agreements, "including the basic precept that arbitration 'is a matter of consent, not coercion.'"[89] Thus, under *Stolt-Nielsen*, agreements that are silent on class actions seemed to preclude class actions by their silence.[90]

III. PROCEDURAL ISSUES

A. Gateway Issues

A critical question is whether a court or an arbitrator should resolve a challenge to the validity of an arbitration agreement. In *Rent-A-Center West v. Jackson*,[91] the US Supreme Court held that under the FAA, where an agreement to arbitrate includes a provision stating that the arbitrator will determine the enforceability of the agreement, if a party challenges the enforceability of the agreement as a whole (such as, for example, a claim that the employee's entry into the entire agreement had been fraudulently induced), the challenge is for the arbitrator.

If, however, the challenge was directed at the validity of the delegation clause, that provision was deemed severable and thus making it subject to a judicial challenge. The entire agreement in *Rent-A-Center* was one simply for arbitration, as opposed to an arbitration clause being contained in an employment or other agreement. The agreement contained a provision that clearly and unmistakably gave to the arbitrator the right to resolve issues of arbitrability. The agreement provided that "[t]he Arbitrator, and not any federal, state, or local court or agency, shall have exclusive authority to resolve any dispute relating to the interpretation, applicability, enforceability or formation of this Agreement including, but not limited to any claim that all or any part of this Agreement is void or voidable."[92] The Court held that in such a circumstance, the type of challenge that a court could hear must be to the validity of the specific provision in the arbitration agreement.[93] However, the Court found that the plaintiff's stated challenge was to the validity of the contract as a whole, not specifically to the delegation provision that was being enforced.[94] Specifically, the plaintiff challenged the entire arbitration agreement as unconscionable and not the delegation provision, the latter being the "written provision" compelling arbitration.[95] Consequently, because

---

89. Stolt-Nielsen S.A. v. AnimalFeeds International Corp. (2010) 559 U.S. 662, 130 S. Ct. 1758, 1773, 176 L. Ed. 2d 605 (citation omitted).

90. The *Stolt-Nielsen* Court also questioned whether *Bazzle* required an arbitrator to decide whether agreements permitted class arbitrations: "[T]he parties appear to have believed that the judgment in *Bazzle* requires an arbitrator, not a court, to decide whether a contract permits class arbitration. . . . In fact, however, only the plurality decided that question." Stolt-Nielsen S.A. v. AnimalFeeds International Corp. (2010) 559 U.S. 662, 130 S. Ct. 1758, 1772, 176 L. Ed. 2d 605.

91. Rent-A-Center, West, Inc. v. Jackson (2010) 561 U.S. 63, 130 S. Ct. 2772, 2778, 177 L. Ed. 2d 403.

92. *Id.*

93. *Id.* at 2779.

94. *Id.*

95. *Id.*

the delegation provision was not challenged as unconscionable, the possible invalidity of the entire contract was for the arbitrator to decide.[96]

B. Standards of Judicial Review: When the Arbitrator Exceeded His or Her Powers

The scope of judicial review of arbitration agreements is extremely narrow.[97] "An arbitrator's decision is not generally reviewable for errors of fact or law, whether or not such error appears on the face of the award and causes substantial injustice to the parties."[98]

Under the FAA, the merits of an arbitration award also can be attacked on the grounds that the arbitrator exceeded his or her powers.[99] "It is not enough for petitioners to show that the panel committed an error—or even a serious error. . . . 'It is only when [an] arbitrator strays from interpretation and application of the agreement and effectively "dispense[s] his own brand of industrial justice" that his decision may be unenforceable.'"[100] Even gross, "painfully clear," or "obvious" errors are insufficient to permit vacatur under 9 U.S.C. § 10(a)(4), which is the relevant statutory vacatur provision.[101]

Whether the parties can create a "designer" standard contemplating greater appellate review is unresolved. Prior to the US Supreme Court's decision in *Hall Street Associates, L.L.C. v. Mattel, Inc.,*[102] the federal courts were split on whether the FAA grounds for judicial review were exclusive. In *Hall Street*, the arbitration agreement provided: "The Court shall vacate, modify or correct any award: (i) where the arbitrator's findings of facts are not supported by substantial evidence, or (ii) where the arbitrator's conclusions of law are erroneous."[103] The US Supreme Court held that the FAA does not permit the parties to expand the scope of review by agreement. The Court held that allowing parties to contract for an expanded scope of review is inconsistent with the FAA's primary goal of ensuring the enforcement of arbitration agreements. "[T]o rest this case on the general policy of treating arbitration agreements as enforceable as such would be to beg the question, which is whether the FAA has textual features at odds with enforcing a

---

96. *Id.* at 2780.

97. 9 U.S.C. § 10(a)(2).

98. Commonwealth Coatings Corp. v. Continental Casualty Co. (1968) 393 U.S. 145, 149, 89 S. Ct. 337, 21 L. Ed. 2d 301.

99. 9 U.S.C. § 10(a)(4).

100. Stolt-Nielsen S.A. v. AnimalFeeds International Corp. (2010) 130 S. Ct. 1758, 1767, 176 L. Ed. 2d 605 (citations omitted); United Paperworkers Intern Union, AFL-CIO v. Misco, Inc. (1987) 484 U.S. 29, 38, 108 S. Ct. 364, 98 L. Ed. 2d 286; United Steelworkers of America v. Enterprise Wheel & Car Corp. (1960) 363 U.S. 593, 597, 80 S. Ct. 1358, 4 L. Ed. 2d 1424.

101. Halim v. Great Gatsby's Auction Gallery, Inc. (7th Cir. 2008) 516 F.3d 557, 563; Bull HN Information Systems, Inc. v. Hutson (1st Cir. 2000) 229 F.3d 321, 330; DiRussa v. Dean Witter Reynolds Inc. (2d Cir. 1997) 121 F.3d 818, 824.

102. Hall Street Associates, L.L.C. v. Mattel, Inc. (2008) 552 U.S. 576, 128 S. Ct. 1396, 170 L. Ed. 2d 254.

103. *Id.* at 579.

contract to expand judicial review following the arbitration."[104] The majority decided that, indeed, those textual features exist. It characterized the statutory grounds for review as remedies for "egregious departures from the parties' agreed-upon arbitration," such as corruption and fraud.[105] It held that the directive in § 9 of the FAA, that the court "must grant" confirmation "unless the award is vacated, modified, or corrected as prescribed in sections 10 and 11," as a mandatory provision leaving no room for the parties to agree otherwise.[106] However, the *Hall Street* majority left the door ajar for alternate routes to an expanded scope of review. "In holding that sections 10 and 11 provide exclusive regimes for the review provided by the statute, we do not purport to say that they exclude more searching review based on authority outside the statute as well. The FAA is not the only way into court for parties wanting review of arbitration awards: they may contemplate enforcement under state statutory or common law, for example, where judicial review of different scope is arguable. But here we speak only to the scope of the expeditious judicial review under sections 9, 10, and 11, deciding nothing about other possible avenues for judicial enforcement of arbitration awards."[107]

C. Effect on EEOC

In *EEOC v. Waffle House, Inc.*,[108] the employee had signed an employment agreement providing for arbitration of employment-related disputes. He was later discharged after suffering a seizure at work. Although he did not initiate arbitration proceedings, he did file a timely discrimination charge with the EEOC alleging that his discharge violated the ADA. The EEOC then filed an enforcement action against the employer in federal court, to which the employee was not a party, requesting injunctive relief, specific relief designed to make the employee whole, including back pay, reinstatement, and compensatory damages, and punitive damages for malicious and reckless conduct.[109] The employer petitioned to stay the EEOC action and compel arbitration. The Fourth Circuit held that the arbitration agreement did not foreclose the enforcement action because the EEOC was not a party to the contract, but that the EEOC was precluded from seeking victim-specific relief in court because the policy goals expressed in the FAA required giving some effect to the arbitration agreement.

The Supreme Court, however, held that the agreement did not bar the EEOC from pursuing victim-specific judicial relief in an enforcement action under ADA.[110] The Court found that following the 1991 amendments to Title VII,[111] the EEOC has

---

104. *Id.* at 586.

105. *Id.*

106. *Id.*

107. *Id.*

108. EEOC v. Waffle House, Inc. (2002) 534 U.S. 279, 122 S. Ct. 754, 151 L. Ed. 2d 755.

109. *Id.* at 284.

110. *Id.* at 296.

111. *See* 42 U.S.C. § 2000e *et seq.*

authority to bring suit to enjoin an employer from engaging in unlawful employment practices, and to pursue reinstatement, back pay, and compensatory or punitive damages. Neither Title VII, nor the ADA, nor case law suggests that the existence of an arbitration agreement between private parties materially changes the EEOC's statutory function or the remedies otherwise available.[112] Further, because the EEOC was not a party to the contract and did not agree to arbitrate its claims, the FAA's pro-arbitration policy goals could not require the agency to relinquish its statutory authority to pursue victim-specific relief, regardless of the forum that the employer and employee have chosen to resolve their disputes.[113]

D. Vacatur of Award

Under § 10 of the FAA, a district court may vacate an arbitration award if any of the following is true:[114]

- The award was procured by corruption, fraud, or undue means.
- There was evident partiality or corruption in the arbitrators.
- The arbitrators were guilty of misbehavior by which the rights of any party were prejudiced.
- The arbitrators exceeded their powers, or so imperfectly executed them that a mutual, final, and definite award upon the subject matter submitted was not made.[115]

Section 10 of the FAA provides the exclusive means by which a court reviewing an arbitration award under the FAA may grant a vacatur of a final arbitration award.[116] Under the FAA, the scope of a confirmation proceeding applying these factors is "extremely limited."[117] The FAA provides no authorization for a merits review.[118] Further, the parties to an arbitration agreement governed by the FAA may not by contract expand the scope of judicial review beyond that which the FAA authorizes.[119] Only when arbitrators

---

112. EEOC v. Waffle House, Inc. (2002) 534 U.S. 279, 296, 122 S. Ct. 754, 151 L. Ed. 2d 755.

113. *Id.* at 298.

114. Johnson v. Gruma Corp. (9th Cir. 2010) 614 F.3d 1062, 1066. *See* 9 U.S.C. § 10(a) (1947).

115. *See* Biller v. Toyota Motor Corp. (9th Cir. 2012) 668 F.3d 655, 665–670 (arbitrator did not manifestly disregard California law in addressing affirmative defenses).

116. Biller v. Toyota Motor Corp. (9th Cir. 2012) 668 F.3d 655, 664.

117. Johnson v. Gruma Corp. (9th Cir. 2010) 614 F.3d 1062, 1066; G.C. & K.B. Invs. Inc. v. Wilson (9th Cir. 2003) 326 F.3d 1096, 1105. *See also* Hall Street Associates, L.L.C. v. Mattel, Inc. (2008) 552 U.S. 576, 585, 128 S. Ct. 1396, 170 L. Ed. 2d 254; Biller v. Toyota Motor Corp. (9th Cir. 2012) 668 F.3d 655, 663–665; Kyocera Corp. v. Prudential-Bache Trade Serv. Inc. (9th Cir. 2003) 341 F.3d 987, 994, 997.

118. Biller v. Toyota Motor Corp. (9th Cir. 2012) 668 F.3d 655, 664.

119. *Id.* at 665; Kyocera Corp. v. Prudential-Bache Trade Serv. Inc. (9th Cir. 2003) 341 F.3d 987, 994.

stray from interpretation and application of the agreement and effectively dispense their own brand of industrial justice may the decision be found to be unenforceable.[120]

In *Hall Street Associates, L.L.C. v. Mattel, Inc.*,[121] the US Supreme Court considered whether an arbitration provision may be vacated when the litigants agree in writing the district court may vacate an award when it is not supported by substantial evidence or when the arbitrator's legal conclusions are erroneous. The Court cast doubt on whether the manifest disregard of the law rule remains viable. In *Stolt-Nielsen S.A. v. AnimalFeeds Intl. Corp.*,[122] the district court judge vacated the award because it was made in manifest disregard of the law, the court of appeals concluded otherwise, and the Supreme Court declined to address the effect of *Hall Street Associates, L.L.C.* on the award, refusing to decide whether manifest disregard survived the decision in *Hall Street Associates, L.L.C.* as an independent ground for review or as a judicial gloss on the enumerated grounds for vacatur set forth in the FAA.[123] Since *Hall Street Associates, L.L.C.*, some federal courts of appeals have declined to decide whether the manifest disregard of the law standard remains legally viable.[124] Some courts have held the manifest disregard of the law standard is no longer an independent legal standard for review of arbitration awards.[125] Other courts of appeals have held that the manifest disregard of the law standard remains viable, not as an independent ground for vacatur, but as a judicial gloss or shorthand for setting aside an award under the FAA.[126] The statutory grounds for vacatur in the FAA may not be waived or eliminated by contract.[127]

---

120. Countrywide Financial Corp. v. Bundy (2010) 187 Cal. App. 4th 234, 249–50, 113 Cal. Rptr. 3d 705.

121. Hall Street Associates, L.L.C. v. Mattel, Inc. (2008) 552 U.S. 576, 579–80, 128 S. Ct. 1396, 170 L. Ed. 2d 254.

122. Stolt-Nielsen S. A. v. AnimalFeeds Intl. Corp. (2010) 130 S. Ct. 1758, 1767, 176 L. Ed. 2d 605.

123. Countrywide Financial Corp. v. Bundy (2010) 187 Cal. App. 4th 234, 250–52, 113 Cal. Rptr. 3d 705. *See* 9 U.S.C. § 10 (1947).

124. *See* Kashner Davidson Securities Corp. v. Mscisz (1st Cir. 2010) 601 F.3d 19, 22.

125. *See* Frazier v. Citifinancial Corp., LLC (11th Cir. 2010) 604 F.3d 1313, 1324; Citigroup Global Markets Inc. v. Bacon (5th Cir. 2009) 562 F.3d 349, 350, 355; Nicholas v. KBR, Inc. (5th Cir. 2009) 565 F.3d 904, 909, n.4.

126. Comedy Club, Inc. v. Improv West Associates (9th Cir. 2009) 553 F.3d 1277, 1290; Stolt-Nielsen S. A. v. AnimalFeeds Intl. Corp. (2d Cir. 2008) 548 F.3d 85, 95, overruled on another ground in Stolt-Nielsen S. A. v. AnimalFeeds Int'l Corp. (2010) 130 S. Ct. 1758, 1766–67, 176 L. Ed. 2d 605.

127. *In re* Wal-Mart Wage & Hour Empl. Practices Litigation (9th Cir. 2013) 2013 U.S. App. LEXIS 24948, *5–14 (in attorney's fees dispute after settlement of multi-district litigation regarding employer's employment practices, nonappealability clause of settlement agreement was unenforceable where it eliminated judicial review under § 10 of FAA, specifying grounds for vacatur).

CHAPTER 8

Multi-Plaintiff Litigation and Class Actions: Plaintiff's Perspective

Maureen S. Binetti and Ashley E. Morin

Imagine the following scenario: You are screening a potential gender discrimination case, and you are meeting face-to-face with the potential plaintiff. Your prospective client informs you that she worked for a large corporation and that during her five years of employment, she suffered continuous unwelcome sexual advances, touching, offensive language, and other improper conduct at the hands of management. She goes on to inform you that the employer's human resources department continually ignored her request for an investigation into the alleged harassment, and that the company ignored her complaints and looked the other way regarding management's misconduct. She also complains that her male peers have substantially higher salaries than her even though she performs the same work that they do.

The facts are egregious, and the plaintiff seems to be a likeable, credible person. As you are a busy lawyer, your first instinct is to take this case and file a "typical" gender discrimination complaint.

However, before deciding to proceed in this fashion, you should consider the following: Is there additional information you could elicit in your initial intake to determine if there are *other* people who were subjected to the same or similar discrimination and employer indifference? Should you even take the time to ask about other instances of discrimination involving other employees? These questions lead to the critical question: "Is there a class action or multi-plaintiff case here?"

Although workplace discrimination cases generally are perceived as involving individualized incidents, plaintiffs' lawyers can be successful in certifying classes of employees or commencing multi-plaintiff litigation that join the claims of several employees in one action. In fact, pay disparity class actions and multi-plaintiff actions have become increasingly popular. Indeed, such actions have been filed against several prominent companies, including the drug manufacturer Merck[1] and internet giant

---

1. Sy Mukherjee, *More Than 400 Women Are Now Suing Merck for Unequal Pay*, FORTUNE, July 21, 2016, *available at* http://fortune.com/2016/07/21/women-suing-merck-sex-discrimination/.

Google.[2] Even law firms are not immune from allegations of pay discrimination.[3] Although many cases involving pay disparity are brought under the Equal Pay Act and equal pay state laws, such claims can also be brought under Title VII, which is the focus of this chapter.[4]

This chapter addresses the rise of class actions and multi-plaintiff litigation in the gender discrimination and retaliation context and the hurdles plaintiffs' lawyers must overcome to successfully bring these types of cases. It seeks to provide useful insights for plaintiff's lawyers into the complexities and ramifications of bringing class and multi-plaintiff actions.

Sections I and II focus on the procedural requirements that must be met in order to bring a class action or multi-plaintiff lawsuit. In particular, the requirements of Federal Rule of Civil Procedure 23, involving class actions, and Federal Rule of Civil Procedure 20, involving party joinder, are discussed.

Section III focuses on retainer arrangements in large-scale multi-plaintiff and class action cases. Because of the unique nature of these types of cases, plaintiffs' counsel's retention implicates ethical and practical issues that must be considered.

Section IV focuses on how to prove a class action/multi-plaintiff gender discrimination case, paying special attention to the two-phase litigation plan followed by courts. These two phases generally are (1) the liability phase, where it is determined if a discriminatory pattern or practice existed in the workplace; and, if liability is established, (2) the recovery phase, where the plaintiffs' recovery is ascertained.

Finally, Section V will discuss settlement of multi-plaintiff/class actions and some of the strategies associated with such settlements. Attorney's fees in these types of actions also are discussed.

I. PROCEDURAL REQUIREMENTS FOR ALL CLASS ACTION LITIGATION

A. Elements of a Class Action

Pursuant to Federal Rule of Civil Procedure 23, a class may be certified (thus allowing one or more members of the class to sue on behalf of others) if the following four prerequisites are satisfied: (1) the class is so numerous that joinder of all class members is impracticable; (2) there are questions of law or fact common to the class; (3) the claims

---

2. Jessica Guynn, *Google Puts Women in Lower Level, Lower Paying Jobs, New Lawsuit Says*, USA TODAY, Sept. 14, 2017, *available at* https://www.usatoday.com/story/tech/2017/09/14/google-hit-gender-pay-gap-lawsuit-seeking-class-action-status/666944001/.

3. Elizabeth Olson, *Lawsuit Presses the Issue of Lower Pay for Female Law Partners*, N.Y. TIMES, May 7, 2017, *available at* https://www.nytimes.com/2017/05/07/business/dealbook/law-firm-pay-gender-bias.html.

4. Obviously, state law as to class certification may provide an additional avenue of pursuit. Because of the widely divergent state law governing class actions and workplace harassment claims, however, this chapter will analyze these issues under federal law. Practitioners are urged to consult their state law for additional guidance.

or defenses of the representative parties are typical of the claims and defenses of the class; and (4) the representative parties will fairly and adequately protect the class's interests.[5] Although the elements of Rule 23 pose a challenge for plaintiffs' lawyers in potential workplace discrimination class actions, they are not insurmountable. Courts have considerable discretion in certifying class actions, but must exercise this discretion within the framework of Rule 23.[6]

1. Numerosity

The first requirement under Rule 23(a) is numerosity, which requires a showing by plaintiffs that joinder of the potential class members is "impracticable." Numerosity is not measured by a strict numerical test.[7] There is no bright line test to satisfy numerosity, but a substantial number of plaintiffs usually satisfies this first prong. However, classes have been certified with as few as nineteen identified members,[8] while others have been denied with sixteen identified members.[9] In fact, one court has stated that "impracticable . . . does not mean impossible,"[10] and courts have suggested utilizing a flexible standard for numerosity in employment discrimination suits, which are cases "particularly fit for class action treatment."[11] Indeed, class certification has been granted in instances where the complaint does not reference by name any potential victims other than the class representative.[12]

2. Commonality

Perhaps the most challenging element of Rule 23(a) for the plaintiffs' attorney is demonstrating that there are common questions of law or fact among the class members. Meeting this requirement is more difficult in employment cases, as there is more emphasis on how the alleged conduct affected the individual plaintiff. Indeed, the usual argument made by defense lawyers in these cases, whether they be discrimination, quid pro quo, or hostile work environment claims, is that the case does not lend itself to class action treatment because it deals with particularized instances of harassment or discrimination that do not satisfy the commonality requirement of Rule 23. They argue that any decisions or conduct relating to class members will vary from individual to individual, facility to facility, and hiring practice to hiring practice. While plaintiffs' attorneys can be successful in demonstrating commonality, the larger the class, the more difficult this becomes.

---

5. FED. R. CIV. P. 23(a) (2018).

6. Randleman v. Fid. Nat'l Title Co., 2008 WL 2323771 (N.D. Ohio 2008) (citing Gulf Oil Co. v. Bernard, 452 U.S. 89, 100 (1981)).

7. *See* Dafflin v. Ford Motor Co., 458 F.3d 549, 552 (6th Cir. 2006).

8. *See* Morgan v. UPS, 169 F.R.D. 349 (E.D. Mo. 1996).

9. Lang v. Kan. City Power & Light Co., 199 F.R.D. 640, 646 (W.D. Mo. 2001).

10. Walsh v. Pittsburgh Press Co., 160 F.R.D. 527 (W.D. Pa. 1994) (ERISA class action of 300 employees).

11. Slanina v. William Penn Parking Corp., 106 F.R.D. 419, 423 (W.P. Pa. 1984).

12. EEOC v. Caterpillar, Inc., 336 F. Supp. 2d 858, 862 (N.D. Ill. 2004).

Wal-Mart v. Dukes[13] demonstrates the challenges plaintiffs' attorneys face in maintaining large, nationwide class actions. In *Wal-Mart*, the proposed class had around 1.5 million plaintiffs who were current and former employees of Wal-Mart. The plaintiffs alleged that Wal-Mart discriminated against them on the basis of gender, arguing that Wal-Mart's "corporate culture permitt[ed] bias against women to infect, perhaps subconsciously, the discretionary decisionmaking of each of Wal-Mart's thousands of managers thereby making every woman at the company the victim of one common discriminatory practice."[14] The Court held that the plaintiffs had not satisfied the commonality requirement because the plaintiffs "provide[d] no convincing proof of a companywide discriminatory pay and promotion policy" and therefore "have not established the existence of any common question."[15] The Court noted that the Wal-Mart policy at issue allowed local supervisors to have discretion over employment practices, which "is just the opposite of a uniform employment practice that would provide the commonality needed for a class action; it is a policy *against having* uniform employment practices."[16] The Court further explained that to demonstrate commonality, the class members' claims "must depend upon a common contention—for example, the assertion of discriminatory basis on the part of the same supervisor. That common contention, moreover, must be of such a nature that it is capable of classwide resolution—which means that determination of its truth or falsity will resolve an issue that is central to the validity of each one of claims made in one stroke."[17]

Wal-Mart has created challenges for plaintiffs' attorneys, especially with respect to establishing commonality; however, the road to certification is not impossible as successful actions have still been brought.

3. Typicality

The typicality requirement of Rule 23(a) seeks to ensure that the named plaintiff's interests are substantially aligned with those of the absent class members. It requires that "claims or defenses of the representative parties [be] typical of the claims or defenses of the class."[18] "[A] plaintiff's claim is typical if it arises from the same event or practice or course of conduct that gives rise to the claims of other class members, and if his or her claims are based on the same legal theory."[19] The claim need not be absolutely identical to those of the potential class members or always involve the same facts or law, provided there is a common element of fact or law.[20]

---

13. 564 U.S. 338 (2011).

14. *Id.* at 345.

15. *Id.* at 359.

16. *Id.* at 355.

17. *Id.* at 350.

18. FED. R. CIV. P. 23(a)(3) (2018).

19. *In re* American Medical Systems, Inc., 75 F.3d 1069, 1082 (6th Cir. 1996) (quoting ALBA CONTE & HERBERT B. NEWBERG, NEWBERG ON CLASS ACTIONS, NEWBERG ON CLASS ACTIONS, § 3:13 (3d ed. 1992)).

20. *Id.*

4. Adequacy of Representation

The final prerequisite to class certification under Rule 23(a) is the adequacy of representation. The rule's requirement is twofold: "(1) the representative must have common interests with the unnamed members of the class; and (2) it must appear that the representatives will vigorously prosecute the interests of the class through qualified counsel."[21]

This element is intertwined with typicality. The main factors identified as bearing on the element of adequate representation are the qualifications, experience, and competency of plaintiff's counsel, and the absence of any antagonistic interests.[22] A representative plaintiff and her counsel should be able to demonstrate that they have the resources to manage the litigation, including sending out notices, communicating and keeping track of the class members, and creating databases and handling voluminous discovery. Responsible named plaintiffs, as well as experienced employment counsel, are critical to this showing.

Although the Rule 23(a) requirements may be satisfied, plaintiffs must also satisfy Rule 23(b).[23]

B. Requirements of Rule 23(B)

Under Rule 23(b), plaintiffs must demonstrate one of the following three elements in order to proceed:

1. The prosecution of separate actions by or against individual members risks inconsistent adjudications or would, as a practical matter, be dispositive of the interests of nonparticipants.
2. The opposing party has acted or refused to act on grounds generally applicable to the class, thereby making injunctive or declaratory relief appropriate to the class as a whole.
3. Common questions of law or fact predominate over questions affecting only individual members, and a class action is superior to other available methods for a proper adjudication of the matter.[24]

Title VII employment class actions were initially brought under 23(b)(2) because the relief sought was typically an injunction.[25] Even when damages became available after the Civil Rights Act of 1991 passed, most Title VII cases were still brought under 23(b)(2) even though they included damages, as well as injunctive relief, and "many courts

---

21. Bremiller v. Cleveland Psychiatric Inst., 195 F.R.D. 1, 22 (N.D. Ohio 2000).

22. *See* Wetzel v. Liberty Mut. Ins. Co., 508 F.2d 239 (3d Cir. 1975), *cert. denied*, 421 U.S. 1011 (1975).

23. *See* Zinser v. Accufix Research Inst., Inc., 253 F.3d 1180, 1186, *amended*, 273 F.3d 1266 (9th Cir. 2001).

24. Fed. R. Civ. P. 23(b)(3) (2018).

25. Michael Selmi & Slyvia Tsakos, *Employment Discrimination Class Actions After Wal-Mart v. Dukes*, 48 Akron L. Rev. 803, 820 (2015).

supported certification under that provision."[26] However, in *Wal-Mart*, the Supreme Court rejected this trend, stating:

> Rule 23(b)(2) applies only when a single injunction or declaratory judgment would provide relief to each member of the class. It does not authorize class certification when each individual class member would be entitled to a *different* injunction or declaratory judgment against the defendant. Similarly, it does not authorize class certification when each class member would be entitled to an individualized award of monetary damages.[27]

The main advantage to certifying a class under Rule 23(b)(2), instead of Rule 23(b)(3) is that "plaintiffs seeking certification under Rule 23(b)(3) must provide individual notice to every prospective class member—including absentee class members—and such notice must contain an opt-out provision."[28] Thus, by limiting the use of Rule 23(b)(2), the Court in *Wal-Mart* added another hurdle for plaintiffs' attorneys.

C. Rule 23(f)

Rule 23(f) permits the immediate appeal of district court rulings certifying or denying class actions. Rule 23(f) permits an appeal within fourteen days of the decision on class certification, with the appellate court having sole discretion to grant or deny permission to appeal.[29] This rule has been utilized by both plaintiffs and the defendants to either obtain or avoid the coveted class certification. Defense lawyers cheer it because it provides them with an avenue by which to immediately challenge class certification and thus delay the almost inevitable road to class settlement discussions. Rule 23(f) also aids plaintiffs' lawyers, however, in that, rather than being forced to await the outcome of litigation, plaintiffs may appeal immediately the denial of certification, thus preserving the hope that a class-wide settlement or verdict may be obtained.

D. Class Action Certification After Wal-Mart

As briefly explained above, *Wal-Mart v. Dukes* created some roadblocks for plaintiffs' lawyers seeking certification of gender discrimination and retaliation cases. With around 1.5 million plaintiffs, *Wal-Mart* is one of the largest employment discrimination class actions in US history.[30] The plaintiffs alleged that Wal-Mart used discriminatory pay and promotion practices. They maintained that "Wal-Mart's strong, centralized

---

26. *Id.*

27. 564 U.S. at 360.

28. Matthew Grimsley, *What Effect Will Wal-Mart v. Dukes Have on Small Businesses?* 8 Ohio State Entrepreneurial Bus. L.J. 100, 103 (2013).

29. Fed. R. Civ. P. 23(f) (2018).

30. 564 U.S. at 342.

structure fosters or facilitates gender stereotyping and discrimination, that the policies and practices underlying this discriminatory treatment are consistent throughout Wal-Mart stores, and that this discrimination is common to all women who work or have worked in Wal-Mart stores."[31] Plaintiffs specifically took issue with Wal-Mart's policy, which left employment decision to local supervisors. Plaintiffs alleged that this policy resulted in a disparate impact on women, and that Wal-Mart was aware of this effect.[32] The plaintiffs sought "injunctive and declarative relief, back pay, and punitive damages."[33] The Northern District of California certified the class, and the certification was upheld by the Ninth Circuit.[34] However, the certification was overturned by the Supreme Court.[35]

First, the Supreme Court explained that commonality is not established by merely showing that the class members "have all suffered a violation of the same provision of law." Indeed, the Court stated:

> [T]he mere claim by employees of the same that they have suffered a Title VII injury, gives no cause to believe that all their claims can be productively litigated at once. Their claims must depend on a common contention—for example, the assertion of discriminatory bias on the part of the same supervisor. That common contention, moreover, must be of such a nature that is capable of classwide resolution—which means that determination of its truth or falsity will resolve an issue that is central to the validity of each one of the claims made in one stroke.[36]

The Court further noted that the plaintiffs need some kind of "glue" to hold the class members together and form "a common answer to the crucial question of *why was I disfavored*."[37] As such, it is not enough to claim that a potential class of plaintiffs all experienced discrimination. Rather, all of the plaintiffs must experience discrimination in the same way so that their claims all have a common answer.

The Court explained that the plaintiffs' claims in Wal-Mart lacked the required "glue" to hold them together as a class action. The Court stated that having a common policy that gave local supervisors power over employment decisions did not satisfy the commonality needed for a class action because plaintiffs did "not identify a common mode of exercising discretion" that was present throughout the entire company.[38] Indeed, the Court explained that even if the plaintiffs were able to use statistics to

---

31. Dukes v. Wal-Mart Stores, Inc., 603 F.3d 571, 577–78 (9th Cir. 2010).

32. *Dukes*, 564 at 345.

33. *Id.* at 345.

34. Dukes v. Wal-Mart Stores, Inc., 222 F.R.D. 137 (N.D. Cal. 20040); Dukes v. Wal-Mart Stores, Inc., 603 F.3d 571 (9th Cir. 2010).

35. 564 U.S. at 362.

36. *Id.* at 350.

37. *Id.* at 352.

38. *Id.* at 356.

show a pattern of promotion and/or pay disparity, they still must point to a specific employment practice that produces the disparity and without this commonality could not be established.[39]

Second, as explained earlier, the Court also rejected the plaintiffs' use of Rule 23(b)(2) because while they were seeking injunctive relief, they were also seeking backpay. The Court stated that it is "clear individualized monetary claims belong in Rule 23(b)(3)" because of the procedural protections of that Rule.[40] As such, claims for back pay should be brought under Rule 23(b)(3), not Rule 23(b)(2).

Lastly, the Court addressed the standard of review for certifications, explaining that certification is only proper after "rigorous analysis."[41] The Court further noted that the "rigorous analysis" may require that Court to go beyond the pleading and consider the merits of the plaintiffs' claims.

Wal-Mart was decided in 2011 and its effect on employment class actions is still being determined. Indeed, while Wal-Mart has resulted in the reconsideration of certification of class actions brought under a similar strategy, such as *Ellis v. Costco*,[42] some argue that it "has not manifested as the death knell for certification."[43] Indeed, while the path to certification may be more difficult, several cases, such as *McReynolds v. Merrill Lynch, Pierce, Fenner & Smith, Inc.*,[44] *Scott v. Family Dollar Stores*,[45] and *Sellars v. CRST Expedited, Inc.*,[46] illustrate that it is still available.[47]

E. Special Considerations

There are some unique procedural advantages for plaintiffs bringing employment discrimination actions. First, plaintiffs benefit with respect to administrative exhaustion. Indeed, to proceed under Title VII in a class action, only *one* of the named class representatives must have filed a timely charge with the Equal Employment Opportunity Commission (EEOC) and must otherwise satisfy the perquisites for suit. It is not necessary that the other class members file a charge with the EEOC to benefit from the final judgment. For example, in *Jenson*, one of the named plaintiffs filed an EEOC charge alleging class-wide discrimination, thus commencing the class action on behalf of all potentially affected plaintiffs.[48] Courts have liberally construed the scope of such

---

39. *Id.* at 357.

40. *Id.* at 362.

41. *Id.* at 351, 356.

42. 657 F.3d 970 (9th Cir. 2011).

43. Michael Selmi & Slyvia Tsakos, *supra* note 25, at 822.

44. 672 F.3d 482 (7th Cir. 2012), *cert. denied,* 133 S. Ct. 338 (2012).

45. 733 F.3d 105 (4th Cir. 2013).

46. 2017 WL 1193730, No. C15-117-LTS, (N.D. Iowa March 30, 2017).

47. Michael Selmi & Slyvia Tsakos, *supra* note 25, at 822.

48. *See* Jenson v. Eveleth Taconite Co., 139 F.R.D. 657, 666 (D. Minn. 1991).

charges to allow the class complaint to include all causes of action that reasonably could be expected to grow out of the charge of discrimination, provided the timely filed charge gives the EEOC and the employer adequate notice of allegations of class-wide discrimination.[49] Thus, it may be relatively easy for one plaintiff to commence a class action on behalf of a large group of employees.

However, some courts have refused to liberally interpret the reasonable nexus requirement. In *Stubbs v. McDonald's Corp.*,[50] the court held that the EEOC charge "did not contemplate claims of hostile work environment."[51] The claimant, an African-American employee, initially filed charges with the EEOC for failure to promote and for constructive discharge. The court found that such charges did not reasonably relate to his later hostile work environment claims.[52]

Additionally, when a class action alleges both discrimination and retaliation claims, plaintiffs' attorneys should exercise caution. If the plaintiff only filed a charge for discrimination and then later experienced retaliation, but did not file a new charge, the retaliation claim may be dismissed for failure to exhaust administrative remedies. Indeed, circuit courts are split on whether retaliation arising after a charge is filed requires a new or amended charge in order to exhaust administrative remedies.[53] Specifically, both the Tenth Circuit[54] and Eighth Circuit[55] require that a new or amended charge be filed. However, the Fourth Circuit[56] and Ninth Circuit[57] have "concluded that a claim of post-charge filing retaliation could be raised for the first time in district court so long as the 'like or reasonably related test is met,'" meaning that the retaliation claim is reasonably related to the claims in the charge.[58] Although these cases are not class actions, plaintiffs' attorneys should be aware of these differing holdings when filing a class action alleging retaliation to avoid dismissal for failure to exhaust administrative remedies.

Second, plaintiffs' attorneys benefit from the opt-out nature of class actions. Indeed, there is little incentive for those affected by discrimination and retaliation in the workplace to decline to participate in class action litigation. Plaintiffs are included in the class unless they specifically elect exclusion. Moreover, if the class

---

49. *See* Griffin v. Carlin, 755 F.2d 1516, 1522 (11th Cir. 1985). *See also* Branum v. United Parcel Serv., 232 F.R.D. 505 (W.D. Pa. 2005).

50. 224 F.R.D. 668 (D. Kan. 2004).

51. *Id.* at 672.

52. *Id.*

53. *See* Jordan Feist, *Discrimination, Retaliation, and the EEOC: The Circuit Split Over the Administrative Exhaustion Requirement in Title VII Claims*, 118 PENN ST. L. REV. 169, 189 (2013).

54. Martinez v. Potter, 347 F. 3d 1208 (10th Cir. 2003).

55. Richter v. Advanced Auto Part, Inc., 686 F.3d 847 (8th Cir. 2012).

56. Jones v. Calvert Grp., 551 F.3d 297 (4th Cir. 2009).

57. Lyons v. England, 307 F.3d 1092 (9th Cir. 2002).

58. Feist, *supra* note 53, at 189.

petition is denied based on the lead plaintiffs' deficiencies as class representatives, a statute of limitations that would bar a Title VII claim may be tolled during the pendency of a putative class action asserting substantially the same claim so that the asserted class members can still invoke their individual Title VII remedies.[59] However, tolling may not apply where certification was denied based on deficiencies in the purported class itself.[60]

F. Class Actions and Arbitration Agreements

A growing problem for plaintiffs' lawyers is the increased use of arbitration agreements in employment contracts. Before accepting a potential class action, plaintiffs' attorneys should be aware of whether the employees signed an arbitration agreement and what the arbitration agreement (if any) covers. Many arbitration agreements require that plaintiffs relinquish their right to pursue class actions, and instead, bring all claims in individual arbitration. While the legality of class action waivers was previously in question with a split between several circuits, the Supreme Court recently addressed the issue and upheld the use of arbitration agreements.[61]

By way of history, the Seventh Circuit and the Ninth Circuit had held that requiring employees to waive their rights to pursue class actions violates the National Labor Relations Act (NLRA) because its prevents employees from engaging in concerted activity.[62] However, the Fifth Circuit held that class and collective action waivers in arbitration clauses do not violate the NLRA as long as they are properly worded.[63] Given this circuit split, the Supreme Court granted certiorari on this issue, consolidating the cases from the Seventh, Ninth, and Fifth Circuits.[64]

In upholding the use of arbitration agreements, the Supreme Court explained: "Congress has instructed that arbitration agreements like those before us must be enforced as written. While Congress is of course always free to amend this judgment, we see nothing suggesting it did so in the NLRA—much less that it manifested a clear intention to displace the Arbitration Act. Because we easily read Congress's statutes to work in harmony, that is where our duty lies."[65] Given the Court's holding, plaintiffs' attorneys should be sure to find out if the employees they intend to represent signed an arbitration agreement and if so, whether the arbitration agreement contains a class action waiver.

---

59. *See* Crown, Core & Seal Co., Inc. v. Parker, 462 U.S. 345, 354 (1983).

60. Yang v. Odom, 392 F.3d 97, 99 (3d Cir. 2004).

61. Epic Systems Corp. v. Lewis, 138 S.Ct. 1612 (2018).

62. *See* Lewis v. Epic Systems Corp., 823 F.3d 1147 (7th Cir. 2016); Morris v. Ernst & Young, 834 F.3d 975 (9th Cir. 2016).

63. *See* Murphy Oil USA, Inc. v. NLRB, 808 F.3d 1013 (5th Cir. 2015).

64. *See* Epic Systems Corp. v. Lewis, 137 S. Ct. 809 (2017).

65. Epic Systems Corp. v. Lewis, 138 S.Ct. 1612, 1632 (2018).

II. MULTI-PLAINTIFF (BUT NOT CLASS) ACTIONS

If the practical realities of handling a class action appear to be too burdensome for your office, or, alternatively, if you have the resources to handle a class action but are unable to meet the requirements of Rule 23(a) or 23(b), a multi-plaintiff action under Rule 20 may be appropriate.

Rule 20 of the Federal Rules of Civil Procedure permits joinder of plaintiffs if their various claims "aris[e] out of the same transaction, occurrence, or series of transactions or occurrences and if any question of law or fact common to all plaintiffs will arise in the action." The joinder rule thus provides an opportunity to bring a multiple-plaintiff claim against an employer whose harassing conduct has affected a group of employees in the workplace.

Although the requirements of Rule 20 are less restrictive than the more burdensome procedural rules for certifying a class under Rule 23, plaintiffs seeking to join multiple plaintiffs must still demonstrate under Rule 20 the existence of common questions of law and fact. As a result, substantive differences among claims can prevent joinder.

For example, in *Curwick v. Ford Motor Company*,[66] the court found that joinder of prospective plaintiffs would not be proper because their claims did not involve the same transaction or occurrence as the original plaintiffs. The original plaintiffs in the action were hourly employees complaining of sexual harassment by supervisors; one plaintiff seeking joinder was a supervisor, and the other potential plaintiff asserted racial harassment and race discrimination claims. Based on the substantial differences between these claims, the court denied joinder. The same result occurred in *Johnson v. Indopco, Inc.*,[67] in which the court refused to join a racial discrimination claim with a sexual harassment claim.

Thus, if there is diversity of claims among the potential plaintiffs, multi-plaintiff litigation may not be the best course of action. However, if the claims involve exclusively harassment/hostile work environment claims, and particularly if the potential plaintiffs are part of the same "group" (that is, all nonsupervisors or all supervisors), the less burdensome requirements of Rule 20 (as opposed to class action prerequisites) may be the means through which to institute multi-plaintiff litigation.

III. THE RETAINER AGREEMENT

If counsel is confident that the group he or she will be representing can meet the requirements of the class action rules, or the joinder rules, the next consideration normally will be entering into a contingency arrangement with the class or multiple plaintiffs. To minimize client misunderstandings and disputes, counsel's ordinary engagement letter must be tailored to meet the needs of the group as a whole.

---

66. 1998 WL 887067, No. 98 C 3755 (N.D. Ill. 1998).

67. 846 F. Supp. 670 (N.D. Ill. 1994).

The first consideration will be communication. The letter should document ground rules for how counsel will communicate with the clients and how group decisions will be made.[68] This part of the letter should discuss counsel's policies regarding joint and separate meetings with clients, how information will be disseminated to the group, and the extent of counsel's duty as an attorney to keep the clients advised of matters concerning the case.[69]

Another important issue will be attorney's fees. It is critical to clarify whether each client is jointly and severally liable for all fees and costs or, alternatively, whether each plaintiff is liable for a share of the fee. Even if clients are legally responsible for the entire payment under the agreement, practically speaking, it may be prudent to choose to bill a portion to each plaintiff. If this is the course taken, it is important to advise the clients as to exactly how counsel is proceeding.[70]

The next crucial consideration will be conflicts of interest. Where there are a diversity of claims regarding discrimination, conflicts can arise regarding settlement strategies, as there could be instances in which one plaintiff has greater damages than another. In this instance, the plaintiffs' lawyer may seek a greater monetary award for the more damaged plaintiff, to the detriment of other plaintiffs. Other conflicts include timing and resolution of litigation, expenditure of fees and costs, nonpayment of fees, and disclosure of confidential communications. These potential, foreseeable conflicts should be addressed in detail in the retainer letter. Clients should be advised to raise the issue of separate representation if and when they feel that conflicts are prejudicing their case.[71] By laying the groundwork early, plaintiffs' lawyers can limit their liability for malpractice, while at the same time making an early attempt to maintain harmony among the class or group of plaintiffs.

Once the attorney has decided that the potential class or group can maintain a class or multi-plaintiff action suit, and after entering into fee agreements with the group, the next (and most important) analysis will be the substantive aspects of proving the multi-plaintiff or class action case.[72]

IV. PROVING THE MULTI-PLAINTIFF CASE

A. Discrimination Class Actions

Title VII class actions are typically proven using a pattern or practice theory of discrimination, which requires plaintiffs "to establish by a preponderance of evidence that . . . discrimination was the company's standard operating procedure the regular rather than the unusual practice."[73] A pattern or practice case proceeds in two stages: the

---

68. *See* Guy Calladine, *You Were Always Lawyer's Pet*, A.B.A. J., Mar. 1999, at 78.

69. *Id.*

70. *Id.*

71. *Id.*

72. *Id.*

73. International Brotherhood of Teamsters v. U.S., 431 U.S. 324, 336 (1977).

liability stage and the recovery stage. The first stage requires the plaintiffs to establish a prima facie case that a discriminatory policy or practice exists. Successful plaintiffs typically do this with "a combination of strong statistical evidence of disparate impact coupled with anecdotal evidence of the employer's intent to treat the protected class unequally."[74] "The burden then shifts to the employer to defeat the prima facie showing of a pattern or practice."[75] This is done by showing that "the plaintiffs' proof is either inaccurate or insignificant."[76] If the employer fails to rebut the employee's prima facie case, the case proceeds to the second stage, which "requires the court to fashion a proper remedy on the presumption that a violation has occurred. If the plaintiff does not provide any additional evidence, the court may impose only prospective remedies. If the plaintiff demonstrates that the employer subjected a particular individual to an adverse employment action, that employee may receive damages."[77] This general framework is applied to pattern-or-practice class actions; however, it is modified slightly for sexual harassment cases, given the unique nature of these claims, as explained in the next subsection.

B. Sexual Harassment Class Actions

The framework for sexual harassment class actions is illustrated in two landmark sexual harassment cases, *Jenson*[78] and *Mitsubishi*.[79]

1. The *Jenson* Case

The plaintiffs in *Jenson* filed a class action against their employer Eveleth Mines, alleging sex discrimination and hostile work environment sexual harassment in violation of Title VII and the Minnesota Human Rights Act. The class was certified by the Minnesota District Court and included those women who worked at Eveleth Mines in Minnesota during a certain period of time.[80]

The environment at Eveleth Mines allegedly was rife with references to sexually inappropriate subjects and to women as sex objects. Discovery revealed that pornographic pictures and graffiti confronted female employees throughout the workplace, and that male employees felt free to display this material wherever they chose. In addition, the work environment allegedly regularly was charged with language reflecting a sexualized, male-oriented atmosphere that exceeded acceptable workplace language in that it crudely referred to women and sex as virtual synonyms. Most of this inappropriate

---

74. EEOC v. Mavis Tire Discount, Inc., 129 F. Supp.3d 90, 103–04 (S.D.N.Y. 2015).

75. 431 U.S. at 362.

76. 129 F. Supp.3d at 336.

77. Semsroth v. City of Withita, 304 Fed. App'x 707, 715 (10th Cir. 2008).

78. 139 F.R.D. 657 (D. Minn. 1991) (sexual harassment hostile work environment class action certified), *judgment entered*, 824 F. Supp. 847 (D. Minn. 1993), *aff'd in part and remanded in part*, 130 F.3d 1287 (8th Cir. 1997).

79. 990 F. Supp. 1059 (C.D. Ill. 1998).

80. *Jenson*, 139 F.R.D. 657.

language was directed at Eveleth women in general, not at a particular woman or group of women. As a result, the *Jenson* court held that this was an environment hostile to women and that it constituted sexual harassment.

The critical aspect of *Jenson* was that it set forth the standard and burden of proof in a class action hostile work environment, sexual harassment case.[81] The court divided the class action into two phases: liability and recovery. The court noted that in the customary pattern or practice case, a determination in the liability phase that the employer engaged in a pattern or practice of discrimination violating Title VII entitles each member of the class to a presumption that she was victimized by the defendant's unlawful discrimination. In the recovery phase, the burden of persuasion shifts to the defendant employer to show that it did not discriminate against individual class members by this pattern or practice.

The *Jenson* court, however, altered the recovery phase, holding that a sexual harassment class member is not entitled to this presumption and resultant burden-shifting.[82] The court reasoned that a showing of pattern or practice of harassment in the liability phase did not automatically establish that a hostile work environment existed that affected each plaintiff as a reasonable woman. Instead, the court held that the burden of persuasion remains on the individual class members and that each class member must show by a preponderance of the evidence that she was as affected as would "the reasonable woman." Under *Jenson*, not until this showing is made will the individual class member be entitled to relief under Title VII and applicable state law.

According to *Jenson*, even though an employee's subjective reaction to acts of sexual harassment is an essential part of proving a claim of hostile work environment, the presumption that the employer discriminated against individual class members does not arise automatically upon the court's determination that a pattern or practice existed. The court therefore held that individual class members should not be allowed to bypass an essential element of a federal hostile work environment claim merely because they were part of a class certified under Rule 23, which, according to the court, involved procedural issues and not the merits of the case.

A subsequent decision in the EEOC's *Mitsubishi* pattern or practice case both follows, and departs from, the *Jenson* rationale.

2. The *Mitsubishi* Case

The *Mitsubishi* case is similar to the *Jenson* case factually and follows part of the *Jenson* analysis, but parts from the *Jenson* rationale on the procedure followed in the recovery phase of a hostile work environment pattern or practice case.

In *Mitsubishi*, the EEOC filed an action claiming that Mitsubishi was liable for a pattern or practice of hostile work environment and quid pro quo sexual harassment. The EEOC alleged, among other things, that it was Mitsubishi's standard operating procedure for its automobile assembly plant in Norma, Illinois, to ignore complaints

---

81. 824 F. Supp. at 875–76.

82. *Id.*

brought by female employees who had been subjected to a sexually hostile and abusive environment.[83]

Mitsubishi moved for partial summary judgment on the grounds that proving an objective and generalized pattern or practice of sexual harassment was impossible because the essence of a sexual harassment claim, as defined in *Meritor* and *Harris*,[84] is that the allegedly offensive conduct was subjectively unwelcome.[85]

The Court reasoned that defendant's argument leads to the conclusion that, so long as the conduct plaintiffs experienced was subjectively unwelcome under *Meritor* and *Harris*, the "commonality" requirement can never be satisfied due to the differences in personal claims. The Court rejected this argument, however, and concluded that this pattern or practice matter was not an individual's case as in *Meritor* and *Harris*, "and the rules of engagement in this context are different."[86] The Court then held that the proofs set out in *Meritor* and *Harris* would have to be modified for a pattern or practice case such as *Mitsubishi*.

Similar to *Jenson*, the *Mitsubishi* court proceeded to divide this action into two phases: phase one, "pattern or practice;" phase two, "individual relief." Phase one focused solely on the company's policy and behavior in terms of discriminating against employees, while phase two focused on the individual victims of harassment in order to satisfy the subjective showings required by *Meritor*.

In phase one, the EEOC was required to establish, by a preponderance of the evidence, that an objectively reasonable person would find the existence of (1) a sexually harassing hostile work environment *or* a situation where individuals within the workplace must accept an environment hostile to their gender to enjoy the tangible benefits of their job (a quid pro quo pattern or practice) and (2) a company policy of tolerating, and therefore condoning, a workforce permeated with severe and pervasive harassment. The Court stressed that subjective proofs would not be considered, nor were they necessary, in this objective first phase of the proceedings. Rather, the focus would be on the totality of the work environment and whether the general pattern or practice of unwanted sexual harassment was severe and pervasive.[87]

If a pattern or practice is found, the burden then shifts under phase two. Phase two, as set forth by the *Mitsubishi* court, differed not only from the traditional pattern or practice phase two, but also from the *Jenson* court's phase two.

As an initial matter, the *Mitsubishi* court agreed with *Jenson* that the presumption of liability, which is traditional to ordinary pattern or practice cases, is inappropriate in sexual harassment hostile work environment pattern or practice cases. Since the *Mitsubishi* court had established that subjective harm was irrelevant to phase one, the court (similar to *Jenson*) refused to presume that the individual plaintiffs' burdens of

---

83. 990 F. Supp. at 1069.

84. *See* 477 U.S. 57 (1986).

85. *Id.*

86. 990 F. Supp. at 1070.

87. *Id.* at 1074.

proof were met in phase two. The *Mitsubishi* court then modified the traditional pattern or practice model, but in a manner different from *Jenson*.

The Court held that, as a result of the phase one pattern or practice finding, the individual victim is provided only with a rebuttable presumption of harm that shifts the burden to the employer in phase two to produce evidence that individual members were *not* subjectively offended by the conduct. However, the ultimate burden remains with the individual plaintiffs to prove to the trier of fact that they were subjectively offended by the pattern or practice. Thus, the liability phase of a pattern or practice hostile environment claim requires objective proof of a hostile work environment, as individual experiences are resolved in the later remedial phase of the trial.[88]

The *Mitsubishi* court noted that once a pattern and practice of harassment is established in phase one, the likelihood is great that a class member will be able to prove the subjective element of his or her claim in phase two. The Court reasoned further that shifting the burden of production to the employer in phase two to show that its conduct was welcomed by a particular individual employee was fair because it is the employer, not the employee, who is likely to possess this evidence.[89]

The *Mitsubishi* court stated that the procedure it was following was more consistent with the essential nature of a pattern or practice case than that followed in *Jenson*. Shifting the burden of production to the employer, according to the *Mitsubishi* court, is essential in a pattern or practice case because a finding of discriminatory conduct in phase one creates a strong presumption that any single discriminatory instance or decision was influenced by the overall pattern of discrimination. The Court also noted that a showing of liability in phase one casts a light on the employer similar to that of a proven wrongdoer.[90] The Court concluded that "[t]o eliminate the presumption [in phase two], as *Jenson* did, ignores the likelihood that the individual decisions a company makes about individuals, consistent with its company-wide pattern or practice, are discriminatory."[91]

Despite their distinctions, both the *Jenson* and *Mitsubishi* decisions set forth thoughtful procedures that have been used in subsequent harassment class actions.[92]

V. SETTLING CLASS ACTION/MULTI-PLAINTIFF CASES

A. General Considerations

As with any other litigation, voluntary resolution of class action or multi-plaintiff cases offers advantages to both sides. The advantage for defendants in settling such actions are numerous, including (1) reducing legal fees; (2) minimizing negative publicity;

---

88. Newsome v. Up-To-Date Laundry, Inc., 219 F.R.D. 356, 361 (D. Md. 2004).

89. 990 F. Supp. at 1078–80.

90. *Id.* at 1079.

91. *Id.* at 1080.

92. *See* EEOC v. Pitre, Inc., 908 F. Supp.2d 1165 (D.N.M. 2012) (applying the *Jenson* model); EEOC v. Dial Corp., 156 F. Supp.2d 926 (N.D. Ill. 2001) (applying the *Mitsubishi* model).

(3) enabling the company to focus on its business instead of costly and distracting litigation; (4) avoiding court-dictated injunctive relief; (5) avoiding the risk of a huge jury verdict, including emotional distress and/or punitive damages; and (6) avoiding court-ordered back pay, front pay and interest.[93]

The advantages to the plaintiff are likewise legion, and include the following: (1) avoiding the risk of receiving little or no monetary compensation; (2) avoiding the mental distress and invasion of privacy of litigation and trial; and (3) obtaining injunctive and/or monetary relief earlier than if the case were to proceed to trial and subsequent appeal.[94]

The timing of settlement discussions will be crucial for plaintiffs' counsel in evaluating the value of a class action case. Between the filing of a workplace discrimination and/or retaliation class action and its ultimate conclusion, several major events touched on already must occur, including class certification, summary judgment motions, phase one liability findings, phase two damages proceedings, and any appeals.[95] As a general matter, the plaintiffs' case will strengthen as they clear each successive hurdle. With each success, plaintiffs normally would demand a higher settlement price, and seek stronger injunctive relief.[96]

Because of the costs involved in defending class action and multi-plaintiff litigation, there is incentive for the defense to settle before a lawsuit is filed. Thus, by gathering evidence early on in the process, and communicating a demand to defense counsel before filing the class action or multi-plaintiff case, plaintiffs' lawyers may pursue a quick resolution without excessive delay, inconvenience, or cost to themselves or their clients. Prefiling mediation is yet another way to achieve an early resolution of a potential class action or multi-plaintiff case.

B. Attorney's Fees

The ability to recover attorney's fees, often in the millions in employment class actions, is another incentive for plaintiffs' lawyers to endure the risks of filing a workplace discrimination class action. For example, in the recent gender discrimination case against Qualcomm, the tech company agreed to pay the plaintiffs $19.5 million to settle the matter, with an additional $5,781,069.50 paid to plaintiffs' attorneys.[97]

Indeed, while the costs associated with class action and multi-plaintiff litigation continue to rise, more firms now are willing to risk the considerable cost outlay for the possibility of an exponentially greater recovery and the application of fee-enhancing formulas that may result in commensurately larger awards if plaintiffs are ultimately successful. Thus, fee awards obviously will be a critical part of settlement discussions.

---

93. *See* James M. Finberg, Settling/Mediating Employment Discrimination Class Actions, in Litigation and Settlement of Complex Employment Class Actions 341 (1998).

94. *Id.* at 342.

95. *Id.* at 343.

96. *Id.* at 344.

97. Pan v. Qualcomm, Inc., No. 3:16-cv-1885-JLS-DHB, slip. op. (S.D. Cal. July 31, 2017).

Therefore, a factor militating in favor of a plaintiff's employment lawyer's decision to commence a multi-plaintiff or class action claim is that the burdens and risks imposed upon defendants by such cases tend to compel large settlements.

VI. CONCLUSION

The lawyer in the hypothetical beginning of this chapter would be wise to inquire whether there were any other employees harmed by the company's pattern or practice of workplace discrimination and retaliation. The more information obtained during an initial client interview, the better counsel will be able to assess whether there is a potential multi-plaintiff or class action claim. By thoroughly screening and investigating potential cases, and developing the proofs necessary to show an overriding pattern and practice that affects numerous employees, counsel may be able to successfully assert a class action or multi-plaintiff litigation and thereby assist a multitude of injured employees.

CHAPTER 9

Multi-Plaintiff Litigation and Class Actions: A Defense Perspective

Kenneth M. Willner[1]

I. INTRODUCTION: HARASSMENT AND RETALIATION CLASS ACTIONS—AN OXYMORON OR THE EXTENSION OF ESTABLISHED LAW?

The US Supreme Court has never approved the certification of a class action under Rule 23 of the Federal Rules of Civil Procedure (FRCP) in a purely harassment context nor in a case solely about retaliation. Nor has any federal appellate court harmonized the harassment cause of action[2] with the requirements of Rule 23, or with the pattern or practice cause of action under any federal discrimination statute. Although some plaintiffs have successfully convinced some district courts to certify class actions in harassment and retaliation cases where the facts were particularly egregious, many courts addressing the issue have recognized that the commonality among class members required by the Rule 23 class action vehicle makes it inherently unsuitable for adjudicating harassment or retaliation actions. They have recognized that several essential elements of harassment and retaliation cases require highly individualized inquiries.

By their nature, harassment claims usually can be resolved only on a case-by-case, plaintiff-by-plaintiff basis. The elements of the cause of action demand individualized treatment. The plaintiff must show that he or she was subjected personally to conduct on the basis of the protected characteristic, for example, gender[3] that was offensive

---

1. Kenneth M. Willner is a partner with Paul, Hastings, LLP and vice-chair of the firm's Employment Law Department. Sarah Besnoff and Christine Cedar are associates in the firm's Employment Law Department who co-wrote portions of this chapter. The authors thank Andrew B. Rogers, formerly a Paul Hastings associate and now with Littler Mendelson, PC, who co-wrote an earlier edition several years ago.

2. Harassment cases in the class action context have primarily focused on sexual harassment, but the principles apply similarly to racial and other forms of harassment. It is worth noting that the Supreme Court crafted the law of sexual harassment from the Court's previous efforts in racial and national origin harassment cases. *See* Faragher v. City of Boca Raton, 524 U.S. 775, 786 (1998) (citations omitted).

3. *Faragher*, 524 U.S. at 787 (citation omitted).

under both objective and subjective standards. In other words, the plaintiff must prove not only that a reasonable person would find the conduct offensive but also that the plaintiff *personally* found it to be so.[4] The conduct must be so severe and pervasive as to alter the conditions of employment, and it also must be *subjectively unwelcome to the plaintiff.*[5] These elements, focusing on the actual state of mind of the plaintiff, are incapable of proof without individualized evidence about each plaintiff. Indeed, even where the alleged conduct is the same for all of the plaintiffs—and it rarely if ever is— individuals often react differently to and participate differently in the conduct. For example, some may be unwilling victims who suffer emotional harm, while others may participate willingly in an affair, may dish out as much as they get, or may otherwise willingly participate in the conduct.

The objective assessments required in a harassment case are nearly as problematic in the class action context as are the subjective elements. When assessing whether the plaintiff has met the "severe and pervasive" prong of the cause of action, the fact finder is charged with "looking at all the circumstances," including the "frequency of the discriminatory conduct; its severity; whether it is physically threatening or humiliating, or a mere offensive utterance; and whether it unreasonably interferes with an employee's work performance."[6] The answers to these questions depend upon the circumstances of each individual's personal work environment and experiences. Often, the conduct experienced by individual plaintiffs differs substantially in terms of content, frequency, alleged participants, and time frame. Employees subjected to different conduct, at different times, by different people, have different claims. Those claims must be assessed and litigated one employee at a time.

Given their fact-intensive nature, retaliation claims also necessitate a highly individualized analysis.[7] Generally, the plaintiff alleging retaliation must show that he or she engaged in "protected" conduct and that, as a result of that conduct, he or she was subjected to a "materially adverse" employment action.[8] However, only certain types of conduct are protected from retaliation. To prevail, the plaintiff must show that he or she *personally* "opposed" an unlawful employment practice, or that he or she *personally* "participated" in an investigation, proceeding, or hearing about an unlawful employment practice. The plaintiff must also show that the particular adverse action to which the particular plaintiff was subjected was sufficient to "dissuade a reasonable worker from making or supporting a charge of discrimination."[9] Without this

---

4. *Id.*

5. Harris v. Forklift Sys., Inc., 510 U.S. 17, 21 (1993) (quoting Meritor Sav. Bank v. Vinson, 477 U.S. 57, 67 (1986)).

6. *Faragher*, 524 U.S. at 787–88 (quoting *Harris*, 510 U.S. at 23).

7. Although the Americans with Disabilities Act and Age Discrimination in Employment Act also contain antidiscrimination provisions and retaliation protections, this chapter will discuss the retaliation standard as codified in and interpreted from § 704(a) of Title VII.

8. Burlington N. & Santa Fe Ry. Co. v. White, 548 U.S. 53, 68 (2006) (defining a "materially adverse" employment action as any action that "might have dissuaded a reasonable worker from making or supporting a charge of discrimination") (citation and quotation omitted).

9. *Id.* at 57.

specific, factual showing, any subsequent employment action cannot be characterized as retaliation.

These personalized inquiries are the antithesis of the class action device set forth in the FRCP. Rule 23 permits class actions where questions of fact or law "common" to all class members predominate over individualized issues. On this basis, employers facing harassment or retaliation class actions ordinarily have been able to present forceful, persuasive arguments in opposition to plaintiffs' motions for class certification. If armed with a thorough understanding of the facts about each plaintiff, the defense may uncover key factual distinctions in each individual putative class member's claim. This is certainly true where the events occurred in different work areas and under different supervisors, and is often true even where the conduct at issue involves the same workplace, the same job description, or the same supervisor but affected the plaintiffs differently. Because of the focus on the individual inherent in the cause of action, harassment and retaliation cases are very different from the types of discrimination cases where class action treatment more often has been found to be appropriate, such as challenges to a pre-employment test or other identifiable employment practices that are administered to all protected class members and affect them the same way.

Another variable undermining the viability of class action mechanisms for harassment cases is the fact-based affirmative defense that the US Supreme Court articulated in *Faragher v. City of Boca Raton*[10] and *Burlington Industries, Inc. v. Ellerth.*[11] The Court held that, as long as the alleged harassment did not cause a "tangible employment action," the employer is not subject to vicarious liability where (1) the employer exercised reasonable care to prevent and correct promptly any harassing behavior, and (2) the plaintiff unreasonably failed to take advantage of those preventive or corrective opportunities.[12] An individualized assessment of each plaintiff's circumstances and actions is required to determine whether each plaintiff suffered a "tangible employment action," "unreasonably" failed to report alleged harassment, or failed to take advantage of other available corrective procedures. Although, one might argue that the existence (or lack) of antiharassment policies and procedures can pose a common question of fact, that issue also often involves individualized questions of whether and how the procedures were published and applied in different branches, divisions, and offices, and by different supervisors, and with respect to different plaintiffs. Moreover, the degree to which the plaintiffs did or did not take advantage of complaint procedures and the existence of a tangible employment action will vary from one plaintiff to the next.

Thus, plaintiffs asserting class-wide claims of sexual harassment face the additional hurdle of showing that the harasser, or harassers, were uniformly supervisors or uniformly not supervisors. In *Vance v. Ball State University*, the Supreme Court clarified that the test for whether an employee is a supervisor is very fact-dependent: "We hold that an employee is a 'supervisor' for purposes of vicarious liability under Title VII if he or she is empowered by the employer to take tangible employment actions against the

---

10. 524 U.S. 775 (1998).

11. 524 U.S. 742 (1998).

12. *Faragher*, 524 U.S. at 777–78.

victim . . . ."[13] In responding to the *Vance* dissent's contention that one of the supervisors in *Faragher* would not have qualified under this test, even though the harasser could impose discipline, the Court responded: "If that discipline had economic consequences (such as suspension without pay) then [the harasser in *Faragher*] might qualify as a supervisor under the definition we adopt today."[14] In *Faragher*, the harassing lifeguard threatened the plaintiff to "[d]ate me or clean the toilets for a year."[15] The Court clarified in *Vance*: "That threatened reassignment of duties likely would have constituted significantly different responsibilities for a lifeguard, whose job typically is to guard the beach. If that reassignment had economic consequences, such as foreclosing Faragher's eligibility for promotion, then it might constitute a tangible employment action."[16] Thus, any plaintiff class must show that the alleged harasser, or harassers, were supervisors, or were not supervisors as to all members of the putative class. Inconsistency as to supervisor status will lead to different defenses among the class members' claims.

Those cases in which plaintiffs have experienced some success in district court on a mass basis almost universally involve sexual harassment and fall into three categories: (1) representative actions brought by the US Equal Employment Opportunity Commission (EEOC); (2) cases involving egregious facts where high-level management ignored or fostered widespread appalling behavior and the district court strained to find a remedy for plaintiffs and punishment for the employer; and (3) cases in which harassment is a "tagalong" claim attached to other issues that were properly brought on a class-wide basis, and that receives little attention from the court. That said, the number of cases in which district courts have certified sexual harassment and retaliation class actions has increased somewhat in the past ten years. Even as the Supreme Court has clarified the narrowness of class action requirements (*Wal-Mart v. Dukes*, *Comcast v. Behrend*), and the concept of supervisory liability (*Vance*), a small number of lower courts faced with a changing political moment have strained to interpret those precedents broadly even while others have applied them consistent with their terms.

Cases in the first category have been able to proceed because EEOC representative litigation is not subject to the strictures of Rule 23 of the FRCP.[17] Nevertheless, even in

---

13. Vance v. Ball State Univ., 570 U.S. 421, 133 S.Ct. 2434, 2439, 118 FEP 1481 (2013). The Supreme Court explained that it was rejecting "the nebulous definition of a 'supervisor' advocated in the EEOC Guidance . . . ." *Id.* at 2443. Under the test set forth, "supervisory status can usually be readily determined, generally by written documentation," *id.*, and, they argued, the test "is easily workable; it can be applied without undue difficulty at both the summary judgment stage and at trial." *Id.* at 2444.

14. *Id.* at 2447 n. 9.

15. *Faragher*, 524 U.S. at 780.

16. *Vance*, 133 S.Ct. at 2447 n. 9; *see also id.* at 2451 ("Contrary to the dissent's suggestions . . . this approach will not leave employees unprotected against harassment by co-workers who possess the authority to inflict psychological injury by assigning unpleasant tasks or by altering the work environment in objectionable ways. In such cases, the victims will be able to prevail simply by showing that the employer was negligent . . . and the jury should be instructed that the nature and degree of authority wielded by the harasser is an important factor to be considered in determining whether the employer was negligent.").

17. Gen. Tel. Co. v. EEOC, 446 U.S. 318 (1980) (the EEOC's statutory authority to bring actions to enforce federal law is separate from the Rule 23 framework); *see also* 42 U.S.C. §2000e-5(f)(1), e-6(a)-(c) (2018).

EEOC cases, courts have struggled to define the elements of the claim in the class context, because of the fundamental inconsistencies between the elements of the harassment cause of action as defined by the Supreme Court and class actions. In decisions falling into the second category, the few district courts allowing such cases have proceeded without full compliance with the commonality and predominance requirements of Rule 23 and the elements of the harassment cause of action. Doubtless, these district courts have been guided by a sense of "rough justice" to find a remedy for victims of outrageous conduct. Surely, they were also aided by the employers' difficulty in securing interlocutory appeal of class certification decisions—and by the resulting frequency of settlements— before the revision of Rule 23 in 1998 to permit interlocutory appeal of class certification orders without permission of the district judge.[18] No federal appellate court has approved a district court decision certifying a purely harassment class action under Rule 23.

In the third category of cases, where harassment claims are intermingled with other issues more appropriate for class treatment, the courts typically have not given substantial analysis to commonality and predominance with regard to the harassment portion of the case. These courts focused instead on issues related to other claims common to the class.[19]

Faced with a harassment or retaliation class action, the employer's initial focus is on preventing class certification. Accordingly, this chapter first discusses the prerequisites to bringing a class action, and then their application in the context of harassment and retaliation litigation. Next, this chapter discusses the related issue of multi-plaintiff litigation in EEOC representative cases and in other cases not certified for class action treatment, including the burdens of proof in mass harassment and retaliation claims. The chapter also examines legal issues arising during precertification discovery.

II. RULE 23: THE CLASS ACTION REQUIREMENTS

In the seminal case involving class certification in employment discrimination cases, the US Supreme Court explained that "a Title VII class action, like any other class action, may only be certified if the trial court is satisfied, after a rigorous analysis, that the prerequisites of Rule 23(a) have been satisfied."[20] The Court reasoned:

> Conceptually, there is a wide gap between (a) an individual's claim that he has been denied a promotion on discriminatory grounds, and his otherwise unsupported allegation that the company has a policy of discrimination, and (b) the existence of a class of persons who have suffered the same injury as

---

18. "A court of appeals may permit an appeal from an order granting or denying class-action certification under this rule if a petition for permission to appeal is filed with the circuit clerk within 14 days after the order is entered. An appeal does not stay proceedings in the district court unless the district judge or the court of appeals so orders." FED. R. CIV. P. 23(f).

19. *See, e.g.*, Martens v. Smith Barney, Inc., 181 F.R.D. 243 (S.D.N.Y. 1998) (focusing on glass ceiling, entry-level barriers, and other indicia of alleged sexual discrimination, rather than commingled sexual harassment claims).

20. Gen. Tel. Co. of Sw. v. Falcon, 457 U.S. 147, 161 (1982).

that individual, such that the individual's claim and the class claims will share common questions of law or fact and that the individual's claim will be typical of the class claims.[21]

Each of the requirements for class action certification, as discussed as follows, flows from this fundamental mandate that to close this "gap" the class representatives' claims and the class members' claims must share common questions of law or fact that are determinative, and those common questions must predominate over individualized inquiries.

A. The Constitutional Requirement of Standing

Plaintiffs in a class action must establish standing. As a threshold matter, plaintiffs in a class action must establish that "a precisely defined class exists, and that the class representatives are members of the proposed class,"[22] that is, that they have standing to assert the claim.[23]

A class action is permissible if one named plaintiff has standing against all defendants.[24] A named the plaintiff must *personally* meet the requirements of constitutional standing; otherwise, the plaintiff may not seek relief on behalf of "persons described in [a] class definition [even if those persons] would have standing themselves to sue."[25] First, there must be an "injury in fact"—an invasion of a legally protected

---

21. *Id.* at 157.

22. Rodriguez v. Berrybrook Farms, Inc., 672 F. Supp. 1009, 1012 (W.D. Mich. 1987) (citation omitted); *see also* Burkhead v. Louisville Gas & Elec., 250 F.R.D. 295 (W.D. Ky. 2008) (denying class certification, inter alia, because proposed representatives were not a sufficient "cross-section" as all lived in the same area and, therefore, were not likely to have claims typical of a broad geographic class); LaBauve v. Olin Corp., 231 F.R.D. 632 (S.D. Ala. 2005) (proposed representative lacked standing because his claim was untimely); Reyes v. Walt Disney World Co., 176 F.R.D. 654 (M.D. Fla. 1998) (declining to certify class because proposed representatives were each employed in different divisions of the company with a different hierarchy of decision-makers); Bromley v. Mich. Educ. Ass'n-NEA, 178 F.R.D. 148 (E.D. Mich. 1998) (certifying class of nonunion members challenging the collection of service fees for political and ideological activities).

23. *See* Griffen v. Dugger, 823 F.2d 1476, 1483 (11th Cir. 1987) ("[A] claim cannot be asserted on behalf of [the] class unless at least one named plaintiff has suffered the injury that gives rise to that claim."); In re Merrill Lynch & Co., Inc. Research Reports Sec. Litig., 375 B.R. 719, 725 (S.D.N.Y. 2007) (stating that a "plaintiff, including one who is seeking to act as class representative, must have individual standing to assert the claims in the complaint against each defendant being sued by him") (citation omitted); Zapata v. IBP, Inc., 167 F.R.D. 147, 157 (D.C. Kan. 1996) ("To proceed as a class action, class claims must be 'fairly encompassed' in the named plaintiff's claims.") (citation omitted).

24. *See* Horne v. Flores, 557 U.S. 433, 446 & n.2, 129 S.Ct. 2579, 174 L.Ed.2d 406 (2009); Arlington Heights v. Metro. Hous. Dev. Corp., 429 U.S. 252, 264 & n.9, 97 S.Ct. 555, 50 L.Ed.2d 450 (1977) ("[W]e have at least one individual plaintiff who has demonstrated standing. . . . Because of the presence of this plaintiff, we need not consider whether the other individual and corporate plaintiffs have standing to maintain the suit."); Simon v. E. Ky. Welfare Rights Org., 426 U.S. 26, 40 n.20, 96 S.Ct. 1917, 48 L.Ed.2d 450 (1976) (class action does not eliminate a class representative's burden of establishing standing); Neale v. Volvo Cars of N. Am., LLC, 794 F.3d 353, 364 (3d Cir. 2015) ("Requiring individual standing of all class members would eviscerate the representative nature of the class action.").

25. *Griffin*, 823 F.2d at 1483 (citations omitted). *See also* Casey v. Lewis, 4 F.3d 1516, 1519 (9th Cir. 1993).

interest, which is (a) concrete and particularized, and (b) "actual or imminent," not "conjectural" or "hypothetical."[26] Thus, the named the plaintiff must show that he or she shares a common injury caused by the same conduct challenged by the putative class. Second, there must be a causal connection between the injury and the conduct complained of—the injury has to be "fairly . . . trace[able] to the challenged action of the defendant, and not . . . th[e] result [of] the independent action of some third party not before the court." Third, it must be "likely," as opposed to merely "speculative," that the injury will be "redressed by a favorable decision."[27] "Although federal courts 'do not require that each member of a class submit evidence of personal standing,' a class cannot be certified if it contains members who lack standing."[28]

Standing is a threshold issue, thus, in theory, the court cannot determine whether a named plaintiff has the proper Rule 23 representative capacity until *after* the plaintiff satisfies the constitutional threshold of proper standing.[29] However, in practice, the Supreme Court has bypassed the standing analysis where class certification will be denied. In *Amchem Products, Inc. v. Windsor* and *Ortiz v. Fibreboard Corp.*, the Supreme Court declined to address the argument that the putative class members had no standing to pursue their class claims and instead began its analysis with Rule 23.[30] The Supreme Court explained that the settlement class's standing issues "'would not

---

26. Spokeo, Inc. v. Robins, 136 S.Ct. 1540, 1547–48 (2016) ("Injury in fact is a constitutional requirement, and '[i]t is settled that Congress cannot erase Article III's standing requirements by statutorily granting the right to sue to a plaintiff who would not otherwise have standing.'"). Moreover, a named plaintiff must establish the existence of a case or controversy between the defendant and herself as to each claim. Naturally, a claim cannot be asserted on behalf of a class unless the named the plaintiff has suffered the injury that gives rise to that claim.

27. Lujan v. Defs. of Wildlife, 504 U.S. 555, 560–61 (1992). *See also Spokeo*, 136 S.Ct. at 1547–48 (emphasizing the need for a showing of both a "concrete and particularized" injury) (quoting *Lujan*, 504 U.S. at 559–60).

28. Avritt v. Reliastar Life Ins. Co., 615 F.3d 1023, 1034 (8th Cir. 2010) (citing Denney v. Deutsche Bank AG, 443 F.3d 253, 263–64 (2d Cir. 2006)); *see also* Halvorson v. Auto-Owners Ins. Co., 718 F.3d 773, 778 (8th Cir. 2013) (denying class certification and holding that "In order for a class to be certified, each member must have standing and show an injury in fact that is traceable to the defendant and likely to be redressed in a favorable decision"); *c.f.* Oetting v. Norton, 795 F.3d 886, 891 (8th Cir. 2015) (holding that certified class representative in main action did not automatically afford said class representative standing in a related, but distinct, action without more); *In re* Celotex Corp., 496 F. App'x 3, 5 (11th Cir. 2012) (finding that certified class representative in national class action did not have standing to assert class action claims against the settlement trust in a bankruptcy adversary proceeding because it did not personally have the claim asserted on behalf of the putative class).

29. *See, e.g.*, Dans v. Coca-Cola Bottling Co. Consol., 516 F.3d 955, 965–66 (11th Cir. 2008), *abrogated on other grounds* Bell Atl. Corp. v. Twombly, 550 U.S. 544, 127 S.Ct. 1955, 167 L.Ed.2d 929 (2009) (holding that "before proceeding to adjudicate as a class action a pattern or practice claim," the court "must determine whether the named plaintiff has standing to prosecute the claim on behalf of similarly-situated employees"); *Casey*, 4 F.3d at 1519 (citations omitted) ("Article III [of the U.S. Constitution] limits the judicial power of the federal courts to 'cases' and 'controversies,'" before they can proceed to a determination of the viability of class certification, the parties initially must address the "fundamental question . . . of jurisdiction."); Jones v. Firestone Tire & Rubber Co., 977 F.2d 527, 531 (11th Cir. 1992) (constitutional standing is a threshold requirement to class certification).

30. 521 U.S. 591, 612–13, 117 S.Ct. 2231, 138 L.Ed.2d 689 (1997); 527 U.S. 815, 831, 119 S.Ct. 2295, 2307 (1999).

exist but for the [class-action] certification'" and that those issues were dispositive "because their resolution [was] logically antecedent to the existence of any Article III issues."[31] Courts have interpreted *Amchem* and *Ortiz* narrowly to apply only where class certification would be dispositive.[32]

B. The Requirements of Rule 23(a): Numerosity, Commonality, Typicality, and Adequacy

As traditionally delineated, plaintiffs must establish numerosity, commonality, typicality, and adequacy of representation to meet the requirements of § 23(a).[33] Like the standing requirement, each of these incorporates the fundamental principle that the class representatives and the putative class members must share common, dispositive issues such that class resolution is preferable to individual claims.

1. Numerosity: The Class Is So Numerous That Joinder of All Members Is Impracticable

The plaintiffs must prove that the proposed class—of people subjected to the same conduct—is sufficiently numerous that joinder of all the plaintiffs would be "impracticable." "Impracticable" does not mean "impossible."[34] Numerosity is a relative concept: "A court is directed to evaluate the type of action, the size of individual claims, the inconvenience of conducting individual lawsuits, and any other factors pertaining to the propriety of joining all class members."[35] While a finding of numerosity may not be

---

31. *Amchem Prods., Inc.*, 521 U.S. at 612 (first alteration in original) (quoting Georgine v. Amchem Prods., Inc., 83 F.3d 610, 623 (3d Cir. 1996)); *see also Ortiz*, 527 U.S. at 831 (reasoning that the question of whether certification of a settlement class under Rule 23(b)(1)(B) on a limited fund rationale presented, as in *Amchem*, an issue of "statutory standing" that "should be treated first").

32. *See, e.g.*, Rivera v. Wyeth-Ayerst Lab., 283 F.3d 315, 319 & n. 6 (5th Cir. 2002).

33. The relevant text of Rule 23(a) is as follows: (a) Prerequisites [to a Class Action]. One or more members of a class may sue or be sued as representative parties on behalf of all members only if: (1) the class is so numerous that joinder of all members is impracticable; (2) there are questions of law or fact common to the class; (3) the claims or defenses of the representative parties are typical of the claims or defenses of the class; and (4) the representative parties will fairly and adequately protect the interests of the class.

34. Cent. States Se. & Sw. Areas Health and Welfare Fund v. Merck-Medco Managed Care, L.L.C., 504 F.3d 229, 244–45 (2d Cir. 2007).

35. Jenson v. Eveleth Taconite, 139 F.R.D. 657, 664 (D. Minn. 1991); *accord* Commander Props. Corp. v. Beech Aircraft Corp., 164 F.R.D. 529, 535 (D. Kan. 1995) ("Numerosity and practicability of joinder are not determined simply by the number of potential class members, but depend on factors like the practical viability of individual suits in terms of inconvenience, inefficiency and the size of the individual claims, requests for injunctive or declaratory relief, and the location and distribution of class members.") (citation omitted); Bacon v. Honda of Am. Mfg., Inc., 370 F.3d 565, 570–71 (6th Cir. 2004) (stating that "[t]here is no automatic cut-off point at which the number of plaintiffs makes joinder impractica[sic], thereby making a class-action suit the only viable alternative. . . . However, sheer number of potential litigants in a class, especially if it is more than several hundred, can be the only factor needed to satisfy [numerosity]."); *see also* Ellis v. Elgin Riverboat Resorts, 217 F.R.D. 415, 421–22 (N.D. Ill. 2003).

based on pure speculation,[36] some courts have allowed plaintiffs to prove numerosity where they are unable to determine the exact number of putative plaintiffs[37] and where a number of potential class members are not interested in the suit.[38] Where the number of putative plaintiffs is not unwieldy, their geographical scope is circumscribed and they are individually identified, certification has been denied for failing to satisfy numerosity.[39]

Although some courts find the use of absolute numerical cut-offs to be inappropriate, others have held that fewer than twenty-one plaintiffs will not satisfy the requirement but more than forty will.[40] Some courts have refused to certify putative classes of fifty or more due to the failure to meet the numerosity requirement.[41] Defendants seeking to challenge certification on this ground must be prepared to set forth a practical plan for the efficient management of a multi-plaintiff case. The failure to do so may serve only to reinforce the plaintiffs' claims that joinder is unworkable.

In many discrimination cases, plaintiffs try to drive up the number of class members by widening the net to capture within the class more departments, more geographic

---

36. Bozes v. Parish of St. Bernard, 252 F.R.D. 313, 316 (E.D. La. 2008) ("While courts do not require evidence of exact size or identity of class members to satisfy the numerosity requirement, a finding of numerosity may not be based on speculation. A plaintiff cannot rely on conclusory allegations that joinder is impracticable, but must show some evidence or reasonable estimate of the size of the class.") (quoting Harrell v. CheckAGAIN, LLC, 248 F.R.D. 199, 206 (S.D. Miss. 2006)).

37. *See* Bremiller v. Cleveland Psychiatric Inst., 898 F. Supp. 572 (N.D. Ohio 1995) (where plaintiff alleged that the potential class consisted of 260 past and present employees whom the plaintiff could not identify, plaintiff's claims of systemic sexual harassment nonetheless met the numerosity requirement).

38. *Jenson*, 139 F.R.D. at 664.

39. *See, e.g.,* Nat'l Ass'n of Gov't Employees v. City Pub. Serv. Bd. of San Antonio, 40 F.3d 698, 715 (5th Cir. 1994) (in discrimination case, only 11 putative class members held claims falling within the limitations period and, therefore, class failed to meet numerosity requirement); *Jones*, 977 F.2d at 534 (in race discrimination case, certification denied for putative class consisting of one manager, five intervenors, a putative intervenor, and five "pivotal employees"); Levels v. Akzo Nobel Salt, Inc., 178 F.R.D. 171, 176 (N.D. Ohio 1998) (class certification denied in race harassment/discrimination case for failure to meet all prongs of 23(a) including numerosity; proposed class had total of only 32 employees and, if divided into work categories, putative classes had less than 20); Gries v. Standard Ready Mix Concrete, LLC, 252 F.R.D. 479, 488 (N.D. Iowa 2008) (class certification denied because all proposed class members were "individually identified" and "geographically concentrated").

40. Harper v. ULTA Salon Cosmetics & Fragrance, Inc., 2005 WL 3542482, at *2 (N.D. Ga. Dec. 23, 2005) (acknowledging that in the Eleventh Circuit, the general rule is that "less than twenty-one is inadequate, more than forty adequate, with numbers between varying according to other factors") (internal citation omitted); *accord* Cima v. WellPoint Health Networks, Inc., 250 F.R.D. 374 (S.D. Ill. 2008) (noting numerosity met with class as law as ten to forty); Marable v. Dist. Hosp. Partners, L.P., 2006 WL 2547992 (D.D.C. 2006) (class of 30 did not satisfy numerosity requirement); Hnot v. Willis Grp. Holdings Ltd., 228 F.R.D. 476, 485 (S.D.N.Y. 2005) (numerosity requirement is satisfied when putative class is larger than 40); Carrier v. JPB Enters., Inc., 206 F.R.D. 332, 334 (D. Me. 2002) ("A class of more than 40 individuals raises a presumption that joinder is impracticable.").

41. Sellars v. CRST Expedited, Inc., 321 F.R.D. 578, 598 (N.D. Iowa 2017) (finding numerosity met where "100 women made sexual harassment complaints"); Lukovsky v. City and County of San Francisco, 2006 WL 140574 (N.D. Cal. Jan. 17, 2006) (class of potentially 50 members does not satisfy numerosity requirement).

areas, and the like.[42] In doing so, however, they risk including individuals who do not share common questions with the class representatives, and thus they place the viability of the class as a whole at risk.

2. Commonality and Typicality: There Are Questions of Law or Fact Common to the Class, and the Claims or Defenses of the Representative Parties Are Typical of the Claims or Defenses of the Class

Litigation is usually "conducted by and on behalf of the individual named parties only."[43] To justify stepping outside that rule, the representative plaintiffs must demonstrate that there are common, dispositive issues applicable to the entire class, and that the plaintiffs' claims are typical of the class members' claims. The first of those requirements, commonly referred to as "commonality," mandates that issues in the putative class action "turn on questions of law [or fact] applicable in the same manner to each member of the class."[44] Not any common question will do. The common questions must be central to the claim and capable of common resolution, and there can be no dissimilarities, which would impede a common resolution. As the Supreme Court explained,

> That common contention, moreover, must be of such a nature that it is capable of classwide resolution—which means that determination of its truth or falsity will resolve an issue that is central to the validity of each one of the claims in one stroke. "What matters to class certification . . . is not the raising of common 'questions'—even in droves—but, rather the capacity of a classwide proceeding to generate common answers apt to drive the resolution of the litigation. Dissimilarities within the proposed class are what have the potential to impede the generation of common answers."[45]

The second requirement, referred to as "typicality," requires that the named plaintiff "must be part of the class and 'possess the same interest and suffer the same injury' as the class members."[46] The "commonality" question has been said to focus on the claims underlying the suit and, therefore, is tied to numerosity and the threshold question of whether there is an aggrieved "class" at all; "typicality," on the other hand, studies the claims of the named plaintiffs and compares their claims to the putative class members' claims.[47] Nevertheless, the commonality and typicality requirements both similarly focus on the existence of common facts and issues among putative class members and class representatives. For this reason, courts' analyses of commonality and typicality

---

42. *See Levels,* 178 F.R.D. at 176 ("Because geographical dispersion adds to difficulty and impracticability of joinder, it is a factor to be weighed in favor of class certification."); *Gries,* 252 F.R.D. at 488.

43. *Gen. Tel. Co.,* 457 U.S. at 155 (internal citation omitted).

44. *Id.*

45. Wal-Mart Stores, Inc. v. Dukes, 564 U.S. 338, 350 (2011) (quoting Nagareda, Class Certification in the Age of Aggregate Proof, 84 N.Y.U.L.Rev. 97, 132 (2009)).

46. *Gen. Tel. Co.,* 457 U.S. at 156 (internal citation omitted).

47. 1 NEWBERG ON CLASS ACTIONS, §3.26 (5th ed.).

often "merge" into an investigation of the common issues in the putative class, including the putative class members and class representatives:

> [C]ommonality and typicality . . . tend to merge [with both serving] as guideposts for determining whether under the particular circumstances, maintenance of a class action is economical and whether the named plaintiff's claim and the class claims are so interrelated that the interests of the class members will be fairly and adequately protected in their absence.[48]

3. Adequacy of Representation: The Representative Parties Will Fairly and Adequately Protect the Interests of the Class

Rule 23(a)'s final prong, adequacy of representation, investigates whether "interests and incentives between the representative plaintiffs and the rest of the class" are adequately aligned.[49] To that end, a plaintiff must establish both that class counsel are qualified[50] and that "the representative's claims are sufficiently interrelated to and not antagonistic with the class's claims as to ensure fair and adequate representation."[51] Courts are charged with ensuring that the named plaintiffs' interests do not conflict with absent class-members' interests, and deny class certification in cases involving such conflicts.[52]

---

48. *Wal-Mart*, 564 U.S. at 349, n. 5 (quoting *Gen. Tel. Co.*, 457 U.S. at 157–58, n. 13).

49. Dewey v. Volkswagen Aktiengesellschaft, 681 F.3d 170, 183 (3d Cir. 2012).

50. On the question of the adequacy of class counsel, plaintiffs' counsel must be "qualified, experienced, and generally able to conduct the proposed litigation." Griffin v. Carlin, 755 F.2d 1516, 1533 (11th Cir. 1985). In addition, the 2003 amendment to Rule 23(g) requires that the district court appoint class counsel when a class is certified unless a statute states otherwise. The district court must consider several factors when making the appointment. Specifically, the court must assess the work counsel has done in identifying or investigating claims in the case, counsel's experience in handling class actions generally and in similar cases specifically or other complex litigation, counsel's knowledge of the relevant law, and the resources counsel can and will commit to representing the class. FED. R. CIV. P. 23(g)(1); *see also* U.S. Trust Co. of N.Y. v. Alpert, 163 F.R.D. 409, 422 (S.D.N.Y. 1995) (stating that "[a]mong the factors generally considered are: the attorney's experience; the attorney's skills and acumen; the attorney's resources, including staff; the attorney's reputation in the field; and the attorney's performance through the litigation to date. In addition, counsel's adequate representation of a class in the past is good evidence that [attorneys] will adequately represent a class now.") (citations omitted). The district court may also consider "any other matter pertinent to counsel's ability to fairly and adequately represent the interests of the class." FED. R. CIV. P. 23(g)(1)(B).

51. *Zapata*, 167 F.R.D. at 160–61 ("We must give particular concern to the adequacy of representation, because inadequate representation would implicate the due process rights of absentee class members bound by the final judgment in the class suit."); Doll v. Chicago Title Ins. Co., 246 F.R.D. 683, 686 (D. Kan. 2007) (same); Berger v. Compaq Comput. Corp., 257 F.3d 475, 479–80 (5th Cir. 2001) (same); Newton v. Merrill Lynch, Pierce, Fenner & Smith, Inc., 259 F.3d 154, 182 n.27 (3d Cir. 2001) (same).

52. *See, e.g.*, Langbecker v. Elec. Data Sys. Corp., 476 F.3d 299, 315 n. 28 (5th Cir. 2007) (holding that district court erred in certifying class without evaluating conflicts within the class); Valley Drug Co. v. Geneva Pharm., Inc., 350 F.3d 1181, 1189–92 (11th Cir. 2003) (class representatives held inadequate where their economic interests and objectives conflicted with those of the absent class members) (citing In re HealthSouth Corp. Sec. Litig., 213 F.R.D. 447, 461–63 (N.D. Ala. 2003)); Pickett v. Iowa Beef Processors, 209 F.3d 1276, 1280 (11th Cir. 2000) (representation inadequate where class includes those "who claim

C. The Requirements of Rule 23(b)

Class plaintiffs must also satisfy one or more of the subsections of Rule 23(b), typically Rules 23(b)(2) or 23(b)(3). Under Rule 23(b)(2), the plaintiffs must establish that the defendant's actions involve common conduct and injury such that injunctive or declaratory relief is appropriately directed toward the class as a whole. Under Rule 23(b)(2), opt-out notice to putative class members is not required, but relief is limited to injunctive relief and to relief that is incidental to the injunctive relief.[53] Rule 23(b)(3) permits broader relief, including damages, but requires substantially greater proof of common questions: Common questions of law or fact must "predominate over any questions affecting only individual members," and proceeding by class action must be "superior to other available methods for fairly and efficiently adjudicating the controversy."[54]

---

harm from the very same acts from which other members of the class have benefitted"); Allied Orthopedic Appliances, Inc. v. Tyco Healthcare Grp. L.P., 247 F.R.D. 156, 177–78 (C.D. Cal. 2007) (adequacy of representation requirement not satisfied where some class members derived a net economic benefit from the very same conduct alleged to be wrongful by named representatives of the class); Broussard v. Meineke Discount Muffler Shops, Inc., 155 F.3d 331 (4th Cir. 1998) (holding that current franchisees with an interest in the ongoing viability of the franchisor had a conflict with former franchisees who sought only to maximize damages); Klotz v. Trans Union, LLC, 246 F.R.D. 208 (E.D. Pa. 2007) (finding that typicality not met because the putative class representative's disputes with the defendant were so atypical of the class that defendant had a valid argument that the named plaintiff's disputes were comparatively frivolous); Alston v. Va. High Sch. League, Inc., 184 F.R.D. 574, 579 (W.D. Va. 1999) (holding that a proposed class of all high school female athletes could not be certified because several of the proposed class members did not share the same objectives or interests of the named plaintiffs because the former were satisfied with and/or benefited from the alleged discriminatory conduct); Cook Cty. Coll. Teachers Union v. Byrd, 456 F.2d 882, 885 (7th Cir. 1972) (denying class certification and dismissing union as party: "The members of the purported class would seem to have interests antagonistic to those of their fellow 'members' and to the Union's. We find it particularly significant that the Union is not recognized as the collective bargaining agent for" the employees); *see also* Sec'y of Labor v. Fitzsimmons, 805 F.2d 682, 697–99 (7th Cir. 1986) (denying class certification where one group of union members' interests conflict with another group's interests); 7A CHARLES ALAN WRIGHT & ARTHUR MILLER, FEDERAL PRACTICE AND PROCEDURE: CIVIL §1768 (3d ed. 2005) ("It is axiomatic that a putative representative cannot adequately protect the class if [his] interests are antagonistic to or in conflict" with other class members' interests); *Kamean v. Local 363, Int'l Bhd. of Teamsters*, 109 F.R.D. 391, 395 (S.D.N.Y. 1986) (in order to satisfy the adequacy requirement, the named plaintiffs must demonstrate that neither they nor their attorneys are subject to extraneous influences that would create a conflict), *dismissed without op.*, 833 F.2d 1002 (2d Cir. 1986). In order to defeat class certification, "'there must be an actual showing of a real probability of a potential conflict which goes to the subject matter of the suit.'" Gilchrist v. Bolger, 89 F.R.D. 402, 409 (S.D. Ga. 1981) (rejecting defendant's claim that antagonistic interests exist between named plaintiff employees and class members consisting of applicants for employment where no showing of conflict made) (quoting *In re S. Cent. States Bakery Prods.*, 86 F.R.D. 407, 418 (M.D. La. 1980), *aff'd in part, vacated in part*, 733 F.2d 1551 (11th Cir. 1984)).

53. *Wal-Mart*, 564 U.S. at 360 (holding that "claims for monetary relief" "may not" be certified under (b)(2) "at least where (as here) the monetary relief is not incidental to the injunctive or declaratory relief"); Allison v. Citgo Petroleum Corp., 151 F.3d 402, 411 (5th Cir. 1998) (citing cases); FED. R. CIV. P. 23(c)(2)(A).

54. In relevant part, Rule 23(b)(2) and 23(b)(3) read as follows: (2) the party opposing the class has acted or refused to act on grounds that apply generally to the class, so that final injunctive relief or

In Rule 23(b)(3) class actions, opt-out notice is required.[55] The circuit courts are split as to whether certification of "hybrid" classes under both 23(b)(2) and (b)(3) is permissible and there is no agreement on the proper standards or analysis to certify such classes.[56]

For common questions of law or fact to predominate over individualized questions under Rule 23(b)(3), "the issues in the class action that are subject to generalized proof,

---

corresponding declaratory relief is appropriate respecting the class as a whole; or (3) the court finds that the questions of law or fact common to class members predominate over any questions affecting only individual members, and that a class action is superior to other available methods for fairly and efficiently adjudicating the controversy. The matters pertinent to these findings include: (A) the class members' interests in individually controlling the prosecution or defense of separate actions; (B) the extent and nature of any litigation concerning the controversy already begun by or against class members; (C) the desirability or undesirability of concentrating the litigation of the claims in the particular forum; and (D) the likely difficulties in managing a class action.

55. FED. R. CIV. P. 23(c)(2)(B).

56. *See Allison*, 151 F.3d 402 (rejecting plaintiffs' request for hybrid class action because class did not meet requirements of (b)(3)); Reeb v. Ohio Dep't of Rehab. & Corr., 435 F.3d 639 (6th Cir. 2006) (holding, in case brought by female employees of a state correctional facility alleging sex discrimination, that individual compensatory damages predominated over injunctive relief, and because such damages are not recoverable under (b)(2), plaintiffs must decide either to proceed under (b)(3) for money damages or under (b)(2) for injunctive relief, but cannot proceed under both theories). In re Allstate Ins. Co., 400 F.3d 505, 508 (7th Cir. 2005) (leaving open the question of whether a hybrid class is appropriate but noting such a merging of requirements would be "complicated and confusing"). Others have approved them. *See* Dukes v. Wal-Mart Stores, Inc., 603 F.3d 571, 622 (9th Cir. 2010), *rev'd on other grounds, Wal-Mart*, 564 U.S. 338 (endorsing "hybrid approach" wherein liability class can be certified under (b)(2), but punitive damages class would be certified under (b)(3); Molski v. Gleich, 318 F.3d 937, 950 (9th Cir. 2003), *abrogated on other grounds by Wal-Mart*, 564 U.S. 338 (endorsing "hybrid certification" in civil rights cases for liability under (b)(2), but monetary damages under (b)(3)); Robinson v. Metro-N. Commuter R.R. Co., 267 F.3d 147 (2d Cir. 2001), *abrogated on other grounds, Wal-Mart*, 564 U.S. 338 (remanding to consider certifying pattern-or-practice liability under (b)(2), and damages under (b)(3)); Lemon v. Int'l Union of Operating Eng'rs, Local No. 139, AFL-CIO, 216 F.3d 577, 581 (7th Cir. 2000) (remanding and instructing the district court to consider certifying class of union workers suing the union for racial and sex discrimination in job referrals under (b)(2) for equitable relief and (b)(3) for damages); Murray v. Auslander, 244 F.3d 807, 812–13 (11th Cir. 2001) (noting with approval that on remand the district court could certify a class of developmentally disabled individuals suing Florida's Medicaid program challenging the administration of the program, under (b)(2) for injunctive relief, and under (b)(3) for damages, so long as the standing requirements are met); Jefferson v. Ingersoll Int'l Inc., 195 F.3d 894, 898 (7th Cir. 1999) ("Divided certification also is worth consideration. It is possible to certify the injunctive aspects of the suit under Rule 23(b)(2) and the damages aspects under Rule 23(b)(3), achieving both consistent treatment of class-wide equitable relief and an opportunity for each affected person to exercise control over the damages aspects."); Eubanks v. Billington, 110 F.3d 87, 96 (D.C. Cir. 1997) (holding, in a case alleging class-wide discriminatory employment practice by the Library of Congress, that where a (b)(2) class seeks monetary and injunctive relief, the district court may certify a (b)(2) class as to the claims for injunctive relief and a (b)(3) class as to claims for monetary relief, "effectively granting (b)(3) protections including the right to opt out to class members at the monetary relief stage"). *See also* Easterling v. State Dept. of Corrections, 278 F.R.D. 41 (D. Conn. 2011) (noting that *Wal-Mart* did not overrule *Robinson's* endorsement of hybrid certification; "The plaintiff's claims for class-wide declaratory and injunctive relief are certified under Rule 23(b)(2), while the plaintiff's claims for monetary and individualized injunctive relief are certified under Rule 23(b)(3)").

and thus applicable to the class as a whole, must predominate over those issues that are subject only to individualized proof."[57] This inquiry is more demanding than the commonality requirement of Rule 23(a).[58]

"Superiority" of the class action procedure over individual suits is weighed against the factors set forth in Rule 23 itself, and is often viewed in terms of the manageability of class action versus individual litigation.[59] In practice, this inquiry often focuses on the question of whether individual issues in the case would cause a class action to devolve into trials of individual issues such that the class action procedure is no better than separate individual suits.[60]

The common thread through all of these Rule 23 requirements is that the class action mechanism depends on the existence and predominance of central common factual and legal issues over individualized inquiries. Whether denominated as commonality, typicality, adequacy of representation (conflict of interest), or predominance, the determining factor in the viability of the class is the degree to which the case will involve common issues with common proof, as opposed to individual issues requiring proof, which differs among class members.[61]

III. APPLICATION OF RULE 23 REQUIREMENTS IN HARASSMENT AND RETALIATION CASES

A. Difficulties Class Representatives Face Using Plaintiffs' Ordinary Tools to Prove Commonality in Harassment Cases

In discrimination putative class action cases, the class representatives typically rely heavily on evidence of a common, allegedly discriminatory policy, and on statistics showing adverse treatment. Neither of these "tools" serves as well in the context of harassment or retaliation cases, as explained as follows.

In *Wal-Mart Stores, Inc. v. Dukes*, the Supreme Court explained the uphill battle facing plaintiffs who seek to establish class-wide liability. In *Wal-Mart*, a putative class

---

57. Rutstein v. Avis Rent-A-Car Sys., Inc., 211 F.3d 1228, 1233 (11th Cir. 2000) (citations omitted).

58. *Amchem Prods., Inc.*, 521 U.S. at 623–24.

59. Several others have raised an interesting addition to the "superiority" analysis in the discrimination/harassment context—the availability of attorney's fees for a prevailing plaintiff. *Zapata*, 167 F.R.D. at 162–63; *Allison*, 151 F.3d at 420; Dukes v. Wal-Mart, Inc., 509 F.3d 1168, 1199 (9th Cir. 2007) (Kleinfeld, J., dissenting). When an award of fees is available even in small cases, attorneys have ample incentive to bring individual suits. Thus, even if the class is not certified, putative plaintiffs are not without recourse.

60. Gregory v. Finova Capital Corp., 442 F.3d 188 (4th Cir. 2006); *In re Genetically Modified Rice Litig.*, 251 F.R.D. 392, 400 (E.D. Mo. 2008); Steering Comm. v. Exxon Mobil Corp., 461 F.3d 598 (5th Cir. 2006); Busby v. JRHBW Realty, Inc., 513 F.3d 1314 (11th Cir. 2008); *In re Conagra Peanut Butter Prod. Liab. Litig.*, 251 F.R.D. 689, 699–701 (N.D. Ga. 2008); Jones v. Jeld-Wen, Inc., 250 F.R.D. 685, 695–96 (S.D. Fla. 2008).

61. There are also risks of class actions under the Equal Pay Act, and collectively actions under the Fair Labor Standards Act. As those are much less common, we limit our analysis to class actions under Title VII.

of female employees argued that a Wal-Mart "policy" that afforded discretion to store managers, with respect to pay and promotions, utilizing their own subjective criteria, amounted to disparate treatment or disparate impact discrimination.[62] Plaintiffs alleged that there was a strong and uniform corporate culture permitting bias against women to infect these discretionary decisions making every woman the victim of a common practice, and that Wal-Mart was aware of statistics indicating that men were favored. The Ninth Circuit *en banc* approved nationwide class certification based on three forms of proof: statistical evidence, anecdotal reports, and a sociologist's testimony. The Supreme Court reversed. The Court held that Rule 23's commonality prerequisite was the "crux of th[e] case."[63] The Court considered whether the named plaintiffs' claims and the class claims were so interrelated that the interests of the class members would be fairly and adequately protected in their absence:

> Quite obviously, the mere claim by employees of the same company that they have suffered a Title VII injury, or even a disparate-impact Title VII injury, gives no cause to believe that all their claims can productively be litigated at once. Their claims must depend upon a common contention—for example, the assertion of discriminatory bias on the part of the same supervisor. That common contention, moreover, must be of such a nature that it is capable of classwide resolution—which means that determination of its truth or falsity will resolve an issue that is central to the validity of each one of the claims in one stroke.[64]

The Court explained that the Rule 23 analysis must be "rigorous," and that it can include merits evidence if relevant to Rule 23 issues.[65]

Having conducted the rigorous analysis, the Court concluded that plaintiffs had failed to show commonality. The crux of the inquiry is the reason for the adverse employment decision; yet, plaintiffs wished to sue about literally millions of different employment decisions at once. "Without some glue holding the alleged *reasons* for all those decisions together, it will be impossible to . . . produce a common answer to the crucial question *why was I disfavored.*"[66] There was no "significant proof that an employer operated under a general policy of discrimination conceivably could justify a class of both applicants and employees if the discrimination manifested itself in hiring and promotion practices in the same general fashion, such as through entirely subjective decision-making processes."[67] The only evidence of a general policy of

---

62. *Wal-Mart*, 564 U.S. 338.

63. *Id.* at 349.

64. *Id.* at 350.

65. *Id.* at 350–52. For example, in this case, "Proof of commonality necessarily overlaps with [plaintiffs'] merits contention [of] a *pattern or practice* of discrimination." *Id.* (emphasis in original). Thus, the Court considered relevant merits evidence.

66. *Id.* at 352 (emphasis in original).

67. *Id.* at 353 (quoting *Falcon*, 457 U.S. at 159, n. 15).

discrimination presented was the testimony of Dr. William Bielby, plaintiffs' sociological expert, who testified that Wal-Mart has a strong corporate culture, which makes it vulnerable to bias. Yet, "[a]t his deposition . . . Dr. Bielby conceded that he could not calculate whether 0.5 percent or 95 percent of the employment decisions at Wal-Mart might be determined by stereotyped thinking."[68] Even if Dr. Bielby's testimony could survive a *Daubert* motion, which remained an open question, the testimony did not provide substantial evidence of a common practice, given that he could not even estimate what percent of employment decisions were infected by stereotypes.

Plaintiffs argued only that the corporate policy allowing discretion by local supervisors was a uniform discriminatory policy, but the Court ruled that it was plainly "a policy *against having* uniform employment practices."[69] The Court held that subjective decision making was common and presumptively reasonable. When different store managers can operate differently, "demonstrating the invalidity of one manager's use of discretion will do nothing to demonstrate the invalidity of another's. A party seeking to certify a nationwide class will be unable to show that all the employees' Title VII claims will in fact depend on the answers to common questions."[70] In conclusion, the Court held that plaintiffs identified no specific, common employment practice that tied together their 1.5 million claims.

Since *Wal-Mart*, courts have continued to show caution in certifying classes where the practices affecting the putative class members differ, whether based on a policy permitting discretion, a purported corporate "culture" or other practices. For example, in *Bolden v. Walsh Constr. Co.*, a putative class of African American employees claimed that by granting discretion to job site supervisors, the company allowed discrimination against them with respect to assigning overtime and in working conditions.[71] The Seventh Circuit found no commonality because the class members worked on at least 262 different construction sites with different superintendents and foremen, each with materially different working conditions. "[W]hen multiple managers exercise independent discretion, conditions at different stores (or sites) do not present a common question."[72] "The sort of statistical evidence that plaintiffs present has the same problem as the statistical evidence in *Wal-Mart*: it begs the question . . . [i]f [the company] had 25 superintendents, 5 of whom discriminated in awarding overtime, aggregate data would show that black workers did worse than white workers—but that result would not imply that all 25 superintendents behaved similarly, so it would not demonstrate commonality."[73] Thus, while plaintiff contended that the company had fourteen policies that present common questions, they all boil down to affording discretion. "*Wal-Mart* tells

---

68. *Id.* at 354.

69. *Id.* at 355 (emphasis in original).

70. *Id.*

71. Bolden v. Walsh Constr. Co., 688 F.3d 893 (7th Cir. 2012).

72. *Id.* at 896.

73. *Id.*

us that local discretion cannot support a company-wide class no matter how cleverly lawyers may try to repackage local variability as uniformity."[74]

In the harassment context, difficulties of proving a common policy or practice related to the elements of the particular cause of action compound these particular challenges, as explained in more detail in the next section. For example, while the plaintiff in a promotion or hiring case may be able to point to centralized hiring or promotion procedures (e.g., pre-employment tests or hiring or promotion standards) that allegedly contribute to the discrimination, analogous policies concerning harassment typically do not exist. Usually the only company policy regarding harassment is the policy prohibiting it—and that is a difficult policy to claim supports a class action harassment claim. Instead, plaintiffs typically point to alleged failures to follow the antiharassment policy. Inevitably, that leads to an individualized inquiry into who followed the policy and who did not, and that in turn leads to the type of manager-specific or location-specific or plaintiff-specific inquiry that undermines the applicability of the class action procedure in employment discrimination cases as described previously. As one court stated:

> [D]iscrimination in employment has an uncomfortable fit with the typicality requirement. Persons are harmed only by virtue of their class membership. Nevertheless, the harm and circumstances of the discrimination may vary widely. *This is especially true for harassment claims.*[75]

An example is *Elkins v. American Showa, Inc.*[76] There, several woman sought to represent a class of all female workers at one of the defendant's facilities alleging, among other claims, a hostile work environment.[77] The court rejected proposed common questions of fact such as "was the environment at the plant hostile."[78] It continued:

> Whether an individual was subjected to a hostile work environment is a highly fact-intensive inquiry which requires consideration of the frequency, severity, and nature of the conduct, including whether it was physically threatening or humiliating or a mere offensive utterance . . . [T]he evidence offered by plaintiffs demonstrates that the factors to be considered varied within the plant and differed for the various female employees. The evidence fails to show a common pattern or practice, or an equally egregious level, of sexual harassment among the various areas of the plant, among the employees supervised by different supervisors and working with different co-workers, and among the employees on different shifts.[79]

---

74. *Id.* at 898.

75. *Levels*, 178 F.R.D. at 178 (emphasis added).

76. 219 F.R.D. 414 (S.D. Ohio 2002).

77. *Id.* at 421.

78. *Id.* at 423.

79. *Id.* at 423–24.

Due to these fundamental differences—"the variations in the frequency and the severity of the behavior to which different female workers were subjected"—the court held that the plaintiffs failed to demonstrate commonality and typicality in satisfaction of Rule 23.[80]

The other primary evidence plaintiffs introduce to support class certification in discrimination cases is statistics, which the plaintiffs argue show that class members were similarly adversely affected with respect to the challenged term or condition of employment.[81] This type of proof is particularly unsuited to harassment cases. In typical discrimination cases involving hiring, promotion, termination, discipline, or compensation, the case centers on employment actions that are well-defined and that are typically tracked by the employer's human resources department. Using readily available data about those discrete events, the class representatives can present statistics purporting to show demonstrable, statistically significant differences in rates of hiring, promotion, or termination or other practices with respect to class members versus individuals outside the class.[82] In contrast, in a harassment case, it would be the truly

---

80. *Id.; see also* Doe v. Unified Sch. Dist. No. 259, 240 F.R.D. 673, 679–80 (D. Kan. 2007). *Doe* exemplifies the difficulty of showing commonality and typicality sufficient under Rule 23 in the harassment context. Plaintiffs, two sisters, sought to represent a class of 20,000 female high school students in Kansas's largest school district in an action for relief under Title IX of the Education Amendments of 1972. The sisters alleged egregious incidents of harassment from other students occurring over their high school tenures. Citing *Falcon*, the court denied the plaintiffs' motion for class certification, holding that they failed to satisfy the requirements of commonality and typicality. It observed that "[w]ith Title IX claims . . . each individual claim is specific . . . [W]hether the conduct rises to the level of actionable harassment . . . depends on a host of circumstances, expectations, and relationships." *Id.* at 680. The court noted that even between the two named plaintiffs, allegations of harassment "took place in different settings, with different students and involving other relationships," making them ill-suited to represent each other—much less 20,000 students. Moreover, the court found class treatment improper because "each allegation needs to be weighed on an individualized basis." *Id.* The differences compelled the court to deny the motion for class certification.

81. *See, e.g.*, Malave v. Potter, 320 F.3d 321, 325 (2d Cir. 2003) (plaintiff may offer statistical evidence to demonstrate a disparity in outcome between groups, but the statistical disparity must be "sufficiently substantial" to raise an inference of causation); Howard v. Gutierrez, 474 F. Supp. 2d 41 (D.D.C. 2007); Attenborough v. Const. & Gen. Bldg. Laborers' Local 79, 238 F.R.D. 82 (S.D.N.Y. 2006); *Hnot*, 228 F.R.D. at 483 ("[P]laintiff[s] must offer statistical evidence of a kind and degree sufficient to show that the practice in question has caused the exclusion of applicants for jobs or promotions because of their membership in a protected group.").

82. Even in ordinary discrimination cases, decentralization of decision-making among locations and managers poses serious challenges for class certification, including the invalidation of the plaintiffs' statistics. Many courts have rejected statistics that lump together departments, offices, supervisors, or other characteristics, especially in cases where relevant employment divisions were not centralized. The courts have rejected the statistics because they were not tailored to the particular units of the employer in which the challenged decisions were made. Where such decision-making is decentralized across different locations, departments, or individuals, the courts have rejected comprehensive statistics. *See, e.g.*, Woodbury v. N.Y. Transit Auth., 832 F.2d 764 (2d Cir. 1987) (finding statistics to be less significant where decision-making is decentralized); Coser v. Moore, 739 F.2d 746 (2d Cir. 1984) (same); Dugan v. Bell State Univ., 815 F.2d 1132, 1137 (7th Cir. 1987) (where decision-making is decentralized, "gross statistics are . . . meaningless absent a departmental breakdown") (quoting Zahorik v. Cornell Univ., 729 F.2d 85, 95 (2d Cir. 1984)); Coates v. Johnson & Johnson, 756 F.2d 525 (7th Cir. 1985) (criticizing statistics for, among other things, not accounting for change in managers).

unusual employer that tracks incidents of harassment in its human resources information system such that statistics could be based on them. Thus, the class representatives are left to argue commonality based on anecdotal evidence.[83] This approach, again, is subject to demonstration of differences based on different locations, supervisors, and so on as described previously.

B. Difficulties Class Representatives Face Because of Proof Specific to Harassment Cases

As described in the introduction to this chapter, the harassment cause of action includes several highly individualized elements that are not necessary in other discrimination cases. These require inquiries into the class members' personal, subjective perceptions of offensiveness and welcomeness. Additionally, harassment cases involve individualized inquiries into the severity and pervasiveness of conduct affecting each person, whether the conduct resulted in a tangible employment action for each person, whether the alleged harasser was a supervisor, whether the employer had reasonable policies and practices in place to avoid harassment, and whether each person took reasonable advantage of the remedial opportunities available to him or her.

Most courts have found that class representatives and putative class members' harassment claims are not common or typical given their distinct factual scenarios.[84]

---

83. *See* Love v. Johanns, 439 F.3d 723 (D.C. Cir. 2006) (absent statistical proof showing differential treatment of women in the award of loans, 662 declarations asserting differential treatment were insufficient to show commonality via a common policy of discrimination).

84. *See* Smith v. Ergo Sols., LLC, 306 F.R.D. 57 (D.D.C. 2015) (denying class certification in suit by female employees against the CEO because representatives did not demonstrate commonality or typicality); Carlson v. C.H. Robinson Worldwide, Inc., No. 02-Civ-3780, 2005 WL 758602, at *13 (D. Minn. 2005) (holding that named plaintiffs failed to meet their burden to establish commonality with respect to sexual harassment claims where anecdotal evidence did not demonstrate the existence of a centralized policy and practice of tolerating or promoting sexual harassment, and the question of whether class members in "decentralized and independent" branches were subjected to severe and pervasive harassment was not "subject to common proof"); Radmanovich v. Combined Ins. Co. of Am., 216 F.R.D. 424, 438 (N.D. Ill. 2003) (holding that "individual issues of: (1) whether the work environment was subjectively hostile; (2) whether a supervisor or coworker exposed the class member to the hostile environment; (3) whether each particular class member suffered an adverse employment action; and (4) the particular class member's steps in taking advantage of possible preventative or corrective opportunities offered by [defendant] predominate over class issues with regard to the hostile work environment claims"); Elkins v. Am. Showa, Inc., 219 F.R.D. 414 (S.D. Ohio 2002) (holding that claims of named plaintiffs and putative class members were not sufficiently similar to satisfy the typicality requirement); Marquis v. Tecumseh Prod. Co., 206 F.R.D. 132, 159–60 (E.D. Mich. 2002) (holding that plaintiffs failed to demonstrate typicality due not only to "substantial differences" between the named plaintiffs and putative class members but also among the named plaintiffs; stating that "claims and allegations of the named [p]laintiffs here, by and large, rest upon discrete misconduct by identifiable bad actors, and not upon a general, pervasive atmosphere of offensive remarks or objectionable materials within a particular area or department"); *Levels*, 178 F.R.D. at 171 (refusing to certify harassment class because named plaintiffs claims were not typical of all the claims of class members because they worked in different areas and were exposed to different supervisors and working conditions); Sheehan v. Purolator, Inc., 103 F.R.D. 641, 656 (E.D.N.Y. 1984) ("[The named plaintiff's] claims of sexual harassment and retaliatory treatment do not present issues suitable for class

In *Smith v. Ergo Sols, LLC*, the female employees alleged that the defendant's CEO and owner made sexual advances on certain female employees, texted graphic pictures to others, and sexually assaulted others.[85] The court held that class certification was not appropriate as "this bare allegation asks the Court to do rather a lot of extrapolating from the personal experiences of a handful of named plaintiffs."[86] The court held that commonality was not met because "the claims of female employees who experienced actual harassment are different from those who experienced only the allegedly hostile workplace environment. Hence, any problems are exacerbated for plaintiffs' quid pro quo harassment claims, which necessarily involve a more individualized experience."[87]

Further, the district court in *Zapata v. IBP*, for instance, held that, in a racial harassment case where the allegations of the potential class members relied on "decentralized, individual conduct of various individual supervisors," no commonality linked their claims: "The majority of the particular work conditions that plaintiffs claim constitute hostile work environment discrimination focus upon the individual actions taken by different individual supervisors, and not on a uniform policy or practice of IBP."[88] The court explained that the claim also failed to meet the predominance test, because "[e]ach class member's exposure to allegedly discriminatory conduct varies in nature

---

actions. The harassment claim rests on a highly personal and individualized set of facts: [plaintiff's] allegation that she was denied a promotion . . . after she rejected the sexual advances of the official selecting the new vice president. In light of the broad class [plaintiff] seeks to represent, it is doubtful that the claim presents common questions of law or fact, or that it is "typical" for [defendant] to condition promotions on the granting of sexual favors."), *aff'd*, 839 F.2d 99 (2d Cir. 1988) (affirming two different decisions by the district court and finding as to the refusal to certify the class that plaintiff had failed to produce evidence sufficient to establish a class of aggrieved individuals); *see also* Keeton v. Hayes Int'l Corp., 106 F.R.D. 366, 372 (N.D. Ala. 1985) (denying class certification where evidence showed that plaintiff was the only employee to ever complain of sexual harassment; "Perhaps the single greatest hurdle which plaintiffs must overcome in this case is the Rule 23(a)(3) requirement that their claims and defenses be typical of those of the class. Both [plaintiffs] have made claims which are peculiar to themselves and which appear to require individualized treatment"); *but see Martens, Inc.,* 181 F.R.D. at 259 (court held that plaintiffs' claims are typical and common where "[t]he various plaintiffs allege essentially the similar wrongdoing: a pattern of discriminatory treatment of women that results in entry barriers, sexual harassment, and glass ceilings, and that traces to a central failure by Smith Barney's management and human resources department to prevent and remedy widespread discrimination"); Meiresonne v. Marriott Corp., 124 F.R.D. 619, 624–25 (N.D. Ill. 1989) (certifying a class of female employees who, among other things, alleged sexual harassment; given the numerous other issues in the case, the court did not dwell on the issues of certification of a harassment class, but it did state that because the plaintiffs were not asking for damages for individual incidents of harassment, but instead were "alleging an atmosphere of sexual hostility that evidences discrimination," the plaintiff's claims were typical of the class). *See also Unified Sch. Dist. No. 259,* 240 F.R.D. at 673 (holding typicality requirement was not satisfied in suit against school district by female high school students alleging a pattern and practice of deliberate indifference to sexual harassment in violation of Title IX because the claims of each proposed class member were factually different from the named plaintiffs' claims with respect to both liability and damages).

85. 306 F.R.D. at 61.

86. *Id.* at 67.

87. *Id.*

88. *Zapata,* 167 F.R.D. at 159.

and degree from that of other named plaintiffs and putative class members"; accordingly, "the class action would devolve into a series of individual trials on issues peculiar to each plaintiff."[89]

Similarly, although the US District Court for the Northern District of Texas in *International Union* did not use the commonality language of Rule 23, the court held that a plaintiff's class claims of sexual harassment, based on unconnected incidents of harassment, were not amenable to class treatment: "as merely reciting the claims of harassment demonstrates, this form of discrimination simply is not amenable to class treatment. The complaints are too individualized, [the employer's] defenses to these varied claims are likely to be very fact-specific, and including these claims in the larger class action would cause the case to devolve into a series of individual trials."[90]

Likewise, in *Hofmann v. AT&T Technologies, Inc.*,[91] the court found that the plaintiffs' allegations of sexual harassment were not sufficiently common or typical to allow class certification. The plaintiffs alleged that they were subjected to sexual harassment during a training program in which different instructors allegedly made offensive comments. The court held, the plaintiffs' circumstances were so different that each one's case would need to be tried separately. At a minimum, the court would be required to conduct a separate analysis for the class members exposed to different instructors.[92]

Levels v. Azko Nobel Salt Co. offers another excellent example of the myriad problems plaintiffs face when attempting to conform the harassment cause of action to the requirements of Rule 23.[93] First, the court found the proposed class of thirty-two was insufficient for numerosity, especially because the class was split into distinct surface and underground worker groups with little or no contact with each other, and different supervisors who, like the employees, did not switch between surface and underground units.[94] Second, the court concluded that these same differences between the underground and surface groups precluded a finding of commonality.[95] Finally, the court held that the plaintiffs had failed to establish typicality because their claims were not the same

---

89. *Id.* at 166.

90. Int'l Union, United Auto., Aerospace, & Agric. Implement Workers of Am., AFL-CIO v. LTV Aerospace and Def. Co., 136 F.R.D. 113, 130 (N.D. Tex. 1991) (holding that the varied harassment complaints by named plaintiffs prohibited their class sexual harassment claims from being certified under Rule 23).

91. 1986 WL 4100 (N.D. Ill. 1986).

92. *Id.* at *4–5 ("Where the claims plaintiffs assert are so highly individualized, class treatment is inappropriate."). *Contra* Markham v. White, 171 F.R.D. 217, 221–22 (N.D. Ill. 1997) (certifying sexual harassment class holding that, although parties were allegedly harassed during different seminars, this distinction does not necessarily destroy commonality or typicality; "Inquiry into each class member's subjective perception and response will of course be relevant to damages. But individual differences in that respect do not detract from the satisfaction of the commonality standard.").

93. 178 F.R.D. 171 (N.D. Ohio 1998).

94. *Id.* at 176.

95. *Id.* at 177.

as those of other putative class members.[96] After concluding that the plaintiffs also could not prevail under § (b) of Rule 23, the court denied the motion for class certification.[97]

In *Elkins v. American Showa, Inc.,* the District Court for the Southern District of Ohio held that the plaintiffs had failed to satisfy the requirements of both Rule 23(a) and 23(b).[98] The court found that the plaintiffs did not demonstrate Rule 23(a) commonality and the evidence showed that "the factors to be considered varied within the plant and differed for the various female employees."[99] The variations of alleged harassment and its severity compelled the conclusion that Rule 23(a) commonality and typicality was lacking.[100] Moreover, citing the same differences among plaintiffs' claims, the court held that the strictures of both Rule 23(b)(2) and (b)(3) had not been met.[101] These cases highlight the inherent problem shared by all sexual harassment putative class actions—they invariably involve a wide variety of allegedly offensive incidents of varying types and severity as well as subjective elements. Plaintiffs have tried to escape the inherently individualized nature of sexual harassment claims by focusing on alleged common practices of ignoring complaints of harassment; however, most courts have declined to gloss over the individualized nature of the proof that nevertheless is required in the first instance to bring a cognizable claim of sexual harassment.[102]

C. *Jenson* and Its Few Progeny: Hard Cases Make Bad Law

Jenson v. Eveleth Taconite Co.[103] is perhaps the best-known decision certifying a class in a harassment case. It is representative of the category of harassment cases into which fall virtually all of the few cases that have been certified as class actions: courts searching for a remedy for egregious harassing conduct of extreme notoriety and a dearth of remedial policies, or a company's utter failure to redress allegedly known, pervasive misconduct.[104] In those cases, the district courts have strained to squeeze the cases into

---

96. *Id.* at 178.

97. *Id.* at 179–80.

98. 219 F.R.D. at 414.

99. *Id.* at 424.

100. *Id.* at 423–25.

101. *Id.* at 425–27; *see also Levels*, 178 F.R.D. 171 (refusing to certify harassment class because the plaintiffs failed to satisfy the numerosity, commonality, or typicality requirements for class certification, and, as the action was primarily one for money damages it could not be certified for declaratory or injunctive relief); Miller v. Hygrade Food Prod. Corp., 198 F.R.D. 638 (E.D. Pa. 2001) (denying motion for class certification under both Rule 23(b)(2) and (b)(3) because injunctive class certification was precluded where plaintiffs were not claiming that each worker was affected by the alleged discriminatory practices in the same manner, and the predominance and superiority requirements for class certification were not satisfied).

102. *See, e.g., Unified Sch. Dist. No. 259*, 240 F.R.D. at 673 (refusing to certify class despite plaintiffs' allegation that defendants failed properly to respond to more than 300 complaints of harassment).

103. 139 F.R.D. 657 (D. Minn. 1991).

104. *See, e.g., Sellars*, 321 F.R.D. at 586 (certifying class where the plaintiffs, female truck drivers, claimed that they consistently sexually harassed, including with threats of bondage, and that the company had a central company policy which only found harassment when the accused confessed or a third-party

the class action mechanism, without faithful adherence to either the Rule 23 standards or the burdens of proof in the harassment cause of action. In these cases, the courts have dealt with Rule 23 commonality requirements, and the individualized aspects of harassment law (such as inquiries into welcomeness, among other things), by ignoring the individualized issues and subjective inquiries and replacing them with class-wide inquiries into what a "reasonable" person would have felt or experienced. No federal appellate court has approved a purely harassment class action, nor has any federal appellate court approved the deviations from the harassment standards of proof used by the few district courts that have allowed such claims to proceed.

In *Jenson*, the district court certified a class of plaintiffs who alleged that their employer knowingly allowed sexually harassing behavior to permeate the workplace and had no policies in place to prevent the offensive conduct.[105] In this case, however, the court heard evidence of pervasive offensive conduct. Sexually explicit graffiti and posters were found on the walls and in lunchroom areas, tool rooms, lockers, desks, and offices. Such material was found in women's vehicles, on elevators, in women's restrooms, in interoffice mail, and in locked company bulletin boards. Women reported incidents of unwelcome touching, including kissing, pinching, and grabbing. Women also reported offensive language directed at individuals as well as frequent "generic" comments that women did not belong in the mines, kept jobs from men, and belonged home with their children.[106]

Notwithstanding the severe conduct alleged,[107] the court noted that "plaintiffs do not seek damages based on individual incidents of harassment, but instead seek class-wide injunctive, declaratory, and financial relief."[108]

The court agreed with the defense that class members' reactions to the alleged profanity and pornography "are highly individualized." However, it strained to avoid that problem by finding a class-wide common link in the question of whether a reasonable woman would find the work environment "hostile," without regard to the putative class members' actual, subjective reactions.[109] Additionally, the court found the defendant's alleged refusal to "institute effective sexual harassment policies or affirmative action policies" to be a prime component of class-wide injury that, if proved, would entitle the class to broad injunctive relief.

---

witnessed the harassment, resulting in constant failure to find evidence of harassment, and thus, widespread failure to impose discipline and retaliation against women who complained); Sims v. Montgomery Cty. Comm'n, 766 F. Supp. 1052 (M.D. Ala. 1991) (certifying class where the plaintiffs, female police officers, claimed that they were subjected to severe and intolerable conditions as a result of pervasive sexual harassment in the department).

105. 139 F.R.D. at 657.

106. *Id.* at 662–63.

107. In one particularly egregious incident, a male employee pretended to perform oral sex on a sleeping female coworker. Further, foremen actually participated in offensive conduct, and management personnel testified that they saw offensive photos and graffiti but, apparently, did nothing. Jenson v. Eveleth Taconite Co., 130 F.3d 1287, 1291–92 (8th Cir. 1997), cert. denied, 524 U.S. 953 (1998).

108. *Jenson*, 139 F.R.D. at 662.

109. *Id.* at 665.

In a later decision, the same court moved beyond the class certification question and defined a brand-new procedure for determining individual plaintiffs' rights to recover for alleged harassment.[110] The court departed from harassment law as outlined by the Supreme Court, and created new burdens of proof in the class context that incorporate some elements of pattern or practice discrimination law, and some elements of harassment law, but not others. The district court first noted, correctly, that, in a traditional pattern or practice discrimination case, the finding of liability entitles a plaintiff to a presumption in her favor.[111] However, the court continued, due to the subjective component of the sexual harassment claim—a component not present in discrimination claims—no such presumption could be applied in a harassment case.[112]

Because the employee's subjective response to acts of sexual harassment is an essential part of proving a claim of hostile environment sexual harassment, a presumption that the employer discriminated against individual class members may not arise from a determination that the reasonable woman would have been affected by the acts of sexual harassment. Individual employees should not be allowed to circumvent an essential element of a hostile environment claim merely because they are permitted to pursue their claims as a class.[113]

Instead, the court held, once a pattern or practice had been found on a class-wide basis, a second phase would explore the individuals' rights to recover and the amount of their damages. In this phase, each plaintiff must show that she was individually subjected to and offended by the hostile environment to "at least" the same extent as the reasonable woman.[114] Nevertheless, in the class context, the court continued, the plaintiffs could prove "unwelcomeness" by showing by a preponderance of the evidence that "women by their conduct indicated that the acts of sexual harassment were unsolicited and regarded as undesirable or offensive."[115] During that phase, however, each

---

110. Jenson v. Eveleth Taconite Co., 824 F. Supp. 847 (D. Minn. 1993) (*Jenson II*).

111. *Id.* at 875–76.

112. *Id.* at 876. In *Harris v. Forklift Systems, Inc.,* 510 U.S. 17 (1993), the Supreme Court held that an alleged victim of sexual harassment must have subjectively perceived the environment to be hostile. The *Jenson II* court stated that the test required "(1) [the plaintiff] belongs to a protected group; (2) that [the plaintiff] was subject to unwelcome sexual harassment; (3) the harassment was based upon sex; (4) the harassment affected a term, condition, or privilege of employment; and (5) the employer knew or should have known of the harassment and failed to take proper remedial action." *Jenson II,* 824 F. Supp. at 875 (citing Burns v. McGregor Elec. Indus., Inc., 955 F.2d 559 (8th Cir. 1992)).

113. *Jenson II,* 824 F. Supp. at 876.

114. *Id.* at 876.

115. In *Jenson II,* the court was persuaded that the plaintiffs had submitted sufficient evidence to support a finding of unwelcomeness. It pointed to the dearth of evidence "that any of the acts of sexual harassment were solicited," minimal evidence that women found the harassment to be unoffensive, and testimony that women had attempted to remove or erase questionable pictures and graffiti. *Id.* at 883. Additionally, the court held that a reasonable woman would find the environment hostile where "the effect, and possibly the intent, of the sexualized environment that existed . . . was to inform women that they were perceived primarily as sexual objects and inferior to men." *Id.* at 885.

individual would retain the burden of proving that she was at least as "affected as the reasonable woman."[116]

In a rush to find a mechanism for class relief, the *Jenson II* court also disregarded the defendant's defense that its responses to complaints were sufficient to relieve the employer of liability. In light of the breadth of the allegations of harassment, the court held, the employer's responses should have addressed the problem as it affected the entire workforce, not just individualized complaints.[117] Decided before *Faragher*, the court did not address the reasonableness of the plaintiff's conduct, nor of the employer's conduct in regard to particular plaintiffs, and it also did not address whether any or all of the plaintiffs had suffered a "tangible employment action." The *Jenson II* focus on the employer's response to the whole workforce, and disregard for the employee's own actions, is inconsistent with *Faragher*'s focus on the employee's own use of the complaint procedures. The district court's class certification and liability decisions in *Jenson* and *Jenson II* were not appealed.

Jenson's progeny are equally troubling with respect to fidelity to the Rule 23 standards and the burdens of proof on the substantive claims. In *Warnell v. Ford Motor Co.*,[118] the US District Court for the Northern District of Illinois certified a class of female workers at Ford's "Chicago area manufacturing facilities" in a case involving egregious alleged conduct. The district court rejected, as a "bold and striking claim, but one quite without merit,"[119] Ford's argument that harassment claims are not suitable for class treatment because they require individualized treatment. The court went on to effectively eliminate the subjective elements of the cause of action, despite Supreme Court precedent requiring them, explaining that the "landscape of the total work environment, rather than the subjective experiences of each individual claimant, is the focus for establishing a pattern or practice of unwelcome sexual harassment which is severe and pervasive."[120] The *Warnell* court elaborated that while it did not expressly hold that a showing of subjective offensiveness was unnecessary, the plaintiffs would not be required actually to prove it, nor would the defendant have the opportunity to

---

116. The court thus apparently followed the "reasonable woman" standard later implicitly rejected by the Supreme Court in both *Faragher*, 524 U.S. 775 (noting that in order to be actionable, an "objectionable environment" must exist that "a reasonable person would find hostile or abusive") and *Oncale v. Sundowner Offshore Services Inc.*, 523 U.S. 75 (1998) (citing the "reasonable person" standard). In neither case did the court make the standard gender-specific, despite the fact that the two cases involved plaintiffs of differing sexes.

117. *Jenson II*, 824 F. Supp. at 887–88. Based on these findings, the district court entered judgment for the plaintiffs and granted injunctive relief. *Id.* at 888. On review, the Eighth Circuit addressed the plaintiffs' challenges to the district court's award of damages; the defendant did not challenge liability. *Jenson*, 130 F.3d 1287. However, although it did not review the question of class certification, the appellate court noted the widespread incidents of harassment and found that "the record requires this court to acknowledge that the sexual harassment conducted against the member class, individually and as a whole, is to say the least, egregious." *Id.* at 1291.

118. 189 F.R.D. 383, 385 (N.D. Ill. 1999), *overruled on other grounds,* Lemon v. Int'l Union of Operating Eng'rs, 216 F.3d 577 (7th Cir. 2000).

119. *Warnell*, 189 F.R.D. at 387.

120. *Id.* (citations omitted).

contest it, because individualized hearings for each person would not be required.[121] The court was also willing to assume away the question of "welcomeness." Quoting a Seventh Circuit decision that "welcome sexual harassment is an oxymoron," the district court found that where there was no evidence of receptiveness to the acts of alleged harassment, "of course it was unwelcome."[122] The court opined that the law did not require "other things being equal, that a woman must introduce further evidence that she finds it subjectively hostile to be . . . subjected to . . . conduct that the plaintiffs here allege."[123] The *Warnell* court found *Faragher* "not to the point."[124] "It cannot be," declared the court without further justification, in a decision that antedates *Dukes*, "that the mere availability of an affirmative defense applicable to some but not all plaintiffs means that individual claims necessarily predominate, or defendants would have an automatic means to deny certification of virtually any class action. That is not the law."[125] The court made no further effort to explain how or why defenses are less relevant than claims to the analysis of whether "claims *or defenses* of the representative parties are typical of the claims *or defenses* of the class," and whether there are "question of law or fact common to the class."[126] That argument was later rejected in *Wal-Mart*.[127] Under the Supreme Court's holding in *Wal-Mart*, typicality requires that *defenses* be typical of the class. Thus, in the end, the *Warnell* district court disregarded the Rule 23 requirements of typicality, commonality, and predominance merely because the court concluded that they stood in the way of class certification. That sort of end-result-driven reasoning in disregard of Rule 23 and the substantive law of harassments claims and defenses is characteristic of the reasoning of *Jenson* and its progeny.

It is also typical of the sort of decisions plainly overruled by the Supreme Court in *Wal-Mart v. Dukes*. In deference to the plain remedial scheme in Title VII, the Court has established a procedure for trying pattern-or-practice cases that "gives effect" to Title VII's statutory requirements; specifically, "When the plaintiff seeks individual relief such as reinstatement or backpay after establishing a pattern or practice of discrimination . . . . the burden will shift to the company, but it will have the right to raise any individual affirmative defenses it may have . . . "[128] In *Wal-Mart*, the plaintiffs advocated and the lower court agreed that this burden-shifting framework based on the statutory requirements could be replaced with "Trial by Formula."[129] Under this "novel project," "[a] sample set of the class members would be selected, as to whom liability for sex discrimination and the backpay owing as a result would be determined

---

121. *Id.*

122. *Id.* (*citing* Carr v. Allison Gas Turbine Div., Gen. Motors Corp., 32 F.3d 1007, 1008 (7th Cir. 1994)).

123. *Id.* at 388.

124. *Id.*

125. *Id.*; *see also* Bremiller v. Cleveland Psychiatric Inst., 195 F.R.D. 1 (N.D. Ohio 2000).

126. FED. R. CIV. P. 23(a)(2) & (3) (emphasis added).

127. *Wal-Mart,* 564 U.S. at 367.

128. *Id.* at 366–67 (citations omitted).

129. *Id.* at 367.

in depositions supervised by a master," "without further individualized proceedings."[130] The court explicitly disapproved of such a class action: "Because the Rules Enabling Act forbids interpreting Rule 23 to 'abridge, enlarge or modify any substantive right,'[131] a class cannot be certified on the premise that Wal-Mart will not be entitled to litigate its statutory defenses to individuals' claims."[132] Rather, Wal-Mart was "entitled to individualized determinations of each employee's eligibility for backpay."[133] Since *Wal-Mart*, courts have rejected certifications that would deny defendants the opportunity to present individualized defenses.[134]

Thus, progeny of *Jenson* which flew past this principle should be viewed as antithetical to *Wal-Mart*. By straining the law in order to permit a class action, the *Jenson* court and those that have followed its example created a procedure that exemplifies the worst of both worlds. Far from fostering judicial efficiency—as the class device is intended to do—the *Jenson* procedure requires both (1) a burdensome Phase I proceeding (in which individualized elements of proof—including exposure to and welcomeness of the alleged conduct, the plaintiff's actual use of complaint procedures, and the employer's response to individual complaints—are sacrificed), and (2) Phase II minitrials for each and every plaintiff, as to whether the plaintiff was exposed to and welcomed the conduct, that are themselves no less burdensome than individual cases would have been had there been no class action in the first place. The *Jenson* court and its followers do not satisfactorily address how this procedure meets the Rule 23 requirements that common questions of law or fact predominate over any questions affecting only individual members and that proceeding by class action is superior to other available methods for the fair and efficient adjudication of the controversy, as specified in *Wal-Mart*.

One of the ironies associated with cases such as *Jenson* is that the district courts need not have strained so hard to create a remedy for affected individuals. No doubt, where the fact patterns are egregious and statutory attorney's fees are available, as in those cases, individual plaintiffs would find no shortage of counsel willing to take their cases based on the very real prospect of large awards in individual cases. An individual remedy was clearly available, and it would not have required any distortion of the applicable legal principles as the district court found necessary to enable class certification. The class action mechanism is not appropriate, much less "superior" in these circumstances. These cases are a far cry from the multi-plaintiff, small-award cases for which the class action mechanism was designed in order to ensure that some remedy existed for such wrongs.

---

130. *Id.*

131. 28 U.S.C. §2072(B); *see* Ortiz v. Fibreboard Corp., 527 U.S. 815, 845, 119 S.Ct. 2295, 144 L.Ed.2d 715 (1999).

132. *Id.*

133. *Wal-Mart*, 564 U.S. at 365.

134. *See, e.g.*, Davis v. Cintas Corp., 717 F.3d 476 (6th Cir. 2013) (denying class certification in a gender discrimination class action; holding that the defendant had a right to present defenses before paying any person an award of backpay, and that plaintiff's "shortfall-based model" to estimate backpay damages to the class "makes no effort to individualize damages at all" and thus, it was "worse than the system that the Supreme Court unanimously rejected in *Dukes*").

D. Difficulties Class Representatives Face Because of Proof Specific to Retaliation Cases

As previously discussed, the cause of action for retaliation necessitates a highly individualized inquiry into whether each plaintiff actually and personally engaged in statutorily protected conduct. This inquiry becomes further complicated in class claims, as protected conduct can take a variety of different forms. For example, if one class member filed an EEOC charge, another participated as a witness in that EEOC proceeding, and yet another member confided in her manager, all three class members may claim to have engaged in protected conduct. Yet none of their scenarios would be the same. Likewise, retaliation claims may be based on different allegedly retaliatory conduct. For example, if one class member is terminated, another is transferred to another job with no loss of pay and another is suspended pending investigation, all three may allege a retaliatory act, but the question of whether the act is severe enough to support a claim may be answered differently.

Because of the distinct factual scenarios in individual retaliation claims, few class retaliation claims have been attempted and most courts have found that class representatives' and putative class members' retaliation claims are not common or typical as required for class certification.[135] The district court in *Elkins v. Am. Showa Inc.*, for instance, held that both commonality and typicality were lacking as to the class representatives' claims of retaliation.[136] In reaching its decision, the court stressed: "[e]ach plaintiff must individually prove the four elements of a retaliation claim."[137] But because the named plaintiffs were unable to identify an underlying retaliation issue which could

---

135. *See* Butler v. Illinois Bell Tel. Co., No. 06C5400, 2008 WL 474367, at *6 (N.D. Ill. Feb. 14, 2008) (denying class certification because "individual issues . . . predominate" in plaintiffs' retaliation claims) ("Ordinarily retaliation claims are not suitable for class certification"); Hohider v. United Parcel Serv., Inc., 243 F.R.D. 147, 222 (W.D. Pa. 2007) (finding that class-wide adjudication of plaintiffs' retaliation claims was not appropriate since "the commonality requirement cannot be met"), *rev'd on other grounds*, 574 F.3d 169 (3d Cir. 2009); Selwood v. Va. Mennonite Retirement Cmty., Inc., No. Civ A, 5:04 CV 00021, 2004 WL 1946379, at *3 (W.D. Va. Aug. 31, 2004) (holding that the class representative's claims are not typical of the class); *Elkins*, 219 F.R.D. at 425 (denying class certification on the basis of both commonality and typicality) ("Plaintiffs' retaliation claims are even less conducive [than discrimination claims] to class-wide adjudication based on a lack of commonality among such claims . . . Similarly, the establishment of a retaliation claim by one plaintiff would not serve to establish any aspect of a retaliation claim brought by another plaintiff. Typicality is therefore lacking as to those claims."); Reid v. Lockheed Martin Aeronautics Co., 205 F.R.D. 655, 676 (N.D. Ga. 2001) ("[T]he court finds that Plaintiffs have failed to demonstrate commonality or typicality with respect to their retaliation claims. As with their hostile environment claims, Plaintiffs' claims of retaliation are fact-intensive and require a showing of intentional discrimination."); *Sheehan*, 103 F.R.D. at 654 ("[C]laims of retaliatory treatment, which require proof of highly individualized facts, generally do not present suitable issues for class actions."); Strong v. Arkansas Blue Cross & Blue Shield, Inc. 87 F.R.D. 496, 511 (E.D. Ark. 1980) (denying class certification on adequacy grounds) ("Plaintiffs' . . . [allegation of] retaliatory selection . . . is clearly not a class issue. Indeed, preoccupation with peculiar retaliatory wrongs allegedly done to one may well make such persons an inadequate representative of the class.") (citations omitted).

136. 219 F.R.D. at 414.

137. *Id.* at 425.

be resolved on a class-wide basis, the court found that the prerequisite of commonality had not been established.[138] Moreover, the court emphasized that "the establishment of a retaliation claim by one plaintiff would not serve to establish any aspect of a retaliation claim brought by another plaintiff."[139] Because of this specific issue of proof, the court found typicality to be lacking as well.[140]

Similarly, in *Hohider v. United Parcel Serv., Inc.*, the district court found that the plaintiffs' allegations of retaliation lacked "sufficient evidentiary support to implicate commonality on a classwide basis."[141] Despite the plaintiffs' showing that several individuals had requested a reasonable accommodation from their employer, and suffered an arguably adverse employment action as a result, the court characterized this evidence as merely "peppered" anecdotes that were insufficiently suggestive of "a *company-wide* policy of retaliation."[142] The court went on to state: "there is little in common among the multiple allegations of retaliation beyond the bare assertion of a policy of retaliation."[143] Thus, because no common issues of fact or law were implicated, the court could not certify the plaintiffs' retaliation claim for class treatment.[144]

These cases highlight the inherent difficulties with presenting proof of class-wide retaliation. It is not enough for one class member to have engaged in statutorily protected conduct, or to have suffered a materially adverse employment action as a result; each class member must have. Given the highly individualized nature of this proof, most courts have declined to certify retaliation claims for class treatment.[145]

E. The Role of Damages in Class Certification

The Supreme Court has held that where there is no credible method as to how to award damages on a basis that may be applied the same way class-wide, without individual calculations, if liability is found, then class certification is inappropriate under Rule 23(b)(3). In *Comcast v. Behrend*, an antitrust case, the Supreme Court explained that class certification requires a single method by which damages can be measured for all class members.[146] The Court explained that the predominance requirement under Rule 23(b)(3)

---

138. *Id.*

139. *Id.*

140. *Id.*

141. 243 F.R.D. 147, 223 (W.D. Pa. 2007), *rev'd on other grounds*, 574 F.3d 169 (3d Cir. 2009).

142. *Id.* at 222.

143. *Id.*

144. *Id.*

145. Certain courts, however, have ignored the fact-intensive nature of this proof, and certified retaliation classes. *See, e.g.*, Holsey v. Armour & Co., 743 F.2d 199, 216–17 (4th Cir. 1984) ("We cannot accept Armour's contention that harassment and retaliation claims are not susceptible of class treatment because they are too individualized. The plaintiffs established a general practice of retaliation against employees who opposed discriminatory practices or exercised rights protected under Title VII, in violation of § 704(a)."); *Sellars*, 321 F.R.D. 578 (certifying a Rule 23(b)(3) class of female truck drivers under hostile work environment and retaliation theories).

146. 569 U.S. 27 (2013).

is not met where damages cannot be calculated on a class wide basis. "If anything, Rule 23(b)(3)'s predominance criterion is even more demanding than Rule 23(a). Rule 23(b)(3), as an adventuresome innovation, is designed for situations in which class action treatment is not as clearly called for."[147] "Without [an adequate] methodology, respondents cannot show Rule 23(b)(3) predominance: Questions of individual damage calculations will inevitably overwhelm questions common to the class."[148] The Court held that while the "[c]alculations need not be exact," "any model supporting a plaintiff's damages case must be consistent with its liability case . . . ."[149] Thus, the legal theory underlying the claim must be capable of being borne out through a damages study.

Several circuit courts have determined that demands for compensatory and punitive damages inevitably result in individualized inquiries that prevent class certification, although some courts will grant certification regardless of some variation regarding the proper amount of damages among class members, provided such questions are not so complicated that they overwhelm the factual and legal commonality of class members. In *Allison v. Citgo Petroleum Corp.*,[150] the Fifth Circuit held that, where the class action seeks damages that are not strictly incidental to injunctive relief, the issues of individual damages will predominate over common questions relating to liability as understood under both Rule 23(b)(2) and 23(b)(3).[151] The court held that "recovery of compensatory

---

147. *Id.* at 34 (citation and internal quotation marks omitted).

148. *Id.*

149. *Id.* at 35 (internal citation and quotation marks omitted).

150. 151 F.3d 402 (5th Cir. 1998).

151. *C.f. Comcast*, 569 U.S. at 34–35 (explaining that individual damage-related questions might destroy predominance). Several circuit courts have agreed that in the Title VII context the individualized nature of the damage claims for each member of the putative class necessarily predominate over common questions. *See* Berry v. Schulman, 807 F.3d 600 (4th Cir. 2015); *Reeb*, 435 F.3d 639; Coleman v. Gen. Motors Acceptance Corp., 296 F.3d 443 (6th Cir. 2002). A number of district courts have ruled on similar issues with varying results. Some cases have sided with *Allison* and found that individualized damages destroy commonality. *See, e.g.*, Dungan v. Acad. at Ivy Ridge, 249 F.R.D. 413 (N.D.N.Y. 2008) (denying class certification to plaintiffs asserting breach of contract and unjust enrichment claims against private boarding school for troubled teens because damages were not susceptible to common proof and were highly individualized); Clausnitzer v. Fed. Exp. Corp., 248 F.R.D. 647 (S.D. Fla. 2008) (presence of 50-variant statutory schemes to be applied to calculate damages weighed against finding that common issues predominate); *Burrell*, 197 F.R.D. 284 (denying certification under 23(b)(3) because the need for individualized damages determinations caused individual issues to predominate over common ones); Parks Auto. Grp., Inc. v. Gen. Motors Corp., 237 F.R.D. 567 (D.S.C. 2006) (holding that individualized damage issues precluded finding of commonality in suit brought by automobile dealerships against vehicle manufacturer); Dodge v. Cty. of Orange, 226 F.R.D. 177 (S.D.N.Y. 2005) (holding that individual issues regarding damages predominated over issues common to proposed class in action against county and sheriff brought by pretrial detainees who had been strip-searched upon arrival at county jail); Kase v. Salomon Smith Barney, Inc., 218 F.R.D. 149 (S.D. Tex. 2003) (issues of law and fact that named plaintiff asserts are common to the class are overshadowed by the existence of many individualized issues relating to both liability and damages); Faulk v. Home Oil Co., 184 F.R.D. 645 (M.D. Ala. 1999) (holding *Allison* controlling and refusing to certify a class action where plaintiffs requested compensatory and punitive damages); Woodell v. Procter & Gamble Mfg. Co., 1998 WL 686767 (N.D. Tex. Sept. 29, 1998) (following *Allison*, refusing to certify a class where plaintiff requested monetary and exemplary damages in product liability case); Marascalco v. Int'l Computerized Orthokeratology Soc'y, Inc., 181 F.R.D. 331 (N.D.

and punitive damages required particularly individualized proof of injury, including how each class member was personally affected by the discriminatory conduct."[152] The court explained:

> [M]onetary relief predominates in (b)(2) class actions unless it is incidental to requested injunctive or declaratory relief. . . . [T]he recovery of incidental damages should typically be concomitant with, not merely consequential to, class-wide injunctive or declaratory relief. Moreover, such damages should at least be capable of computation by means of objective standards[153] and not dependent in any significant way on the intangible, subjective differences of each class member's circumstances. Liability for incidental damages should not require additional hearings to resolve the disparate merits of each individual's case.[154]

Miss. 1998) (holding in contract case that because plaintiffs requested a large amount of compensatory damages, *Allison* precluded the case from proceeding as a class action); Saunders v. Bellsouth Adver. & Publ'g Corp., 1998 U.S. Dist. LEXIS 20523, at *4–5 (S.D. Fla. 1998) (denying class certification where plaintiffs sought compensatory and punitive damages); Pickett v. IBP, Inc., 182 F.R.D. 647, 657 (M.D. Ala. 1998) ("convinced that the Eleventh Circuit would also apply similar analysis," the district court followed *Allison* to deny class certification where compensatory and punitive damages were sought); Abrams v. Kelsy-Seybold Med. Grp., Inc., 178 F.R.D. 116, 134 (S.D. Tex. 1997) (in race discrimination case where the plaintiffs' claims involved different jobs, managers, and clinics, court held that "[b]ecause the predominant relief sought in this class is economic—compensatory damages, including back pay and future pay, and punitive damages—rather than injunctive and/or declaratory, certification under Rule 23(b)(2) is inappropriate"). Conversely, other cases reasoned that, where common questions of discrimination exist, individual issues as to damages do not predominate. *See, e.g.,* Cavin v. Home Loan Ctr., Inc., 236 F.R.D. 387 (N.D. Ill. 2006) (granting class certification in part in Fair Credit Reporting Act action because named plaintiffs sought only statutory damages and those putative class members seeking actual damages could opt out of class); Cicilline v. Jewel Food Stores, Inc., 542 F. Supp. 2d 831 (N.D. Ill. 2008) (certifying class in case alleging violations of Fair and Accurate Credit Transactions Act despite minor differences in damages among class members); Flanagan v. Allstate Ins. Co., 242 F.R.D. 421 (N.D. Ill. 2007) (noting individual assessments regarding causation and damages in breach of contract action did not prevent finding of commonality); Murray v. Cingular Wireless II, LLC, 242 F.R.D. 415 (N.D. Ill. 2005) (finding commonality element of Rule 23 satisfied despite potential for individualized damages because of one legal question common to class); Zeno v. Ford Motor Co., Inc., 238 F.R.D. 173 (W.D. Pa. 2006) (holding that while individualized inquiry may be required with respect to causation or with respect to damages, such did not preclude the court from certifying a class for the purpose of deciding the common issues underlying breach of contract claims); Orlowski v. Dominick's Finer Foods, Inc., 172 F.R.D. 370 (N.D. Ill. 1997) (in race discrimination suit, limiting district court's holding in *Allison* to cases where court finds that monetary damages are the principal relief sought).

152. *Allison*, 151 F.3d at 416.

153. Although some courts hold that where damages can simply be calculated by reference to a formula, class certification is not precluded, where "individual damages cannot be determined by reference to a mathematical or formulaic calculation, the damages issue may predominate over any common issues shared by the class." *Steering Comm.*, 461 F.3d at 602.

154. *Allison*, 151 F.3d at 415; *see also* Bell Atl. Corp. v. AT&T Corp., 339 F.3d 294, 308 (5th Cir. 2003) ("[C]lass certification is not appropriate" because plaintiffs "failed to demonstrate that the calculation of individualized actual economic damages, if any, suffered by the class members can be performed in accordance with the predominance requirement"); O'Sullivan v. Countrywide Home Loans, Inc., 319 F.3d 732, 745 (5th Cir. 2003) (holding that district court abused its discretion in certifying class "[i]n light of the individual calculation of damages that is required").

The court in *Allison* also refused to certify a "hybrid" class action or bifurcate the trial because, under either scenario, individual issues would ultimately predominate.[155]

Allison poses an even larger obstacle in harassment cases than in other types of discrimination cases. In cases involving termination, promotion, hiring, or compensation, the plaintiff either lost the job or was denied a benefit with a defined monetary value. Therefore, in those cases there are issues of reinstatement and equitable back pay that may be viable. That differs markedly from many harassment cases, in which the plaintiff was neither terminated nor denied monetary benefits, and the primary remedies sought are compensatory and punitive damages. Often in such cases, differences between class members' claims for damages preclude certification. For example, in *Adler v. Wallace Computer Services*, the court refused to certify a class of women alleging sex discrimination and harassment in the employer's sales force.[156] It held that the plaintiffs could not maintain a (b)(2) class because the compensatory and punitive damages required individualized proof.[157] The court explained:

> Even with a finding of class-wide discrimination, each plaintiff in the present case must, at the very least, show that she suffered an adverse consequence as a result of discrimination. . . . Wallace's pattern and practice of discrimination may be relevant in a particular case, but it does not establish that the company discriminated against each member of the putative class. Individual issues still exist in this case. . . . Additional plaintiff-specific issues could be raised with regard to the claim of hostile work environment sexual harassment, especially since that claim requires a showing that the employee perceived the environment to be abusive. The predominance problem here is compounded by the fact that the compensatory and punitive damages requested require individualized proof. Since so many issues in this case cannot be determined on a class-wide basis, the superior method of adjudicating these controversies is separate actions.[158]

The court rejected the plaintiffs' proposal for a hybrid class and denied the motion for class certification.[159]

Likewise, in *Armstrong v. Whirlpool Corporation*, the court found that a purported class of plaintiffs satisfied the Rule 23(a) prerequisites but nevertheless denied certification on the ground that the plaintiffs had failed to meet the standards required by (b)(2) or (b)(3).[160] Plaintiffs were a group of African-American employees at a single facility of the defendants and alleged "a gauntlet of racial discrimination, verbal abuse, racist graffiti and hostile treatment." Applying the Sixth Circuit's decision in

---

155. 151 F.3d at 418.

156. 202 F.R.D. 666 (N.D. Ga. 2001).

157. *Id.* at 670–71.

158. *Id.* at 672–73 (internal citations omitted).

159. *Id.* at 673–74.

160. 2007 WL 676694, at *8–14 (M.D. Tenn. Mar. 1, 2007).

Reeb, the court found that a (b)(2) class was inappropriate because the damages calculations were highly individualized and were less designed to "inure to the group" but rather amounted to individual compensatory damages.[161] Moreover, the court also determined that common issues did not predominate over differences between the claims of individual class members, and that the class action device was not superior to individualized adjudication, due the different allegations of harassment in different locations to which the defendant would raise different affirmative defenses.[162] These dissimilarities persuaded the court to deny plaintiffs' motion for certification.[163]

Although plaintiffs in some discrimination cases have sought to circumvent *Allison* by waiving their claims for compensatory and punitive damages, that is often infeasible in harassment cases because those are the primary relief sought.[164] Moreover, the waiver by a class representative of absent class members' damages claims in order to support class certification (and a larger award of attorneys' fees for class counsel) raises troubling issues of conflict of interest, adequacy of representation and superiority of the class mechanism, all of which militate against certification.

F. Tag-Along Harassment or Retaliation Claims

Although courts have occasionally certified classes that include sexual harassment claims, such courts have typically based the certification on the nonharassment claims.[165] Those courts seemed to view the harassment claims as no more than a buttress to the primary discrimination claims, rather than as a stand-alone cause of action.[166] In contrast, nearly all courts that have considered harassment claims separately for certification purposes have found that the harassment claims were inappropriate for class certification.[167]

---

161. *Id.* at *9–10.

162. *Id.* at *11–14.

163. *Id.*

164. This waiver of damages by the representative plaintiffs in order to try to achieve class representation itself raises serious conflict of interest and adequacy of representation issues. *See* Colindres v. QuitFlex Mfg., 235 F.R.D. 347, 375–76 (S.D. Tex. 2006) (noting that adequacy of representation requirement was not met insofar as waiver of compensatory damages might create conflict of interest between current and former employees).

165. *See, e.g., Martens*, 181 F.R.D. 243 (certifying class for discriminatory treatment including promotion and hiring claims, and only mentioning sexual harassment claims in passing, focusing instead on barriers to entry and glass ceiling facts).

166. *See, e.g., Meiresonne*, 124 F.R.D. at 624–25 (certifying class and noting that plaintiffs were not claiming damages for all class members for sexual harassment, but instead "they are alleging an atmosphere of sexual hostility that evidences discrimination").

167. *See, e.g., Marquis*, 206 F.R.D. 132 (holding that plaintiffs failed to demonstrate typicality because of "substantial differences" between the named plaintiffs and putative class members and among the named plaintiffs); *Unified Sch. Dist. No. 259*, 240 F.R.D. 673 (holding typicality requirement was not satisfied in suit against school district by female high school students alleging a pattern and practice of deliberate indifference to sexual harassment in violation of Title IX); *Zapata*, 167 F.R.D. 147 (holding that the subjective nature of sexual harassment analysis would require a series of individual trials and thus weighed

IV. OPPOSING CLASS CERTIFICATION IN HARASSMENT AND RETALIATION CASES

Plaintiffs advancing harassment or retaliation allegations on a class basis pin their hopes on *Jenson* and its progeny. Yet none of those cases has properly applied the Rule 23 requirements, as required by *General Telephone Company of the Southwest v. Falcon*, *Dukes v. Wal-Mart*, and *Comcast v. Behrend*, nor has any adhered to the harassment cause of action in *Harris/Meritor* and *Faragher/Ellerth* or the pattern or practice claim in *Teamsters*.

Employers are well-positioned to respond—unlike plaintiffs—based on precedent of the Supreme Court and courts of appeals. As described already in greater detail, defendants can challenge the proposed certification of harassment and retaliation class actions on the grounds that the plaintiffs' claims are individualized, not common to the class, and therefore fail the Rule 23(a) requirements of commonality and typicality under *Dukes v. Wal-Mart* and *Comcast v. Behrend*, and the Rule 23(b) requirements of predominance and superiority. Under *Harris* and *Meritor*, the harassment cause of action requires inherently individualized determinations of subjective questions such as whether each individual perceived the conduct as offensive and unwelcome, as well as objective questions such as whether the conduct directed at each putative class member was severe or pervasive and affected the terms of employment.[168] The *Faragher* affirmative defense also requires individualized inquiries into whether the alleged harasser is a supervisor, the steps taken by each putative class member to use the employer's internal remedies to put an end to harassing behavior, as well as the availability to that person of such remedies.[169] The employer should explore the differences in treatment of individual class members (and their involvement in and perception of the conduct), and variations in the availability and use of remedial procedures.

In most if not all harassment suits, the defendant will be able to show that the alleged harassment of each individual putative class member differed in severity, involved different acts and alleged harassers, and was perceived in different ways by the putative

---

against a finding of commonality); Int'l Union, United Auto., Aerospace, & Agic. Implement Workers of Am., AFL-CIO v. LTV Aerospace and Def. Co., 136 F.R.D. 113 (N.D. Tex. 1991); Hofman v. AT&T Techs., Inc., No. 84C 7893, 1986 WL 4100, at *3 (N.D. Ill. 1986) (noting that a "myriad" of differences in the circumstances of the plaintiffs' claims cast doubt on the existence of a common company policy of discrimination); *Keeton*, 106 F.R.D. 366 (holding that plaintiffs' claims required too much individualized proof to be treated as a class action).

168. Harris v. Forklift Sys., Inc., 510 U.S. 17, 21–22 (1993) ("Conduct that is not severe or pervasive enough to create an objectively hostile or abusive work environment—an environment that a reasonable person would find hostile or abusive—is beyond Title VII's purview. Likewise, if the victim does not subjectively perceive the environment to be abusive, the conduct has not actually altered the conditions of the victim's employment, and there is no Title VII violation."); Meritor Sav. Bank v. Vinson, 477 U.S. 57 (1986) ("For sexual harassment to be actionable, it must be sufficient severe or pervasive to alter the conditions of the victim's employment and create an abusive working environment," and noting that "the question whether particular conduct was indeed unwelcome presents problems of proof and turns largely on credibility determinations committed to the trier of fact") (internal citations and quotation marks omitted).

169. *Faragher*, 524 U.S. at 777–78.

class member. The employer will then be able to rely on a wealth of authority that such differences in factual circumstances cause individual issues to predominate, and render the case unsuitable for class treatment.[170]

Similarly, in retaliation cases, the defendant will be able to show that the putative class members did not engage in the same protected activities, that the putative adverse employment actions differed in scope, and in timing vis-à-vis the protected activities, and that different managers, teams, or offices were involved in the decision-making around the putative adverse employment action. The employer can rely on the strength of case law from around the country that has held that plaintiffs could not meet the commonality requirement needed for class certification for a retaliation claim, nor suffered the same adverse actions.

The employer also should examine whether the claims of the named plaintiffs harbor internal conflicts with the interests of the remainder of the class. Courts have precluded named plaintiffs from representing putative class members whose interests may differ from theirs.[171] For example, where supervisor knowledge of or response to harassment, or supervisory participation in or knowledge of retaliation, is an issue, a supervisor may not be an adequate representative of nonsupervisory putative class members (nor would the claims and defenses involving the supervisor be typical of

---

170. *See, e.g.,* Armstrong v. Whirlpool Corp., 2007 WL 676694, at *8–14 (holding that Rule 23(b)(3) certification was improper because of vastly different allegations of harassment in different employer facilities to which the court anticipated the defendant would raise different affirmative defenses); *Adler,* 202 F.R.D. 666 (holding that even assuming class-wide discrimination, significant individual issues foreclosed class certification); *Radmanovich,* 216 F.R.D. at 438 (holding that "individual issues of: (1) whether the work environment was subjectively hostile; (2) whether a supervisor or coworker exposed the class member to the hostile environment; (3) whether each particular class member suffered an adverse employment action; and (4) the particular class member's steps in taking advantage of possible preventative or corrective opportunities offered by [defendant] predominate over class issues with regard to the hostile work environment claims"); *Elkins,* 219 F.R.D. at 414 (claims of named plaintiffs and putative class members were not sufficiently similar to satisfy the typicality requirement); *Doe,* 240 F.R.D. 673 (holding typicality requirement was not satisfied in suit against school district by female high school students alleging a pattern and practice of deliberate indifference to sexual harassment in violation of Title IX); *Marquis,* 206 F.R.D. at 159–60 (holding that plaintiffs failed to demonstrate typicality because of "substantial differences" between the named plaintiffs and putative class members and among the named plaintiffs); *Zapata,* 167 F.R.D. at 163 (class action was not superior method for adjudicating either discrimination claim or hostile environment harassment claims; given right to attorney's fees to prevailing plaintiffs, attorneys will have incentive to bring suits for individuals and, further, "manageability problems exist with respect to calculating the compensatory damages plaintiffs claim. Courts have held that claims for compensatory damages unique to each individual greatly complicate management of a class.").

171. *See Levels,* 178 F.R.D. 171 (holding that harassment class would not be certified because the named plaintiffs allege only a hostile work environment, not adverse employment action, and as such they could not represent a class including victims of discrimination in hiring); *Elkins,* 219 F.R.D. 414 (claims of named plaintiffs and putative class members differed to such an extent that certification of class was not proper under Rule 23); Watkins v. Publix Super Mkt., Inc., 1996 U.S. Dist. LEXIS 13123 (M.D. Fla. 1996) (noting that plaintiff was an inadequate representative where she attempted to represent a promotion class while she had been promoted to a high-level position within the company); *see also Jenson,* 139 F.R.D. at 665–67 (plaintiffs, hourly employees, could not adequately represent the interests of salaried workers where they were "vigorous advocates of their claims as hourly employees").

the class).[172] Similarly, where the named plaintiffs were spurred to suit by an outside organization such as a union, with its own separate agenda, a conflict with the putative class may be found.

The employer also should explore the individual issues inherent in the damages sought by the plaintiff class, and question whether injunctive relief is appropriate or the prime focus of the putative class action.[173] In *Comcast*, the Supreme Court held that a methodology for calculation of damages that could not be applied class-wide was not sufficient to support certification.[174] A class cannot be certified using a damages model with "nearly endless" permutations of liabilities that do not account for said individualized defenses.[175] Where the bulk of the relief sought is compensatory or punitive damages, the magnitude of these damages detracts from the plaintiff's ability to show that injunctive relief is the primary focus of the suit. As explained already, the *Allison* court concluded that, where the putative class seeks compensatory or punitive damages that are not incidental to equitable relief, the issues of individual damages will predominate over common questions as understood under both Rules 23(b)(2) and 23(b)(3).

Certifying the case as a hybrid class action or bifurcating the trial would not solve the key problem identified in *Allison* or *Comcast*. The plaintiff in *Allison* also asked the court to certify the class as a "hybrid" class action whereby the compensatory and punitive damages would be certified under Rule 23(b)(3) and all other relief would be certified under Rule 23(b)(2).[176] The Fifth Circuit, citing *Jackson*, held that, even if the compensatory and punitive damages were certified under 23(b)(3), the issues pertaining to individual damages still would predominate, preventing certification of the class.[177] The court rejected the argument that bifurcating the trial into liability and damages phases would eliminate the problem, on the ground that it merely postpones, and would not avoid, decertification. The same problem the *Allison* court foresaw—the lack of efficiency or savings by use of the class mechanism—is not limited to the facts of that case. For example, in a sexual harassment class action, as long as the court correctly applies the subjective element of proof, inevitably every plaintiff will need a separate minitrial to prove her individual claim.[178] The same is true in a retaliation case. Thus,

---

172. *See, e.g., Watkins*, 1996 U.S. Dist. LEXIS 13123 (supervisor is not an appropriate representative of lower-level employees).

173. *See, e.g., Levels*, 178 F.R.D. at 180 (putative racial harassment class action primarily sought money damages; certification denied under 23(b)(2)); *contra Jenson*, 139 F.R.D. at 666 (failure to implement effective sexual harassment policies or procedures was a failure to act on "grounds" applicable to the class under 23(b)(2)); *Martens*, 181 F.R.D. 243 (common questions satisfied rule 23(b)(2) or 23(b)(3) where the challenges relied on issues such as an arbitration agreement and centralized failure to comply with Title VII).

174. *Comcast*, 569 U.S. at 36–38.

175. *Id.* at 38.

176. 151 F.3d at 418.

177. *Id.* at 419–20.

178. In *Jackson*, the Eleventh Circuit held in a discrimination case that, even where plaintiffs alleged a common pattern or practice of discrimination, "as a practical matter, the resolution of this overarching common issue breaks down into an unmanageable variety of individual legal and factual issues."

the hybrid class action or bifurcation is of little use in overcoming the predominance and manageability problems.

The class certification issues associated with harassment and retaliation allegations should not be forgotten in cases that include "tagalong" harassment or retaliation claims. In fact, those allegations give the employer additional ammunition to oppose certification of all types of claims in those cases. First, the individuals allegedly subject to harassment or retaliation are often fewer than or different from those allegedly subjected to other forms of discrimination such as lack of promotions or reduced compensation. Thus, the representative plaintiffs may encounter difficulty with the class definition, and with commonality and typicality, because some putative discrimination class members also have potential harassment or retaliation claims and others do not, and some putative harassment or retaliation class members also have potential discrimination claims and others do not.[179] Similarly, typicality issues may arise, because class representatives who have harassment claims may not be typical of those who lack them, and vice versa.[180] Manageability and superiority of the class action mechanism also present potential problems, because the differences between the elements of proof under the discrimination pattern or practice and adverse impact claims and the harassment and retaliation claims, and the different trial "phases" as defined by some courts, could prevent trying of the different claims together, even as subclasses. Similarly, trial of harassment and retaliation claims together with discrimination claims may unduly prejudice the employer by inserting inflammatory issues from each claim into the trial of the other.

Finally, in the event that a district court certifies a class in a harassment or retaliation case, the employer should request an appeal within ten days thereafter pursuant to Rule 23(f) of the FRCP. Such an appeal will stand a substantial chance of success, as no federal appellate court has yet approved a purely harassment or retaliation class action. Additionally, where a class has been certified, the employer has the opportunity to seek decertification of the class at a later time, such as when further progress in the case makes its unmanageability clear. A class certification order may be altered or amended at any time before final judgment.[181]

Jackson v. Motel 6 Multipurpose, Inc., 130 F.3d 999, 1006 (11th Cir. 1997). *See also Int'l Union*, 136 F.R.D. at 130 (where the claims of the named plaintiffs were factually unique, the court refused to certify a class as to plaintiffs' sexual harassment claims, stating that "[t]he complaints are too individualized, LTVAD's defenses to these varied claims are likely to be very fact-specific, and including these claims in the larger class action would cause the case to devolve into a series of individual trials"); *Keeton*, 106 F.R.D. at 372 (holding that named plaintiffs who made sexual harassment claims "peculiar to themselves" lack typicality and are unlikely to result in efficiency through the class action mechanism).

179. *See Levels*, 178 F.R.D. 171 (denying motion for class certification because putative class representatives alleged only hostile environment claims, but did not suffer any adverse employment action on the basis of race; therefore, named plaintiffs could not represent a class including those who were victims of discrimination in hiring).

180. *Id.*

181. FED. R. CIV. P. 23(c)(1)(C).

V. *MITSUBISHI*: THE EEOC REPRESENTATIVE ACTION ANOMALY

EEOC v. Mitsubishi Motor Manufacturing of America, Inc.[182] likely will be cited by every plaintiff seeking class certification of a harassment claim. However, a key distinction bears repeating—*Mitsubishi* was not a class action. The court expressly so held, noting that cases involving class action analysis were "uncontrolling," and further stated that the prerequisites of the FRCP that govern class actions did not apply to its analysis.[183] Instead, the court held that the case could proceed without a class certification under the EEOC's authority to prosecute in the public interest.[184] In *General Telephone Co. v. EEOC*, the Supreme Court held that the EEOC's statutory authority to bring actions to enforce federal law is separate from the Rule 23 framework and the EEOC need not meet the same commonality and typicality requirements as private plaintiffs.[185] Because *Mitsubishi* did not concern the Rule 23 standard, it cannot be cited as precedent in support of class certification under that rule.

A case of first impression, *Mitsubishi* simply held, without substantial analysis, that "Title VII authorizes a pattern or practice suit for sexual harassment."[186] The court then outlined a three-phase proof scheme for such cases, based on a combination of elements articulated by the Supreme Court in *International Brotherhood of Teamsters v. United States*[187] for pattern or practice discrimination (nonharassment) cases and elements of the sexual harassment cause of action set forth in *Harris* and *Meritor*.[188] Because of fundamental differences between the two paradigms, the court was unable to adhere fully to either.

Under the *Mitsubishi* proof scheme, in Phase I, the EEOC could prove "the existence of: (1) a hostile environment of sexual harassment within the company . . . or a situation where individuals within the workplace, as a whole, must accept a gender-hostile environment to enjoy the tangible benefits of their jobs . . . and (2) a company policy of tolerating (and therefore condoning and/or fostering) a workforce permeated with severe and pervasive sexual harassment."[189] Put simply, the court reasoned that "the landscape of the total work environment, rather than the subjective experiences of each individual claimant, is the focus for establishing a pattern or practice of unwelcome sexual harassment which is severe and pervasive."[190] If the "landscape" showed a pattern or practice of harassment, then in Phase II the individual claimants would enjoy a

---

182. 990 F. Supp. 1059 (C.D. Ill. 1998).

183. *Id.* at 1069 n.4.

184. *Id.* at 1070.

185. *Gen. Tel. Co*, 446 U.S. 318.

186. 990 F. Supp. at 1070.

187. 431 U.S. 324 (1977).

188. *Harris*, 510 U.S. 17; *Meritor*, 477 U.S. 57.

189. 990 F. Supp. at 1073.

190. *Id.* at 1074.

rebuttable presumption that they were subjected to sexual harassment.[191] In Phase III, the court would examine individual damages.[192]

The *Mitsubishi* court recognized that a showing of pattern or practice liability "does not give rise to any obvious presumptions with regard to individual liability for sexual harassment."[193] Nevertheless, it substituted a rebuttable presumption for the subjective prong of the long-established *prima facie* case for hostile environment sexual harassment.[194] Accordingly, the *Mitsubishi* court shifted the burden of production on the subjective prong to the defendant, forcing the defense to come forward with evidence that the alleged harassment was not unwelcome.[195] As to the issue of employer notice, Mitsubishi was not permitted to defend its practices during Phase I by showing individualized responses to employee complaints, but, rather, was required to show that it responded to the problem company wide. According to this analysis, the fact that the company may have responded to individual complaints it received on a case-by-case basis did not suffice to prove that it properly responded to the sexually harassing environment. In Phase II, the court again shifted the burden to the employer to prove that it was not on notice of harassment, requiring the plaintiff merely to "*assert* that the employer had notice and was negligent with regard to the harassment she suffered."[196]

In reaching these conclusions, the court departed from fundamental precepts of harassment law that the individual who is complaining must show that (1) he or she was personally subject to severe and pervasive harassment, (2) he or she personally found the conduct offensive and unwelcome, (3) he or she personally took reasonable measures to alert her employer as to the conduct, and (4) the employer did not respond adequately to the complaint. The court effectively eliminated the subjective elements of the harassment cause of action by shifting the burden of proof from the individual plaintiff—who has the evidence about his or her state of mind—to the defendant—who does not have that evidence but who nevertheless under the *Mitsubishi* scheme must overcome a presumption. The notice and response elements of the *Mitsubishi* scheme also depart substantially from the *Harris/Meritor* format and from the *Faragher* defense (although it should be mentioned that *Mitsubishi* antedates *Faragher*). Under *Mitsubishi*, the plaintiff is relieved of the obligation to prove that the employer had notice and was negligent. Moreover, by preventing the employer from relying on its reasonable and appropriate response to individual complaints in Phase I, the *Mitsubishi* court departed

---

191. *Id*. This phase would require the employer to produce evidence showing that some women were not subjectively offended by the pervasive environment, thus allowing the court to determine who belonged in the "affected class." *Id*. at 1079. Once the employer presented this proof, the affected class members carried the ultimate burden of proving that they were subjectively affected. For all other individuals, a finding of liability would be automatic.

192. *Id*. at 1082.

193. *Id*. at 1078.

194. *Id*. at 1078–79.

195. *Id*. at 1079.

196. *Id*. at 1080 (emphasis added).

entirely from the terms of *Harris, Meritor,* and *Faragher*—all of which incorporate the employer's ability to rely on such individual responses.

While failing to follow the harassment burdens of proof, the *Mitsubishi* court also departed substantially from the pattern and practice method of proof approved by appellate courts in nonharassment discrimination cases. Generally, plaintiffs, or the EEOC, make this showing with a combination of (1) statistics demonstrating widespread disparities in treatment of a protected class and (2) anecdotal evidence of discriminatory animus that ties the disparities to discrimination.[197] In contrast, the *Mitsubishi* court found a pattern or practice of discrimination without any quantitative, statistical evidence showing a company-wide practice—the court essentially accepted purely anecdotal evidence as the basis for the alleged "pattern and practice" of harassment without any quantitative evidence of the pervasiveness of the harassment. In contrast, numerous courts have rejected class claims of discrimination where they were not supported by statistics.[198] In *Dukes v. Wal-Mart,* the Supreme Court found that anecdotes of discrimination cannot support class certification in the absence of statistics that are not properly disaggregated if the anecdotes do not represent a large proportion of the workforce.[199] Thus, *Mitsubishi*'s analysis is contrary to the established proof standard for both harassment and pattern and practice discrimination cases.

The *Mitsubishi* approach has been applied in several EEOC enforcement cases, although some courts have modified or partially rejected it.[200] For example, in *EEOC v. Dial Corporation,* the district court added a Phase IV in which the court apportions any punitive damages "guided" by the verdicts in Phases II and III.[201] The court had applied the *Mitsubishi* model in other respects in an earlier opinion.[202] The US District Court

---

197. *See, e.g.,* Sperling v. Hoffman-La Rouche, Inc., 924 F. Supp. 1346, 1379 (D.N.J. 1996) ("In order to prove a pattern or practice of discrimination, plaintiffs generally must demonstrate widespread differences in treatment (usually through statistical evidence) and must also produce sufficient evidence of intentional discrimination (usually, but not always, through testimony regarding intentional discrimination against individual members of the class)."); Graffam v. Scott Paper Co., 870 F. Supp. 389 (D. Me. 1994) (holding that company-wide statistics were relevant, but finding for the employer because none of the 11 plaintiffs proved their individual cases), *aff'd,* 60 F.3d 809 (1st Cir. 1995).

198. *See, e.g.,* Stambaugh v. Kan. Dep't of Corr., 151 F.R.D. 664, 676 (D. Kan. 1993) (class certification denied on sex discrimination/harassment claims of law enforcement officers because, among other reasons, plaintiffs offered anecdotal rather than statistical evidence: "Without statistics or at least anecdotal evidence from a statistically significant group, the court is left to assume" the existence of discrimination; such assumptions "cannot substitute for the rigorous analysis required by Rule 23"); *see* Gonzales v. Brady, 136 F.R.D. 329, 331 (D.D.C. 1991) ("Statistics generally are offered at the certification stage of litigation to show that a class-wide problem exists.").

199. *Wal-Mart,* 564 U.S. at 358, n. 9 ("A discrimination claimant is free to supply as few anecdotes as he wishes. But when the claim is that a company operates under a general policy of discrimination, a few anecdotes selected from literally millions of employment decisions prove nothing at all.").

200. *See, e.g.,* EEOC v. Burlington Med. Supplies, Inc., 536 F. Supp. 2d 647 (E.D. Va. 2008); EEOC v. Dial Corp., 259 F. Supp. 2d 710, 715 (N.D. Ill. 2003); EEOC v. Foster Wheeler Constructors, Inc., 1999 WL 528200 (N.D. Ill. 1999).

201. *Dial Corp.,* 259 F. Supp. 2d at 715.

202. EEOC v. Dial Corp., 156 F. Supp. 2d 926, 947 (N.D. Ill. 2001). The *Dial* court applied the *Mitsubishi* framework. *Id.* at 958.

for the Eastern District of Virginia "applied" the framework in *EEOC v. Burlington Medical Supplies, Inc.*, finding the approach "persuasive and consistent with Title VII" before *Wal-Mart v. Dukes*.[203] The district court began with the observation that EEOC enforcement actions brought pursuant to §707 of Title VII need not conform to Rule 23.[204] The *Burlington* court outlined the following order of proof:

> In Phase I, the EEOC must demonstrate harassment that is (1) based on sex; (2) sufficiently severe or pervasive to alter the terms or conditions of a reasonable person's employment and to create an abusive work environment; (3) unwelcome from the standpoint of a reasonable woman; and (4) imputable on some factual basis to the employer. . . . Demonstrating a pattern or practice of sexual harassment in this manner may entitle the EEOC to appropriate declaratory and injunctive relief authorized by Title VII. . . . In Phase II, the burden of production shifts to *Burlington* to demonstrate a former employee seeking individual relief welcomed the sexually harassing conduct. . . . To recover damages for an individual, however, the EEOC must carry the ultimate burden of proving that the sexual harassment was unwelcome to the individual for whom relief is sought and that the individual subjectively found the harassment so severe or pervasive as to alter her employment and create an abusive work environment.[205]

The *Burlington* court found the *Mitsubishi* "burden-shifting approach persuasive and consistent with Title VII," and so shifted the burden of production to the defendant to come forward with evidence that the alleged harassment was not unwelcome.[206] However, the court departed from *Mitsubishi* by placing the ultimate burden of proof on the plaintiffs, affirming that in Phase II the EEOC must prove for each individual plaintiff that sexual harassment was unwelcome and that each plaintiff found the harassment so severe as to amount to actionable harassment.[207]

In the final analysis, the combination method of proof in *Mitsubishi* and its progeny honors neither the harassment law nor the pattern or practice method of proof on which it purports to rely. For no apparent reason other than the convenience of proof for plaintiffs, it largely eliminates the harassment law elements involving the state of mind of individual plaintiffs, as well as the *Faragher* notice–response defense. Similarly, while it purports to incorporate the *Teamsters* requirement of proof of an overarching policy of discrimination, it eliminates the requirement of an actual discriminatory policy or quantitative proof of a pattern of discrimination, accepting instead mere anecdotal evidence that is regularly rejected without statistics in discrimination cases under

---

203. *Burlington Med. Supplies*, 536 F. Supp. 2d at 658.

204. *Id.* at 655.

205. *Id.* at 658 (internal citations omitted).

206. *Id.* The court noted that "in the absence of an employer's individual defense, one can presume from an objective pattern or practice finding that the working environment, as a whole, is hostile, and that most women would also find such an environment subjectively hostile." *Id.* (internal quotations omitted).

207. *Id.*

Teamsters. No appellate court has approved this method of proof. In fact, no court has yet found an effective method of resolving the individualized harassment issues on a mass basis.

VI. PRECERTIFICATION NUTS AND BOLTS: DISCOVERY AND SUMMARY JUDGMENT

Because a favorable decision on class certification reduces a defendant's exposure considerably, the defense to class certification is a major focus of pretrial activity. Key issues for the defense on which evidence must be found are (1) the individuality of the named plaintiffs' and class members' allegations, and reactions to and involvement in the challenged conduct; (2) the defendant's efforts to investigate and resolve complaints of harassment or retaliation, or at least the uneven failure to do so; (3) differences in the plaintiffs' and class members' use of complaint procedures; and (4) limiting the allegations of harassment or retaliation to "pockets" within the company, such that the experience of putative class members outside of them is inconsistent with that of the named plaintiffs.

A. Discovery

The defendant's precertification discovery plan should focus on preparing for and taking thorough depositions of all named plaintiffs and a sampling of putative class members.[208] Although taken at the precertification stage—and intended to garner information necessary for challenging certification—the depositions will cover many of the same topics explored with the plaintiff in a single-plaintiff harassment or retaliation lawsuit. Thus, the employer should seek to exhaust the plaintiff's knowledge and recollection of each alleged act of harassment or retaliation; the plaintiff's response to each act; the impact each act had on job performance, working conditions, and psychological well-being; the employer's nonharassment or nonretaliatory explanation for any adverse action; the extent if any of the alleged harasser's supervisory responsibilities; the steps the plaintiff took to communicate the unwelcome nature of the conduct to the employer; the plaintiff's attempts to report the conduct to higher levels at the company; and the steps the company took to investigate and remedy any alleged harassment.

Obtaining such detailed testimony serves three major purposes. First, it will reveal details that create the basis for the employer's arguments that each plaintiff tells a unique story and brings unique claims. This testimony will probably include different alleged

---

208. As with the deposition in any other sexual harassment case, the deposition notices for the named plaintiffs should include a document production demand requesting production of all documents germane to the plaintiff's contentions and damages. At a minimum, the document demand should (1) track the language of the complaint, requesting all documents in plaintiff's possession, custody, or control that support each allegation in the complaint; (2) seek all documents given to or received from any governmental agency; (3) seek documentation of any treatment the plaintiff received for emotional distress; and (4) seek documents in the plaintiff's possession, custody, or control that relate to other employees' claims of sexual harassment.

harassers, different types of harassment or allegations of retaliation, different times and locations of harassment, different reactions to or involvement in the challenged conduct by the plaintiff, different supervisors or nonsupervisors, and different reactions by the company to reports of harassment. It will enable the employer to argue at class certification that the claims of the named plaintiffs are not common to each other—much less "typical of" or "common to" the claims of others in the purported class.

Second, by locking down the testimony of each named plaintiff, the employer will be able to evaluate its prospects for summary judgment on the named plaintiffs' individual claims. For example, the employer may be able to establish that the conduct alleged by a particular named plaintiff is not "severe and pervasive," and, therefore, cannot constitute a legally cognizable claim of hostile-environment harassment. Likewise, the employer may be able to prove that the alleged adverse action on which a plaintiff's retaliation claim rests is not sufficiently adverse to support a claim. Similarly, the employer may establish that the plaintiff knew of the company's procedures for reporting harassment and refused to avail herself of them, resulting in the possibility of summary judgment under the Supreme Court's decisions in *Faragher* and *Ellerth*.

To the inevitable argument that broad discovery and motions for summary judgment are premature at the certification stage, the answer is simple. Broad discovery uncovers differences between class members' claims, which bear obvious relevance to class certification. The Supreme Court affirmed in *Wal-Mart* that the class certification inquiry overlaps with the merits.[209] Dispositive motions also can play a decisive role in answering the threshold question in the certification inquiry, by determining each named plaintiff's standing to sue.[210] Thus, a defendant should consider a motion for summary judgment (or partial summary judgment), to focus the court on cognizable claims in analyzing whether a class will be certified (and, if so, in analyzing the appropriate scope and composition of such a class).

Third, as with any sexual harassment or retaliation plaintiff, locking down the plaintiff's testimony early in the case serves to prevent the plaintiff from adding to or fabricating new types of harassment or retaliation as the lawsuit progresses and the plaintiff becomes more familiar with the claims of co-plaintiffs and others.

In addition to examining the plaintiff as to the substance of his or her underlying claims, the employer also should cover a number of issues that relate directly to class certification and to the dynamics of the lawsuit. The employer should ask whether the named plaintiff understands his or her role as a class representative and what that role entails. What does the plaintiff know about the claims of co-plaintiffs? A class representative is expected to become familiar with the claims of those he or she purports to represent. If

---

209. *Wal-Mart*, 564 U.S. at 352 ("[P]roof of commonality necessarily overlaps with respondents' merits contention that Wal-Mart engages in a *pattern or practice* of discrimination . . . Here respondents wish to sue about literally millions of employment decisions at once. Without some glue holding the alleged *reasons* for all those decisions together, it will be impossible to say that examination of all the class members' claims for relief will produce a common answer to the crucial question *why was I disfavored*.") (internal citation omitted).

210. *See supra* §I (discussion of constitutional standing to sue).

the named plaintiff has failed to become familiar with the claims of co-named plaintiffs, the employer may argue that the named plaintiff has abandoned or neglected his or her role and therefore must not be allowed to serve as a representative. What does the plaintiff know about the claims of nonnamed plaintiffs? If the plaintiff knows nothing about such claims, it strengthens the employer's argument that the employee cannot be allowed to serve as a class representative. If, on the other hand, the employee provides testimony regarding the claims of others, that testimony will give the employer a road map for investigating those claims during the early discovery phase of the lawsuit.

The employer also should explore the dynamics of the named plaintiff's involvement in the lawsuit. How did the plaintiff get involved? Did he or she contact lawyers or did they contact the plaintiff? What prompted that contact? Are other entities (such as unions or political action organizations) involved in or overseeing the named plaintiffs' participation in the lawsuit? Any such outside influences raise potential conflicts of interests.[211]

If plaintiffs seek certification of a class that involves more than one work unit or facility, the employer should establish the named plaintiff's lack of knowledge regarding much of what occurred in facilities or work units other than his or her own. Therefore, the employer should seek to have each named plaintiff admit that he or she personally knows no employees other than those in his or her work unit (or, alternatively, establish a list of such employees). Similarly, the employer will seek to establish that plaintiff rarely, if ever, set foot in any facility other than the facility or facilities where he or she physically worked. To the extent that the plaintiffs' theory of class certification is grounded upon a company-wide failure to police the workplace, the employer will want to establish the plaintiff's lack of knowledge of the names, qualifications, and harassment-related actions of human resources officials other than those at the plaintiff's facility.

Finally, the employer should ask the named plaintiff to admit that he or she is seeking monetary damages, and then obtain a detailed description of those damages and the basis for them. Such admissions will be important to establish the individualized nature of the requested monetary relief.

After all named plaintiffs' depositions have been completed, the employer should propound interrogatories requesting detailed information regarding the names, job titles, and nature of claims of any purported class members who are known to plaintiffs or to their attorneys. The interrogatories also should seek a detailed description of damages claimed in the lawsuit and the basis for claiming them.

The employer also should request all declarations obtained by plaintiffs or their counsel to support the lawsuit and all documents in plaintiffs' possession that relate to the individuals identified as potential claimants or fact witnesses during the named plaintiff depositions. In this way, the "universe" of potential allegations against the employer can be determined. In addition, all, or a representative sample of, declarants should be deposed on the same issues as the named plaintiffs. This will help not only to show the lack of commonality but also may demonstrate that the allegations in the declarations are overblown.

---

211. *See supra* § II.B.3.

CHAPTER 10

Discovery and Deposing the Plaintiff and Plaintiff's Witnesses: Defense Perspective

Sandra R. McCandless

I. THE OVERRIDING SIGNIFICANCE OF THE PLAINTIFF'S DEPOSITION

The most crucial pretrial event in the defense of a workplace harassment case is the plaintiff's deposition. How successful the plaintiff's deposition is for the defense determines whether the case will settle and the range of settlement value. If the case will be tried, the deposition is the single most important factor in the preparation for the cross-examination of the plaintiff. Workplace harassment cases are highly fact-specific, and the plaintiff and defense pre-lawsuit versions of the facts are typically very different. The outcome of the workplace harassment case hinges on how well defense counsel prepares for and takes the plaintiff's deposition and how much persistence defense counsel has in limiting the plaintiff's claims and obtaining admissions in the deposition process.

In other types of lawsuits it is sometimes possible to take a narrow deposition focusing on a few specific events in the knowledge of a particular witness. In an employment case—and in a workplace harassment case in particular—the successful plaintiff's deposition may cover the details of the plaintiff's entire life in the relevant time period. Plaintiff's counsel will try to narrow the plaintiff's deposition to the events to which the plaintiff and the alleged harasser were parties. The successful deposition for the defense will elicit in detail the other events, both work-related and personal, that may have contributed to any emotional distress the plaintiff claims.

No matter how well prepared for the rigors of deposition by plaintiff's counsel, the workplace harassment plaintiff typically arrives for deposition eager for the chance to finally tell the story of offending conduct at work but somewhat unprepared for the unpleasantness of the process. A well-prepared and thorough plaintiff's deposition allows the plaintiff to truly understand for the first time the stamina needed to take the case through to trial. Sitting at trial as the plaintiff in a workplace harassment case is not for the faint of heart. Often it is only the firsthand experience of sitting through extensive deposition questioning by experienced defense counsel that convinces the plaintiff to become more realistic about case value and the vagaries of a jury trial.

Defense counsel should take the deposition of the plaintiff in a workplace harassment case as seriously as a trial. Nothing drives up the cost of a defense case more than a plaintiff's deposition that maximizes, rather than limits, what the plaintiff is actually claiming in the particular case..

II. PREPARATION FOR THE PLAINTIFF'S DEPOSITION

A. Obtain All Relevant Documents and Electronic Information

The plaintiff's deposition testimony is carefully coached by plaintiff's counsel. Interrogatory responses are written by plaintiff's counsel from a one-sided point of view. The memories of witnesses are often faulty. Therefore, documents recording events contemporaneously as they occurred are often the best source of information to the defense in preparing for the plaintiff's deposition. Defense counsel should use all available means to obtain as much of the documentation relevant to the case as possible before the plaintiff's deposition begins. This can include formal methods, such as requests to produce and subpoenas, and various informal methods. The defense must review the relevant documents before the deposition. If certain highly relevant documents are not available on the first day of deposition, there should be additional time during which the plaintiff may be examined about the contents of subsequently uncovered documents.

Documents can be obtained from numerous sources that obviously vary from case to case. However, as a rule of thumb, defense counsel should seek documents from the company and the accused supervisor or co-worker, from the plaintiff, from administrative agencies with which the plaintiff filed charges, from prior and subsequent employers, from other court cases or administrative claims to which the plaintiff has been a party, and from the plaintiff's doctors.

1. Client Documents and Electronically Stored Information

Defense counsel should begin to collect and review the client company's documents and electronically stored information when the client first notifies the attorney of a potential claim. These include the personnel files of the plaintiff and the accused, personnel handbooks and any memoranda containing policies, the investigative file, complaint files involving other employees, the medical and/or workers' compensation files maintained by the company on the employee, and emails and other correspondence (electronic or otherwise) written or received by the plaintiff during the course of his or her work. Defense counsel should also obtain records, such as time cards, security records, computer use logs, and attendance logs, which could disprove plaintiff's claims that others were present as witnesses or some other aspect of the plaintiff's claims. Often, the client will not immediately provide defense counsel with all documentation relevant to the defense, either because of a misunderstanding about what is needed, a reluctance to divulge its internal affairs, or a desire to avoid spending time gathering the information requested. Defense counsel may need to make several requests before the documentation and electronic information provided by the client is as complete as possible.

The means of obtaining relevant documents and electronic information from the accused supervisor or co-worker will depend on whether defense counsel jointly represents the accused along with the company or the accused has separate counsel.[1] If the accused has not been sued personally or if there is joint representation, defense counsel should request that the accused turn over all relevant information in his or her possession when the initial request to the company is made. As in the case of the company, it may take several requests to obtain complete disclosure. If the accused has his or her own counsel, the request for information from the accused should be made through that individual's counsel early in the case.

The prevalence of electronic communication and data storage in the workplace has placed an entirely new gloss on the retrieval of evidence from the client and client-friendly witnesses. In the early days of workplace harassment lawsuits, the documents generated by parties and witnesses consisted of company documents, diaries, and calendars. Defense counsel must now cast a very wide net for electronically stored information as well as paper documents and deal with numerous corresponding e-discovery issues, including the use of an experienced e-discovery provider.

The communication by employees using text and instant messaging presents yet another source of potentially relevant information for the workplace harassment suit. The tone and content of text and instant messaging conversations resemble the tone and content of telephone conversations; they are often informal and much less guarded than other forms of written communication. However, unlike telephone conversations, some or all of the contents of these types of communications may be retrievable. Thus, a thorough information review necessarily entails a search of the means of communication used by the particular employer and its employees, such as a search for relevant text and instant messages in addition to email messages.

In the modern workplace, electronically stored information is rarely irretrievably destroyed. Businesses typically back up data—though retrieving such data can be prohibitively expensive. Similarly, even deleted data without backup can often be recovered—again at considerable cost. Because of these potential costs and the independent legal obligation to do so, defense counsel should instruct the client and employees of the client with information about the plaintiff and his or her claims to preserve that information as soon as the client notifies the attorney of a potential claim.

Defense counsel should also be well aware that electronic documents often contain information not included when those communications are printed. Metadata, which are attached to most common electronic documents, may include information such as the document's creation date, edit dates, and access dates, as well as the names of users who created, edited, and viewed the document. Printed "hard copies" of electronic documents generally will not contain this metadata information, nor will documents that have been converted to an electronic file format different from their original format.

---

1. *See* Chapter 6.

If the metadata might be helpful, counsel should request electronic documents written by or to an employee in their original electronic format.[2]

The employer's review of employee-generated electronic communications and use of such communications in a workplace lawsuit may sometimes result in an employee claim of a violation of his or her privacy rights. The employer should of course maintain a policy that the information contained on the company's electronic communication systems belongs to the employer and may be searched at the employer's discretion to forestall and/or to provide a defense to any such claim. However, even absent such a policy, courts have found no reasonable expectation of privacy in employee email communications.[3]

2. Plaintiff's Documents

The defense should request documents and information from the plaintiff as early in the case as the applicable rules allow. Nothing wastes more time during a deposition than having counsel thumbing or paging through previously unseen documents and/or electronic information. The plaintiff's own documents and information should be received well in advance of the deposition and thoroughly reviewed for lines of questioning, possible admissions, identification of other witnesses, and a variety of other purposes.

The request for plaintiff's documents and electronic information should be very broad. Among the items that should be included are the following:

- All documents and electronic information that support each and every specific allegation of the complaint
- Documents and electronic information received or generated by the plaintiff in the course of and/or related to his or her employment
- All company personnel documents in the possession of the plaintiff
- All diaries maintained by the plaintiff during the relevant time period
- All postings to the internet written by the plaintiff during the relevant time period in any way related to his or her employment, including but not limited to postings on blogs, social networking sites, or other public or private websites
- All writings or electronic communications between the plaintiff and any other employee of the company
- All documents or statements submitted by the plaintiff to any administrative agency
- All printouts of emails, text messages, instant messaging conversations, cell phone photos, and transcriptions of voice mails in any way related to employment and in the plaintiff's possession or control
- All documents in the plaintiff's possession relating to visits to or treatment by the plaintiff's doctors in the relevant time period

---

2. For an overview of metadata, *see* MICHAEL OVERLY, OVERLY ON ELECTRONIC EVIDENCE IN CALIFORNIA § 2:8 (2007).

3. *See, e.g.,* Smyth v. Pillsbury Co., 914 F. Supp. 97, 101 (E.D. Pa. 1996); McLaren, Jr. v. Microsoft Corp., No. 05-97-00824-CV, 1999 WL 339015, at *5 (Tex. App. May 28, 1999).

- All documents related to the plaintiff's educational history and work history with other employers, including résumés and performance appraisals
- All documents relevant to damage claims, such as documents related to attempts to obtain other employment

Since plaintiff's counsel is likely to object strenuously to a defense attempt to obtain documents and information covering the plaintiff's entire life, defense counsel should limit the requests for certain types of information to specified time periods. For example, the request for plaintiff's records of medical visits could be limited to a period two to three years before the inception of employment with the company or the onset of alleged harassment.

The use of technology by employees has exponentially increased the number of potentially relevant plaintiff's documents, including emails, cell phone photos, text messages, instant messaging conversations, and internet postings, whether the information has been printed out or remains only in electronic storage form, than was the case at the time when sexual harassment cases first became prevalent. Much of this information may reside on the plaintiff's personal computer or cell phone. Counsel should send the plaintiff a preservation notice and consider seeking a preservation order to prevent the plaintiff from deleting discoverable information. In certain cases defense counsel may consider seeking court permission to examine the plaintiff's computer and cell phone rather than trusting the plaintiff to locate and produce all the relevant information.

The plaintiff may have posted relevant information on public and private websites such as blogs or social networking sites like Facebook and MySpace. Defense counsel should run an internet search of the plaintiff's name to locate postings. However, because information posted on nonpublic websites will not be accessible to defense counsel, counsel should request copies of internet postings, public and private, written during the relevant time period. Additionally, because internet posts attributed to a writer may have been written by another party, defense counsel should be prepared for the possibility that the plaintiff will deny the authenticity of the posting in deposition.

3. Administrative Agency Files

The workplace harassment plaintiff has almost always filed a charge with a local or federal administrative agency, since doing so is generally a procedural prerequisite to filing a lawsuit. Defense counsel should obtain copies of all documents contained in the investigative file of any administrative agencies with which the plaintiff has had contact. The employer defendant in a workplace harassment lawsuit may obtain a copy of the U.S. Equal Employment Opportunity Commission file as a matter of right, and state administrative agencies generally provide the same right. If counsel is unclear as to how to obtain the file of a particular agency, a simple telephone call to the agency will elicit the procedure for obtaining the investigation file. Deferral jurisdictions permit a plaintiff to cross-file a charge with more than one agency. Defense counsel should obtain the investigative files of all agencies where a charge was filed by the plaintiff.

Documents obtained from agency files are often helpful because they provide the defense with immediate information that may differ in material respects from the plaintiff's court complaint and/or any supplementary information. For example, the plaintiff may have told the administrative agency the identity of potential witnesses with information as to expected testimony. This information may not otherwise be available before the deposition. The plaintiff's administrative complaint may be more limited than the allegations he or she is making in court. As part of the strategy for determining how to narrow the plaintiff's allegations in a deposition, it is helpful to review any variations between earlier allegations in other proceedings and the allegations of the court complaint.

4. Prior and Subsequent Employers

The case at hand is sometimes the plaintiff's first claim of unfair and harassing treatment by an employer. In other cases, however, the plaintiff's work history at the client company bears critical similarity to his or her work history at one or more other employers. The plaintiff may even have filed other claims against prior employers. Where the defense asserts that no workplace harassment occurred and that plaintiff responded to work-related problems with a supervisor or co-workers by claiming harassment, a pattern of similar claims in prior employment may be helpful to the defense.

Defense counsel should subpoena documents related to plaintiff's employment with other employers as early as possible in the case. Typically, the defense obtains only the personnel files of the most recent employers. Older personnel files have often been destroyed, and seldom has another employer maintained any information on the plaintiff other than his or her personnel file. Although electronically stored information is rarely irretrievably destroyed, the cost of recovering the information may be prohibitive.

Even where only limited documentation is obtained, however, the files of other employers often provide fertile ground for questioning by the defense. A workplace harassment plaintiff typically claims an absence of prior or subsequent problems with other employers. A personnel record from another employer to the contrary will make it impossible for the plaintiff to make such a claim. Ideally, the defense will ask the plaintiff about other employment and elicit a denial of any problems. If defense counsel has obtained records that show a contrary story, those records may then be used to impeach the plaintiff in further deposition or at trial.

5. Other Court Cases and Administrative Claims

In addition to issuing subpoenas for employment records from prior and subsequent employers, the thorough defense lawyer will search court records and administrative filings for other disputes involving the plaintiff. These filings are not limited to employment claims. Often, divorce or other public litigation records provide a fertile ground for information on the plaintiff.

6. Plaintiff's Doctors

The identity of one or more of the plaintiff's doctors may be available in the initial stage of a lawsuit from company workers' compensation files and/or from medical notes or certifications received in the course of the plaintiff's employment. Subsequently, interrogatory responses and/or the early hours of the plaintiff's deposition will clarify and confirm the identities of the plaintiff's medical providers and what treatment was provided. As soon as this information is known, the defense should subpoena plaintiff's medical providers for any and all documents in the medical provider's possession regarding the plaintiff.

The request for medical records on the plaintiff is one area in which plaintiffs' counsel typically attempts to limit the information obtained by the defense. Defense counsel should anticipate an attempt by plaintiff's counsel to prohibit the production of this information and/or to limit the information provided. Since a claim for emotional distress damages should allow the defense access to the records showing the stressors to which the plaintiff was subjected, the defense should continue in its necessary effort to obtain these relevant records.

Like any documentation prepared contemporaneously with events, plaintiff's medical records may contain helpful admissions not available to the defense from other sources. Consider a scenario in which a plaintiff claims that harassment by two supervisors was witnessed by a third supervisor who was supportive of her claims. Other witnesses believe that the third supervisor is biased because he was having an affair with the plaintiff. The plaintiff initially vigorously denies the affair. However, when subsequently faced with the notes of her psychiatrist recording her recollection of the affair, she may be forced to admit on the record that she had lied earlier in the deposition.

B. Use Interrogatories to Obtain "Hard" Information

Early interrogatories designed to elicit the nuances of a plaintiff's case, such as the contents of significant conversations, are a mistake in an employment case. The plaintiff's deposition, not interrogatory responses prepared by plaintiff's counsel, is the mechanism to narrow and limit the plaintiff's case.

Propounding a set of interrogatories seeking "hard" data before the plaintiff's deposition is, however, a necessary tool to enable the defense to prepare adequately for the deposition. Such a set of interrogatories can provide information as to potential witnesses whom the plaintiff claims support her case, identify the plaintiff's prior employers and medical providers, identify the plaintiff's job search efforts, and provide initial information as to damages claimed. An initial interrogatory should simply set the stage for information to be acquired in detail in the plaintiff's deposition.

Rule 26(a)(1) of the Federal Rules of Civil Procedure requires the plaintiff to provide to the defense the name, address, and telephone number of individuals likely to have discoverable information—along with the subjects of that information—that the disclosing party may use to support its claims or defenses, unless solely for impeachment. The plaintiff must also provide a copy or description by category and location of all documents, electronically stored information, and tangible items in the plaintiff's possession as well as a computation of relevant damages. Some state courts, such as California, use "form" interrogatories to enable the parties to ascertain certain information as a matter of right early in a case. The use of interrogatories in a given jurisdiction, whether state or federal, will require detailed knowledge of the rules and procedures of that jurisdiction and any limits on the information obtainable.

Later in the case counsel may wish to propound "contention" interrogatories that require plaintiff's counsel to restate plaintiff's claims as refined by intervening discovery or requests for admissions on essential points that are not yet clearly admitted on the record. However, counsel should be careful in the postdeposition discovery process not to expand a case that has already been successfully limited by plaintiff's deposition admissions.

C. Interview Critical Fact Witnesses

By the time defense counsel asks the court reporter to swear the witness, defense counsel should have a detailed understanding of the relevant events in the plaintiff's work history. Such an understanding requires interviews and, where necessary, re-interviews of as many witnesses and potential witnesses to the critical events as predeposition time and company resources will allow. Interviews should not be limited to the most important players in the drama, such as the accused and the individual who conducted the internal investigation. Defense counsel should also interview co-workers and outside parties who may have observed alleged events, had relevant discussions (in person or electronically) with the plaintiff, or had experiences of their own that may be important to the case.

It is important to conduct these interviews in a manner that does not detract from the defense theory of the case. This does not mean that the defense should be putting words into the mouths of witnesses or asking them to slant their view of events. But interviews should be conducted in a manner that encourages the witnesses to be forthcoming and cooperative. The hostile or overly "cold" defense interviewer will not only fail to get the information needed from the witness but may also create reluctance in a witness who would otherwise be supportive of the defense.

In the process of interviewing witnesses, defense counsel should also "view the scene." Counsel should visit the work areas in which relevant events allegedly occurred to look for helpful information. For example, the plaintiff may claim inappropriate comments were made in her desk area but that no one else ever heard any such comments. If her desk area was in close proximity to that of numerous other employees who were within earshot, defense counsel's site visit may be helpful to case preparation.

III. THE PLAINTIFF'S DEPOSITION

A. Preparation and Content

By the first day of the plaintiff's deposition, the well-prepared defense counsel should know the alleged conversations and events better than the plaintiff who participated in them. Defense counsel has had the benefit of talking to the defense witnesses in detail, reviewing documents and electronic information, and interviewing other employees who were present for relevant events but who viewed the events in a different way from the plaintiff.

Counsel should prepare for the examination of the plaintiff by preparing a case time-line of relevant events. Placing all of the case documents and information into chrono-logical order is critical to this process. Witness interview notes should be reviewed, and their contents included in the case timeline. The timeline should not be limited to the period of the plaintiff's employment but should include relevant pre- and post-employment events.

Counsel should have complete mastery of the documents, information, and lists that reflect the timeline of events. The relevant information should be read and reread in sufficient detail so that nothing is missed. Often, the best case defense is not apparent until counsel masters this timeline. For example, if the defense believes that a work-place harassment plaintiff filed suit primarily because she hated her supervisor, only review of the detailed sequence of work-related events can reveal when and why the plaintiff first became sufficiently angry that an overstated claim became her tactic. In the process of attempting to elicit a helpful admission in deposition, counsel will need to know all of the documents well enough to avoid the need to thumb through them during the questioning process.

Employment plaintiffs come to deposition prepared to assert broad-ranging claims, sometimes with little factual support. Typically, a highly detailed treatment of all of the relevant events of a plaintiff's work history is very helpful to the defense. Defense counsel must know the exact record of the plaintiff's work history and relevant events and have a detailed plan for obtaining confirmation of that information in deposition. The plan should be modified in light of the actual testimony as the deposition proceeds. For example, if the plaintiff makes generalized claims of harassment over a period of time and the defense position is that the offending conduct was limited to two minor incidents, defense counsel will need to have a plan for bringing the plaintiff to the point of admission that she remembers nothing other than the two incidents of which the defense is aware. The timeline prepared for the deposition is very helpful in this process: The plaintiff who asserts continued harassment over an extended period of time may be forced to concede a memory of only a handful of incidents when questioned month by month or even week by week about actual events.

As the plaintiff's deposition begins, defense counsel should also know the relevant case law, what will be required for a credible summary judgment motion, and pro-spective jury instructions well enough that the questioning of the plaintiff can lay the groundwork for potential summary judgment and/or trial. Defense counsel need not read each and every case that will form the basis for summary judgment or jury instructions in great detail before the deposition. However, counsel should at least be well-informed about the applicable law and its application to the defense theory of the case before embarking on the all-important plaintiff's deposition.

Topic lists and a checklist of items not to be missed are more helpful in deposing workplace harassment plaintiffs than formalized lists of precisely worded individ-ual questions. Some individual questions can be prepared to keep the questioner on track and to begin each new topic or chronological area of questioning. The ques-tioner should know what is needed for each topic and item. A free flow of informa-tion between questioner and deponent is generally a more successful technique for the deposition of a workplace harassment the plaintiff than a rigid list of prewritten questions. The best deposition questioner in employment cases is one who "goes with the flow," listening to the testimony, strategizing where to take the questioning based on responses already provided, following up all lines of questioning suggested by the responses, and determining when to ask a particular question that is likely to elicit a crucial admission.

The topics for questioning a workplace harassment plaintiff will vary from case to case, depending on the allegations and the employer's defenses. Potential topics include the following:

- Educational history
- Prior employment history, including any claims asserted against prior employers, supervisors, or co-workers, problems in prior employment, and reasons for leaving prior employment
- Incidents of alleged harassment and plaintiff's reactions to each incident
- Plaintiff's complaints about harassment
- Plaintiff's knowledge of events of any investigation of his or her internal harassment claim
- Examination of plaintiff from any notes or writing (electronic or otherwise) he or she made either contemporaneously with events or thereafter
- Other contacts with the accused (in addition to incidents of alleged harassment)
- Facts related to plaintiff's work performance or other reasons for discharge (if applicable)
- Plaintiff's reasons for leaving employment (if applicable) and any actions taken to resolve plaintiff's situation prior to leaving
- Conduct or comments by plaintiff negating the claim of harassment
- Subsequent employment and job search efforts (if applicable)
- Plaintiff's knowledge of company procedures, including its workplace harassment policy

Where retaliation is a component of the plaintiff's case, the defense will need to build appropriate questions into the topic outline. Here, too, timing and detail is everything. If the defense truly did not retaliate but, instead, took its actions for legitimate business reasons, the best technique to defeat a retaliation claim is questioning that demonstrates complete mastery of the timeline and the facts.

B. Organization, Technique, Pace, Timing, and Approach

Although no two cases, plaintiffs, or depositions are ever the same, defense counsel should be aware of various techniques in conducting the deposition of a workplace harassment plaintiff.

The use of a chronological questioning technique makes it more difficult for a plaintiff to assert generalized claims that are difficult to defend. The plaintiff who worked at a company for nine months should be questioned about the relevant events in a month-by-month chronological fashion. (For example: Do you remember the first month of your employment? What, if anything, happened to which you objected? Do you remember the second month? What, if anything, happened to which you objected?) The plaintiff with six years of employment might be questioned year by year for the first four years and month by month for the last two years. Although the method and technique will vary, forcing the plaintiff to organize the events in chronological fashion will necessarily limit the events to those truly remembered and therefore be beneficial to the defense.

A technique that often proves helpful when time allows is to go through the relevant events with the plaintiff twice, once probing the plaintiff's memory without documents and a second time using the documents, arranged chronologically, to retest the plaintiff's memory. Often, the plaintiff impeaches himself or herself when faced with documents prepared at the time, having earlier testified to events more favorable to the plaintiff's case but belied by the documentation.

Similarly, questioning as to incidents and conversations should be structured to avoid allowing the plaintiff to ramble on in a manner damaging to the defense. The plaintiff should be pinned down to his or her exact memory of incidents and discussions. The plaintiff should be asked: What happened first? What happened next? What happened after that? Is that all? Who else was present? Where did the conversation take place? When did the conversation take place? Who spoke first? What did he say? Who spoke next? What did she say? Is that all? What was your response or reaction? Again, this type of questioning forces the plaintiff to stick to what is actually remembered and prevents the plaintiff from presenting a scripted rendition of abuse and mistreatment over an extended period of time with little support to the rendition.

The "funnel" approach, always advisable in deposition, works well in ascertaining and limiting all of the plaintiff's claims. Start with general, open-ended questions and end with specifics. Follow up in detail and tie everything down. Defense counsel should ask the plaintiff to list all objectionable incidents and conversations. When the incidents have been listed, a detailed inquiry should be conducted until the witness's memory of each incident is exhausted. The technique is to listen carefully, follow up on all leads, and be persistent and thorough. The objective is to leave no room for later addition of more incidents and claims.

Defense counsel should pose the questioning in a manner that requires the witness to answer who, what, when, where, why, and how questions and/or to describe and explain. Always ask the witness who else was present for each and every event or conversation. The witness should provide direct knowledge of events and discussions. Except in limited circumstances, speculation by the plaintiff creates an unclear and unhelpful record.

There may be times in the plaintiff's deposition when it is advisable and appropriate to allow the witness to ramble. The witness's rambling, particularly when the witness is tired late in the day, may lead to helpful admissions or to the provision of information he or she had intended not to disclose. It is acceptable to allow the witness to ramble so long as the detailed, fact-specific information that the defense must obtain is not precluded elsewhere in the deposition.

Priority is important. The defense should take the plaintiff's deposition as early as the rules allow to avoid having any defense witnesses deposed first. Priority allows the defense witnesses to prepare for deposition having had the benefit of reviewing the transcript of the plaintiff's deposition.

Plaintiff's counsel will try to force defense counsel to take a brief, quick deposition. Defense counsel should persist in taking as much time as needed, assuming the applicable rules allow. Splitting up the plaintiff's deposition into more than one day is helpful, in that it enables the defense to regroup, examine the earlier record, and better prepare for the latter part of the deposition.

Defense counsel is well advised to adopt a manner that is most appropriate to the witness and to the stage of the deposition. A cross-examination approach would be a mistake with an open, friendly, talkative plaintiff. Often, the best tactic is to use a relatively informal approach at first so that the plaintiff is forthcoming and to be more formal later. The use of both approaches at different times is more likely to elicit admissions than the use of only one mode of questioning.

The pace of a deposition is also important. Obviously, if there is a choice between asking a plaintiff a crucial question right after a break when the plaintiff has just been coached by opposing counsel or late in the day when the plaintiff is eager to end the questioning, the latter is the better time. Counsel should look for times in a deposition when the witness is less guarded or when there seems otherwise to be an opening to obtain a major admission.

By the conclusion of the plaintiff's deposition, defense counsel should have covered all of the allegations and issues raised by the complaint. The plaintiff's claims, the plaintiff's knowledge of an investigation of the claims, the plaintiff's discussions with others about the claims, similar instances that allegedly happened to others—all should be probed in depth. Before concluding the deposition, defense counsel should have examined the plaintiff regarding the contents of the complaint and any interrogatory responses, the contents of any documents contained in any administrative agency file, the contents of any emails or documents written or received by the plaintiff, and any information written by the plaintiff. Using case documents and pleadings in this manner often enables defense counsel to inquire about the same information more than once, thereby obtaining inconsistent testimony or later admissions that could not be obtained earlier in the deposition.

As is the case in every aspect of litigation, thorough preparation and persistent, well-thought-out technique are the keys to effectively taking the plaintiff's deposition in a workplace harassment or other employment case. Once the defense preparation has been done, it is the job of the defense practitioner to "box the witness" to his or her story: Boxing in the witness is a two-step process. The first step is to measure the contents; the second is to build the box around it.

Measuring the contents—learning what the witness does and doesn't know—involves more than just asking open-ended questions. It means asking follow-up questions, exploring what the witness hasn't said as well as what he has said. It is one of the reasons why writing out your questions in advance almost guarantees disaster—it tends to cut off follow-up questions. . . .

The next step is building the box. The point is to establish that the witness has gone to the end of the line on every inquiry—that there is nothing left. And the technique is never to do this by implication, but always to make it explicit. "Is there anything else that happened?"[4]

"Boxing the witness" prevents a plaintiff from alleging additional events in a subsequent affidavit or declaration or in a subsequent proceeding. At the end of a line of questioning on a particular event or conversation, defense counsel should ask, "Was there anything else said or done during this conversation?" The intent of this question is to demonstrate on the record that the plaintiff's description of events was completely exhausted. Similarly, at the end of questioning regarding a specific block of chronological time, defense counsel should ask "Were there any other offensive incidents during that time?" or "Have you told me all of the incidents that offended you during that time period?" At the conclusion of the deposition, defense counsel should once again close any potential loopholes in testimony by follow-up questions such as "Have you told me all of the incidents in which offensive comments were made by X?" These questions should be asked regarding every generalized allegation made. Keeping the record as tight as possible will preempt the plaintiff's attempt to add factual allegations later in the case.

Nowhere is "building the box" more important than in the workplace harassment case. Such cases often rise and fall with limiting the plaintiff's testimony to isolated instances and making the plaintiff recall "everything" that supports the claim. The defense practitioner must be mindful of "building the box" at every step of the preparation and effectuation of its defense.

Defense counsel must decide whether to video record the plaintiff's deposition in the process of "building the box." A video recording will show the plaintiff's demeanor and any long pauses before answers—two things a transcript conceals. Video depositions are commonly taken by default today on the assumption that the addition of video to a deposition will always be beneficial to the party taking the deposition. But it is nonetheless possible that, in a particular harassment case, video recording the deposition can cause defense questioning to be more formal and to put the plaintiff on guard, thereby causing the plaintiff to limit volunteered information.

IV. PREPARATION OF DEFENSE WITNESSES FOR THEIR DEPOSITIONS

It is a truism that defense cases need not be won in deposition; they need only not be lost. In general, preparing a critical defense witness for deposition should take three times as long as the deposition itself will take. Defense witnesses should follow a few simple rules, which should be communicated to those witnesses on several occasions.

First and foremost, the witness should be told to tell the truth at all times. Apart from the ethical reasons for this advice, no one gets into trouble more quickly than

---

4. James W. McElhaney, McElhaney's Litigation 48 (Am. Bar Ass'n 1995).

the witness who lies. It is easy to remember the truth when asked about it on a second occasion. It is not as easy to tell the same lie twice.

The witness should be made to understand the importance of conveying only what he saw, heard, and spoke. The witness should be told not to speculate about what one individual told another or what someone else was thinking. The witness should be instructed not to speculate at all. Speculation is almost always wrong, and, next to lying, it is the worst thing a witness can do in a deposition.

The witness should be told that "I don't know" and "I don't remember" are perfectly good answers if that is the case. Despite this advice, many witnesses are uncomfortable with "I don't know" answers and have to be given this advice again during the course of the deposition.

The defense witness should be told to listen to the question, to pause to allow defense counsel time for objection if such is appropriate, and to answer only the question asked. The witness should know that when he or she hears an objection, the witness may be in a danger area and should be particularly careful about the testimony to be rendered. If the deposition is to be video recorded, the effect of a pause in testimony before answering should be discussed.

The defense witness should understand that questions ending with "isn't that true?" or that paraphrase the witness's responses are often trick questions, however seemingly innocuous the question.

It is important for the defense deponent to understand the plaintiff's material allegations and how the deponent's testimony will fit into the plaintiff's claims and the defense presentation. The deponent should be told that, when asked a question, he should try to understand its relevance and not answer in a vacuum.

The witness should be made to understand that opposing counsel is neither friend nor foe. The witness should be made wary of seemingly friendly opposing counsel and advised of how to forestall anger in the case of hostile opposing counsel.

The witness should also be advised

- to tell defense counsel if there is a mistake on the record so that it can be corrected;
- to be prepared to respond affirmatively to the question of whether the witness prepared with counsel for the deposition; and
- to leave documents at home, but to be prepared to answer truthfully which documents the witness reviewed in preparation for the deposition.

The witness and counsel should spend substantial time in role-playing expected questions and answers as thoroughly as possible until the witness is good at responding using the appropriate techniques (avoid speculation, listen to the question, answer only the question asked, and so on).

The witness should be prepared for questions typically asked in employment cases. For example, if asked if he ever received management training and no formal training was received, the witness may refer to informal on-the-job training.

V. DEPOSITIONS OF PLAINTIFF'S DOCTORS AND OTHER EXPERTS

Many of the same rules that apply to the deposition of the plaintiff in a workplace harassment case apply to the depositions of plaintiff's treating doctor and any other medical or other experts. Inquiry should be made in a chronological fashion that provides a framework for the organization of the deposition, particularly where counsel is examining a treating doctor about various sessions he had with the plaintiff. Defense counsel should proceed from the general to the specific and should ask the who, what, where, and how questions, again tying down the expert witness to the extent possible under the circumstances.

Areas of inquiry of experts should include full identification of files, documents, and reports; education and employment background; prior experience as an expert; any published writings by the expert; nature of the assignment in the present case; bases for any expert opinions; and all information relied on by the expert.

Before deposing any treating physician or other expert, counsel should retain the defense's own expert for thorough and knowledgeable assistance in the preparation process. A useful reference source for attorneys seeking to depose a psychiatric or psychological treating doctor or testifying expert is the American Psychiatric Association's *Diagnostic and Statistical Manual of Mental Disorders* (most recently, the *DSM-5*), which is widely accepted as the "common language" of mental health practitioners.[5] In addition, defense counsel should be aware that Rule 35 of the Federal Rules of Civil Procedure allows the defendant to move for a physical or mental examination of the plaintiff when the physical or mental condition of the plaintiff is in controversy.[6]

---

5. The *DSM-5* was published in 2013.

6. For further discussion on Rule 35 examinations, *see* Chapter 20.

CHAPTER 11

Discovery and Deposing the Alleged Harasser and Defense Witnesses: The Plaintiff's Perspective

Cynthia N. Sass[1]

I. ALWAYS CONSIDER THE GOAL OF DISCOVERY IN HARASSMENT AND/OR RETALIATION SUITS

From the very beginning and throughout the course of litigation, it is extremely important to keep focused on the purpose of discovery. The plaintiff's counsel should identify what needs to be shown in the case, and craft discovery that is designed to obtain evidence to make that showing. Counsel should conduct every litigation with the assumption that the case is going to trial. The plaintiff's counsel should develop a litigation outline to use as a framework for the case. A litigation outline should include each element that the plaintiff will need to prove for each claim as it will help ensure that the plaintiff gets adequate discovery on each element needed for each claim. It should also help focus the plaintiff's discovery requests.

At the very least, the plaintiff's counsel will need to gather sufficient discovery to demonstrate a prima facie case. The specific requirements of a prima facie case can vary with context and were "never intended to be rigid, mechanized, or ritualistic."[2] Therefore, while the framework set out in *McDonnell Douglas*[3] and *Price Waterhouse*[4] can be useful, the ultimate issue is simply whether the evidence would permit a reasonable fact finder to conclude that the plaintiff's gender or protected activity caused the discharge or other adverse employment action.[5] One way this showing can be made is through

---

1. Special recognition to Joshua R. Kersey and Jennifer D. Zumarraga of the Sass Law Firm for their assistance and contributions to this chapter.

2. Furnco Constr. Corp. v. Waters, 438 U.S. 567, 577 (1978).

3. McDonnell Douglas Corp. v. Green, 411 U.S. 792 (1973).

4. Price Waterhouse v. Hopkins, 490 U.S. 228 (1989).

5. The anti-retaliation provisions under Title VII encompass a broader range of actions than adverse actions subject to challenge under the nondiscrimination provisions of that statute. The anti-retaliation provision contemplates any employer action that "might well deter a reasonable employee from complaining about discrimination." Burlington Northern & Santa Fe Railway Co. v. White, 548 U.S. 53, 69 (2006).

demonstration of a "convincing mosaic of circumstantial evidence" that discrimination has occurred.[6]

Often in an employment discrimination or retaliation case, the defendant submits a statement of position to an administrative agency that investigates the plaintiff's claims prior to the filing of a lawsuit. This statement usually provides far greater insight into the defendant's defenses than its answer to the complaint. These statements can usually be obtained prior to the filing of a lawsuit (e.g., from the Equal Employment Opportunity Commission [EEOC] or Occupational Safety and Health Administration).

The plaintiff's counsel should review the statements of position closely and identify discovery needed to show a genuine issue of material fact that may be used to defeat summary judgment, or to show pretext in general. This can be done in many ways. For example, evidence of pretext can exist if the employer allegedly based its adverse action on the plaintiff's performance problems, but performance evaluations were positive;[7] if the employer provides shifting explanations for its actions;[8] if the employer departs from its normal policies in taking action against the plaintiff;[9] or if the timing of the employer's action is suspect.[10]

Craft discovery designed to evaluate the strengths and weaknesses in both the defendant's case and the plaintiff's case. Be honest about any negative aspects of the plaintiff's case. The plaintiff should use interrogatories and corporate representative depositions to ask questions about the factual bases of denials and affirmative defenses in the defendant's answer. Remember, the ultimate goal is to obtain a good settlement of the plaintiff's claims, or to try a winning case. Every attempt should be made to gain leverage for a favorable settlement. Discovery should look for evidence of a pattern of a hostile work environment or retaliation to support expanding the case into a class action. Discovery should cast the widest net possible for potential evidence that might support the plaintiff's claim. If the trail of evidence leads far up the corporate ladder, the plaintiff should not hesitate to climb each rung of the ladder. If discovery shows the defendant may be guilty of other wrongdoing (false claims, Fair Labor Standards Act violations,

---

An action need not be materially adverse standing alone, so long as the employer's retaliatory conduct, when considered as a whole, would deter protected activity. Vega v. Hempstead Union Free Sch. Dist., 801 F.3d 72 (2d Cir. 2015) (holding that a high school teacher stated a claim for retaliation based on the combination of "his assignment of notoriously absent students, his temporary paycheck reduction, and the District's failure to notify him of a curriculum change"); Sanford v. Main St. Baptist Church Manor, Inc., 327 F. App'x 587, 599 (6th Cir. 2009) (holding that although some of the incidents alone may not rise to the level of an adverse action, "the incidents taken together might dissuade a reasonable worker from making or supporting a discrimination charge"); Ortiz v. Werner Enterprises, Inc., 834 F.3d 760, 765 (7th Cir. 2016).

6. Burns v. Johnson, 829 F.3d 1, 16 (1st Cir. 2016); Holland v. Gee, 677 F.3d 1047, 1062 (11th Cir. 2012); James v. N.Y. Racing Ass'n, 233 F.3d 149, 157 (2d Cir. 2000) ("[T]he way to tell whether a plaintiff's case is sufficient to sustain a verdict is to analyze the particular evidence to determine whether it reasonably supports an inference of the facts plaintiff must prove—particularly discrimination.").

7. Williams v. Time Warner Operation, Inc., 98 F.3d 179, 183 (5th Cir. 1996) (Title VII).

8. Cleveland v. Home Shopping Network, Inc., 369 F.3d 1189, 1194–95 (11th Cir. 2004).

9. Doebele v. Sprint/United Management Co., 342 F.3d 1117, 1138 (10th Cir. 2003).

10. Daoud v. Avamere Staffing, LLC, 336 F. Supp. 2d 1129, 1137 (D. Or. 2004).

and so on), the plaintiff should consider adding new causes of action to the complaint. Discovery can develop evidence supporting punitive damages. It can also delve into relevant but potentially embarrassing areas for the alleged harasser, the defendant's key executives, and/or its key witnesses. The plaintiff should be prepared to defend the basis for such discovery and should not undertake it without a good faith basis to do so.

The plaintiff should also consider, within ethical norms, the publicity factor of the case. Who is harmed more by potential publicity, the plaintiff or the defendant? Will publicity hurt or help the chances of a settlement? The best leverage for settlement will always be discovery that shows the plaintiff is likely to win the case and be awarded substantial damages. For example, interrogatories might ask, "Identify each person who has knowledge of the defendant's investigation of the plaintiff's complaint, each person who has ever complained of harassment while employed with the defendant, each person who claims to have witnessed the events alleged in the complaint, and each person who the defendant believes has knowledge pertaining to its asserted defense of prompt remedial action," or "Identify each document that the defendant believes supports its claim that the plaintiff welcomed the conduct of the alleged harasser."

II. UNLAWFUL HARASSMENT AND RETALIATION CASES: WHAT FACTS DOES THE PLAINTIFF NEED TO EXPLORE?

A. Basics About Employer

The plaintiff needs to obtain basic information about the employer and the actors in the suit. Depending on the specific basis of the suit, an employer may need to meet certain requirements to be covered by the statute. The plaintiff should seek discovery to determine whether the employer has the requisite number of employees, or revenue, or any other prerequisite to liability. The plaintiff should also determine whether the key players in the suit are employees or agents of the employer, as the status of actors can also affect liability.

The plaintiff should obtain discovery as to the defendant's financial condition if there is any concern that the defendant may be insolvent or otherwise unable to pay any judgment in the case. This includes determining whether a potential defendant is in bankruptcy, as there may be significant consequences for initiating an action against such a defendant. This discovery should be done prior to, or very early on in, litigation if it is necessary.

Information regarding any applicable insurance policies should be obtained as well. Federal Rule of Civil Procedure 26(a)(1)(A) requires that ". . . a party must, without awaiting a discovery request, provide to the other parties: [. . .] for inspection and copying under Rule 34, any insurance agreement under which an insurance business may be liable to satisfy all or part of a possible judgment in the action or to indemnify or reimburse for payments made to satisfy the judgment." There may be state statutes that provide a means for obtaining insurance information as well. For instance, Florida Statute § 627.4137(1) requires an insurer, in certain circumstances, to provide the plaintiff with (a) the name of the insurer; (b) the name of each insured; (c) the limits of the liability coverage; (d) a statement of any policy or coverage defense, which such insurer reasonably believes is available to such insurer at the time of filing such statement; and (e) a copy of the policy. Insurance information may also be important should the plaintiff prevail and obtain a judgment. For instance, in Florida, a prevailing plaintiff must move to include the insurer on the judgment.[11]

B. Policy and Procedure of Employer Regarding Harassment Reporting and Prevention

Generally, an employer may avoid liability for harassment under Title VII if it can prove the two elements of the affirmative defense set forth in *Faragher v. City of Boca Raton*[12] and *Burlington Industries, Inc. v. Ellerth*,[13] commonly referred to as the *Faragher-Ellerth* defense. Those two elements include (1) that the employer exercised reasonable care to prevent and correct promptly any sexually harassing behavior, and (2) that the plaintiff employee unreasonably failed to take advantage of any preventive or corrective opportunities provided by the employer or to otherwise avoid harm.[14]

However, to maintain a *Faragher-Ellerth* defense, certain things must be true about the defendant employer's sexual harassment policy. For example, the employer's complaint mechanism must provide a clear path for reporting sexual harassment.[15] Therefore, the plaintiff should seek discovery of the employer's sexual harassment policy to determine whether there is a clear path for reporting complaints. Moreover, the plaintiff should seek discovery regarding whether the policy is effective in general—have others complained about harassment? Has the harassment, in the plaintiff's case and in others, been investigated promptly? Is everyone aware of the harassment policy? Was the plaintiff aware of the policy? Was the harasser? This information goes directly to determining whether a *Faragher-Ellerth* defense is available to the employer.[16]

---

11. Fla. Stat. § 627.4136(4) (2018).

12. 524 U.S. 775 (1998).

13. 524 U.S. 742 (1998).

14. There are some instances where this defense is not applicable. Indeed, the "mere existence" of an official policy against harassment, by itself, is not sufficient to invoke the *Faragher-Ellerth* defense. The defendant must distribute the policy to all employees and it must be shown to have actually worked. Star v. West, 237 F.3d 1036 (9th Cir. 2001). Where a defendant promulgates different versions of its harassment policy, the issue of whether it had an "effective" harassment policy becomes a question of fact. Moreover, the complaint procedure should not require an employee to complain first to the alleged harasser. Madray v. Publix Supermarkets, Inc., 208 F.3d 1290 1299 (11th Cir. 1999), *cert. denied*, 121 S.Ct. 303 (2000). Should management fail to take remedial action upon an employee's initial complaint, his or her claim cannot be defeated for a failure to report subsequent conduct. Miller v. Kenworth of Dothan, Inc., 277 F.3d 1269, 1276 (11th Cir. 2002). Of course, any action taken against an employee for reporting such harassment may give rise to an actionable retaliation claim.

15. EEOC v. Mgt. Hosp. of Racine, Inc., 666 F.3d 422, 436 (7th Cir. 2012).

16. *See, e.g.,* Miller v. Kenworth of Dothan, Inc., 277 F.3d 1269, 1280 (11th Cir. 2002) ("a policy must be found ineffective when company practice indicates a tolerance towards harassment or discrimination.").

C. Training Undertaken by Employer to Prevent Harassment

Although not dispositive, whether an employer exercised reasonable care to prevent and correct promptly any harassing behavior is also evidenced by the existence or lack of harassment training.[17] Seek discovery regarding any harassment or discrimination training the employer requires of its employees or provides. Determine how often the training occurs, the extent of the training, and whether the employer requires its employees to verify that they have completed the training and understand it. This can be done through requests for production, interrogatories, and depositions of the employer's corporate representatives.

D. Complaints

The plaintiff should seek discovery regarding actual complaints of gender harassment. This includes documentation from any investigation into the plaintiff's complaint. The employer may have notes from an investigation and may have statements from witnesses. This information will help determine whether the plaintiff's complaints were corroborated or disputed. The plaintiff should also seek to discover information regarding the harasser's history with the employer.[18]

Determine whether there have been other complaints of harassment made against the same individual, and whether the individual was disciplined for those previous complaints.[19] It is also important to determine whether the harasser had supervisory authority over the plaintiff for purposes of vicarious liability. The plaintiff's counsel should also investigate whether the harasser has any relevant criminal record, and ethically review all of the harasser's available social media for useful information.

E. Witnesses

The plaintiff will be the first source of information regarding potential witnesses. Ideally, nonparty witnesses should be interviewed informally, prior to their deposition. However, the plaintiff's counsel must be sure to comply with the applicable rules of professional conduct regarding contact with represented parties. Whether ex parte communication with an individual is permissible under such rules can depend on whether

---

17. Thornton v. Fed. Express Corp., 530 F.3d 451, 456–57 (6th Cir. 2008) (stating that an effective sexual harassment policy should, among other things, provide for training regarding the policy, but then observing that there was no dispute regarding the reasonableness of the employer's prevention efforts where the employer distributed its policy via an employee handbook and the plaintiff received more than one copy of the handbook during his or her employment).

18. Goldsmith v. Bagby Elevator Co., 513 F.3d 1261 (11th Cir. 2008) ("me too" evidence admissible as relevant to the plaintiff employee's claim of hostile work environment, to rebut employer's "good faith" defense and as probative of intent of the common decision maker).

19. Once such discovery is obtained, it may be important to determine through discovery whether those individuals also asserted a subsequent complaint of retaliation.

the witness is a current or former employee, whether they held a managerial role, or whether they have or had the authority to bind the defendant.

The plaintiff should question witnesses about their observations of the defendant employer's company culture as it relates to harassment and retaliation. With respect to the plaintiff's harassment claim, the plaintiff's obligation to report harassment is eliminated where the harassment is sufficiently pervasive.[20] The plaintiff should also question witnesses about their observations of the harasser's actions and comments as it relates to the harassment alleged. When deposing members of management, determine what knowledge they have of the harasser's actions and comments. The plaintiff also needs to determine whether management performed any investigation into the plaintiff's complaint, and the details of the investigation, such as who was interviewed, what each person said, whether notes were taken, whether witness statements were obtained, etc. With respect to the plaintiff's retaliation claim, the plaintiff should determine whether management made it clear to the harasser and others in his or her chain of command, as well as the plaintiff's co-workers, that no retaliatory conduct would be tolerated.

The plaintiff must also determine the results of management's investigation and whether any action was taken as a result. The plaintiff's counsel should also ask witnesses whether they were interviewed by management as part of any investigation into the plaintiff's complaints and, if so, what they were asked and how they responded. Ultimately, the plaintiff's counsel should determine whether the witnesses' accounts are going to corroborate or negate the plaintiff's claims.

When deposing the defendant's witnesses, the plaintiff's counsel should not hesitate to ask questions to which they do not already know the answers. It is better to find out the answers and the full import of the witnesses' testimony in discovery rather than at trial. When deposing nonparty witnesses who may or may not be available for trial, and for whom there is a good chance that the only testimony from that witness will be in the deposition, greater caution is required.

Courts generally will allow at least limited requests for information designed to find witnesses to corroborate the plaintiff's testimony. In one case, the plaintiff sought production of co-workers' personnel file information, specifically date of birth, residence telephone number, and job title. The plaintiff also sought information from the personnel files of eight persons alleged to have witnessed or been involved in harassing conduct. The defendant was ordered to provide the information.[21]

The plaintiff should seek to discover information about the alleged harasser's former employers, especially if the information is relatively recent. The harasser's former personnel file and former supervisors, co-workers, and subordinates could yield information indicating the harasser had a history of prior conduct similar to that alleged by the plaintiff.

---

20. Ford v. West, 222 F.3d 767, 776 (10th Cir. 2000) (an employer may be deemed to have constructive knowledge of harassment where the pervasiveness of the harassment supports an inference of employer knowledge).

21. Hoskins v. Sears, Roebuck and Co., No. 96-1357-MB, 1997 WL 557327, at *1 (D. Kan. Sept. 2, 1997).

F. The Plaintiff's History

The plaintiff's history is as important as that of any other witness. The plaintiff's personnel file is a good place to start when seeking this discovery.[22] The plaintiff should seek information regarding hire date, raises, promotions, demotions, performance reviews, discipline, and the value of all compensation (monetary and nonmonetary) for damages purposes. The plaintiff's counsel should also investigate the plaintiff's personal history to discover any prior litigation or criminal history. The plaintiff's counsel should also review all available social media from the plaintiff so as to avoid being blindsided by defense counsel down the road.

G. Location and Format of Information

In the modern workplace, most nonverbal evidence of harassment and retaliation is going to exist in emails, text messages, instant messaging programs, and other forms of electronic communication. At the outset of the case, before litigation begins, the plaintiff's counsel should send a litigation hold letter to the employer requesting preservation of evidence related to specific documents and individuals involved, as well as for more general and encompassing information. The litigation hold letter should request its dispersal to all relevant individuals, the company's IT department, and any relevant third-party vendor. Once litigation commences, the plaintiff should make sure to craft discovery requests that specifically seek this type of information, in its native format, with all metadata intact. Similarly, most modern-day investigative reports are created in an electronic word-processing program like Microsoft Word. The plaintiff should request all iterations of any investigative report in their native format, including all versions and their metadata, to determine when the report was created, and whether and to what extent it has been edited.

H. The Plaintiff's Damages

The plaintiff should do extensive discovery into his or her own damages. Relevant information will include compensation history such as pay stubs, raises, bonuses, compensation plan documents, and commissions. The plaintiff's pecuniary damages can also include moving expenses, job search expenses (travel, resume preparation, postage, employment agency fees), medical expenses (doctor visits, loss of health insurance, Consolidated Omnibus Budget Reconciliation Act expenses, prescriptions, transportation costs to see mental health counselor, psychiatric or counseling expenses, physical therapy expenses), property losses (loss of home, loss of car), fringe benefits, seniority

---

22. **PRACTICE POINTER**: Consider requesting files generally, as opposed to "personnel files," because some defense counsel will intentionally interpret "personnel file" to include only a subset of the relevant information. For example, the plaintiff might request: "The complete files, including but not limited to personnel files, the records pertaining to the job duties for each position held, salary, bonuses, promotions, evaluations, discipline, benefits, demotions, discharge, layoff or retirement, for the following individuals: ..."

benefits, or the loss of vacation or sick time. Depending on the extent and complexity of emotional damages, the plaintiff may need to obtain medical records including those showing a mental health history in addition to any medications being taken. The plaintiff's counsel should determine whether an expert will be necessary to calculate the plaintiff's pecuniary damages, or to testify to the severity of the plaintiff's medical- or health-related damages. The plaintiff should also maintain records showing any mitigation of damages. However, the defendant ultimately carries the burden of proof on that issue.[23] If the plaintiff is seeking an award of punitive damages, the employer's financial records are discoverable. This is true even though punitive damages are capped under the Civil Rights Act of 1991.[24]

III. PRE-SUIT DISCOVERY

Important discovery must be performed prior to the filing of a lawsuit as well, such as researching the defendant employer and finding out if the plaintiff has filed for bankruptcy.[25] Review any recent press clippings regarding the employer for relevant information. See, for instance, whether the employer is involved in any current litigation or is going through a sale. The plaintiff's counsel should also issue Freedom of Information Act or public records requests for any applicable EEOC or state agency files. Again, as discussed already, the plaintiff should contact witnesses and get affidavits (while making sure to comply with all ethical rules of professional responsibility).

The plaintiff's counsel should also conduct all appropriate bankruptcy, criminal background, and social media searches prior to filing suit. With respect to social media, the plaintiff's counsel should ensure the plaintiff preserves relevant information, and assist the plaintiff in doing so to avoid claims of spoliation. The plaintiff should turn all social media privacy settings to the highest degree of privacy to prevent the defendant from obtaining that discovery informally.[26] The plaintiff should avoid posting *anything* about the case on social media, or discussing the case with anyone without first talking to his or her counsel. Again, the plaintiff should also check the social media profiles of the harasser for any relevant information. If any is found, the plaintiff should preserve the information

---

23. Booker v. Taylor Milk Co., Inc., 64 F.3d 860, 864 (3rd Cir. 1995) (although the statutory duty to mitigate damages is placed on the plaintiff, the employer has the burden of proving a failure to mitigate).

24. EEOC v. Klockner H & K Machs., Inc., 168 F.R.D. 233, 236 (E.D. Wis. 1996).

25. It is important to research any prior bankruptcy filings by the plaintiff before pursuing an employment claim. Most circuits hold that, under the doctrine of judicial estoppel, a debtor's failure to disclose pending or anticipated litigation claims can bar the debtor from filing a subsequent lawsuit based upon that undisclosed claim. Whether or not a plaintiff can pursue an initially undisclosed claim often turns on the facts of the individual's case. *See., e.g.*, DeLeon v. Comcar Industries, Inc., 321 F.3d 1289, 1290–91 (the plaintiff was judicially estopped from prosecuting his complaint of employment discrimination because he had not disclosed the existence of the claim prior to petitioning for bankruptcy) to Bejarano v. Bravo! Facility Servs., Inc., 251 F.Supp.3d 27 (D.D.C. 2017) (where the plaintiff amended her bankruptcy schedules before filing suit against the defendant on her own volition, the plaintiff did not attempt to conceal claims from her creditors and judicial estoppel thus did not apply to bar her discrimination claim).

26. EEOC v. Honeybaked Ham Co. of Ga., Inc., 2012 WL 5430974 (D. Colo. Nov. 7, 2012).

as well as possible, and send a pointed letter to defense counsel requesting specifically that the information be preserved. The plaintiff should consider hiring an expert to download and properly preserve the plaintiff's emails, text messages, and social media information.

Prior to filing suit, the plaintiff's counsel should also identify other litigation that the pertinent individuals have been involved in. The plaintiff should search Public Access to Court Electronic Records or the internet in general for the defendant employer's other litigation. It may be useful to obtain the deposition transcripts of the witnesses in those prior litigations for purposes of impeachment. The plaintiff should also obtain any information from unemployment hearings, such as documents provided or sworn testimony that was recorded. The plaintiff's counsel should also try to participate in any unemployment proceedings if that option is available. The plaintiff's counsel should also obtain the filings and other documents from any workers' compensation claim filed by the plaintiff, as well as any pleadings related to the harasser, such as divorce pleadings and bankruptcy, if available.

IV. DISCOVERY UNDER FEDERAL RULES OF CIVIL PROCEDURE (AND LOCAL RULES)

A. The Rule 26(F) Conference and Case Management Reports

The importance of the Rule 26(f) conference and subsequent case management report or discovery plan is often overlooked. A meaningful Rule 26(f) conference and case management report can greatly reduce future headaches in litigation. For example, counsel should request that the parties provide a minimum of ten days' notice before serving a nonparty subpoena, so that all other parties have an opportunity to object, and if an objection is served the subpoena in question will not be served absent agreement of the parties or a court order. This may help curb a common defense tactic of sending subpoenas to the plaintiff's current employer requesting irrelevant documents, simply to put the current employer on notice that the plaintiff is involved in employment litigation.

In the weeks prior to the Rule 26(f) conference, consider giving defense counsel notice of the items you want to discuss, as specifically as possible so that he or she can be prepared to discuss those items at the conference. For instance, consider letting defense counsel know ahead of time that at the conference you intend to discuss issues such as

- if information was preserved in accordance with the litigation hold letter and the date of preservation;
- the date ranges for any electronically stored evidence (ESI) to be produced;
- the description of ESI from sources that are not reasonably accessible because of undue cost or burden and that will not be reviewed for responsiveness or produced, but that will be preserved in accordance with Federal Rule of Civil Procedure 26(b)(2)(B);

- the number and names or general job titles or descriptions of custodians for whom ESI will be preserved;
- the list of systems, if any, that contain ESI not associated with individual custodians that will be preserved;
- descriptions and locations of systems in which potentially discoverable information is stored;
- how potentially discoverable information is stored;
- how discoverable information can be collected from systems and media in which it is stored;
- the formats in which discoverable information will be produced; and
- any other disputes related to the scope or manner of preservation.

If defense counsel will not agree to discuss these matters, the plaintiff's counsel should file a motion requesting a pretrial hearing with the judge under Rule 16(a) to resolve the disputed issues, and to address with the court those issues that defense counsel refuses to discuss. The joint discovery plan should also address how potentially responsive information will be searched (e.g., use of search terms).

Be wary of overly restrictive confidentiality agreements regarding discovery production. Difficult defendants will over-designate discovery production as "confidential." Down the road, the use of discovery designated "confidential" in support of or in defense to motions can be extremely time-consuming and burdensome if much of the information has to be filed under seal.

Difficult defense counsel will use discovery obstruction as a litigation tactic. For defendants who drag their feet, are nonresponsive, or are otherwise deliberately difficult, the plaintiff's counsel should request periodic case management conferences. Also, when dealing with these defendants, be sure to get specific dates for responses and provide hard deadlines. It is a common defense tactic to stall and obstruct discovery by providing vague responses to the plaintiff's conferral requests using statements such as "we are looking into it" or that they "hope" to have a response by early next week, or that they will get a response "soon." Unfortunately, a plaintiff who accepts these types of responses will quickly find him- or herself behind the eight ball in discovery. The plaintiff's counsel should be cooperative in discovery and understanding in providing extensions of deadlines, but make clear to defense counsel that they will take action by a date certain if the issue is not resolved. And always follow up any verbal conferrals in writing so that there is a record of what was discussed.

Along those lines, do not hesitate to file motions to compel as soon as possible. There simply is no time to delay. When there is a discovery dispute, the parties' counsel may arrange for a conferral conference in five days. If, after the conferral, the plaintiff files a motion to compel, defendant may have fourteen days or more to respond to the motion—the plaintiff may then have even more time to file a reply. The judge might then set a hearing on the plaintiff's motion to occur two weeks or more after the final date to reply. After the hearing, the judge might provide the defendant twenty days or more to produce the information that has been compelled. In sum, even if the plaintiff acts immediately to address disputed discovery, it might take two months or more for the plaintiff to actually receive that discovery—that can constitute more than one-quarter of the entire discovery period.

B. Depositions in Relation to Written Discovery

Once the initial disclosures are received from the defendant, a background check, including a criminal background check, should be done on each witness listed by both the plaintiff and the defendant to alleviate any surprises down the road.

The plaintiff should serve written discovery as soon as permissible in litigation, preferably at the Rule 26(f) conference. The plaintiff's counsel should obtain as much relevant discovery production as possible prior to depositions. This will help to minimize situations where a deponent refers to relevant discovery that has not been produced and, therefore, cannot be discussed in detail as an exhibit to the deposition. The sooner the plaintiff obtains discovery, the sooner the plaintiff can schedule depositions. Ideally, the plaintiff should schedule depositions far enough before the discovery cutoff deadline, so that additional discovery requests can be served if the depositions reveal the existence of additional relevant discovery.

1. Fact Witnesses

Fact witnesses should be used to corroborate the plaintiff's claims. Prior to the deposition, the plaintiff should be able to list which facts a particular witness should know. However, the plaintiff's counsel should ask open-ended questions and allow the witness to expand on the answers to potentially discover unexpected information—whether good or bad for the case. Fact witnesses should be asked about any harassment or retaliatory action they observed, as well as observations they made of the plaintiff's behavior, and the plaintiff's interactions with the harasser and management. Fact witnesses may also be able to testify as to any complaints the plaintiff made, and whether an investigation or any other action was taken as a result of those complaints. Even if a witness did not observe the harassment, he or she may have knowledge of the harassment by other means, such as hearing others discuss it. The witness may also have been harassed or retaliated against for complaining about such harassment and should be asked about his or her personal experiences. Fact witnesses should also be asked about their knowledge of the employer's policy regarding harassment and retaliation, and their effectiveness.

2. Rule 30(b)(6) Corporate Representative Deposition

The deposition of an employer defendant's corporate representative under Rule 30(b)(6) is an excellent discovery tool for obtaining information known generally by the employer. It is a discovery device designed to avoid the bandying about by an employer where individual officers or employees disclaim knowledge of facts clearly known to the company.[27] Therefore, one purpose of the special corporate representative deposition is to curb any temptation by the employer to shunt a discovering party from "pillar to

---

27. United States v. Taylor, 166 F.R.D. 356, 361 (M.D.N.C. 1996).

post" by presenting deponents who each disclaim knowledge of facts known to some-one in the company.[28]

Rule 30(b)(6) imposes burdens on both the discovering party and the designating party. The party seeking discovery must describe the matters with reasonable par-ticularity and the responding employer must produce one or more witnesses who can testify about the company's knowledge of the noticed topics.[29] As a corollary to the employer's duty to designate and prepare a witness, it must perform a reasonable inquiry for information that is reasonably available to it.[30]

A plaintiff's attorney can expect to meet substantial resistance from defense coun-sel to many questions during the deposition. The plaintiff's counsel should study the applicable case law regarding corporate representative depositions in the jurisdiction prior to the deposition, and have the case law on hand at the deposition. For instance, a corporate designee must provide responsive answers even if the information was transmitted through the corporation's lawyers.[31]

Rule 30(b)(6) requires that in its notice of corporate deposition, the plaintiff "must describe with reasonable particularity the matters for examination." Neither the Fed-eral Rules of Civil Procedure nor the Advisory Committee notes define "reasonable particularity." Moreover, courts differ as to what constitutes "reasonable particularity."[32]

The plaintiff should try to serve the notice of corporate representative deposition *duces tecum*, and provide requests for production to accompany the notice. To do so, the plaintiff needs to serve the duces tecum notice at least thirty days prior to the sched-uled deposition. If no date for the deposition is scheduled and a deadline is approach-ing, serve the duces tecum notice with a date and time to be determined, along with a footnote that the notice is being served to comply with the thirty-day requirement, and that the parties will continue to work toward a mutually agreeable date.

Potential areas of inquiry for corporate representative depositions include company policies, the details of any previous complaints, the conduct of any investigation into complaints, how they handle the electronic retrieval of emails, or authentication of

---

28. Great Am. Ins. Co. v. Vegas Constr. Co., Inc., 251 F.R.D. 534, 539 (D. Nev. 2008), *Cf.* Ierardi v. Loril-lard, Inc., No. 90-7049, 1991 WL 66799 at *2 (E.D. Pa. Apr. 15, 1991) (without the rule, a corporation could "hide behind the alleged 'failed' memories of its employees").

29. Great Am. Ins. Co. v. Vegas Constr. Co., Inc., 251 F.R.D. 534, 539 (D. Nev. 2008).

30. Fowler v. State Farm Mut. Auto. Ins. Co., 2008 WL 4907865, at *5 (D. Haw. 2008); Marker v. Union Fidelity Life Ins. Co., 125 F.R.D. 121, 127 (M.D.N.C. 1989).

31. Great Am. Ins. Co. v. Vegas Constr. Co., Inc., 251 F.R.D. 534, 542 (D. Nev. 2008).

32. Prokosch v. Catalina Lighting, Inc., 193 F.R.D. 633, 638 (D. Minn. 2000) ("[T]he requesting party must take care to designate, with painstaking specificity, the particular subject areas that are intended to be questioned and that are relevant to the issues in dispute."); Young v. United Parcel Serv. of Am., Inc., 2010 WL 1346423, at *9 (D. Md. Mar. 30, 2010) (explaining that the topics for "the 30(b)(6) deposition must not be overbroad and must be limited to a relevant time period, geographic scope, and related to claims"); Omega Patents, LLC v. Fortin Auto Radio, Inc., 6:05CV1113 ORL 22DAB, 2006 WL 2038534 (M.D. Fla. July 19, 2006) (noting that the court ordered the defendant in a patent case to produce a witness to answer questions on "(1) The factual basis for [defendant's] defenses or denials of the allegations raised in Plaintiff's Complaint; (2) The factual basis for [defendant's] counterclaims; (3) [defendant's] claims of invalidity; and (4) [defendant's] claims of non-infringement").

employer documents for trial. The plaintiff's counsel should also try to obtain admissions as to disputed issues of material fact—for example, whether the alleged harassment was severe or pervasive.

3. Deposing the Harasser

When deposing the harasser, go through each allegation of harassment and obtain his or her position regarding same. A common defense to sexual harassment is that the harassment was welcomed, that is, that it was not subjectively offensive. If the defendant claims the harassment was welcomed, ask for each fact that supports the defense as well as the identity and location of any documents or electronic evidence that support the defense. Determine the harasser's general view on harassment, and whether he or she has ever used such language or jokes, or engaged in such conduct in the past. Often, the other fact witnesses will contradict the harasser on these issues. It is unlikely that the harasser will admit to the harassment, but the details of the story will still be important to surviving the employer's inevitable motion for summary judgment. Ask the harasser for any pictures, text messages, or emails with the plaintiff or with other employees that may be relevant to the allegations in the complaint or to the defendant's defenses. Also, inquire into the harasser's relationships with other co-workers in the plaintiff's protected class.

The deposition of the alleged harasser should be painstakingly thorough. Clear testimony and explicit admissions or denials of key facts must be elicited by the plaintiff's counsel. It is highly unlikely the harasser will be led into an admission that his or her conduct was harassing or, to the extent relevant, retaliatory.[33] More probable is testimony that denies the alleged harassing conduct, that the conduct was meant in jest, or that the plaintiff welcomed or consented to the conduct.

The two main goals of the harasser's deposition are to show lack of corroborating evidence for the harasser's version of events and to nail down testimony from the harasser that squarely conflicts with the plaintiff's or another witness's testimony. Along the way, the plaintiff's counsel should gain an understanding of the harasser's views on the plaintiff, on personal relationships in the workplace, and on working women (or men) in general if it is a sexual harassment case. The harasser should also be asked whether he or she has ever used a sexist epithet at any point in his or her life, whether at work or at home, and whether in jest or seriously. Harassers will often deny ever using such language and can later be contradicted by other witnesses, including witnesses who are otherwise friendly to the employer. Often, the harasser's own words can be used by counsel to portray the individual as power-hungry, arrogant, or untrustworthy. Such a portrayal makes it easier for the jury to view the harasser as abusive and as one who would have engaged in the harassing conduct with which he is charged.

---

33. To the extent the harasser is also the retaliator, the plaintiff's counsel will have to review thoroughly the alleged legitimate business reasons for the adverse action taken against the plaintiff. Otherwise, such questions can be conducted directly with the person(s) who took the adverse action as well as with the corporate representative.

Inquiry should be made of any peculiar aspects of the case. For example, one court permitted the plaintiff to question the alleged harasser about his sexual relationships with other female employees. The court noted that a supervisor's sexual relationship with his subordinates is potentially relevant to the plaintiff's hostile-environment claim, especially when the harasser was the owner of the company.[34]

C. Interrogatories and Requests for Production

As stated already, the plaintiff should send out written discovery as soon as permissible. Interrogatories and requests for production can be hand-delivered to the opposing party at an in-person Rule 26(f) conference or served via email immediately after a telephonic Rule 26(f) conference. Grant extensions of time to respond to discovery as a courtesy, but do not do so repeatedly. When granting a discovery extension, the plaintiff's counsel should let defense counsel know that if the information is not produced by the extended deadline, he or she will move the court to hold a status conference under Rule 16(a) so that the court is aware of the delay in production. That way, if the defendant continues to delay and an extension of the discovery cutoff date becomes necessary, the plaintiff's counsel can show the court that the plaintiff's counsel was diligent in trying to obtain the requested discovery, but that the defendant did not cooperate. Do not let the defendant drag its feet throughout the discovery process.

The plaintiff's counsel should use interrogatories to discover information such as the names of all individuals who were involved in, or otherwise have knowledge of an investigation into the complaint of harassment and the reasons for the alleged retaliatory action. Insofar as requests to produce, the plaintiff should request all versions of documents, including ESI. Specify what format of documents the plaintiff's counsel seeks, such as text messages, emails, documents in native form, Excel charts, etc. Also, counsel should request the defendant to specify which documents, if any, it refuses to produce, including those withheld based on the attorney-client privilege.[35] If necessary, counsel should request an inspection of the premises and have an IT expert conduct mirroring of computers and examine servers.

The plaintiff's counsel should also seek the plaintiff's employment history through requests to produce. It is important to request all files on the plaintiff, not just personnel files. Requests should include all manager files, human resources files, or any other such file regarding the plaintiff. Likewise, counsel should request all files on the harasser's employment history, not limited to his or her personnel files. A request of this nature should include complaints made by other employees regarding the harasser and any investigations, conclusions, or corrective action made thereafter.

Similarly, interrogatories should be used to seek information about each person who has ever complained about a similar type of harassment or subsequent retaliation within

---

34. Plaisance v. Beef Connection Steakhouse, No. CIV. A. 97-0760, 1998 WL 214740, at *4 (E.D. La. Apr. 30, 1998).

35. Fed. R. Civ. P. 26(b)(5)(A).

a reasonable time. Courts generally will permit such discovery for smaller employers where the information requested closely relates to the underlying facts asserted by the plaintiff. However, when the defendant is a large corporate employer operating nationwide, courts may limit the inquiry by location, a particular department or division or to certain categories of employee.[36]

That said, the plaintiff's counsel may find some success in seeking nationwide discovery where the plaintiff asserts that the defendant failed to properly enforce its harassment policy. As noted already, the seminal decisions of *Ellerth*[37] and *Faragher*[38] establish that employers have the responsibility to try to prevent harassment. If the defendant does not have a harassment policy or fails to enforce it effectively, the defendant loses an important defense to liability. Thus, discovery regarding the defendant's receipt of other complaints of harassment and how it handled such complaints is relevant to whether the defendant effectively implemented its own policy.[39]

With respect to a plaintiff's retaliation claim, the plaintiff's counsel will want to use discovery to establish the prima facie case of the plaintiff's claim, namely that he or she engaged in protected activity, that he or she suffered adverse action, and that there was a causal connection between those first two elements. A plaintiff may engage in "protected activity" by either "participating" in an Equal Employment Opportunity (EEO) process or "opposing" unlawful sexual harassment. To participate in an EEO process, the plaintiff must raise a claim, testify, assist, or participate in an investigation, proceeding, or hearing under the EEO laws. Courts interpret the participation clause expansively as providing protection for those who file or serve as a witness in an administrative proceeding or lawsuit alleging discrimination. The participation clause is applicable even if the underlying allegation of discrimination or harassment is not meritorious.[40]

Like the participation clause, a retaliation claim based upon the opposition clause is actionable even where the underlying discrimination claim is found lawful. However, unlike the protections of the participation clause, the opposition clause will only protect a plaintiff if he or she acted with a reasonable, good faith belief that an EEO violation exists.[41]

---

36. Longo v. Dayton Hudson Corp., 1996 WL 219702, at *2 (N.D. Ill. 1996) (severely limiting discovery of complaints against a large, nationwide employer to just the specific retail store where the plaintiff was employed).

37. Burlington Indus., Inc. v. Ellerth, 524 U.S. 742 (1998).

38. Faragher v. City of Boca Raton, 524 U.S. 775 (1998).

39. DeSilva v. Bluegreen Corp., 1997 WL 375748 (N.D.N.Y. 1997) (where the plaintiff alleged that employer failed to enforce its company-wide policy prohibiting harassment, court permitted the plaintiff's requests for information for the previous five years on prior complaints of harassment against any of the defendant's employees, at any of the offices across twenty states).

40. Johnson v. Univ. of Cincinnati, 215 F.3d 561, 582 (6th Cir. 2000).

41. Trent v. Valley Elec. Ass'n, Inc., 41 F.3d 524, 526 (9th Cir. 1994) ("[A] plaintiff [in an opposition case] does not need to prove that the employment practice at issue was in fact unlawful under Title VII . . . [A plaintiff] must only show that she had a "reasonable belief" that the employment practice she protested was prohibited under Title VII.").

Thus, prior to filing suit, the plaintiff's counsel should have a clear idea what "type" of protected activity the plaintiff is asserting and then develop a discovery plan to establish the existence of such activity. Although a document request may be sufficient to establish activity protected under the "participation" clause, further discovery may be necessary to establish protection under the "opposition" clause. The opposition clause imposes both a subjective and objective component upon the plaintiff in establishing the claim. Thus, in addition to finding applicable case law that mirrors the facts of the underlying discrimination (i.e., to establish that the complaint of harassment was "objective"), discovery should be made to establish the severity and pervasiveness of the harassment in question (i.e., to establish the complaint of harassment was reasonably "subjective"). The plaintiff's counsel also should seek discovery that the decision-maker knew of the plaintiff's protected activity. To the extent this is not a clearly established fact, counsel may consider requesting documents affirming receipt of the plaintiff's complaint of discrimination.

The plaintiff's counsel should also utilize discovery to establish the second prong of the plaintiff's retaliation claim, that is, whether the plaintiff suffered an adverse action. Unlike discrimination cases, the anti-retaliation provisions under Title VII encompass a broader range of actions than materially adverse actions. In fact, any retaliatory action that "deters a reasonable employee from complaining about discrimination" constitutes an adverse action.[42] When drafting discovery, consider that retaliation is not limited to a single retaliatory action, but instead contemplates a pattern of conduct that, when considered as a whole, could be deemed retaliatory.[43]

Such actions could include threatening reassignment, scrutinizing the employee's work or attendance more closely, removing supervisory authority, requiring reverification of work status, making false reports to government agencies, etc.[44] Therefore, discovery requests should address each possible retaliatory action that make up the pattern of retaliatory conduct, including emails or other memorandums between the decision-maker and other key witnesses regarding each possible retaliatory action.

Finally, with regard to the third prong of the prima facie case, discovery should be used to establish a "causal connection," which is often established by evidence of a close temporal proximity between the protected activity and the adverse action (or pattern

---

42. Burlington Northern & Santa Fe Railway Co. v. White, 548 U.S. 53, 69 (2006).

43. Vega v. Hempstead Union Free Sch. Dist., 801 F.3d 72 (2d Cir. 2015) (holding that a high school teacher stated a claim for retaliation based on the combination of "his assignment of notoriously absent students, his temporary paycheck reduction, and the District's failure to notify him of a curriculum change"); Sanford v. Main St. Baptist Church Manor, Inc., 327 F. App'x 587, 599 (6th Cir. 2009) (holding that although some of the incidents alone may not rise to the level of an adverse action, "the incidents taken together might dissuade a reasonable worker from making or supporting a discrimination charge").

44. *See. e.g.,* Geleta v. Gray, 645 F.3d 408, 412 (D.C. Cir. 2011) (ruling that fact issue for jury existed as to material adversity when, among other things, the plaintiff went from supervising twenty employees to supervising none), Bartolon-Perez v. Island Granite & Stone, Inc., 108 F. Supp. 3d 1335, 1340–41 (S.D. Fla. 2015) (holding that a fact finder could conclude an employer engaged in retaliation under the Fair Labor Standards Act where it knew about the plaintiff's immigration status but waited until after he engaged in protected activity to "hold it . . . over his head"); Greengrass v. Int'l Monetary Sys., Ltd., 776 F.3d 481, 485–86 (7th Cir. 2015) (ruling that employer's listing of employee's name in public filing with the Securities and Exchange Commission was materially adverse).

of adverse action).[45] Courts will presume a causal connection where the temporal proximity is extremely close.[46] Counsel should not rely solely on the date the adverse action actually occurred. Indeed, discovery of when the defendant first contemplated the adverse may bolster the plaintiff's attempts to establish a causal connection. Counsel should therefore be sure to request that disciplinary actions, poor performance evaluations, or other documentary adverse actions be produced in their native format, with all metadata intact. Such documentation will insure that the plaintiff's counsel can determine the exact date and time the defendant first drafted, and subsequently revised the adverse action in question.[47]

When conducting discovery, it is important to be aware that the causation standard in Title VII retaliation cases differs from Title VII harassment cases. Where the defendant is a private sector employer or a state or local government, the plaintiff must show that "but for" a retaliatory motive, the employer would not have taken the adverse action(s).[48] This "but-for" standard, however, does not require that retaliation be the "sole cause" of the action. Indeed, there can be multiple "but-for" causes, so long as retaliation was "a but-for" cause for the adverse action.[49] Although a defendant certainly will not attest to such retaliatory motives via interrogatory responses, counsel should be sure to request documents that relate to the plaintiff's complaint of harassment (or participation in a co-worker's complaint) from all of the key players. The fact that such objection or participation irked the decision-makers is relevant to establishing that the employee's protected activity played "a but-for" role in the decision to retaliate against the plaintiff.

Another area the plaintiff's counsel will want to explore is the defendant's affirmative defenses. With regard to interrogatories, counsel will want to ask the employer to state, with specificity, the factual basis for each denial and affirmative defense. Counsel will also want to include a request for production seeking any document relied upon and/or used to support any such defense. Additionally, the plaintiff will want to confer with defense counsel regarding any affirmative defenses that are insufficiently pled prior to

---

45. However, it is important to note that temporal proximity is not necessarily the only way to establish a causal connection. Evidence that the proffered reason for the adverse action is pretextual may also establish a causal link. Abbott v. Crown Motor Co., 348 F.3d 537 (6th Cir. 2003) (causation established, notwithstanding eleven-month interim, because supervisor stated his intention to "get back at" those who had supported the discrimination allegations).

46. Gilliard v. Georgia Dept. of Corrections, 500 Fed. Appx. 860, 864 (11th Cir. 2012) (temporal proximity may establish causal connection by itself where it is "very close"); Higdon v. Jackson, 393 F.3d 1211, 1220 (11th Cir. 2004) (timespan of one month is sufficient to establish causal connection by itself).

47. If Microsoft Word documents are produced electronically, counsel can determine the date the document in question was created by examining the document's properties.

48. Univ. of Tex. Sw. Med. Ctr., v. Nassar, 133 S.Ct. 2517, 2534 (2013) (holding that "but-for" causation is required to prove Title VII retaliation claims).

49. Kwan v. Andalex Grp., 737 F.3d 834, 846 (2nd Cir. 2013) (but-for causation "does not require proof that retaliation was the only cause of the employer's action, but only that the adverse action would not have occurred in the absence of a retaliatory motive").

filing a motion to strike the defense. This process will either provide additional information from the defendant or eliminate affirmative defenses that have no bases.[50]

Finally, the plaintiff's counsel should serve interrogatories and requests to produce regarding the plaintiff's damages. Requests to produce should include records reflecting the compensation the plaintiff earned, benefits such as retirement plan benefits, stock, fringe benefits, benefit summary plan descriptions, and so on, during the plaintiff's employment. Of course, this request should be limited to the relevant period. For the plaintiffs who had an employment agreement, a copy of the agreement would certainly be relevant. Moreover, if the plaintiff is seeking punitive damages, the defendant's financial records are discoverable and should be sought.[51]

D. Requests for Admissions

Though often overlooked, requests for admissions can be an effective tool to simplify litigation. Such requests can reduce the cost of litigation by establishing undisputed facts and authenticating documents without the expense of more traditional discovery methods. In harassment cases in particular, the plaintiff's counsel can use request for admissions to establish that the defendant was aware of the plaintiff's complaint of harassment and that the plaintiff properly followed the defendant's harassment policy. With regard to the plaintiff's retaliation claim, the plaintiff can establish that the defendant was aware of the plaintiff's protected activity, thus eliminating any burden of proving this prima facie element any further. Moreover, requests for admission can be used to establish insurance coverage or benefits. Like other discovery devises, requests for admissions are expansive in nature.[52]

When responding to a request for admission, the defendant must admit or deny each request or "state in detail why [it] cannot truthfully admit or deny it."[53] Such responses must be straightforward and specific. If the defendant denies only part of a request, it must specify the part admitted and qualify or deny the rest.[54] If, for some reason, the defendant does not know the answer, it must state that it made a "reasonable inquiry" into finding the answer but was unable to obtain the information to answer the request.[55] If the defendant fails to timely respond to a request for admission, the

---

50. Ashcroft v. Iqbal, 129 S.Ct. 1937 (2009) (setting forth a heightened pleading standard); Bell Atlantic Corp. v. Twombly, 550 U.S. 544 (2007) (same); Holtzman v. B/E Aerospace, Inc., 2008 WL 2225668 (S.D. Fla. 2008) (the Iqbal-Twombly heightened pleading standard applies to the defendant's defenses, such that the defendant must plead sufficient facts to establish that defenses are plausible on their face. Mere conclusory statements without sufficient factual support are deficient).

51. EEOC v. Klockner H&K Machs, Inc., 168 F.R.D. 233, 236 (E.D. Wis. 1996) (employer's financial records are relevant to punitive damages and are thus discoverable, even though such damages are capped under the Civil Rights Act of 1991).

52. FED. R. CIV. P. 36(a)(1).

53. FED. R. CIV. P. 36(a)(4).

54. *Id.*

55. *Id.*

request will be presumed admitted.[56] Also, if a defendant fails to admit a matter and the plaintiff's counsel later proves the matter through other discovery tools, the court may order the defendant to pay the reasonable expenses incurred in proving the matter, including attorney fees.[57] Thus, requests for admissions can be a powerful tool when dealing with defendants who otherwise drag their feet during the discovery process.

E. Common Discovery Issues for Plaintiffs

One issue that seems to arise continually is the defendant's claim that either no documents are responsive to the plaintiff's requests or that it was unable to locate any such responsive documents. In such an instance, the plaintiff's counsel should work closely with defense counsel to set forth an agreed list of search terms for the defendant to use when seeking to respond to the plaintiff's discovery requests. When counsel agrees on the terms to be used, such terms should be recorded in writing so there is no confusion in the future.

Defendants also frequently seek copies of the plaintiff's retainer agreement with counsel at the outset of litigation. The plaintiff's counsel should object to such requests on the basis of the attorney-client privilege, the work product doctrine, and relevancy.[58]

Likewise, counsel should object to any request for affidavits obtained from witnesses before or during litigation based on the work-product doctrine.[59]

Defendants often request the plaintiffs' bank statements, including monthly account statements, for a period of years. The plaintiff's counsel should object to these types of requests as they are typically overbroad, constitute an invasion of privacy, and are entirely irrelevant given the fact that such relevant information can be sought using less intrusive means. A request for bank statements would show all financial activity of the plaintiff, not just the information needed for mitigation purposes. Moreover, any income or benefits the plaintiff may have received from sources other than subsequent employment (e.g., unemployment, workers' compensation and/or social security benefits) likely have no relevance to any claim or defense. The only potentially relevant information contained in such financial information can almost always be obtained through less intrusive means, for example, through W-2s.

Similarly, defendants often request expansive medical records when such records are not relevant to the plaintiff's claims. Where the plaintiff seeks only "garden variety" emotional damages, the defendant is not entitled to information relating to the

---

56. Fed. R. Civ. P. 36(a)(3).

57. Fed. R. Civ. P. 37(c)(2).

58. Banks v. Off. of Sen. Sergeant-at-Arms, 222 F.R.D. 7, 13 (D.D.C. 2004) (holding that a fee arrangement becomes relevant "at best" after the plaintiff prevails and seeks attorneys' fees, and that knowing what one's opponent is paying counsel is not a legitimate use of discovery; discovery seeks relevant evidence, not ammunition for settlement discussions . . .").

59. Castle v. Sangamo Weston, Inc., 744 F.2d 1464 (11th Cir. 1984) (affidavits or documentation containing questions formulated by counsel and directed to potential witnesses in anticipation of litigation or after litigation constitute work product); FDIC. v. Cherry, Bekaert & Holland, 131 F.R.D. 596 (M.D. Fla. 1990) (same); Cohen v. Gulfstream Training Acad. Inc., 249 F.R.D. 385 (S.D. Fla. 2008) (same).

plaintiff's health.[60] Where the plaintiff seeks extensive emotional damages or sought medical treatment as a result of the discriminatory conduct, a defendant may be entitled to the plaintiff's medical records that are relevant to those claims.

Sometimes, defendants will seek third-party subpoenas directed at the plaintiff's former or current employers. In most cases, counsel should move to quash any such subpoenas on the basis that they are overbroad or not proportional to the needs of the case. The likely benefit of obtaining such records will almost always outweigh the burden to the plaintiff and/or the responding third party, especially where such information can be obtained through less intrusive means.[61] The plaintiff's counsel may also want to argue that the subpoenas should be quashed on the basis that they are designed to embarrass, harass and/or interfere with the plaintiff's current employment.[62]

---

60. Laboy v. Emeritus Corp., 2014 WL 1293440, at *1 (M.D. Fla. Mar. 28, 2014) (the plaintiff's claim does not extend beyond the "garden variety" claim for emotional distress warranting the defendant's request for a HIPAA release for medical records relating to the plaintiff's mental health).

61. DeJesus et al v. Tender Touch Health Care Services, Case No. 5-16-cv-00049 (N.D. Fla. Dec. 1, 2016) (granting motion to quash/for protective order of overly broad subpoena to the plaintiff's former and current employers where the defendant failed to narrowly tailor the subpoena to any issue in the case); Graham v. Casey's General Store, 206 F.R.D. 251, 256 (S.D. Ind. 2002) (holding that a less intrusive means of obtaining discovery rather than serving a subpoena to a current employer will balance the interests of burdening the party/employee and the benefit of the records).

62. FED. R. CIV. 26(c)(1).

CHAPTER 12

Motion for Summary Judgment: Defense Perspective

Zascha Blanco Abbott

I. INTRODUCTION

A motion for summary judgment may provide the employer the best opportunity for winning its case. This procedure allows the defendant's case to be evaluated on its merits without regard to the sympathy for the employee, and minimizes the emotional perspective that interplays in decisions before a jury. Given the importance of a motion for summary judgment, the process must be planned well before the motion is filed, and the assessment on whether a motion for summary judgment should be filed begins soon after the complaint is served on the defendant.

In 1986, the US Supreme Court issued a trilogy of decisions addressing summary judgment.[1] With those decisions came a new, more favorable view on entering summary judgments.[2] These cases changed the landscape of motions for summary

---

1. Celotex Corp. v. Catrett, 477 U.S. 317 (1986); Anderson v. Liberty Lobby, Inc., 477 U.S. 242 (1986); Matsushita Elec. Indus. Co. v. Zenith Radio Corp., 475 U.S. 574 (1986). In Celotex Corp. v. Catrett, the US Supreme Court held that the moving party is not required to support its motion with affidavits or other like materials negating the nonmovant's claim. The US Supreme Court emphasized that Rule 56 is not limited to isolated and extraordinary circumstances, and it is an integral part of the federal rules designed "to secure the just, speedy, and inexpensive determination of every action." 477 U.S. at 324. In Matsushita Electric Industrial Co. v. Zenith Radio Corp., the US Supreme Court held that when a moving party has carried its burden under Rule 56 of showing that no disputed material facts exist, the nonmovant must do more than simply show that there is some "metaphysical doubt as to the material facts" because where the record as a whole could not lead a rational trier of fact to find for the non-moving party, there is "no genuine issue for trial." *Id.*

2. *See,* e.g., City of Mt. Pleasant, Iowa v. Associated Elec. Coop., Inc., 838 F.2d 268, 273 (8th Cir. 1988) ("In any case, whatever the meaning of our earlier cases, [after the *Celotex* trilogy] ... we should be somewhat more hospitable to summary judgments than in the past."); Cal. Architectural Bldg. Prods. v. Franciscan Ceramics, Inc., 818 F.2d 1466, 1468, 1470 (9th Cir. 1987) (noting that the *Celotex* trilogy "increased the utility of summary judgment"); Raynor v. Richardson-Merrell, Inc., 643 F. Supp. 238, 240–41, 245 (D.D.C. 1986) (explaining that after the 1986 Supreme Court decisions, summary judgment motions would be a "bulwark against claims based on speculation and ... inference").

judgment and made it easier for defendants to obtain summary judgment in employment cases. But in some circuits sexual harassment and retaliation cases have resulted in reluctance from the courts to grant summary judgment. Summary judgments are an integral part of litigating gender harassment and retaliation claims, and are a useful tool for disposing of meritless cases. It is therefore important that when presented with these issues, defense employment counsel evaluate and focus their cases on potentially prevailing on a motion for summary judgment.

II. THE FEDERAL STANDARD FOR MOTION FOR SUMMARY JUDGMENT

The summary judgment procedure is a method for promptly disposing of actions in which there is no genuine issue as to any material fact. When preparing the motion for summary judgment, the movant should keep in mind elements and criteria required under the federal rules for a proper and a well-supported motion for summary judgment. Rule 56 of the Federal Rules of Civil Procedure provides for the filing of a motion for summary judgment in advance of trial.

According to the rule, a party may file a motion any time until thirty days after close of all discovery, unless a different time is set by local rules of the court.

> (a) MOTION FOR SUMMARY JUDGMENT OR PARTIAL SUMMARY JUDGMENT. A party may move for summary judgment, identifying each claim or defense—or the part of each claim or defense—on which summary judgment is sought. The court shall grant summary judgment if the movant shows that there is no genuine dispute as to any material fact and the movant is entitled to judgment as a matter of law. The court should state on the record the reasons for granting or denying the motion.
>
> (b) TIME TO FILE A MOTION. Unless a different time is set by local rule or the court orders otherwise, a party may file a motion for summary judgment at any time until 30 days after the close of all discovery.
>
> (c) PROCEDURES.
>> (1) Supporting Factual Positions. A party asserting that a fact cannot be or is genuinely disputed must support the assertion by:
>>> (A) citing to particular parts of materials in the record, including depositions, documents, electronically stored information, affidavits or declarations, stipulations (including those made for purposes of the motion only), admissions, interrogatory answers, or other materials; or
>>> (B) showing that the materials cited do not establish the absence or presence of a genuine dispute, or that an adverse party cannot produce admissible evidence to support the fact.

As can be seen in the Federal Rule, it is crucial that the motion for summary judgment include citations to particular parts of the material on the record, including depositions, documents, electronically stored information, affidavits or declarations, stipulations, admissions, interrogatory answers, or other materials obtained in the case. The motion should show that the materials cited do not establish the presence of a genuine dispute or that an adverse party cannot produce admissible evidence to support that a genuine issue of fact exists.

The standard for determining summary judgment pursuant to Rule 56 mirrors the standard for determining whether a directed verdict is appropriate under Rule 50 (a). The courts must review the record taken as a whole and the nonmoving party may not rest on mere allegations or denials of the adverse party's pleading, but must set forth specific facts: by affidavit or other admissible evidence; that demonstrate that there is no genuine issue for trial. In general, summary judgment is appropriate if no genuine issue of material fact exists and the moving party is entitled to judgment as a matter of law.[3] The defendant movant bears the burden of identifying those portions of the record it believes demonstrate the absence of a genuine issue of material fact.[4] If the burden of proof at trial lies with the nonmoving party, the movant may satisfy its initial burden by pointing out to the district court that there is an absence of evidence to support the nonmoving party's case.[5] Although the party moving for summary judgment must demonstrate the absence of a genuine issue of material fact, it does not need to negate the elements of the nonmovant's case.[6] A fact is "material" if the resolution in favor of one party might affect the outcome of the lawsuit under governing law.[7] For a motion for summary judgment, if the moving party fails to meet its burden, the motion for summary judgment must be denied, regardless of the response from the nonmoving party.[8] Courts agree that a plaintiff cannot defeat a motion for summary judgment by resting upon conclusory allegations in the pleadings.[9] Nor may summary judgment be defeated merely on the basis of a "metaphysical doubt" about material facts or on the basis of "conjecture or surmise."[10]

Lastly, when the decision is made to file the summary judgment motion, local court rules should always be reviewed in the research process. If Rule 56 stated the only requirements for a motion for summary judgment, the moving party might be able to submit nothing more than a motion, and the motion might not even have to be in writing.[11] Of course, the ordinary practice is to file a written motion with supporting documents. But the specific form of the documents can vary significantly among the

---

3. FED. R. CIV. P. 56(c).

4. Rimkus Consulting Group, Inc. v. Cammarata, 688 F. Supp. 2d 598 (S.D. Tex. 2010); Triple Tee Golf, Inc. v. Nike, Inc., 485 F.3d 253, 261 (5th Cir. 2007).

5. *See* Celotex, 477 U.S. at 325.

6. *See* Boudreax v. Swift Transp. Co., 402 F.3d 536, 540 (5th Cir. 2005).

7. *See* Sossamon v. Lone Star State of Texas, 560 F.3d 316, 326 (5th Cir. 2009).

8. United States v. $92,203.00 in U.S. Currency, 537 F.3d 504, 507 (5th Cir. 2008).

9. FED. R. CIV. P. 56(e); Anderson v. Liberty Lobby, Inc., 477 U.S. 242, 248 (1986).

10. Matsushita Elec. Indus. Co. v. Zenith Radio Corp., 475 U.S. 574, 585 (1986); Bryant v. Maffucci, 923 F.2d 979, 982 (2d Cir.), *cert. denied,* 502 U.S. 849 (1991).

11. Andrea Doreen Ltd. v. Building Material Local Union 282, 299 F. Supp. 2d 129, 143 (E.D. NY 2004).

federal districts. For example, the brief can be limited to as little as ten pages[12] or as much as fifty pages,[13] depending on the applicable local rules.

In addition, it is a good idea to research case law by the particular judge assigned to your case to understand any prior analysis that has been used in the particular court for your case.

In sum, when deciding that a motion for summary judgment is appropriate in a case, attorneys should understand the applicable standards and procedures and prior written opinions and preferences of the assigned judge. It is also important that the attorney be familar with any pertinent state or local rules that may apply to such motions.

III. THE FAILURE TO EXHAUST ADMINISTRATIVE REMEDIES

It is crucial that employment law attorneys have a complete understanding of the various procedural prerequisites and administrative exhaustion schemes that apply to claims of harassment and retaliation under Title VII as the failure of the plaintiff to comply with these prerequisites may be a basis for granting summary judgment in favor of the defendant. And, the plaintiff's failure to comply with the requirements surrounding the filing of an Equal Employment Opportunity Commission (EEOC) charge may cause the plaintiff to lose the case in its entirety.

Generally, a plaintiff seeking to bring a lawsuit for employment gender harassment or retaliation must first file a charge of discrimination with the EEOC before being able to initiate a civil action. Defense counsel should verify that the defendant was previously named in a timely filed EEOC charge, because a timely EEOC charge is a prerequisite to filing a private cause of action under Title VII.[14] Determining timeliness, however, depends upon (1) the state in which the claim is filed; (2) the relationship, if any, between the EEOC and any existing state or local agency in existence to address the claim; and (3) the precise nature of the claim. In this regard, attorneys should be prepared when arguing the timeliness requirements, that courts have protected plaintiffs by liberally applying the doctrines of waiver, estoppel, and equitable tolling in these cases.[15] And in harassment cases, in particular, courts have permitted the continuing violation doctrine.[16]

In order to pursue a claim for gender harassment or retaliation under Title VII, a plaintiff must file an EEOC charge contesting the alleged conduct within 300 days of the alleged violation in deferral states.[17] The plaintiff must include the scope of the

---

12. N.D. Ohio R. Civ. P. 71(g).

13. D. Alaska R. Civ. P. 5.1 (L).

14. *See* 42 U.S.C. § 2000e-5(b), (c), (d), (e), & (f).

15. Zipes v. Trans World Airlines, Inc., 455 U.S. 385 (1982).

16. Mandel v. M & Q Packaging Corp., No. 11-3913 (3d Cir. 2013); National Railroad Passenger Corp. v. Morgan, 536 U.S. 101 (2002).

17. 42 U.S.C.A 2000e-5(e) (deferral state claimant must file EEOC Charge within 300 days of alleged unlawful employment practice.); Griffin v. Air Products and Chemicals, Inc. 883 F.2d 940, 941 (11 Cir. 1989).

allegations within the EEOC charge and do so in a timely manner.[18] The statute of limitations for filing a charge of discrimination depends on state and local law. Generally, an employee has 180 days from the date the alleged discrimination or retaliation took place to file a charge. If a state or local agency enforces a law prohibiting the same type of discrimination, the time limit is extended to 300 days.[19]

In many states, the EEOC has entered into a work-sharing agreement with the state fair employment practices agency. If a charge of discrimination is filed with either the EEOC or the state agency in one of these states, it will automatically be filed with the other agency, too. If the state does not have a work-sharing agreement, and a claimant wants to preserve his or her rights under both federal and state law, a charge should be filed with both agencies.

Legitimate grounds for granting a motion for summary judgment exist where a plaintiff is late filing either a charge with the EEOC or a subsequent complaint with the court or where the plaintiff fails to bring the claim before the EEOC prior to filing a complaint in court for sexual harassment or retaliation. For example, sometimes a complaint in a civil action will allege facts or claims that were not asserted by the plaintiff in his or her charge of discrimination. Under those circumstances, the question becomes whether the scope of the charge of discrimination is determined by the facts and claims that can reasonably be expected to grow out of the EEOC's investigation of the charge.[20]

The EEOC has attempted to coordinate federal, state, and local charge filing requirements by entering into contractual agreements with state and local Fair Employment Practices Agencies (FEPA) known as work-sharing agreements.[21] When a state or local agency has the authority to address sexual harassment or retaliation claims, the state is a "deferral state." The term applies because Congress wanted to give state and local agencies "an opportunity to address the evil at which the federal legislation was aimed, and to avoid federal intervention unless its need was demonstrated."[22] 42 U.S.C. § 2000e-5(c) prohibits any charge from being "filed with the EEOC until sixty days have elapsed from initial filing of the charge with an authorized state or local agency unless that agency's proceedings have been earlier terminated."[23]

Frequently, part of the work-sharing agreement provides for a waiver of the sixty-day deferral. With that waiver in place, a charge filed with the EEOC within the 300-day period is timely.[24] From the employer's perspective, the "deferral" purpose and the plain

---

18. *See* Chanda v. Engelhard/ICC f.k.a Ciba-Geigy Corp., 234 F.3d 1219 (11th Cir. 2000) (plaintiff failed to meet the initial jurisdictional requirement for this Title VII retaliation claim by not including it in his EEOC charge).

19. 42 USCA 2000e-5(e)(deferral state claimant must file EEOC charge within 300 days of the alleged unlawful employment practice).

20. *See* Chanda v. Engelhard/ICC f.k.a Ciba-Geigy Corp., 234 F.3d 1219 (11th Cir. 2000).

21. The criteria for being known as a FEPA for the purposes of Title VII are set forth at 29 C.F.R. Part 1601, subpart H.

22. Mohasco Corp. v. Silver, 447 U.S. 807, 821 (1980).

23. EEOC v. Commercial Office Prods. Co., 486 U.S. 107, 111 (1988).

24. Commercial Office Prods. Co., 486 U.S. 107.

language of 42 U.S.C. § 2000e-5 would seem to suggest that if a plaintiff fails to file a charge with a deferral agency, the plaintiff should not have the benefit of the extended 300-day limitation.

Even if the plaintiff satisfies the timeliness requirements for filing the EEOC charge, additional requirements exist for filing a complaint. Assuming that the EEOC elects not to litigate the matter, it will issue a right-to-sue letter to the plaintiff. Then, within ninety days of receiving that letter, the plaintiff must file the civil complaint.[25] If the ninety-day deadline is missed for filing a complaint under Title VII, the action may be ripe for an employer's summary judgment.

Therefore, when drafting a motion for summary judgment, attorneys should be aware of the requirements for filing the charge of discrimination and whether the state is a deferral state and has work-sharing agreements.

IV. THE HARASSMENT CAUSE OF ACTION

The lawyer representing a defendant and preparing a motion for summary judgment must be careful to analyze the allegations in a dispute at the earliest stage in the litigation to ascertain the elements necessary to prepare and prevail in its motion for summary judgment. For an employer to establish that it is entitled to a motion for summary judgment, counsel must also be familiar with the law and factual circumstances in the case law that have permitted and disallowed motions for summary judgment.

Title VII does not specifically prohibit sexual harassment, but the US Supreme Court has held that harassment because of a person's sex is a form of sex discrimination that violates Title VII.[26] The case law analyzing harassment claims has continually evolved. The law addressing sexual harassment claims is also applicable to other types of illegal harassment such as harassment based on retaliation.[27] More specifically, Title VII does not specifically prohibit "harassment" or "hostile work environment" as worded in the statute; however, such discrimination is covered by the "terms, conditions and privileges" language of the statute.[28] Title VII is violated when the workplace is permeated with discriminatory (based on a protected category) intimidation, ridicule, and insult that is sufficiently severe or pervasive to alter the conditions of the victim's employment and create an abusive working environment.[29]

---

25. 42 U.S.C. § 2000e-5(f)(1).

26. Harris v. Forklft Systems, 510 U.S. 17 (1993).

27. *See, e.g.,* Herrera v. Lufkin Indus., 474 F.3d 675, 681 (10th Cir. 2007) (Title VII's prohibition on race or national origin discrimination includes claims of a hostile work environment based on race or national origin; to survive summary judgment on a claim alleging a racially hostile work environment, the plaintiff "must show that a rational jury could find that the workplace is permeated with discriminatory intimidation, ridicule, and insult, that is sufficiently severe or pervasive to alter the conditions of the victim's employment and create an abusive working environment," and that the victim "was targeted for harassment because of [his] . . . race or national origin."); Carpenter, 2005 U.S. Dist. App. LEXIS 35453 (applying Harris to racial harassment context).

28. Harris v. Forklift Systems, 510 U.S. 17, 21 (1993).

29. Meritor Savings Bank v. Vinson, 477 U.S. at 67.

Title VII's prohibition against sex discrimination in the workplace includes two forms of sexual harassment: quid pro quo and hostile work environment.[30] In either case, a prevailing plaintiff must have suffered disadvantages in employment that members of the other sex did not.[31] But the likelihood of an employer obtaining summary judgment may depend on whether the claim is characterized as quid pro quo or hostile environment. Lastly, each has separate elements, and the defendant should show in the motion for summary judgment how the plaintiff is unable to establish at least one of any of the elements of the prima facie case.

A. Quid Pro Quo Claim

To prevail on a quid pro quo claim, a plaintiff must prove the following four elements: (1) she was a member of a protected class; (2) she was subjected to unwelcome sexual harassment in the form of sexual advances or requests for sexual favors; (3) the harassment was based on her sex; and (4) her submission to the unwelcome advances was an express or implied condition for receiving job benefits or her refusal to submit resulted in a tangible job detriment.[32] Quid pro quo harassment occurs when a work-related benefit is considered expressly or impliedly on the granting of a sexual favor. For example, "If you don't go out with me you will be fired." The prima facie case in a quid pro case is whether a tangible job benefit was conferred or a tangible job detriment was imposed based on a discriminatory or prohibited criteria.[33] A quid pro quo claim arises when a tangible employment action results from an employee's refusal or acquiescence to a supervisor's sexual demands.[34] A tangible employment action has been described as "a significant change in employment status, such as hiring, firing, failing to promote, reassignment with significantly different responsibilities, or a decision causing a significant change in benefits."[35] On the other hand, many actions have been found not to be

---

30. Meritor Sav. Bank v. Vinson, 477 U.S. 57 (1986); *see also* 42 U.S.C. § 2000e-2(a)(1); *accord* Burlington Indus. v. Ellerth, 524 U.S. 742 (1998).

31. Oncale v. Sundowner Offshore Servs., Inc., 523 U.S. 80 (acting Harris at 25) (1998).

32. Soto v. John Morrell & Co., 285 F. Supp. 2d 1146 (N.D. Iowa 2003).

33. The EEOC's guidelines state that unwelcome sexual advances constitute sexual harassment if submission to such conduct is made a condition of employment or if employment decisions are based on submission or rejection of such conduct. *See* 29 CFR 1604.11(a)(1)-(2).

34. *Ellerth*, 524 U.S. at *751–754*.

35. *Id.* at 652–53; *Ellerth*, 524 U.S. at 765; *see also* EEOC Guidance on Vicarious Employer Liability for Unlawful Harassment by Supervisors § IV(B)(1) (1999), http://www.eeoc.gov/policy/docs/harassment .html (a tangible employment action, inter alia, "is usually documented in official government records," "may be subject to review by higher level supervisors" and "often requires the formal approval of the enterprise and use of its internal procedures"); *see, e.g.,* Burlington Northern and Santa Fe Railway Co. v. White, 364 F.3d 789 (6th Cir. 2004) ("reassignments without salary or work hour changes do not ordinarily constitute adverse employment decisions," although a reassignment can do so if it constitutes a demotion evidenced by a "less distinguished title, a material loss of benefits, significantly diminished material responsibilities or other indices that might be unique to a particular situation"); Pa. State Police v. Suders, 542 U.S. 129 (2004) (listing transfer to a position with unbearable working conditions constitutes a tangible employment action); Virostek v. Liberty Twp. Police Dep't, 2001 U.S. App. LEXIS 15909

"tangible employment actions," such as denial of a bonus,[36] receiving negative performance evaluations,[37] being placed on probation or a performance improvement plan,[38] receiving a change in schedule,[39] and being submitted to psychological examinations and internal investigations.[40]

It is important to determine whether a tangible employment action has occurred, because the description precludes a co-worker from being a quid pro quo harasser, as co-workers lack the necessary authority to make an employment decision (a requisite element of the claim). Conversely, a supervisor[41] can only make the decision on behalf of the employer; and therefore, the decision cannot be made outside the scope of the supervisor's employment. As a result, when a supervisor creates quid pro quo harassment, the employer has no substantive defense and will be vicariously liable.

(6th Cir. 2001) (reassignment from detective to patrol officer required more dangerous and physical duties and deprived plaintiff of more desirable "intellectual" tasks); *cf.* Tran v. Trs. of State Colls., 355 F.3d 1263 (10th Cir. 2004) (transfer to a job that required plaintiff to develop new computer programming skills without a cut in pay or benefits is not a tangible employment action); EEOC v. Rest. Co., 490 F. Supp. 2d 1039 (D. Minn. 2007) (extra duties not a tangible employment action where all duties related to plaintiff's job as a cook).

36. *See, e.g.,* Hunt v. City of Markham, 219 F.3d 649 (7th Cir. 2000) (bonus is generally irregular and discretionary, as opposed to pay raises, which are normal for an employee performing satisfactorily).

37. *See, e.g.,* Lucas v. Chicago Transit Auth., 367 F.3d 714 (7th Cir. 2004); Primes v. Reno, 190 F.3d 765, 767 (6th Cir. 1999); Kohler v. Inter-Tel Techs., 244 F.3d 1167 (9th Cir. 2001).

38. *See, e.g.,* Thompson v. Naphcare, Inc., 2004 U.S. App. Lexis 23697 (5th Cir. 2004) (mere increased criticism of an employee's work performance is not a tangible employment action); Agnew v. BASF Corp., 286 F.3d 307, 310 (6th Cir. 2002); Stewart v. Mo. Pac. R.R. Co., 2005 U.S. App. LEXIS 1841 (5th Cir. 2005) (year-long probation in job with same pay and responsibilities was not an adverse employment action); *cf.* Rachel-Smith v. FT Data Inc., 247 F. Supp. 2d 734 (D. Md. 2003) (plaintiff was placed on probation that would result in termination if any "lack of performance or meeting objectives" occurred during that period. Because plaintiff's performance was to be reviewed on a weekly basis, the court held that the placement on probation constituted an adverse employment action.).

39. *See, e.g.,* Thornton v. Fed. Express Corp., 2008 U.S. App. LEXIS 13294 (6th Cir. 2008) (change in schedule in same job that was personally inconvenient one day per week without an increase in responsibilities, demotion, or loss of pay or benefits was not an adverse employment action).

40. *See, e.g.,* Harrison v. City of Akron, 43 Fed. Appx. 903, 2002 U.S. App. LEXIS 16263 (6th Cir. 2002) (unpublished).

41. On June 24, 2013, the US Supreme Court issued its opinion in Vance v. Ball State University, No. 11-556, 133 S.Ct 2432 (2013), holding that an employee is a "supervisor" for purposes of vicarious employer liability under Title VII of the Civil Rights Act of 1964 ("Title VII") only if he or she is permitted by the employer to take tangible employment actions against the employee. The Supreme Court upheld a narrow definition of "supervisor" that had been affirmed by the Seventh Circuit. The Supreme Court held that a supervisor is an individual who has authority to take a tangible employment action, meaning "a significant change in employment status, such as hiring, firing, failing to promote, reassignment with significantly different responsibilities, or a decision causing a significant change in benefits." The US Supreme Court noted that, in Faragher v. City of Boca Raton, 524 U.S. 775 (1998), and Burlington Industries Inc. v. Ellerth, 524 U.S. 742 (1998), a split theory of liability was established for employers in Title VII harassment cases depending on whether the alleged harasser is a "supervisor" or a "co-worker" in relation to the employee complaining of harassment. If the harasser is a coworker, an employer will only be liable for the harassing behavior if the employee can prove negligence on the part of the employer. In other words, the employer failed to take reasonable measures to prevent and correct the offending behavior.

In quid pro quo sexual harassment cases employers are strictly liable for the acts of their supervisors, despite a lack of notice by the employer of the harassment. Thus, in order to prevail, the employee need not prove that the employer knew or should have known of the alleged harassment.

B. Hostile Work Environment Claim

Unlike a quid pro quo cause of action, a hostile environment can be created by either a supervisor or a co-worker, and the difference is significant. If the alleged harasser is a co-worker, the employer will not be liable for the alleged conduct unless the employer knew or should have known about it.[42] But if the alleged harasser is a supervisor, the employer will be vicariously liable unless it can prove an affirmative defense. The affirmative defense requires that the employer show that (1) the employer exercised reasonable care to prevent[43] and promptly correct the alleged hostile environment,[44] and (2) the employee unreasonably failed to take advantage of the preventative or corrective opportunities provided by the employer; or the employee otherwise unreasonably failed to avoid the harm.[45] Obviously, when the alleged harasser is a supervisor, the employer has a much more difficult defense.

Counsel should not lose sight of the distinction between a supervisor and co-worker as the alleged harasser. Often, the facts will not draw these lines clearly, and in those cases, defense counsel must work to shape the facts in the light most favorable to the defendant, that is, a co-worker rather than a supervisor, and a hostile environment rather than a quid pro quo claim. The result will be the application of a more lenient standard, for example, negligence rather than strict liability and the availability of an affirmative defense rather than automatic liability.

---

42. Meritor Sav. Bank v. Vinson, 477 U.S. 57 (1986).

43. *See, e.g.*, Clark v. United Parcel Serv., 400 F.3d 341, 349 (6th Cir. 2005) (employer's efforts to prevent harassment can include a comprehensive sexual harassment policy that should at least "(1) require supervisors to report incidents of sexual harassment; (2) permit both informal and formal complaints of harassment to be made; (3) provide a mechanism for bypassing a harassing supervisor when making a complaint; and (4) provide for training regarding the policy").

44. *See, e.g.*, Collette v. Stein-Mart, Inc., 2005 U.S. App. LEXIS 2093 (6th Cir. 2005); Kennedy v. Wal-Mart Stores, Inc., 15 Fed. Appx. 755 (10th Cir. 2001) (unpublished) (plaintiff complained repeatedly to managers about the harasser's behavior, yet, for ten months, management did not fire him, demote him, move him, or move the plaintiff).

45. Faragher v. City of Boca Raton, 524 U.S. 775 (1998); Burlington Indus. v. Ellerth, 524 U.S. 742 (1998); see e.g., Walton v. Johnson & Johnson Serv., Inc., 347 F.3d 1272 (11th Cir. 2003) (summary judgment for employer affirmed when, after initial sexual advances by her supervisor, employee both failed to follow the harassment policy and returned to supervisor's apartment on three occasions, drank alcohol, agreed to a massage, and was assaulted again by him. The employer reacted by terminating the supervisor after receiving complaint three months later.); cf. Hardy v. Univ. of Ill. at Chicago, 328 F.3d 361 (7th Cir. 2003) (six-week delay in reporting sexual harassment by supervisor reasonable when plaintiff-employee tried to first work it out and talk with her supervisor before reporting); *see also* Barrett v. Applied Radiant Energy Corp., 240 F.3d 262 (4th Cir. 2001) (the "inevitable unpleasantness" inherent in making a report cannot excuse an employee from taking advantage of her employer's complaint procedure).

Harassment that is based on a protected category, including gender or retaliation, is illegal. Harassment that is based on a general dislike of another person is not illegal.[46] Title VII does not prohibit profanity alone, however profane. It does not prohibit harassment alone, however severe and pervasive. Instead, Title VII prohibits discrimination, including harassment that discriminates based on a protected category such as, for example, sex or retaliation.[47] To establish that an employer's hostile work environment violated the law, a plaintiff must prove that: (1) he or she belongs to a protected group; (2) she or he was harassed because of his or her sex or other protected characteristic; (3) the harassment was sufficiently severe or pervasive to alter the terms and conditions of employment; (4) he or she was subjected to unwelcome harassment; and (5) there is some basis for holding the employer liable.[48]

Each of the prongs in the sexual harassment prima facie case may form the basis for the motion for summary judgment. With the prima facie case, defendants may also move for summary judgment by attempting to demonstrate that the plaintiff cannot show a genuine issue of material fact, which precludes the establishment of the affirmative defense. There are key issues to consider when drafting the motion for summary judgment on behalf of the employer to support that granting of the motion is appropriate. For example, Title VII is not violated in cases in which the conduct complained of is equally offensive to male and female employees. Conduct directed to both male and female employees negates the contention that it is based on sex.[49]

In proving harassment was unwelcome, a plaintiff must show that he neither solicited nor incited it and that she regarded the conduct as undesirable or offensive.[50] An employee must prove that he or she was subjected to conditions that were sufficiently severe or pervasive to alter the terms and conditions of employment and create a discriminatorily abusive working environment.[51] Courts have determined that comments that do not interfere with an employee's job performance or cause an employee to feel physically threatened are not sufficiently severe or pervasive to create a hostile working environment.[52] The conduct must be viewed from both an objective and subjective perspective. A plaintiff must show that the alleged incidents are sufficiently severe or pervasive enough to create an objectively hostile work environment and that a reasonable person would find the conduct offensive.

---

46. *See, e.g.*, Baldwin v. Blue Cross/Blue Shield of Alabama, 480 F.3d 1287, 1300, 1301–02 (11th Cir. 2007).

47. Jensen v. Potter, 435 F.3d 444, 449 (3d Cir. 2006) ("Many may suffer . . . harassment at work, but if the reason for that harassment is one that is not proscribed by Title VII, it follows that Title VII provides no relief."); Carpenter v. Kelley Foods of Ala., Inc., 2005 U.S. Dist. LEXIS 35453 at *17 (M.D. Ala. 2005) ("the three statements about which the plaintiffs complain fall under the rubric of offensive conduct which is outside the scope of Title VII") (citing Harris v. Forklift Sys, 510 U.S. 17 (1993)); Gowski v. Peake, 682 F.2d 1299 (11th Cir. 2012).

48. *See* Baldwin v. Blue Cross/Blue Shield, 480 F.3d 1287 (11th Cir. 2007); Miller v. Kenworth of Dothan, 277 F.3d 1269, 1275 (11th Cir. 2002).

49. *See* Scusa v. Nestle USA Co., Inc., 181 F.3d 958 (8th Cir. 1999).

50. Henson v. Dundee, 682 F.2d 897, 903 (11th Cir. 1982).

51. Mendoza v. Borden, Inc., 195 F.3d 1238, 1245 (11th Cir. 2000).

52. *See* Harris v. Forklift Systems, Inc., 510 U.S. 17, 21 (1993).

In 1998, the US Supreme Court issued two decisions regarding the standards for imposing liability for illegal harassment.[53] Under the *Ellerth/Faragher* analysis, harassment liability now depends on the identity and status of the harasser, rather than the specific type of harassing conduct. According to these decisions, where a *supervisor* engages in harassment that results in a tangible employment action, the employer is strictly liable for the conduct.[54] If there is no tangible employment action, the employer is not liable if it can show that it used reasonable care to prevent and promptly correct the harassment and that the complaining party unreasonably failed to take advantage of any preventative or corrective opportunities provided by the employer.[55]

Not all tangible employment actions are adverse employment actions.[56] An adverse employment action is a tangible employment action, such as a demotion or termination, which a reasonable person in the plaintiff's position would view as adverse. Although typical adverse employment actions (failure to hire, discharge, demotion, reduction in pay) are easily recognizable, others may not be (transfers, loss of prestige, or diminishment of responsibilities). An employment action is not adverse merely because an employee dislikes or disagrees with it. Generally, courts will not look to an employee's subjective feelings regarding an employment action to determine if it is adverse. The standard is an objective one, that of a reasonable person in like or similar circumstances.[57]

1. Employer's Affirmative Defense to a Hostile Work Environment Claim

If the actionable hostile work environment harassment is perpetrated by a supervisor, but the harassment does not culminate in a tangible employment action, a defending employer may avoid liability where it proves: "(a) that the employer exercised reasonable care to prevent and correct promptly any sexually harassing behavior, and (b) that the plaintiff employee unreasonably failed to take advantage of any preventive or corrective opportunities provided by the employer or avoid harm otherwise."[58]

---

53. *See* Faragher v. City of Boca Raton, 524 U.S. 775 (1998), and Burlington Indus. v. Ellerth, 524 U.S. 742 (1998).

54. *See id.*

55. *See id.*

56. The EEOC has taken the position that a tangible employment action does not have to be adverse to be actionable. *See* EEOC Guidance Number 915.002 (June 18, 1999). A nonadverse tangible employment action includes the job benefit provided to an employee who consents to unwelcome harassment by a supervisor. Seemingly beneficial conduct toward an employee, if conditioned upon a request for sexual favors, can subject the employer to strict liability. Under either theory of proving harassment, employees need not be terminated or demoted to sue for harassment. *See* Townsend v. Indiana Univ., 995 F.2d 691 (7th Cir. 1993).

57. *See* Dedner v. Oklahoma, 42 F. Supp. 2d 1254 (E.D. Okla. 1999) (failure to allow desired days off is not a tangible employment action).

58. *Faragher,* 524 U.S. at 807.

a. The employer exercised reasonable care to prevent and correct promptly any harassing behavior

In creating the first prong of the affirmative defense, which requires in part that the employer exercise reasonable care to prevent sexual harassment, the Supreme Court sought to give effect to Title VII's deterrent purpose.[59] Accordingly, the Supreme Court implied that employers could meet the initial burden in determining whether they had exercised reasonable care to prevent sexual harassment by promulgating an antiharassment policy.[60] To determine reasonable care, the courts consider whether the employer has an established and disseminated antiharassment policy that allows multiple reporting opportunities other than the employee's immediate supervisor.[61] If the employer cannot show that it acted reasonably in response to a complaint of harassment; however, having a policy in place may not be sufficient to establish the first prong of the affirmative defense.[62]

b. The plaintiff employee unreasonably failed to take advantage of any preventive or corrective opportunities provided by the employer or avoid harm otherwise

The affirmative defense set forth in *Faragher* and *Ellerth* is two-pronged. Not only must the employer have acted reasonably to prevent and promptly correct illegal harassment, the plaintiff must have unreasonably failed to take advantage of preventative or corrective opportunities provided by the employer.[63]

Where employees were aware of the employer's complaint procedure and knew to whom they should complain if they felt they were being harassed, but instead complained to low-level managers not identified in the procedure, they unreasonably failed to take advantage of preventative or corrective measures provided by the employer.[64] The Eleventh Circuit has rejected an employee's sexual harassment claim where the employee failed to take advantage of the employer's offered remedy.[65] The court also

---

59. *See* Madray v. Publix Supermarkets, Inc., 208 F.3d 1290, 1297 (11th Cir. 2000) (citing Faragher, 524 U.S. at 806 ("it would therefore implement clear statutory policy and complement the Government's Title VII enforcement efforts to recognize the employer's affirmative obligation to prevent violations and give credit here to employers who make reasonable efforts to discharge their duty")).

60. *Id.*

61. *Id.*

62. *See* Frederick v. Sprint/United Management Co., 246 F.3d 1305 (11th Cir. 2001) (reversing summary judgment for the employer, holding that issues of fact existed as to what the employer's policy was and whether it was properly posted or disseminated to employees); Cadena v. Pacesetter Corp., 224 F.3d 1203 (10th Cir. 2000) (upholding jury verdict in favor of a sexual harassment plaintiff and rejecting the employer's argument that the jury's verdict should be overturned because the employer had an antiharassment policy in place because there was evidence that the company was aware of the harasser's conduct before the plaintiff complained and failed to take action against him).

63. Walton v. Johnson & Johnson Services, Inc., 347 F.3d 1272, 1289 (11th Cir. 2003) (to succeed on the *Faragher/Ellerth* affirmative defense, the employer also bears the burden of proving the second element of that defense—"that the employee unreasonably failed to take advantage of any preventive or corrective opportunities provided by the employer or to otherwise avoid harm").

64. *Madray*, 208 F.3d at 1302.

65. *See* Baldwin v. Blue Cross/Blue Shield, 480 F.3d 1287, 1306 (11th Cir. 2007).

held that even if the plaintiff had not refused to cooperate with the employer's offered corrective measures, her failure to report the alleged harassment sooner would establish the second element of the *Faragher/Ellerth* defense.[66]

C. Co-Worker Harassment

The *Faragher* and *Ellerth* decisions dealt with situations in which the alleged harasser was the complaining party's supervisor. These decisions did not alter the liability analysis in cases in which the alleged harasser is a co-worker.[67] Where the actionable hostile work environment harassment is perpetrated by co-workers, the employer will be held liable for the harassment where it knew (actual notice) or should have known (constructive notice) of the harassment and failed to take prompt remedial action reasonably calculated to end the harassment.[68]

1. Whether the Employer Knew or Should Have Known

For an employee to demonstrate actual knowledge he must prove that the employee complained to higher management of the problem.[69] As to constructive knowledge or that an employer should have known, an employee must prove that the harassment was so severe *or* pervasive that an inference of constructive knowledge to the employer arises. In a case of co-worker harassment, failure of an employee to complain of sexual harassment may result in a finding of no employer liability if the employer had no other reason to know about the alleged harassment.[70]

---

66. *Id.* at 1306–07.

67. *See* Swinton v. Potomac Corp., 270 F.3d 794 (9th Cir. 2001) (*Faragher/Ellerth* affirmative defense does not apply in cases of co-worker harassment but employer can avoid liability by showing that it took prompt remedial action to remedy the harassment).

68. *See* 29 C.F.R. § 1604.11(d) (1992); Dudley v. Metro-Dade County, 989 F. Supp. 1192, 1200 (S.D. Fla. 1997); Baldwin v. Blue Cross/Blue Shield, 480 F.3d 1287, 1302 (11th Cir. 2007) (When a plaintiff alleges that her employer is liable for the harassing conduct of co-workers instead of supervisors, the employer will be held liable only if it "knew or should have known of the harassing conduct but failed to take prompt remedial action."); Hitchens v. Montgomery County, 2008 U.S. App. LEXIS 10688 (3d Cir. May 19, 2008) (unpublished decision) (affirming order entering judgment as a matter of law on plaintiff's allegations of co-worker harassment where plaintiff failed to show that the employer knew or should have known of the alleged harassment since she failed to report the harassment until she filed her EEOC charge; "because her employer did not know or have reason to know of the alleged sexual harassment, there was no opportunity for her employer to promptly remedy the situation and defendants cannot be held liable.").

69. Kilgore v. Thompson & Brock Management, Inc., 93 F.3d 752, 754 (11th Cir. 1996).

70. *See, e.g.*, Kouri v. Liberian Services, Inc., 55 Fair Empl. Prac. Cas. (BNA) 124 (E.D. Va. 1991) (employer not liable where employee never told anyone in management that she was being sexually harassed and produced no evidence that complaints were ignored); Tindall v. Housing Authority of Ft. Smith, 762 F. Supp. 259 (W.D. Ark. 1991) (plaintiff had presented no credible evidence of discriminatory verbal harassment due to her failure to report harassment to manager who had "open door" policy); Neville v. Taft Broadcasting Co., 42 Fair Empl. Prac. Cas. (BNA) 1314, 1317 (W.D.N.Y. 1987) (plaintiff's failure to fully report more than one alleged instance of sexual harassment led to inference that harassment either did not occur or was not considered by plaintiff to be significant until time of suit), *aff'd*, 857 F.2d 1461 (2d Cir. 1987).

In some situations, a plaintiff's failure to utilize an available harassment procedure despite knowledge of it may insulate an employer from liability.[71] The following factors have also been considered with regard to the issue of constructive knowledge of harassment: (1) the remoteness of the location of the harassment as compared to the location of management; (2) whether the harassment occurs intermittently over a long period of time; (3) whether the victims were employed on a part-time or full-time basis; and (4) whether there were only a few discrete incidents of harassment.[72]

2. Prompt Remedial Action

Prompt remedial action is action reasonably designed to end the harassment.[73] The employer is not required to take the action the complaining party wants, nor is it always necessary to discharge the alleged harasser.[74] To be reasonably calculated to end the harassment, the employer's action need not end the harassment instantly.[75]

The employer usually will not be considered to have taken prompt remedial action where it does nothing, but the harasser voluntarily ceases the harassing conduct.[76]

---

71. *See* Harvill v. Westward Communications, L.L.C., 433 F.3d 428 (5th Cir. 2005) (employee unreasonably failed to take advantage of the employer's corrective opportunities where she delayed in complaining to upper level management even though she was not satisfied with the way her supervisor handled her complaint; after employee complained to upper level management, the harassment stopped); Farley v. American Cast Iron Pipe Company, 115 F.3d 1548 (11th Cir. 1997) ("once a company has developed and promulgated an effective and comprehensive anti-harassment policy, aggressively and thoroughly disseminated the information and procedures contained in the policy to its staff, and demonstrated a commitment to adhering to this policy, it has fulfilled its obligation to make reasonably diligent efforts to 'know what is going on' within the company").

72. Benn v. Florida East Coast Railway Co, 12 Fla. L. Weekly Fed. D 498 (S.D. Fla. 1999); *see also* Allen v. Tyson Foods Inc., 121 F.3d 642, 647 (11th Cir. 1997).

73. Ellison v. Brady, 924 F.2d 872, 882 (9th Cir. 1991).

74. *See* Barrett v. Omaha Nat'l Bank, 726 F.2d 424 (8th Cir. 1984).

75. *See* Kreamer v. Henry's Towing, 150 Fed. Appx. 378, 382 (5th Cir. 2005) (unpublished opinion) (employer's action in warning and then transferring alleged harasser was sufficient prompt remedial action because it ended the harassment; employer was not required to discharge the alleged harasser) (citing Dornhecker v. Malibu Grand Prix Corp., 828 F.2d 307, 309 (5th Cir. 1987)). The reasonableness of the employer's actions is determined on a case-by-case basis. Courts focus on the employer's ability to stop the harassment. Steele v. Offshore Shipbuilding, Inc., 867 F.2d 1311 (11th Cir. 1989) (female employees failed to establish constructive discharge because the evidence showed that harassment stopped after officials of the parent company reprimanded the harasser); *compare with* Loughman v. Malnati Organization, Inc., 395 F.3d 404 (7th Cir. 2005) (finding issue of fact for jury regarding effectiveness of employer's actions against harasser accused of physically assaulting plaintiff; testimony of other employees who claimed to have been assaulted together with the recurring nature of the harassment against the plaintiff could lead a reasonable jury to find the employer was negligent in addressing its clear sexual harassment problems).

76. *See, e.g.,* Crowley v. L.L. Bean, Inc., 303 F.3d 387 (1st Cir. 2002) (affirming jury verdict in favor of plaintiff on her harassment claim based on the harasser's "stalking" actions where employer did not discharge the harasser until after the plaintiff obtained a court protection order against him); Wilson v. Tulsa Junior College, 164 F.3d 534 (10th Cir. 1998) (holding employer liable for compensatory damages despite supervision and move of harasser).

In light of the foregoing, in the motion for summary judgment, counsel should show that it is undisputed that the plaintiff cannot establish one or more elements of the prima facie case and that it is undisputed that the employer's affirmative defenses are satisfied and that the plaintiff unreasonably failed to take advantage of the anti-harassment policy that was available.

V. CAUSE OF ACTION FOR RETALIATION

Court cases regarding harassment have often turned to allegations of retaliation. In Burlington Northern & Santa Fe Railway Co. v. White, the US Supreme Court expanded the grounds under which an employee can successfully sue for retaliation.[77] The US Supreme Court explained that for conduct to become actionable as retaliation, "[a] plaintiff must show that a reasonable employee would have found the challenged action materially adverse which in this context means it well might have dissuaded a reasonable worker from making or supporting a charge of discrimination."[78]

Accordingly, the court in Burlington found that when plaintiff White complained of sexual harassment by her co-worker, and was transferred to a less desirable position where she was later suspended for getting into a disagreement with her supervisor, but then reinstated with back pay, the employer violated Title VII and committed retaliation. The court reasoned that even if a transfer resulted in no diminution of wages and all lost pay was eventually reimbursed, a transfer to a less desirable position and a thirty-seven-day suspension after opposing discrimination would tend to discourage other employees from opposing discriminatory conduct.

Claims of retaliation constitute close to half of the charges of discrimination filed with the EEOC and are common with harassment claims. Treatment of an employee who has claimed discrimination, or who has supported another employee's claim of discrimination, could give rise to a separate claim of retaliation. The protection also extends to former employees who have been retaliated against by postemployment actions for having filed a claim with the EEOC.[79]

In *Thompson v. North American Stainless L.P.*, the US Supreme Court held that Title VII permits third parties within the "zone of interests" of the statute to bring a claim for retaliation because punishing of such people would deter individuals from bringing complaints of discrimination.[80] In *Thompson*, the US Court did not limit the types of relationships entitled to protection, but it drew a general distinction between close family members and casual acquaintances.

When analyzing a harassment complaint, therefore, not only should you be aware of the distinctions between quid pro quo and hostile environment causes of action,

---

77. 548 U.S. 53 (2006).

78. *Id.* (citing Rochon v. Gonzales, 438 F.3d 1211, 1219 (D.C. Cir. 2006)).

79. Robinson v. Shell Oil Co., 519 U.S. 337 (1997).

80. Thompson v. North American Stainless L.P., 131 S. Ct. 863 (2011) (holding that fiancé of employee who had filed a charge of discrimination and who was also employed by the same employer had cause of action for retaliation after he was fired).

but you should also be aware of whether a retaliation claim is present. This is a commonly litigated issue that could substantially affect your case and may be an issue in the motion for summary judgment as well.

VI. USING DISCOVERY TO SET UP THE SUMMARY JUDGMENT

Focused discovery is key to developing the story and undisputed material facts of the case, and discovery conducted with an aim toward summary judgment requires constant attention to both the standards applicable to the harassment claim and to summary judgments. A realistic assessment of the potential success on a motion for summary judgment is determined during the discovery stage of the case. From the moment that defense counsel receives a complaint, the plan for the investigation and discovery for materials necessary to support a motion for summary judgment should be undertaken. Furthermore, the discovery process including the plaintiff's deposition should be scheduled. It is important that the deposition of the plaintiff be taken as soon as possible so that the plaintiff does not have the opportunity to change his story around regarding the allegations that he or she is bringing against the defendant.

The deposition of the plaintiff should be used to get the plaintiff to acknowledge that the harassment was not ongoing and not severe or pervasive. The deposition can also be used to show that the plaintiff is aware that likely the harasser did not like the plaintiff and it was unrelated to any protected category or that the alleged harasser treated everyone poorly (unrelated to any protected characteristic). And for the plaintiff to admit that she understood and received the anti-harassment policy but failed to use or otherwise take advantage of the procedures therein to avoid the harm. This can also be used to get the plaintiff to admit that she or he did not object to the alleged harassing conduct and in fact may have welcomed such alleged harassment.

Significantly, the antiharassment policy and acknowledgement form should be used during the deposition as well as any documents reflecting that any complaints were investigated. In addition, communications with the plaintiff regarding the investigation and resolution of any alleged harassment complaints should be included.

The discovery process should also be used to clarify if an employee is a co-worker or a supervisor as this will establish the burden and defenses relating to the claims. For example, relevant portions of the job description and hierarchal relationships between employees should establish that a plaintiff is a co-worker of the harasser. The discovery process including the interrogatories could help establish that the statute of limitations was violated.

The discovery process helps show that the anti-harassment and anti-retaliation policy was disseminated, understood, and received and acknowledged by the plaintiff. And any antiharassment trainings should also be acknowledged. Of course, all of these subjects can be addressed through formal discovery, but an opportunity to gain an admission on a material fact should not be missed.

As mentioned already, after the pleading stage, a defendant should move quickly to schedule the plaintiff's deposition. If the jurisdiction is not one that requires automatic disclosures,[81] a defendant should time the issuance of interrogatories and requests for production of documents to the plaintiff with a view toward receiving the answers and responses before the deposition. It is a good practice not to delay the deposition on account of the written discovery. And, the deposition of the plaintiff should be requested and taken before the deposition of the employer is taken. By deposing the plaintiff first, the risk of hearing a coached response designed to defeat a dispositive motion is greatly reduced. In fact, the ability to conduct the early deposition usually is much more important than any written discovery. Nevertheless, that deposition will probably be more fruitful if written discovery has been conducted first.

Ideally, the statement of facts presented in a summary judgment motion will be derived almost entirely from the complaint and the plaintiff's deposition testimony. Using the plaintiff's own words to set forth the facts makes it much more difficult for the plaintiff to oppose the motion on the grounds that there are factual disputes. To accomplish this feat, however, defense counsel must be extraordinarily well prepared. First, defense counsel should be familiar with relevant case law. Mere knowledge of applicable law and dicta will not suffice. Defense counsel should be familiar with the particular facts of favorable cases and how those facts were relied upon by courts reaching favorable outcomes. Then, defense counsel's preparation should focus on eliciting testimony from the plaintiff that will offer facts indistinguishable from those that gave rise to favorable rulings before.

In addition, defense counsel should prepare to ask questions that will obtain single answers in full context. In other words, the deposition should be conducted to produce a transcript filled with concise, powerful excerpts that will be quoted in the statement of undisputed facts and memorandum of law to support the motion for summary judgment. Likewise, to keep the brief clear and concise, prepare to ask many leading questions for the purpose of establishing the "mundane" material facts. These leading questions are not likely to draw any resistance from the plaintiff; they will keep the deposition moving quickly; they will later make for easy record citation when the statement of facts is drafted.

In many cases, more information about the "mundane" facts will be obtained at other points in the deposition through the use of more open-ended questions. But those portions of the deposition will not be the parts to use in the summary judgment brief. Nevertheless, defense counsel should take care to prevent eliciting testimony harmful to the motion.

Despite the goal of obtaining all the material facts from the plaintiff's deposition testimony, many times a plaintiff's deposition will be near its conclusion when defense counsel realizes that the defendant or the defendant's witnesses will be the source for material facts. When this happens, if possible, the plaintiff should be examined to make sure that the plaintiff does not have evidence to contradict the material facts. In response to a summary judgment motion, the plaintiff will have the burden of pointing

---

81. *See* FED. R. CIV. P. 26(a)(1).

to specific portions of the record that raise genuine issues of material fact.[82] A plaintiff who cannot remember certain material facts and cannot rebut the same material facts offered by the defendant, has failed to present evidence, and in that case, the defendant should prevail as a matter of law.[83]

VII. THE AFFIDAVIT OF EMPLOYER

When the defendant must provide additional facts to support a motion for summary judgment, frequently an affidavit or declaration will be used. In federal courts, declarations can be used in lieu of an affidavit pursuant to 28 U.S.C. § 1746, and unlike affidavits, declarations do not require a notary's signature.[84] Thus, supporting the motion with a declaration is easier than using an affidavit, but regardless of which is used, the facts presented must be admissible evidence.[85]

Both testimony and documents can be entered into the record by declaration. Indeed, a declaration or affidavit must be used if the motion is to be supported by documents other than the Rule 56(c) enumerated discovery documents. Rule 56(c) limits the record on which a summary judgment decision can be rendered to pleadings, depositions, answers to interrogatories, admissions on file, and affidavits. Therefore, failing to accompany a nonenumerated document with a declaration can be fatal to the motion.[86] In addition, for the documents to be admissible, the declarations should be sufficient to authenticate the documents.[87] Obviously, to properly authenticate the documents, the declaration must be by a person competent to provide the authentication.[88]

Likewise, when a declaration is offered for the primary purpose of introducing the declarant's testimony, that testimony must be admissible. As provided in Rule 56(e): "A supporting or opposing affidavit must be made on personal knowledge, set out facts that would be admissible in evidence, and show that the affiant is competent to testify on the matters stated." Thus, the declarations must comport with the Federal Rules of Evidence. The affidavits must not be conclusive or based on hearsay. These include any

---

82. Celotex Corp. v. Catrett, 477 U.S. 317 (1986).

83. *See* Healy v. N.Y. Life Ins. Co., 860 F.2d 1209, 1220 (3d Cir. 1988).

84. *E.g.*, Hameed v. Pundt, 964 F. Supp. 836 (S.D.N.Y. 1997).

85. FED. R. CIV. P. 56(e); Jacobsen v. Filler, 790 F.2d 1362, 1367 (9th Cir. 1986); Villasenor v. Sears, Roebuck & Co., 2011 U.S. Dist. Lexis 4301 (C.D. Cal. 2011); CMG Fin. Servs. V. Pac. Trust Bank, FSB, 50 Supp. 3d 1306 (S.D. Cal. 2014).

86. *See* FED. R. CIV. P. 56(e) ("a sworn or certified copy must be attached to or served with the affidavit"); *see also* Peterson v. United States, 694 F.2d 943, 945 (3d Cir. 1982) (denying motion because movant failed to attach important documents).

87. Hal Roach Studios, Inc. v. Richard Feiner & Co., 896 F.2d 1542, 1551 (9th Cir. 1989); Cummings v. Roberts, 628 F.2d 1065 (8th Cir. 1980); Rill v. Trautman, 950 F. Supp. (D.C. Mo. 1996).

88. Garcia v. Sprint PCS Caribe, 841 F. Supp. 2d 538 (D.P.R 2012); Arroyo-Perez v. Demir Group Intern, 762 F. Supp. 2nd 374 (D.P.R. 2011); Goguen ex rel. Estate of Goguen v. Textron, Inc. 234 F.R.D. 13 (D. Mass. 2006).

rules such as the exception to hearsay requirements for using any business records to support the motion for summary judgment.[89]

When drafting declarations, counsel should ensure not to introduce evidence that will give rise to genuine issues. If the declaration contradicts the plaintiff's testimony with regards to a material fact, summary judgment may be lost because of the dispute. Similarly, the declaration should not contradict any prior testimony given by the declarant. Thus, to maintain the greatest likelihood of avoiding any conflict, declarations should be kept as concise as possible.

VIII. THE TIMING FOR THE MOTION FOR SUMMARY JUDGMENT

In any case, the timing for filing the motion may differ depending on the defendant's goals, but as a general rule, the motion should not be filed before the plaintiff has conducted meaningful discovery. But the patience in filing the motion may need to be balanced against the desire to use it as a settlement tool. If the case seems particularly favorable to the defendant, serving a motion for summary judgment early may provide the quickest means to a settlement. A defendant with a strong case may be able to obtain the most settlement leverage by serving a persuasive summary judgment motion before the mediation. After the litigants become aware of the facts, the summary judgment motion provides their attorneys with the opportunity to advocate the law not only to the court but also to their clients and opposing parties.

Motions for summary judgment, however, should be served after the discovery is completed. Once discovery is completed, the facts should be known to both parties, and the facts should not change significantly from that point forward. In this manner, the defendant has all of the evidence on the record completed at the time the motion is filed and if the plaintiff attempts to bring in new evidence to support a genuine issue of fact, it may be deemed waived. Further, the parties and the court have the highest degree of confidence that any decision will result from evaluating all the relevant facts when the motion is filed after the completion of discovery.

IX. HOW TO WRITE A PERSUASIVE MOTION

When drafting a motion for summary judgment, it is important that the motion be persuasive throughout, and it should be drafted in the most persuasive way possible. The motion should be based on the facts that are undisputed and in favor of the defendant's position that the plaintiff cannot state a cause of action for its claims. This includes the presentation of the facts in the undisputed material facts, the motion and all legal arguments. It is important to focus on the facts that are material as the plaintiff will attempt to confuse issues by arguing facts that are not material to establishing any of the claims or defenses. In addition, attorneys should keep the legal argument concise and the key

---

89. Fed. R. Evid. 803.

facts should be incorporated in the memorandum of law. Counsel seeking summary judgment will want to avoid using facts that are in dispute in the drafting of the motion for summary judgment. Counsel should argue that even if opposing counsel's version of the facts were established as true, summary judgment should be granted because the plaintiff is relying on facts that are not material to the cause of action.

After drafting a clear and persuasive statement of facts, the legal arguments should be addressed. The motion for summary judgment should demonstrate to the judge that the case boils down to undisputed facts that are simple and should lead to judgment as a matter of law in favor of the defendant. By drafting the facts first, the focus on the legal issues should appear simple. Indeed, when presenting the legal issues and authorities, clarity is the advocate's greatest weapon. In addition, with a firm grasp on the core legal issues, counsel can draft an argument that will be much more concise. And that combination of clear and concise writing is the key to persuading the court.

The brief should focus on only the strongest arguments. Summary judgment is proper if the plaintiff cannot point to evidence that will raise a genuine issue of material fact on every element of the plaintiff's claim. In addition, the defendant may argue that the plaintiff cannot raise genuine issues of material fact regarding elements of the prima facie case. The argument will be considerably more forceful if it is focused on only the elements that obviously have no genuine issues of material fact. In the end, the defendant only has to convince the court that one element cannot be satisfied by the plaintiff's evidence, and the defendant will prevail.

In addition, one should cite to the portions of the record with specificity. The court is not obligated to sift through the record to find evidence. And, "the designated portions of the record must be presented with enough specificity that the district court can readily identify the facts upon which the nonmoving party relies."[90] The motion for summary judgment should also get to the heart of the argument and minimize boilerplate descriptions of summary judgment standards. The best means to avoid that problem is to get right to the substance. Begin your argument with a succinct paragraph that sets forth the overall issue presented in the motion. Use the first words of your argument to focus the judge's attention and gain the judge's interest in the dispute.

Following the opening paragraph that sets forth the key facts and legal principles, the most persuasive authority should be immediately cited and discussed. To keep the argument concise and clear, the material undisputed facts of the case before the court should be incorporated in the statement of law. The brief should then continue by citing and discussing the most current cases, preferably from the controlling jurisdiction, that offer closely analogous facts. The analogies should be clearly identified to the court, and the best language from those decisions should be quoted to the court and applied to the facts currently before the court.

In jurisdictions where a reply in support of a motion for summary judgment is not permitted, if space permits, the brief should address the most obvious weaknesses in the defendant's case and demonstrate that these are not relevant or being misrepresented by

---

90. Guarino v. Brookfield Township Trustees, 980 F.2d 399, 405 (6th Cir. 1992).

plaintiff. The argument could then be strengthened by a discussion of relevant supporting authority. Similarly, if the plaintiff is certain to rely on a particular case law, the brief in support of the motion may include a portion directed toward distinguishing the case.

X. REPLY

A reply in support of a motion for summary judgment will usually be helpful to create further support of the motion's arguments and should be used to address and counter all of the conclusions and assertions in the response to the motion for summary judgment. In only rare circumstances should a defendant choose not to serve a reply in response to the plaintiff's response in opposition. The reply allows the defendant to address any remaining issues that may appear to create a genuine issue of material fact. The response in opposition will nearly always contain one or more of the following problems that warrant a reply: (1) reliance on nonmaterial facts; (2) reliance on speculative and conclusory statements; (3) inaccurate statements of law; (4) misrepresentation of evidence in the record; (5) reliance on case law that is easily distinguishable; (6) misrepresentation of holdings in case law; (7) inclusion of inadmissible evidence in declarations filed in opposition to the motion; and (8) filing declarations inconsistent with prior deposition testimony.

Each of these issues can be discussed in a reply to support the motion for summary judgment. Certainly, little trouble should be encountered when seeking authority to demonstrate why reliance on nonmaterial facts or a declaration containing inadmissible evidence cannot withstand a motion for summary judgment.[91] Likewise, cases that have been misrepresented or at least to favorably cast against defendant should be clearly distinguished in the reply. Finally, a declaration inconsistent with prior deposition testimony can be readily addressed by focusing on the deposition testimony to highlight the inconsistencies and by citing those authorities that hold that a genuine issue of fact cannot be created by a nonmoving party's affidavit that conflicts with the same party's earlier deposition testimony.[92]

The reply in support of the motion for summary judgment should be limited to addressing only those arguments that were raised in the plaintiff's response. A summary judgment movant should not use its reply to amend its motion for summary judgment or to raise new and independent summary judgment grounds. Consideration should be given as to whether additional declarations should be provided in support of a reply. If the declaration addresses facts raised in the plaintiff's response, an equally

---

91. *E.g.*, Fed. R. Civ. P. 56(e).

92. *See, e.g.*, S.W.S. Erectors, Inc. v. Infax, Inc., 72 F.3d 489 (5th Cir. 1996); Darnell v. Target Stores, 16 F.3d 174 (7th Cir. 1994); Sinskey v. Pharmacia Opthalmics, Inc., 982 F.2d 494 (Fed. Cir. 1992); Trans-Orient Marine Corp. v. Star Trading & Marine, Inc., 925 F.2d 566 (2d Cir. 1991); Davidson & Jones Dev. Co. v. Elmore Dev. Co., 921 F.2d 1343 (6th Cir. 1991); Clay v. Equifax, Inc., 762 F.2d 952 (11th Cir. 1985); Schuyler v. United States, (S.D. Cal. 1997); Slowiak v. Land o'Lakes, Ic., 987 F.2d 1293, 1296 (7th Cir. 1993) (Plaintiff may not avoid summary judgment by submitting an affidavit that conflicts with earlier deposition testimony).

good chance exists that the defendant's newly submitted declaration will be viewed as raising issues of fact rather than quelling any issue of fact. Furthermore, if the declarant's deposition has not been taken, the door may be opened for new discovery to be conducted at a time when the defendant certainly does not want any more to be done.

In sum, the reply should be concise and focused on the matters that will strengthen defendant's position. The reply should demonstrate that the facts are undisputed that there is no genuine issue of material fact and show that the response brief has mere conclusory assertions without support in the record, or immaterial allegations and distinguishable law.

XI. EMPLOYERS SHOULD BE AWARE OF BEST PRACTICES TO POSITION THEIR COMPANIES FOR A PREVAILING MOTION FOR SUMMARY JUDGMENT

The US Supreme Court imposes strict liability for harassment by supervisors unless the employer can prove an affirmative defense.[93] This defense is only available where the harassment does not result in a tangible action, and even if available, the affirmative defense is filled with various requirements regarding the proper implementation and dissemination of the policy. As to claims of retaliation, it is crucial for employers to be sensitive to the fact that the treatment of an employee who has claimed harassment or who has supported another employee's claim of harassment, may give rise to a wholly separate claim of retaliation. And, this protection also extends to former employees who have been retaliated against by post-employment actions for having filed a claim with the EEOC.[94]

In light of the case law referenced herein, employers must incorporate business policies and practices to prevent sexual harassment and position the employer to obtain summary judgment before any litigation occurs. Attorneys should counsel their clients on the development of policies, awareness and investigative procedures that go into creating the structure for the proper policy dissemination and implementation. An employer's best defense is to have in place, before any claims arise, a sound policy that prohibits sexual harassment and offers a concise and understandable avenue for addressing concerns of harassment or retaliation in the workplace. Although summary judgment can be obtained in the absence of a properly disseminated anti-harassment policy, it is much more difficult to obtain without it.

---

93. Faragher v. City of Boca Raton, 524 U.S. 775 (1998); Burlington Indus. v. Ellerth, 524 U.S. 742 (1998); Oncale v. Sundowner Offshore Servs., Inc., 523 U.S. 75 (1998).

94. See Robinson v. Shell Oil Co., 519 U.S. 337 (1997).

XII. CONCLUSION

As shown herein, the courts have developed the standards and case law for prevailing on motions for summary judgment in retaliation and gender harassment claims and counsel should be familiar with these and continue to stay up to date with these standards for opportunities in prevailing motions for summary judgment. Regardless of whether a motion for summary judgment is granted or denied, it can be a useful tool in the litigation process. In addition to the obvious objective of winning the case with a summary judgment motion, the motion can be used to obtain additional discovery of an opponent's facts and legal theories; it can be used as leverage in settlement negotiations, as well as to educate the judge anticipating trial.

CHAPTER 13

Opposing Motions for Summary Judgment: Plaintiff's Perspective

William C. Jhaveri-Weeks and Shajuti T. Hossain

Employers often move for summary judgment in sexual harassment and retaliation cases. This chapter addresses how to oppose such motions. Simply put, the plaintiff must gather and present to the court evidence showing that a genuine issue of material fact exists, such that a reasonable jury could rule in the plaintiff's favor.

Section I of this chapter discusses how plaintiffs' counsel can lay the groundwork to create an evidentiary record that will maximize the chances of defeating summary judgment. Section II discusses strategies for writing the opposition brief itself. Section III discusses the relationship between summary judgment and settlement.

I. CREATING A RECORD TO DEFEAT SUMMARY JUDGMENT

At the summary judgment stage, the court will be deciding whether a genuine issue of material fact exists that requires resolution by a fact finder to decide liability. To establish that there is such an issue, plaintiffs should give careful thought far in advance about how they will build a strong record of evidence to use in opposing a summary judgment motion, as well as at trial. As a rule of thumb, the more facts a plaintiff can gather before the defendant's summary judgment motion is filed, the better prepared the plaintiff will be to defeat the motion. Such gathering should be driven by the elements of the claims and defenses. This section begins by describing typical sources of facts that plaintiffs often cite in opposing summary judgment motions, and then describes the elements of sexual harassment and retaliation claims, with discussion about gathering evidence supporting particular elements.

A. Sources of Proof

Plaintiffs can build a record through various sources, including: the plaintiff's own written discovery responses, deposition testimony, and affidavit; testimony from the plaintiff's co-workers, the defendant, and others; and documents, either in the plaintiff's possession or obtained through discovery.

1. The Plaintiff's Written Discovery Responses

When responding to discovery requests—particularly interrogatories—attorneys often have an inclination to reveal only the minimum amount of information required by the discovery rules. But verified responses to interrogatories can be a useful source of admissible evidence supporting the plaintiff's claims. Unlike a deposition, in which the plaintiff must answer questions immediately without talking through the answers with her attorney, plaintiffs responding to interrogatories can discuss the facts with counsel and state the facts exhaustively and in the most advantageous light.[1]

2. The Plaintiff's Deposition

The plaintiff's deposition is one of the most important days of the case for defeating a later motion for summary judgment. Thorough preparation with that goal in mind is essential. Counsel may want to explain to the plaintiff the elements of her legal claims and the employer's defenses in a way that will allow the plaintiff to understand and remember them. For example, if the employer is likely to assert as a defense that it was not on notice of the harassing conduct (discussed further as follows), the client would be well-served to understand the importance of giving full testimony about the various ways the employer was on notice.

During preparation, counsel should emphasize the importance of giving comprehensive answers, and prepare the plaintiff to recount all specific instances of harassing or retaliatory conduct with as many details as possible. Additionally, counsel should be sure that the plaintiff understands the breadth of what constitutes such conduct.[2] Counsel should caution plaintiffs against providing answers that limit their ability to put before the court each and every incident they suffered when opposing summary judgment. For example, the defense lawyer taking the deposition may conclude a line of questioning about harassing conduct with: "Have you told me about every incident that bothered you?" If the plaintiff answers "yes," the court may hold her to that admission, even if the plaintiff had not, in fact, given a comprehensive list of relevant incidents. The plaintiff should be prepared to recognize the danger of such questions, and to respond to them by listing all additional incidents. Plaintiffs should avoid inaccurately "limiting" their own useful facts—for example, if the facts in a particular case bear it out, the plaintiff should be prepared to give testimony such as: "Those are the specific comments

---

1. *See, e.g.,* Iweala v. Operational Techs. Servs., Inc., 634 F. Supp. 2d 73, 83 (D.D.C. 2009) (relying on plaintiff's interrogatory responses about temporal proximity between complaints and termination to deny summary judgment of retaliation claim); Carpenter v. Miss. Valley State Univ., 807 F. Supp. 2d 570, 595 (N.D. Miss. 2011) (relying on plaintiff's interrogatory responses about his complaints and supervisor's response to deny summary judgment of retaliation claim).

2. Hoyle v. Freightliner, LLC, 650 F.3d 321, 326–37 (4th Cir. 2011) (vacating district court's grant of summary judgment on hostile work environment claim where plaintiff recounted in her deposition several specific instances of sexual harassment, such as the tampon she found tied to a key ring on a truck in her work area, the inappropriate photos of women on a toolbox and on computer screensavers, and the sexually inappropriate calendars a co-worker brought to share with other employees).

I can recall at this time, but the comments were made regularly over many years, so it is difficult to recall every single comment off the top of my head."[3]

Practice Tip: For most lay witnesses, a crucial component of deposition preparation is practicing answering deposition questions in advance of the deposition. The closer the circumstances mimic the real experience of a deposition, the better. The plaintiff's attorney may wish to role-play by asking the questions that the defendant's attorney is likely to ask. By stepping out of role from time to time, the plaintiff's attorney can help the plaintiff learn how to listen carefully to the questioning and give accurate testimony that will ensure that the record includes the most advantageous, truthful testimony possible. If a plaintiff practices answering the same hard questions multiple times in advance of the deposition, the actual deposition record is more likely to include the key facts that the plaintiff needs to place in the record.

If the witness gives incomplete testimony during the deposition (e.g., falls into the trap of inaccurately limiting her own testimony), the plaintiff's counsel should consider whether to elicit complete testimony through re-direct examination (i.e., the plaintiff's attorney's opportunity to ask questions after the defense counsel finishes cross-examining the witness). The benefit of this approach is that the defense counsel will then have the right to cross-examine the plaintiff about the additional testimony. If, instead, the plaintiff submits a later affidavit or errata to attempt to correct the record, the defendant will not have an opportunity to cross-examine the additional testimony, and the affidavit or errata may run afoul to the "sham affidavit" doctrine (discussed as follows).

Testifying about certain incidents of harassment or retaliation will be traumatic for some plaintiffs. Particular styles of deposition-taking may exacerbate the experience. Plaintiffs' counsel should do their best to prepare the witness to testify fully, even about traumatic subject matter, when the testimony will provide facts that are important to the plaintiff's case. Again, practicing under realistic conditions is typically the most effective form of preparation. Courts may be unsympathetic when plaintiffs later assert the fear of unpleasantness or retaliation as justification for incomplete deposition testimony.[4]

3. The Plaintiff's Declaration

Plaintiffs often submit affidavits, also known as declarations, in opposition to summary judgment. If the declaration is made after the plaintiff has already been deposed, plaintiff's counsel will need to be aware of the sham affidavit doctrine. This doctrine applies specifically at the summary judgment phase, and allows courts to disregard declaration testimony that is inconsistent with the declarant's prior deposition testimony.

---

3. *See, e.g.*, Hernandez v. Valley View Hosp. Ass'n, 684 F.3d 950, 956 n.3 (10th Cir. 2012) (where plaintiff mentioned two incidents as well as "stuff like that"; she was not precluded from describing additional incidents in a declaration opposing summary judgment).

4. *See, e.g.*, Johnson v. Watkins, 803 F. Supp. 2d 561, 578 (S.D. Miss. 2011) (instructing jury to disregard pro se plaintiff's argument that her witnesses did not testify about plaintiff's supervisor striking her for fear of retaliation absent evidence to support this justification).

The rule is intended to prevent a plaintiff from generating a triable issue of fact through the use of declaration testimony that contradicts the plaintiff's deposition testimony. Different circuits differ on how strictly they apply the sham affidavit doctrine.[5] If the declaration is not contradictory, but is merely explanatory or supplemental, the court may rely on it, but any such declaration should be drafted with the governing circuit's sham affidavit case law in mind.

Even without other evidence, the plaintiff's deposition and affidavit may be sufficient in some cases to defeat summary judgment, and such sources are particularly important when the alleged harassment occurs behind closed doors without witnesses or a paper trail.[6]

Although the general rule is that a plaintiff's declaration should be comprehensive and detailed when describing the relevant, supportive facts, some courts have held that when the conduct in question has persisted for multiple years, it is unreasonable to require specific details of each instance in a plaintiff's affidavit.[7] If a plaintiff cannot remember every particular instance because there were so many, he or she should note that fact in the affidavit and should give a detailed description of the duration, frequency, and circumstances of the history of incidents.

4. Co-Worker Testimony

Favorable testimony from co-workers can help defeat an employer's summary judgment motion.[8] Plaintiffs can obtain co-worker testimony through declarations or depositions. Current employees may hesitate voluntarily to submit a declaration for fear of retaliation. However, if the co-worker is noticed to appear for a deposition, the co-worker will be able to provide truthful testimony without having voluntarily stepped forward, which may reduce the fear of retaliation.

---

5. For stricter application of the doctrine, *see* France v. Lucas, 836 F.3d 612, 622, 632 (6th Cir. 2016); Meuser v. Fed. Exp. Corp., 564 F.3d 507, 515, 523 (1st Cir. 2009); Pourghoraishi v. Flying J, Inc., 449 F.3d 751, 759 (7th Cir. 2006). For more flexible approaches, *see* Furcron v. Mail Centers Plus, LLC, 843 F.3d 1295, 1306 (11th Cir. 2016) ("[A]n opposing party's affidavit should be considered although it differs from or varies [from] his evidence as given by deposition or another affidavit and the two in conjunction may disclose as issue of credibility."); Knitter v. Corvias Military Living, LLC, 758 F.3d 1214, n.3 (10th Cir. 2014) ("[A]n affidavit may not be disregarded solely because it conflicts with the affiant's prior sworn statements" " . . ." (internal citations omitted)); Moll v. Telesector Resources Grp., Inc., 760 F.3d 198, 206 (2d Cir. 2014) (where plaintiff had been terminated between deposition and declaration, court considered contradictory declaration testimony based upon employee's explanation that his deposition testimony had been limited by fear of retaliation); Van Asdale v. Int'l Game Tech., 577 F.3d 989, 999 (9th Cir. 2009) (". . . the sham affidavit rule does not automatically dispose of every case in which a contradictory affidavit is introduced to explain portions of earlier deposition testimony.") (internal citations omitted); EBC, Inc. v. Clark Bldg. Systems, Inc., 618 F.3d 253, 268 (3d Cir. 2010).

6. *See, e.g.*, Fields v. Atlanta Independent Sch. Sys., 916 F. Supp. 2d 1348, n.40 (N.D. Ga. 2013); Hawkins v. County of Oneida, N.Y., 497 F. Supp. 2d 362, 375–76 (N.D.N.Y. 2007) (relying on the plaintiff's deposition and affidavit, which detail employer's racist remarks to deny summary judgment on hostile work environment claim).

7. *Hawkins*, 497 F. Supp. 2d at 375.

8. McKinley v. Salvation Army, 192 F. Supp. 3d 678, 682, 687, 690 (W.D. Va. 2013).

Practice Tip: As the plaintiff's attorney, when having investigative discussions with potential witnesses, it can be helpful to explain the difference between providing a declaration and appearing for a deposition, so that the co-worker is informed about the options, and so the attorney can gauge the witness's preferences. In addition, attorneys should familiarize themselves with the governing ethical rules before contacting witnesses. For example, ethics rules governing communication with "represented parties" may preclude speaking with certain employees of the defendant.

Co-workers can provide helpful testimony at the summary judgment phase if they witnessed the harasser's actions toward the plaintiff.[9] Co-workers can also provide testimony that reflects the company's inappropriate response to the plaintiff's complaints of harassment.[10] In retaliation cases, co-worker testimony may be useful to prove that the plaintiff was a good performer and that the employer's proffered reasons for an adverse employment action are pretextual.[11]

So-called "me too" testimony from co-workers who experienced similar harassment or retaliation can help create a fact issue that survives summary judgment. Different jurisdictions take varying approaches to "me too" evidence at the summary judgment stage. The Third Circuit has stated that "me too" evidence is neither *per se* admissible nor *per se* inadmissible and that district courts have discretion whether to consider the evidence when ruling on a summary judgment motion, taking into account, for example, how closely the evidence relates to the plaintiff's own experience.[12] The Eleventh Circuit permits admissibility of "me too" evidence to prove retaliation.[13] In the Sixth Circuit, "me too" evidence may be inadmissible as unduly prejudicial unless the plaintiff can show that it concerns the same actors or circumstances as her own claim.[14]

Plaintiff's counsel should be aware that Rule 26(a) of the Federal Rules of Civil Procedure (FRCP) requires parties to identify in their initial disclosures anyone likely to have discoverable information about the case.[15] Rule 26(e) requires supplementation of initial

---

9. *Furcron*, 843 F. 3d at 1308–10 (vacating district court's grant of summary judgment and requiring the lower court to consider co-worker's declaration about seeing the harasser rubbing against plaintiff); McKinley, 192 F. Supp. 3d at 682, 687, 690.

10. Ariz., Dept. of Law, Civil Rights Div. v. ASARCO, L.L.C., 844 F. Supp. 2d 957, 970–71 (D. Ariz. 2011) (admitting evidence from supervisor about his own experience as a victim of the same type of harassment that plaintiff had experienced and complained about previously because it shows the employer failed to take remedial action after plaintiff's complaint).

11. Foster v. Univ. of Maryland-Eastern Shore, 787 F.3d 243, 253–54 (4th Cir. 2015); E.E.O.C. v. Boeing Co., 577 F.3d 1044, 1051 (9th Cir. 2009).

12. Mandel v. M & Q Packaging Corp., 706 F.3d 157, 167–68 (3d Cir.2013).

13. Furcron v. Mail Centers Plus, LLC, 843 F.3d 1295, 1309 (11th Cir. 2016).

14. Jones v. St. Jude Med. S.C., Inc., 823 F. Supp. 2d 699, 734 (S.D. Ohio 2011) (citing Schrand v. Fed. Pac. Elec. Co., 851 F.2d 152, 156 (6th Cir. 1988)); Coy v. County of Delaware, 993 F. Supp. 2d 770, 784–85 (S.D. Ohio 2014) (considering parts of co-workers' deposition testimony because plaintiff was aware of the harassment toward her co-workers, their testimony involved harassment by the same supervisor, and their testimony supplemented plaintiff's testimony, instead of forming the entire basis of her claim).

15. Fed. R. Civ. P. 26(a)(1)(A)(i).

disclosures. The failure to timely identify witnesses may have adverse consequences, including the striking of declarations.[16]

5. Employer's and Harasser's Testimony

Plaintiff's counsel will likely rely on testimony from the harasser and the employer to oppose summary judgment. Plaintiff's counsel should plan their depositions of defendants and harassers carefully with an eye toward responding to a summary judgment motion. If the plaintiff testifies about specific instances of harassment and the harasser denies that such instances occurred, that fact dispute should defeat summary judgment if a reasonable jury could believe the plaintiff and if liability would be established by the plaintiff's assertions.

In federal court, depositions of employers can be taken under FRCP 30(b)(6). Rule 30(b)(6) testimony binds the company. In the deposition notice, plaintiffs must "describe with reasonable particularity the matters for examination," and the company has an obligation to prepare the witness to testify about those topics on the company's behalf. Plaintiff's counsel should prepare the topics and questions with the elements of the plaintiff's claims in mind.

6. Documentary Evidence

Relevant documents may be in the plaintiff's control or the employer's control. The strongest documentary evidence at the summary judgment stage is direct evidence of harassment or retaliation.[17] Plaintiffs should try to determine whether any written documents substantiate the allegations of harassment or retaliation, such as contemporaneous emails, texts, or notes from the harasser or plaintiff illustrating, recounting, or alluding to the allegations, contemporaneous notes taken by the plaintiff, emails to or from higher-level managers or human resources personnel, or any other document tending to prove that the harassing or retaliatory acts took place.[18]

A plaintiff may want to use medical records to show she consulted a therapist or doctor about sexual harassment. Counsel should give careful thought to whether doing so will open the door to discovery into otherwise nondiscoverable confidential matters.[19]

---

16. *See, e.g.*, Cruz v. Bristol Myers Squibb Co. PR, Inc., 777 F. Supp. 2d 321, 329 (D.P.R. 2011); Poitra v. Sch. Dist. No. 1 in Cnty. of Denver, 311 F.R.D. 659, 664 (D. Col. 2015) (mentioning names in passing in deposition is not sufficient).

17. Mayes v. WinCo Holdings, Inc., 846 F.3d 1274, 1280, 1282 (9th Cir. 2017) (finding that plaintiff's direct evidence of supervisor's sexist comments alone is sufficient to defeat summary judgment).

18. *See, e.g.*, E.E.O.C. v. Air Liquide USA LLC, 692 F. Supp. 2d 658, 662 (S.D. Tex. 2010) (denying summary judgment based partially on emails from plaintiff to the human resources department in which she detailed and complained about the harassment); Lindsey v. Clatskanie People's Util. Dist., 140 F. Supp. 3d 1077, 1085 (D. Or. 2015) (denying summary judgment of retaliation claim in part based on text messages and emails between multiple employees expressing frustration with their sexually hostile work environment).

19. Johnson v. Shinseki, 811 F. Supp. 2d 336, 346 (D.D.C. 2011) (denying summary judgment in part based on plaintiff's medical records that show that the workplace harassment led her to seek mental health counselors).

Other helpful documents that plaintiffs may want to seek from the employer through the discovery process to prepare for opposing summary judgment include: any complaints to the employer relating to the allegations, the harasser's personnel file, the plaintiff's personnel file, documents that describe the employer's complaint system and anti-harassment or anti-retaliation policies, and other emails, letters, or memoranda that may concern the allegations and the employer's response.[20]

Plaintiff's counsel should keep in mind that these are not exhaustive lists, and should consider all other documents that may support the plaintiff's claims.

B. Tailoring Your Evidence to the Elements of the Claims

To defeat summary judgment, the plaintiff must be able to show that a reasonable jury could rule in the plaintiff's favor on each element of the plaintiff's claim(s). Discovery should be planned accordingly. The subsections below will detail the elements of sex- and gender-based harassment and retaliation claims, and suggest ways of generating evidence to establish a material question of fact as to each element.

Under Title VII of the Civil Rights Act of 1964 (Title VII), there are two types of sexual harassment claim: hostile work environment and quid pro quo sexual harassment. Title VII retaliation claims arise when a plaintiff suffers an adverse employment action for engaging in protected activity.

1. Hostile Work Environment

In general, to establish a hostile work environment claim on the basis of sex, a plaintiff must prove that (1) he or she belongs to a protected group; (2) he or she was subjected to unwelcome harassment; (3) the harassment was based on the sex of the employee; (4) the harassment was sufficiently severe or pervasive to alter the terms or conditions of employment and create a discriminatorily abusive working environment; and (5) the employer is liable.[21]

To create a record that supports the "based on sex" element, the plaintiff should discover and place into the record all available evidence showing that the hostile comments or acts were "because of" the plaintiff's sex.[22] The conduct need not be "sexual"—it only need be harassment that occurred because of the victim's gender.[23] In some cases,

---

20. *Air Liquide USA LLC*, 692 F. Supp. 2d at 664, 671, 678 (denying summary judgment based partially on emails among plaintiff's supervisors about her pending termination).

21. *See, e.g.,* Smith v. Rock-Tenn Servs. Inc., 813 F.3d 298, 307 (6th Cir. 2016); Trask v. Sec'y, Dep't of Veterans Affairs, 822 F.3d 1179, 1195 (11th Cir. 2016); *see also* Meritor Sav. Bank, FSB v. Vinson, 477 U.S. 57, 67 (1986) (The sex-based harassment was "sufficiently severe or pervasive to alter the condition of [the victim's] employment and create an abusive working environment."). Various circuits apply differing versions of the test. *See, e.g.,* Arizona ex rel. Horne v. Geo Grp., Inc., 816 F.3d 1189, 1206 (9th Cir. 2016) (elements are: (1) subjected to verbal or physical conduct of harassing nature; (2) conduct was unwelcome; (3) conduct sufficiently severe or pervasive to alter the conditions of the victim's employment and create an abusive working environment).

22. 42 U.S.C. § 2000e-2(a)(1) (2018).

23. *See, e.g.,* Williams v. Gen. Motors Corp., 187 F.3d 553, 564–66 (6th Cir. 1999).

the comments will explicitly pertain to sex or gender, making the causal connection between sex and harassment obvious. In other cases, the causation will be less apparent. For example, evidence may show that even though explicitly gendered language was not used, members of one gender or sex were subject to conduct or language that members of the other gender were not.[24] Offensive conduct that does not, in isolation, appear to be based on gender or sex may plausibly be "because of sex" when viewed in the full context of the workplace.[25]

Practice Tip: The plaintiff's counsel should learn from the plaintiff everything that the plaintiff experienced that was negative, and then consider whether there is evidence that the negative experiences the plaintiff had were shared by other members of the protected class but not by employees of the other gender. Then, learn from the plaintiff and other witnesses about good things that other employees of the other gender experienced but the plaintiff and other employees of the plaintiff's gender did not. This may help identify additional data points that would support a jury in finding a causal link.

To prove the severe or pervasive element, the plaintiff must show that the work environment was both objectively and subjectively hostile.[26] The plaintiff's counsel should ensure that the facts demonstrating the extent and severity of the harassing conduct are all in the record. A single, sufficiently severe act can create hostile work environment.[27] More often, a totality of numerous comments or acts will be proffered as rising to the level of severe or pervasive. For example, if the conduct in question is sexual advances, the plaintiff's counsel should adduce any existing evidence about: sexual advances, such as flirtations, propositions, invitations to sexual activity, late-night nonwork related communications, invitations to engage in intimate (even if nonsexual) out-of-work activities; verbal conduct of sexual nature, such as graphic sexual language, innuendos, jokes, emails; physical conduct of sexual or suggestively sexual nature, such as kissing, touching, patting, rubbing, and brushing against; visual conduct of sexual nature, such as sexually suggestive gestures and inappropriate eye contact; and any persistence in engaging in the foregoing actions even after being told that they are unwelcome. Actions that take place away from the workplace may have contributed to the hostile work environment the plaintiff experienced at the workplace.[28]

To determine whether the harassment altered the conditions of employment and created a hostile or abusive work environment, the trier of fact must consider the totality of

---

24. *See, e.g.*, Harsco Corp. v. Renner, 475 F.3d 1179, 1186–87 (10th Cir. 2007) (In addition to some gendered comments, there were nongendered comments to which the plaintiff was subject but male peers were not, supporting jury finding on "because of" sex.).

25. Bird v. West Valley City, 832 F.3d 1188, 1206 (10th Cir. 2016) (We have held that "[f]acially neutral abusive conduct can support a finding of gender animus sufficient to sustain a hostile work environment claim when that conduct is viewed in the context of other, overtly gender-discriminatory conduct ". . . The question then becomes whether [p]laintiffs can use a substantial amount of arguably gender-neutral harassment to bolster a smaller amount of gender-based conduct on summary judgment. Our precedents say that they can.") (internal citations and quotations omitted).

26. Harris v. Forklift Sys., Inc., 510 U.S. 17, 21 (1993).

27. *See, e.g.*, Fuller v. Idaho Dep't of Corrs., 865 F.3d 1154, 1166–67 (9th Cir. 2017).

28. *See, e.g.*, Nichols v. Tri-Nat'l Logistics, Inc., 809 F.3d 981, 985–86 (8th Cir. 2016).

circumstances.[29] Relevant factors include: quantity, frequency, severity of the incidents, extent of physical threat or humiliation, and extent of interference with the plaintiff's work performance.[30]

The plaintiff must have a clear theory about why the employer is liable for the hostile work environment, and must ensure that the record at summary judgment contains evidence that would allow a fact finder to hold the employer liable. If the harasser is a "supervisor" (defined as someone with authority to take tangible employment actions against the victim), then the employer is vicariously liable for the harasser's actions.[31] However, if the supervisor's harassment does *not* involve a tangible employment action (i.e., "a significant change in employment status, such as hiring, firing, failing to promote, reassignment with significantly different responsibilities, or a decision causing a significant change in benefits") then the employer may assert a so-called "*Faragher-Ellerth* defense" to liability under Title VII. To establish the defense, an employer must prove "(a) that the employer exercised reasonable care to prevent and correct promptly any sexually harassing behavior, and (b) that the plaintiff employee unreasonably failed to take advantage of any preventive or corrective opportunities provided by the employer or to avoid harm otherwise discussed below."[32]

If the harasser is a nonsupervisor co-worker and there was no tangible employment action, then the employer will not be vicariously liable, but may be liable under a negligence theory. Such liability exists if the plaintiff proves that the company's management had actual or constructive knowledge of the harassment but failed to take appropriate action.[33] Actual knowledge exists if the employee reported to management officials (or those officials otherwise learned) about the conduct in question.[34] Constructive knowledge exists if the harassment is so pervasive that the employer can be charged with knowledge of it.[35] An employer's response is inadequate if it simply advises the harasser of the existence of anti-harassment policy without disciplinary action, if the harasser continues the conduct in question after the plaintiff reported it up, or if it delays investigation.[36]

---

29. *Meritor,* 477 U.S. at 69.

30. *See* Harris v. Forklift Systems, Inc., 510 U.S. 17, 23 (1993); Fuller v. Idaho Dep't of Corrs., 865 F.3d 1154, 1161 (9th Cir. 2017).

31. *Ellerth,* 524 U.S. at 765; Vance v. Ball State Univ., 133 S. Ct. 2434, 2439 (2013).

32. *Ellerth,* 524 U.S. at 765.

33. *Id.*

34. Dunlap v. Spec Pro, Inc., 939 F. Supp. 2d 1075, 1085 (D. Col. 2013).

35. Kramer v. Wasatch County Sheriff's Office, 743 F.3d 726, 757 (10th Cir. 2014).

36. *See, e.g.,* Freeman v. Dal-Tile Corp., 750 F.3d 413, 424 (4th Cir. 2014) (finding an employer's three-year delay in responding to harassment complaints creates a genuine issue of material fact of whether employer took prompt remedial action); Radmer v. OS Salesco, Inc., 218 F. Supp. 3d 1023, 1030–31 (D. Minn. 2016) (finding that the existence of an anti-harassment policy is not dispositive to satisfy the elements of its affirmative defense); Pitter v. Community Imaging Partners, Inc., 735 F. Supp. 2d 379, 392 (D. Md. 2010) (denying summary judgment in part because harasser continued harassing the plaintiff after she reported him); Reagan v. City of Knoxville, 692 F. Supp. 2d 891, 899 (E.D. Ten. 2010) (granting summary judgment in part because plaintiff had no evidence of defendants delaying the sexual harassment investigation).

Although Title VII does not allow individual harassers to be held personally liable,[37] some state laws do.[38] If the plaintiff is asserting state law claims seeking to hold the harasser liable, the plaintiff should ensure that the record contains evidence that would allow a reasonable jury to find such liability.

2. Quid Pro Quo Harassment

Different courts articulate the elements of a quid pro quo harassment claim differently, but a common formulation is: (1) the plaintiff experienced a tangible employment action as a result of (2) his or her refusal or acceptance of a sexual advance from the harasser.[39]

The tangible employment action requirement refers to a "significant change in employment status, such as hiring, firing, failure to promote, reassignment with significantly different responsibilities, or significant change in benefits."[40] Although economic harm usually occurs, courts have disagreed about whether it is required.[41]

The "as a result of" requirement may be easily met if, for example, a supervisor explicitly conditioned a change in employment status on acceptance of a sexual advance. In other cases, evidence will be required to support the inference of a causal connection between the plaintiff's response to a sexual advance and a subsequent adverse employment action. Temporal proximity can help draw the inference. The plaintiff's counsel should gather any other evidence that tends to support the causal link or to rule out other potential explanations for the adverse action.

3. Retaliation

The elements of a retaliation claim under Title VII are: (1) the plaintiff engaged in protected activity (i.e., opposed a practice made unlawful by Title VII or "made a charge, testified, assisted, or participated in" a Title VII proceeding or investigation); (2) the plaintiff suffered a materially adverse employment action (i.e., one that would dissuade

---

37. *See, e.g.*, Miller v. Maxwell's Intern'l Inc., 991 F.2d 583, 587–88 (9th Cir. 1993); Wathen v. Gen. Elec. Co., 115 F.3d 400, 405 (6th Cir. 1997).

38. *See, e.g.*, Fitzsimons v. Cal. Emergency Physicians Med. Grp., 205 Cal. App. 4th 1423, 1427–28 (2012) (California law); Arthur v. Whitman Cnty., 24 F. Supp. 3d 1024, 1037 (E.D. Wa. 2014) (Washington law).

39. *See* Jones v. Needham, 856 F.3d 1284, 1292 (10th Cir. 2017); Hawkins v. Avalon Hotel Group, LLC, 986 F. Supp. 2d 711, 721 (M.D. La. 2013). Another formulation of the elements is: (1) the plaintiff was a member of a protected class; (2) she was subjected to unwelcome harassment in the form of sexual advances or requests for sexual favors; (3) the harassment was based on sex; and (4) her submission to the unwelcome advances was an express or implied condition for receiving job benefits or her refusal to submit resulted in a tangible job detriment. Moberly v. Midcontinent Commc'n, 711 F. Supp. 2d 1028, 1038 (D.S.D. 2010).

40. *Ellerth*, 524 U.S. at 761.

41. Mormol v. Costco Wholesale Corp., 364 F.3d 54, 57 (2d Cir. 2004) ("A tangible employment action in most cases inflicts direct economic harm, but there is no requirement that it must always do so . . . ") (internal citations and quotations omitted); *but see* Lutkewitte v. Gonzales, 436 F.3d 248, 268, 271 (D.C. Cir. 2006) (rejecting Second and Ninth Circuit opinions that do not require economic harm because they "removed the requirement of tangibility from the definition of a tangible employment action").

a reasonable worker from making or supporting a charge of discrimination); and (3) the plaintiff's engagement in protected activity was the but-for cause of the adverse action.[42]

A materially "adverse employment action that would dissuade a reasonable worker from making or supporting a charge of discrimination" is not limited to adverse actions that are directly related to employment or that occur at the workplace.[43] Some examples of adverse employment actions include reassignment to more arduous and less popular position, termination of employment, a less distinguished title, a material loss of benefits, and significantly diminished material responsibilities.

The third prong—causation—requires the plaintiff to prove that his or her protected conduct was the "but for" cause of the adverse action—a higher standard of causation than applies to Title VII discrimination claims.[44] Again, temporal proximity can be probative.[45] Of particular importance, when it comes to causation, is the *McDonnell Douglas* framework that applies to retaliation claims (*see infra*). This framework may make it easier for plaintiffs to prove that retaliatory animus was the real cause of the adverse action. The plaintiff should try to pin down the employer and its witnesses in discovery concerning the purported legitimate, nondiscriminatory reasons that the employer will proffer as the explanation for the adverse action. The plaintiff's counsel should be sure to gather and put into the record evidence showing that the explanation is pretextual. For example, if the employer is going to argue that the plaintiff was fired not for engaging in protected activity but for low sales numbers, the plaintiff and her counsel will need to give careful thought to what evidence will demonstrate that the proffered explanation is pretextual. In a retaliation case, this evidence can make the difference between a grant and a denial of summary judgment.

Practice Tip: The plaintiff's lawyer should work closely with the plaintiff to develop a response to the employer's claims of pretext. Employer explanations that may sound reasonable to the attorney may be subject to major flaws that only someone with the plaintiff's intimate knowledge of the facts and workplace will understand. Work with the client early on to discuss ways in which the employer's explanations can be undermined, and develop a plan for obtaining the supporting evidence.

4. Defenses
In addition to the *Faragher-Ellerth* defense, plaintiff's counsel should be sure that the record contains evidence to address any other likely defenses, such as a failure to exhaust administrative remedies, a statute of limitations defense, and the like.

---

42. *See* 42 U.S.C. § 2000e-3(a) (2018); Burlington Northern & Santa Fe Ry. Co. v. White, 548 U.S. 53, 54 (2006); Univ. of Tex. Sw. Med. Ctr. v. Nassar, 133 S. Ct. 2517, 2533 (2013).

43. *Burlington Northern*, 548 U.S. at 53–54.

44. *See* Univ. of Tex. Sw. Med. Ctr. v. Nassar, 133 S. Ct. 2517, 2533 (2013).

45. Fye v. Oklahoma Corp. Comm'n, 516 F.3d 1217, 1228 (10th Cir. 2008).

II. PREPARING THE OPPOSITION

To defeat a defendant's summary judgment motion, the plaintiff must demonstrate that the record contains evidence allowing a reasonable jury to rule in the plaintiff's favor—in other words, that there is, at the very least, a genuine issue of material fact as to each element of the plaintiff's claim and each of the defendant's defenses. This section will discuss strategies and suggestions for preparing an effective summary judgment opposition brief.

A. Summary Judgment Standard

Courts will grant summary judgment if the "pleadings, depositions, answers to interrogatories, and admissions on file, together with the affidavits, if any, show that there is no genuine issue as to any material fact and that the moving party is entitled to a judgment as a matter of law."[46] A material fact is one that could affect the outcome of the case, and a genuine issue of material fact exists if a reasonable jury could resolve the fact question in a way that results in a finding of liability for the nonmoving party. A defendant can win summary judgment either by offering proof that negates an element of the plaintiff's cause of action, or by showing that the plaintiff does not have enough evidence to prove an element of his or her cause of action. The defendant can also win summary judgment by showing that there are no material fact disputes regarding one of the defendant's defenses, and that no reasonable jury could rule in plaintiff's favor on the defense. It is important to remember that to prevail on summary judgment, the defendant only needs to make the required showing on a single element of the plaintiff's cause of action or on a single defense that negates liability.[47]

In response, the plaintiff has the burden to proffer "significant probative evidence" to support the essential elements of his or her argument.[48] The plaintiff can meet this burden with either direct evidence or circumstantial evidence—anything that would allow a reasonable jury to find in his or her favor. When courts consider a summary judgment motion, they must view the evidence and draw reasonable inferences in the light most favorable to the plaintiff.[49] The bottom line is that if a reasonable jury could believe the plaintiff's evidence, disbelieve the defendant's evidence, and hand down a verdict in favor of the plaintiff, the case should be decided by a jury, not resolved by a judge at summary judgment.

---

46. Fed. R. Civ. P. 56(c).

47. Parties may also move for partial summary judgment, sometimes called "summary adjudication," on a discrete issue or claim in the case, even if resolving that issue does not resolve the entire action.

48. E.E.O.C. v. Creative Networks, LLC, 912 F. Supp. 2d 828, 834 (D. Ariz. 2012); Chan v. Wells Fargo Advisors, LLC, 124 F. Supp. 3d 1045, 1053 (D. Haw. 2015).

49. Crawford v. Carroll, 529 F.3d 961, 964 (11th Cir. 2008); *Chan*, 124 F. Supp. 3d at 1053.

B. The Statement of Facts

The statement of facts should tell the story of what happened to the plaintiff in a way that will allow the court fully to appreciate the wrongs that she or he experienced. Generally, the statement of facts should consist of factual assertions, not legal arguments. The plaintiff's counsel should strive to include only those facts that are necessary to win the legal arguments briefed in the argument section and to tell a coherent story. The facts should be stated objectively and fairly, but in a compelling way calculated to leave the judge with the feeling that the plaintiff deserves to win the case. Generally, the facts section should not take up the court's time and attention with facts that are not relevant to the summary judgment decision—doing so may also confuse the legal analysis. Each factual assertion, without exception, should be supported by a precise citation to the record—if an assertion is not supported, the court may disregard it, and may be frustrated with the brief-writer. The facts section should be user-friendly for the court: When the judge or clerk comes to a fact citation, the nature of the factual source and its location should immediately be clear. If the cite is to deposition testimony, it is often preferable to use a citation convention that includes the name of the deponent, and if it is not clear from the sentence to which the cite is appended exactly what the court will find upon turning to that page, consider adding a parenthetical. For example, after initially giving the full citation for a deposition transcript, subsequent cites might say "*See* Pl. Dep. at 100:3-101:16 (describing manner in which supervisor looked at her)." If, instead, the fact cite gives no hint of what is being cited (for example, "See Ex. D at 100–01"), then the reader may have to stop reading the brief to figure out what Exhibit D contains and why it is being cited, and the reader's attention will be diverted from the story being told in the brief.

In the course of laying out the facts, it is important to highlight the key factual disputes. For example, it is helpful to directly contrast the plaintiff's and the harasser's account of what happened during a particular incident. Then, in the argument section, the brief can refer back to those facts when explaining that a jury could believe the plaintiff's account, and thus could rule in the plaintiff's favor.

Local court rules often require summary judgment motions to be accompanied by a "separate statement of undisputed facts." Be sure to review the local rules carefully. Under a typical rule, the moving party will be required to file a list of each factual assertion that the moving party claims is an undisputed fact supporting the motion, accompanied by citations to the record supporting that fact. As a practical matter, moving parties often write the fact section of their brief, and then copy and paste the facts into the separate statement, breaking them up into single facts. The opposing party typically must file a response to the separate statement, in which the opposing party responds to each factual assertion by either admitting that the fact is undisputed, or by stating that the fact is disputed and citing the evidence demonstrating the dispute. Depending on the jurisdiction, the opposing party may also submit a statement of additional disputed facts, and the moving party may have an opportunity to respond to those facts in its reply submission. It is often good practice for the opposing party to include every fact in his or her fact section in his or her counterstatement of undisputed and disputed facts.

In deciding the motion and writing the opinion, the judge and clerk will likely work directly from the counterstatement of undisputed facts. The court will treat each undisputed fact as a given, and will assume that a reasonable jury would find the undisputed fact to be true. It is therefore extremely important for the party opposing summary judgment to be very precise and to avoid admitting that facts are undisputed unless they are truly and fully undisputed. It is also important for the party opposing summary judgment to be exhaustive when providing record citations to the evidence showing that particular factual contentions are disputed. For example, if the movant's statement of facts asserts that the plaintiff heard offensive comments on only three occasions, the opposing party should marshal any and all evidence countering that assertion. Of course if there were more than three occasions, or if some of the three "occasions" consisted of multiple interactions, the plaintiff should identify each and every offensive comment and provide fact cites for them. But the plaintiff should also consider whether this is an appropriate place to remind the court that the plaintiff also saw offensive behavior, heard sexually suggestive overtones, received communications that, although not explicitly offensive, were nonetheless offensive in tone or circumstance—or any other facts that might be necessary to ensure that the court does not accept as undisputed the simple assertion that the plaintiff only heard offensive comments on three occasions if, in fact, that is not the whole story.

C. The Argument Section

In the opening brief, the defendant will have laid out the attacks it is making on the plaintiff's case—either arguing that the evidence negates certain elements of the cause of action, or that the record lacks evidence to satisfy certain elements of the cause of action, or that certain defenses apply as a matter of law given the facts in the record. One good way of organizing the argument section of the opposition is to tackle the most significant arguments first. Those are the arguments that will get the most attention from the court, and addressing them first and giving them plenty of space in the brief will show the court that you are tackling the hard argument head-on and that you want the judge to focus on the reasons why those arguments fail. If the opening brief has failed to provide the court with a correct description of the cause of action and its elements, the opposition must point this out and provide the court with the correct framework. Then, the goal is to show the court, simply and directly, that the evidence in the record would allow a jury to rule in the plaintiff's favor on whichever element the motion attacks.

Although it is important to keep the proper summary judgment standard in mind when framing and describing your arguments, it is typically a waste of space to brief the basic summary judgment standard to the court in any more than the most succinct terms—the court will be intimately familiar with the standard. Similarly, federal courts decide cases under the *McDonnell Douglas* burden-shifting framework (discussed below) all the time—therefore, there is typically little need to devote significant space to explaining how the test works. The main task, again, is to show the court that the facts discussed in the facts section provide a jury with the evidence it needs to rule in the plaintiff's favor on the challenged element. In other words, a key function of the argument section is to map the critical facts to the elements of the plaintiff's cause of action, and to show how those facts, if the jury believes the plaintiff's evidence, would allow the jury to decide that element in the plaintiff's favor.

The structure of the opposition brief must depend on the nature of the defendant's attacks in the opening brief. If, for example, the opening brief challenges only the "severe or pervasive" element of the plaintiff's hostile work environment claim, establishing that a fact issue exists on that element should be the near-exclusive focus of the opposition. The brief can remind the court quickly that the moving papers do not challenge the plaintiff's ability to raise a material fact dispute on the other elements of the cause of action; to be safe, the plaintiff may wish to cite the court very succinctly to evidence in the record demonstrating that the other elements are met.

The brief should also be sure to frame clearly the key fact disputes. To continue the "severe or persuasive" example, if the defendant argues that certain incidents did not occur or that a physically intimidating encounter was less severe than the plaintiff claims, the brief should forcefully argue that the question at the summary judgment phase is whether the jury could find the "severe or persuasive" prong to be met *assuming* that the jury believes the plaintiff and disbelieves the defendant about whether the various incidents occurred, and *assuming* that the jury believes the plaintiff's description of what happened during the physically intimidating encounter. The brief may wish to illustrate how strong the plaintiff's case will appear if every factual dispute is resolved in the plaintiff's favor.

In general, the plaintiff's counsel should write the argument section in a clearly organized, logical way, supported by citations to binding authority and tying all arguments to the elements of the plaintiff's case that the motion is challenging. The tone should be persuasive but not overbearing—a helpful tip is to write the brief in such a clear, credible, and well-supported way that the court could copy and paste your brief into the decision.

1. Using Case Law Effectively

An effective way to use case law in opposing a summary judgment motion is to lay out the evidence raising a fact dispute on the element of the cause of action that the defendant is challenging, and then to cite cases in which a similar or even less persuasive factual showing was held to be sufficient to raise a material issue of fact on that element.

The plaintiff's counsel should be mindful of the fact that authority from the US Supreme Court and the circuit court in the applicable circuit are binding on federal district courts, while district court decisions—even from the same court—are merely persuasive. Citing to favorable prior decisions authored by the judge presiding over the plaintiff's case can be effective, and plaintiffs' counsel should be sure to search for any such decisions.

Distinguishing the moving party's cases is important, and the plaintiff's counsel should read each such case carefully in an effort to identify characteristics of the case that make it less persuasive or applicable to the plaintiff's case. For example, if the key issue is whether the incidents of harassment were severe or pervasive, and the defendant cites a case in which the evidence of such incidents was held to be insufficient to raise a material fact dispute, the plaintiff's counsel should explain, if possible, why the totality of the circumstances in that case gave rise to a showing of harassment that was less severe and/or pervasive than the plaintiff's showing. If that is not possible, the plaintiff could explore whether the case is an outlier in that many other courts have reached a different conclusion on similar facts, or whether the judge in that case relied on flaws in the employee's evidence or strengths in the employer's evidence that do not exist in the plaintiff's case. The plaintiff's counsel should be sure to check whether the cases the movant cites have been criticized or reversed by subsequent courts.

2. Briefing the *McDonnell Douglas* Burden-Shifting Framework

Some Title VII discrimination claims are governed, at least in part, by the *McDonnell Douglas* burden-shifting framework. This framework provides an alternative way of proving discrimination or retaliation by *inference*, in addition to the traditional method of proof, that is, by simply offering proof that unlawful discrimination occurred.[50] The basic *McDonnell Douglas* framework, which differs slightly depending on the claim at issue (i.e., retaliation, termination, failure to hire or promote, etc.), consists of three steps. In a retaliation case, first, the plaintiff must establish a prima facie case of retaliation by showing (i) that she engaged in protected activity, (ii) that she was then subjected to an adverse employment action, and (iii) that a causal connection existed between the two. The level of causation required at this stage is "less onerous" than the plaintiff's ultimate burden to prove but-for causation.[51] Once the plaintiff makes a prima facie showing, the burden of production shifts to the defendant to come forward with evidence that its employment action was based on a legitimate, nonretaliatory reason. This shifting of the burden was adopted in recognition of the problems of proof that plaintiffs often face in discrimination cases, given that the employer controls the evidence and knowledge about why certain employment actions were taken. If the employer articulates a nonretaliatory reason, the burden of production then shifts back to the plaintiff to provide evidence that the defendant's proffered reason is pretextual—that is, that it was not the real reason for the action. If an employer cannot meet its burden to come forward with a legitimate, nonretaliatory reason, or if the plaintiff provides evidence that the reason is false, a jury is permitted to conclude that retaliation was the real reason for the adverse action.[52] Although the burden of production shifts, the burden of persuasion—that is, the burden to convince the jury by a preponderance that the employer committed unlawful retaliation—always remains with the plaintiff.

Although circuit courts are in agreement that the *McDonnell Douglas* framework applies to retaliation claims, some circuit courts have held that the framework does not apply to hostile work environment claims or quid pro quo sexual harassment claims,

---

50. *See, e.g.*, Shirrell v. St. Francis Med. Ctr., 793 F.3d 881, 887 (8th Cir. 2015) (describing these two avenues of proof); Foster v. Univ. of Md.-Eastern Shore, 787 F.3d 243, 249 (4th Cir. 2015) (same).

51. *See, e.g.*, Foster v. Univ. of Md.-Eastern Shore, 787 F.3d 243, 251 (4th Cir. 2015).

52. *See, e.g.*, Foster v. Univ. of Md.-Eastern Shore, 787 F.3d 243, 250 (4th Cir. 2015).

or have not conclusively addressed the issue.[53] Courts taking the position that *McDonnell Douglas* does not apply to such claims have pointed out that there is no legitimate business reason for permitting the employer conduct of creating a hostile work environment or demanding sexual favors in exchange for benefits at work.[54] The plaintiff's summary judgment opposition should rely on the law of the governing circuit, and should be wary of citing cases from other circuits in which a different rule may govern.

If the governing authority permits the use of the *McDonnell Douglas* framework, the plaintiff can, but need not, rely on it, in addition to or instead of a straightforward argument that she has introduced evidence satisfying each of the elements of a retaliation cause of action. In general, the framework was adopted to assist plaintiffs, so plaintiffs should generally make use of the framework if it is available and helpful to their claims. Courts sometimes find that even if summary judgment is merited on a straightforward theory of retaliation, summary judgment should be denied under the *McDonnell Douglas* framework.[55] At the summary judgment phase, the plaintiff need only show that the record contains evidence that would allow a jury to apply the framework and to find liability for the plaintiff. For example, in a retaliation case, if a reasonable jury could find that the evidence supports each element of a prima facie case, and if a reasonable jury could conclude that the defendant's reason for the adverse employment action is not the real reason, summary judgment should be denied, and the jury should be permitted to resolve the factual disputes.

III. SUMMARY JUDGMENT AND SETTLEMENT

The point in the case just before summary judgment is decided may be a point of uncertainty for both sides that is conducive to settlement. The defendant will understand that if the plaintiff prevails at summary judgment, the case may proceed to a jury trial, resulting in the certainty of significant legal fees and a large time commitment, and the risk of an adverse verdict. The plaintiff will understand that if the defendant prevails at summary judgment, the plaintiff's case is over at the trial level. For both sides, preparing an effective summary judgment submission will not only increase their chances of prevailing on the motion, but will provide a powerful message to the other side about the strength of their case. Plaintiffs' counsel should explain this dynamic to their clients, and should determine whether the point just before summary judgment is decided is a time when the client would be interested in attempting to resolve the case through settlement.

---

53. *See* Moody v. Atl. City Bd. of Educ., 870 F.3d 206, 213 n. 11 (3d Cir. 2017) (framework does not apply to hostile work environment claims); Pollard v. E.I. DuPont de Nemours Co., 213 F.3d 933, 943 (6th Cir. 2000), *rev'd on other grounds*, 532 U.S. 843 (2001); Martin v. Nannie & The Newborns, Inc., 3 F.3d 1410, 1417 n. 8 (10th Cir. 1993); Johnson v. Booker T. Wash. Broad. Serv. Inc., 234 F.3d 501, 510–11 (11th Cir. 2000); *but see* Okoli v. City of Baltimore, 648 F.3d 216, 222–23 (4th Cir. 2011) (applying framework to quid pro quo analysis); Farrell v. Planters Lifesavers Co., 206 F.3d 271, 286 (3d Cir. 2000) (noting that circuit had not yet decided extent to which framework applies to quid pro quo claims).

54. *See* Moody v. Atl. City Bd. of Educ., 870 F.3d 206, 213 n. 11 (3d Cir. 2017); Pollard v. E.I. DuPont de Nemours Co., 213 F.3d 933, 943 (6th Cir. 2000), *rev'd on other grounds*, 532 U.S. 843 (2001).

55. *See, e.g.*, Jacobs v. N.C. Admin. Office of the Courts, 780 F.3d 562, 578–79 (4th Cir. 2015).

CHAPTER 14

Work, Sex, and the Morning News: An Updated Look at Discovering Juror Attitudes in Sexual Harassment Cases

Susan G. Fillichio, Steven J. Son, and Thi Quang[1]

Today is jury selection in your sexual harassment case. You grab your briefcase, your jury seating chart, and your sticky notes. Some of you will have already met with your jury consultant to plan your strategy. But wait: Did you remember to check the news this morning? Have you been following the latest on the talk show circuit? You may want to put these items on your to-do list, since you can be sure that some percentage of the venire will have done so. Not since the days of Clarence Thomas and Anita Hill has the topic of sexual harassment so dominated the headlines. The recent verdict that Bill Cosby was found guilty of sexual assault is indicative of juror willingness to apply the law to anyone accused, even one of the most popular father figures and comedians in the history of television.

In addition to the headlines, since our first chapter on jury selection in harassment cases, there have been several other developments that have changed the dynamics of juror thinking in these cases. The #MeToo movement took off in October 2017 after revelations of sexual harassment in the workplace were reported in the entertainment and media industries. The movement was viewed by many as creating a forum for publicly discussing the issue of sexual harassment, extending empathy for those who have experienced it, and summoning a call to action for increased accountability against acts of sexual harassment. There is no safe harbor in any industry, including business, sports, politics, and even some of the most respected members of the judiciary. The roster of the accused includes Harvey Weinstein, Roger Ailes, Steve Wynn, Charlie Rose, Bill O'Reilly, Matt Lauer, Al Franken, and even Donald Trump, to name just a few. The initial frequency of media reports of these allegations, coupled with the fact

---

1. The authors are resident in the Los Angeles office of DecisionQuest and are grateful to their trusted clients for allowing them the privilege of participating in hundreds of sexual harassment cases across the country.

that they have been leveled against well-known and prominent individuals and those in roles of public trust, prompted discussion and policy reviews in companies across the country. The issue of sexual harassment has garnered so much recent attention that it even prompted the American Bar Association (ABA) in February of 2018 to pass Resolution 302, which expanded the 1992 ABA anti-harassment policy and ". . . urges employers in the legal profession to adopt and enforce policies that prohibit, prevent and redress harassment and retaliation based on sex, gender, gender identity, sexual orientation."[2]

Given the spotlight on the topic, it is critical to revisit how these developments have impacted jurors' perceptions and beliefs, and how these perceptions and beliefs may influence juror attitudes and decision-making in sexual harassment cases. Just as companies are adjusting the manner in which they respond to sexual harassment claims, counsel too needs to address the change in the mindset of jurors and their reactions and expectations of companies investigating and handling these claims. In this chapter update, we will explore recent nationwide data on issues that are central to jury selection in sexual harassment cases, including increased juror openness to listening to claims of sexual harassment, and how attitudes and beliefs may have changed since our first publication on the topic in 2010. We will also provide some suggestions for questions that may be integrated in voir dire strategy in sexual harassment cases.

I. TIMES THEY ARE A-CHANGIN': JUROR ATTITUDES AND EXPERIENCES

As discussed in the original chapter, while every effective jury selection requires identifying and deselecting the most dangerous jurors, the process can be especially critical in sexual harassment cases, which often are accompanied by (and in juror minds, bolstered by) retaliation and/or discrimination claims. Fundamentally, jurors in all employment cases generally express a high level of commitment to their positions; the subject matter of sexual harassment, however, often raises an even higher level of emotion. In particular, testimony in these cases is typically sexually suggestive, explicit, and even graphic. Witnesses on both sides of the dispute often testify about deeply personal experiences and they may be completely emotionally exposed throughout the process. Consequently, such cases affect the lives and careers of accuser and accused far beyond the courtroom.

Our work with jurors since the inception of the #MeToo movement validates that many jurors have had experiences (whether as a victim, friend, or acquaintance of a victim, or even as a witness) with discrimination and harassment both within and outside of the workplace. Such experiences affect their attitudes in these cases and it is thus no surprise that those personal experiences are often referenced both in response to voir dire questioning and, importantly, later on in deliberations. Additionally, jurors

---

2. https://www.americanbar.org/news/reporter_resources/midyear-meeting-2018/house-of-delegates-resolutions/302.html

are becoming far more familiar with workplace policies against discrimination, sexual harassment, and retaliation as they continue to garner attention, evolve in scope, and become more widely implemented. Jurors today are even more likely to have expectations of how employers should create, implement, and enforce these policies.

As counsel is doubtless aware, it is critical to understand these extremely relevant experiences during the course of voir dire to select an unbiased jury. However, what makes voir dire in these sensitive cases even more challenging is that jurors are frequently reluctant to discuss their own experiences, especially if they have been victims of, or accused of, discrimination or harassment. There is a natural tension between the need to explore a juror's potential bias and respecting a juror's privacy. Nonetheless, uncomfortable though it may be, counsel selecting a jury in a sexual harassment case must explore both the experiences a juror has had that may relate to the case, and the attitudes that result from the juror's pertinent life history.

Importantly, learning of a juror's experience through voir dire or the use of a written juror questionnaire alone does not allow counsel to understand whether that juror is predisposed against her client's case. First, just knowing about a particular juror experience does not indicate what that juror's attitude about that experience is. Jurors' perceptions of their experiences dictate the attitudes they form from those experiences. Second, in light of increased coverage of high-profile cases through television and social media, wherein women and men alike demonstrate willingness to come forward about perceived compensation disparities and sexual harassment, jurors today are consistently exposed to a greater variety of experiences implicating workplace harassment. Unable to avoid the topic, counsel can embrace media stories as a way to break the ice and allow jurors to talk about the central issues in the public cases and their views of such issues, while asking jurors how such views might affect the juror's service in your case. Such a strategy allows counsel and her consultant to identify juror perceptions that may impact juror decision-making in the case.

II. DECISIONQUEST 2018 RESEARCH SURVEY DATA

A. Comparison of Data from the DecisionQuest Surveys in 2008 and 2018

In the original chapter, we explored DecisionQuest's 2008 research survey data of surrogate jurors' attitudes relating to harassment cases. The 2008 study surveyed 1,120 jury research participants in various regions of the country[3] regarding the attitudes we had found most pervasive in sexual harassment cases. The purpose of the study was to assess how prevalent these attitudes were in the venues in which we were conducting our research. Subjects were recruited using a stratified sample that creates panels of participants that demographically resembled typical jury panels in those venues.

---

3. Although the results of both the 2008 and 2018 surveys are informative, they cannot be taken as an accurate representation of juror attitudes in the areas in question; instead, the data should be viewed as an indication of trends on the issues.

In the last decade, especially given the recent attention in the media to sexual harassment and assault reports, we hypothesized that certain juror attitudes on the topic have changed. In an effort to assess those changes and the impact of the recent media reports on the topic of sexual harassment, at the beginning of 2018, we conducted a nationwide survey of 1,093 jury-eligible respondents, again from various regions across the country. Respondents were residents of California, Colorado, the District of Columbia, Florida, Georgia, Illinois, Massachusetts, New York, Pennsylvania, Texas, and Washington State, as detailed in the chart below. What follows is a comparison of the attitudes reported in 2008 with those in 2018, as well as a discussion of new issues addressed in the most recent survey.

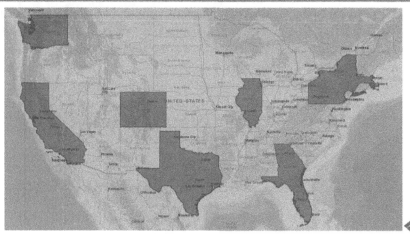

**2018 National Survey:
Respondents' State of Residence**

© DecisionQuest 2018

DECISIONQUEST

1. Increase in the Number of People Who Have Experienced Sexual Harassment

The most notable difference between the 2008 and 2018 responses is in the number of respondents who indicated that they, or someone close to them, had experienced sexual harassment in the workplace. In fact, the percentages of those who experienced sexual harassment in the workplace doubled. Specifically, in 2008, only 9.5 percent reported that they had experienced sexual harassment in the workplace; another 8.7 percent reported that someone close to them had such experiences and another 3.1 percent reported that both they, and someone close to them, had experienced sexual harassment in the workplace. Fast-forward to 2018, when 21.1 percent reported that they had experienced sexual harassment in the workplace, another 21.0 percent reported that someone close to them had experienced sexual harassment in the workplace, and another 5.5 percent reported that both they and someone close to them had experienced sexual harassment in the workplace.

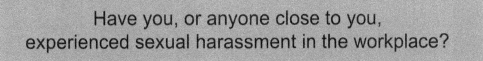

Have you, or anyone close to you, experienced sexual harassment in the workplace?

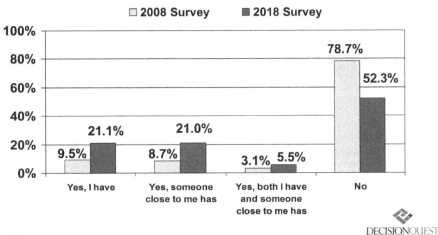

□ 2008 Survey   ■ 2018 Survey

	Yes, I have	Yes, someone close to me has	Yes, both I have and someone close to me has	No
2008	9.5%	8.7%	3.1%	78.7%
2018	21.1%	21.0%	5.5%	52.3%

© DecisionQuest 2018

DECISIONQUEST

2. Mixed Perceptions of Corporate Response

At the same time that the percentages of those who experienced sexual harassment in the workplace doubled, the data suggest that there is a perception of only minimal progress by corporations to address workplace harassment. Preliminarily, and on the positive side, there has been increased training on the topic. In 2008, 46.7 percent reported having been trained on the topic of sexual harassment in the workplace (38.6 percent had attended a live training session and 8.1 percent had attended an internet training session). Compare that to 2018, where 56 percent reported that they had been trained on the topic (38.6 percent had attended a live training session and 17.4 percent had attended an internet training session).

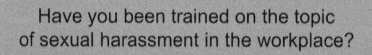

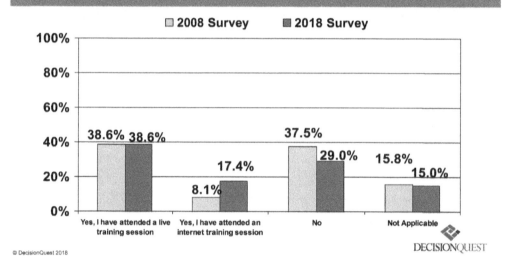

© DecisionQuest 2018

DECISIONQUEST

Notwithstanding the increase in internet training, however, survey respondents expressed skepticism about the quality of that training, as well as investigations and disciplinary action for violation of sexual harassment policies. Importantly, the percentage of respondents who believed that corporations provide sexual harassment training merely for show doubled: The percentage of those who agreed that when an employer trains its employees on the issue of sexual harassment, it is merely trying to "look good" (rather than show it actually cares about its employees) rose from 23.1 percent in 2008 to 51.3 percent in 2018.

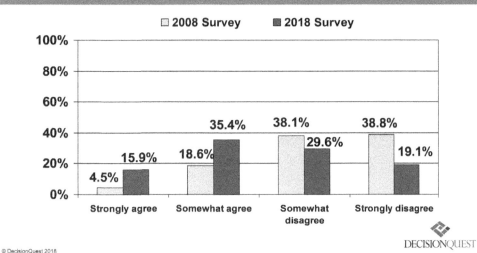

When an employer trains its employees on the issue of sexual harassment, it is merely trying to "look good," rather than caring about its employees.

□ 2008 Survey   ■ 2018 Survey

© DecisionQuest 2018

DECISIONQUEST

Second, respondents were slightly more critical of corporations' efforts to address claims of sexual harassment. Specifically, the percentage of those who agreed that companies do an inadequate job of investigating claims of sexual harassment rose from 59.9 percent (7.3 percent strongly) in 2008 to 67.8 percent (18.4 percent strongly) in 2018.

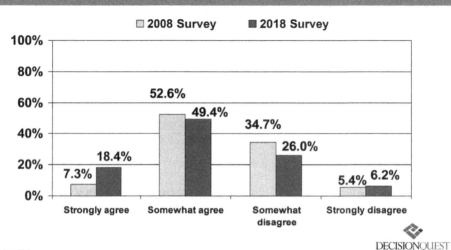

© DecisionQuest 2018

DECISIONQUEST

Third, respondents were more critical of corporate response to employees who engage in the harassing conduct. Specifically, the percentage of those who agreed that typically employees who engage in conduct considered to be sexual harassment get only a "slap on the wrist" from their employer rose from 55 percent (9 percent strongly) in 2008 to 76.1 percent (21.5 percent strongly) in 2018.

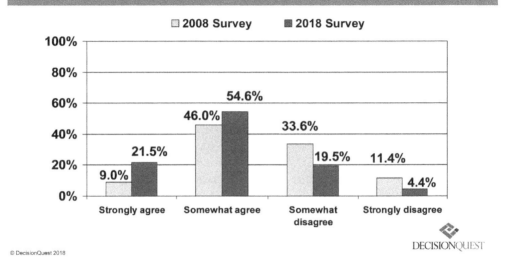

Typically, employees who engage in conduct considered to be sexual harassment get only a "slap on the wrist" from their employer.

☐ 2008 Survey   ■ 2018 Survey

© DecisionQuest 2018

DECISIONQUEST

The increase in jurors' perceptions of a lack of a significant response by corporations might be surprising at first, given the many media reports of individuals being immediately suspended or fired after an allegation of sexual harassment. However, it is likely that jurors' perceptions are based on the logic that if more and more instances of reported long-term sexual harassment are just now coming to light, then those in charge have not taken complaints seriously over the last several years, nor have they taken action necessary to curtail the behavior.

Not surprisingly, respondents were more critical of how good a job corporate America has done in fighting harassment in the workplace. Specifically, in 2008, only 5.4 percent of respondents believed that corporate America had done a very good job in fighting harassment in the workplace, 29.8 percent believed corporate America had done a good job, 51.4 percent believed corporate America had done an adequate job, 12.3 percent believed corporate America had done a poor job, and only 1.1 percent believed corporate America had done a very poor job in fighting harassment in the workplace. In 2018, when asked the same question, a slightly increased percentage (10 percent) believed corporate America had done a very good job and 16.6 percent believed corporate America had done a good job; however, 32 percent believed corporate America had done an adequate job, 33.9 percent believed corporate America had done a poor job, and 7.6 percent believed corporate America had done a very poor job. Again, the data likely reflect the sentiment in many jurors' minds that corporations allowed the pattern of behavior to occur and are now reacting too little, too late.

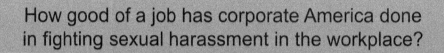

How good of a job has corporate America done in fighting sexual harassment in the workplace?

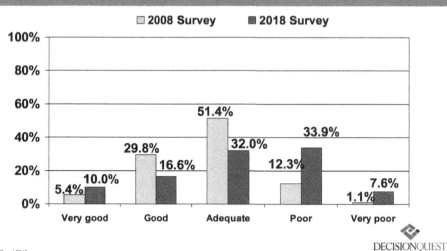

© DecisionQuest 2018

DECISIONQUEST

3. Perceptions of the Claimants

Interestingly, respondents were more critical of the women who make sexual harassment claims. Specifically, the percentage of those who agreed that women who make a sexual harassment claim often provoke the behavior rose slightly from 25.4 percent in 2008 to 31.3 percent in 2018.

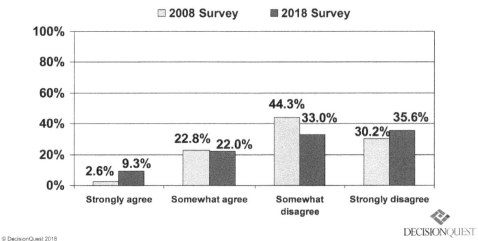

© DecisionQuest 2018

DECISIONQUEST

Ultimately, the percentage of jurors who believed that most sexual harassment law-suits filed against companies are justified remained high and relatively unchanged: from 74.7 percent in 2008 to 77.4 percent in 2018. That is, jurors are not yet ready to hold a plaintiff entirely blameless, but at the same time continue to believe that one would not make such a claim without proof.

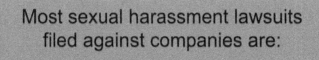

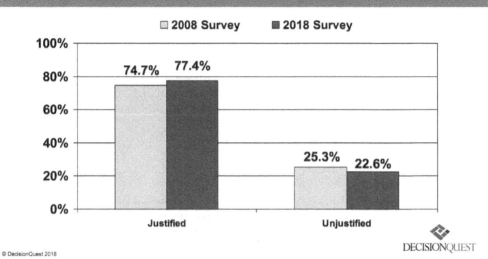

© DecisionQuest 2018

B. Current Issues: The Media, Same-Sex Harassment, and Beyond

1. Impact of the Media

In addition to assessing changing opinions over the past decade, the recent survey was designed to gauge the level of attention respondents have paid to the recent media reports on the issue of sexual harassment, as well as the effects of the media attention on respondents' attitudes. The data show that people are indeed paying significant attention to the publicity surrounding sexual harassment. Specifically, when asked, "How closely do you follow media and social media reports on sexual harassment?" 22.5 percent said very closely, 44.8 percent said somewhat closely, 25.3 percent said not very closely, and 7.3 percent said not at all closely.

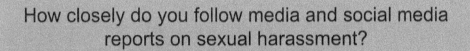

How closely do you follow media and social media reports on sexual harassment?

2018 Survey

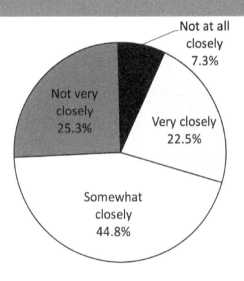

Not at all closely
7.3%

Not very closely
25.3%

Very closely
22.5%

Somewhat closely
44.8%

© DecisionQuest 2018

DECISIONQUEST

Not surprisingly, given that respondents are paying close attention to the publicity about sexual harassment, an overwhelming majority, 76.1 percent, indicated that they had heard of the #MeToo movement.

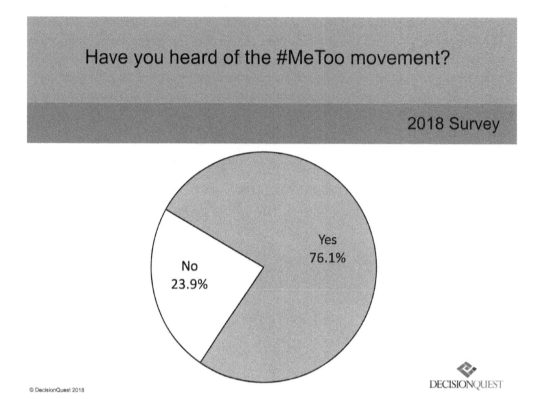

© DecisionQuest 2018

Further, over two-thirds of recent respondents indicated their belief that the issue of sexual harassment seems to have garnered a lot more attention recently than it has in the past. Specifically, 68.2 percent believed that there has been much more coverage recently on the topic of sexual harassment than in the past; 18.4 percent believed there has been a little more coverage recently, 8.9 percent believed the coverage has been about the same, and only 4.6 percent believed there has been less or much less coverage recently than in the past.

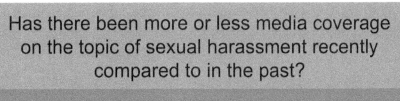

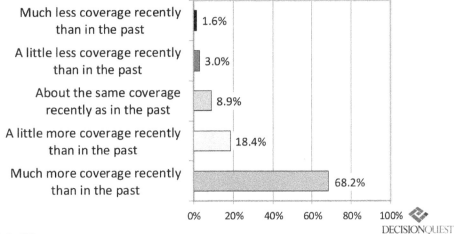

© DecisionQuest 2018

But most importantly, especially as it relates to jury selection, beyond just a perceived increase in reporting on the issue of sexual harassment, a very high percentage of respondents believe in the validity of the reported cases. In fact, 80.1 percent of the respondents indicated that the recent media and social media reports of sexual harassment cases have led them to believe that sexual harassment has occurred in those cases.

Do the recent media and social media reports of sexual harassment cases lead you to believe that sexual harassment has occurred in those cases?

2018 Survey

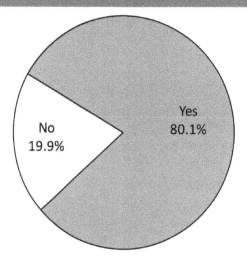

© DecisionQuest 2018

DECISIONQUEST

Interestingly, despite acknowledging the increased media attention on the issue of sexual harassment, respondents had mixed opinions as to whether sexual harassment was a bigger problem now than it was in the past. Although the vast majority of respondents (55.3 percent) believed that sexual harassment is as big a problem today as it was in the past, 23.1 percent believed that it was a bigger problem today; somewhat surprisingly, there is a still a fairly large percentage of respondents (21.6 percent combined) who believed that it was not as big a problem today than it was in the past, is no longer a problem today, or has never been a problem.

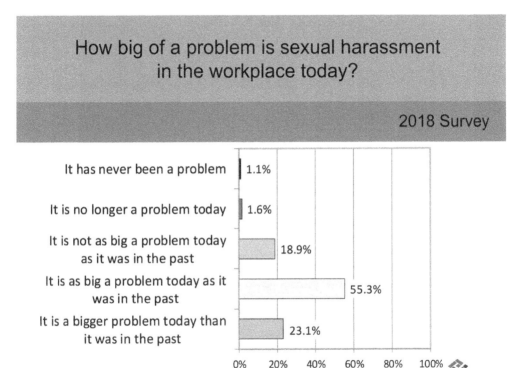

2. Men as Victims and Same-Sex Harassment

In the most recent survey, respondents were also questioned about the idea of men being victims of sexual harassment in the workplace. Rather overwhelmingly, 95.2 percent agreed (63.9 percent strongly) that men can be the victims of sexual harassment in the workplace.

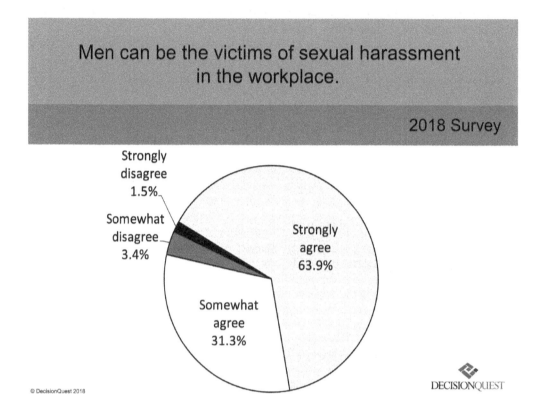

Men can be the victims of sexual harassment in the workplace.

2018 Survey

Strongly disagree 1.5%

Somewhat disagree 3.4%

Strongly agree 63.9%

Somewhat agree 31.3%

© DecisionQuest 2018

DECISIONQUEST

However, similar to the issue of whether sexual harassment generally was a bigger problem now than it was in the past, respondents had mixed opinions about same-sex harassment. Specifically, 48.7 percent of respondents believed that it is as big a problem today as it was in the past, 26.4 percent believed that it is a bigger problem today than it was in the past; only 24.9 percent combined believed that it is not as big a problem today than it was in the past, is no longer a problem today, or has never been a problem.

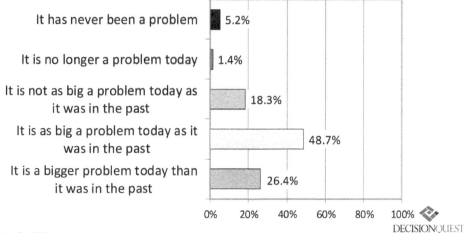

How big of a problem is same-sex sexual harassment (when the harasser and the victim are the same sex) in the workplace today?

2018 Survey

© DecisionQuest 2018

DECISIONQUEST

3. Retaliation

Lastly, respondents were questioned on the issue of retaliation. As observed in countless sexual harassment cases, these claims survive dispositive motions and are very often present at the trial phase. Materially, a significant majority of respondents believe that employees are often retaliated against after making a complaint of sexual harassment or discrimination.

Specifically, 72.1 percent of the respondents agreed that it is common for employees who complain about sexual harassment or discrimination to experience retaliation after they make a complaint. It might surprise you to learn that our additional analyses of the data revealed that 72.7 percent of respondents who held management or supervisory level positions with formal authority to discipline, hire, or fire other employees agreed with this notion that retaliation against employees for making complaints is common.

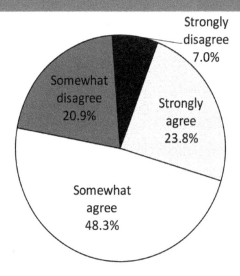

It is common for employees who complain about sexual harassment or discrimination to experience retaliation after they make a complaint.

2018 Survey

Strongly disagree 7.0%

Somewhat disagree 20.9%

Strongly agree 23.8%

Somewhat agree 48.3%

© DecisionQuest 2018

DECISIONQUEST

C. Deep Dive into the Data: Knowing the Attitude, Not Just the Experience, Is Critical

Although the results of the most recent survey data are interesting on the surface, a deeper analysis of the data revealed additional compelling results:

- Of the 26.6 percent who reported having experienced sexual harassment in the workplace, 38.1 percent were men, and 42.6 percent held management or supervisory level positions with formal authority to discipline, hire, or fire other employees.
- Perhaps not surprising, 62.4 percent of those who believed that corporate America has done a very good job in fighting sexual harassment in the workplace were men, and 67.9 percent held management or supervisory level positions with formal authority to discipline, hire, or fire other employees.
- Also perhaps not surprising, 63.7 percent of those who strongly agreed that women who make a sexual harassment claim often provoke the behavior were men, and 61.8 percent held management or supervisory level positions with formal authority to discipline, hire, or fire other employees.
- Additionally, 71.3 percent of those who strongly agreed that when an employer trains its employees on the issue of sexual harassment, it is merely trying to "look good" rather than show it cares about its employees, had themselves attended a training session on the topic of sexual harassment in the workplace (59.2 percent had attended a live training session). This finding suggests that employees perhaps question the motivation employers have in sponsoring sexual harassment training sessions as well as the intended outcomes.

More importantly, our multivariate analysis of the data revealed a perfect example of how knowing the experience a juror has had is not enough; counsel must understand the resultant attitudes as well. To illustrate, respondents who had personally experienced sexual harassment in the workplace were no more likely to believe that corporate America had done a poor or very poor job of fighting sexual harassment in the workplace than those who had never personally experienced sexual harassment in the workplace, nor knew someone close to them who had (42.6 percent compared to 40.0 percent, respectively). In fact, counterintuitively, those who had personally experienced sexual harassment in the workplace were more than two and a half times as likely to believe that corporate America had done a very good job of fighting sexual harassment in the workplace than those who had never personally experienced sexual harassment in the workplace, nor knew someone close to them who had (18.6 percent compared to 7.0 percent, respectively). This finding is noteworthy in that counsel might reasonably assume that a person who had experienced sexual harassment in the workplace would be much less likely to believe that corporate America had done a very good job of fighting it, compared to a person who had not.

Additionally, respondents who had personally experienced sexual harassment in the workplace were more than three times as likely to say that women who claim they have been sexually harassed often provoke the behavior than those who had never person-ally experienced sexual harassment in the workplace, nor knew someone close to them who had (18.2 percent compared to 5.6 percent, respectively). However, respondents who had personally experienced sexual harassment in the workplace were far more likely to agree that companies do an inadequate job of investigating claims of sexual harassment than those who had never personally experienced sexual harassment in the workplace, nor knew someone close to them who had (73.5 percent compared to 64.9 percent, respectively). And those who had personally experienced sexual harass-ment in the workplace were nearly twice as likely to strongly agree that typically, employees who engage in conduct considered to be sexual harassment get only a "slap on the wrist" from their employer than those who had never personally experienced sexual harassment in the workplace, nor knew someone close to them who had (30.6 percent compared to 16.6 percent, respectively).

As this example illustrates, not only is knowing the attitudes that accompany the experiences more important than the experience itself, but it is important to consider the totality of those attitudes when assessing a prospective juror's suitability for service in your case.

III. EXPERIENTIAL AND ATTITUDINAL QUESTIONS FOR JURY SELECTION

Our national survey data discussed here has been validated by our experiences support-ing counsel in jury selection on sexual harassment cases across the country. An effec-tive voir dire on the topic of sexual harassment requires asking prospective jurors about a variety of relevant experiences and attitudes so that counsel and your consultant may obtain an overall assessment of the juror. Juror questionnaires and follow-up voir dire should focus on exposing not only a juror's workplace experiences, and their attitudes and beliefs, but also their expectations of a company's obligations and responsibilities to employees in sexual harassment and discrimination cases. The following questions may be considered as part of your voir dire strategy to elicit information to understand both juror experiences and perceptions of those experiences; your consultant can assist you in formulating the sequencing and composition of a voir dire strategy to fit your case:

- Have you ever held a management or supervisory level positions with formal authority to discipline, hire, or fire other employees?
- Have you ever attended a training session on the topic of sexual harassment in the workplace? If so, was it a live training session or a web-based training session?
- Have you ever worked at a company where the culture or atmosphere was unfriendly or hostile to employees based on their age/race/religion/gender/sexual orientation or to those who complained or filed grievances?
- Have you worked in a company where there were allegations of discrimination, harassment, or retaliation? Can you describe what that was like? How did you feel about that?

- Experience with offensive behavior (even as a witness): Have you or someone close to you ever experienced discrimination, sexual harassment, or retaliation? What was the behavior that you found improper, illegal, or offensive? What was the nature of the behavior? Was there profanity involved? Was the alleged perpetrator in a position of authority? Was it an isolated event or was it commonplace? Were there complaints made and investigated? Were the complaints taken seriously?
- Do any of you believe that you have been treated unfairly in connection with your employment, either current or former? Do you believe that any member of your family or someone close to you has been treated unfairly? (Follow up about when, who was involved, and the specific circumstances involved.)
- Are most (age/gender/race/religion/sexual orientation) discrimination/sexual harassment/retaliation lawsuits justified?
- How successful has corporate America been in fighting (age/gender/race/religion/sexual orientation) discrimination/sexual harassment/retaliation in the workplace?
- How often do you think women/older employees/a particular race/a particular religion/a particular sexual orientation are treated unfairly in the workplace?
- How often do you think women/older employees/a particular race/a particular religion/a particular sexual orientation are denied opportunities to advance to management or supervisory positions, even when they are qualified for such positions?
- When you hear that someone has been demoted or fired, do you tend to believe that that person was treated unfairly?
- Do you believe that individuals who claim that they have been sexually harassed provoke the behavior?
- Do companies do an adequate job of investigating claims of discrimination/sexual harassment/retaliation?
- Do you believe that the employer in discrimination/sexual harassment/retaliation lawsuits has the obligation to prove the harassment did not take place?
- Do you think that employees who engage in conduct considered to be discriminatory/sexual harassment/retaliation get only a "slap on the wrist" from their employer?
- How often do you think that employees make up lawsuits against their employers solely as a means to get money?
- Do you think that women/older employees/a particular race/a particular sexual orientation often use discrimination/harassment/retaliation accusations to get back at their employers and/or boss?
- Do you have any philosophical problem with the type of claim involved in this case, that is, a claim by an employee against her current/former supervisor for alleged discrimination/sexual harassment/retaliation?
- Do you closely follow media and social media reports on sexual harassment? Has the #MeToo movement affected how you view sexual harassment in the workplace?

- Have you ever been fired from a job?
- Have you ever filed a complaint with your employer?
- Are most lawsuits filed by employees who claim they have been fired in retaliation for making complaints justified?
- Do you agree that it is common for employees who complain about sexual harassment (or discrimination) to experience retaliation after they make a complaint?

IV. CONCLUSION

Exploring juror attitudes is the key to effective jury selection in sexual harassment cases. In light of the current media focus on the #MeToo movement, it is even more imperative to manage the jury selection process in a manner that will allow a better understanding of jurors' beliefs and perspectives. As illustrated in the previous example of the perhaps surprising and varying opinions of respondents who had personally experienced sexual harassment in the workplace, the totality of juror's attitudes must be assessed and considered. The overall increasing scrutiny by jurors of corporate responses to such claims and an overall greater belief in the validity of those claims (even among those who have held management or supervisory positions) has changed the landscape. DecisionQuest will continue to track trends in juror decision-making in sexual harassment cases. With well-planned and strategic voir dire questioning, counsel and your jury consultant can assist in drawing out more complete responses from jurors to allow a more thorough assessment of whether the juror will be helpful or harmful to your case.

CHAPTER 15

Voir Dire and Plaintiff's Opening Statement: Plaintiff's Perspective

Marian H. Birge

I. PREPARING FOR VOIR DIRE

A. Voir Dire—Definition and Purpose

The term *voir dire,* as defined by Black's Law Dictionary, means "to speak the truth." The group of people from among whom a jury will be selected is sometimes referred to as the venire. Voir dire refers to the preliminary questioning of prospective jurors, a process used to determine whether each of them is qualified to sit on the jury of a particular case, the word "qualified" referring, under these circumstances, to a potential juror's ability to be neutral and objective; those sometimes elusive attributes are critical to protecting the parties' rights to a fair trial on the merits of a case.

All of us, throughout our unique life experiences, form attitudes, beliefs, and personality characteristics that may have an effect—sometimes unconsciously—on our ability to be fair and impartial under certain circumstances. Because we all harbor conscious or unconscious biases to varying degrees, any prospective juror may be qualified to serve on some jury panels, but not on others. It is crucial, during voir dire, for Bench and Bar to convey the utmost respect and consideration to every potential juror, and to communicate that every citizen who answers the call to jury service, whether he/she serves or is dismissed, plays an important role in ensuring a fair civil justice system. Unless provided by state law or company policy, an employer is not required to pay an employee for serving on a jury, and people must sometimes make arrangements for child care, or to handle other aspects of daily life, in anticipation of serving on a jury for an unknown number of days, so responding to a call to jury service can be inconvenient and costly. It can also be discomfiting for people who sometimes must answer questions about their personal lives, and reveal things about themselves in the presence of strangers. The venire should be reminded that being released from service is routine, and not in the least an indictment of anyone's fitness or character. It's a privilege to practice in the court of a judge who is particularly mindful of a prospective panel's time, efforts, and unease, and who is adept at facilitating the process. When attorney voir dire is structured properly and efficiently, it can help maximize juror candor, cognizance, involvement, and performance, as well as respect for the justice system.

The process of voir dire is important in three distinct ways. First, it gives parties and their lawyers the opportunity to discover as much as they can, under necessarily limited circumstances, about each juror's life experiences, backgrounds, expertise, opinions, inclinations, and biases; all the criteria that will influence each juror's abilities to weigh and decide critical issues. This information must be elicited in a relatively short time span; some courts place unusually strict time or other limits on voir dire, begging the question of how to accomplish as much as one would like within restricted parameters. In short, a well-prepared attorney needs to focus not merely on questions and short answers, but on drawing out narratives, or conversations between jurors, which can reveal receptivity or intolerance toward theories or elements of your client's case, all while monitoring nonverbal behavior and interactions with other jurors. Second, voir dire gives prospective jurors the first opportunity to evaluate the attorneys and to gain a first impression of parties and counsel. The initial impression a juror has of a lawyer, and the lawyer's relationship with the judge, his client, and opposing counsel, will set the tone for the entire trial. The venire will look closely at counsel's outward appearance, manner, and nonverbal signals; they will observe all interactions with the judge and client/plaintiff, and they will look to whether counsel listens and understands their responses. Jurors want to know whether counsel is someone they can trust, so part of the job at voir dire is to give an organized, attentive presentation, in other words, to demonstrate indicators of your reliability. Similarly, everything counsel states in an opening statement must be established by evidence during trial, and echoed at closing argument as a reminder that counsel did exactly what he/she said they would do. Your initial contact with the finders of fact can affect the outcome of trial, because a bad first impression can be nearly impossible to reverse. Third, voir dire presents an opportunity to educate jurors about your case; it's never to indoctrinate, which would likely result in an objection, and not to argue, but rather to present information as part of the voir dire information gathering process.

To do a good job, it is essential for counsel to give significant thought and planning to the process of jury selection, in line with the courtroom, local, state, or federal procedures used in the particular court where the case will be tried. A word of caution: attorneys must be judicious about using peremptory challenges. Many times, lawyers will use all their peremptory challenges in the first round, only to find that they have exhausted these challenges just when they need it most in a second round.

An interesting phenomenon arises from the many televised and streamed courtroom dramas that are available for viewing; most prospective jurors watch television, and people tend to think that dramatic portrayals of lawyers and courtroom situations are realistic. Often, these shows are the only information people have upon which to base their ideas and perceptions about the legal system. Once a panel is picked, if one or more jurors have unreasonable expectations of how attorneys, clients, and witnesses can speak and act, or of how evidence should be introduced, they may be confused or harbor an erroneous belief that the lawyers they are watching are less than competent than a favorite character, or that counsel are obtuse, inaccessible, unentertaining, or worse. Disappointed expectations can affect perceptions and deliberations, but they can also be negated early on by letting a prospective panel know that television shows do not accurately portray how trials are conducted. Another benefit of distinguishing reality from drama or "reality courtroom TV" may be that jurors will be more open-minded to, and curious about, the actual process of trial. A bored juror can be expected to zone out during testimony, so the more interested and invested the panel members are, the better. One of counsel's goals should be to immediately present a confident, trustworthy image to those who will make up the jury.

Juries are charged with the responsibility of reaching a verdict based on the facts of a case, as presented in open court, and by applying the law as it is explained by the trial judge. There will always be people who find the process interesting, and some people who appreciate the opportunity to serve. There will be some who seek attention. Some will be reluctant to serve for various reasons. For yet others, jury service is an uncomfortable, intimidating, or challenging prospect. In any given large cross-section of humanity, it's likely there will be some especially difficult, bullying, or "high conflict" personalities. Observe members' interactions with each other, and be cautious about a juror who uses voir dire as a way to hold forth or self-dramatize; these personalities may prove caustic or difficult for other members of the panel to take, especially during a long trial. Jurors are only human, and while a person may genuinely express a belief that he or she is capable of deciding a case in an impartial manner, the questioning process can sometimes disclose a deep-seated bias or prejudice that makes authentic neutrality unlikely or impossible. To skillfully use the voir dire process, a lawyer should (1) question potential jurors in a respectful, encouraging manner, seeking to (2) reveal juror orientations that are not immediately apparent, and which could negatively, or positively, impact the outcome of trial. It is a serious mistake to give short shrift to jury selection; the choices attorneys make from any given pool of potential jurors can have a crucial impact on how issues of liability and damages are decided. A single, strong-willed person's opinion can change the course of deliberations.

B. Early Preparation for Jury Selection

It's advisable to prepare for voir dire from the very beginning of the case. A trial note-book should be started early on, and as discovery progresses, counsel can begin and hone the analysis of major and minor themes, issues, and defenses, as well as consider the personality traits of the parties and key witnesses. This material can be used for multiple purposes along the trajectory of litigation, and will greatly help counsel to develop profiles of potentially favorable and unfavorable jurors. The profiles, in turn, may be used to formulate questions for potential jurors. If this is accomplished months before trial, and refined in the weeks leading up to trial, perhaps with extra time taken to attend jury selection in the courtroom where the trial will be held, the result will be a well-thought-out presentation, made with confidence and executed without fumbling, leaving jurors with a positive first impression, and counsel with a detailed juror profile chart.

There are numerous ways to begin a juror profile chart. One method is to list major issues, elements, themes, strengths, weaknesses, and theories for plaintiff and defendant, along with spaces to list good and bad juror characteristics. See Appendix 15A of this chapter for a sample form.

Certain personality, background, family, employment, or other characteristics are likely to feed either a pro-plaintiff or pro-defendant orientation. Start with a general picture of what positive and negative jurors may look like, then refine your analysis. Consider what personality types and what kinds of life experiences or employment experiences may cause a hypothetical juror to harbor a negative or positive predisposition to a plaintiff's claims. As an example, a service employee and an executive may have dissimilar responses to certain phraseology, such as references to the "rights of employees" in the workplace. Watch juror facial reactions and body language. A person who works in a traditionally male-dominated environment, like construction, may be inclined to minimize how workplace harassment can affect an employee or a group of employees. A small business owner who once experienced conflict with an employee may feel aggrieved, and more sympathetic toward a defendant in a disparate pay case. If the case involves sexualized harassment in the workplace, it may be useful to develop questions that can reveal what that person believes about high-profile cases and verdicts. The initial analysis and profile of favorable and unfavorable juror characteristics may change over time, as new facts come to light or as the case theory develops. Consider the jury pool, and consult other trial lawyers in your area, or publications containing information (such as verdicts and settlements) that may help you better understand the general make-up of the population the court draws from, whether conservative or more liberal. Cases involving sex-based discrimination and pay disparity may, in some states, include wage and hour claims that carry a potential for significant punitive damages, so if a prospective juror has ever been on the receiving end of an administrative citation, he/she may be inclined to think statutory penalties are unjust. A standard, stodgy query like, "Do you feel you can put aside personal feelings and follow the law as given to you in this case?" may be somewhat insulting, and would be less likely to elicit a thoughtful, honest response than a question that invites a narrative: "Have any of you ever filed a claim with the Labor Commissioner, or had one filed against you? Did you think it was resolved fairly? Why/why not?" Some supervisors may feel, based on personal experience or on perceptions about lawsuits and greedy plaintiffs, that insubordinate employees are likely to complain falsely of illegal retaliation, or that small business owners are unfairly targeted by one-sided and destructive laws. If a lawyer were to successfully kindle a brief exchange between jurors by asking, "Does anyone else feel the same way, or feel differently?", then not only might deep-seated feelings be revealed, but the discussion might also cue an opportunity to get the venire thinking about issues of fairness in the context of the case that some (or all of them) will be hearing.

It can take practice for even the best of trial lawyers to learn to confidently and comfortably draw out jurors. In the context of lesbian, gay, bisexual, transsexual, and queer (LGBTQ) issues, it would be wise to expect a wide variety of sometimes conflicted, sometimes unshakable, beliefs grounded in tinderbox areas of inquiry such as religion, culture, familial conflicts, freedom of association, and personal preferences. The nature of cases involving sex and gender identity presents a need to carefully develop questions that will not cause counsel to be perceived as engaging in impermissible argument, and that will likely draw out the kind of discussion that can establish bias. Practice with a focus group could be particularly helpful in this respect. In some cases or in some jurisdictions, it may be preferable to determine well ahead of trial whether some questions should be presented in writing. Prospective jurors tend to strongly respect and admire their judge, and many judges recognize that some questions are best asked by a judge, rather than counsel. These include questions that may elicit embarrassing responses such as whether any person or close family member has been convicted of a felony.

Counsel should also practice and be prepared in the event a juror's response appears unclear, evasive, or confusing. Rather than letting an unclear answer lie, as too often happens, a vague response should generate an invitation to clarify, which may lead a lawyer to catch the brass ring of voir dire: a dialogue between jurors. The most simple, honest question, "I'm sorry, I don't quite understand. Could you explain that a little bit more?" can open the door to a sudden wealth of juror information. Lines of questioning that probe prospective jurors' negative experiences and invite disclosure of special sensitivities and dispositions can be done in a manner that is minimally intrusive, and the best way to get jurors to loosen up is often with humor. As an example, in a legal malpractice action, the question, "Anyone know some good lawyer jokes?" may invite a little uncomfortable laughter, then lead into the question of whether anyone has ever been represented by a lawyer. A positive response leads to the next question, whether it was a good experience, and on to opening the same questions to the entire panel. (That question works because it is self-deprecating but, obviously, it would not work in the context of harassment.) The best way to reduce discomfort is to make jurors feel that the lawyer questioning them is skilled, respectful of them and of their time, trustworthy, and open. The key is not only to prepare well-crafted questions, but to listen to and observe jurors closely, then follow up on responses that are ambiguous, or which reveal serious discomfort or hidden emotions concerning a topic. Unscrewing the lid to juror emotions and beliefs all begins with that first impression.

If plaintiff's counsel has the resources, he or she may consider retaining the services of a private company or jury consultant. Professional jury investigation companies offer a variety of experts, including statisticians, psychologists, and behavioral scientists, along with several types of services in anticipation of voir dire, including evaluation of venue, taking community surveys, helping with the creation of effective case themes, and facilitating discussions about the personalities of the parties and witnesses who will testify. It can be helpful to produce a mock voir dire. Jury experts may also be retained to monitor juror responses and attitudes during voir dire, and to propose supplemental juror questions. These services can be expensive, and many firms conduct their own pretrial research. If cost is an issue, then make use of colleagues and office personnel as mini-focus groups, or to gather a group of people for a mock voir dire to ascertain, among other things, attitudes and responses to how the questions and the case are presented. This kind of information is not only useful for general trial preparation, but it can also open new synergies. In addition, many lawyers videotape voir dire practice sessions to review and analyze their own presentation. The routine of practicing, identifying problem areas, rethinking, and adjusting a presentation can increase counsel's level of confidence and enhance counsel's communication skills.

Another useful preparation tool to consider is a "position analysis." This involves a live presentation, or the preparation of a video that is shown to a panel of community members, immediately followed by the distribution of a questionnaire, with an ensuing discussion. The video should consist of a concise, neutral statement of the case, with brief presentations of the parties' positions. After the panelists view the video, they respond to written questions about the themes, legal issues, facts, and concepts presented. A discussion period can help draw out the community members' reactions, thoughts, and opinions to the parties' positions, which helps counsel to gauge potential jurors' responses to the case. This kind of feedback can disclose the existence of general and specific opinions and sentiments that were not previously considered.

Too often, lawyers wait until the last minute to prepare for voir dire. It takes time and effort to plan, prepare, try out, and reframe potential juror questions. However, practice and planning can make a significant difference in performance during jury selection, and an added benefit is that counsel will make a positive impression on jurors and the court.

Remember that jury trial procedures vary among federal and state courts and even between individual judges in the same county. In some courts, the general practice is for the judge to conduct voir dire. In these cases, a judge may also instruct attorneys to submit written questions for the judge's approval prior to voir dire. In other courts, the judge conducts an initial voir dire, then provides an allotted time frame for attorneys to ask supplementary questions. If more is required than is customary in a particular court or jurisdiction, discuss the matter with the judge, consider a motion for extended voir dire, and look to helpful case law holdings to the effect that trial courts should permit a reasonably extensive examination of prospective jurors so that the parties have a basis for an intelligent exercise of the right to challenge.[1] As early as possible, determine what practice is typically used in the trial court at hand, and develop a voir dire plan.

C. Electronic Social Media and Internet Searches

Electronic social media (ESM) can be a powerful tool to help counsel learn about prospective jurors' prejudices, biases, opinions, and preferences. However, the use of social media by trial lawyers is controversial and has generated a number of concerns, not the least of which revolve around intrusions into juror privacy. Courts have also articulated the danger of "facilitat[ing] improper personal appeals to particular jurors" in a manner that would be destructive to the integrity of trial, and have further expressed that the one-sidedness of "allowing lawyers to do to the venire what the venire cannot do to the lawyers will likely have a corrosive effect on fidelity to the no-research admonition."[2]

---

1. "The voir dire examination plays a critical role in securing the right to an impartial jury in civil, as well as criminal, trials." Darbin v. Nourse, 664 F.2d 1109, 1981 U.S. App. LEXIS 14902, 33 Fed. R. Serv. 2d (Callaghan) 154, 72 A.L.R. Fed. 62.

2. Oracle Am., Inc. v. Google Inc. (2016) 172 F. Supp. 3d. 1100, 1102, U.S. Dist. LEXIS 39675 (N.D. Cal. 2016) [Order Re Internet and Social Media Searches of Jurors].

Some courts have called for voluntary consent to a ban on internet research, and others have adopted somewhat of a Solomon's approach of ordering delimited research and informing the venire of the limits while reinforcing the standard no-research admonition. Still other courts accept the value of the internet's role in securing the right to an impartial jury, and recognize that this genie will not go gently back into its bottle. Lawyers now typically scour Facebook, Twitter, LinkedIn, and other sites, for the purpose of researching the venire. However, it would be a mistake to do this research in the courtroom during voir dire, as a screen may be visible to potential jurors, who may view such investigations to be disrespectful snooping at best. The better approach is to have an associate perform the searches outside the courtroom, and to inconspicuously provide information to lead counsel in the courtroom as needed.

The American Bar Association (ABA) clarified its position on the use of electronic social media in Formal Opinion 466, dated April 24, 2014, wherein judges and lawyers are encouraged to discuss parameters pursuant to local rules, department rules, standing orders, case management orders, and the applicable Rules of Professional Conduct. The opinion states, in part, as follows:

> Unless limited by law or court order, a lawyer may review a juror's or potential juror's Internet presence, which may include postings by the juror or potential juror in advance of and during a trial, but a lawyer may not communicate directly or through another with a juror or potential juror.

In line with ABA model Rule 3.5 and similar rules of professional conduct, lawyers may not cause any sort of *ex parte* communication with a juror, or seek to influence a juror. The opinion addresses three levels of lawyer review of juror internet presence: (1) passive review of a website or ESM; (2) active review where there is a request for access to ESM; and (3) passive review where a juror becomes aware of the identity of a lawyer/viewer. Review applicable state bar ethics opinions for important information, including about whether an indirect communication to a juror, such as a network-generated notice to subscriber of the identity of a viewer, is an "impermissible communication" within the meaning of the state Bar association's professional rules. It is important for lawyers to be current with ever-changing technology.

What remains abundantly clear is that the principles of respect and deference to juror privacy remain intact:

> Trial judges have such respect for juries—reverential respect would not be too strong to say—that it must pain them to contemplate that, in addition to the sacrifice jurors make for our country, they must suffer trial lawyers and jury consultants scouring over their Facebook and other profiles to dissect their politics, religion, relationships, preferences, friends, photographs, and other personal information.[3]

---

3. Oracle Am., Inc. v. Google Inc,. *supra,* 172 F. Supp. 3d at 1101.

A final word on ESM is in the nature of a caveat: social media presents a tremendous temptation to those who use it daily, including jurors. Some courts have developed instructions to jurors on the use of social media during trial to emphasize the prohibitions against doing research on a pending case and discussing or electronically communicating information about a case before the trial is concluded.[4] Our collective romance with ESI is often spoken of as addictive, so daily instructions may prove most effective.

D. Assign Jury Selection Duties

During planning for jury selection, the lead attorney may wish to assign specific tasks to be handled by associates and staff. As an example, one attorney will address jurors and ask them questions, while associates assist by taking detailed notes including juror names, seating positions, and verbal responses, and by flagging challenges for cause. Other tasks might include the careful, continual observation of the panelists' facial expressions and body postures, or performing a public records search online outside the courtroom. It may be wise to designate someone to suggest on-the-spot follow-up questions. The voir dire team should agree on a simple, systematic rating system for panel members. Inexperienced voir dire team members will find it helpful to observe jury selection at other trials, and to practice presentations through role-playing. Counsel might consider including one or more nonlawyers on the jury selection team, since nonlawyers can bring useful perspectives and insights into prospective jurors' apparent attitudes.

As with everything else, it is critical to review the law, including local and courtroom rules, regarding voir dire, and to be organized before a pretrial conference. If unfamiliar with the courtroom, counsel might consult with the courtroom clerk, the bailiff, or the court reporter to acquire information about a particular judge's procedural preferences, style, and the expected courtroom etiquette. Alternatively, contact colleagues who have practiced before a particular judge to inquire about particular or favored procedures. As an example, counsel will want to determine whether the judge typically uses juror questionnaires, and if so, when and whether they are to be received from jurors and provided to counsel. Ask whether attorneys are required or invited to submit supplemental questions. Find out how much time is customarily permitted for attorney voir dire, and whether the scope of questioning is limited. Where attorney voir dire is permitted, counsel is sometimes strictly limited to ten, twenty, or thirty minutes total. Ask if original and replacement jurors are questioned separately, or if replacement jurors are examined simultaneously with the jurors seated in the jury box. Scrupulous preliminary preparations will help ensure efficient and constructive selection efforts. Early planning will also help determine whether an attorney needs to file a motion for improved or altered voir dire conditions.

Before voir dire begins, counsel should have a premade jury box diagram to ensure notation of the correct names and pronunciation for each prospective juror. Small sticky notes can be used to shift positions as members of the venire are dismissed. Attorneys

---

4. ABA Formal Opinion 466 notes, at page 6, the findings of a three-year study, which found that jury instructions were the most effective tool to mitigate the risks of inadvertent but harmful juror misconduct.

practicing in an unfamiliar court might also determine, ahead of time, how the seats will be numbered. In many courtrooms, before voir dire begins the clerk prepares and provides lawyers with a jury box form showing how the seats are numbered and filled. Some clerks will provide a revised form to attorneys after the jurors are selected, with correctly spelled names and seating numbers. The amount of latitude a judge typically allows during voir dire can vary greatly, so if time permits, attorneys should observe the judge during voir dire in a different trial to familiarize themselves with courtroom procedure.

E. Seeking Improved or Altered Voir Dire Conditions

Cases involving harassment, and cases involving LGBTQ clients may comprise provocative or disquieting facts that give rise to a need for a more prolonged, or strategic, examination of opinions and sentiments. This may give cause for counsel to seek improved or altered voir dire conditions.

Owing in part to increased strains on court resources, some argue that voir dire should be conducted only by judges, or that the time allotted to attorneys should be limited. However, the competing concern is that overly restrictive limitations may unfairly hinder the ability of counsel to detect jurors who have biases and prejudices, and may deny prospective jurors an opportunity to make disclosures or accurately respond to lines of inquiry, as they might prefer. Further, absent well-informed bases for exercising peremptory challenges, qualified jurors may unintentionally be deselected. In cases where the facts are tinged with politically or socially explosive issues, attorneys need to consider how to question potential jurors about "hot button" facts and issues without inadvertently alienating some. Of course, hot button issues may also reveal attitudes that give rise to for-cause challenges. These particularly difficult cases may generate a need to seek more time, or greater latitude in asking questions than the court typically permits. Counsel can work with the court to contour the process, and given that it can be time-consuming to develop a plan, this should be brought to the court's attention long before trial call. Few courts would delay jury selection and trial, thereby further inconveniencing jurors, to accommodate an unpunctual motion or request.

A pretrial motion seeking improved or altered voir dire conditions is usually based on grounds that the requested, expanded voir dire is reasonably necessary to obtain certain information about jurors to permit plaintiff to meaningfully exercise the challenges to which the plaintiff is legally entitled. As an example, counsel may need to have additional time to explore areas of potential bias on sensitive, embarrassing, or otherwise emotionally charged topics, because people's responses may (understandably) be colored by feelings of embarrassment, self-consciousness, or an inclination to keep certain feelings private. Meaningful selection requires the opportunity to hear not only a potential juror's initial response to a question, but also explanation and magnification on a pivotal topic. People are not always able to view themselves objectively, and are sometimes reluctant to admit they misspoke, even when they recognize an answer was incomplete or unclear. A potential juror may be responding in good faith when she or he states that she or he feels able to judge a case impartially, but a juror is unlikely to volunteer information without adequate inquiry. A motion for improved voir dire conditions must provide a factual basis showing why a particular case raises particular problems of juror bias, and should specify the issues and attitudes that the "improved" voir dire will address. The motion must cite legal authorities and applicable (if possible, factually similar) case law supporting the grounds upon which the motion is based. Depending upon what is routinely permitted by the court, a motion for improved voir dire might address: (1) the necessity for lawyer-conducted voir dire; (2) a request for an introduction to set the stage for voir dire; (3) a request for submission of a written questionnaire or a supplemental questionnaire to prospective jurors; (4) the need to ask extensive questions during jury voir dire; (5) the need for time to ask open ended questions and probing questions; (6) whether to conduct individual questioning or small group questioning; and (7) use of the "struck system" for seating and replacing prospective jury members (in which an adequate number of prospective jurors are struck "for cause" before peremptory challenges are exercised).

Another type of motion relating to voir dire requests that the court issue an order to preclude certain types of inquiries, or a line of questioning by opposing counsel during voir dire. The purpose of this motion is to prevent counsel from attempting to precondition, or prejudice the jury against the plaintiff. Under some circumstances, counsel might also consider whether partial sequestration (in-camera questioning) is appropriate to insulate the panel from the influence and potentially prejudicial effect of negative attitudes and inflammatory remarks expressed by a fellow prospective juror in response to voir dire questions. The latter motion might, for example, address pre-trial publicity, or the need to avoid the inappropriate "education" of jurors in matters involving highly complex facts and issues.

F. Written Questionnaires

Written juror questionnaires are increasingly being used as courts discover that the administrative burden can be relatively minor in comparison with the benefit derived. However, written questions should never be viewed as a substitute for asking questions in open court, which is the only way to experience the immediacy of a person's personality, reactions, and feelings. Some courts customarily ask prospective jurors to fill out short questionnaires asking very basic demographic information, and others do not.

One example of a standard juror questionnaire provided by a judge, to be answered verbally by each juror at the start of voir dire, asks the following questions:

1. What is your name?
2. What part of [name of] county do you live in?
3. What is your occupation, or the last occupation you had before you retired?
4. What is the occupation of your spouse or anyone with whom you have a significant personal relationship who lives with you? Or if retired, what was their occupation before they retired?
5. Do you have any children?
   a. What are their ages?
   b. If they are employed what do they do?

6. Have you ever been a party to a lawsuit?
7. Do you, any close relative, or close personal friend, have any special training in the law, or law enforcement?
8. Do you, any close relative, or close personal friend, have any special training in medicine?
9. Have you had prior jury duty?
   a. Was it civil, criminal, or both?
   b. Was the jury able to reach a verdict?
   c. What was the case about?
10. Is there anything that would prevent you from being fair and impartial in this trial?

Although the foregoing is not a written questionnaire in the sense of allowing jurors to fill in boxes and write more descriptive answers for perusal before verbal voir dire, it provides some basic information that would enable the court or counsel to obtain supplemental information more efficiently, and it exemplifies how basic written questions can give counsel the ability to develop follow-up questions. It is easy to extrapolate how an expanded written questionnaire would save time and generate follow-up questions where necessary, as well as thoughtful responses.

A proposal to use a questionnaire should be raised with the judge early on. In most cases, the questionnaire should be short enough that jurors can complete it within twenty to thirty minutes. Ideally, prospective jurors should receive the questionnaires days or even weeks before they must appear in court to give counsel enough time to review the responses before jury selection. Failure to provide adequate time for counsel's review would undercut the value of the questionnaire.

One way to approach seeking judicial approval to submit written questions is to first ask opposing counsel if he/she/they will join your request. A court may be more inclined to grant permission when both sides agree and jointly submit the questionnaire. If an opponent declines to join, then counsel may file a motion to permit submission of a written questionnaire. Such a motion may be based on grounds including that the use of a questionnaire will: (1) elicit more candid and considered responses to fundamentally important questions than can be expected in oral voir dire; (2) assist counsel in detecting potential bias on emotionally charged topics; (3) provide crucial information that will better enable counsel to intelligently exercise peremptory and for cause challenges; (4) help protect the privacy of jurors; and (5) promote judicial economy by streamlining the oral voir dire process. The use of a questionnaire recognizes that it is fair to explore potential areas of bias, but sometimes difficult to do so without causing embarrassment or reticence. If a potential juror has had a disturbing or painful experience that could affect his or her attitude toward certain witnesses or issues, he or she may be reluctant to reveal it in the presence of a group. People may be reluctant to mention or discuss strong feelings of prejudice in the presence of a judge, lawyers, and other potential jurors. People may feel nervous or intimidated by the process, which can impact the quality and tone of a response. Jurors see lawyers as people who have an agenda; the use of a questionnaire may mitigate concerns about which lawyer is asking which question, and for what purpose. When jurors know a written questionnaire will be reviewed only by counsel and the court, and feel their privacy is protected, that can only encourage more thoughtful and frank responses on particularly sensitive issues. As one example, if a member of the venire is opposed to any or all women or members of the LGTBQ community working in private or national security industries, then this information may be more readily elicited through a questionnaire, where the juror can focus on the answer rather than on the surrounding crowd, and the lawyer can engage in a circumspect follow-up. A prospective juror may worry about being "judged" by officers of the court or peers, but a questionnaire can give each respondent time to reflect, in private, on his or her answers, while eliminating the pressure or discomfort of answering questions in a public setting. That said, even without a questionnaire, a juror's facial expressions and body language can provide significant clues about his or her feelings, and that is why having an associate present to monitor the panel can be important. As another example, the use of a questionnaire will likely enable attorneys and the court to quickly identify persons who may be excused for hardship or for cause, and will save time by eliminating the need to repeat the same questions to individual jurors. Using written questionnaires can significantly improve the quantity and the quality of the information obtained through voir dire, as long as the questions are relevant and substantially likely to expose strong attitudes and beliefs that make impartiality unlikely or impossible. Where it is not possible to submit the written questions to the panel well before trial, counsel might ask that the court administer a proposed juror questionnaire to the venire while court and counsel are engaged in arguments on motions in limine and other proceedings, and may also ask that permission be granted to analyze the responses overnight on grounds that having time to review the written answers will shorten the length, and improve the quality, of the oral voir dire process because it will enable counsel to be better prepared and able to concentrate only on matters that need clarification or elaboration. Always address any applicable state and local laws relating to the use of questionnaires.

G. Pretrial Conference

Judicial practices vary, and even after determining what is normally permitted in voir dire, attorneys should discuss and confirm the selection procedures at a pretrial conference. In some jurisdictions, the trial judge conducts the initial examination of prospective jurors, after which attorneys are permitted to directly question prospective jurors. If the judge will permit attorneys to directly question potential jurors, then the judge may ask attorneys to provide an estimate of the time each requires for voir dire for the purposes of scheduling, or the judge may establish time or other limitations. Another issue to discuss is whether each side will question the prospective panelists in turn, or whether they will be asked to alternate questions to the panel. Determine whether jurors are to be questioned separately, or in groups, or if everyone on the panel is questioned simultaneously.

Judges have the power to impose time limits on voir dire and many exercise this power as the result of progressively limited court resources. Some judges act as the sole questioner, and do not normally permit lawyers to directly question potential jurors.

If that is the case, attorneys should determine whether the judge will ask standard questions or questions submitted by lawyers, or both. Some courts have prospective jurors complete short, written questionnaires asking for basic background information before commencement of voir dire. If questionnaires are used, attorneys should confirm whether they may submit prospective questions, and whether the attorneys will receive copies of the completed questionnaire forms.

Other procedural issues to be clarified include: (1) the number of jurors and alternates who will be seated; (2) how the panelists will be seated in the jury box; (3) the manner in which jurors' hardship pleas are handled; and (4) how alternates will replace excused jurors. A traditional order of questioning in civil cases allows plaintiffs to voir dire twelve potential jurors, followed by defendants. At the completion of questioning, peremptory challenges begin and as members of the original panel are replaced, each of the replacement jurors called is examined separately. Another method, sometimes referred to as the "six-pack" method, calls for a number of replacement jurors (commonly six, but sometimes more) to be randomly selected and listed in the order in which they will be called as replacements. The replacement jurors are examined simultaneously with the original twelve prospective jurors seated in the jury box. Thus, if an original juror is excused, the next replacement juror steps in to take the excused juror's seat in the jury box without the need for additional questioning. (If all of the replacement jurors are used, another group of replacement jurors is called and examined separately.)

Attorneys should also determine the procedure for making challenges "for cause," including ascertaining which side goes first, and whether challenges should be exercised openly or outside the presence of the jury, orally, or in writing.

Statutes and court rules typically set the number of peremptory challenges afforded to each party. It is important to know the number of peremptory challenges each side will have for jurors and for alternates, to confirm the procedure for presenting these challenges, and to keep careful count of the number of peremptories exercised by counsel for all parties as the number of available challenges grows smaller. If there are multiple defendants, determine whether defense counsel will exercise defendants' peremptories jointly or separately. As one example, in some jurisdictions parties may have six peremptory challenges, plus one for each alternate appointed, unless there are two defendants, in which case the defendants may share eight, plus one for each alternate.

It will also be necessary to discuss the duration of questioning periods, when breaks will be taken, and whether the court will permit attorneys to take time to consult with voir dire team members during or after voir dire.

Do not fail to confirm the procedure for making voir dire objections and requests for admonitions. In the event opposing counsel asks improper questions on voir dire, which seek to influence jurors through improper argument or references, counsel must challenge the questions by objection. To preserve the issue for appeal it may also be necessary to request that the jury be admonished to disregard the improper question, the matters referred to in the question, and the inferences to be drawn therefrom, and to ask that opposing counsel be admonished not to pursue the line of questioning.

Counsel must object, on the record, to improper limitations placed on voir dire examination before the jury is sworn. Otherwise, the objection may be deemed waived.

II. VOIR DIRE: PRACTICE TIPS

A. Establishing Rapport and Control

Most jurors will have no experience with the legal process or civil trials. Up to the point of voir dire, they may feel part of a crowded herd, with little or no idea of what happens next. People in new situations thirst for information, and potential jurors tend to look to counsel to determine which of them will become a trustworthy guide to the case. Expect people to pick a "favorite" lawyer, so it is wise to decide what it is you want your jurors to see in you, such as a good communicator, someone who cares about the jurors, someone the judge respects, someone who has confidence in her/his case, someone who is completely prepared, and someone who likes and believes in her/his client. If counsel can find a common ground with jurors, and alleviate their natural apprehensions, they will appreciate it. Use people's names, rather than calling them "juror number two." Give them information they can use, such as what time they will break for lunch. Let the members of the venire know that you respect their privacy; if a person needs to say or explain something, he/she may do that in private with the judge. Tell jurors that there are no right or wrong answers to questions, and that no one is making any judgments about their responses. The goals are to establish trust from the outset, to facilitate juror conversations, and to discover enough to be able to make careful juror selections or deselections, and where possible, to educate jurors about case issues. That is a lot on one plate, and one common recommendation is to "be yourself," because jurors know when someone is being superficial.

Whatever the time frame, counsel should concentrate on essential questions. A lawyer wastes the court's time and the venire's time at the peril of squandering the opportunity to make a good first impression. In the debate about the efficacy of lawyer-conducted voir dire, some argue that lawyers can be invasive of jurors' privacy, tedious, time-consuming, expensive, and frivolous. Many people, lawyers included, believe that judge-conducted voir dire conserves judicial resources and increases juror candor because of the formal demeanor of the judge. However, a different school of thought argues that jurors may be less candid out of a desire to please the judge. Concerns about shrinking court resources and increasing backlogs of cases are as valid as concerns about ensuring the right to a fair and neutral jury panel. Counsel's objective should be to implement voir dire procedures that are appropriate to the particular case, approved by the court, and calculated to efficiently accomplish the task of screening and selecting a jury. When the preparation is done in advance, jurors see and respect the control and confidence.

Remember that jurors can be tired, bored, unhappy, and uneasy in a courtroom; do what you can to make their jobs easier. Instead of legal lingo and terms of art, use conversational language. Be clear and careful with words; as an example, use "before" and "after" instead of "prior to" and "subsequent to," because some people may mistakenly reverse the meaning of the latter words. Instead of stating a rule, and asking if jurors can "comply with" the rule, which is a way of telling people what to say, be approachable, and formulate a question that addresses real life. Do not ask questions that appear patronizing, such as: "Do you understand that the law says . . . ?" If a lawyer asks a panel whether it is inappropriate for a supervisor to comment on an employee's clothing, the response is likely to be a less informative "yes" or "no;" but a question that is framed to invite a narrative response may facilitate a conversation, and create a sense of ease and friendliness with the lawyer. As an example, "What kind of comment by a supervisor about an employee's clothes would cross the line into inappropriate territory?" Another way to invite dialog would be to give an example, and say, "Some people think that is inappropriate, and some don't. Which side are you closer to?" Ask who feels the same way, or who sees things a little differently. If questions are asked in a gentle, inviting way, with curiosity, people are likely to respond in an open, neighborly way, and will appreciate being treated respectfully. If you are lucky enough to open prospective jurors up to an exchange of opinions, thank them for a good discussion.

Many lawyers dislike jury selection and give it short shrift, or rely on experts, because of discomfort with the dynamic. People in large groups act differently than they normally do in their daily lives, and it can be difficult to squeeze the reliable data lawyers always look for from a restricted process. Then, there is always the fear that a "wrong" juror will be admitted to the panel, and that the case may be lost before the trial begins. These concerns should not dissuade a lawyer from focusing on voir dire as a critical element of trial. The reality is that jurors will always be observing and picking counsel, just as counsel are observing and picking jurors, and one of them will win.

B. Articulating the Case Theme

Because the purpose of the selection process is to obtain a fair, impartial jury, voir dire questions must be neutral and phrased in a nonargumentative manner. It is improper for an attorney to misuse the voir dire process by arguing the case, or by trying to instruct the jury in matters of law. Nor is it proper to put a spin on voir dire questions in a manner that seeks to prejudice the jury for, or against, a particular party. However, although one may not try to educate the jury panel about the *facts* of the case, one may take the opportunity to subtly educate the jurors about the *themes* of your case.

Courts and individual judges vary in the extent to which they will permit counsel to articulate her case themes during voir dire. Some do not permit any attempt to preview case themes, while others allow it, even to the extent of permitting a mini-opening statement at the beginning of voir dire, or during introductory remarks. Where permitted, counsel typically introduces his or her client, and tells the jurors "a little bit about the case." A more subtle method is to embed themes in the questions directed to the panel. Sometimes, the primary objective is less to gather information about a prospective juror than to make a point. An example is the straightforward question, "How many of you believe that women should be paid the same as men for doing the same job?" The question does more to drive home a point, than to invite a negative response, although the negative response would be enlightening. Another example might be the question, "How many of you believe that a transsexual person has the same right to be considered for a job as a fireman as anyone else who can pass the physical test?" Whether and to what extent a court will allow this kind of questioning varies from one venue to the next, and even from one courtroom to the next, and opposing counsel may well object to such a preview.

C. Use Basic Biographical Information as a Launching Pad

It is a mistake to make stereotypical assumptions about how someone thinks. Moreover, the similarly situated juror may feel unique, and attribute faults to your client that confirm the juror's own singular identity. Basic biographical information (which include age, citizenship, residency, hobbies, etc.) can be revealing, but it is not enough. In addition, potential jurors sometimes distort replies to questions, whether intentionally or unintentionally, and it is often that case the further voir dire exposes relevant experiences, values, and emphatically held opinions that go to the heart of the facts and issues of a case. Logical "follow-up" questions can identify those jurors with favorable or unfavorable traits or personal predispositions regarding social status, ethnicity, religion, sexual orientation, or other class attributes at issue in harassment cases. Fact scenarios and allegations relating to class-based discrimination can evoke strongly held convictions and powerful emotions, just as the presence of non-English speaking parties and witnesses may tap into potent beliefs concerning immigration and patriotism. That is not to say that everyone who has an opinion necessarily harbors prejudice, but only that it is fair to question panel members about subjects that could reveal immutable preconceptions and opinions that demonstrate a juror is unable, or unlikely, to be impartial. In harassment cases, jurors will often have to grapple with sensitive issues relating to cultural and social stereotypes, and potential jurors may be hesitant to fully disclose intensely personal experiences or beliefs out of embarrassment, or out of fear of being labeled intolerant, or simply because the questioning process feels unpleasant and invasive. Plaintiffs' counsel must prepare for ways to address unpleasant, but relevant, topics and to probe further into some responses when it appears reasonably necessary.

Prejudice may be defined as an unwillingness to grant other people social rights, or an unwillingness to accept other viewpoints. Depending upon the facts, and the *type* of harassment case, a few general examples of the many potential areas of inquiry include

- perceptions about whether anti-harassment laws work well;
- perceptions about whether a party or witness should be considered more credible or less credible owing to their profession, occupation, or association;
- perceptions about whether gender/sex/religious/race/etc., prejudice is a problem in society or in the community;
- addressing whether a potential juror's strongly held religious beliefs are likely to inhibit true impartiality under the circumstances (how might that affect your feelings as a juror in this case?);
- asking whether intolerance is a problem in society;
- determining whether someone is inclined to disfavor or distrust people who look and dress differently;
- addressing attitudes about LGTBQ;
- addressing attitudes about women in the workforce or in male-dominated workplaces;
- asking about attitudes regarding gender identity;
- asking whether a different gender identity is abnormal;

- addressing the fact that jurors must hear crude language or hear about sexual conduct;
- assessing attitudes about whether sexual or other types of jokes or pranks are harmless or humorous;
- addressing attitudes about dating in the workplace;
- asking about women's or men's roles in society;
- exploring jurors' empathy for, or identification with, business owners and supervisors;
- exploring attitudes concerning the general obligations of corporations, employers, and supervisors;
- inquiring about attitudes regarding noncitizens or non-English speaking persons having access to state or federal laws and courts;
- exploring attitudes about how society has changed in the past decade;
- determining whether any potential juror has had any experience involving, or relating to, a claim of harassment or discrimination;
- asking if the fact that a party or witness is from a particular background will affect the credibility jurors will give their testimony, or will affect their judgment;
- addressing perceptions and attitudes about lawsuits, "greedy" lawyers, and plaintiffs;
- asking how people feel regarding a person who seeks damages for emotional distress, or about perceptions regarding emotional distress damage awards;
- determining which jurors are business owners or managers, or have experience hiring and firing employees;
- determining if any juror or family member has been involved, even peripherally, in any sort of workplace harassment dispute;
- asking whether any juror has ever been accused of acting unfairly toward a co-worker;
- delving into immediate family members' experiences or expressions about a particular issue;
- determining whether family members or friends discussed a relevant experience with the juror;
- if any recent (or otherwise notable) news stories or televised shows featured facts and issues similar to a particular case, then it may be wise to take the opportunity to ask whether jurors are familiar with the event or show, and to ask about the potential juror's opinions and beliefs concerning the topic; and
- asking if it matters how people choose to dress.

Courtesy and respect are essential, but if counsel is to accurately assess juror bias and prejudice, she or he must find a way to explore these areas in ways that will facilitate candor.

It is important to remember that questions that appear discriminatory (such as asking women significantly different questions than men) are objectionable.

D. The Process

1. Preliminary Considerations

Attorneys, clients, and team members should stand when the prospective jurors are brought in and should meet their eyes. After prospective jurors are selected at random and seated in the jury box, the jury panel is sworn in and voir dire commences. The judge may then consider jurors' hardship requests, read the statement of the case, explain the need for fairness and impartiality, and generally explain the voir dire process. In some courts, it is the trial judge's duty to conduct the initial examination of prospective jurors. The judge may ask questions that are general in nature, or may follow a standard set of questions. In other cases, jurors may already have answered background questions provided on questionnaires.

When addressing the panel, counsel should never talk down to jurors. Instead, convey that jury selection questioning is not intended to be invasive or embarrassing, and that it is solely the result of efforts by each side to select a jury that is as impartial and unbiased as possible. Let jurors know that their candor in responding to questions is what protects the parties' rights to select a jury that can be fair and impartial, and that a decision to excuse a juror is not a negative reflection on that person. Ideally, prospective jurors should feel positive about being an essential part of the justice system. Counsel's respectful demeanor also makes a good first impression on the panel.

2. Basic Background Questions

If the court permits counsel to conduct voir dire, then lawyers may wish to start with (or follow up on) basic biographical or background questions, which "break the ice." Valuable information may be gleaned by asking about marriage, children, work history, education, relevant experiences, areas of study, favorite newspapers and other publications, associations, hobbies, recreational activities, and about family members, friends, and co-workers. Responses to these kinds of questions can be useful in evaluating jurors' personality characteristics, and often cue follow-up questions to expand upon answers. However, if time for voir dire is very limited, it may be wise to focus only on the questions that will elicit the most useful information. During group and individual questioning, counsel and team members should pay close attention to raised hands and nodding heads, to accurately attribute the responses to each juror. Counsel and team members should focus on the disclosure of the several attitudes and biases previously identified as inimical to plaintiff.

3. Open-Ended and Probing Follow-Up Questions

A poorly worded question, or a failure to follow up on an ambiguous or partial response, may generate misleading answers. A potential juror may genuinely not recognize her or his own biases, and jurors may even be intentionally deceptive as, for example, where a case has been heavily publicized and a prospective juror wishes to function as a jurist for self-serving reasons. Counsel should, when possible, take time to probe further into background responses and to encourage prospective jurors to talk more. Certainly, when a response is muddled or ambiguous, counsel should follow up with a question that encourages explanation or amplification. That means that the questioner must maintain his or her focus on juror responses, rather than on asking the next prepared question. People tend to say more revealing things about themselves in the context of a narration, anecdote, or explanation. However, voir dire should not be the equivalent of an interrogation. Counsel can make the process more conversational, and a little less inquisitional, by using verbal and nonverbal cues such as nodding to invite further explanation, or by encouraging a narrative account with a look of expectation and the tactical deployment of the word "and . . . ?" stated as a question. Another way to invite explication is to repeat a person's last words, and wait for the response. People tend to respond when others listen carefully, with genuine interest, and invite detail. The voir dire team should look for body language, facial expressions, and evidence of receptivity or discomfort as voir dire proceeds.

Probing follow-up questions are also an excellent way to prompt prospective jurors to give narrative. Probing questions include the following:

"Would you please tell me more about that?"
"Would you please give an example?"
"I'm not certain that I understand. Can you explain what you mean?"
"How did you feel about . . . "
"Why do you think that is?"
"How did that impact you?"
"Why?"
"Do you agree with that?"

Counsel might ask what the other jurors think to encourage discussion. However, this method can take valuable time and may overlook potential jurors who fail to speak up. If counsel can understand the experiences that inform a juror's stated opinions and views, and the bases for a juror's perceptions, the resulting information will help counsel make meaningful choices when making peremptory challenges or challenging jurors for cause.

4. Hypothetical and Leading Questions

Hypothetical questions may be permitted on voir dire, as when prospective jurors are asked to assume certain facts to gauge their willingness to apply the relevant principles of law, or for the purpose of assessing their attitudes regarding the hypothetical fact pattern. However, if a question is lengthy, or needs to be answered in parts, the risk is that a juror will be confused or give an incomplete response. It is also unwise to invite confusion and misleading responses by asking questions that are overly abstract. Leading questions are sometimes permitted, but are generally thought to be less revealing of any hidden partiality or prejudice.

5. Evaluating Personalities

As questioning proceeds, counsel and the voir dire team can "rate" what kind of person the respondent is to determine whether he or she may tend to identify more with plaintiffs or defendants. The following types of questions can elicit general and specific viewpoints, and the forthrightness with which jurors respond to questions may help identify positive and negative traits:

- Satisfaction with life—Clearly, people who feel a sense of fulfillment and satisfaction about their lives, families, and futures have a greater tendency to be generous toward others. Prospective jurors who exhibit an outlook of happiness, hope, creativity, curiosity, and a sense of perspective generally make more magnanimous jurors. On a hypothetical "kind-hearted" to "hard-hearted" scale, people at the far end who appear bitter, angry, and disappointed or fearful in life tend to be less compassionate and more begrudging.
- Empathy—From the Greek word *empatheia*, from *em* (meaning "from") and *pathos* (meaning "feelings" or "emotion"). Does the prospective juror have the ability to see things from another perspective by reading and understanding another person's emotions? Does the juror value other people's opinions and experiences? Or does the juror tend to view situations only through his or her own personal lens? Is the juror cynical or incredulous? Does the juror favor a world of absolutes and certainties? Is the juror inclined to listen to what others think?
- Flexible, critical thinking—Does the prospective juror exhibit an analytic mind? Does he or she like puzzles? Is there an evident willingness to tackle challenging problems and find constructive solutions, or openness to new experiences and ideas? Or does the juror appear to favor a "black-and-white," "all-or-nothing," or simplistic approach to issues? Is the juror stubborn or closed to other points of view? Is he or she self-centered, pompous, or smug?
- Leader or follower—Does the prospective juror demonstrate self-confidence? Will she or he be able to make constructive decisions on his or her own? Is he or she overly strong-willed or egotistical? Or does the juror value the opinions of others too much and show a tendency to be led by the opinions or preferences of others?
- Accountability—This is a concept in ethics that is often characterized synonymously with responsibility, enforcement, blameworthiness, and liability. Does the prospective juror recognize that group and organizational dynamics can be complex, and that accountability can be shared? Or does the person identify more with the principle that personal responsibility means accepting full responsibility for the choices we make, as well as the vagaries of life? Does the person appear to feel indignant about "complainers" or does he or she have perceptions about the harm litigation does to business? Will she or he tend to resent the plaintiff or any plaintiff?

Look for jurors' special skills, and observe how each potential juror processes information. Be aware of generational differences, but do not make assumptions about how people really feel and think. Follow up with the less talkative jurors. Find out which persons just want to get out of jury service and back to work, and which will perform the job with a sense of duty.

6. Rating Potential Jurors

Many people find it useful to keep track of jurors using a jury box form and small sticky notes with juror names and numbers. A scale for rating jurors might include five points, with the lowest number indicating a heavily defense-oriented person with a strong personality, and the highest number indicating someone who appears to be pro-plaintiff, with a strong enough personality to be a possible advocate in the jury room.

7. Challenges

A. For Cause

The questioning attorneys are generally permitted to dismiss a limited number of jurors for cause, as when a juror's answer reveals bias, prejudice, or preconceived notions of guilt or innocence. Potential jurors may be challenged for cause by giving a reason why they might be unable to reach a fair verdict. Procedures vary, but challenges for cause may be made on grounds including for general disqualification based on age (minority), limited language skills, hearing disability, a felony conviction without restoration of rights, or residency. A "for cause" challenge may also be based on implied or actual bias, when a prospective juror evidences a state of mind that would prevent her or him from acting impartially as a juror. Examples of implied bias include: if a juror is related by blood or marriage to party or witness; the existence of a business or fiduciary relationship; a tenant–landlord relationship; an agency relationship; service as a prior juror or witness in litigation involving a party; and service on a trial involving the same causes of action, along with indications that the juror has prejudged the case. Examples of actual bias include friendship with a party, overt hostility to plaintiff's claims, and prejudice to a class member. Tainting of the entire jury pool (through inappropriate voir dire questioning of comments by a juror) may be grounds for a pretrial challenge to the panel as a whole.

B. Peremptory Challenges

Questioning attorneys are also generally permitted a limited number of peremptory challenges that may be used to dismiss a juror for any reason, or for no particular reason. Sometimes prejudice and bias may be perceivable, but not demonstrable. Therefore, peremptory challenges permit counsel to reject a certain number of potential jurors who appear to have an unfavorable bias. A peremptory challenge may be based on a prospective juror exhibiting partiality by giving a nod or encouraging smile to, or appearing more friendly or sympathetic toward, an opposing party. A peremptory challenge may be based on a prospective juror looking tired or bored, or appearing very critical of the plaintiff, or of having a defensive body posture during voir dire. One principle underlying peremptory challenges is that if both parties have contributed toward the composition of the jury, they will find its verdict more acceptable.

III. OPENING STATEMENTS

"Evidence itself is eloquence, and the facts, if properly arranged . . . will shout louder than you possibly could," Lloyd Paul Stryker once said.[5]

After the jury has been selected, counsel give their opening statements. These statements comprise the jurors' introduction to the parties' competing theories of the case, and a primary goal is to help jurors understand the nature of the dispute, and what they are about to see. A good opening helps the finders of fact anticipate and track key evidence as it is presented over the course of the trial. That means, of course, that everything you say must accurately represent what jurors will see and hear. It is not hyperbole to state that a strong and effective opening statement is a critical component of a successful outcome to a plaintiff's case. In fact, research and voluminous amounts of anecdotal evidence show that jurors often form strong opinions about a case after opening statements are made. This is your opportunity to tell jurors what you will prove and, other than in a limited way in voir dire, it will be your first opportunity to connect with the jury and to establish your, and your client's, credibility. If you are well prepared and appropriately confident (not arrogant), this will strengthen the jurors' trust in you, and in what you say. Though your opening should be powerful and hit upon the key details of your case, take care not to overstate your case. Jurors will remember your representations and promises and, if they don't, defense counsel will be sure to remind them during closing arguments.

The best opening statements start with a hook, are reasonably short, and should resemble a story to the greatest possible extent. Placing facts and events in chronological order can help accomplish that task. Let the evidence speak. There are three primary goals to be accomplished, the first being to describe the case to the panel, presenting a clear picture of relevant events, the participants, their contentions, and the dispute itself, all the while weaving in the theme of the case. Once jurors are empaneled, they begin to wonder what to expect during the next hours, days, or weeks of jury service, and will be grateful for helpful guidance. The second purpose is to kindle jurors' interest and curiosity in your case. Ideally, your presentation will awaken an enthusiasm to hear your evidence. Engaged jurors keep track. Bored jurors tend to blank out during testimony, or miss blocks of critical evidence. Third, this is another opportunity to build rapport with jurors by speaking directly to them, demonstrating your sincerity, and by communicating a genuine confidence in your client and the case. Jurors will be evaluating you and your command of the opening statement so, as with everything else, preparation is vital.

By the time you make your opening statement, you should have practiced it several times. Practice alone and with an audience, preferably of nonlawyers. This will assist you in honing your presentation and will allow for a confident, strong opening with as little use of notes as possible. It will also help you to identify and eliminate, or minimize, any distracting or annoying habits you may have, including those you do not even realize you have. It is important to be well organized and to avoid fumbling with notes or shuffling papers while you are speaking. Although it is fine to refer to notes during your opening, or to refer to an outline with keywords or phrases that can jog

---

5. LLOYD PAUL STRYKER. THE ART OF ADVOCACY 53 (1954).

your memory, reading your opening statement to the jury as though you are reading from a book can have the undesired effect of boring and annoying jurors. If the court permits you to use visual aids during opening, such as a photograph, a key document, or timeline of events, you should do so—people love visuals, and any time you can engage jurors on a level besides auditory, interest will spike. Today's jurors are enthusiastic consumers of visual technology, and will often respond very positively to visual presentations, especially given that they will be proscribed from using personal devices for (relatively) long periods of time over the course of trial.

You will make your opening statement during the initial stage of proceedings, when jurors are most attentive and receptive. Jurors will be waiting to hear what the case is about and who the players will be. As plaintiff's counsel, you will have the first opportunity to tell your client's story, and the more effectively you do that, the more you improve your client's chances for a successful outcome. There are limits on what you can or should say, although the extent to which these limits are enforced is typically left to the discretion of the trial judge. Some judges permit the attorneys a fair bit of latitude, while others strictly enforce the general rules. In general, argument is improper during opening statements. This is not the time to argue about how to resolve conflicts in the evidence, or to discuss how to apply the law to the facts. This is not the time to try to arouse the emotions of the jurors. In addition, an attorney should not mislead by reference to inadmissible evidence, express personal opinions, comment outside the evidence, make statements regarding the credibility of any party or witness, or refer to facts of the case not substantiated by evidence. The goal is to make the plaintiff's story come alive, so jurors will understand why what happened to your client was wrong, and why your client is deserving of compassion and compensation. A good opening describes the key witnesses and evidence to be presented so the jury will understand what to expect during the trial, and can follow your case even if witnesses are presented out of order.

An effective opening statement will convey the case theme and the facts you intend to present at trial in such a way that the jury understands that an injustice was done to your client, and that they have an opportunity to remedy that injustice. You must not ask jurors to put themselves in your client's shoes, or to deliver the verdict they would wish to receive if they were in that person's position (the Golden Rule), but whenever possible, you want them to naturally identify with your client and see the case from the plaintiff's perspective or, at a minimum, to understand why your client believes he or she was wrong. Do your best to introduce the case to the jury in the most vivid, interest-producing way possible.

IV. ANATOMY OF AN OPENING STATEMENT

A. Introduction and Case Theme

By this time, jurors will have had at least some opportunity to meet counsel, and you will have built some rapport with them. The judge may have explained to the jury the purpose of opening statements and the normal procedure of the trial. If not, then it may be useful to begin the opening statement by introducing yourself and your client, by explaining the procedural order of the trial, and by briefly telling the jury that what is said in opening statements is not evidence—it is a preview of what is to come. Giving a brief explanation about the trial process may help a nervous lawyer get more comfortable, and may allow you to play up your confidence while giving jurors helpful information. However, you should not allow an introduction of this kind to supplant or lessen the strategy of starting off with a solid "hook" that launches the plaintiff's case by emphasizing the case theme.

When you accept the case, it's important to develop a case theme early in the process. The theme may change or evolve as the case progresses through the litigation process, but deciding on a theme near the outset will assist you in creating an effective discovery plan. Although you want the case theme to be short, you also want it to allow a jury to understand what your case is about from the beginning. Think about what would you want each juror to say if someone asked, "What is the case about that you just heard?" For example, in a retaliation case where your client was terminated after reporting sexual harassment, your scene might be: "This case is about an employee who did the right thing, but was punished for doing it." A case theme might include reference to someone who believes they can operate above the law, or begin with someone who courageously spoke out despite daunting financial and emotional risks. A good case theme appeals to the juror's sense of right and wrong. It has to naturally emerge from your client's story, and it has to ring true. And, the opening statement must paint a clear picture of events, participants, instrumentalities, and disputes. If jurors find your case theme memorable, and accept it, then they will naturally look for evidence throughout trial that supports it.

You want the jury to listen to your opening statement attentively, and jurors are likely to be more receptive when you maintain good eye contact with them and give a strong showing that you are completely at ease with your presentation and with the facts of your client's case. Jurors will be curious about, and open to, any indications that you like, and have confidence in, your client. It is important to capture the attention of the jury, and to hold it through opening until the end; beware of making an overlong statement that may cause jury members to lose attention, watch the clock, or focus on something other than what you are saying. Even for seasoned lawyers, it is tremendously beneficial to practice the opening as many times as possible before the trial begins. Practice in front of associates, colleagues, family members, and then videotape or record the presentation. Smooth out the rough edges, be cohesive, integrate the case theme, and make sure the audience is interested. Commit enough to memory that you can work with an outline, feel confident, and look directly at jurors as you speak. The finders of fact, who will decide your case, may still be forming their first impression of you, and this is an opportunity to solidify their confidence in you as the person who will guide them throughout the case. Because jurors are consumers of entertainment, and perceive trial as a contest, they often want to identify with the lawyer whom they view as the one with the most conviction and the kind of skill that comes from solid preparation.

B. Telling the Story

During the opening statement, the jury begins to form a visual image of what took place. Two concepts, the primacy effect and the and recency effect, are important to opening statements. When asked to recall a list of items in any order, people tend to best remember those items at the end of the list (the recency effect). Among earlier list items, the first few items are recalled more frequently than the middle items (the primacy effect). You get a psychological advantage if you start strongly, and end strongly, on your case theme. A story narrative can be the best way to keep a jury's attention, and your opening should tell your client's story in a way that explains, in simple terms, why you should win and your adversary should lose. The objective is to fire people's imaginations and make them want to hear your case, and want to be on your client's side. Many lawyers overuse the phrase, "the evidence will show," as they move through the story, but repetition is not an ideal way to hold a panel's attention. As you move through the story, present an overview of the case and use a narrative to help the jury to understand and focus on the key evidence that will build to a conclusion. Help jurors by defining any important terms to be used during trial. Personalize the client, so the jury has some basis for knowing who the plaintiff is, liking them, and believing in the client's claims. Show your own enthusiasm and compassion, which will help jurors identify with your client, and will create a sense of injustice that needs to be reversed.

Opening statement may also provide an opportunity for plaintiff's counsel to describe how the evidence will demonstrate weaknesses or inconsistencies in the defense's case or relative to a particular witness. However, keep in mind that your opening statement is for the purpose of discussing your own evidence and, clearly, you do not know what your opponent is going to present. Although you want to show how the evidence proves your client was wronged, you do not want to appear to be slinging mud at, as an example, a corporate defendant, or at employees who have been individually named. This kind of tactic could easily backfire and create sympathy for the defense. You must not attempt to give the jury any personal opinions about the credibility of witnesses, as this is improper. You may, however, use the facts to demonstrate why the jury may find a witness or defendant less than credible (as an example, by describing how the evidence will show that certain witnesses have told inconsistent stories before, and during, the litigation.) If, for example, you are representing the client in sexual harassment case, and the facts warrant it, you will want to point out the defendant's failure to have basic anti-harassment policies, or to provide any training to its supervisors, or to follow its own policies and procedures. You can paint a picture showing the ways in which plaintiff, who was being harassed, was left without protection. If the plaintiff complained to no avail, emphasize how the employer failed to ensure that its employees complied with its own anti-harassment policies, or otherwise failed to act reasonably to remedy or stop the harassment. If the plaintiff was retaliated against for reporting harassment, emphasize how you will show that the defendants punished your client for simply doing the right thing.

Any weaknesses in your case should be disclosed in the opening statement, by bringing them out in the most positive manner possible. The goal is to appear honest, and to lessen the negative impact when your opponent, inevitably, points them out. Stick to the main story and key points—opening statement is not the time to get bogged down in all manner of minutia and in the complexities of your case. This is not the time to burden the jury with multiple dates and events. While emphasizing and focusing on your case theme, point out the relevant and salient facts. You do not want to lose the jury in a long recitation of facts, it is enough to give sufficient factual information to establish an understanding of how your client was wronged as well as to establish a client's reasonableness, and more importantly, your client's credibility. Use the power of a good story to stimulate memory retention.

Never in an opening statement make promises to bring forth evidence or facts that have been excluded in pretrial motions, or facts that are clearly inadmissible or without evidentiary support. ABA Model Rules of Professional Conduct 3.4(e) provides, in relevant part, that a lawyer shall not, "in trial, allude to any matter that the lawyer does not reasonably believe is relevant or that will not be supported by admissible evidence, assert personal knowledge of facts in issue except when testifying as a witness, or state a personal opinion as to the justness of a cause, the credibility of a witness, the culpability of a civil litigant or the guilt or innocence of an accused." Failure to heed this rule creates the risk of admonishment from the judge or, worse, a finding of contempt that would subject counsel to embarrassment and a loss of credibility with the jury. Never promise anything you cannot deliver. Jurors will not forget what you said at opening, and will almost certainly consider missing evidence during closing and in deliberations. There is also the risk of giving defense counsel the opportunity to remind jurors during closing that you (and your client) failed to deliver what you promised.

C. Procedural Considerations

To be effective, a good opening needs to be reasonably brief. A jury's attention is at its peak during the first few minutes of the opening statement, so try not to waste that valuable time. The length of an opening statement may vary, according to local rules and depending on the complexity of the case. In most cases, an opening statement should be no more than twenty minutes. The court may ask in a pretrial conference what the expected length of your opening statement is, and some courts will provide preset limits. Generally, it is within each judge's discretion to set time limits, but as long as your request is reasonable, judges generally permit leeway in allowing counsel sufficient time to present an opening statement. As always, check local rules and your judge's personal preferences to determine the court's trial policies and practices. Most jurisdictions do not permit the law to be discussed in any detail in an opening statement; however, many will permit a statement about the main legal issues or an applicable statute.

It is customary to wait until the judge acknowledges you to begin. Some judges require counsel to use a fixed lectern, and some allow counsel to move the lectern to a more favorable spot, or to walk to a space toward the front of the jury box, which allows free movement. Rather than holding a speech or outline, it is best to be near enough to your table to be able to quickly refer to notes or retrieve an exhibit. It is not good to be so uncomfortably close to the jury box that you are invading jurors' space.

In most jurisdictions, counsel is permitted to use demonstrative evidence during an opening statement. If counsel can stipulate to exhibits, such as diagrams, charts, or models that will help the jury understand the case, they may be permitted at the court's discretion. It is always wise to obtain the advance approval of the judge before using exhibits.

If, during the opening statement, opposing counsel makes an objection, remember that jurors are still evaluating you, as well as your case. Rather than generating an argument, either with the judge or your opponent, which could create a negative appearance, keep your response simple. As an example, "I am only stating what I expect the evidence to show." If the objection is sustained, apologize and move on. However, if an objection is overruled, return to what you were saying and repeat it for any jurors who became distracted, then continue. The goal is to give jurors a cohesive picture of your case, and if you allow opposing counsel to engage you in an argument, that will only distract from this primary goal.

D. Discussion of Damages

Opening statement is not the time to present a detailed description of your client's damages; that discussion is best saved for the closing argument after the panel has had the opportunity to assess the defendants' egregious conduct and how that conduct affected your client. A focus on money and figures during the opening creates the risk of boring, or even alarming, jurors, as it can invoke a suggestion of greed. Throwing out numbers that jurors may, at the outset, find overreaching or excessive could color a juror's perception of a plaintiff's motives and the case before the first real shot is fired. Certainly, a brief discussion is in order about how your clients were damaged and, most importantly, how their damages will relate back to the defendant's conduct. You will want to explain how the events will demonstrate that the defendant's improper conduct affected your client financially and emotionally, and jurors need to know that you will ask, at the end of trial, that the defendants be held financially responsible for the consequences of their wrongful conduct. After the close of evidence, you will have a better idea of how the case is going, and how best to present plaintiff's damages in numbers.

E. Conclusion

Because first impressions are so important, you should rarely, if ever, waive or reserve the opening statement. The beginning and conclusion of your opening statement should be equally strong, and should repeat or invoke the case theme. Mention that your client will be looking to the jury for justice, and thank the jurors for their attention and anticipated service. Capture the jurors' attention from the beginning and make them want to make your client whole. In all cases, the key is to begin to prepare the voir dire and opening statement from the beginning of the case.

Appendix 15A

Sample Form to Record Juror Characteristics at Voir Dire

Aspects of Case	Favorable Jury Characteristics	Unfavorable Juror Characteristics
Major Issues		
a.	a.	a.
b.	b.	b.
Theme of Plaintiff's Case		
a.	a.	a.
Strengths of Plaintiff's Case		
a.	a.	a.
b.	b.	b.
Weaknesses of Plaintiff's Case		
a.	a.	a.
b.	b.	b.
Profile of Plaintiff		
a.	a.	a.
Profile of Defendant		
a.	a.	a.
Profile of Key Witnesses		
a.	a.	a.
b.	b.	b.

CHAPTER 16

Voir Dire and Opening Statement: Defense Perspective

Nadia P. Bermudez, Greg A. Garbacz, and Patrick J. Goode II

I. INTRODUCTION[1]

American poet Robert Frost is attributed with the quotation: "A jury consists of twelve persons chosen to decide who has the better lawyer." Frost implied that style inevitably prevails over substance in a court of law. The truthfulness of that statement can be the subject of reasonable debate among trial lawyers. However, no lawyer can deny the importance of effective communication and advocacy, along with presentation of evidence. There is no better showcase for such skills than during voir dire examination and opening statements, when the jury—arguably—is most attentive and captivated by the proceedings.

Indeed, voir dire is often the earliest opportunity for a defense attorney to communicate directly to potential jurors. It is important for the defense attorney to focus on both jury selection and subtle advocacy during voir dire. Ignoring either of these components neglects a golden opportunity to garner the trust of the jury and start the process of persuasion. Following jury selection, opening statements provide another crucial opportunity for the defense. Because the plaintiff's case in chief begins immediately following the defense's opening statement, it is particularly important for defense lawyers to make a strong, positive impression so that the jury is inclined to keep an open mind as the plaintiff's case presentation begins.

There is significant variation among states, counties, and even courtrooms as to whether to allow the attorneys to conduct voir dire and, if so, to what extent. This chapter (and the previous one) assumes that a right to jury trial exists in the type of case involved and that a jury trial has been timely demanded and has not been waived. In this chapter, we discuss a defense-oriented process by which prospective jurors are

---

1. This chapter includes content written by authors of previously published versions of this chapter that may or not be credited herein.

examined about their backgrounds and any actual or potential biases before being chosen to sit on a jury. Following jury selection, opening statements provide an opportunity to introduce the jury to the facts of the case and the parties' theories of the case to a jury.

For the defense, voir dire is an important time to speak to the jury because a jury could go days listening to the plaintiff's case in chief before hearing any defense theories. In the context of claims of workplace harassment and/or disputes, many jurors will have firsthand experiences with a less than desirable workplace or will know someone who has made complaints against an employer. In addition to personal experience, media exposure about harassment cases, especially high-profile cases, can predispose a jury against alleged harassers or accusers. Similarly, the juror pool is likely to consist of few individuals with ownership or management experience or with subordinates reporting to them. Thus, voir dire is a window into the biases of potential jurors who may have prejudices against employers.

As with voir dire, the defense's opening statement provides an opportunity to diffuse harmful information presented during a plaintiff's opening statement and to counter with issues of factual dispute that a jury will ultimately resolve.

Voir dire and opening statements mark the beginning of the presentation of a trial to a jury. By this time, all discovery has been concluded and motions in limine have been decided. The presentation to the jury must adhere to the evidence and the limitations imposed by law or the judge; however, the style and tone of the presentation of evidence may affect the trust and credibility of the advocate, ultimately impacting the decision-making process of a jury.

II. VOIR DIRE AND JURY SELECTION

The term voir dire means "to speak the truth." Indeed, at the inception of voir dire, prospective jurors are sworn to speak truthfully in response to a jury questionnaire or direct questioning from a judge or lawyer. After the judge instructs the courtroom deputy to call a panel of prospective jurors from the jury assembly room, the prospective jurors are sworn in using an oath similar to the following: "You and each of you do solemnly swear that you will truthfully answer the questions put to you concerning your qualifications to sit as jurors in the cause now before this court. So help you God."

Once the panel swears to tell the truth, defense counsel can solicit other promises, such as a promise to keep an open mind in the case until actual evidence is presented. Some judges will pre-instruct a jury that the attorney's comments and arguments should not be considered as evidence. In a workplace harassment or discrimination case, voir dire serves other objectives for the defense: (1) to indirectly educate the jury about your side of the case; (2) to glean information about any prejudices or experiences that may yield a more favorable attitude toward management or the defense themes; (3) to ascertain whether grounds exist for the exercise of a challenge for cause; and (4) to assist counsel in the strategic exercise of preemptory challenges.

A. Before Voir Dire Begins

It is highly recommended that you seek guidance from the court in advance to understand the scope of voir dire, how and when prospective juror challenges or strikes are to be handled, and whether such challenges can be made outside of the presence of the panel. Another option is to contact a trial attorney who has recently tried a case in your judge's courtroom.

A party can request voir dire from the trial judge, and if the request is denied, the party can request that a written questionnaire be prepared.

In *Fietzer v. Ford Motor Co.*,[2] the Seventh Circuit Court of Appeals stated that a trial court "should permit a reasonably extensive examination of prospective jurors so that the parties have a basis for an intelligent exercise of the right to challenge."

The following are important questions to consider during the pre-voir dire conference:

- Whether the court will use a jury questionnaire and to what extent counsel will have input in the development of it
- Whether the court has guidelines for the use of the juror questionnaire
- Whether the court will permit supplemental questions to be propounded to the panel by questionnaire
- The extent of the court's oral inquiry of the panel
- The extent of oral questioning by counsel
- The court's procedures for challenges: how many jurors will be seated, and in what order
- Whether challenges for cause will be discussed in open court, in the presence of the prospective jury, or both
- How the court will handle replacing jurors after challenges are exercised
- Under what circumstances alternate jurors will be used

Even if the judge permits sidebars or recesses for the exercise of challenges, it is important that such proceedings remain on the record. Frequently, counsel may be asked to waive the reporting of voir dire or jury selection, but many experienced counsel will decline such a request. While the record of voir dire may rarely be needed, it is recommended because the absence of a record may be painful to an appellant. For instance, if a juror signals strong bias against a defendant, yet the judge declines to exercise a challenge for cause, it may be very difficult for a party to use the juror's bias to overturn a subsequent, adverse verdict.

The pre-voir dire conference is an important time to ask questions about the process outside the presence of your prospective jury.

---

2. 622 F.2d 281, 284, relying on Kiernan v. Van Schaik, 347 F.2d 775 (3d Cir. 1965).

B. Jury Questionnaire

In many cases, judges will ask prospective jurors to complete written questionnaires before the commencement of voir dire. Voir dire questionnaires typically ask for basic information regarding each prospective juror's age, occupation, previous jury experience, whether the juror has a spouse and his or her occupation, acquaintance with parties or counsel, and knowledge of the case. Parties are usually given an opportunity to review the questionnaire before it is submitted to the panel. Thereafter, the questionnaire answers can be used by the judge or counsel, or both, while examining individual jurors in oral voir dire.

Jury questionnaires have some advantages, such as making the voir dire more efficient and protecting the privacy of the prospective juror, which may result in more candid responses. Jury questionnaires may also solicit more honest answers if jurors are permitted time to reflect on the question, as opposed to answering it in live time in open court. By the same token, challenges can be considered in a more meaningful and reflective way because of the additional time to intellectually digest the information provided. Because more intrusive, and potentially embarrassing, questions are often better presented through questionnaires (as opposed to live questioning), defense lawyers can leverage the neutral source of the questions to avoid creating the impression that they are invading the juror's privacy while still obtaining answers to more direct and probing questions.

Jury questionnaires also have disadvantages: Jurors may use the questionnaire to identify a reason to be excused from service, the voir dire process is prolonged, and jurors may find the process tedious, especially if questions are repetitive and the questionnaire is extensive. Further, the questionnaire may provide a cunning juror more time to fashion an evasive, yet literally truthful, response that could hinder detection of bias.

C. Defense Voir Dire Examination

In the heat of the moment, jury selection can move quickly. Therefore, it is important to delegate responsibilities to other members of the defense team, including taking notes, observing, and suggesting follow-up. If you are the lead trial counsel, it is likely more important for you to watch the jury and establish a rapport, instead of jotting down a yes/no answer.

Most federal judges do not allow any voir dire by counsel.[3] It is therefore important to research your judge in advance of trial to determine whether and to what extent your trial judge will allow attorney voir dire. Assuming attorney-conducted voir dire is permitted, the court has discretion to determine appropriate limits on length and content. This can be limited to as little as twenty to thirty minutes in federal court.[4]

---

3. District courts are not required to allow attorneys to conduct any voir dire at all. *See* FED. RULES CIV. PROC. R. 47(a); *see also* Perry v. Allegheny Airlines, Inc., 489 F.2d 1349, 1352 (2d Cir. 1974).

4. *See* Luera v. Snyder, 599 F. Supp. 1459, 1463–64 (D. Co. 1984); Nanninga v. Three Rivers Elec. Co-op., 236 F.3d 902, 906–07 (8th Cir. 2000).

In *Darbin v. Nourse*, the Ninth Circuit Court of Appeals ruled that while it is within the court's discretion to control the length of attorney-conducted voir dire, such limitations cannot go so far as to preclude the parties from effectively exercising peremptory and cause challenges:

> The trial court must conduct voir dire in a manner that permits the informed exercise of both the peremptory challenge and the challenge for cause. Questions which merely invite an express admission or denial of prejudice are, of course, a necessary part of voir dire because they may elicit responses which will allow the parties to challenge jurors for cause. However, such general inquiries often fail to reveal relationships or interests of the jurors which may cause unconscious or unacknowledged bias. For this reason, a more probing inquiry is usually necessary. In some lawsuits the nature of the case itself suggests that a more specific inquiry is required with respect to particular matters. The nature of the controversy or the relationship and identity of the parties may involve matters on which a number of citizens may be expected to have biases or strong inclinations. If an inquiry requested by counsel is directed toward an important aspect of the litigation about which members of the public may be expected to have strong feelings or prejudices, the court should adequately inquire into the subject on voir dire. The court must not be niggardly or grudging in accepting counsel's requests that such inquiries be made.

The court need not use the question in the precise form suggested by counsel. Nor need a particular question be asked if the substance of the inquiry is covered in another question, differently phrased, or in the voir dire as a whole. Certainly the trial court need not conduct an inquiry which is cumulative.[5]

Typically, lawyers for both sides will delve into a potential juror's employment background and experience in the workplace. It is also important to learn about the experiences of your prospective juror's close family members, friends, or fellow household members. Useful questions may include the following:

- What are the most important duties in your current position?
- What do you like about your current job? What do you dislike, and why?
- Have you ever been a union member? (Because of the labor-vs.-management perspective, union members may have a less favorable view toward members of management and supervisors.)
- Have you ever been self-employed? (This can be a useful tool in determining whether the prospective juror has any management experience, and thus might be more likely to sympathize with the employer and decision-makers.)
- Have you ever been unemployed for an extended time, and if so, what were the circumstances? (Such a question may illicit bias against employers in general or gaps in employment history caused by a past conflict with an employer.)

---

5. Darbin v. Nourse, 664 F.2d 1109, 1113 (9th Cir. 1981).

Questions regarding a loss of employment can be sensitive. Thus, you could ask generally about loss of work due to merger, lack of work, layoff, termination, and resignation. When defending an employer, it may also be useful to ask questions to determine whether prospective jurors have a bias against corporations or businesses in general by asking more open-ended questions about how the jurors feel about corporate America or whether corporations value employees, which may solicit answers indicative of bias or negative precepts. You can then solicit promises from prospective jurors to be fair and impartial, while noting jurors that you may want to challenge to avoid the potential for bias.

Other questions pertaining to previous management experience may include the following:

- Have you ever worked as a manager or supervisor of other employees? If so, how many employees did you supervise? What were your responsibilities?
- Have you ever recommended or been involved in a termination?
- Have you ever recommended or been involved in the hiring or promotion of an employee?
- Have you ever recommended or been involved in the disciplining of an employee? (It is equally important to find out the circumstances of these occasions, for example, firing, hiring, promotions, and discipline, and identify the rules or policies on which the potential juror relied.)
- Have you been asked to evaluate another employee's job performance?

In addition, questions related to any training in human resources or management are important, as are questions about any work experience in the same industry as the position at issue. It may also be appropriate to ask about attitudes toward supervisors and managers.

Additionally, ask questions about specific employment situations that may be the subject of the litigation:

- Have you ever worked for the government as a civil servant? (This question can be particularly important because public employees might have experienced "civil service protection," requiring certain steps and procedures in advance of a termination or adverse employment action.)
- Have you ever heard of someone at work being accused of harassment (or discrimination)? What were the circumstances? Do you think the situation was resolved properly? Why or why not? (It is often easier to delve into this area instead of directly asking someone if they have ever been discriminated against or harassed at work.)

Another area worth exploring is general conflict resolution:

- Have you ever sued anyone? Have you ever been sued? What were the circumstances? How do you feel about the result? Were you satisfied?

- Have you ever been laid off from a position? If so, what were the circumstances? How do you feel about how the situation was handled?
- Have you ever observed an employment decision that you believe was unfair? If so, describe the circumstances.
- Have you (or a family member) ever filed any type of employment complaint or lawsuit against an employer? Were you satisfied with how the issue was resolved? Why or why not?

One technique for deselecting members of the venire who are likely to be the most unfavorable to your client's defense is to identify "leaders" in the panel and to eliminate those leaders that are likely to have a forceful point of view that is contrary to your client's interests. Prospective jurors who are identified as "followers" are less likely to influence other jurors and are potentially less of a concern during voir dire—particularly if you only have thirty minutes to ask questions.

Finally, it is important to identify and integrate the defensive themes of your case into voir dire. Every trial is ultimately a story, with characters and evidentiary support. Every story has a theme. In addition to asking stock questions designed to identify favorable or unfavorable witnesses, voir dire presents a unique opportunity to subtly communicate themes that will be important to your defense, evaluating how jurors respond to those themes and planting themes in jurors' minds, which may influence the lens through which they later view the evidence and witnesses.

D. Challenging Plaintiff's Improper Voir Dire

Voir dire questions may be challenged by objection or followed by a request for an admonition. The objection should be made as soon as possible because objections to the nature and extent of voir dire that are not made before commencement of testimony are treated as waived.[6]

Note that an objection alone may not avoid prejudice to the defendant's case. To preserve the issue for appeal, the objecting party should also request that the jury be admonished to disregard the statement and/or question. An admonition given by a judge is also a more effective means to curb an opposing counsel's overreach, causing the counsel to question further aggressive voir dire, while causing the jurors to perceive the admonished lawyer as having crossed a line set by the judge.

If you anticipate highly prejudicial voir dire by your opposing counsel, motions in limine should also be drafted to encompass your opponent's voir dire examination. Frequently, speaking with other counsel who have tried cases against your opposing counsel will provide an ability to learn in advance the nature of your opposing counsel's voir dire style and whether advance steps should be taken to control that style.

---

6. United States v. Diez, 736 F.2d 840, 844 (2d Cir. 1984); *see also* United States v. DeFiore, 720 F.2d 757, 765 (2d Cir. 1983).

E. Challenges to the Panel

1. Challenges for Cause

Traditionally, challenges for cause have been divided into two categories: (1) those based on actual bias and (2) those grounded in implied bias.[7] Actual bias is demonstrated by a prospective juror's inability to act impartially or refusal to weigh the evidence properly.[8] Nonetheless, a judge has the discretion to reject a challenge for bias provided that the juror commits to "lay aside those feelings and reach a verdict based on the evidence presented and the court's instructions."[9]

It is important to note that the number of challenges based on cause is unlimited.[10] Again, in case of an unsuccessful challenge for cause, defense counsel can still consider peremptorily striking a juror.

2. Peremptory Challenges

After both plaintiff and defendant have passed on cause challenges, the parties can opt to exercise peremptory challenges. This begins with the plaintiff's counsel and then alternates to the defense counsel and back to plaintiff, until all peremptory challenges are exhausted or both sides consecutively decline further peremptory challenges.

In federal court, each party is entitled to three peremptory challenges.[11] State procedures can vary. Keep in mind that co-parties are sometimes considered a single party for these purposes, but the court still has discretion to allow additional peremptory challenges. The number of challenges and alignment of the parties is an excellent topic for pretrial conferences.

Because, in employment cases, issues often are based on identifiable characteristics such as race, gender, or disability, the appearance of the defense's exercise of challenges to exclude jurors with those same characteristics can draw a *Batson* objection. Systematic exclusion of persons of a particular race, gender, or other cognizable group from jury service is impermissible.[12] Defense trial lawyers are advised to treat prospective jurors similarly regardless of race, gender, or other protected characteristics and, if exercising a challenge against a juror in a protected status, to be prepared to offer a genuine, nondiscriminatory reason for the challenge.

---

7. United States v. Torres, 128 F.3d 38, 43 (2d Cir. 1997).

8. Image Technical Servs., Inc. v. Eastman Kodak Co., 125 F.3d 1195, 1220 (9th Cir. 1997); *see also* Staley v. Bridgestone/Firestone, Inc., 106 F.3d 1504, 1514 (10th Cir. 1997).

9. Image Technical Servs., 125 F.3d at 1220.

10. United States v. Annigoni, 96 F.3d 1132, 1138 (9th Cir. 1996).

11. 28 U.S.C. §1870.

12. Batson v. Kentucky, 476 U.S. 79, 89 (1986); J.E.B. v. Alabama *ex rel.* T.B., 511 U.S. 127, 129 (1994). These rules apply in the context of civil cases as well. *See* Edmonson v. Leesville Concrete Co., Inc., 500 U.S. 614, 616 (1991) ("We must decide in the case before us whether a private litigant in a civil case may use peremptory challenges to exclude jurors on account of their race. Recognizing the impropriety of racial bias in the courtroom, we hold the race-based exclusion violates the equal protection rights of the challenged jurors. This civil case originated in a US District Court, and we apply the equal protection component of the Fifth Amendment's Due Process Clause.").

In *Alverio v. Sam's Warehouse Club, Inc.*, a Seventh Circuit case involving allegations of sexual harassment, the Court of Appeals held that it was not error to allow the employer to exercise a peremptory strike against all three women in the jury panel. The court opined that as a preliminary matter, juries in sexual harassment trials need not include female jurors.[13] In *Alverio*, the employer proffered nondiscriminatory credible explanations for the challenges, which were unrelated to the sex of the prospective juror. The Court of Appeals concluded:

> Finally, we decline [plaintiff's] invitation to find that sexual harassment trials must necessarily include female jurors. The idea that one gender is better suited to hear a class of cases than another, is itself a sexist concept. [Plaintiff] contends that this trial involved "women's issues." We disagree. This trial concerned an allegedly hostile work environment created by sexually explicit comments and gestures. Productive work environments, free of harassment, are not merely a woman's worry, they are a national concern. [Plaintiff's] assumption that women, by virtue of their gender, are better suited to adjudicate these cases falls prey to the very stereotypical generalizations that the Court sought to eradicate in J.E.B. v. Alabama ex rel. T.B., 511 U.S. at 132–33, 114 S. Ct. 1419 (documenting "romantic paternalism" that justified exclusion of women from polluted atmosphere of courtrooms). Moreover, protection from gender-based discriminatory strikes is not a one-way street. It is a right that extends to both genders.[14]

If you are required to exercise challenges in the presence of the prospective jury members, it is important to be polite, thank the juror for his or her cooperation, and not provide the reason for the dismissal unless it is required.

F. Picking a Jury in the Digital Age

Currently, lawyers and parties have nearly immediate access to expansive information about potential jurors at the speed of keystrokes. Without much expertise in investigatory methods, a mere Google search can yield significant information about a person's identity and background. Indeed, social media profiles can disclose wide-ranging information about a person's political leanings, interests, and other important life experiences that may or may not have been sought through traditional voir dire.

It is likely for this reason that in 2014, the America Bar Association (ABA) issued a formal opinion regarding the ethics surrounding use of the internet in jury selection. ABA Formal Opinion 466 includes four guideposts for attorneys:

> Unless limited by law or court order, a lawyer may review a juror's or potential juror's Internet presence, which may include postings by the juror or potential

---

13. Alverio v. Sam's Warehouse Club, Inc., 253 F.3d 933 (7th Cir. 2001).

14. *Id.* at 942.

juror in advance of and during a trial, but a lawyer may not communicate directly or through another with a juror or potential juror.

A lawyer may not, either personally or through another, send an access ["friend"] request to a juror's electronic social media. An access request is a communication to a juror asking the juror for information that the juror has not made public and that would be the type of ex parte communication prohibited by Model Rule 3.5(b).

The fact that a juror or a potential juror may become aware that a lawyer is reviewing his Internet presence when a network setting notifies the juror of such does not constitute a communication from the lawyer in violation of Rule 3.5(b).

In the course of reviewing a juror's or potential juror's Internet presence, if a lawyer discovers evidence of juror or potential juror misconduct that is criminal or fraudulent, the lawyer must take reasonable remedial measures including, if necessary, disclosure to the tribunal.

Additionally, various states and voluntary bar associations have also issued opinions and guidance on this issue. In a lawsuit involving two internet giants,[15] District Court Judge William Aslup issued an order asking the parties to voluntarily refrain from scouring social media sites for information on potential jurors.

G. Trial Readiness Support: Focus Groups, Mock Trials, and Jury Consultants

In general, a trial court judge is going to have wide discretion on what types of courtroom graphics and technology can be introduced at trial. No litigator should count on a court providing access to much equipment, if any, for use in the courtroom. This is also an excellent topic for a pretrial conference: what equipment is available and what will be allowed.

Countless studies support the notion that a person is more likely to remember what they saw as opposed to what they heard in a courtroom. Demonstrative exhibits can be key to explaining a point, illustrating a theme, or creating a favorable impression of evidence or arguments in a juror's mind that will be called upon during jury deliberations.

Trial attorneys have mixed opinions on the use of jury consultants. Such consultants and experts offer a wide range of services in trial, including advice regarding jury selection and presentation of themes and issues. Jury consultants can help trial counsel on specific tasks, such as preparing voir dire questions for potential jurors. Additionally, during the jury selection process, the jury consultant can observe the body language, reactions and responses of the prospective jurors and can opine, based on their experience and studies, about which jurors would be most likely to return a favorable verdict for your client.

---

15. Oracle America, Inc. v. Google, Inc. (No. C 10-03561 WHA).

Some services a jury consultant can provide during trial include the following:

- Analysis of the community from which potential jurors are selected, including relevant issues, publicity, and attitudes toward the client
- Case issue focus groups
- Advice on case theme selection
- Suggesting oral questions and assisting in formulating juror questionnaires
- A "third chair" to evaluate other nonverbal communications from the jury panel during voir dire
- Trial simulation and mock juries
- Real-time response feedback, which enables consultants to observe mock jurors' immediate response to evidence being presented at that moment
- Posttrial interviews

Because of the cost and time associated with jury consultants, they are typically only used in major cases. Assuming that jury decisions are driven by facts and evidence, as opposed to the jurors' predisposed attitudes, a jury consultant might be used for a narrower purpose, such as developing a clear and persuasive way to present evidence to a jury. In sum, it is important to note that the field of jury consulting is not an exact science, and people are, by nature, unpredictable.

H. Final Considerations About Defense Voir Dire Examination

In employment cases dealing with sensitive issues of race, sex, and religion, perspectives can often defy stereotypes. Potential jurors will bring various experiences to the courtroom including previous service as a juror, familiarity with the courts, and vastly different experiences in their personal work history. Equally important as the attorney's advocacy and communicative style is the attorney's ability to listen. Voir dire is as much about listening as it is about speaking. Voir dire is the one opportunity for the parties and lawyers to hear from the jury about their past experiences and attitudes.

III. OPENING STATEMENTS

Envision an opening statement as offering a roadmap to the evidence, as well as an opportunity to highlight important themes and evidence key to your defense. From the defense perspective, the opening statement is crucial because, quite possibly, the following days of trial will paint an extremely negative portrayal of the employer and put a microscope on the conduct of the decision-makers leading to the adverse employment action at issue.

The jurors want to make the "right" decision. They are looking for someone to assist them in arriving at the correct decision. It makes sense that the jurors will, thus, place their trust in a lawyer who speaks plainly, is straightforward, and is well-organized.

Tell the jurors why your story is different and more credible than the plaintiff's version of events. Humanize your witnesses through specific anecdotes that frame their perspective. You can begin by succinctly stating the theme of the case followed by the chronology of events that supports your defense strategy. If your case has an affirmative defense, you must be able to discuss it in common terms, without giving into the temptation of relying on statements of law. Avoid legal terms and jargon that are unfamiliar to jurors.

Case themes in a jury trial are important because they are easy reminders of your arguments in the case and they help a jury understand the evidence in the context you have offered. It seems obvious, but it merits restating here: You want the jury to understand the facts from the perspective of the theme by which you've asked them to consider them.

A. Purpose of Opening Statements: Back to Basics

In *Testa v. Village of Mundelein, Illinois*, the Seventh Circuit supplied its own do's and don'ts about opening statements in response to an appeal based on an improper opening statement:

> Because of the widespread belief that juries typically make up their minds about a case after the opening statements, attorneys often find it tempting to convert their statements into improper opening arguments. The purpose of an opening statement is to state what evidence will be presented, to make it easier for the jurors to understand what is to follow, and to relate parts of the evidence and testimony to the whole. It is not an occasion for argument. . . .

First impressions count, but even in an era of courtroom cameras, short attention spans, and newsworthy sound bites, trial lawyers are well served when they follow the Broadway adage and "save a little for the last act."[16]

The *Testa* opinion implies that an effective opening statement is a product of style and substance. Both are equally important. Most trial attorneys agree on at least the following: Be succinct, keep it energetic, and keep it short.

In summary, a jury should also be told what they can expect with respect to the evidence favorable to your side or a defense to the claims. Giving jurors a "heads up" on what to expect allows them to focus on what is most relevant to the issues to be tried. If they have a clear picture of the issues of the case, they will not be so easily distracted by other harmful, yet nonprobative, evidence or argument that plaintiff's counsel may attempt to offer into evidence.

Finally, it is important to recognize the difference between opening statements and closing arguments. In opening statements, parties are restricted to describing and stating the evidence to be introduced at trial; for example, "Plaintiff's co-workers will testify that she regularly was asleep on the job." In contrast, in closing arguments, parties

---

16. Testa v. Vill. of Mundelein, Ill., 89 F.3d 443, 446 (7th Cir. 1996).

are free to argue the merits of the case. For example, as we know from the plaintiff's own co-workers, the plaintiff's lack of productivity caused others to routinely miss deadlines, giving the company a legitimate reason to terminate her employment."

B. The Rules and Strategy of Effective Defense Openings

An opening statement should outline the factual issues and forthcoming evidence. In general, it is improper to argue the applicable law during opening statement.[17] If the plaintiff's counsel discusses legal principles in his or her opening statement, defense counsel should object because (1) an objection will prevent the jurors from getting the impression that the plaintiff's counsel is better informed about the applicable law, and (2) the plaintiff may skew the applicable law or, worse, misstate the law altogether.

In very limited circumstances, counsel can request and receive a preliminary jury instruction in advance of opening statements.[18] Depending on the jurisdiction, other possible grounds for objection to plaintiff's opening argument include an attorney engaging in argument, referring to an irrelevant or highly prejudicial matter, or referring to matter that the attorney knows could not be admitted into evidence. Further, most courts, as well as the ABA Model Rules of Professional Conduct, preclude an attorney from stating personal opinions or beliefs as to the justness of a cause, the credibility of a witness, or the culpability of a civil litigant.[19]

The primary objective for a defense opening is to open minds and keep them open. Defense counsel's window of opportunity to begin the opening statement is a moment in time that cannot be duplicated: Jurors' interest is piqued, jurors have not yet decided whose counsel is more credible, and you have the opportunity to provide the defendant's perspective on the issue in the case. A successful opening statement assists jurors' understanding of what really happened in the case, as well as decreasing jurors' resistance to your evidence and arguments. Thus, an effective opening statement helps convince the jury to wait for the rest of the story and persuades the jurors to be patient and follow their natural inquisitiveness in the fact-finding process.

---

17. As stated by the Seventh Circuit: "Since it was the province of the district court to pass upon the law . . . it was entitled to tell plaintiff's counsel to refrain from legal argument in his opening statement." Schwartz v. Sys. Software Assocs., Inc., 32 F.3d 284, 288 (7th Cir. 1994); *see also* United States v. Dinitz, 424 U.S. 600, 612 (Burger, C.J., concurring) ("An opening statement has a narrow purpose and scope. It is to state what evidence will be presented, to make it easier for the jurors to understand what is to follow, and to relate parts of the evidence and testimony to the whole; it is not an occasion for argument. To make statements which will not or cannot be supported by proof is, if it relates to significant elements of the case, professional misconduct.").

18. *See* Saffold v. McGraw-Edison Co., 566 F.2d 621, 623 (8th Cir. 1977) ("[T]he proper procedure would have been for the trial court to judicially notice the statutes, instruct the jury as to their applicability, and prohibit the reading of the statutes or reference to their criminal aspects." (footnote omitted)).

19. Model Rules of Prof'l Conduct R. 3.4 ("A lawyer shall not: . . . (e) in trial, allude to any matter that the lawyer does not reasonably believe is relevant or that will not be supported by admissible evidence, assert personal knowledge of facts in issue except when testifying as a witness, or state a personal opinion as to the justness of a cause, the credibility of a witness, the culpability of a civil litigant or the guilt or innocence of an accused. . . .").

Nonetheless, it is important to be practical and take a read of the mood of the courtroom. If plaintiff's counsel has just delivered an impassioned statement about how badly his client was treated by his or her employer, the jury might be emotionally connected to the plaintiff by sympathy. In this situation, it is important to acknowledge the humanity of the situation and move on. It is foolish to disregard that jurors are experiencing a sensitive emotional state. However, time might be well spent humanizing the defendant or its managers and discussing the difficult situation that the plaintiff's behavior put them in. It is important for jurors to hear both sides of the story and not accept the plaintiff's perspective as the only perspective that they will be asked to consider.

C. Case Themes in Defending a Workplace Harassment Lawsuit

The effectiveness of an opening statement in an employment harassment case can be enhanced through practice and preparation. By zeroing in on certain themes and minimizing peripheral negative evidence, a defense lawyer can put his or her strongest argument forward and hold the jury's focus. Creating a case theme may be more difficult for the defense, but it is nonetheless important to be prepared to rebut anticipated plaintiff-oriented themes by explaining that "there are always two sides to the story" or by discussing plaintiff's personal responsibility, if applicable. An effective defense opening statement will neutralize the plaintiff's opening statement and halt the plaintiff's momentum.

Case themes should be simple and memorable. In an opening statement, an employer must have a convincing, plausible explanation for whatever adverse action was taken against the plaintiff employee. The defense lawyer should also show that the employer was as fair and reasonable as possible in light of the plaintiff's conduct, performance shortcomings, or issues out of the employer's control such as a business downturn. Case themes are important for several reasons:

- During the presentation of evidence, a case theme can help jurors organize and remember key facts. In other words, themes facilitate evidence comprehension favorable to your position.
- A persuasive theme allows jurors to minimize peripheral evidence and to pay close attention to the documents and testimony that best conforms to the theme.
- Jurors deliberate in themes, meaning that when finally given the opportunity to discuss the merits of the case, jurors may find themselves repeating applicable concepts offered by the defense.

In cases alleging a wrongful termination, defense case themes can deflect the attention back to the plaintiff and focus attention on his or her conduct leading to the adverse employment action:

- Plaintiff's conduct negatively affected his co-workers.
- Plaintiff acted unreasonably.
- Plaintiff acted without any provocation.

- "No good deed goes unpunished." You can apply this saying in a case theme asserting that even after the employer gave the plaintiff opportunities to advance or improve, plaintiff instead turned to litigation to resolve the case.

Recent reports note an uptick in age discrimination litigation, due in part to an aging Baby Boomer workforce. The plaintiff's counsel may attempt to use an emotion-based case theme that the plaintiff "gave them the best years of her life" and "then was tossed out like. . . ." Such sympathetic ploys can be diffused with some commonsensical themes in the news: "It was the bad economy, and not discrimination, that led to the plaintiff's layoff."

A case theme can also suggest sympathy for the individual decision makers, as opposed to a large corporate employer: "The human resources personnel (or supervisors) were doing the best they could with the facts they had at the time." At all times, it is important to humanize the employer with the faces and names of credible, likeable representatives, especially those who function in a decision-making capacity.

In cases of sex or gender discrimination, defense lawyers can consider a case theme that turns the focus away from the alleged wrong-doer's acts and onto the plaintiff-employee's performance or own misconduct:

- This is about job performance; it is not about sex discrimination.
- The plaintiff should not be able to get away with poor performance just because she is a woman.
- Other women working for this employer are getting the job done.

Case themes that involve vilifying the plaintiff as an opportunist or greedy should be carefully considered and deployed judiciously. Defense counsel should carefully evaluate whether the jury will like the plaintiff and, if so, attacking the plaintiff may not be the best defense and may alienate the jury. However, saying that a case is "about money" or that certain claims are being used as a "bargaining chip" may be justified in the appropriate circumstances.

More general defense themes may be applicable with proper adaptation to the facts of the case. You may want to suggest that the plaintiff wanted special treatment or that the plaintiff did not want to abide by the rules that everyone else had to follow in the workplace. The baseball metaphor of three strikes is an old standard: first, an oral warning; second, a written warning; and then the third strike, which is termination. In the case where "progressive discipline" is at issue, establishing that the plaintiff was informed of the policies or deficiencies, had a genuine opportunity to improve or correct her behavior, and did not do so is important.

D. Promising Only What You Can Deliver

An obvious consideration in preparing an opening statement is contouring the opening statement to present facts and evidence that you are certain the jury will have an opportunity to consider. In the sales context, we all know the concept of underpromising and overdelivering and that maxim should be applied to opening statements.

In the pretrial phase, you have the opportunity to review deposition testimony, frame and outline the expected witnesses' testimony, and select the necessary exhibits to be presented. As a result of this preparation, you should be able to anticipate evidence that may not be admitted or that may be limited. As a result, you should be prepared to modify your opening statement to conform to anticipated evidentiary objections and in limine rulings, precluding or limiting certain facts or arguments. Failure to carefully outline your opening statements in light of this guidance may open the door for the plaintiff's counsel to highlight broken promises about evidence that would be presented. As a result you may lose the trust of your jury.

E. Beyond PowerPoint: Courtroom Technology

By the time a case finally reaches the courtroom for trial, parties have invested significant resources and time to the proceeding and the stakes are high. Vendors providing trial assistance have increased significantly over the last decade. This includes: jury consulting, facilitated focus groups, a mock trial, litigation graphics, and courtroom trial technology support. When considering whether to incur the additional expenses of video depositions, live transcripts, court reporters, and so on, it is almost always advisable to do so.

However, before deploying expensive technology or slick graphics, consider carefully the impact upon the jury in light of the facts and realities of your case. Expensive demonstrative exhibits may be effective to illustrate your points. But they may also be construed as overkill or create a "David and Goliath" impression that highlights the parties' disparity in economic resources or alienates a jury. As part of your consideration, determine to what extent your opposition plans to deploy technology and fancy graphic displays. A jury will be less inclined to hold expensive or elaborate presentations against one party when both parties are fully engaged in such displays.

F. Final Considerations About Opening Statements

A plaintiff is likely to discuss the most harmful facts to your case in his opening statement. Therefore, a defense lawyer should be prepared to provide a credible explanation to take the sting out of the evidence or, if mistakes were made, to consider credibly acknowledging them while changing the focus of the discussion. Be prepared to highlight key evidence and witness testimony that the plaintiff's counsel is not discussing with the jury. Highlighting what your opposition has avoided discussing may undermine the jury's trust for your adversary and may help identify the defense as the party that tells the "whole story."

As suggested by the Seventh Circuit in the *Testa* decision, "save a little for the last act." In other words, hold back some ammunition to keep the jury focused on your defense. Presenting evidence of some of the plaintiff's misconduct for the first time during cross-examination or through other witnesses can be more impactful. Teasing the evidence during opening statement, only to have it more fully drawn out and explained during a particularly credible witness' testimony may better hold your jury's attention during trial, allowing them to better identify with defense witnesses and come to their aid with a defense verdict.

The importance of practice cannot be overstated. If you are trying this case in a locality that is unfamiliar, it is advisable to practice your opening statement with locals and follow local issues in the newspaper. Practicing in front of a relative or friend who knows nothing about the case may lead to some insightful questions that you would not otherwise have identified. But the best advice is to keep it short and keep it simple. The best and most credible story is the one that can be told simply and without convoluted explanations and elaborate details.

CHAPTER 17

Evidentiary Issues in Workplace Harassment and Retaliation Litigation

Harriet E. Cooperman and Gillian A. Cooper

I. INTRODUCTION

The admissibility of evidence in workplace harassment cases often hinges on the degree to which the evidence will encroach upon a party's legitimate interests in preserving privacy and avoiding undue prejudice. In deciding questions of admissibility, courts balance the need for complete information against the privacy rights of the individual parties and the degree of undue prejudice that may result.

Sexual harassment litigation presents numerous unique evidentiary issues. Two common themes frequently emerge in proving or defending against the claims: Did the plaintiff welcome the alleged harassing conduct and has the alleged harasser ever done it before?[1] For example, to prove that the plaintiff welcomed the alleged conduct, defendants often try to introduce evidence that (1) the plaintiff's relationship with the accused was consensual; (2) the plaintiff was not offended by the alleged hostile environment; or (3) the plaintiff's past sexual conduct indicates sexual promiscuity to the extent that the alleged conduct is not harassment. Similarly, in proving that the defendant "has done it before," plaintiffs often try to introduce evidence that the alleged harasser is a "womanizer," who has been the focus of prior sexual harassment complaints.

This chapter examines: (1) a general review of the Federal Rules of Evidence (FRE) with respect to workplace harassment cases; (2) effective use of motions *in limine*; (3) changes in the FRE regarding admissibility of evidence of both parties' past sexual conduct; (4) how case law has applied FRE 412 and 415 to sexual harassment cases; (5) the use of social media evidence; (6) the impact of using counsel to investigate harassment claims and the applicable privileges that may be used to exclude the introduction

---

1. Throughout this chapter the female pronoun refers to the plaintiff and the male pronoun to defendant. Although the vast majority of sexual harassment cases reflect that assignment of sexes, the US Supreme Court's decision in Oncale v. Sundowner Services Inc., 523 U.S. 75 (1998) (recognizing same-sex harassment under Title VII) indicates that is not always the case. The gender assignment used throughout this chapter is used to make the analysis easier to read and follow.

of investigative results from trial; and finally, (7) the use of expert witnesses to testify as to the adequacy of an employer's harassment policies.

II. THE PARTIES' PASTS: WHAT ARE THE PERMISSIBLE EVIDENTIARY PARAMETERS?

Unless otherwise prohibited, a party may introduce any evidence relevant[2] to any element of a harassment claim or defense. FRE 401 (Rule 401) defines relevant evidence as information that has a tendency to make the existence of any fact that is of consequence to the determination of the action more or less probable than it would be without such evidence.[3] In a workplace harassment case, this could include evidence of a party's past offensive conduct, discriminatory animus, a party's former sexual partners, medical history, experiences of childhood sexual abuse, adultery, or the content of sexual conversations or activity the plaintiff or defendant or alleged harasser may have had.

A. Evidentiary Rules Typically Used in Motions *in Limine*

Given the sensitive and potentially embarrassing nature of the information elicited in harassment cases, motions *in limine* are useful tools to prevent unnecessary disclosures. A motion *in limine* is a request that the court exclude certain evidence from trial due to irrelevance, prejudice, or another impropriety provided in the FRE.[4] Typically, FRE 401 through 404 form the basis for motions *in limine*. As previously noted, Rule 401 defines what evidence is relevant and Rule 402 provides that, unless otherwise prohibited, all relevant evidence is admissible.

Rule 403 permits the exclusion of relevant evidence when its probative value is substantially outweighed by the danger of unfair prejudice, confusion of the issues, or misleading the jury, or by considerations of undue delay, waste of time, or needless presentation of cumulative evidence.[5] Under Rule 403, district courts must assess the relevance of the evidence and conduct their own balancing of the probative value and potential prejudicial effect explicitly and on the record.[6]

Rule 404(a) excludes character evidence whether in the form of reputation, opinion, or evidence of past acts to prove that the person acted in conformity therewith on a particular occasion.[7] Although the probative value of such evidence may be high, the evidence is excluded because the risk of unfair prejudice outweighs the probative value.

---

2. Under FED. R. EVID. 402, all relevant evidence is admissible unless otherwise provided by federal law.

3. FED. R. EVID. 401.

4. Conversely, a Rule 412 motion is a request to admit sensitive information that would otherwise be prohibited by the rules of evidence. The procedural requirements for a Rule 412 Motion are outlined *infra*.

5. FED. R. EVID. 403.

6. Sprint/United Mgmt. Co. v. Mendelsohn, 552 U.S. 379 (2008).

7. FED. R. EVID. 404(a) ("Evidence of a person's character or trait of character is not admissible for the purpose of proving accident conformity therewith on a particular occasion.").

The risk is that the finder of fact will rule against the party because it believes that he or she is a bad person based on such character evidence, regardless of the facts in the case before it.

Rule 404(b) excludes evidence of other crimes, wrongs, or acts to prove the character of a person and to show the person acted in conformity therewith.[8] Such evidence, however, is admissible to show proof of intent, opportunity, preparation, plan, knowledge, identity, or absence of mistake or accident.

B. Motions *in Limine* Regarding Character or Bad Act Evidence

In harassment cases, the most frequent topic for a motion *in limine* is the exclusion of bad act and character evidence. Plaintiffs generally attempt to introduce this type of evidence through testimony that other co-workers were also harassed or that there were prior complaints made to the employer about the alleged harasser. Typically, the plaintiff's counsel will claim that evidence of alleged harassment by others is offered as proof of the defendant or alleged harasser's intent or motive, employers' notice (the employer knew or should have known), or the pervasive nature of the hostile work environment. Although such evidence is likely to be considered by the jury as proof of conformity, a motion *in limine* will force plaintiff's counsel to assert a proper basis for admission of the evidence. In situations where no such basis exists, the evidence should be excluded.

Whether character or bad act evidence is admissible is highly fact specific. Defense counsel should determine whether the claimed purpose for the evidence is among those listed under Rule 404(b) (i.e., motive, intent, opportunity, preparation, plan, knowledge, identity, or absence of mistake or accident) and at issue in the case. Moreover, where evidence is offered to prove that the work environment was hostile, the defense should file a motion *in limine* to exclude all acts of which the plaintiff was unaware or in which the plaintiff was not involved.

If the plaintiff asserts that the evidence is offered for a permissible purpose, the defense should focus on Rule 403, and may be able to have such evidence excluded on the basis that it is unfairly prejudicial, or that it will result in confusion of the issues or in a waste of time. The Advisory Committee's notes state in pertinent part: "Exclusion for risk of unfair prejudice, confusion of issue, misleading the jury, or waste of time, all find ample support in authorities. 'Unfair prejudice' within its context means an undue tendency to suggest decision on an improper basis, commonly, though not necessarily, an emotional one."[9]

In *El-Bakly v. Autozone, Inc.*,[10] the court denied plaintiff's motion *in limine* to exclude evidence that, on prior occasions, the plaintiff had made anti-Semitic comments and spoken favorably about the Nazis.[11] In this hostile work environment case, plaintiff

8. FED. R. EVID. 404(b).
9. FED. R. EVID. 403. Advisory Committee's notes.
10. No. 04-C-2767, 2008 WL 1774962 (N.D. Ill. Apr. 16, 2008).
11. *Id.* at *13.

asserted that evidence of his prior conduct was being offered as improper character evidence under Rule 404 and that it was highly prejudicial under Rule 403.[12] Defendant argued that these statements were relevant to show that plaintiff also engaged in harassing conduct, and therefore, could not have been subjectively offended by the racist comments of others that formed the basis of his hostile work environment claim.[13] The court rejected plaintiff's argument and held that such evidence was relevant to both the subjective and objective elements of a hostile work environment and the prejudicial effect of the evidence was not outweighed by the probative value of plaintiff's conduct in the face of the alleged harassment.[14]

Similarly, in *Hernandez Loring v. Universidad Metropolitana,*[15] defendant filed a motion *in limine* seeking to exclude testimony from several witnesses prepared to testify that they also had been sexually harassed by the defendant.[16] The defendant contended that the testimony of these witnesses was irrelevant since it did not relate to the alleged sexual harassment of plaintiff.[17] The court denied the defendant's motion, holding that testimony about the alleged sexual harassment of other women could be used to prove the existence of a generalized hostile work environment, to establish motive or intent, and to evidence that the defendant knew or should have known that the alleged harasser created a hostile work environment.[18]

The court in *Vandiver v. Little Rock School District*[19] similarly denied the defendant's motion *in limine* seeking to exclude evidence of prior bad acts and sexually harassing statements made by the alleged harasser.[20] In her deposition, the plaintiff did not reveal that she had any knowledge of the specific instances of harassment that were identified in the defendant's motion. The court, nevertheless, advised that if plaintiff testified at trial that she was aware of those specific occurrences, the court would allow such evidence to show the alleged hostile work environment.[21] Moreover, even if the plaintiff lacked contemporaneous knowledge of the prior incidents of harassment, the court stated that the evidence would be admissible under Rule 404(b) to show the defendant's discriminatory motives and intent.[22]

In contrast, in *McCleland v. Montgomery Ward Co.,*[23] the court granted the defendant's motion *in limine* to exclude evidence of prior sexual complaints. In that case, the

---

12. *Id.*

13. *Id.* at *15.

14. *Id.*

15. 190 F. Supp. 2d 268 (D.P.R. 2002).

16. *Id.* at 271.

17. *Id.* at 272.

18. *Id.*

19. No. 4:03-cv-00834 GTE, 2007 WL 2806928 (E.D. Ark. Sept. 25, 2007).

20. *Id.* at *4.

21. *Id.*

22. *Id.*

23. No. 95-C-237, 1995 WL 571324 (N.D. Ill. Sept. 25, 1995).

defendant sought to exclude evidence of prior complaints made by another employee and involving a different harasser as irrelevant and unfairly prejudicial. The court granted the defendant's motion, reasoning that evidence of the prior complaint did not make plaintiffs' complaints more or less probable. Further, the court noted that even if the evidence was relevant, its probative value was substantially outweighed by "the danger of unfair prejudice to Montgomery Ward, the likely confusion of the issues, and the significant litigation time that would be expended on trying a collateral issue."[24]

Accordingly, motions *in limine* can be effective tools for both a plaintiff and defendant in preventing prejudicial and embarrassing explorations into the party's past.

III. DID SHE WELCOME IT? THE ADMISSIBILITY OF THE PLAINTIFF'S PAST SEXUAL CONDUCT

To prove that the plaintiff welcomed the allegedly sexually harassing conduct, defendants often desire to delve into the plaintiff's past sexual conduct looking for evidence to undermine the claims against them. The first reported case to squarely confront the admissibility of the plaintiff's sexual history was *Priest v. Rotary*.[25] In *Priest*, the defendant sought the names of each person the plaintiff had had sexual relations with in the prior ten years to demonstrate that the plaintiff was fired for flirting with customers and not for refusing her supervisor's sexual advances. The defendant argued that this evidence would show that the plaintiff had a habit of living with men for the purpose of deriving economic benefits from them.[26] The court interpreted this argument as nothing more than a "thinly disguised attempt to seek character evidence" and upheld the magistrate judge's denial of the defendant's motion to compel discovery.[27] The court based its holding, in part, on Rule 404 and noted that evidence of an individual's prior acts is not admissible to prove she engaged in similar conduct on a particular occasion.[28] From this holding, it appeared that it shut the door to a plaintiff's sexual past.

Three years later, in *Meritor Savings Bank, FSB v. Vinson*, the US Supreme Court thrust that door open.[29] The court held that in a sexual harassment suit brought under Title VII, a plaintiff is required to prove that her alleged harasser's conduct was "unwelcome." Consequently, "the correct inquiry is whether [the plaintiff] by her conduct indicated that the alleged sexual advances were unwelcome."[30] By turning the focus to the plaintiff's conduct, her speech and dress are now discoverable areas of inquiry. In fact, the *Meritor* court concluded that evidence of plaintiff's sexually provocative

---

24. *Id.* at *11.

25. 634 F. Supp. 571 (N.D. Cal. 1983).

26. *Id.* at 759.

27. *Id.*

28. *Id.*

29. 477 U.S. 57 (1986).

30. *Id.* at 68.

clothing and speech was not only discoverable, but "obviously relevant" and admissible as to whether she indicated that her supervisor's conduct was unwelcome.[31]

Meritor, therefore, established not only that a Title VII sexual harassment plaintiff must demonstrate that her harasser's conduct was unwelcome, but also that courts can consider the plaintiff's own sexual conduct to determine whether she truly considered her alleged harasser's conduct unwelcome. As long as the evidence of a sexual harassment plaintiff's prior conduct falls within the permissible parameters of the FRE, employers are permitted to introduce evidence at trial of plaintiff's on- and off-the-job sexual behavior to demonstrate that she welcomed her harasser's conduct.[32] Although *Meritor* has been interpreted broadly, it is applicable only in hostile work environment sexual harassment claims and its holding has not been interpreted to include the admissibility of speech or dress that was not sexual in nature.

A. Amended FRE 412: An Attempt to Shield the Admissibility of Plaintiff's Past Sexual Conduct

In an effort to afford a sexual harassment plaintiff some degree of privacy, on December 1, 1994, the US Congress amended Rule 412, effectively altering the landscape and the evidence admissible in sexual harassment cases.[33] The amended rule extended the "rape shield"[34] protection to civil actions that claim sexual misconduct, including sexual harassment. The rule expanded privacy protections to alleged victims of sexual misconduct by limiting evidence regarding the past sexual behavior of a plaintiff or other harassment victims.[35]

1. A Closer Look at Rule 412: What Conduct Is In, What Conduct Is Out

According to the legislative history discussing the effect of the amendments, Rule 412 was amended to diminish the confusion engendered by the original rule and to expand

---

31. *Id.*

32. Christina A. Bull, The Implications of Admitting Evidence of a Sexual Harassment Plaintiff's Speech and Dress in the Aftermath of Meritor Savings Bank v. Vinson, 41 UCLA L. Rev. 117 (1993).

33. (a) Evidence generally admissible—The following evidence is not admissible in any civil or criminal proceeding involving alleged sexual misconduct except as provided in subdivisions (b) and (c):

    (1) Evidence offered to prove that any alleged victim engaged in other sexual behavior.

    (2) Evidence offered to prove any alleged victim's sexual predisposition.

  (b) Exceptions.

    * * *

    (2) In a civil case, evidence offered to prove the sexual behavior or sexual predisposition of any alleged victim is admissible if it is otherwise admissible under these rules and its probative value substantially outweighs the danger of harm to any victim and of unfair prejudice to any party. Evidence of an alleged victim's reputation is admissible only if it has been placed in controversy by the alleged victim.

34. Prior to its amendment, FRE 412 prohibited evidence of the past sexual behavior of victims only in rape prosecutions.

35. FED. R. EVID. 412(2)(b).

the protection afforded to alleged victims of sexual misconduct.[36] The revised rule is aimed at safeguarding alleged victims against invasion of privacy, potential embarrassment, and unwarranted sexual stereotyping that is associated with public disclosure of intimate sexual details and the injection of sexual innuendo into the fact-finding process.[37] To that end, the rule is intended to prohibit the introduction of evidence that involves actual physical activities (i.e., sexual intercourse or contact); activities connected to, or that result from, physical conduct (i.e., abortions, use of contraceptives, and venereal diseases); and mental activities (i.e., sexual dreams and fantasies).[38] In addition, the rule prohibits evidence of plaintiff's reputation unless it has been placed in controversy by plaintiff.[39]

Despite the legislative intent, the court's application of Rule 412 has yielded mixed results. Although courts are skeptical about broad inquiries into a plaintiff's sexual history, they nevertheless are finding new relevance for such evidence when evaluating damage claims. For example, in *Judd v. Rodman*,[40] a woman brought suit against basketball player Dennis Rodman, alleging that he infected her with genital herpes. At trial, Judd filed a motion *in limine* to exclude evidence that she worked as a nude dancer. The district court denied her motion. On appeal, the court agreed with the district court that evidence that Judd worked as a nude dancer was relevant to her claim for damages. In her testimony, Judd stated that she felt "dirty" after she contracted the disease. The court determined that her employment before and after she contracted herpes was relevant to her damages claim for emotional distress because it suggested an absence of change in her body image after contracting the disease.[41]

In *Sublette v. Glidden Co.*,[42] the plaintiff filed an action against her former employer for retaliatory discharge, intentional infliction of emotional distress, and back pay. At trial, the defendant sought to introduce evidence of the plaintiff's subsequent employment at a massage parlor as relevant to her claim for damages. The court noted that while the potential for unfair prejudice was high, the plaintiff's choice to work at a

---

36. Fed. R. Evid. 412 Advisory Committee's note (1994 amendment).

37. *Id.*

38. *Id.*; United States v. Galloway, 937 F.2d 542 (10th Cir. 1992), *cert. denied*, 506 U.S. 957 (1992) (use of contraceptives). *See also* State v. Carmichael, 727 P.2d 918, 925 (Kan. 1986) (evidence of venereal disease inadmissible). *See* 23 Charles Alan Wright & Kenneth W. Graham, Jr., Federal Practice and Procedure §5384 at p. 548 (1980) ("[W]hile there may be some doubt under statutes that require 'conduct,' it would seem the language of Rule 412 is broad enough to encompass the behavior of the mind.").

39. It should be noted that while Rule 412 applies to evidence offered to prove that a victim of sexual misconduct in a civil case engaged in other "sexual behavior" or had a "sexual predisposition," neither of the terms are defined. The Advisory Committee's notes, however, include a further analysis by stating under subdivision (a), "unless the (b)(2) objection is satisfied, evidence such as that relating to alleged victims mode of dress, speech, or lifestyle will not be admissible." Advisory Committee notes accompanying Rule 412(c) state that in sexual harassment actions, for instance, while some evidence of the alleged victim's sexual behavior and/or predisposition in the workplace may perhaps be relevant, nonworkplace conduct will usually be irrelevant.

40. 105 F.3d 1339 (11th Cir. 1997).

41. *Id.* at 1343.

42. No. 97-CV-5047, 1998 U.S. Dist. LEXIS 15692 (E.D. Pa. Oct. 1, 1998).

parlor massaging men was probative of the actuality and severity of her emotional distress and her claim that she was unable to work with men.[43] Accordingly, the court admitted the evidence.

2. The Rule 412 Balancing Test

For evidence to be admissible under Rule 412(b)(2), the proponent must convince the court that the probative value of the evidence substantially outweighs the danger of harm to any victim and does not unfairly prejudice any party.[44] This rule differs in three respects from the procedure provided for in Rule 403[45] governing the admissibility of evidence. First, it shifts the burden to the proponent to demonstrate the admissibility of the evidence, rather than requiring the opponent to justify its exclusion. Second, 412(b)(2) raises the threshold for admission by requiring that the probative value of the evidence substantially outweigh the specified damages. Finally, Rule 412(b) requires consideration of "harm to the victim" in addition to prejudice to the parties.[46] By placing the burden on the proponent of the evidence to establish its admissibility rather than on the opponent, and by requiring consideration of harm to the victim, the Advisory Committee intended to further shield the alleged victim's sexual past from unnecessary exposure.[47]

In *Fedio v. Circuit City Stores*,[48] plaintiff filed a post-trial motion for a new trial on the basis that the trial court improperly admitted evidence of her sexual past. At trial, the defendant introduced evidence that, at work, the plaintiff told her co-workers: (1) that she was going to wear a finger ring until she "got laid" and that she subsequently removed the ring; (2) that she kept a delivery truck waiting outside her apartment while she had sex with her roommate; and (3) that she had been date-raped prior to obtaining employment with the defendant. The district court concluded that this information was highly probative of "how little plaintiff would be offended by [her supervisor's] alleged sexual innuendos when she felt comfortable publicizing her own sex life."[49] The evidence, therefore, was found to be admissible. The court acknowledged that while the Rule 412(b)(2) balancing test places a significant burden on the party seeking to introduce the sexual evidence, Circuit City had met its burden. The balancing test tipped in favor of admitting evidence of Fedio's sexual past, in large part because she had volunteered the information to her co-workers. The court noted that while the purpose of Rule 412 is to protect an alleged victim's most intimate secrets, to "allow an alleged

---

43. *Id.* at 13–14.

44. FED. R. EVID. 412(b)(2).

45. FED. R. EVID. 403 states: Exclusion of Relevant Evidence on Grounds of Prejudice, Confusion, or Waste of Time: Although relevant, evidence may be excluded if its probative value is substantially outweighed by the danger of unfair prejudice, confusion of the issues, misleading the jury, or by consideration of undue delay, waste of time, or needless presentation of cumulative evidence.

46. FED. R. EVID. 412(b)(2).

47. FED. R. EVID. 412 Advisory Committee's note (1994 amendment).

48. No. 97-5851, 1998 U.S. Dist. LEXIS 21144 (E.D. Pa. Nov. 4, 1998).

49. *Id.* at *18.

victim to publicly flaunt her sexual behaviors and yet remain protected by Rule 412 would be tantamount to a complete disregard of this rule's purpose."[50]

In *Seybert v. Int'l Grp., Inc.*,[51] the plaintiff filed a motion *in limine* to exclude certain email exchanges containing sexual content. Although the emails at issue included sexual content, none of them expressly involved the plaintiff's sexual behavior or predisposition. However, the court applied Rule 412 to analyze evidence involving attempted sexual humor and innuendo. The court ultimately denied the plaintiff's motion *in limine* because the content of the plaintiff's emails involved content similar to that which the plaintiff complained about.

In contrast, in *Howard v. Historic Tours of America*,[52] the District Court for the District of Columbia applied the Rule 412(b)(2) balancing test and refused a discovery request seeking the names of co-workers, other than the defendant, with whom the plaintiff had had sexual relations. Noting that such evidence would be inadmissible at trial, the court stated as follows:

> Since permitting the defendants to demand plaintiff tell them in discovery about their sexual behavior with other co-workers is as inhibitory of their exercising their legal rights as answering the same question at trial, the Court is convinced that compelling an answer which the amended rule may not permit and protecting it from further disclosure until trial nevertheless violates the clear intendment of Fed. R. Evid. 412.[53]

In *EEOC v. New Breed Logistics*,[54] the court granted plaintiff's motion *in limine* to exclude the claimant's social media postings. Defendant argued that claimant's social media postings were relevant to whether she subjectively found the alleged harasser's comments offensive. Applying a Rule 412 analysis, the court found that "context matters," reasoning that comments the claimant may welcome from friends on social media are not connected to whether she would find such comments offensive from a supervisor or co-worker.

3. Procedural Requirements

Rule 412(c) sets forth the procedure for offering evidence pursuant to Rule 412(b). Specifically, it requires that the party intending to offer the evidence file a written motion at least fourteen days before trial specifically describing the evidence and stating the purpose for which it is offered. The rule further requires that the court hold a hearing *in camera* at which the alleged victim and any party must be afforded the right to be present and to be heard. All papers connected with the motion and any record of the hearing must be kept under seal.

---

50. *Id.* at *20.

51. CIV.A. 07-3333, 2009 WL 3297304, at *1 (E.D. Pa. Oct. 14, 2009).

52. 177 F.R.D. 48 (D.D.C. 1997).

53. *Id.* at 51.

54. 10-2696-STA-TMP, 2013 WL 10129293, at *1 (W.D. Tenn. Apr. 29, 2013).

Sheffield v. Hilltop Sand & Gravel Co.[55] emphasized the importance of complying with all the procedural requirements of Rule 412(c)(2). There, defense counsel admitted that when it filed its Rule 412 motion, the defense failed to place the motion under seal. As a sanction, the court held that the defendant could not introduce evidence of the plaintiff's participation in sexually explicit discussions with her co-workers. The court justified its ruling by citing that the primary purpose of Rule 412 was "to protect alleged victims against invasion of privacy, potential embarrassment, and sexual stereotyping."[56] By ignoring the procedures set forth in the rule, defendant "frustrated Rule 412's objectives and presumptively inflicted harm upon the plaintiff."[57]

The importance of complying with the procedural requirements of Rule 412(c) was reaffirmed in *B.K.B. v. Maui Police Department*.[58] The defendants had offered Rule 412 testimony without filing the requisite Rule 412 motion and represented to the judge that testimony elicited would not implicate Rule 412.[59] Defendants offered offending testimony about the plaintiff's past sexual conduct without filing the required motion at least fourteen days prior to trial.[60] Upon consideration of the arguments, the judge stated, "I think this was a violation of Rule 412," yet denied plaintiff's motion for a mistrial, issued curative instructions to the jury, and ordered the offending testimony stricken from the record.[61] On appeal, the Ninth Circuit held that defendants flouted the procedural guidelines of Rule 412(c), misrepresented the nature of the testimony,[62] and failed to establish that the probative value of the testimony substantially outweighed its prejudicial effect.[63] The case was remanded for a new trial.

It is important to note, however, that the procedures contained in Rule 412(c) do not apply to discovery of the plaintiff's past sexual conduct or predisposition in civil cases. Rather, discovery in civil cases continues to be governed by Federal Rule of Civil Procedure (FRCP) 26, which provides for the issuance of protective orders.[64] The Advisory

---

55. 895 F. Supp. 105 (E.D. Va. 1995).

56. *Id.*

57. *Id.* at 109.

58. 276 F.3d 1091 (9th Cir. 2002).

59. *Id.* at 1106.

60. *Id.* Defendants offered testimony from one of the plaintiff's former colleagues that following a party at the plaintiff's house, he and a fellow officer were too drunk to drive home and decided to spend the night at the plaintiff's home. *Id.* The officer testified that after others had left the party, the plaintiff turned the conversation to sex, described her use of a sexual device to stimulate herself, and that the plaintiff admitted to having had an orgasm while using the device and thinking of him at work. *Id.* The judge overruled the plaintiff's objections to the testimony, and the officer testified that the plaintiff then modeled lingerie and stated that she liked younger men, that she thought he would be fun in bed, and that she wanted to teach him things and hurt him. *Id.*

61. *Id.* at 1098–99.

62. *Id.* at 1105. The testimony was offered to impugn plaintiff's moral character and establish that sexual advances by her supervisor and sexual misconduct at the workplace were not unwelcome. *Id.*

63. *Id.* at 1106.

64. Fed. R. Civ. P. 26(c) states: A party may obtain discovery of documents and tangible things otherwise discoverable under subdivision (b)(1) of this rule and prepared in anticipation of litigation or for trial by or for another party or by or for that other party's representative (including any party's attorney,

Committee's note to Rule 412 urges judges to make liberal use of Rule 26(c) protective orders and not to undermine the intent of the rule through the discovery process.[65] In pertinent part, the note states:

> Courts should presumptively issue protective orders barring discovery unless the party seeking discovery makes a showing that the evidence sought to be discovered would be relevant under the facts and theories of the particular case, and cannot be obtained except through discovery.[66]

4. Evidence Not Covered by Rule 412

The Advisory Committee's notes reference specific instances in which Rule 412 does not apply. Those instances include: (1) when the underlying case does not involve sexual misconduct or evidence relating to a third-party witness's alleged sexual activities; (2) evidence offered against a person not reasonably characterized as a "victim" of sexual misconduct (e.g., in a defamation action involving allegedly defamatory statements regarding sexual misconduct, evidence supporting truth of statement will be allowed); and (3) evidence offered to prove allegedly false prior claims by the alleged victim.[67]

B. Cases Involving the Admissibility of Plaintiff's Past Sexual Conduct

Despite the language of Rule 412 and the commentary provided by the Advisory Committee, there is a lack of uniformity in its application by district courts. This is a result of the highly fact-specific nature of the cases and the fact that appellate courts have provided little guidance regarding Rule 412.[68] As a practical matter, a practitioner must fully review sexual harassment decisions rendered in the applicable circuit. As the following cases indicate, no standard interpretation exists.

---

consultant, surety, indemnitor, insurer, or agent) only upon a showing that the party seeking discovery has substantial need of the materials in the preparation of the party's case and that the party is unable without undue hardship to obtain the substantial equivalent of the materials by other means. In ordering discovery of such materials when the required showing has been made, the court shall protect against disclosure of the mental impressions, conclusions, opinions, or legal theories of an attorney or other representative of a party concerning the litigation.

65. Fed. R. Evid. 412 Advisory Committee's note (1994 amendment).

66. *Id.*

67. *Id.*

68. In Excel Corp. v. Bosley, 165 F.3d 635 (8th Cir. 1999), plaintiff filed suit that her ex-husband sexually harassed her while she was at work and that she was wrongfully discharged. Her former employer sought to introduce evidence that: (1) the plaintiff and ex-husband were having sexual relations outside of work during the same period as the alleged harassment; and (2) the plaintiff told a clinical psychologist that she may be sending her ex-husband "mixed signals." The Eleventh Circuit acknowledged that the applicability of Rule 412 to a Title VII claim was one of first impression. Although the court affirmed the district court's decision finding the evidence inadmissible, it did so by "assuming, without deciding, that Rule 412 [was] applicable to the evidence proffered." *Id.* at *14.

1. Cases Excluding Evidence of Plaintiff's Past Sexual Conduct

A number of district courts have applied Rule 412 to exclude evidence of a plaintiff's past sexual conduct involving posing for nude magazines,[69] abortions, viewing pornography,[70] former sexual partners,[71] sexual conduct outside of work,[72] illicit affairs,[73] and moral character/promiscuity.[74]

The district court for Utah held that evidence regarding plaintiffs' sexual history was inadmissible character evidence and not discoverable in *Mitchell v. Hutchings*.[75] The defendant had argued that the degree of the plaintiffs' emotional distress and damages would be affected by their degree of sexual promiscuity, and also that their sexual activity was relevant "habit" evidence. The court reasoned that evidence of sexual activity of which the defendants were unaware was unrelated to the alleged sexual harassment, and also was unlikely to lead to the discovery of admissible evidence. The court further

---

69. Burns v. McGregor Elec. Indus., Inc., 989 F.2d 959, 963 (8th Cir. 1993). The court determined that evidence that the plaintiff had posed nude for a magazine outside work hours was not material to the issue of whether she found her employer's work-related conduct offensive. The court noted "[plaintiff's] private life, regardless of how reprehensible . . . did not provide lawful acquiescence to unwanted sexual advances at her work-place by her employer. To hold otherwise would be contrary to Title VII's goal of ridding the work-place of any kind of unwelcome sexual harassment." *Id.*

70. Kelly-Zurian v. Wohl Shoe Co., Inc., 64 Fair Empl. Prac. Cas. (BNA) 603 (Cal. Ct. App. 1994). The court granted plaintiff's motion *in limine* excluding evidence concerning: (1) the viewing of X-rated videotapes by the plaintiff and her husband; (2) plaintiff's abortions; and (3) her prior sexual history and sexual conduct with individuals other than the alleged harasser or other co-workers. The court determined that the plaintiff's viewing of videotapes with her husband and her abortions were irrelevant. The court further noted that excluding evidence of plaintiff's past sexual behavior served to narrow the case, to the extent possible, to what happened between the plaintiff and the alleged harasser.

71. Howard v. Historic Tours of Am., 177 F.R.D. 48 (D.C. 1997). The court denied defendants' pretrial discovery request for the names of any prior sexual partners of the two plaintiffs. Defendants claimed that plaintiffs' prior sexual conduct was relevant to whether alleged offensive conduct was welcomed. The court noted that the fact that a plaintiff may have had consensual sex with one co-worker does not in any way justify an assumption by another co-worker that his workplace advances would be welcomed.

72. Barta v. City and County of Honolulu, 169 F.R.D. 132 (D. Haw. 1996). The court held that evidence of plaintiff's sexual conduct while off duty and outside of the workplace was not discoverable because it did not involve the named defendant. "The fact that the plaintiff may welcome sexual advances from certain individuals has absolutely no bearing on the emotional trauma she may feel from sexual harassment that is unwelcome. Past sexual conduct does not allow one to subsequent unwelcomed sexual advancements." *Id.* at 136.

73. Truong v. Smith, 183 F.R.D. 273 (D. Colo. 1998). The court denied the defendant's discovery request regarding the plaintiff's history of extramarital affairs. Defendant claimed this evidence was relevant to his defense that the consensual relationship was initiated by the plaintiff. The court held that the plain meaning of Rule 412 mandated the exclusion of such evidence.

74. Socks-Brunot v. Hirschvogel Inc., 184 F.R.D. 113, 117 (S.D. Ohio 1999). The employer was not permitted to offer evidence that the employee had engaged in sexual conduct with co-workers. Rodriguez-Hernandez v. Miranda-Velez, 132 F.3d 848 (1st Cir. 1998) (holding that evidence concerning plaintiff's moral character or promiscuity and evidence that her boyfriend was a married man was inadmissible under Rule 412).

75. 116 F.R.D. 481 (D. Utah 1987). This case was decided prior to the amendment of Rule 412.

noted that "[p]ast sexual conduct does not . . . create emotional calluses that lessen the impact of sexual harassment."[76]

In *Cacciavillano v. Ruscello, Inc.*,[77] the defendant sought to introduce evidence that the plaintiff: (1) grabbed her breasts and asked a sixteen-year-old busboy whether he liked them; (2) unbuttoned her blouse, exposed her cleavage, and put a banana in the front of her pants; (3) engaged in sexual discussions with her co-workers; and (4) waited on a table with her blouse partially unbuttoned to embarrass customers into leaving. The defendant asserted that this evidence was relevant to establish that the allegedly harassing behavior was welcomed. The Eastern District of Pennsylvania found the evidence to be inadmissible under Rule 412. The court explained that none of the behavior was probative of the plaintiff's receptiveness to the conduct to which she had been subjected. Specifically, the court found that by touching herself in a sexually suggestive manner and partaking in sexual banter, the plaintiff did not give the impression that she would welcome her supervisors touching, grabbing, and flashing her. Accordingly, the court concluded that this evidence was of little to no probative value as to how the "reasonable woman" would react to such behavior.[78]

The *Cacciavillano* court also found the evidence to be unfair and prejudicial to the plaintiff. In referencing the Advisory Committee's notes, the court observed that the purpose of Rule 412 is to protect victims against potential embarrassment and unwarranted sexual stereotyping. As a result, the court held that evidence of plaintiff's sexually related conduct could sidetrack the fact finder. The court cautioned that admission of such evidence could result in the jury punishing plaintiff for her behavior, by finding that the plaintiff is somehow undeserving of Title VII protection because she is "immoral."[79] Finally, the court concluded that defendant's attempt to introduce questionable and embarrassing evidence would be a waste of the court's time and resources.[80]

In *Wolak v. Spucci*,[81] the Second Circuit reversed a district court's decision allowing the defendant to inquire about the plaintiff's sexual behavior outside of the workplace, including permitting the defendant to ask questions about two parties that the plaintiff attended where pornographic videos were shown and occasions where the plaintiff watched others perform sexual acts.[82] In concluding that the evidence was inadmissible under Rule 412, the court emphasized that in the context of sexual harassment litigation, "whether a sexual advance was welcome, or whether an alleged victim in fact perceived an environment to be sexually offensive, does not turn on

---

76. *Id.* at 485.

77. No. 95-5754, 1996 U.S. Dist. LEXIS 16528 (E.D. Pa. Nov. 4, 1996).

78. *Id.*

79. *Id.*

80. *Id.*

81. 217 F.3d 157 (2d Cir. 2000).

82. *Id.* at 159. A federal magistrate denied defendant's discovery request for allegedly sexually explicit photographs of the plaintiff and her boyfriend.

the private sexual behavior of the alleged victim."[83] Similarly, in *Basile v. Spagnola*,[84] the court denied the defendant's attempt to introduce evidence that the plaintiff had flashed her breasts at the workplace while off-duty. The defendant did not witness the event himself. The court found that the prejudicial effect of the evidence outweighed the probative value.

In *Chamblee v. Harris & Harris, Inc.*,[85] plaintiff moved to exclude evidence that she worked as a call girl/escort prior to being employed by McDonald's.[86] The court granted the plaintiff's motion *in limine*, concluding that plaintiff's history as a call girl was irrelevant except to prove her sexual disposition, which is a "purpose plainly prohibited by Rule 412."[87]

2. Cases Admitting Evidence of Plaintiff's Past Sexual Conduct

Courts have held that evidence regarding a plaintiff's sexual discussions with co-workers and managers,[88] her past sexual partners and activity,[89] and previous jobs are admissible.[90] Evidence regarding the plaintiff's sexual orientation, moreover, has been admitted to show that other facts could have contributed to a plaintiff's psychiatric condition.[91]

---

83. *Id.* at 160.

84. 346 Fed. Appx. 687, 690 (2d Cir. 2009).

85. 154 F. Supp. 2d 670 (S.D.N.Y. 2001).

86. *Id.* at 679.

87. *Id.* at 680. The court, however, permitted the introduction of Rule 412 evidence regarding plaintiff's speech and sexual conduct with and in the presence of the alleged harasser. The court also concluded that it was too premature to rule on the admissibility of discussions with co-workers about starting an escort service without the *in camera* hearing required by Rule 412(c). *Id.*

88. Sheffield v. Hilltop Sand & Gravel Co., 895 F. Supp. 105 (E.D. Va. 1995). The court held that evidence of plaintiff's conversations with her manager and co-workers in which she discussed her sex life with her husband and in which she used vulgar language was admissible. The court reasoned that this evidence was relevant to whether her manager's conduct was welcome. *See also* Herchenroeder v. Johns Hopkins Univ. Applied Physics Lab., 173 F.R.D. 179 (D. Md. 1997) (discovery into whether plaintiff ever discussed engaging in any sexual activity with a particular business associate found permissible, conditioned on the issuance of a protective order).

89. *Barta v. City & County of Honolulu*, 169 F.R.D. 132 (D. Haw. 1996). The court determined that the plaintiff's sexual conduct on duty, at the workplace, or with the named defendants was relevant to the resolution of her claims and discoverable evidence. The court also permitted discovery of plaintiff's social relationships and of individuals with whom she had sexual contact. *See also* Sanchez v. Zabihi, 166 F.R.D. 500 (D.N.M. 1996) (plaintiff's past romantic or sexual conduct/actions in the workplace over a three-year period held discoverable, provided that the interrogatory answer be placed under seal and reviewed solely by defendant's attorney).

90. *See* Judd v. Rodman, 105 F.3d 1339 (11th Cir. 1997).

91. Gretzinger v. Univ. of Haw. Prof'l Assembly, No. 97-15123, 1998 U.S. App. LEXIS 15370 (9th Cir. July 7, 1998). Evidence of the plaintiff's extramarital affair and lesbianism held admissible to rebut the plaintiff's claim that she suffered posttraumatic stress disorder because of the defendant's alleged assault on her. The court reasoned the affair and the plaintiff's sexual orientation also could have been sources of her emotional distress.

In *Sublette v. Glidden Co.*,[92] the plaintiff filed a motion *in limine* to exclude evidence of her past sexual conduct. The court denied her motion, stating that it had little difficulty in finding evidence of the plaintiff's conduct relevant. It then turned its attention to the Rule 412 balancing test. The court held that evidence indicating that the plaintiff (1) wore a sign saying "Best Blow Job on the #8 line"; (2) wet her t-shirt and stood in front of a large industrial fan to show off her breasts; and (3) ripped her t-shirt and exposed her cleavage was not barred by the Rule 412 balancing test.[93] The court explicitly noted that while other district courts may find such evidence unfairly prejudicial, those cases are not binding precedent.[94]

In *Woodward v. Metro I.P.T.C.*,[95] the court determined that the probative value of evidence that plaintiff worked at a lingerie shop, which she advertised and marketed at Metro, and her invitations to male co-workers to come to the shop for private shows for a $40 fee substantially outweighed any potential unfair prejudicial effects on her harassment claims.[96] Similarly, evidence that the plaintiff distributed topless and naked pictures of herself to co-workers, as well as pictures of herself modeling lingerie, and the plaintiff's sexualized banter and flirtations were not barred by Rule 412.[97]

Rule 412 has also been relied upon to permit discovery of a plaintiff's sexual past. In *Holt v. Welch Allyn*,[98] a federal magistrate granted discovery of a photograph showing the plaintiff attending a party with co-workers where a nude erotic dancer performed. The photographs allegedly were brought to the workplace and shown to the plaintiff's co-workers. In upholding the magistrate judge's decision to allow discovery of the photographs, the district court stated that the magistrate judge correctly concluded that these photographs may be relevant to show the perception of the plaintiff's co-workers regarding her workplace behavior.[99] Similarly, in *Rodriguez-Hernandez v. Miranda-Velez*,[100] the First Circuit affirmed the district court's admission of evidence of the plaintiff's sexual relationship outside of the workplace. The court determined that the evidence was relevant to the defendant's contention that the plaintiff's work performance deteriorated because of that relationship.[101] The court further permitted evidence of the plaintiff's allegedly flirtatious behavior at work as relevant to whether the alleged harasser's advances were welcomed.[102]

---

92. No. 97-cv-5047, 1998 U.S. Dist. LEXIS 15692 (E.D. Pa. Oct. 1, 1998).

93. *Id.* at *12.

94. *Id.* at *10–12.

95. No. IP 98-646-c, 2000 WL 684101 (S.D. Ind. Mar. 16, 2000).

96. *Id.* at *7.

97. *Id.* at *13.

98. No. 95-CV-1135 WL 210420, at *7–8 (N.D.N.Y. Apr. 15, 1997).

99. *Id.* at *7.

100. 132 F.3d 848, 855–56 (1st Cir. 1998).

101. *Id.* at 855.

102. *Id.*

In *EEOC v. Simply Storage Mgmt., LLC*,[103] the defendant sought discovery of the claimants' social media content, arguing that it is relevant to the nature of the claimants' injuries. The court first addressed that the content was not shielded from discovery simply because it is "private." The court ordered discovery finding that the claimants' emotional or mental injury may "manifest itself" in some of the content, and was, therefore, relevant.

The Nevada district court applied a Rule 412 analysis in *Mackelprang v. Fid. Nat. Title Agency of Nevada, Inc.*,[104] and ruled that social media content was discoverable. The court however, excluded content containing sexually explicit communications between the plaintiff and third persons, which were unrelated to her employment.

IV. WAS IT SEVERE OR PERVASIVE?

To prevail on a sexual harassment claim, the plaintiff must prove that the alleged harassment was sufficiently severe or pervasive to alter the terms and conditions of employment and create an abusive environment.[105] Whether the conduct rises to this level is judged by both an objective and subjective standard.[106] This means that *both* the plaintiff and a reasonable person would find the conduct abusive.

The determination of whether the behavior is sufficiently severe or pervasive is made by examining all of the circumstances, including "the frequency of the discriminatory conduct; its severity; whether it is physically threatening or humiliating, or a mere offensive utterance; and whether it unreasonably interferes with an employee's work performance."[107] The social context surrounding the particular behavior is considered.[108] This requires "common sense" and an "appropriate sensitivity to social context."[109] Incidents that would objectively give rise to bruised or wounded feelings will not satisfy the "severe" or "pervasive" standard.[110] Rather, the challenged conduct must be so objectively offensive as to alter the "conditions" of the victim's employment.[111] The US Supreme Court has emphasized that "[a] recurring point in [our] opinions is that simple teasing, offhand comments, and isolated incidents (unless extremely serious) will not amount to discriminatory changes in the 'terms and conditions of employment.'"[112]

---

103. 270 F.R.D. 430, 432 (S.D. Ind. 2010).

104. 2:06-CV-00788-JCM, 2007 WL 119149 (D. Nev. Jan. 9, 2007).

105. *Meritor*, 477 U.S. at 67.

106. *Oncale*, 523 U.S. at 81.

107. Harris v. Forklift Sys., Inc., 510 U.S. 17, 23 (1993).

108. *Oncale*, 523 U.S. at 81.

109. *Id.*

110. Faragher v. City of Boca Raton, 524 U.S. 775, 778 (1998).

111. *Oncale*, 523 U.S. 75, 81 (1998).

112. Clark County School District v. Breeden, 532 U.S. 268 (2001). Courts repeatedly have refused to find the existence of a hostile work environment where the alleged conduct consists of a handful of isolated comments or even a few incidents of minor physical touching. *See* Wolf v. Northwest Indiana Symphony Society, 250 F.3d 1136 (7th Cir.) *cert. denied*, 534 U.S. 1028 (2001) (incidents including female boss telling

In *Barrett v. Omaha Nat. Bank*,[113] the plaintiff alleged that she had been sexually harassed by a co-worker during an out-of-town seminar attended by the plaintiff and two colleagues. The harassment consisted of multiple incidents of physical and verbal conduct, including the co-worker touching the plaintiff's thighs, pressing his arm into her breast, and grabbing the plaintiff in her crotch area.[114] The court found the challenged conduct sufficiently abusive to establish a *prima facie* case of sexual harassment.[115] Although the court noted that the plaintiff was not "a mere bystander when it came to talk of sexual activity" and believed it "doubtful that the general sexual talk shocked [the] plaintiff as much as she would have [the] [c]ourt believe,"[116] the co-worker, nevertheless, had "overstepped the bounds of decency in his conversation and physical contact with plaintiff." [117]

The employer, in *Aryain v. Wal-Mart Stores Texas LP*,[118] contended that the plaintiff could not establish a *prima facie* case of sexual harassment because she did not subjectively perceive her working environment to be hostile or abusive. In support of its position, Wal-Mart noted that the plaintiff had failed to complain to the harasser about his offensive comments and continued to work alongside him for four months. The court rejected the employer's contention. Citing the plaintiff's rating of the harassing conduct (which included almost daily sexual comments and advances) as a "ten on a scale of one to ten," her statements that she was "happy to be away" from the harasser, did not want to work alone with the harasser, and that she felt humiliated every time he made one of his sexually charged comments,[119] the court found there to be sufficient evidence to allow a jury to conclude that the plaintiff subjectively perceived her working environment to be hostile or abusive.[120]

---

male employee that she was glad to have muscle in the office, calling him late at night to tell him she was lonely, informing him that she had not been with a man in several years, when considered together, were not sufficiently severe and pervasive to constitute a hostile work environment); Alfonso v. Costello, 294 F.3d 365 (2d Cir. 2002) (incidents including instructing plaintiff that she not eat carrots, bananas, hot dogs, or ice cream because she did so in a "seductive" manner and had allegedly simulated oral sex when eating a carrot, the plaintiff's discovery in her work mailbox of a carrot and two potatoes arranged to suggest male genitalia, a sham notice posted barring carrots in the visiting area due to the plaintiff's strong liking for them; and a hand-drawn cartoon depicting a male subordinate making vulgar sexual remarks, fell "well below the threshold" for a hostile environment claim); Russell v. Board of Trustees of University of Illinois at Chicago, 253 F.3d 336 (7th Cir. 2001) (supervisor's reference to the plaintiff as "bitch" and "grandma," telling her that she was hired based on her appearance, and that she dressed "sleazy" is insufficient to create a hostile work environment); Bowman v. Shawnee State Univ., 220 F.3d 456 (6th Cir. 2000) (rubbing employee's shoulders, grabbing buttocks, and placing finger on employee's chest not enough to create hostile work environment).

113. 584 F. Supp. 22, 23 (D. Neb. 1983), aff'd, 726 F.2d 424 (8th Cir. 1984).

114. *Id.*

115. *Id.* at 24.

116. *Id.* at 29.

117. *Id.*

118. 534 F.3d 473, 480 (5th Cir. 2008).

119. *Id.*

120. *Id.*

Isolated instances of harassment are typically not regarded as creating a hostile work environment unless they are very severe.[121] For example, in *Morales Evans v. Admin. Office of the Courts of New Jersey*,[122] an employee kissed the plaintiff on the cheek on four occasions, joked about another employee who forcibly tried to kiss the plaintiff, commented the plaintiff was voluptuous, commented after the plaintiff sneezed that the noise a woman makes while sneezing correlates with the noise she makes during intercourse, discussed his anatomy and his visit to a nude beach, and commented on the plaintiff's breasts to another co-worker. The court, however, held no reasonable juror could conclude these few scattered events over an extended period of time were sufficiently "severe or pervasive" such that a reasonable woman would consider the working environment hostile.[123] On the other hand, in *Lockard v. Pizza Hut, Inc.*,[124] the court found an isolated incident where a customer pulled the plaintiff to him by her hair, grabbed her breast, and put his mouth on her breast sufficiently severe to create an abusive environment.[125]

V. HAS HE EVER DONE IT BEFORE? THE ADMISSIBILITY OF THE ACCUSED'S PAST CONDUCT AND PRIOR COMPLAINTS

A. Rule 415: Plaintiff's New Sword?

Rule 415 was promulgated to allow the introduction of evidence of a defendant's prior commission of similar acts. The rule permits a plaintiff to use this evidence in her attempt to prove that the defendant is the kind of person who engages in sexual misconduct, and that he engaged in such activity on the occasion(s) in question.[126]

Rule 415 applies to civil actions in which a claim for damages or other relief is based on the defendant's alleged commission of an offense of sexual assault or child molestation.[127] The definition of sexual assault for the purposes of Rule 415 includes "any conduct proscribed by chapter 109A of Title 18, United States Code," which is the section of the criminal code relating to sexual abuse.[128] This definition substantially expands the range of admissible behavior in sexual misconduct cases. For example, in addition

---

121. *See Faragher,* 524 U.S. at 788.

122. 102 F. Supp. 2d 577, 588 (D.N.J. 2000).

123. *Id.* at 590.

124. 162 F.3d 1062 (10th Cir. 1998).

125. *Id.* at 1067.

126. FED. R. EVID. 415.

127. FRE 415 provides in pertinent part that "[i]n a civil case involving a claim for relief based on a party's alleged sexual assault or child molestation, the court may admit evidence that the party committed any other sexual assault or child molestation." Pursuant to Rule 413, "[t]he evidence may be considered on any matter to which it is relevant."

128. FED. R. EVID. 413(d)(1).

to aggravated sexual abuse, the definition of sexual assault also includes nonaggravated sexual abuse—causing or attempting to cause another to engage in a sexual act by placing the person in fear.[129]

The United States Code also criminalizes abusive sexual contact. Sexual contact is defined as "intentional touching, either directly or through the clothing, of the genitalia, anus, groin, breast, inner thigh, or buttocks of any person with an intent to abuse, humiliate, harass, degrade, or arouse or gratify the sexual desire of any person."[130] Although this definition, notably, does not include all the behavior that may occur in a sexually hostile work environment, such as sexual comments and propositions, it may be used in sexual harassment cases that include allegations of unwanted sexual touching (e.g., buttocks pinching, hands on breasts).[131]

Prior to the adoption of Rule 415, sexual character evidence in the form of prior bad acts often was restricted to the time frame in which the plaintiff's complaints were made and was limited to acts in the workplace.[132] Rule 415, in contrast, provides no time limit on the uncharged conduct[133] and does not require a workplace nexus for the admissibility of evidence of prior acts of sexual assault.[134]

1. Procedural Steps

For a plaintiff seeking to introduce evidence of the alleged harasser's past sexual conduct, Rule 415 only requires her to establish that the evidence is relevant.[135] The threshold governing relevancy is extremely low and encompasses all "evidence having any tendency to make the existence of any fact that is of consequence to the determination of the action more probable or less probable than it would be without the evidence."[136] On its face, Rule 415 admits evidence of prior sexual assaults that is relevant to character. The legislative history of Rule 413 and Rule 414[137] indicates that Congress determined that the need to aggressively crack down on crimes of sexual abuse was greater than the risks associated with allowing sexual character evidence.

---

129. 18 U.S.C. §2246.

130. *Id.* at §2246(3).

131. *Id.*

132. Fed. R. Evid. 415.

133. The absence of a time limit was challenged by opponents of the amendment. Then-Senator Joseph Biden noted, "to allow total, uncorroborated, unsubstantiated testimony about something that could have happened—anything—from the day before to 50 years before into a trial . . . absolutely violates every basic tenet of our system." 140 Cong. Rec. S1U277 (daily ed. Aug. 2, 1994) (statement of Sen. Biden).

134. *See, e.g.*, Frank v. County of Hudson, 924 F. Supp. 620, 625 (D.N.J. 1996) (rejecting evidence of molestation of stepdaughter in sexual harassment case on grounds it was inflammatory, but impliedly accepting that conduct fell within Rule 415).

135. Fed. R. Evid. 415.

136. Fed. R. Evid. 401.

137. Rule 415 is part of the same legislative package as Rules 413 and 414.

2. Judicial Ambivalence to Rule 415

Notwithstanding this legislative intent, Rule 415 has been met with resistance by the courts. Many judges simply refuse to admit sexual character evidence offered to show general propensity.[138] When encountering such evidence in civil cases, courts invoke their discretionary authority to exclude it. This approach substantially limits the rule's impact.

In *Frank v. County of Hudson*,[139] employees brought a sexual harassment action against the county sheriff's office and several officers. The defendants sought a protective order to prevent the plaintiffs from using the statement of the stepdaughter of the defendant supervisor that he had sexually abused her for nearly ten years. The plaintiffs, whose allegations against the defendants included claims that their supervisor forced them to view him masturbating and that he sexually touched the plaintiffs' buttocks, made gratuitous sexual comments, and intimidated them through the use of a shotgun, offered a number of theories in an attempt to establish relevance of the stepdaughter's statement. These theories included the general propensity of the supervisor to engage in sexual assaults, the supervisor's motive and intent, and that the County of Hudson and sheriff's office had prior knowledge of the supervisor's conduct. The court assigned a low degree of probative value to these theories and stated that there was a great risk of unfair prejudice.[140] Specifically, the court determined that the emotional response that the evidence of child abuse was likely to elicit from the trier of fact was too great. In granting the defendant's protective order, the court emphasized that the "purpose of the evidence rules' general prohibition against propensity evidence is to address the danger that a jury might convict the defendant not for the offense charged but for the extrinsic offense presented."[141]

Another example of judicial aversion to applying Rule 415 was exhibited in *Jones v. Clinton*.[142] Paula Jones had attempted to introduce evidence of President Clinton's relationship with Monica Lewinsky to prove a pattern and practice of sexual behavior with subordinates. The court acknowledged that while evidence concerning the president's relationship with Lewinsky may be relevant, it determined that the prejudicial effect of these acts was "too great" and barred the evidence pursuant to Rule 403.[143]

---

138. United States v. Sumner, 119 F.3d 658, 661–62 (8th Cir. 1997) (in a prosecution for criminal sexual assault, evidence indicating defendant had previously assaulted young girls was not admissible because general propensity evidence is unfairly prejudicial); United States v. Guardia, 955 F. Supp. 115, 117 (D.N.M. 1997) (testimony of other patients alleging inappropriate acts during a gynecological exam not admissible under Rule 403), *aff'd*, 135 F.3d 1326 (10th Cir. 1998). Shea v. Galaxie Lumber & Constr. Co., No. 94 C 906, 1996 U.S. Dist. Lexis 2904 (N.D. Ill. Mar. 12, 1996) (Rule 403 requires exclusion of sexual character evidence).

139. 924 F. Supp. 620, 627 (D.N.J. 1996).

140. *Id.*

141. *Id.*

142. 993 F. Supp. 1217 (E.D. Ark. 1998).

143. *Id.*

3. The Significance of Defendant's Past Sexual Conduct in the Wake of *Faragher* and *Ellerth*

The US Supreme Court's *Faragher v. City of Boca Raton*[144] and *Burlington Industries v. Ellerth*[145] decisions diminished the significance of an alleged harasser's prior conduct where the allegations involve the conduct of a supervisor.[146] *Faragher* and *Ellerth* established that an employer may be found vicariously liable for the actions of its supervisory personnel in creating a hostile work environment. The court created an affirmative defense to the claim where the employer has exercised reasonable care to prevent and promptly correct any sexually harassing behavior, and the employee has unreasonably failed to take advantage of preventative or corrective opportunities provided by the employer or to otherwise avoid harm.[147] The affirmative defense, however, is available only in cases where the plaintiff has not suffered an adverse job action.

Nevertheless, the value of evidence of the alleged harasser's prior acts or prior complaints to the employer about the alleged harasser should not be dismissed. Such evidence is helpful to show the pervasiveness of the harassment and the employer's failure to take reasonable care to prevent or correct harassing behavior. This evidence may preclude the employer from establishing the first prong of the affirmative defense.[148] In addition, in cases where the plaintiff alleges that the sexual harassment was perpetrated by a nonsupervisory co-worker, the plaintiff must establish that the employer knew or should have known about the harassment.[149]

B. Common Objections to the Admissibility of the Accused's Past Sexual Conduct and Prior Complaints

Invariably, employers and alleged harassers will object to admitting evidence concerning prior complaints of harassment in the workplace. Employers often object to the admissibility of such evidence on the basis of relevance, purpose, and danger of unfair prejudice.

Defendants also may object to the evidence of prior complaints that were made beyond the limitations period for the plaintiff's claim. Such evidence, however, generally

---

144. 524 U.S. 775 (1998).

145. 524 U.S. 742 (1998).

146. *Id.*

147. Prior to *Ellerth* and *Faragher*, hostile environment plaintiffs primarily used prior complaints and lawsuits filed against the employer or the particular harasser as evidence that the employer knew or should have known of the harasser's behavior due to prior incidents, and negligently failed to stop it. *See, e.g.*, Davis v. U.S. Postal Serv., 142 F.3d 1334 (10th Cir. 1998) (evidence that defendant was aware of prior complaints against the alleged harasser showed that defendant should have been on notice of the harassing behavior); Hirase-Doi v. U.S. W. Commc'ns, Inc., 61 F.3d 777, 785–86 (10th Cir. 1995) (evidence of employer knowledge of previous harassment by co-worker raised issue of material fact regarding employer's negligence).

148. *Ellerth*, 524 U.S. 742.

149. *See, e.g.*, Fall v. Ind. Univ. Bd. of Trs., No. 96-CV-205, 1998 U.S. Dist. LEXIS 12174, at *32–33 (N.D. Ind. July 23, 1998) (analysis of first prong of affirmative defense similar to negligence analysis).

is discoverable and admissible at trial if it is relevant background evidence to later discriminatory acts[150] or part of a continuing violation.[151] For example, in *Hurley v. Atlantic City Police Department*,[152] the court admitted evidence of complaints occurring both before and after the plaintiff's allegations as relevant background information and relevant to assist the jury in placing the plaintiff's experience in context. For evidence beyond the limitations period to be admissible as part of a continuing violation, it must be closely connected to later events that form the basis of the claim.[153] Such evidence also may be relevant to prove the employer's knowledge of harassment and its continuing failure to remedy it, or to prove a continuing pattern of pervasive and severe conduct.[154] Clearly discrete acts, however, cannot be combined to allege a continuing violation.[155]

C. Cases Admitting Evidence of Prior Complaints and the Accused's Past Sexual Conduct

In *Minshew v. Brown*,[156] the court determined that two prior sexual harassment complaints against the defendant were relevant because they tended to show his attitude toward women, his treatment of others in similar circumstances, and the general work environment created by his actions.[157] The court held that this evidence was admissible under the Rule 404(b) exceptions, which allow evidence of prior incidents to prove motive and intent. This evidence, moreover, was found to be close enough factually and in time to survive a Rule 403 balancing test.

In *Heyne v. Caruso*,[158] the court held that the district court improperly granted defendant's motion *in limine* excluding testimony from six other female employees who also claimed to be sexually harassed by the same person.[159] The court explained that the testimony was admissible to prove the defendant's motivation or intent behind the

---

150. Evans v. United Airlines, Inc., 431 U.S. 533 (1977); Kimzey v. Wal-Mart Stores, Inc., 107 F.3d 568, 573 (8th Cir. 1997).

151. Bazemore v. Friday, 478 U.S. 385, 395 (1986) (affirming the First Circuit's analysis of continuing violations insofar as liability may be imposed for systematic violations in discriminatory policy or practice that continue beyond the limitations period).

152. 933 F. Supp. 396, 410 (D.N.J. 1996).

153. *See, e.g.*, Governale v. Airborne Express, 1997 U.S. Dist. LEXIS 7562, at *8–9 (E.D.N.Y. May 12, 1997) (claims of substantially similar acts of harassment including making propositions and sexual suggestions to plaintiff constituted continuing violation).

154. *See, e.g.*, Rorie v. United Postal Serv., Inc., No. 97-3678, 1998 U.S. App. LEXIS 17102, at *8 (8th Cir. July 23, 1998); Galloway v. Gen. Motor Serv. Parts Operations, 78 F.3d 1164, 1166 (7th Cir. 1996).

155. *See, e.g.*, Koelsch v. Belton Elec. Corp., 46 F.3d 705, 707 (7th Cir. 1995) (court found company president's advances toward plaintiff not closely related to his telling jokes in the workplace); Choi v. Chem. Bank, 939 F. Supp. 304, 311 (S.D.N.Y. 1996) (discrete incidents of nonpromotion over a nineteen-year period did not constitute continuing violation).

156. No. Civ. A. 95-2507, 1996 WL 601436 (E.D. La. Oct. 18, 1996).

157. *Id.* at *1.

158. 69 F.3d 1475 (9th Cir. 1995).

159. *Id.* at 1481.

adverse employment action.[160] Specifically, the sexual harassment of other employees, if shown to have occurred, is relevant and probative of the alleged harasser's general attitude of disrespect and sexual objectification of females in the workplace.[161]

The court in *Forrest v. Dynamic Sec., Inc.*,[162] denied the defendant's motion to exclude evidence of sexual harassment despite the fact that the plaintiff's claim alleged gender discrimination, not sexual harassment. The court found that evidence of sexual harassment was relevant and admissible to show the workplace conditions and environment.

Similarly, in *Woolner v. Flair Communications Agency, Inc.*,[163] the court allowed the plaintiff to introduce evidence of three instances of alleged sexual harassment of other female employees for purposes outlined in Rule 404(b).[164] In that case, the court highlighted that the other instances of sexual harassment were similar to the conduct experienced by the plaintiff and occurred near the time of her alleged harassment.[165] Accordingly, evidence of the alleged harasser's prior conduct was relevant and admissible to show intent, motive, or absence of mistake and to support whether the alleged sexual harassment was pervasive.[166]

Rule 412 also has been interpreted to apply to discovery requests. In *Governale v. Airborne Express, Inc.*,[167] the defendant was compelled to produce documents concerning claims of sexual harassment by other employees. The court noted that such information was likely to lead to probative information regarding the defendant employer's responsiveness to the plaintiff's complaint. Courts also have admitted evidence of prior complaints on the basis that such complaints may be relevant to the adequacy of an employer's harassment policy[168] and to an employer's own knowledge of the alleged harassment.[169]

D. Cases Admitting Evidence of Past Conduct and Prior Complaints in Other Types of Workplace Harassment Litigation

In *Cruz v. Coach Stores, Inc.*,[170] the court considered evidence of the alleged harasser's treatment of other employees to support plaintiff's hostile work environment claims.[171] Specifically, plaintiff offered testimony from current and former employees that the

---

160. *Id.* at 1480.

161. *Id.*

162. CIV.A. 00-3423, 2002 WL 246401, at *2 (E.D. La. Feb. 19, 2002).

163. No. 01 C 6043, 2004 WL 2032717 (N.D. Ill. Aug. 30, 2004).

164. *Id.* at *5–6.

165. *Id.* at *6.

166. *Id.*

167. No. 95-CV-0541 (CBA), 1997 U.S. Dist. LEXIS 7562, at *19–21 (E.D.N.Y. May 12, 1997).

168. Butta-Brinkman v. FCA Int'l Ltd., 164 F.R.D. 475, 476 (N.D. Ill. 1995).

169. De Silva v. Bluegreen Corp., No. 96-CV-0683, 1997 U.S. Dist. LEXIS 9532, at *6–7 (N.D.N.Y. Jun. 24, 1997). The court compelled the defendant to produce information regarding all sexual harassment complaints by employees of defendant brought to management's attention during a specified period of time.

170. 202 F.3d 560 (2d Cir. 2000).

171. *Id.* at 570–71.

alleged harasser constantly made derogatory statements and directed racial epithets at minority employees.[172] The court held that with this evidence, plaintiff satisfied her burden of demonstrating a work environment of racial and sexual hostility sufficient to survive the defendant's motion for summary judgment.[173]

Madani v. BHVT Motors, Inc.[174] involved claims of race and national origin harassment. The defendant filed a motion *in limine* to prohibit the plaintiff from introducing evidence of alleged harassment against persons of other races and national origins.[175] Specifically, the defendant sought to exclude evidence and testimony regarding alleged comments made by former managers about a Bosnian salesperson; African-American, Asian-American, Hispanic-American, and Indian-American customers; and an African-American baseball player.[176] The defendant also sought to exclude evidence that the alleged harasser knocked the turban off the head of a customer and called him a derogatory name.[177] The court denied the defendant's motion, explaining that in making the determination of whether the harassment was severe or pervasive enough to be actionable, the trier of fact must look at the workplace as a whole.[178] Accordingly, evidence of comments targeting minorities may contribute to a hostile work environment for a minority employee and, therefore, is relevant and admissible in harassment litigation.[179]

VI. EVIDENTIARY ISSUES IN RETALIATION CLAIMS

Title VII prohibits an employer from both (1) discriminating against an employee on the basis of sex and (2) retaliating against an employee for complaining about prior discrimination or retaliation.[180]

Title VII of the Civil Rights Act of 1964 (Title VII) is not, however, a general civility code for the workplace.[181] Rather, Title VII's "antiretaliation provision seeks to prevent employer interference with 'unfettered access' to Title VII's remedial mechanisms."[182] The statute prohibits employers from actions that are likely to deter discrimination

---

172. *Id.* at 571.

173. *Id.*

174. No. Civ. 04-1897 PHX RCB, 2006 WL 1127149 (D. Ariz. Apr. 27, 2006).

175. *Id.* at *1.

176. *Id.*

177. *Id.*

178. *Id.* at *2.

179. *Id.*

180. 42 U.S.C. §2000e-2(a)(1); 42 U.S.C. §2000e-3(a).

181. Burlington N. & Santa Fe Ry. Co. v. White, 548 U.S. 53, 68, 126 S. Ct. 2405, 2415, 165 L. Ed. 2d 345 (2006).

182. *Id.* (citations omitted).

victims from complaining to their employers, the Equal Employment Opportunity Commission, and the courts.[183] "[N]ormally petty slights, minor annoyances, and simple lack of good manners will not create such deterrence."[184]

A. When Is an Employment Action Materially Adverse?

Generally, a "plaintiff sustains an adverse employment action if he or she endures a 'materially adverse change' in the terms and conditions of employment."[185] A materially adverse change requires more than a "mere inconvenience or an alteration of job responsibilities."[186] Rather, a materially adverse change might include employment termination, demotion and decrease in wage or salary, or a material loss of benefits.[187] Failure to promote may also be an adverse employment action.[188]

However, "changes in duties or working conditions that cause no materially significant disadvantage" are not actionable.[189] In *Harlston*, the plaintiff was reassigned but suffered no diminution in her title, salary, or benefits.[190] Rather, the plaintiff alleged that her reassignment involved fewer "secretarial duties and was more stressful in that she had to watch the door, listen for the fax, and be in charge of security for people coming in and out of the area."[191]

An unfulfilled threat of an employment action that did not result in any material harm is not actionable.[192] Written reprimands that do not result in loss of pay or benefits is not an adverse employment action.[193]

Ultimately, whether an employment action is "materially adverse" is an objective question.[194] The test is whether the employer's conduct might have dissuaded a reasonable employee from the protected conduct.[195]

---

183. *Id.*

184. *Id.*

185. Galabya v. New York City Bd. of Educ., 202 F.3d 636, 640 (2d Cir. 2000).

186. *Id.*

187. *Id.*

188. Allen v. Michigan Dep't of Corr., 165 F.3d 405, 410 (6th Cir. 1999) (adverse employment action requirement means that the employee "must establish that he has suffered a 'materially adverse' change in the terms or conditions of employment because of the employer's actions").

189. Harlston v. McDonnell Douglas Corp., 37 F.3d 379, 382 (8th Cir. 1994).

190. *Id.*

191. *Id.*

192. Ajayi v. Aramark Bus. Servs., Inc., 336 F.3d 520, 531 (7th Cir. 2003).

193. Medearis v. CVS Pharmacy, Inc., 646 Fed. Appx. 891, 898 (11th Cir. 2016).

194. Burlington N. & Santa Fe Ry. Co. v. White, 548 U.S. 53, 67, 126 S. Ct. 2405, 2415, 165 L. Ed. 2d 345 (2006).

195. *Id.*

B. Establishing the But-For Causation Standard

A plaintiff may prove a Title VII violation through either (1) direct and indirect evidence of retaliatory animus or (2) the burden-shifting framework of *McDonnell Douglas Corp.*[196] An employee alleging retaliation under the direct evidence framework must prove that the employer's retaliatory motive was the but-for cause of the adverse employment action. In *Univ. of Texas Sw. Med. Ctr. v. Nassar,*[197] the plaintiff resigned his position after alleging harassment by his supervisor stemming from "religious, racial and cultural bias against Arabs and Muslims."[198] The plaintiff sent a letter to the chair of the plaintiff's former department, as well as others, stating the reason for his departure.[199] The employer had offered the plaintiff a different job; however, after receipt of the plaintiff's letter, the department chair protested the offer, which the employer ultimately withdrew.[200] The plaintiff alleged that the chair's actions were in retaliation for his complaints about his supervisor.[201]

The US Supreme Court held that Title VII retaliation claims must be proved under the traditional but-for causation standard rather than the less onerous causation standard applicable to race, sex, religion, and national origin discrimination claims under § 2000e-2(m).[202] The court explained that the statutory language of Title VII's retaliation provision differs significantly from that of Title VII's discrimination provision. Specifically, § 2000e-2(m) provides that "an unlawful employment practice is established when the complaining party demonstrates that race, color, religion, sex, or national origin was a *motivating factor* for any employment practice, even though other factors also motivated the practice."[203] In contrast, § 2000e-3(a), which prohibits retaliation by an employer, provides that an employer may not retaliate against an employee "*because* he has opposed any practice made an unlawful employment practice by this subchapter, or because he has made a charge, testified, assisted, or participated in any manner in an investigation, proceeding, or hearing[.]"[204] Thus, the US Supreme Court held the but for causation test applies in retaliation claims, which requires proof that the unlawful activity would not have occurred *in the absence* of the alleged wrongful actions of the employer.[205]

Since *Nasser*, some circuits have held that *Nasser* modifies the *McDonnell Douglas* framework as applied to retaliation cases by requiring plaintiff to show retaliation was

---

196. McDonnell Douglas Corp. v. Green, 411 U.S. 792, 93 S. Ct. 1817, 36 L. Ed. 2d 668 (1973).

197. 133 S. Ct. 2517, 186 L. Ed. 2d 503 (2013).

198. *Id.* at 2523–24.

199. *Id.* at 2524.

200. *Id.*

201. *Id.*

202. *Id.* at 2533.

203. *Id.* at 2526 (quoting § 2000e-2(m) (emphasis added)).

204. *Id.* at 2528 (quoting § 2000e-3(a) (emphasis added)).

205. *Id.* at 2533.

the but-for cause for the adverse employment action.[206] Other circuits have held that *Nasser* does not modify the *McDonnell Douglas* framework.[207]

C. Evidence Required to Prove the Employer Knew or Should Have Known

Employer liability turns on the harasser's position and basic agency principles.[208] Employers can be strictly liable for harassment by supervisors under agency principles.[209] In contrast, employers are not strictly liable for a co-worker's harassing behavior because a co-worker is not considered an agent of the employer. An employer, however, may be held liable for co-worker harassment under negligence principles where the employer knew or should have known of the harassment and failed to take adequate steps to address it.[210] For example, in *EEOC v. Prospect Airport Servs., Inc.*,[211] the court found the employer knew about the harassment because the employee repeatedly complained to his employer and was told to console himself by saying "I'm too sexy for my shirt." In determining whether the employer should have known of the harassment, courts will look at whether the harassment complained of is so severe or pervasive that the employer would have known "had it but opened its corporate eyes."[212] Courts also will consider the existence and effectiveness of an anti-harassment policy and complaint procedure.[213]

VII. OTHER EVIDENTIARY ISSUES

A. Counsel as the "Investigator"

The question of whether counsel should conduct the investigation of a harassment complaint has been hotly debated. Frequently, employers will have either their in-house or outside counsel conduct the investigation because they believe that attorneys are more skilled in investigating a harassment matter than any of the company's employees and/or because they feel more comfortable with their own lawyer than with an outside

---

206. EEOC v. Ford Motor Co., No. 12-2484, 2015 WL 1600305 at *14 (6th Cir. Apr. 10, 2015); Ward v. Jewell, 772 F.3d 1199, 1203 (10th Cir. 2014); Smith v. City of Fort Pierce, Fla., 565 F. App'x 774, 778–79 (11th Cir. 2014).

207. Hague v. Univ. of Tex. Health Sci. Ctr. at San Antonio, 560 F. App'x 328, 336 (5th Cir. 2014); Kwan v. Andalex Grp. LLC, 737 F.3d 834, 845 (2d Cir. 2013); Foster v. Univ. of Maryland-E. Shore, 787 F.3d 243 (4th Cir. 2015).

208. 42 U.S.C. §2000e(b).

209. *Vance v. Ball State Univ.,* 570 U.S. 421 (2013).

210. 29 C.F.R. §1604.11(d).

211. 621 F.3d 991, 1001 (9th Cir. 2010).

212. Sharp v. City of Houston, 164 F.3d 923, 930 (5th Cir. 1999).

213. *Id.*

investigator. Before embarking on this course, the employer must be advised that there is a substantial possibility that the information uncovered by the attorney during the course of the investigation, including conversations between the company and attorney, may not be protected by either the attorney-client privilege or the work-product doctrine. This evidence, therefore, may be discoverable by the plaintiff and admissible at trial.

1. Attorney-Client Privilege

FRE 501 protects from disclosure communications made to an attorney in confidence for the purpose of obtaining, seeking, or providing legal assistance to the client.[214] In asserting the attorney-client privilege, several factors need to be present. First, the client or prospective client must claim a communication is privileged. Second, the communication sought to be protected must have been between a client or prospective client and an attorney, an attorney's employee, or a nonlawyer assistant. Third, the communication must have been made for the purpose of securing legal advice or assistance and not made in the presence of any nonessential third parties. Finally, the communication must have been made in good faith and not for the purpose of committing a crime or perpetrating a fraud.[215]

In *Upjohn Co. v. United States*,[216] the US Supreme Court explained that

> [T]he privilege exists to protect not only the giving of professional advice to those who can act on it but also the giving of information to the lawyer to enable him to give sound and informed advice. The first step in resolution of any legal problem is ascertaining the factual background and sifting through the facts with an eye to the legally relevant.[217]

The adequacy of the employer's internal investigation may be an important component in its defense to the harassment charge. Evidence regarding the conduct of the investigation, information disclosed, analysis of the information, and the conclusion reached is relevant and admissible at trial. This may include the investigator's notes and conversations with company officials. Courts have held that where the investigation is conducted by counsel, this evidence is admissible, and the attorney-client privilege is waived.

For example, in *Harding v. Dana Transport, Inc.*,[218] outside counsel investigated a sexual harassment complaint on behalf of the employer and the employer raised the investigation as a defense to liability. Plaintiff sought discovery of documents relating to the investigation and to take the deposition of the attorney who conducted the

---

214. FED. R. EVID. 501.

215. MODEL RULES OF PROF'L CONDUCT R. 1.6.

216. 449 U.S. 383 (1981).

217. *Id.* at 391 (citations omitted).

218. 914 F. Supp. 1084 (D.N.J. 1996).

investigation. The court rejected the employer's contention that such discovery was protected by the attorney-client privilege, stating:

> By asking [the attorney] to serve multiple duties, the defendants have fused the roles of internal investigator and legal advisor. Consequently, Dana cannot now argue that its own process is shielded from discovery. Consistent with the doctrine of fairness, the plaintiffs must be permitted to probe the substance of Dana's alleged investigation to determine its sufficiency. Without having evidence of the actual content of the investigation, neither the plaintiffs nor the fact-finder at trial can discern its adequacy. Consequently, this court finds that Dana has waived its attorney-client privilege with respect to the content of [the attorney's] investigation of the plaintiff's allegations. This waiver extends to documents which may have been produced by [the attorney] or any agent of Defendant Dana that concern the investigation.[219]

Employers need to be aware that while any legal advice provided may be privileged,[220] the factual investigation may not be deemed to be privileged, particularly if the employer intends to raise the adequacy of the investigation as a defense to the claim. For example, in *Brownell v. Roadway Package System, Inc.*,[221] the court found that when defendant asserted the adequacy of the investigation into plaintiff's allegations of sexual harassment conducted by outside counsel as a defense, defendant waived the right to invoke the attorney-client privilege.[222] First, by claiming that it "fully and fairly" investigated plaintiff's allegations while objecting to the production of statements obtained in the course of that investigation, the court stated that the defendant attempted to use the privilege as both a "sword and a shield." Second, the court explained that by arguing the adequacy of the investigation, defendant placed the investigation "in issue," making the reasonableness of defendant's response to plaintiff's allegations critical to the issue of liability.[223] Accordingly, defendant had to produce all statements taken from employees by outside counsel in the course of its investigation into plaintiff's harassment complaint. Ultimately, where an employer "affirmatively invokes a *Faragher-Ellerth* defense that is premised, in whole [or in] part, on the results of an internal investigation, the defendant waives the attorney-client privilege and work product protections for not only the report itself, but for all documents, witness interviews, notes and memoranda created as part of and in furtherance of the investigation."[224]

---

219. *Id.* at 1096.

220. *See* United States v. Adlman, 134 F.3d 1194 (2d Cir. 1998).

221. 185 F.R.D. 19 (N.D.N.Y. 1999).

222. *Id.* at 25.

223. *Id.*

224. Angelone v. Xerox Corp., 09-CV-6019, 2011 WL 4473534, at *2 (W.D.N.Y. Sept. 26, 2011).

2. Work-Product Doctrine

Rule 26(b)(3) of the FRCP establishes parameters of the work-product doctrine. This rule prohibits discovery of documents and tangible things otherwise discoverable and prepared in anticipation of litigation or trial.[225] The rule, moreover, expressly protects against disclosure of "mental impressions, conclusions, opinions, or legal theories of a party's attorney or other representative concerning the litigation."[226]

The principle governing the work-product doctrine is that it is essential that a lawyer work with a certain degree of privacy, free from unnecessary intrusion by opposing parties and their counsel. To properly prepare the client's case, the attorney must be able to assemble information, sift through what he considers relevant facts from irrelevant facts, prepare legal theories, and plan his strategy without undue and needless interference.[227]

The federal courts have recognized that litigants need not make an "extraordinary showing of necessity that would be required to remove the work product privilege."[228] A claim of work-product privilege may be challenged under the doctrine of implied waiver. The court applied this doctrine in *Harding*, explaining that litigants should not be permitted to manipulate the work-product doctrine for their own benefit by attempting to selectively disclose their attorney's work product.[229] The court emphasized that the fact that the defendant employer's attorney acted as both investigator and attorney cannot change the significance of the employer placing the investigation at issue by asserting it as an affirmative defense. Concluding that the principles of fairness and consistency require the employer to produce all of the underlying documentation, the court emphasized that "[i]t would be fundamentally unfair for the plaintiffs to be required to meet an element of their *prima facie* case without sufficient information regarding the factual substance of that element."[230]

Similarly, in *Brownell*, the court concluded that plaintiff demonstrated a "substantial need" to overcome the work-product privilege, requiring the production of the written statements given to defendant's counsel in connection with his investigation.[231] The court also stated that by asserting the adequacy of an investigation as an affirmative defense to a harassment claim, defendant impliedly waived the protections of the work-product doctrine.[232]

In *Musa-Muaremi v. Florists' Transworld Delivery, Inc.*,[233] the court concluded that documents created by the employer during the investigation in the plaintiff's claims of

---

225. Fed. R. Civ. Proc. 26(b)(3)(A).

226. Fed. R. Civ. Proc. 26(b)(3)(B).

227. Harding v. Dana Transp., Inc., 914 F. Supp. 1084, 1097 (D.N.J. 1996).

228. *In re* Sealed Case, 676 F.2d 793, 811 (D.C. Cir. 1982).

229. *Harding*, 914 F. Supp. at 1098.

230. *Id.* at 1099.

231. Brownell v. Roadway Package Sys., Inc., 185 F.R.D. 19, 26 (N.D.N.Y. 1999).

232. *Id.*

233. 270 F.R.D. 312, 316 (N.D. Ill. 2010).

hostile work environment were not communications for the purpose of obtaining legal advice. Rather, the attorney's comments were "editorial," and therefore, not protected.[234]

It is important to note, however, that even where reliance on an investigation as a defense waives the attorney-client and work-product privileges, courts have remained willing to protect portions of the investigative reports that reflect the attorney's intra-litigation advice or analysis.[235]

B. Self-Critical-Analysis Doctrine

Employers also have sought to avoid disclosure of their investigative files under the self-critical-analysis privilege. This doctrine first was recognized in *Bredice v. Doctors Hospital, Inc.*,[236] when a plaintiff in a medical malpractice case sought discovery of a hospital's peer review committee minutes and reports. The court denied such discovery. It explained that "self-analysis" plays a critical role in ensuring the continual improvement of patient care in hospitals, and that the peer review process was conducted with the expectation that the communications would remain confidential.[237]

Shortly thereafter, the federal district court in Georgia applied the privilege in the employment discrimination case of *Banks v. Lockheed-Georgia Co.*[238] There, the court denied the plaintiff access to internal reports prepared by employees regarding the employer's compliance with Title VII and Executive Order 11246. The court reasoned that access to internal affirmative action materials would "discourage frank self-criticism and evaluation in the development of affirmative action programs of this kind."[239]

Despite these holdings, extension of this privilege to employment litigation has been hotly disputed. Courts that have endorsed the privilege in the employment context maintain that the privilege promotes the public interest in encouraging voluntary compliance by employers with federal equal employment opportunity laws.[240] In *Webb v. Westinghouse Elec. Corp.*,[241] the court explained that

> Employers must be encouraged to be candid and forthright in assessing their employment practices and setting goals and timetables for eradicating policies deemed to be discriminatory in operation or effect. If subjective materials constituting "self-critical analysis" are subject to disclosure during discovery, this

---

234. *Id.*

235. Walker v. County of Contra Costa, 227 F.R.D. 529, 535 (N.D. Cal. 2005).

236. 50 F.R.D. 249 (D.D.C. 1970), *aff'd mem.*, 479 F.2d 920 (D.C. Cir. 1973).

237. *Id.* at 250.

238. 53 F.R.D. 283 (N.D. Ga. 1971).

239. *Id.* at 285.

240. Dickerson v. U.S. Steel Corp., 1976 WL 640, 14 Fair Empl. Prac. Cas. (BNA) 1450 (E.D. Pa. 1976); Sanday v. Carnegie-Mellon Univ., 1975 WL 294, 12 Fair Empl. Prac. Cas. (BNA) 101 (W.D. Pa. 1975); Banks v. Lockheed-Ga. Co., 53 F.R.D. 283 (N.D. Ga. 1971).

241. Webb v. Westinghouse Elec. Corp., 81 F.R.D. 431 (E.D. Pa. 1978).

disclosure would tend to have a "chilling effect" on an employer's voluntary compliance with equal employment opportunity laws.[242]

Most employment cases examining the self-critical-analysis privilege involve discovery of affirmative action plans, rather than the applicability of the privilege to investigatory files.[243] However, in *Harding*, the court refused to apply the privilege to discovery of documents and information relating to the investigation of the plaintiff's sexual harassment and discrimination complaint.[244]

Courts that recognize the privilege in employment discrimination cases typically require the existence of four factors for the application of the self-critical-analysis doctrine: (1) materials protected generally have been those prepared for mandatory governmental reports; (2) only subjective, evaluative materials have been protected; (3) objective data in those same reports have not been protected; and (4) in sensitivity to plaintiffs' need for such materials, courts have denied discovery only where the policy favoring exclusion clearly has outweighed plaintiffs' need.[245] For example, in *Clark v. Pennsylvania Power & Light Co.*,[246] the court held that the self-critical-analysis privilege applied to the subjective components of the defendant's affirmative action plans required by the candid self-evaluation process, and limited discovery to the portions of the plans containing exclusively factual information.[247] The court similarly extended this privilege to Equal Employment Opportunity reports prepared as part of a confidential self-evaluation intended to be distributed solely to certain members of the board of directors.[248] The plaintiff failed to show a compelling need sufficient to overcome the privilege, and defendant did not need to produce portions of the reports containing evaluative and analytical data.[249]

Many courts, however, have refused to extend the self-critical-analysis doctrine to employment cases.[250] Declining to recognize the privilege, the court in *Cherefant v. Nationwide Credit, Inc.*, stated "a self-critical analysis privilege is questionable when one considers the possibility that, if a company engages in a self-critical analysis, and then does nothing as a result of damaging findings, highly relevant evidence of an

---

242. *Id.* at 433.

243. McDougal-Wilson v. Goodyear Tire & Rubber Co., 232 F.R.D. 246 (E.D.N.C. 2005) (concluding that self-critical-analysis privilege did not protect the defendant's affirmative action plan because its contents were relevant and discoverable).

244. Harding v. Dana Transp., Inc., 914 F. Supp. 1084, 1101 (D.N.J. 1996).

245. Witten v. A.H. Smith & Co., 100 F.R.D. 446, 450–51 (D. Md. 1970), *aff'd mem.*, 785 F.2d 306 (4th Cir. 1986); O'Connor v. Chrysler Corp., 86 F.R.D. 211, 217 (D. Mass. 1980).

246. No. 98-3017, 1999 WL 225888 (E.D. Pa. Apr. 14, 1999).

247. *Id.* at *2.

248. *Id.* at *3.

249. *Id.*

250. *See, e.g.*, Cherefant v. Nationwide Credit, Inc., No. CIV 03-60655, 2004 WL 5313965 (S.D. Fla. May 10, 2004) (declining to recognize a self-critical-analysis privilege in the employment discrimination context); Johnson v. United Parcel Serv., Inc., 206 F.R.D. 686 (M.D. Fla. 2002).

employer's intent would be excluded from discovery and impede the public's important interest in enforcement of this nation's equal employment opportunity laws."[251]

In *Witten v. A.H. Smith & Co.*,[252] the court refused to apply the privilege, concluding that disclosure would not necessarily greatly deter future self-evaluations or substantially reduce their thoroughness. The court further noted that there are reasons to believe that deterrents to candid self-evaluation by the employer already exist.[253] Other courts have emphasized that when balancing the interests protected by nondisclosure against the possible benefits flowing from disclosure, the privilege should not be recognized in employment discrimination litigation.[254]

C. Use of Experts Regarding Sufficiency of Employers' Harassment Policies

Litigants in harassment cases may seek to introduce expert testimony regarding the adequacy and effectiveness of an employer's anti-harassment policies and procedures. A critical prerequisite to the admissibility of an expert's opinion is that the testimony is beyond the knowledge of the jury.[255] Proponents of such evidence typically argue that workplace harassment and the elements of an effective intervention and prevention program are not common knowledge that a typical juror would possess.

In *Shrout v. Black Clawson Co.*,[256] a female employee had a sexual relationship with her supervisor. After ending the affair, the supervisor continued to taunt the plaintiff and make sexually explicit offers to her on a daily basis. One of the issues in the case was whether an adequate sexual harassment policy was in place at the time of the harassment. A human resources consultant was qualified as an expert by the court and opined as to the adequacy of the defendant's corporate policies and procedures with respect to sexual harassment in the workplace. The expert concluded that the defendant had no policy regarding sexual harassment.[257] The expert stated that the defendant's

> "[O]pen-door policy" did not qualify as a sexual harassment policy because it
> was too broad, it was not adequately communicated to the employees, it did
> not specifically mention sexual harassment, it did not assure employees that no

---

251. No. CIV 03-60655, 2004 WL 5313965, at *5 (citing Freirmuth v. PPG Indus., 218 F.R.D. 694, 698 (N.D. Ala. 2003)).

252. 100 F.R.D. 446 (D. Md. 1984), *aff'd mem.*, 735 F.2d 306 (4th Cir. 1986).

253. *Id.* at 451–53.

254. *See* Tharp v. Sivyer Steel Corp., 149 F.R.D. 177, 182 (S.D. Iowa 1993) and cases cited therein.

255. FED. R. EVID. 702 (a witness who is qualified as an expert may testify in the form of an opinion if the expert's scientific, technical, or other specialized knowledge will help the trier of fact understand the evidence or to determine a fact in issue).

256. 689 F. Supp. 774, 777–78 (S.D. Ohio 1988).

257. *Id.* at 777.

retaliation would occur, and it was intimidating for lower-echelon women who were harassed . . . to complain directly to the (male) President.[258]

Similarly, in *Kimzey v. Wal-Mart Stores, Inc.*,[259] the plaintiff was constantly subjected to sexual harassment from both her supervisor and store manager. The plaintiff used an expert witness to opine that Wal-Mart's "open-door policy" was completely inadequate for a company the size of Wal-Mart. Evidence of Wal-Mart's failure to train its employees on sexual harassment policy implementation and how to properly conduct investigations of harassment complaints also was introduced.

In *Neil v. District of Columbia Department of Corrections*,[260] the Department of Corrections retained an expert witness to opine as to the sufficiency of its sexual harassment training and retraining programs. Although defendants ultimately did not prevail on their claim, the court permitted and credited the defendants' expert testimony. Notably, in *Hurley v. Atlantic City Police Department*, the court advised that in a sexual harassment case, "the sufficiency of the defendants' sexual harassment policy" is a critical issue that properly calls for expert evaluation and testimony.[261]

The court excluded the plaintiff's expert in *Arjangrad v. JPMorgan Chase Bank, N.A.*[262] The expert was being offered to testify about generally accepted human resources practices for large US companies and the employer's human resources policies and practices. The court found that the expert to be qualified about standard human resources practices, however, concluded that the expert report was unreliable and irrelevant as the expert's testimony consisted of legal conclusions.[263]

Despite these holdings, the use of human resource experts to opine on an employer's personnel policies and practices remains a controversial and unsettled issue.

258. *Id.*

259. 107 F.3d 568 (8th Cir. 1997).

260. No. CIV A 93-2420, 1995 WL 517244 (D.D.C. Aug. 9, 1995).

261. No. CIV A 93-260, 1996 WL 549298, at *8 (D.N.J. Sept. 17, 1996).

262. 3:10-CV-01157-PK, 2012 WL 1890372 (D. Or. May 23, 2012).

263. *Id.*

CHAPTER 18

Cross-Examining the Plaintiff in a Workplace Harassment Case

Wayne E. Pinkstone

I. INTRODUCTION

The plaintiff has just finished testifying about the harassment he or she endured at the hands of the alleged harasser and the complicity and lack of remedial action by the employer defendant.

It is now your turn as the employer's counsel to cross-examine the plaintiff. The examination is critical. You know this could make or break the case. Although the plaintiff testified clearly and persuasively, information gathered during the discovery process revealed that the plaintiff failed to follow company procedures in reporting harassment and has a personal history with the alleged harasser. A number of the plaintiff's coworkers also told you that the plaintiff regularly engaged in joking and banter. Should you question the plaintiff on these issues? If so, how should you do it? You want the cross-examination to be respectful of the court and of the plaintiff, especially in front of the jury. You know, however, that in order for the examination to be effective, you will have to attack the plaintiff's credibility. The most important and often most difficult goal of the cross-examination of a harassment plaintiff is undermining the plaintiff's credibility.

In a harassment case, there are four primary tools for undermining the plaintiff's credibility on cross-examination:

1. Classic impeachment with prior inconsistent statements or actions
2. Examining the plaintiff's other agendas or motives for bringing or exaggerating charges
3. Establishing the plaintiff's role and responsibility for the alleged bad acts
4. Establishing the plaintiff's failure to follow company procedures on reporting harassment

II. CLASSIC IMPEACHMENT

During the discovery phase, you have deposed the plaintiff and deposed or obtained statements from pertinent witnesses. By the time of trial, you will have conducted a thorough investigation of all public records pertaining to the plaintiff, including all statements the plaintiff made to agencies such as the Equal Employment Opportunity Commission (EEOC), the National Labor Relations Board, the Department of Labor, unemployment compensation boards, state and local fair employment practice agencies, workers' compensation agencies, and police authorities. You will have obtained copies of any similar lawsuits or charges filed by the plaintiff against employers or other entities and obtained public records pertaining to collateral matters that may bear upon the case, such as records of bankruptcy, divorce, child custody, or personal injury.

If the case involves allegations of severe emotional harm, you may have also gathered pertinent medical records, deposed the plaintiff's psychiatrist or psychologist, and conducted an independent medical examination of the plaintiff, if possible.

Before trial, you will have examined the information gathered during discovery and scrutinized the best evidence that is inconsistent with the plaintiff's claims. Lack of credibility is one major theme of the defense cross-examination if the plaintiff has told different stories at different times to different people.

A. Areas to Examine for Inconsistencies

1. Compare written and oral statements made to
   a. co-workers
   b. human resources personnel
   c. family and friends
   d. therapists or physicians
   e. EEOC or other agencies
   f. at deposition
   g. on social media
2. Review contemporaneous notes or diaries with later statements made in the complaint or deposition.
3. Identify any areas in which the plaintiff embellishes earlier statements or positions.
4. Focus on the destruction or loss of any evidence and the timing of such destruction or loss.
5. Look critically for inconsistencies between the plaintiff's deposition and declarations filed in the case.
6. With respect to damage claims, look for inconsistencies between the plaintiff's claim that she was emotionally healthy before the alleged harassment and another case or claim in which she alleges that some other factor, such as an automobile accident, caused significant stress and depression.

7. Examine plaintiff's initial complaint of alleged harassment with that set forth in the court complaint.
8. Examine plaintiff's initial reaction to the alleged harassment with that alleged in the complaint.
9. Check the medical records and depositions to determine whether the plaintiff described her alleged emotional damages differently to her psychiatrist than she did in her complaint and deposition.
10. Discover whether the plaintiff has filed previous complaints or charges of discrimination against prior employers.
11. Examine plaintiff's postings on social media sites such as Facebook or Instagram for statements that are inconsistent with allegations in the complaint or deposition testimony.

If the case is going to trial, it is usually because the defense denies the facts alleged by the plaintiff. Therefore, the case will turn on whom the jury believes. Credibility is key.

B. Methods of Classic Impeachment

The most common type of impeachment will be from prior testimony by the plaintiff. Counsel has two choices: (1) confront the plaintiff with prior inconsistent testimony and give the plaintiff an opportunity to respond; or (2) simply read the inconsistent testimony. In either case, defense counsel must set up the prior inconsistency so the jury can follow the fact that there has been a change. Counsel should initiate the impeachment by having the plaintiff confirm the testimony that can be proven to be inconsistent:

Q. You testified yesterday on direct that when Mr. Samson walked into your office, he hugged you and tried to kiss you, right?
A. Yes.
Q. You testified that you were sitting at your desk and he came up to you from behind, right?
A. Yes.
Q. In fact, you told your psychiatrist, Dr. Jones, that you were standing and facing Mr. Samson when he approached you and hugged you. Isn't that true?
A. Yes.
Q. And you never said anything to Dr. Jones about Mr. Samson trying to kiss you, correct?
A. Yes.
Q. You were present at Dr. Jones's deposition when she testified about your statement to her about Mr. Samson, weren't you?
A. Yes.

Q. Let me read you what Dr. Jones said you told her about Mr. Samson when you met right after the incident [read excerpt].[1]

It is critical to keep the cross-examination controlled so the plaintiff does not have an opportunity to offer an explanation for the difference between her two statements. The goal after cross-examination should be to leave the jury with the inconsistencies in the plaintiff's testimony. Any explanation should be avoided and left for redirect.

How do you handle the witness who asks to explain? Defense counsel must make a judgment. Defense counsel's preference is to curb the plaintiff's effort to explain damaging inconsistencies. Defense counsel should, however, permit an explanation if it is likely the jury will view curtailment as unfair or if the judge is likely to permit an explanation. You do not want to appear to the jury as if you are purposely trying to avoid having them hear evidence.

If possible, the cross-examination should string together a whole series of inconsistencies. In each case, it is imperative that the prior inconsistency be laid out clearly. If defense counsel is using audiovisual aids, any prior inconsistent statements or documents should be highlighted for the jury on an overhead projector or large posterboard or distributed if the court will permit. You will likely use excerpts from plaintiff's deposition testimony. Have those excerpts ready to show the jury by highlighting those areas that are inconsistent with the plaintiff's testimony. Defense counsel will want to use either the written statement on a projector or large posterboard. If possible, defense counsel should play the video recording of the plaintiff's testimony, particularly if the plaintiff's demeanor was very assertive, belligerent, or defiant about the subject. Video-recorded impeachment of the plaintiff is a powerful tool.

III. EXAMINATION OF THE PLAINTIFF'S OTHER AGENDAS OR MOTIVES FOR BRINGING FALSE OR EXAGGERATED CHARGES

Another avenue for cross-examination of the plaintiff in a sexual harassment case is highlighting other factors that may have led the plaintiff to bring false or exaggerated charges. Giving the jury information on which to base a belief that this particular plaintiff may have made false allegations is helpful.

The following is a checklist of common agendas that arise in harassment claims.

1. The plaintiff's job was in danger or the plaintiff perceived that his or her job was in danger.
   a. The company has announced plans to downsize but has not revealed who will be affected.

---

1. Review Federal Rule of Civil Procedure 32(a) and the thoughtful discussion of the rule in the context of employment cases by Kerry Notestine, "Cross-Examination in Employment Cases," in *The Practical Litigator* (Mar. 1999).

    b. The plaintiff recently received a bad performance review.

    c. A new supervisor made new demands on the plaintiff, and the plaintiff was insecure as a result.

    d. The new supervisor is strictly enforcing rules and policies that the plaintiff previously ignored or even violated.

2. The plaintiff and the alleged harasser had a romantic relationship that ended or that, to plaintiff's dismay, never began.

    a. The plaintiff is vindictive.

    b. The plaintiff anticipates that the alleged harasser will be vindictive.

    c. In jurisdictions that permit individual liability: The plaintiff believes the alleged harasser will be uncomfortable working with her after the relationship ends and believes that the individual defendant would prefer to pay the plaintiff off rather than continue to work together.

3. Something external has caused a change in how the plaintiff interacts with others in the workplace.

    a. The plaintiff is involved in a separation or divorce.

    b. The plaintiff has suffered some other blow to his or her self-esteem and coping skills.

4. Something external has caused the plaintiff to make a claim so he or she does not have to work.

    a. The plaintiff has had a child or children.

    b. The plaintiff has gotten married.

    c. The plaintiff is suffering from unrelated health problems.

    d. The plaintiff is starting a new business or trying to complete a degree.

    e. The plaintiff's work schedule was changed and he or she prefers the old schedule.

5. The plaintiff is someone who makes these types of claims.

    a. The plaintiff has a history of suffering or anticipating job losses with claims against other employers.

    b. The plaintiff has a history of making complaints at the same workplace.

    c. The plaintiff has a history of trying to preempt impending disciplinary issues by making claims of harassment.

6. Other external factors.

    a. The plaintiff has been caught by a spouse or significant other in a sexual relationship with a co-worker or supervisor and, to avoid conflict in the primary relationship, claims it was forced.

IV. PLAINTIFF'S ROLE IN THE ALLEGED HARASSMENT

Another area for cross-examination is the plaintiff's role in causing or encouraging the alleged problem to occur. It is axiomatic that sexual harassment exists only where there is unwelcome sexual conduct. Any conduct by the plaintiff that suggests that she was actually involved in a consensual relationship is fair game for cross-examination, subject to the restrictions of Rule 412 of the Federal Rules of Evidence.

To establish that the sexual conduct in question was not unwelcome, defense counsel may consider whether the plaintiff displayed any of the following types of behavior:

- Provocative behavior toward the alleged harasser, such as inviting him or her to social activities outside the workplace
- Voluntary conversations with the alleged harasser about his or her sexual experiences, history, or relationships with others
- More broadly, treating the alleged harasser as a confidante or intimate
- History of complaining about problems in the workplace
- Sexual aggressiveness toward others in the workplace, subject to the potential limitations of Rule 412 of the Federal Rules of Evidence[2]
- Telling or transmitting jokes of a sexual nature or use of sexually explicit language
- Sending text messages or emails to the alleged harasser showing participation in the complained-of conduct
- Social media postings reflecting a consensual relationship
- Pursuit of the alleged harasser
- Encouragement of the defendant's sexual overtures
- Failure to complain to the alleged harasser
- Failure to complain or to complain in a timely way to others, formally or informally, within the organization, especially if the employer has written policies prohibiting harassment and retaliation and the plaintiff has signed a written acknowledgment of receipt
- Failure to complain or disclose the problem in other appropriate circumstances, such as in a worker's compensation proceeding relating to stress, or to a therapist or close friends or family members
- General participation in the conduct plaintiff now claims was harassing or offensive

Evidence of the plaintiff's sexual history with others or sexual predisposition might also be probative of whether the sexual conduct was welcome, but may be subject to the constraints of Rule 412 of the Federal Rules of Evidence. If the particular evidence in question falls under Rule 412 and is the subject of a pretrial motion in limine, counsel should assume that the plaintiff will be well prepared for the subjects of cross-examination, if the court permits the cross-examination. Even assuming the court permits evidence of sexual history with others or sexual predisposition, counsel must exercise judgment about whether the jury will consider such evidence fair. If the evidence appears unrelated to the dispute in time or content, the jury may view its use as unnecessary and even harassing.

---

2. *See* Rule 412 of the Federal Rules of Evidence.

V. PLAINTIFF'S FAILURE TO FOLLOW COMPANY POLICY

You know that, as a result of your advice and guidance, your client has adopted and distributed to its employees a clear policy prohibiting harassment in the workplace. This policy is distributed to all employees upon hire and has been updated and republished regularly. The policy also contains a procedure whereby employees are informed that should they experience what they believe is harassment, they should report it to their immediate supervisor or to the director of human resources. All employees have also received instructions through regular training on the policy on what they should do if they believe they have been subjected to harassment.

Contained in the plaintiff's personnel file is a signed acknowledgment form showing that the plaintiff received and read the company's anti-harassment policy, including the company's procedure on reporting harassment. During her deposition, the plaintiff was shown the acknowledgement form and admitted that it was her signature and that she reviewed the policy and was aware of the process for reporting harassment. The plaintiff also admitted that she did not follow the reporting procedure and never told anyone at the company that she experienced harassment.

This provides you with a critical piece of evidence that you can use for cross-examining the plaintiff. Indeed, the plaintiff's failure to complain made it impossible for your client to take appropriate action and remedy the alleged harassment. This may provide your client with a significant legal defense to the plaintiff's harassment claim.[3] It also provides you with an opportunity to cross-examine the plaintiff on why she failed to report the harassment internally. It could raise serious doubts as to whether the harassment even occurred and whether the plaintiff is now motivated by other factors in pursuing her claims.

VI. OTHER CONSIDERATIONS

Other issues to consider in conducting the cross-examination of a plaintiff in a harassment case are the following:

1. Do not think that the longer the examination the better. Make your points quickly and clearly. The jury has already heard a lot of information. There is no need to rehash what they have already heard.
2. Lead the plaintiff with your questions. Although such questions are not permitted on direct examination, they are allowed when cross-examining a witness. You should already know where you want to go with the examination. By asking leading questions of the plaintiff, you can effectively direct the testimony to the answer that supports your defense theme.

---

3. *See* Faragher v. City of Boca Raton, 524 U.S. 775 (1998) and Burlington Indus., Inc. v. Ellerth, 524 U.S. 742 (1998) (in certain circumstances, an employer can raise as a defense to a harassment claim that it exercised reasonable care to prevent and correct promptly any sexually harassing behavior and the employee unreasonably failed to take advantage of those preventative or corrective opportunities).

3. Do not get angry or lose your temper. The jury will not like a bully. You can get the information you want in a calm and respectful manner. You can emphasize your point with a pause or repeating the answer. If the witness is being difficult, you can press for the answer but do not be abusive toward the witness.
4. Be prepared. The key to an effective cross-examination is preparation and organization. Know the facts and make sure your questions are designed to elicit answers that are supported by the record.

CHAPTER 19

Cross-Examination of the Alleged Harasser and Decision-Maker

Joseph Y. Ahmad

The ability to cross-examine the potential harasser and decision-maker presents the plaintiff's attorney with a unique opportunity to strengthen his client's case and to weaken the opposing party's defenses. Generally, an attorney can strengthen his client's case by using the cross-examination to establish or strengthen damages, to admit facts establishing liability, or to create an emotional response in the jury.[1] Similarly, an attorney can weaken the defendant's arguments by using cross-examination to damage the testimony previously offered on behalf of the defendant or by engendering dislike of the defendant by the jury.[2]

In employment cases, cross-examination is particularly important. First, you often have to prove your case in whole or in part with evidence controlled by the defendant, including the testimony of witnesses who are either openly hostile or employed by the defendant, and therefore must be presumed defense-friendly. Second, in almost all employment cases, the employer's state of mind is the critical liability issue. You often must prove a discriminatory animus, which you can rarely do completely with friendly witnesses. Third, in cases involving employment actions like demotions or terminations, you must show that the employer's reason for taking the action is pretextual, and therefore you will have to cross-examine defense witnesses who were involved in making the decision.

Outside of family courts, gender harassment and retaliation cases are often some of the most contentious cases in the courthouse. You will rarely have a completely unbiased witness, whether it is a former employee (typically referred to as "disgruntled" employees by defense counsel), current employees who may feel their job is on the line when they testify, and company management. Of course, at the same time most jurors either are or have been employed and know from experience what is fair and what is not in the employment setting. If an employer is trying to appear fair but actually is not,

---

1. *See* John Alan Appleman, *Cross-Examination of Defendant*, 6 Am. Jur. Trials 297, § 3 (2008).
2. *Id.*

your best time to expose the lie is during cross-examination. Whether you are trying to show that a company's CEO vengefully retaliated for a sexual harassment complaint against him or that an employer targeted female workers in a layoff, your case is often won or lost during cross-examination of the defendant's witnesses.

Cross-examining the potential harasser or the decision-maker also bears some risks. The jury may decide it finds the defendant more credible than the plaintiff.[3] Overzealous cross-examination may evoke a negative response from the jury to the plaintiff's attorney.[4] Cross-examination of the defendant additionally allows him or her to reiterate the testimony he may have offered on direct examination. That reiteration may establish, in the minds of the jury, the veracity of the defendant's story.[5]

I. THEME OF LITIGATION

During cross-examination, the plaintiff's attorney should reiterate and strengthen the case theme and argue his or her case through the witnesses. Without a theme, you cannot have a cross-examination with purpose. The facts of any case are crucial: The facts win the case while the lawyers may lose it. The theme, however, allows the jurors to tie the facts together coherently and to determine the essence of the attorney's story. The theme provides the jurors with a memorable short statement they can use to interpret the defense's statements and to explain the motivations of the participants in the case. It becomes, in essence, the shorthand method for the attorney to reference a major argument or key element of the case.[6] The theme can also create an emotional response in the jurors; it can cause them to identify with your client by considering how they have undergone similar situations or have witnessed similar acts.

However, your cross-examination does not have to prove every aspect of your case, and you should not try to prove too much with one witness. In addition, you should not ask a question that states all or part of the case theme, regardless of the answer you expect. Some lawyers think that as long as they make a statement ("You discriminated against my client because of her sexual orientation, didn't you?"), even if it is denied, a jury will find it believable. This technique rarely works.

II. PREPARING FOR CROSS-EXAMINATION

To successfully argue your case through cross-examination, focus on making small points that connect to form an inevitable conclusion. For example, you are trying to prove that your client was a good employee. Rather than ask "Ms. Jones was a hard

---

3. *Id.* § 4.

4. *Id.*

5. *Id.*

6. Allan Kanner & Tibor L. Nagy, *Legal Strategy, Storytelling and Complex Litigation*, 30 AM. J. TRIAL ADVOC. 1, 15–16 (Summer 2006).

worker, who came in early, left late, and always volunteered for additional work?" It is far better to split the question as follows: "Ms. Jones came early;" "She worked late frequently;" and "She regularly volunteered for additional work." If you want to drive the point home even further, you can sum up the line of questioning with "She was a very hard worker, was she not?"

Your outline should contain no more than one fact in a statement that the witness made during his deposition or that appeared in an exhibit. An outline structured this way will help you formulate questions based on each fact. It will also allow you to quickly refer to the deposition or exhibit when the witness tries to fight you.

As an example, here is an excerpt of an outline of the cross-examination of the chair of a university's sexual harassment board. The theme in this case was that the harasser was so well-regarded that the employer did nothing to stop the harassment and retaliation of the plaintiff:

Reference	Fact
Exhibit_, p._	He was the chair of the sexual harassment board.
Exhibit_, p._	The plaintiff complained about continually being retaliated against after complaining about sexual harassment.
Depo, p._	He and the sexual harassment board had no duty to prevent or correct any sexual harassment.
Depo, p._	He did nothing to stop the harassment.
Depo, p._	He did nothing to stop the retaliation
Depo, p._	Only the president can stop the harassment and retaliation.
Depo, p._	He knows of nothing the president did to stop the harassment or retaliation.

Here is an edited transcript of the cross-examination as it played out at trial.

Q: You were the head of the sexual harassment board that investigated my client's complaint.

A: I was the head of the panel of the sexual harassment board.

Q: During the investigatory process, my client complained that he was still being subjected to harassment, correct?

A: When I interviewed him, yes, he did.

Q: Can you look at Exhibit 153—do you see that document, sir?

A: Yes. This is a letter dated June 9, 1997.

Q: And I see at the bottom that you received a copy of this letter. Is that correct?

A: That's what it says.

Q: Okay. Now, in it, my client mentions that he had on several occasions subsequent to his complaint asked for protection from further harassment and retaliation. Do you see that?

A: Yes.

Q: And you remember him mentioning this to you?
A: During the interview. Yes.
Q: Sir, the board could do nothing to stop the harassment or the retaliation?
A: That's correct.
Q: Board members had no duty to correct or prevent harassment, did they?
A: That's correct.
Q: They had no power to do that?
A: That is correct.
Q: And the only person you know that had that power was the university president?
A: That is correct.
Q: And you don't know of anything he did to stop the harassment?
A: That's correct.
Q: Or prevent the retaliation?
A: That's correct.

The university president later testified that it was not his responsibility to stop the sexual harassment and retaliation either. The jury found the university liable for sexual harassment and retaliation, and the verdict was affirmed on appeal.

III. SETTING UP CROSS-EXAMINATION

During cross-examination, the plaintiff's attorney is trying to develop rapport with both the jury and the alleged harasser. Adopting a conversational style is crucial to achieving these two goals. It helps the witness to be more comfortable with being cross-examined and he may become more forthcoming. Additionally, it allows the attorney the opportunity to engage in a conversation with the witness that may help the attorney gauge and understand the witness's personality. If the attorney keeps a moderate tone, the court will also likely view him as more confident in the plaintiff's case and unflappable. Professor Susan Rutberg asks attorneys to envision the effects of a conversational style of cross-examination:

> Is there another way to cross-examine? Visualize the conversational cross-examiner, a charming disarmer, in place of the attack dog. Picture a lawyer building trust with the witness through the tone and content of the initial questions. Watch the lawyer first establish trust, then see the witness let down his guard and answer the cross-examination questions more responsively. A lawyer who treats the witness respectfully and who asks controlled, leading questions without projecting hostility succeeds in more effectively communicating the client's position than does the swashbuckling gladiator.[7]

---

7. Susan Rutberg, *Conversational Cross-Examination*, 29 Am. J. Trial Advoc. 353, 356 (2005).

IV. PRELIMINARY QUESTIONS

The first necessary step in cross-examining an alleged harasser is ensuring that he understands the questions and letting him know that if he does not understand them, he should not answer but should ask the attorney to rephrase. Beginning the cross-examination by establishing these parameters ensures that the witness cannot later alter his testimony and claim that he was confused or misunderstood the original question.

As part of making the witness comfortable and willing to answer questions openly and honestly, the plaintiff's attorney should next solicit background information from the witness concerning his position at the employer's company, how long he has held that position, and the requirements of the position. The attorney may also find it useful to determine the amount of the witness's compensation in their current position. For example, in *[Plaintiff] v. Nicholson,*[8] a case involving a plaintiff who alleged sexual harassment as a police officer and sexual assault by co-workers during a workplace training, the plaintiff's attorney Michele Fisher began the cross-examination of the plaintiff's supervisor by finding out his background in his current position:

Q. You currently work for the St. Cloud Department of Veterans Affairs; is that correct?
A. That's correct.
Q. And that's their medical center in St. Cloud, right?
A. That's correct.
Q. How long have you held that position?
A. I've been at the VA thirty-four years.
Q. How long have you held—you are currently the chief of police; is that right?
A. That's correct.
Q. How long have you held that position?
A. Four years.
Q. As chief of police, is it your job to supervise the St. Cloud VA police officers?
A. Correct.

After establishing the details of the "bad actor" or potential harasser's work position and the length of time holding that position, the plaintiff's attorney may find it helpful to next determine the circumstances surrounding the plaintiff's hire and how the potential harasser views the work environment. Continuing in the aforementioned case, Ms. Fisher next inquired about the gender composition of the department and the details of the plaintiff's employment:

Q. [Plaintiff], my client here, [the plaintiff], worked as a police officer for the St. Cloud VA; is that correct?
A. Correct.

---

8. Civil No. 04-1369, 2006 WL 2830021 (D. Minn. Sept. 29, 2006).

Q. And during that time you were her supervisor, right?

A. Correct.

Q. She started her employment on January 6, 2003; is that correct?

A. Correct.

Q. And her employment ended on June 30, 2006 when—or 2003 when she was terminated; is that correct?

A. That's correct.

Q. So she was there about six months, right?

A. Correct.

Q. When [Plaintiff] was there, she was the only female police officer, right?

A. Correct.

Q. There were six male officers at the time?

A. Correct.

A. Definitional Questions

After establishing what position the potential harasser held, his relationship to the plaintiff within the workplace environment, and the duration of time he has held the position, the plaintiff's attorney may next turn to the issue of harassment or retaliation. During this period of cross-examination the most important information the attorney can elicit from the witness is how the witness would define sexual harassment or retaliation. No matter how the witness answers that question, the plaintiff's position is strengthened. If the witness offers an incomplete definition, then the plaintiff is positioned to argue that the employer is liable since it failed to provide adequate training regarding sexual harassment. If the witness offers a complete and accurate definition of sexual harassment or discrimination, then the plaintiff may argue that the potential harasser knew that his behavior was within the legal definition of harassment. In the [Plaintiff] case, Ms. Fisher quickly moved into asking the witness definitional questions:

Q. You understand that [Plaintiff] has brought a claim for gender discrimination, sex harassment, and retaliation relating to her employment with the St. Cloud VA; you understand that, right?

A. Yes.

Q. And you understood while you were [Plaintiff's] supervisor what gender discrimination was; is that correct?

A. Correct.

Q. What did you understand that to be?

A. Not treating a female like a male.

Q. And you understood that that was illegal; is that right?

A. Correct.

Q. You understood that the VA had its own policies that set forth that gender discrimination was wrong and that it was against VA policy; is that right?

A. Correct.

Q. I am showing you what's been marked as Exhibit Number 9, which is the equal employment opportunity program slide show that we received from the VA. Have you seen that before?

A. Yes.

Q. And you recall that one of the objectives of the St. Cloud VA—Under the objectives, you see there that it's one of the objectives of the VA that it stresses the importance of a work environment free from discrimination and sexual harassment. Did you understand that?

A. Yes.

Furthermore, the attorney can expand the definitional questions of the witness by drawing connections to the witness's definition of or the employer's policies concerning sexual harassment. Asking these questions later precludes the bad actor from claiming ignorance or uncertainty. In the [Plaintiff] case, Ms. Fisher directly asked the witness whether he understood that firing someone for reporting harassment was illegal:

Q. You know it's illegal to terminate an employee for reporting sexual harassment, don't you?

A. Correct.

Q. And you knew that at the time that [Plaintiff] was working for you, right?

A. Correct.

Q. You know it's illegal to terminate somebody for reporting a sexual assault, right?

A. Correct.

Q. You knew that at the time you terminated [the plaintiff]?

A. Correct.

Q. And you know that it's illegal to terminate an employee for participating in an investigation into those matters, right?

A. Correct.

Q. You knew that when you fired her, right?

A. Correct.

V. ISOLATE THE HARASSER

One of the most successful strategies for cross-examination is to isolate the alleged harasser from his colleagues and co-workers. This approach allows the attorney to separate the company or employer, which may have extensive sexual harassment policies and training, from the individual wrongdoer. Additionally, documenting the employer's response to the claims also supports the plaintiff's assertion of harassment if the alleged harasser was disciplined by his employer or if the employer found evidence of wrongdoing. In the [Plaintiff] case, the witness's attempt to discredit all of his colleagues resulted in him appearing difficult to get along with and lacking in judgment.

Q. You understood that [Plaintiff] made some complaints about her termination and there was a board convened in St. Cloud to investigate that, correct?

A. Correct.

Q. And they also investigated some other—some sex harassment allegations at the facility in St. Cloud, right?

A. Correct.

Q. And you met with the board and provided some testimony, right?

A. Correct.

Q. And after you provided that testimony you were aware that they were talking with some of your police officers about you, right?

A. Correct.

Q. And you were worried about what those police officers were going to say to you—say about you?

A. It was brought to my attention that they were saying wrongful things, yes.

Q. And these are the six police officers besides [the plaintiff], right, that we talked about earlier?

A. Correct.

Q. And in response—I'm showing you Exhibit Number 58. This is a document you gave the board, right?

A. Sent it to them.

Q. It was an email and then attached to that email—I'll flip to the next page—it talks about investigation comments and it goes on to talk about several of the police officers who were being interviewed, right?

A. Correct.

Q. Let's see here. It looks like you talk about Pam Krueger in the first paragraph and you're talking—you're giving the reasons why you think she would be negative about you, right?

A. Correct.

Q. You also go on to talk about Connie Powell, who was a female police officer who was interviewed, right?

A. Correct.

Q. You also say that she doesn't care for you due to the fact that you don't agree with her rapport, right?

A. Correct.

Q. You go on to say—you talk about Craig Jacobs?

A. Correct.

Q. You talk about that he's been disturbed about some personal incident with you for years and I think you say in the last sentence, I don't know how—he thinks that you don't know how to treat women equally. Do you recall that?

A. Because I'm not married, correct.

A. No.

Q. And you gave that to the board so they could see why all these people have it out for you, right?

A. Correct.

Ms. Fisher continued the cross-examination by asking about the employer's investigation of the witness's behavior and the discipline imposed on him. While continuing to isolate the witness, this strategy also effectively separates the progressive discipline that the witness received from the witness's abrupt firing of the plaintiff. As one scholar noted, "Proof that the usual disciplinary procedures were not utilized suggests that this decision was not properly motivated."[9] When the jury recognizes that the alleged harasser has also violated the employer's progressive discipline policies, it will likely lead the jury to not trust the witness and to respond skeptically to his testimony. In the following section from the [Plaintiff] case, Ms. Fisher asks the witness about the result of his employer's investigation of him and the subsequent discipline:

Q. I'm going to go back to this board investigation in St. Cloud. They ended up reaching some findings, right?

A. Correct.

Q. Showing you Exhibit Number 43, have you seen that before, some of the findings of the board?

A. No, I have not.

Q. During that board investigation were you informed that the board was concerned about the way that [Plaintiff] was fired so quickly?

A. No.

Q. You weren't informed that they were concerned about the swiftness of her termination and that they were very troubled by it?

A. No.

Q. Were you aware that the board recommended your termination?

A. No.

Q. And you were just put on leave and you were called back after that leave, right?

A. Correct.

Q. You only received a performance improvement plan and no further disciplinary action, right?

A. Correct.

Q. Were you aware that the board found that the termination of [Plaintiff] wasn't proper in its findings?

A. No.

Q. I'm showing you Exhibit Number 44, which is a document dated September 22, 2003, and it's addressed to you, John Schreifels. Have you seen this document before?

A. Yes.

Q. And this is a document where they told you that—is this the performance improvement plan you were talking about?

A. Yes.

---

9. Mack Player, *Employment Discrimination Law* § 5.44(4) (1988).

Q. And down under paragraph 2, I will highlight a portion of it. It says, "Based on the findings of a recent Administrative Board of Investigation, your performance as reviewed against the performance standards for the critical elements of your position has been as follows," and it talks about personnel management. Do you see that?

A. Correct.

Q. It says that the standard at the VA is that—it says, "Is supportive of management's affirmative action goals for hiring and promoting minorities and women, the handicapped and disabled veterans, and shows evidence of encouragement by supervisor to his or her employees to participate in the EEO program." You understand that that was the standard?

A. Correct.

Q. And it says below, "Regarding this standard, your performance has been unacceptable as it relates to support of the equal employment opportunity/affirmative employment program," right?

A. Correct.

Q. And you understood that they were disciplining you for that, correct?

A. I wasn't disciplined.

Q. You understood that, you read that?

A. Right, but I wasn't disciplined.

Q. Okay. You weren't disciplined, you were called back and put on a performance plan?

A. Correct.

Q. Did anybody tell you that you would have to reapply for your job after you came back from being on leave?

A. No.

Q. Did you ever tell [Plaintiff] that, that she could come back at some point and reapply for her job?

A. No.

Q. You never gave her any opportunity, you just fired her, right?

A. We terminated her, yes.

An attorney can also successfully isolate the potential harasser from his employer and other co-workers by asking about the witness's relationships with his colleagues. Along with isolating the witness, this strategy can help reveal whether the witness has ever been accused of harassment or discrimination, has had a workplace relationship, or has been accused of making female co-workers uncomfortable. In the following examples from the [Plaintiff] case, Ms. Fisher sets up an argument that the witness has engaged in patterns of harassment of many of his female subordinates.

Q. And isn't it true that Connie Powell quit her job right after receiving that promotion because of you?

A. No.

Q. Isn't it true that she didn't want to work with you and that's why she quit that job as sergeant?

A. No.

Q. Isn't it true that she took—she transferred to another department?

A. Yes.

Q. And she went from, I believe, a grade 7 to a grade 4. Does that sound right?

A. I can't say what grade, but she did take a downgrade, yes.

Q. Pam Krueger was another female police officer who had worked just prior to [Plaintiff]; is that right?

A. No. She was probably seven, eight years prior, I would say.

Q. She transferred to a different department so she wouldn't have to work with you; is that right?

A. No.

Q. Did you ever make comments to Pam Krueger: You're a girl, you can type better, so you type up the report or anything like that?

A. No.

VI. RETALIATION

According to attorney Douglas Hedin, six factors influence the size of the jury's award to the plaintiff in a sexual harassment case: (1) the plaintiff's loss of wages and benefits; (2) the extent of the plaintiff's emotional distress and resulting medical care; (3) whether the harasser touched or assaulted the plaintiff; (4) whether the employer knew of the harassment and what its response was to the harassment; (5) whether the employer or harasser engaged in reprisal against the plaintiff; and (6) whether the harasser himself was the plaintiff's employer.[10] In this excerpt from the [Plaintiff] case, Ms. Fisher questions the witness to establish whether his stated reason for firing the plaintiff was pretextual and attempts to prove that the witness engaged in reprisal against the plaintiff.

Q. Showing you Exhibit Number 7, the police officer job description, do you recognize that as the police officer job description?

A. Correct.

Q. I'm going to go a few pages into that document where it says, "Each otherwise qualified VA police officer will be provided appropriate training and a reasonable period of time to achieve weapons qualification." Do you recall that as or do you know that to be the VA policy?

A. Correct.

Q. Isn't it true that when VA police officers are going through training and don't qualify the first time on the range, it's VA policy to give them another chance?

A. Correct.

---

10. Douglas A. Hedin, *Cross-Examination of the Alleged Sexual Harasser and Other Defense Witnesses*, *in* Litigating the Sexual Harassment Case 354, 355 (Matthew B. Schiff et al., eds., 2000).

Q. And that's after there's proof that they didn't qualify, right?
A. Correct.
Q. And [Plaintiff] was never even given the opportunity to qualify; is that right?
A. Correct.

The strategies employed by the attorneys in the [Plaintiff] case were ultimately successful. The jury awarded the plaintiff damages in excess of $440,000 and found in favor of the plaintiff on the sexual harassment and reprisal claims. The strategies employed by Ms. Fisher in cross-examination of the plaintiff's supervisor helped to set up the theme of the litigation, establish that the witness knew the legal definition of sexual harassment, isolate the witness from the policies of the workplace and his colleagues, and demonstrate that the witness engaged in reprisal against the plaintiff.

VII. DEALING WITH THE HOSTILE WITNESS

In contentious employment cases you will often encounter hostile witnesses. Keep in mind that having a witness fight you on cross-examination while you are asking short, simple, leading questions is probably your best way to score points with the jury. Just as an admission by a hostile witness is more valuable than one made by a friendly witness, an admission by a witness who fights you every step of the way is even more valuable. A hostile witness's admission underscores the importance of the admitted fact. At the same time, it is important not to react to an unfavorable answer. Simply act naturally and continue on with your cross-examination without delay as if nothing has happened. The jury takes a cue from the lawyers, and if a lawyer acts as if the witness has hurt the plaintiff, the jury will conclude that as well.

A witness's need for control on the stand can reveal something about his or her conduct in the workplace. Jurors who watch a witness refuse to answer short, direct questions are more likely to view that witness as being willing to take advantage of an employer's power over employees. Such a display at trial can motivate a jury to right a wrong and to award punitive damages. One particular type of hostile witness you will often encounter in a gender discrimination or retaliation case is the CEO or other high-level employee who is rarely challenged. Two techniques for controlling this type of witness are repeating the question verbatim and asking if the opposite is true. Once you have asked the same question twice, you can say, "My question is about [subject]." Then repeat the question once more. If the witness refuses to answer at this point, the jury can conclude only that he or she is being evasive. By asking if the opposite of your first question is true, the witness will appear uncooperative and evasive because he or she will not agree or disagree with a sample, direct, factual assertion.

Here is an example of how both of these techniques might work at trial:

Q: Mr. CEO, Ms. Jones never missed a day of work in the ten years that she worked for ABC Corp., correct?
A: ABC Corp. has an extensive sick leave and vacation leave policy. We are very good to our employees about that. For example, we are one of the few

companies that gives employees four weeks of leave from their first day of work. No other company in our business is so generous to their employees in terms of time off. And, frankly, it does not matter to me whether an employee takes one day here or there, or four weeks of leave at one time.

Q: Sir, Ms. Jones never missed a day of work in the ten years that she worked for ABC Corp., did she?

A: Again, I don't think that matters. Whether they miss one day or four weeks is irrelevant under our policies.

Q: Sir, my question is not about your company's policies. My question is about how many days of leave Ms. Jones took in her ten years of employment with ABC Corp. She never missed a day of work in the ten years that she was there, did she?

A: Well, I know there were times when she was gone, so you have to understand this is not a situation in which your client was there every minute of every day.

Q: Are you testifying that there were days in which Ms. Jones did not show up to work?

A: Look, there were times when she was gone. That's what I'm saying.

Q: Was she ever away from the office for an entire day?

A: She was gone for hours.

Q: Sir, I am handing you what has been marked as Exhibit 5. That is Ms. Jones's personnel file, is it not?

A: It looks like it.

Q: And it looks like she has never missed a day in the ten years that she worked there at ABC?

A: Looks like it.

Q: Ms. Jones never missed an entire day of work in the ten years she was there, did she?

A: Not an entire day, no.

How does the witness come off in this exchange? By refusing to concede the smallest point to help the plaintiff's case—that she never missed a day of work—the witness appears evasive and even dishonest. An exchange like this can only help reinforce your claim that the defendant is lying about why your client was terminated.

CHAPTER 20

Damages Issues in Title VII Cases: Plaintiff's Perspective

Robert B. Fitzpatrick

I. INTRODUCTION

A plaintiff who proves that the employer is liable for violation of Title VII of the Civil Rights Act of 1964 (Title VII), as amended by the 1991 Civil Rights Act, including sex (gender) harassment and retaliation, may be awarded reinstatement, back pay, front pay, compensatory and punitive damages, attorney's fees and costs, and interest.[1] The practitioner who represents a plaintiff should document and discover information about potential damages from intake and up to the time of trial. Applicable circuit model jury instructions should be consulted for guidance; reported decisions on damages in the relevant circuit should be researched. Thought should be given to requesting other equitable relief since courts have the discretion to award a variety of equitable remedies where Title VII violations are established, such as injunctions barring future unlawful behavior by an employer and orders mandating changes in an employer's policies or practices. This chapter provides an understanding of the scope of relief available so that a plaintiff's potential recovery of damages can be maximized.

II. REINSTATEMENT

A. Overview

Reinstatement is an obvious form of relief to make the plaintiff whole and to relieve the plaintiff of the effects of discrimination. Reinstatement for wrongful termination or instatement for a wrongful denial to a position is the "basic remedy under Title VII."[2]

---

1. 42 U.S.C. § 2000e-5(g) (2000).

2. *See, e.g.,* Darnell v. City of Jasper, 730 F.2d 653 (11th Cir. 1984); EEOC v. Century Broad. Corp., 957 F.2d 1446, 1463 (7th Cir. 1992); Goldstein v. Manhattan Indus., Inc., 758 F.2d 1435, 1448 (11th Cir.), *cert. denied*, 474 U.S. 1005 (1985); Dickerson v. Deluxe Check Printers, Inc., 703 F.2d 276, 280 (8th Cir. 1983); Ellis v. Ringgold Sch. Dist., 832 F.2d 27 (3d Cir. 1987).

Although within the discretion of the district court, the reinstatement order should be considered when requested by the plaintiff and when circumstances warrant its award. In *Bruso v. United Airlines, Inc.,* the Seventh Circuit engaged in the following discussion on reinstatement as a suitable remedy:

> The equitable remedy of reinstatement requires the court to strike a delicate balance. On the one hand, reinstatement is the preferred remedy for victims of discrimination, and the court should award it when doing so is feasible. *See* McKnight v. General Motors Corp., 973 F.2d 1366, 1370 (7th Cir. 1992) (quoting Coston v. Plitt Theatres, Inc., 831 F.2d 1321, 1330 (7th Cir. 1987), vacated on other grounds, 486 U.S. 1020 (1998)). On the other hand, a court is not required to reinstate a successful plaintiff where the result would be a working relationship fraught with hostility and friction. *See* Hutchison v. Amateur Elec. Supply, Inc., 42 F.3d 1037, 1045–46 (7th Cir. 1994). Reinstatement in such situations could potentially cause the court to become embroiled in each and every employment dispute that arose between the plaintiff and the employer following the plaintiff's reinstatement. *See id.* at 1046. A court must be careful, however, not to allow an employer to use its anger or hostility toward the plaintiff for having filed a lawsuit as an excuse to avoid the plaintiff's reinstatement. *See* Century Broad. Corp., 957 F.2d at 1462. . . . [R]einstatement may become particularly infeasible if the plaintiff would no longer enjoy the confidence and respect of his superiors once reinstated. *See* Tennes v. Massachusetts Dep't of Revenue, 944 F.2d 372, 381 (7th Cir. 1991). Reinstatement may also be more problematic when the plaintiff holds a management position, *see* Avitia, 49 F.3d at 1230, or would be supervised by the same individuals who discriminated against him in the first place, *see* Price v. Marshall Erdman & Assocs., Inc., 966 F.2d 320, 325 (7th Cir. 1992).[3]

Factors that a court may consider in determining whether reinstatement is an appropriate remedy might include:

- whether any other form of relief is possibly available to fully compensate the plaintiff.[4]
- whether reinstatement is feasible in the case at hand.[5]
- whether reinstatement would be in the best interests of the employee.[6]
- whether the employer is likely to comply with the court's order.[7]

---

3. 239 F.3d 848, 861–62 (7th Cir. 2001).

4. *See, e.g.,* Hopkins v. Price Waterhouse, 920 F.2d 967, 976 (D.C. Cir. 1990).

5. *See, e.g.,* Palasota v. Haggar Clothing Co., 2005 U.S. Dist. LEXIS 1242 (N.D. Tex. Jan. 28, 2005).

6. *See, e.g.,* McGinnis v. Ingram Equip. Co., 685 F. Supp. 224 (N.D. Ala. 1988).

7. *Id.*

- whether hostility between the parties would result from reinstatement, including consideration of the antagonism generated by the litigation at hand, such that it will be unlikely that an effective employment relationship can be reestablished.[8]
- whether the plaintiff has found other work.[9]
- whether reinstatement would require displacement of a nonculpable employee.[10]

When courts find that reinstatement is an inappropriate remedy, they strive to make the plaintiff whole by awarding other remedies, usually in the form of a reasonable amount of back pay and front pay.[11]

B. Bumping

"Bumping" occurs when a court orders reinstatement, and the plaintiff effectively bumps another employee from his or her position. Many courts continue to award front pay rather than bump someone out of a job in an attempt to provide "make whole" relief to the plaintiff. The court in *Hicks v. Dothan City Board of Education*[12] reviewed seven factors that should be considered in determining whether to bump or not: (1) effect on the plaintiff of the refusal to displace; (2) culpability of the incumbent; (3) disruption to the incumbent; (4) degree of culpability of the employer; (5) uniqueness of position and availability of comparable positions; (6) the plaintiff's diligence in taking steps to assure that the position remains available should the plaintiff prevail; and (7) undue disruption of the employer's business.[13]

In *Lander v. Lujan*,[14] the court, when asked to decide whether and under what circumstances a court may order bumping as a remedy for Title VII violations, held:

Reinstatement to a job from which a plaintiff was discriminatorily denied need not require the displacement of an incumbent. The necessity for the bumping remedy only arises with unique, typically higher-level, jobs that have no reasonable substitutes.

---

8. *See, e.g.*, Fitzgerald v. Sirloin Stockade, 624 F.2d 945, 957 (10th Cir. 1980); EEOC v. Pac. Press Publ'g Ass'n, 482 F. Supp. 1291 (1979), *aff'd*, 676 F.2d 1272 (9th Cir. 1982); Henry v. Lennox Indus., 768 F.2d 746 (6th Cir. 1985); EEOC v. Red Baron Steak Houses, 1988 U.S. Dist. LEXIS 12425 (N.D. Cal. June 3, 1988); Rabkin v. Or. Health Scis. Univ., 350 F.3d 967, 977 (9th Cir. 2003).

9. *See, e.g.*, Henry v. Lennox Indus., 768 F.2d 746 (6th Cir. 1985).

10. *Id.*

11. *See, e.g.*, McGinnis v. Ingram Equip. Co., 685 F. Supp. 224 (N.D. Ala. 1988); EEOC v. Red Baron Steak Houses, 1988 U.S. Dist. LEXIS 12425 (N.D. Cal. June 3, 1988).

12. 814 F. Supp. 1044, 1050 (M.D. Ala. 1993).

13. *See also* Walters v. City of Atlanta, 803 F.2d 1135, 1148–49 (11th Cir. 1986); Brewer v. Muscle Shoals Bd. of Educ., 790 F.2d 1515, 1522–23 (11th Cir. 1986); Parker v. Wallace, 596 F. Supp. 739, 746 (M.D. Ala. 1984) (refused to bump because incumbent was innocent party).

14. 888 F.2d 153, 155–56 (D.C. Cir. 1989).

One case, *Kraemer v. Franklin & Marshall College*,[15] held that bumping is not a suitable remedy in nearly all situations, and cited numerous cases in explanation:

> Reinstatement is not an appropriate remedy if it requires bumping or displacing an innocent employee in favor of the plaintiff who would have held the job but for illegal discrimination. *See* Spagnuolo v. Whirlpool Corp., 717 F.2d 114, 119–122 (4th Cir. 1983) (although district court initially entered a judgment in accordance with the "rightful place" theory whereby the employee who suffered past discrimination will be given full seniority rights and permitted to obtain the next available vacancy by means of that seniority, district court erred in amending that judgment to require the defendant corporation to bump the innocent incumbent who held the position originally in dispute so that plaintiff could be reinstated); Ray v. Iuka Special Mun. Separate Sch. Dist., 51 F.3d 1246, 1254 (5th Cir. 1995) (district court did not abuse its discretion in denying reinstatement where there were no existing vacancies in school district and where reinstating plaintiff would require displacement of an existing employee); Deloach v. Delchamps, Inc., 897 F.2d 815, 822–23 (5th Cir. 1990) (applying ADEA precedent to interpret the Louisiana Age Discrimination in Employment Act, court upheld district court's order that reinstatement was not feasible because plaintiff had been replaced and reinstatement would disrupt the employment of others); Shore v. Federal Express Corp., 777 F.2d 1155, 1157–59 (6th Cir. 1985) (affirming district court's order that reinstatement of successful Title VII plaintiff was not feasible because reinstatement of plaintiff would displace the person who had held the position since plaintiff's termination and there were no comparable positions available); EEOC v. Century Broadcasting Corp., 957 F.2d 1446, 1463 (7th Cir. 1992) (denial of reinstatement of radio announcers terminated in violation of ADEA was properly based upon one strong and solid reason; there were a limited number of announcing positions at the radio station and each position was filled at the time and granting reinstatement to even one announcer would have required defendant to displace a currently employed announcer); Graefenhain v. Pabst Brewing Co., 870 F.2d 1198, 1208–09 (7th Cir. 1989) (in ADEA case, reinstatement is properly denied and front pay awarded where the employee's position exists but is not available because someone else currently occupies the employee's former position).

The court in Kraemer did recognize, however, that there are cases in which bumping is acceptable; it cited both Walters[16] and Lander[17] for this proposition, in addition to *Reeves v. Claiborne County Board of Education*:[18]

---

15. 941 F. Supp. 479, 483 (E.D. Pa. 1996).

16. 803 F.2d at 1148–50.

17. 888 F.2d at 155–56.

18. 828 F.2d 1096, 1101–02 (5th Cir. 1987).

[W]here [the] district court denied reinstatement because defendant had hired a successor to plaintiff's position who would be bumped, appellate court reversed noting that successor to plaintiff's position was hired just two months before trial and that "if the existence of a replacement constituted a complete defense against reinstatement, then reinstatement could be effectively blocked in every case merely by hiring an innocent third party after the retaliatory purpose was achieved."[19]

Thus, although rare, at times courts will use their discretion and award reinstatement despite the consequence that another employee is bumped. For instance, in Walters,[20] the court held that while bumping was an extraordinary remedy to be used sparingly, when an applicant for the position of director of the city's Cyclorama had been repeatedly and discriminatorily denied the position, the plaintiff's remedy would be "unjustly inadequate" absent reinstatement to the position. The court also noted that the bumped employee took the position long after the plaintiff brought suit, and other suitable employment was available to the employee with the city.

III. BACK AND FRONT PAY DAMAGES

A. Back Pay Damages

1. Availability of Back Pay Awards Generally

Back pay includes lost earnings and other elements of wages such as lost overtime, shift differential, premium pay, sales commissions, cost-of-living increases, raises, bonuses, promotional increases, tips, vacation and sick pay, pension and retirement benefits, profit-sharing, insurance, and other amounts the plaintiff would have received had she continued working. Front pay is defined as an award for future lost earnings to make the plaintiff whole.

> Back pay is not an automatic entitlement. Rather, the court will exercise its discretion in determining what is equitable. Nonetheless, the court should not deny back pay except in the most limited of circumstances. The US Supreme Court stated this principle in *Ford Motor Co. v. EEOC*: "[B]ackpay is not an automatic or mandatory remedy; . . . it is one which the courts 'may invoke in the exercise of their sound discretion [which] is equitable in nature. . . .' Nonetheless, while 'the power to award backpay is discretionary power,' . . . a 'court must exercise this power in light of the large objectives of the [relevant statute or cause of action at hand],' and, in doing so, must be guided by 'meaningful standards' enforced by "thorough appellate review. . . ."[21] Thus, a Title

---

19. *Kraemer*, 941 F. Supp. at 483–84.

20. 803 F.2d at 1148–50.

21. 458 U.S. 219, 227 (1982) (quoting Albemarle Paper Co. v. Moody, 422 U.S. 405, 415, 476 (1975) (citations omitted).

VII plaintiff is presumptively entitled to a back pay award.[22] Under the Age Discrimination in Employment Act (ADEA), one court even referred to back wages as a mandatory element of damages.[23]

"The purpose of back pay is to completely redress the economic injury the plaintiff has suffered as a result of discrimination."[24] Therefore, the award should consist of lost wages, including any anticipated raises or benefits.[25] Most Title VII cases awarding back pay involve the plaintiff being wrongfully terminated, and usually the plaintiff is entitled to an award of back pay from the date of wrongful termination until the date of judgment.[26]

There are a number of conditions under which the plaintiff can be denied back pay or where back pay may be reduced or otherwise modified. For example, plaintiffs securing equal or greater pay through subsequent employment are not entitled to back pay.[27] When the defendant has relied upon the terms of legislative enactments, courts waive liability for retroactive compensation.[28] Additionally, interpretive rulings by regulatory agencies may defeat the plaintiff's entitlement to back pay.[29] Unexcused delay may toll back pay accrual.[30] Back pay also may be reduced as a result of a pre-termination record of absenteeism.[31] Back pay is normally reduced by any interim earnings, regardless

---

22. Walters v. City of Atlanta, 610 F. Supp. 715 (N.D. Ga. 1985), *aff'd in part, rev'd in part*, 803 F.2d 1135 (11th Cir. 1986) (a Title VII claimant is presumptively entitled to back pay); *see also* Rasimas v. Mich. Dep't of Mental Health, 714 F.2d 614, 626 (6th Cir. 1983), *cert. denied*, 466 U.S. 950 (1984); EEOC v. Hacienda Hotel, 881 F.2d 1504 (9th Cir. 1989) (awarding back pay to undocumented alien victims of sexual harassment that resulted in loss of pay); Wheeler v. Southland Corp., 876 F.2d 16 (6th Cir. 1989) (in view of evidence that plaintiff could have continued work for successor company, defendant was liable for back pay even after entity for which plaintiff had worked was sold to third party).

23. Maxfield v. Sinclair Int'l Corp., 766 F.2d 788 (3d Cir. 1985), *cert. denied*, 474 U.S. 1057 (1986).

24. Saulpaugh v. Monroe Cty. Hosp., 4 F.3d 134, 145 (2d Cir. 1993) (citations omitted).

25. *Id.*

26. *Id.* at 144–45. *See also* Molina v. J. F. K. Tailor Corp., 2004 U.S. Dist. LEXIS 7872, at *11–12 (S.D.N.Y. Apr., 30 2004); Johnson v. Spencer Press of Me., Inc., 364 F.3d 368, 379 (1st Cir. 2004) ("Generally, a plaintiff is entitled to back pay," which "compensates plaintiffs for lost wages and benefits between the time of the discharge and the trial court judgment.").

27. Blum v. Witco Chem. Corp., 829 F.2d 367 (3d Cir. 1987) (when plaintiffs in Age Discrimination in Employment Act (ADEA) action secured jobs with higher salaries before trial, severance pay received by plaintiffs compensated for their unemployed period).

28. Alaniz v. Cal. Processors, Inc., 785 F.2d 1412 (9th Cir. 1986) (denial of back pay where defendant had relied in good faith on a state commission order).

29. Albemarle Paper Co. v. Moody, 422 U.S. 405 (1975) (denial of back pay where defendant had relied in good faith upon an EEOC interpretative ruling).

30. Kamberos v. GET Automatic Elec., Inc., 603 F.2d 598 (7th Cir. 1979), *cert. denied*, 454 U.S. 1060 (1981) (because the plaintiff allowed an Equal Employment Opportunity Commission complaint to lie dormant for four years before a right-to-sue letter was issued, the plaintiff's wages were denied for the period the plaintiff was awaiting the right-to-sue letter); Lynn v. W. Gillette, Inc., 564 F.2d 1282 (9th Cir. 1977) (plaintiff's lack of diligence in seeking a right-to-sue letter from the EEOC may be taken into account in determining the amount of back pay to be awarded).

31. *See, e.g.*, Swock v. Milwaukee Boiler Mfg. Co., 665 F.2d 149, 161 (7th Cir. 1981) (plaintiff's projected earnings were reduced because of his 12 percent average absenteeism rate).

of the type of work involved.[32] The burden is on the employer to prove any offsets to damages.[33]

2. Calculation of Back Pay

The amount of back pay is the amount the plaintiff would have earned less the amount actually received by the plaintiff. The components of back pay are lost wages and lost fringe benefits. Any fringe benefit determined to have a cash value must be considered in the formula used to calculate total retroactive pay due.[34] The amount the plaintiff would have earned is often calculated using the average earnings of employees of the defendant with comparable seniority and job assignments during the relevant time period.[35] Many courts apply the United States fifty-two week treasury bill rate, referred to in 28 U.S.C. § 1961, to awards of back pay under Title VII.[36] Some courts require

---

32. Merriweather v. Hercules, Inc., 631 F.2d 1161 (5th Cir. 1980).

33. *See, e.g.* Rhodes v. Guiberson Oil Tools, 82 F.3d 615 (5th Cir. 1996) (holding that because plaintiff failed to assert entitlement to damages based on loss of fringe benefits, the district court's determination not to award such damages was not clearly erroneous); Davis v. Odeco, Inc., 18 F.3d 1237 (5th Cir. 1994) (holding that when an employee has bargained for a fringe benefit as additional consideration for employment, compensation received by the employee under that fringe benefit should not be deducted from damages awarded to the employee as a result of the employer's conduct); Rodriguez v. Tailor, 569 F.2d 1231, 1243 (3d Cir. 1977), *cert. denied*, 436 U.S. 913 (1978).

34. Bempah v. Kroger Co., 1989 U.S. Dist. LEXIS 6345 (S.D. Ga. June 5, 1989) ("plaintiff [in a Title VII case] is entitled to 'fringe benefits that could be turned into cash by the employee'"; Crabtree v. Baptist Hosp., 749 F.2d 1501, 1502 (11th Cir. 1985).

35. *See* Merriweather v. Hercules, Inc., 1979 U.S. Dist. LEXIS 15326 (N.D. Ala. Jan. 2, 1979), *aff'd*, 631 F.2d 1161 (5th Cir. 1980).

36. *See, e.g.*, EEOC v. Gurnee Inn Corp., 914 F.2d 815 (7th Cir. 1990) (applying the IRS rates and compounding interest); EEOC v. Wooster Brush Co. Employees Relief Ass'n, 727 F.2d 566, 579 (6th Cir. 1984) (summarizing the use of IRS and other rates); Welch v. UNUM Life Ins. Co. of Am., 2008 U.S. Dist. LEXIS 73308 (D. Kan. Aug. 18, 2008) (applying the IRS interest rate to a damages award under the Employment Retirement Income Act of 1974); Great-West Life & Annuity Ins. Co. v. Dana Credit Corp., 2006 U.S. Dist. LEXIS 77118 (D. Ill. 2006) (applying the IRS interest rate, but noting that the parties can agree to another interest rate); Devore v. City of Philadelphia, 2004 U.S. Dist. LEXIS 8993 (D. Pa. 2004) (applying the IRS rate to a postjudgment interest accrual calculation); Shannon v. Fireman's Fund Ins. Co., 136 F. Supp. 2d 225, 231 (D.N.Y. 2001); Albahary v. City & Town of Bristol, 96 F. Supp. 2d 121, 123 (D. Conn. 2000) (applying the IRS rate to a postjudgment interest award); Ware v. ABB Air Preheater, Inc., 1995 U.S. Dist. LEXIS 14159, No. 91-CV-37S, 1995 WL 574464, at *9–10 (W.D.N.Y. 1995); Rao v. N.Y. City Health & Hosps. Corp., 882 F. Supp. 321, 327–29 (S.D.N.Y. 1995); McIntosh v. Irving Trust Co., 873 F. Supp. 872, 882–84 (S.D.N.Y. 1995); Frank v. Relin, 851 F. Supp. 87, 91 (W.D.N.Y. 1994); Russo v. Unger, 845 F. Supp. 124 (S.D.N.Y. 1994) (holding that it was more appropriate to award compound interest in order to assure that the plaintiff is made whole); United States v. City of San Francisco, 55 EPD (CCH) ¶ 40,345 (N.D.Cal. 1990) (rejecting argument that state simple interest rate should be applied and adopting § 621 rate); Maturo v. Nat'l Graphics, 722 F. Supp. 916 (D. Conn. 1989) (using § 621 rate); Pegues v. Miss. State Employment Serv., 1984 U.S. Dist. LEXIS 24116 (N.D. Miss. Aug. 24, 1984) (using § 621 rate and compounding annually); Davis v. Constr. Materials, Inc., 558 F. Supp. 697, 699–700 (N.D. Ala. 1983); EEOC v. St. Joseph Paper Co., 557 F. Supp. 435, 442 (W.D. Tenn. 1983); Fadhl v. Police Dep't of San Francisco, 553 F. Supp. 38, 45 (N.D. Cal. 1982); EEOC v. Stone Container Corp., 548 F. Supp. 1098, 1106 (W.D. Mo. 1982); Lilly v. Harris-Teeter Supermarket, 545 F. Supp. 686, 715 (W.D.N.C. 1982); EEOC v. Wooster Brush Co., 323 F. Supp. 1256, 1268 (N.D. Ohio 1981); Richardson v. Rest. Mkt. Assocs., 527 F. Supp. 690 (N.D.

that the calculation of back pay be done in quarterly periods;[37] other courts calculate back pay based on an annual basis.[38] Back pay awards cannot be based on speculation.[39] The Equal Pay Act must be complied with in calculations used to support back pay agreements.[40]

When lower expenses offset a lower salary in a new job, the defendant is not liable for retroactive compensation to bring to par the loss in salary.[41] Interim earnings are to be offset from back pay regardless of whether the employment was comparable to the position at issue.[42] "Moonlighting earnings"—money that the plaintiff earned at a second job—should not reduce plaintiff's back pay award unless the defendant demonstrates that the plaintiff could not moonlight in the position from which she was terminated.[43]

On the specific issue of whether overtime compensation should be deducted from a back pay award, most courts agree that it should not, as long as the plaintiff could have earned the compensation even if he had not been wrongfully terminated, had

---

Cal. 1981) Chisholm v. U.S. Postal Serv., 516 F. Supp. 810, 881 (W.D.N.C. 1980); EEOC v. Pac. Press Publ'g Ass'n, 482 F. Supp. 1291 (N.D. Cal. 1979) (adopting § 621 rate, which encourages timely compliance, discourages unlawful discrimination, and more fully compensates victims for economic losses).

37. *See, e.g.,* Bufco Corp. v. NLRB, 331 U.S. App. D.C. 150 (D.C. Cir. 1998); Kendrick v. Jefferson County Bd. of Educ., 13 F.3d 1510 (11th Cir. 1994).

38. *See, e.g.,* Leftwich v. Harris-Stowe State Coll., 702 F2d 686, 693 (8th Cir. 1983).

39. For instance, in Bonura v. Chase Manhattan Bank, N.A., 629 F. Supp. 353, 361 (S.D.N.Y. 1986), the court refused to award lost bonuses as back pay because bonuses were not mandatory on the part of the employer and any award would be "rearview fortune-telling"; the court declined to award salary bonuses on the ground that they were too speculative. *See also* Hodgson v. Ideal Corrugated Box Co., 1974 U.S. Dist. LEXIS 12474 (N.D. W. Va. Jan. 31, 1974). In Goldstein v. Manhattan Indus., Inc., 758 F.2d 1435, 1446–47 (11th Cir. 1985), the court rejected the defendant's argument that damages were too speculative. The court allowed a discharged salesman to recover damages for his lost income from "outside lines" of noncompeting products that the employer had allowed the plaintiff to sell along with the employer's products; the court rejected an argument by the defendant that such damages were compensatory (and thus unrecoverable), finding that the opportunity to sell such outside products was in the nature of a fringe benefit.

40. Crabtree v. Baptist Hosp., 749 F.2d 1501 (11th Cir. 1985) (back pay amount under Title VII cannot be calculated upon salary that violates Equal Pay Act).

41. *See* Mitchell v. W. Feliciana Parish Sch. Bd., 507 F.2d 662, 666 n.7 (5th Cir. 1975) (although plaintiff's salary was somewhat lower in new job, her lower travel expenses offset decreased salary).

42. *See* Merriweather v. Hercules, Inc., 631 F.2d 1161, 1168 (5th Cir. 1980), Brown v. A.J. Gerrard Mfg. Co., 715 F.2d 1549 (11th Cir. 1983).

43. *See* NLRB v. Ferguson Elec. Co., 242 F.3d 426, 433 (2d Cir. 2001); Gaworski v. ITT Commercial Fin. Corp., 17 F.3d 1104, 1111–12 (8th Cir. 1994); Chesser v. State of Ill., 895 F.2d 330 (7th Cir. 1990); Kossman v. Calumet County, 800 F.2d 697, 703 (7th Cir. 1986), *rev'd on other grounds,* Coston v. Plitt Theatres, Inc., 831 F.2d 1321, 1336 (7th Cir. 1987); Lilly v. City of Beckly, 797 F.2d 191, 196 (4th Cir. 1986); Whatley v. Skaggs Cos., Inc., 707 F.2d 1129 (10th Cir.), *cert. denied,* 464 U.S. 934 (1983); Behlar v. Smith, 719 F.2d 950 (8th Cir. 1983); Thorton v. E. Tex. Motor Freight, 497 F.2d 416, 422 (6th Cir. 1974); Bing v. Roadway Express, 485 F.2d 441, 454 (5th Cir. 1973); Lewis v. City of Chicago, 2007 U.S. Dist. LEXIS 24378 (D. Ill. 2007); Jordan v. City of Cleveland, 2006 U.S. Dist. LEXIS 76400 (D. Ohio 2006); Menchaca v. Am. Med. Response of Ill., Inc., 2002 U.S. Dist. LEXIS 405 (N.D. Ill. Jan. 14, 2002); Mendoza v. City of New Orleans, 2001 U.S. Dist. LEXIS 20586 (E.D. La. Dec. 5, 2001); Willis v. Watson Chapel Sch. Dist., 749 F. Supp. 923 (W.D. Ark. 1990).

been properly promoted, and so on.[44] There is an obvious analogy between overtime and moonlighting earnings. Both allow individuals to accumulate earnings additional to what their normal working hours provide and both do so because normal working hours do not exhaust the working capabilities of the workers involved. A job that does not exhaust its workers' time or energies permits the accumulation of earnings from secondary employment, which can easily be considered a benefit of such a job. But moonlighting and overtime are different in that overtime hours are required to meet the needs of the employee's primary employer; by looking at the experiences of other employees of the employer involved, it is possible to come up with a reasonable estimate of the likely overtime hours that a given employee would have worked.[45]

In determining the salary/wages that the plaintiff would have earned, expert testimony may be introduced to estimate the plaintiff's salary projections.[46]

3. Duration of Back Pay

Courts vary in their decisions as to when back pay accrual terminates. Variations include the date of trial (either commencement or termination), the date the jury returns a verdict, or the date of any damages settlement.[47] Other courts hold that back pay liability is ended as of the date of judgment or the date judgment is entered, not the date on which the court announced its factual findings from the bench.[48]

---

44. Mendoza v. City of New Orleans, 2001 U.S. Dist. LEXIS 20586 (E.D. La. Dec. 5, 2001); Nordstrom v. NLRB, 299 U.S. App. D.C. 349, 984 F.2d 479 (D.C. Cir. 1993); Behlar v. Smith, 719 F.2d 950 (8th Cir. 1983); Welborn v. Hunt, 929 F.2d 1341 (8th Cir. 1991); Floyd v. Mellon Bank, N.A., 1991 U.S. Dist. LEXIS 2599, 1991 WL 30755 (E.D. Pa. Mar. 6, 1991); Anderson v. Phillips Petroleum Co., 736 F. Supp. 239 (D. Kan. 1990). In *Mendoza*, the court concludes that the majority of the relevant case law supports a finding that plaintiff's overtime earnings should be deducted from any back pay award, because it is undisputable that plaintiffs would have been unable to earn that compensation if they had been working as captains. While plaintiffs clearly could have worked overtime hours as captains, they could not have earned any extra compensation for doing so; they could only earn the extra compensation while they were still lieutenants. Plaintiffs would, in fact, be made "more than whole" if the overtime earnings were not deducted, as their earnings as lieutenants being compensated for both mandatory and voluntary overtime work were greater than their earnings would have been had they been promoted to captains. *Mendoza*, 2001 U.S. Dist. LEXIS 20586, at *9–10 (D. La. 2001).

45. Lewis v. City of Chicago, 2007 U.S. Dist. LEXIS 24378, at *26–27 (D. Ill. Mar. 20, 2007).

46. *See, e.g.*, Blum v. Witco Chem. Corp., 829 F.2d 367 (3d Cir. 1987); Goldstein v. Manhattan Indus., Inc., 758 F.2d 1435, 1438 (11th Cir. 1985), *cert. denied*, 474 U.S. 1005 (1985); Pollard v. E.I. Dupont de Nemours, 338 F. Supp. 2d 865, 882 (D. Tenn. 2003).

47. *See, e.g.*, Cassino v. Reichhold Chems., Inc., 817 F.2d 1338, 1348 (9th Cir. 1987); Wehr v. Burroughs Corp., 619 F.2d 276, 283 (3d Cir. 1980) (date of trial); Loeb v. Textron, Inc., 600 F.2d 1003, 1021 (1st Cir. 1979) (date of trial); Watlington v. Univ. of P.R., 751 F. Supp. 318, 330 (D.P.R. 1990) (date of jury verdict); Coston v. Plitt Theatres, Inc., 44 F.E.P. Cas. (BNA) 1717 (N.D. Ill. 1986), *aff'd in part & rev'd in part on other grounds*, 831 F.2d 1321 (7th Cir. 1987), *vacated*, 486 U.S. 1020 (1988) (date of jury verdict); Kolb v. Goldring, Inc., 694 F.2d 869, 874 n.4 (1st Cir. 1982) (date of damages settlement); Loubrido v. Hull Dobbs Co., 526 F. Supp. 1055, 1058 (D.P.R. 1981) (date of damages settlement).

48. Nord v. U.S. Steel Corp., 758 F.2d 1462, 1473 (11th Cir. 1985). *See also* Dunlap-McCuller v. Riese Org., 980 F.2d 153, 159 (2d Cir. 1992), *cert. denied*, 510 U.S. 908 (1993); Weaver v. Casa Gallardo, Inc., 922 F.2d 1515, 1528 (11th Cir. 1991); Shorter v. Hartford Fin. Servs. Group, Inc., 2005 U.S. Dist. LEXIS 19902 (D. Conn. 2005); Greene v. Union Mut. Life Ins. Co., 635 F. Supp. 1437, 1438 (D. Me. 1986), Merkel v. Scovill, Inc., 570 F. Supp. 141, 145 (S.D. Ohio 1983).

If judgment is stayed pending appeal, back pay continues until the date of vacation of the stay.[49]

Back pay periods do not necessarily end when the employee would have eventually been laid off or when the place of employment was scheduled to close down. For example, in *Bonura v. Chase Manhattan Bank*,[50] the court found that the back pay period was not terminated when the defendant sold the division in which the plaintiffs worked, particularly when there was evidence that the plaintiffs would have retained their positions after the division had been acquired or would have relocated to other positions with the defendant. Further, retroactive pay is not terminated when the defendant closes one place of operation, especially when the defendant has other locations in the area and it is plausible that the plaintiff could be employed at such other locations.[51]

The duration of back pay can sometimes be affected by the source of the funding for the employee's payroll. For example, in *Welch v. University of Texas & Its Marine Science Institute*,[52] it was determined that if the program in which the plaintiff is employed is funded under subsidy, back pay eligibility is ended upon expiration of such subsidy.

4. Offsets to Back Pay for Collateral Source Payments

Back pay awards serve both purposes of civil rights laws: compensation for victims of discrimination and deterrence of future discrimination.[53] In some cases, plaintiffs who leave a workplace that has violated their Title VII rights have serious psychological consequences that impair their ability to work. If they then receive collateral payments from the government or other sources, an issue arises as to whether the award should offset those payments. The burden is on the employer to prove any offsets to back pay awards from collateral sources.[54]

The collateral source rule "is a substantive rule of law that bars a tortfeasor from reducing damages owed to a plaintiff by the amount of recovery the plaintiff receives from sources that are collateral to the tortfeasor."[55] The purpose of the collateral source rule is not to avoid overcompensating the plaintiff, but to prevent the tortfeasor from paying twice.[56] The rule focuses on what the tortfeasor and collateral source should

---

49. Stewart v. Gen. Motors Corp., 542 F.2d 445 (7th Cir. 1976), *cert. denied*, 433 U.S. 919 (1977) (holding that the cutoff of back pay turns on whether the district court stays the decree pending appeal; if the judgment is not stayed, the cutoff is the date of the decree, but if the judgment is stayed pending appeal, back pay continues until the date of vacation of the stay).

50. 629 F. Supp. 353 (S.D N.Y. 1986), *aff'd*, 795 F.2d 276 (2d Cir. 1986).

51. *See* Gibson v. Mohawk Rubber Co., 695 F.2d 1093, 1097 (8th Cir. 1982).

52. 659 F.2d 531, 535 (5th Cir. 1981).

53. *See* Albermarle Paper Co. v. Moody, 422 U.S. 405, 421 (1975); Gaworski v. ITT Commercial Fin. Corp., 17 F.3d 1104, 1113 (8th Cir. 1994).

54. *See* Rodriguez v. Taylor, 569 F.2d 1231, 1243 (3d Cir. 1977), *rejected on other grounds*, 746 F.2d 998 (3d Cir. 1984).

55. Jackson v. City of Cookeville, 31 F.3d 1354, 1359 (6th Cir. 1994).

56. *See* EEOC v. O'Grady, 857 F.2d 383, 389 (7th Cir. 1988).

pay, not on what the plaintiff should receive.[57] This rule has particular importance in employment discrimination cases where employers attempt to reduce their damages by offering proof that the plaintiff received public assistance or pension benefits after being terminated.

The court in *Toro v. Sanchez* described the collateral source rule in some detail and noted some policy reasons for its existence. Under the collateral source doctrine a plaintiff need not offset his/her recovery from the defendant by the amount of any benefits received from sources independent of those who wronged him/her.[58] In other words, this rule generally allows recovery against a wrongdoer for the full amount of damages even though the injured party is also compensated for some or all of the same damages from a different source independent of the tort-feasor.[59]

Hence, "the collateral source rule is an exception to the general rule that damages in tort should be compensatory only."[60] The purpose behind such a rule or doctrine is to lessen the danger of the jury finding no liability or reducing a damage award "'when it learns that plaintiff's loss is entirely or partially covered.'"[61] Traditionally the rule that collateral benefits are not subtracted from the plaintiff's award of damages has been applied to benefits paid under: (1) an insurance policy or by a relief association; (2) employment benefits; (3) gratuitous payments; (4) social legislation benefits such as social security, welfare, pensions; and (4) benefits received under certain retirement acts. The basic argument advanced for the rule's application is that a tortfeasor should not be allowed to escape the consequences of his wrongful act merely because his/her victim has received a benefit from a collateral source, which would constitute a windfall to the defendant wrongdoer.

Another argument in its favor is that in many instances the plaintiff has paid for these benefits in the form of insurance premiums or concessions in the wages he received because of such fringe benefits. If such considerations are not present and the payments are gratuitous, it is maintained that the maker of the payments did not intend to relieve the tortfeasor of any liability, but rather to aid the plaintiff by doing him/her a favor. It is also argued that the collateral source rule is designed to offset the inability of ordinary damages to adequately compensate an injured accident victim.[62,63]

---

57. *Id.* at 390.

58. *See* England v. Reinauer Transportation Companies, L.P., 194 F.3d 265, 273–74 (1st Cir. 1999); McGrath v. Consolidated Rail Corp., 136 F.3d 838, 839 (1st Cir. 1998) (citing Lussier v. Runyon, 50 F.3d 1103, 1107 (1st Cir. 1995).

59. *See* Reilly v. U.S., 863 F.2d 149, 165 (1st Cir. 1988).

60. Joel K. Jacobsen, *The Collateral Source Rule and the Role of the Jury,* 70 Or.L.Rev. 523, 524 (1991).

61. *Id.* (quoting Moses v. Union Pac. R.R., 64 F.3d 413, 416 (8th Cir. 1995). *See also* Tipton v. Socony Mobil Oil Co., 375 U.S. 34, 36–37, 84 S. Ct. 1, 2–3, 11 L. Ed. 2d 4 (1963) (per curiam).

62. *See* Clausen v. Sea-3, Inc., 21 F.3d 1181, 1192–94 (1st Cir. 1994).

63. 141 F. Supp. 2d 195, 196–97 (D.P.R. 2001).

As a general rule, evidence of income from collateral sources is inadmissible and cannot be offset against damages in an employment discrimination case.[64] One key factor in determining whether funds are collateral is whether the payment is from the employer itself. Payments from a separate and distinct entity supported partly by contributions from the defendant are collateral and may not be offset against a damage award.[65] This means that payments pursuant to state or federal social policy are collateral.[66] However, payments that the employer assumes voluntarily and intends to avoid later are not.

The collateral source rule, however, is difficult to apply in practice. Whether income from other sources is collateral, and thus immune from offset, depends on the jurisdiction, the source of the income, and, sometimes, on whether the defendant seeks an offset to an award of back pay or front pay.

a. Government Assistance

The collateral source rule arises most frequently in Title VII cases where constructively discharged or intentionally discharged employees receive government assistance payments as a result of the discharge. The federal courts are badly splintered on whether government assistance payments may be offset against a plaintiff's recovery. None, however, appear to require that such payments be offset. Instead, the issue is whether the district court retains the discretion to deduct collateral benefits from back pay awards or whether deduction is prohibited as a matter of law.

i. Whether the Decision to Offset Is a Matter for the District Court's Discretion

A brief survey reveals that the Court of Appeals for the Second, Fifth, Seventh, Ninth, Tenth, and D.C. circuits leave the decision to offset income received from government assistance programs to the district court's discretion.[67] The Court of Appeals for the First Circuit has not definitively ruled, but has expressed a willingness to leave this

---

64. *See Gaworski*, 17 F.3d at 1112–13; Thurman v. Yellow Freight Sys., Inc., 90 F.3d 1160 (6th Cir. 1996).

65. *Id.*

66. *See* NLRB v. Gullett Gin Co., 340 U.S. 361, 364 (1951) (rejecting argument that unemployment insurance is direct rather than collateral benefit because "payments . . . were not made to discharge any liability or obligation . . . but to carry out a policy of social betterment for the benefit of the entire state"); Clark v. Burlington N., Inc., 726 F.2d 448, 450 (8th Cir. 1984).

67. *See* Dailey v. Societe Generale, 108 F.3d 451 (2d Cir. 1997) (leaving decision to deduct unemployment from Title VII back pay within discretion of district court); Swanks v. Wash. Metro Area Transit Auth., 325 U.S. App. D.C. 238 (D.C. Cir. 1997) (holding that deduction of collateral courses of income from a back pay award is a matter within the trial court's discretion); Naton v. Bank of Cal., 649 F.2d 691, 700 (9th Cir. 1981) (holding that a district court has the discretion to deduct in ADEA cases); Hunter v. Allis-Chalmers Corp., 797 F.2d 1417, 1429 (7th Cir. 1986) (acknowledging discretion as Seventh Circuit rule but stating that it "may be unduly favorable to defendants"), *abrogation on other grounds recognized by* Manhotra v. Cotter & Co., 885 F.2d 1305, 1312 (7th Cir. 1989); Green v. Denver & Rio Grande W. R.R. Co., 59 F.3d 1029, 1032 (10th Cir. 1995) (noting that Tenth Circuit placed decision to offset funds involving state treasury in district court's discretion but acknowledging that some confusion may result from this approach); Guthrie v. J.C. Penney Co., 803 F.2d 202, 209 (5th Cir. 1986) (discretionary decision).

decision to the discretion of the district court.[68] As a result, precedent within these circuits is often conflicting and determination of whether an offset is appropriate is exceedingly difficult.

However, other courts retain per se rules as to what type of benefits a trial court can or must deduct from back pay.[69] For example, the Third, Sixth, Eighth, and Eleventh circuits hold as a matter of law that government assistance payments may not be deducted.[70] Although Ninth Circuit precedent is conflicting on this issue, the more recent cases withdraw discretion from the district court.[71] These circuits opt for a per se rule to avoid the arbitrary and inconsistent outcomes arising from leaving the matter to the discretion of the district courts.

ii. Offsets for Government Assistance Payments

Courts disagree whether social security benefits should be deducted from back pay. The "per se" circuits prohibit offset of these payments against back pay awards.[72] Not surprisingly, precedent in those circuits that give district courts discretion to offset social security payments is inconsistent.[73]

The per se circuits generally refuse to deduct unemployment compensation benefits from back pay awards.[74] These holdings derive from the US Supreme Court's decision in *NLRB v. Gullett Gin Co.*, which held that the National Labor Relations Board (NLRB) did not abuse its discretion by refusing to offset state unemployment benefits against

---

68. *See* Lussier v. Runyon, 50 F.3d 1103, 1109 (1st Cir. 1995).

69. *See* Thurman v. Yellow Freight Sys. Inc., 90 F.3d 1160, 1171 (6th Cir.); Maxfield v. Sinclair Int'l, 766 F.2d 788, 793–95 (3d Cir. 1985) (holding that social security benefits could not offset an ADEA award); Arneson v. Callahan, 128 F.3d 1243, 1247–48 (8th Cir. 1997); Doyne v. Union Elec. Co., 953 F.2d 447, 451 (8th Cir. 1992); Salitros v. Chrysler Corp., 306 F.3d 562, 573 (8th Cir. 2002) ("Our circuit has treated the reduction of pay awards by other benefits as a legal question, rather than as something entrusted to the district court's discretion.").

70. *See* Hamlin v. Charter Twp. of Flint, 165 F.3d 426, 433 (6th Cir. 1999); Dominguez v. Tom James Co., 113 F.3d 1188, 1191 (11th Cir. 1997); Gaworski v. ITT Commercial Fin. Corp., 17 F.3d 1104, 1114 (8th Cir. 1994); Maxfield v. Sinclair Int'l, 766 F.2d 788, 795 (3d Cir. 1985).

71. *Compare* Kauffman v. Sidereal Corp., 695 F.2d 343, 346–47 (9th Cir. 1982), *with* Nation v. Bank of Cal., 649 F.2d 691, 700 (9th Cir. 1981) (holding that district court possesses discretion to deduct collateral benefits from back pay awards in ADEA case).

72. *See, e.g., Dominguez*, 113 F.3d at 1191 ("Social Security benefits should not be deducted from [a plaintiff's] damage award."); Maxfield v. Sinclair Int'l, 766 F.2d 788, 795 (3d Cir. 1985).

73. *Compare* EEOC v. Wyo. Ret. Sys., 771 F.2d 1425 (10th Cir. 1985) (approving, where state was defendant, trial court's decision to offset back pay by amounts received from social security because otherwise the state treasury would have to finance a windfall for plaintiffs), *with* Whatley v. Skaggs Cos., 707 F.2d 1129, 1138 & n.8 (10th Cir.) (affirming trial court's refusal to deduct social security from back pay awards; finding that the plaintiff would not have suffered the injury had defendant not terminated him and thereby forced him to take job performing manual labor).

74. *See, e.g.,* Brown v. A.J. Gerrard Mfg. Co., 715 F.2d 1549 (11th Cir. 1983) (*en banc*) (unemployment compensation, even if supported by tax on employers, may not be deducted from Title VII back pay); Thurman v. Yellow Freight Sys., Inc., 90 F.3d 1160 (6th Cir. 1996) (same); Craig v. Y & Y Snacks, Inc., 721 D.2d 77, 81–85 (3d Cir. 1983) (same).

back pay awards.[75] The Court of Appeals for the Ninth Circuit would apparently follow suit.[76] Once again, there is conflicting authority in those circuits that grant the district court discretion to offset unemployment benefits.[77] These circuits have not developed general rules to guide the district courts in exercising their discretion, and there is often little to distinguish the cases.

At least one court has required that the portion of workers' compensation benefits attributable to lost wages be deducted from a back pay award.[78] However, many more courts have refused to deduct such benefits, arguing that workers' compensation benefits are collateral in nature and hence not deductible.[79]

Courts are similarly torn on whether disability benefits are to be deducted from back pay liability.[80]

At least one court has found that welfare benefits are not part of a claimant's interim earnings for purposes of deducting from back pay.[81] Retroactive wages, however, are subject to deductions based upon the claimant's receipt of food stamp allowances.[82]

Even in the circuits that have adopted per se rules against offsetting government assistance payments, such an offset may be appropriate for government employers if a statute authorizes the state to recoup its public assistance payments.[83] In these cases,

---

75. 340 U.S. 361, 364 (1951).

76. *See* Kaufman v. Sidereal Corp., 695 F.2d 343, 347 (9th Cir. 1982) (holding in a Title VII case that "unemployment benefits received by a successful plaintiff . . . are not offsets against a back pay award"); *but see* Nation v. Bank of Cal., 649 F.2d 691, 700 (9th Cir. 1981) (earlier case holding that district court possesses discretion to deduct collateral benefits from back pay awards in ADEA case).

77. *Compare* Dailey v. Societe Generale, 108 F.3d 451 (2d Cir. 1997) (upholding refusal to deduct unemployment from Title VII backset), *with* EEOC v. Enter. Ass'n Steamfitters Local No. 638, 542 F.2d 579, 591–92 (2d Cir. 1976) (allowing district courts to offset public assistance payment against a Title VII back pay award). *Also compare* Hunter v. Allis-Chalmers Corp., 797 F.2d 1417, 1429 (7th Cir. 1986), *abrogation on other grounds recognized by* Malhotra v. Cotter & Co., 885 F.2d 1305, 1312 (7th Cir. 1989) (not abuse of discretion to refuse to deduct unemployment benefits from back pay), *with* Orzel v. City of Wauwatosa Fire Dept, 697 F.2d 743, 756 (7th Cir.) (approving decision to deduct unemployment and retirement pension benefits).

78. EEOC v. Blue & White Serv. Corp., 674 F. Supp. 1579 (D. Minn. 1987) (Title VII case).

79. *See, e.g.*, Moysis v. DTG Datanet, 278 F.3d 819, 828 (8th Cir. 2002); Thurman v. Yellow Freight Sys., Inc., 90 F.3d 1160, 1171 (6th Cir. 1996); Brownlow v. Edgecomb Metals Co., 1987 U.S. Dist. LEXIS 15081 (N.D. Ohio 1987); Adams v. Doehler-Jarvis, 144 Mich. App. 764, 376 N.W. 2d 406 (1985); Eide v. Kelsey Haves Co., 154 Mich. App. 142, 397 N.W. 2d 532 (1986).

80. *E.g., compare* Whatley v. Skaggs Co., 707 F.2d 1129 (10th Cir.), *cert. denied*, 464 U.S. 938 (1983) (holding that disability benefits are from a collateral source and are not to be deducted from back pay liability), *with* Smith v. Office of Pers. Mgmt., 778 F.2d 258 (5th Cir. 1985) (deducting plaintiff's disability compensation from his recovery under the ADEA).

81. Falls Stamping & Welding Co. v. Int'l Union. United Auto.. Workers, 485 F. Supp. 1097, 1148 (N.D. Ohio 1979), *aff'd without opinion*, 667 F.2d 1026 (6th Cir. 1981).

82. *Id.*

83. *See, e.g.,* Gaworski v. ITT Commercial Fin. Corp., 17 F.3d 1104, 1114 (8th Cir. 1994) (offset may be appropriate if state seeks to recoup its payments); Dillon v. Coles, 746 F.2d 998 (3d Cir. 1984) (proper to offset back pay by amounts received from public assistance where employer was state and had the right to recoup benefits it had paid); Gelof v. Papineau, 829 F.2d 452 (3d Cir. 1987) (state could not set off unemployment benefits where statute did not provide for recoupment).

allowing an offset improves efficiency by eliminating the need for a separate action for recoupment. However, this does not mean that state the defendants may automatically offset public assistance payments.[84]

b. Offsets for Insurance Benefits

The availability and value of lost insurance benefits (health, disability, and life) is a hot litigation issue today. A number of courts have held that the plaintiff should be reimbursed for any health, life, or other insurance premiums that the employer would have paid, in whole or in part, but for the plaintiff's termination. When the plaintiff has not purchased alternative coverage, some courts have held that the trial court had discretion to decline to include health insurance premiums in the plaintiff's award.[85]

Some courts have held that the plaintiff is entitled to recover medical expenses that would have been covered by the defendant's medical insurance had the plaintiff remained employed.[86] The Fourth Circuit, however, has taken a contrary view, even when the employee had died and there was, accordingly, a loss under a life insurance policy. In *Fariss v. Lynchburg Foundry*,[87] the plaintiff, the wife of a deceased employee, claimed that she was entitled to recover the proceeds of a life insurance policy that she would have received had her husband not been terminated by the defendant. The defendant argued that the plaintiff was only allowed to recover the premiums she or her husband would have paid because of the discharge. In rejecting the plaintiff's argument, the court noted that the deceased employee had the option to convert his group life insurance to an individual policy, but declined to do so, and there was no evidence introduced to show that the employee had attempted to secure other coverage. The court reasoned that it was unfair to penalize an employer for lost benefits in any amount beyond the cost of the premiums because the employer elects to limit its insurance liability by paying premiums to a third-party carrier. From a plaintiff's standpoint,

---

84. *Compare* Gelof v. Papineau, 829 F.2d 452 (3d Cir. 1987) (no offset for state defendant where no statute provided for recoupment), *with* EEOC v. Wyo. Ret. Sys., 771 F.2d 1425 (10th Cir. 1985) (approving state defendant's offset of social security payments to save state treasury from financing a windfall for plaintiffs, even though there was no indication of a state statute allowing recoupment).

85. *See, e.g.*, Swock v. Milwaukee Boiler Mfg. Co., 665 F.2d 149 (7th Cir. 1981); Bucholz v. Symons Mfg. Co., 445 F. Supp. 706 (E.D. Pa. 1978); Coston v. Plitt Theatres, 831 F.2d 1321 (7th Cir. 1987); Merriweather v. Hercules. Inc., 631 F.2d 1161 (5th Cir. 1980) (Title VII case).

86. *See, e.g.*, Davis v. Ingersoll Johnson Steel Co., 628 F. Supp. 25 (S.D. Ind. 1985) (medical expenses incurred by plaintiff were recoverable in ADEA action); Bempah v. Kroger Co., 51 FEP Cases(BNA) 195, 202 (S.D. Ga. 1989) ("if plaintiff purchased substitute insurance coverage . . . or if he incurred uninsured, out-of-pocket medical expenses for which he would have been reimbursed under defendant's insurance plan, then he is entitled to recover any funds he expended as a result of defendant's failure to accord him full-time status"); Merkel v. Scovill. Inc., 570 F. Supp. 141 (S.D. Ohio 1983), *aff'd in part, rev'd in part*, 787 F.2d 174 (6th Cir.); Spagnuolo v. Whirlpool Corp., 550 F. Supp. 432 (W.D.N.C. 1982), *aff'd in part, rev'd in part on other grounds*, 717 F.2d 114 (4th Cir. 1983); Foster v. Excelsior Springs City Hosp. & Convalescent Ctr., 631 F. Supp. 174, 175 (W.D. Mo. 1986) (medical bills recoverable when plaintiff is uninsurable except through defendant's group insurance plan).

87. 769 F.2d 958 (4th Cir. 1985).

this argument misses the mark: the make-whole remedy of the Age Discrimination in Employment Act (ADEA) was not intended to keep the employer whole, but to compensate the plaintiff for what she has incurred as a result of the job loss.

c. Offsets for Pension Payments

The courts are split on the question of whether pension benefits should be offset against damages awards. The employer's contribution to the pension fund is often more direct than other collateral sources such as public assistance payments, making the collateral source inquiry more problematic. However, the important question is not solely whether the funds come directly from the employer. Instead, the court must ask whether the funds are fringe benefits that are effectively part of the employee's compensation or whether the benefit was intended to relieve the employer of future liability.[88] The cases suggest that pension benefits should be offset only when failure to do so would result in double-payment by the employer.

The Court of Appeals for the Third Circuit has adopted a per se rule that pension benefits are collateral and may not be offset against back pay awards.[89] The rationale for these holdings is that pension plans are indistinguishable from forms of government assistance because both "are designed to serve social policies independent of those served by back pay awards. The employer contributes to both forms of benefits either directly or indirectly."[90]

Cases in other circuits generally prohibit offset of pension payments against an award of back pay unless an offset is necessary to prevent the employer from paying twice. In *Glover v. McDonnell Douglas Corp.,* the court held that regardless of how the pension plan was funded, an offset was appropriate to prevent the plaintiff from being placed in a better position than if he had never been terminated.[91] The plaintiff in Glover began receiving payments after his discharge. The district judge ordered reinstatement and back pay, and also ordered the employer to supplement the plaintiff's pension plan so that the plaintiff, upon retiring, would receive benefits as though he had never been discharged.[92]

The Court of Appeals for the Eighth Circuit held that unless the employer could reduce the back pay award by the amount paid from the pension plan, the plaintiff would be placed in a better than whole position. Although this language suggests that the crucial inquiry is whether the plaintiff is recovering twice, the likely basis for the decision is that requiring the defendant to make a fully compensatory back pay award

---

88. *See* Clark v. Burlington N., Inc., 726 F.2d 448, 450 (8th Cir. 1984).

89. *See, e.g.,* Maxfield v. Sinclair Int'l, 766 F.2d 788, 795 (3d Cir. 1985) ("There are no significant discernible differences between Social Security benefits, unemployment benefits and pension benefits. . . ."); McDowell v. Avtex Fiber, Inc., 740 F.2d 214, 217 (3d Cir. 1984), *vacated and remanded on other grounds,* 469 U.S. 1202 (1985).

90. *McDowell,* 740 F.2d at 217.

91. 12 F.3d 845, 848 (8th Cir.) (referring to discussion in earlier opinion at 981 F.2d 388, 396).

92. *Id.*

and augment the employee's pension plan to offset the benefits paid as a result of the termination forces the defendant to pay twice.[93]

Cases from the Court of Appeals for the Seventh Circuit also support the notion that pension funds should not be offset against damages awards unless failing to do so would force the defendant to pay twice. In *EEOC v. O'Grady,* for example, the Seventh Circuit approved the district court's refusal to offset pension benefits against a back pay award.[94] The plaintiff was employed by the county, which contributed to the county retirement fund. Payments from the fund, however, were supported by contributions from many employers.[95] The Seventh Circuit allowed a fully compensatory back pay award without setoff, because the county would have had to contribute to the fund and pay the employee's salary even if it had not discriminated.[96]

The court noted, however, that the county did not appeal the district court's order to compensate the pension fund so that the plaintiff would receive the same pension he would have received had he not been terminated.[97] Thus, there remains the possibility that an award similar to that awarded by the Eighth Circuit in Glover would require an offset of pension benefits. The Sixth Circuit has likewise disapproved offsetting pension benefits against damages awards, at least where the employer is not the direct source of the pension benefits.[98]

Appellate courts rarely reverse a district court's decision not to offset pension benefits. The few cases that do are limited to pension and severance payments made directly and solely by the employer.[99]

d. Improper Use of Evidence of Collateral Source Payments

In all cases the judge should determine whether the collateral sources should be offset, and no evidence of collateral sources should be shared with the jury. The proper analogy here is to Rule 411 of the Federal Rules of Evidence. This rule rejects evidence of liability insurance to prove fault to avoid the possibility that juries would "decide cases on improper grounds."[100] Courts should view evidence of recovery from other sources with similar skepticism, because this evidence is typically offered to color the jury's

---

93. *Id.* at 396–97; *accord* Doyne v. Union Elec. Co., 953 F.2d 447, 451 (8th Cir. 1992) (holding that pension payments were collateral and could not be offset against an ADEA judgment, because an independent retirement plan, rather than the employer, was responsible for the payments).

94. 857 F.2d 383 (7th Cir. 1988).

95. *Id.* at 388–91.

96. *Id.*

97. *Id.*

98. Hamlin v. Charter Twp. of Flint, 165 F.3d 426, 433–35 (6th Cir. 1999) (distinguishing Sixth Circuit cases to the contrary as dependent on peculiar facts).

99. *See, e.g.,* EEOC v. Sandia Corp., 639 F.2d 600, 626–27 (10th Cir. 1980) (setoff for "law off allowances" coming directly from employer); Guthrie v. J.C. Penney Co., 803 F.2d 202 (5th Cir. 1986) (setoff for payments received from defendant's own retirement fund).

100. *See* FED. R. EVID. 411 cmt.

determination of the defendant's fault. As the Court of Appeals for the Eighth Circuit recently stated:

> [A] plaintiff's collateral sources of compensation cannot be inquired into as part of a defendant's case, because of the danger that the jury may be included to find no liability, or to reduce a damage award, when it learns that plaintiff's loss is entirely or partially covered.[101]

e. Vacation and Paid Leave

Depending on the defendant's vacation policy, lost vacation may be compensated in an ADEA suit. A defendant should argue that vacation pay beyond what occurred before the termination date is not recoverable because a back pay award would cover any lost vacation pay since an employee is only compensated for a total of fifty-two weeks per year. This argument loses its merit, however, if the defendant has a policy of allowing employees to work in lieu of vacation, or if the plaintiff has secured employment after termination but earns less vacation.[102] But a plaintiff still must prove, with reasonable certainty, entitlement to the benefit claimed.[103]

5. Adjusting Back Pay Awards to Compensate for Tax Consequences

Both back pay and front pay awards are ordinarily taxable events.[104] Where back pay awards are taxable,[105] plaintiffs should request an adjustment to the jury's verdict to compensate for the increased tax burden resulting from a lump sum payment. This burden results from the high tax bracket in which the lump sum is taxed, as opposed to the lower bracket that would have applied had the plaintiff received wages as scheduled. Although there is little law in this area, especially regarding the method for computing such an adjustment, the majority of the courts that have addressed this issue have concluded that such "gross up" or "tax bump" relief is an appropriate way to adjust for adverse consequences and to ensure the plaintiff is, in fact, made whole by the damages award.[106]

---

101. Porchia v. Design Equip. Co., 113 F.3d 877, 882 (8th Cir. 1997).

102. *See, e.g.*, Bonura v. Chase Manhattan. N.A., 629 F. Supp. 353 (S.D.N.Y 1986), *aff'd*,795 F.2d 276 (2d Cir. 1986).

103. *See* Sennello v. Reserve Life Ins. Co., 667 F. Supp. 1498, 1517 (S.D. Fla. 1987), *aff'd*, 872 F.2d 393 (11th Cir. 1989) (court refused to award plaintiff $4,000 for claimed lost "vacation and conventions," even in absence of an objection from the defendant, when plaintiff could not substantiate the amounts claimed).

104. *See, e.g.*, Comm'r of Internal Revenue v. Schleier, 515 U.S. 323 at 330, (1995) (noting that damages awards under the ADEA are ordinarily taxable); United States v. Burke, 504 U.S. 229 at 241, (1992) (noting that Title VII damages compensate aggrieved plaintiffs for "wages that, if paid in the ordinary course, would have been fully taxable."); Novak v. Andersen Corp., 962 F.2d 757 (8th Cir. 1992); Tanaka v. Dep't of Navy, 788 F.2d 1552, 1553 (Fed. Cir. 1986); Blim v. W. Elec. Co., 731 F.2d 1473, 1479 (10th Cir. 1984); Volkman v. United Transp. Union, 826 F. Supp. 1253 (D. Kan. 1993). Rev. Rule. 78–336, 1978-2C.B.255.

105. Comm'r of the Internal Revenue v. Schleier, 515 U.S. 323 (1995).

106. *See, e.g.*, Norfolk & W. Ry. Co. v. Liepelt, 444 U.S. 490, 494 (1980) ("It follows inexorably that the wage earner's income tax is a relevant factor in calculating the monetary losses suffered by his dependent's when he dies."). In *Liepelt*, the Supreme Court expressed a concern that the jury might incorrectly

In *Gelof v. Papineau,* for example, the district court included as an element of damages an amount to compensate plaintiff for the increased tax burden of a lump sum back pay award.[107] The defendant contested only the amount of the award. The Court of Appeals for the Third Circuit approved the award, but reserved judgment as to whether such an award is appropriate in all back pay cases. The court vacated and remanded, however, for a more accurate determination of the amount necessary to compensate for the increased tax.[108]

As Gelof makes clear, an income tax adjustment due to a lump sum payment is warranted only where the court has sufficient evidence to calculate an appropriate adjustment.[109] Where the plaintiff fails to present evidence of the increased income tax liability resulting from a lump sum damage award, a trial court's denial of a tax enhancement will rarely be overturned.[110] Some courts, however, may be willing to adjust for the increased tax by computing prejudgment interest on gross instead of net back pay. Thus the court relieves plaintiffs of the need to specify a method for

---

assume that its award was taxable and hence "gross up" its award accordingly without any instruction to do so. In sum, the Supreme Court concluded that the tax effect should be presented to the jury in making its damage assessment. Explaining this decision, the Court observed: "[I]t surely is not proper for the Judiciary to ignore the demonstrably relevant factor of income tax in measuring damages. . . ." 444 U.S. at 495–96. *See also* Eshelman v. Agere Sys., Inc., 554 F.3d 426 (3d Cir. 2009) (holding a trial judge may gross up a back pay award in order to offset additional taxes that the plaintiff will owe due to a lump sum award); Starceski v. Westinghouse Elec. Corp., 54 F.3d 1089 (3d Cir. 1995); Gelof v. Papineau, 829 F.2d 452 (3d Cir. 1987) (allowing damages to compensate plaintiff for increased tax burden caused because of a single lump sum award); Sears v. Acheson, Topeka & Kan. City Ry. Co., 749 F.2d 1451, 1456 (10th Cir. 1984) (allowing an increase in award for back pay in order to compensate for the resultant tax burden from receiving a lump sum of more than 17 years in back pay); Jordan v. CCH, Inc., 230 F. Supp. 603 (E.D. Pa. 2002); O'Neill v. Sears Roebuck & Co., 108 F. Supp. 2d 443 (E.D. Pa. 2000) (holding that plaintiff was entitled to an award in the amount of the negative tax consequences on his back pay and front pay awards); EEOC v. Joe's Stone Crab, Inc., 15 F. Supp. 2d 1364 (S.D. Fla. 1998) (citing *Sears* with approval but holding that such a tax bump required a sufficient evidentiary foundation); Cooper v. Paychex, Inc., 960 F. Supp. 966, 975 (E.D. Va. 1997) (citing *Gelof* and *Sears* with approval); Gregg D. Polsky & Stephen F. Befort, *Employment Discrimination Remedies and Tax Gross Ups*, 90 Iowa L. Rev. 67 (2004); Laura Sager & Stephen Cohen, *How the Income Tax Undermines Civil Rights Law*, 73 So. Cal. L. Rev. 1075 (2000). *But see* Fogg v. Gonzales, 492 F.3d 447 (D.C. Cir. 2007) (reversing the trial court's award of a tax gross-up because it failed to consider a relevant factor when it did not distinguish *Dashnaw*, "a facially applicable precedent of this circuit"); Dashnaw v. Pena, 12 F.3d 1112 (D.C. Cir. 1994) (holding that, despite the multitude of cases listed above, there was a "complete lack of support in existing case law for tax gross-ups" and therefore declining to grant one in this case); *cf.* Porter v. U.S. Agency for Int'l Dev., 29 F. Supp. 2d 152 (D.D.C. 2003) (holding that the court could enter "a gross-up order in the exercise of the 'full equitable powers' I have to effectuate the purposes of Title VII." The court distinguished this case from *Dashnaw* because *Dashnaw* involved a lump sum back pay award and in this case the tax gross-up related to an award of attorney's fees.).

107. 829 F.2d 452, 455–56 (3d Cir. 1987).

108. *Id. See also* Sears v. Acheson, Topeka, & Kan. City Ry. Co., 749 F.2d 1451, 1456 (10th Cir. 1984) (approving increase in back pay award to compensate for additional taxes resulting from receiving more than 17 years of back pay in one award).

109. *See* Hukkanen v. Int'l Union of Oper. Eng'rs, 3 F.3d 281, 287 (8th Cir. 1993).

110. *Id.* (trial court did not abuse its discretion in denying a request for an enhanced monetary award where plaintiff did not prove the amount of the tax burden).

computing the tax adjustment.[111] If at all possible, however, plaintiffs should present evidence of the amount of or means to calculate the award.

Not all courts consider such an adjustment to be appropriate relief, holding that "the general rule that victims of discrimination should be made whole does not support 'gross-ups' of back pay to cover tax liability."[112] Nonetheless, it behooves plaintiffs to request a damages adjustment to ensure that back pay awards are fully compensatory.

Further, since both back pay and front pay awards are ordinarily taxed, juries and courts should not deduct from back pay and/or front pay awards the amounts that the plaintiff would have ordinarily paid in income, social security, and similar taxes, because such a ruling would effectively tax the plaintiff's award twice.[113]

B. Front Pay Damages

1. Availability of Front Pay Awards Generally

In *Pollard v. E.I. du Pont de Nemours & Co.,* the US Supreme Court stated, "In cases in which reinstatement is not viable because of continuing hostility between the plaintiff and the employer or its workers, or because of psychological injuries suffered by the plaintiff as a result of the discrimination, courts have ordered front pay as a substitute for reinstatement."[114] The court went on to say that "Front pay is simply money awarded for lost compensation during the period between judgment and reinstatement or in lieu of reinstatement."[115] Several courts have made explicit reference to the fact that front pay is an equitable remedy, granted as an alternative to reinstatement.[116]

Absent reinstatement, the trial court has discretion to award front pay based on a reasonable prediction of the plaintiff's continued employment expectancy. The court's sound discretion is subject to common sense limitations, as noted in *Davis v. Combustion Engineering, Inc.:*

---

111. *See* Cooper v. Paychex, Inc., 960 F. Supp. 966, 975–76 (E.D. Va. 1997), *aff'd*, 163 F.3d 598 (4th Cir. 1998) (applying prejudgment interest to the gross, rather than net, damage award, in part to compensate plaintiff for the additional tax burden of receiving a lump sum payment); Artis v. U.S. Indus., 822 F. Supp. 510 (N.D. Ill. 1993).

112. Dashnaw v. Pena, 12 F.3d 1112, 1116 (D.C. Cir 1994).

113. *See, e.g.,* Robinson v. SEPTA, 982 F.2d 892 (3d Cir. 1993) (noting that back pay awards under Title VII are taxable, and noting the potential double taxation potential of not taking federal income tax into account for damages purposes); Rasimas v. Mich. Dep't of Mental Health, 714 F.2d 614, 627 (6th Cir. 1983) ("backpay awards should not be reduced by the amount of income and social security taxes which would have been deducted from the wages the plaintiff would have received but for the discrimination"); EEOC v. Ky. State Police Dep't, 80 F.3d 1086 (6th Cir. 1996).

114. 532 U.S. 843, 846 (2001).

115. *Id.; see also* Abuan v. Level 3 Commc'ns, Inc., 353 F.3d 1158, 1176 (10th Cir. 2003).

116. *See* Rogers v. AC Humko Corp., 56 F. Supp. 2d 972, 978 (D. Tenn. 1999); Cline v. Wal-Mart Stores, Inc., 144 F.3d 294, 307 (4th Cir. 1998) (holding that under the FMLA front pay is an equitable remedy substitutable for reinstatement).

For example, the award of front pay to a discriminatorily discharged 41 year old employee until such time as he qualifies for a pension might be unwarranted. On the other hand, the failure to make such an award for an employee age 63, likewise discriminatorily discharged, might be an abuse of discretion.[117]

Front pay may be awarded in lieu of reinstatement "only after reinstatement is dismissed as a realistic alternative."[118] Although front pay sometimes is an appropriate remedy, it is not a mandatory remedy.[119] Normally, the courts consider whether there is a position available and whether the relationship between the parties has been irreparably damaged by animosity or extreme hostility so that reinstatement is impracticable.[120] Reinstatement may not be appropriate, for instance, because of a hostile working environment.[121] However, the Second Circuit held that hostility generated from the heat of litigation is not a sufficient reason to deny reinstatement.[122] The fact that the plaintiff did not hold a position that was unique or unusually sensitive argues in favor of reinstatement.[123]

Among the situations that have been deemed appropriate for an award of front pay are as follows:

- "The employer has exhibited such extreme hostility that, as a practical matter, a productive and amicable working relationship would be impossible."[124]
- No comparable positions are available.[125]
- A promotion will be delayed,[126] or a job opening is not immediately available.[127]
- The employer-employee relationship has been irreparably damaged by animosity caused by the lawsuit.[128]
- The fact finder can reasonably predict that the plaintiff has no reasonable prospect of obtaining comparable alternative employment.[129]
- The time period for which front pay is to be awarded is relatively short (that is, the plaintiff is very close to retirement).[130]

---

117. 742 F.2d 916, 922 (6th Cir. 1984).

118. O'Donnell v. Ga. Osteopathic Hosp., Inc., 748 F.2d 1543, 1551–52 (11th Cir. 1984).

119. Starrett v. Wadley, 51 FEP Cases (BNA) 608, 619 (10th Cir. 1989); Shore v. Fed. Express Corp., 777 F.2d 1155, 1159 (6th Cir. 1985).

120. *See, e.g.,* Maxfield v. Sinclair Int'l, 766 F.2d 788, 796 (3d Cir. 1985).

121. *See, e.g.,* Thome v. City of El Segundo, 802 F.2d 1131 (9th Cir. 1986).

122. Whittlesey v. Union Carbide Corp., 742 F.2d 724, 728–29 (2d Cir. 1984).

123. *See, e.g.,* Dickerson v. Deluxe Check Printers, Inc., 703 F.2d 276, 281 (8th Cir. 1983); Armsev v. Nestle Co., 631 F. Supp. 717 (S.D. Ohio 1985).

124. EEOC v. Prudential Fed. Sav. & Loan Ass'n, 763 F.2d 1166, 1172 (10th Cir. 1985).

125. Whittlesey v. Union Carbide Corp., 742 F.2d 724, 728 (2d Cir. 1984).

126. EEOC v. Safeway Stores, Inc., 634 F.2d 1273 (10th Cir. 1980), *cert. denied.* 451 U.S. 986 (1981).

127. Nord v. U.S. Steel Corp., 758 F.2d 1462 (11th Cir. 1985).

128. *Id.*

129. McNeil v. Econ. Lab., Inc., 800 F.2d 111, 118 (7th Cir. 1986).

130. *Id.* at 118.

A plaintiff has the burden of proving that front pay should be awarded and of producing evidence necessary for the jury or court to make an award. Evidence presented should include the plaintiff's prospects for future employment, how long such employment would last, and, if bonuses and commissions are elements of damage, how those would be forecast. Moreover, the plaintiff should introduce evidence on availability of liquidated damages and the appropriate discount rate.[131]

Of necessity, evidence introduced by plaintiffs on the propriety of a front pay award and factors supporting that award will be speculative. Such speculation is no defense to the employer, and the vigilant defendant will introduce countervailing evidence in an attempt to minimize or defeat front pay.

2. Offsets to Front Pay Awards

Some courts may be more willing to offset payments from collateral sources against front pay awards. The leading case in this area is *Lussier v. Runyon*. In this case, the Court of Appeals for the First Circuit upheld a decision to offset an award of front pay by the increased amount of disability benefits the plaintiff would receive due to his discriminatory discharge.[132] In doing so, the court held that deducting collateral benefits from front pay is within the equitable discretion of the trial court. The court noted that the appellate courts are split on whether the treatment of collateral benefits in determining back pay should be left to the district court's discretion. It stated that to confer discretion on the trial courts in awarding front pay is "an easier call" because of the speculative nature of front pay.[133]

The fact that front pay is an equitable remedy suggested to the court "that the logically derivative question of whether a front pay award, if granted, may be tailored to take collateral benefits into account is also within the court's equitable discretion."[134] Finally, the court downplayed the decreased deterrent effect resulting from allowing an offset of pension benefits:

> [A]s between the two primary statutory purposes, the goal of compensation, and not deterrence, is likely the more important in regard to front pay. . . . For that reason, an abuse of discretion ordinarily will not lie when the trial court, in the process of making the plaintiff whole—no more, no less—happens to produce a marginal diminution of deterrence.[135]

---

131. Coston v. Plitt Theatres, Inc., 831 F.2d 1321 (7th Cir. 1987), *cert. denied*, 485 U.S. 1007 (1988), *vacated on other grounds*, 486 U.S. 1020 (1988). *See generally* Jones & Laughlin Steel Corp. v. Pfeifer, 462 U.S. 523 (1983) (determining discount rates).

132. 50 F.3d 1103 (1st Cir. 1995).

133. *Id.* at 1109.

134. *Id.* at 1108.

135. *Id.* at 1112 n.10; *see also* Johnson v. Chapel Hill Ind. Sch. Dist., 853 F.2d 375, 382 (5th Cir. 1988) ("The district court has discretion to decide whether unemployment compensation should be deducted from a back pay or front pay award."). The court in *Lussier* relied on a series of holdings from other circuits. On closer look, however, these cases do not support the First Circuit's opinion. *Lussier* cited *Hukkanen v. Int'l Union of Operating Eng'rs*, 3 F.3d 281, 286 (8th Cir. 1993), as Eighth Circuit precedent allowing deduction of collateral income from front pay, citing language that "calculation of front pay . . . is a matter

The collateral source rule does not exist to limit what plaintiffs may recover in any way. Instead, the rule ensures that defendants do not pay twice for their wrongdoing.[136] The proper focus is on what the tortfeasor should pay, not on what the plaintiff should receive.[137] Defendants who contribute to state or federally mandated benefit programs should not benefit from the collateral source rule, because these plans "are designed to serve social policies independent of those served by back pay awards."[138] Defendants are required to make these payments. Offsetting these payments against a plaintiff's damages actually allows the defendant to benefit from his or her own wrongdoing.

Plaintiffs should emphasize that even cases citing double recovery as a reason for offsetting pension or government assistance benefits are actually ensuring that the defendant does not double-pay. *Glover v. McDonnell Douglas Corp.*, for example, contains language suggesting the court was concerned with the plaintiff's double recovery, but the defendant in that case had been ordered to restore the plaintiff's pension plan to its original state and make a fully compensatory back pay award.[139] Allowing the plaintiff to retain the pension benefits already paid would effectively have resulted in double payment by the defendant.

3. Calculation of Front Pay

As a prospective make-whole remedy, front pay at best "can only be calculated through intelligent guesswork."[140] The defense will contend that the amount of front pay sought by the plaintiff is speculative and that there is not an adequate basis in the record for the amounts sought. The speculative nature of future damages is a valid reason to deny

---

of equitable relief within the district court's sound discretion." That front pay is equitable, however, does not necessarily imply that collateral income may be deducted, and more specific Eighth Circuit precedent refuses to deduct pension benefits from an ADEA front pay award. *See* Doyne v. Union Elec. Co., 953 F.2d 447, 451–52 (8th Cir. 1992).

Lussier also interprets *Jackson v. City of Cookeville*, 31 F.3d 1354, 1360 (6th Cir. 1994) as applying an abuse-of-discretion test to evaluate a district court's deduction of pension benefits from an ADEA front pay award. The Sixth Circuit has subsequently rejected *Lussier*'s holding and its interpretation of *Jackson*. In Hamlin v. Charter Twp. of Flint, 165 F.3d 426, 433 (6th Cir. 1999), the Sixth Circuit explained that its opinion in *Jackson* announced a general rule prohibiting deduction of pension payments from front pay awards but allowed a deduction based on the peculiar facts of that case. *Hamlin* also rejected *Lussier*'s reliance on the equitable nature of the front pay remedy and on the inherently subjective nature of front pay determinations. Instead, the Sixth Circuit focused on the fact that "[a]pplying the collateral source rule in the employment discrimination context prevents the discriminatory employer from avoiding liability and experiencing a windfall, and also promotes the deterrence functions of discrimination statutes." *Id.* at 434. The Sixth Circuit's language indicates that setoffs of income from collateral sources are inappropriate regardless of whether back or front pay is at issue.

136. *See* EEOC v. O'Grady, 857 F.2d 383, 389 (7th Cir. 1988).

137. *Id.* at 390.

138. McDowell v. Avtex Fiber, Inc., 740 F.2d 214, 217 (3d Cir. 1984), *vacated and remanded on other grounds*, 469 U.S. 1202 (1985).

139. 12 F.3d 845, 848 (8th Cir.), *cert. denied*, 511 U.S. 1070 (1994).

140. Sellers v. Delgado Coll., 781 F.2d 503, 505 (5th Cir. 1986).

an award of front pay.[141] The Sixth Circuit has discussed the factors that the jury should consider in calculating front pay damages. Those factors include

- an employee's duty to mitigate;
- the availability of comparable employment opportunities;
- the period within which one by reasonable efforts may be re-employed;
- the employee's life expectancy (mortality);
- the employee's work-life expectancy; and
- the discount tables to determine the present value of future damages.[142]

For example, in *Wulach v. Bear Stearns & Co.*,[143] the court limited front pay to two years, finding that given the plaintiff's impressive experience and proven ability to attract offers of lucrative employment, it was reasonable to expect the plaintiff to obtain comparable employment within two years.[144]

4. Taxation of Front Pay Awards

As noted already in the back pay taxation section, front pay awards, like back pay awards, are ordinarily taxable events.[145] Thus, the same issues mentioned already in the back pay section regarding "tax bump" or "gross up" adjustments, and the need to properly instruct the jury or brief the court as to the tax consequences of damage awards, also equally apply to front pay awards.

C. Who Decides Back Pay and Front Pay: The Judge or Jury?

1. Back Pay as a Judge or Jury Issue

Although back pay awards in Title VII cases have traditionally been analogized to restitution and thus considered equitable matters for the trial court, the recent trend

---

141. Loeb v. Textron. Inc., 600 F.2d 1003, 1013 (1st Cir. 1979); Fite v. First Tenn. Prod. Credit Assn. 861 F.2d 884, 893 (6th Cir. 1988) (court found there was sufficient evidence to support the jury's award of front pay).

142. Shore v. Fed. Express Corp., 777 F.2d 1155, 1160 (6th Cir. 1985). *See also* Barbour v. Merrill, 48 F.3d 1270 (D.C. Cir. 1995) (a factor included "whether an award of front pay would be unduly speculative") (internal citation and quotation omitted); Shorter v. Hartford Fin. Servs. Group, Inc., 2005 U.S. Dist. LEXIS 19902 (D. Conn. May 31, 2005) (considering the plaintiff's age, education and training, work experience, skills, the job market, and reasonable prospects for comparable employment); Fernandez v. N. Shore Orthopedic Surgery & Sports Med., P.C., 79 F. Supp. 3d 197, 204 (E.D.N.Y. 2000).

143. 1990 U.S. Dist. LEXIS 2386 (S.D.N.Y. Mar. 8, 1990).

144. *See also, e.g.*, Deloach v. Delchamps, Inc., 897 F.2d 815 (5th Cir. 1990) (five years); Dominic v. Consol. Edison Co., 822 F.2d 1249, 1258 (2d Cir. 1987) (two years); Snow v. Pillsbury Co., 650 F. Supp. 299 (D. Minn. 1986) (three years).

145. *See, e.g.*, Comm'r of Internal Revenue v. Schleier, 515 U.S. 323 at 330 (1995) (noting that damages awards under the ADEA are ordinarily taxable); United States v. Burke, 504 U.S. 229 at 241 (1992) (noting that Title VII damages compensate aggrieved plaintiffs for "wages that, if paid in the ordinary course, would have been fully taxable."); Novak v. Andersen Corp., 962 F.2d 757 (8th Cir. 1992); Tanaka v. Dep't of Navy, 788 F.2d 1552, 1553 (Fed. Cir. 1986); Blim v. W. Elec. Co., 731 F.2d 1473, 1479 (10th Cir. 1984); Volkman v. United Transp. Union, 826 F. Supp. 1253 (D. Kan. 1993); Rev. Rule. 78–336, 1978-2C.B.255.

in Title VII cases is to treat back pay as a legal remedy triable to the jury.[146] The courts seldom explain the rationale for this treatment. When they do, courts usually reject the analogy to restitution because back pay does not rectify any unjust enrichment of the employer and does not restore something lost by the plaintiff.[147] Despite the unclear doctrine underlying the treatment of back pay awards, "as a matter of practice, back pay claims now seem routinely to be submitted to juries."[148]

2. Front Pay Awards as an Alternative to Reinstatement

Because front pay is a substitute for the equitable remedy of reinstatement, the decision to award front pay is to be made by the court.[149] Front pay is appropriate where reinstatement is impractical, because of the employer's hostility to the plaintiff or for other reasons.[150] The circuits are divided on the question of whether a jury can determine the amount, as opposed to the availability, of front pay. The Courts of Appeals for the Third, Fifth, Sixth, and Ninth circuits hold that the district court must initially determine whether a plaintiff is entitled to front pay in lieu of reinstatement, but that the jury must determine the amount of front pay to award.[151] In contrast, the Courts of Appeals for the Second, Fourth, Seventh, Eighth, and Tenth circuits hold that the determination of whether to award front pay and how much to award are questions for the district court's equitable direction. In these circuits, the court decides the amount of front pay.[152] The rationale for these decisions is that "[t]here is much overlap between the facts relevant to whether an award of front pay is appropriate and those relevant to the size of the award."[153]

---

146. *See* Waldrop v. S. Co. Serv. Inc., 24 F.3d 152, 157 (11th Cir. 1994); 2 KENT SPRIGGS, REPRESENTING PLAINTIFFS IN TITLE VII ACTIONS § 30.03 (2d ed.).

147. *See Waldrop*, 24 F.3d at 159. *But see* Schwartz v. Gregori, 45 F.3d 1017, 1022–23 (6th Cir. 1995) (categorizing back pay under ERISA as equitable, because it restores to the plaintiff something that would have been enjoyed had she not been terminated).

148. SPRIGGS, *supra* note 141, § 30.03 at 30-14 (citing *Waldrop*, 24 F.3d 152 (11th Cir. 1994)); Hutchison v. Amateur Elec. Supply, 42 F.3d 1037 (7th Cir. 1994); Dailey v. Societe Generale, 889 F. Supp. 108 (S.D.N.Y. 1995), *aff'd* 108 F.3d 451 (2d Cir. 1997).

149. *See, e.g.*, Shore v. Fed. Express Corp., 42 F.3d 373 (6th Cir. 1994) (front pay under Title VII is equitable); Cooper v. Asplundh Tree Expert Co., 836 F.2d 1544 (10th Cir. 1988) (ADEA); McNeil v. Econs. Lab., 800 F.2d 111 (7th Cir. 1986), *overruled on other grounds*, 860 F.2d 834 (7th Cir. 1988) (same).

150. *See* Berndt v. Kaiser Aluminum & Chem. Sales, Inc., 789 F.2d 253 (3d Cir. 1986).

151. *See* Hansard v. Pepsi-Cola Metro. Bottling Co., 865 F.2d 1461, 1470 (5th Cir. 1989); Fite v. First Tenn. Prod. Credit Ass'n, 861 F.2d 884, 893 (6th Cir. 1988), *abrogated on other grounds*, 6 F.3d 367 (6th Cir. 1993); Cassino v. Reichhold Chem. Inc., 817 F.2d 1338, 1347 (9th Cir. 1987); Maxfield v. Sinclair Int'l, 766 F.2d 788, 796 (3d Cir. 1985).

152. *See* Williams v. Pharmacia, Inc., 137 F.3d 944 (7th Cir. 1998); Fortino v. Quasar Co., 950 F.2d 389, 398 (7th Cir. 1991); Newhouse v. McCormick & Co., 110 F.3d 635 (8th Cir. 1997); Denison v. Swaco Geolograph Co., 941 F.2d 1416, 1426 (10th Cir. 1991); Duke v. Uniroyal, Inc., 928 F.2d 1413, 1424 (4th Cir.); Dominic v. Consol. Edison Co., Inc., 822 F.2d 1249, 1257 (2d Cir. 1987).

153. *Dominic*, 822 F.2d at 1257.

3. Front Pay as a Component of Future Emotional Distress Damages: A Jury Question?

Regardless of whether the judge or jury decides the amount of front pay, it is often argued that the appropriateness and amount of future emotional distress damages should be decided by the jury. Emotional distress is a subset of compensatory damages authorized by the Civil Rights Act of 1991, and a party is entitled to a jury trial when seeking such damages.[154] Compensatory damages do not include "any other type of relief authorized under . . . [42 U.S.C.A. § 2000e-5(g)]."[155] Reinstatement is an equitable remedy authorized by § 2000e-5(g). Whether to award front pay as an alternative to reinstatement is also an equitable decision.[156] Those circuits treating the amount of front pay as equitable do so because that question and the question of whether to award front pay at all are decided based on the same facts.[157]

At least one case supports the position that future emotional distress damages should be decided by a jury. In *Kientzy v. McDonnell Douglas Corp.*, a jury awarded $125,000 for mental anguish under the Missouri Human Rights Act, and also awarded $25,000 for future mental anguish.[158] The jury awarded actual and emotional distress damages, and a magistrate judge awarded $75,000 in front pay in lieu of reinstatement.[159] The issue was merely whether the plaintiff had presented sufficient evidence to justify the award of emotional distress damages, and neither party nor the court suggested that calculation of these damages belonged to the court.[160]

Although there are good arguments for giving the determination of front pay to the jury when it is a part of compensatory damages, and not an alternative for reinstatement, trial courts more often than not seem to view front pay awards as the sole province of the court.

D. Plaintiff's Duty to Mitigate

The principle of mitigation of damages, or as it is called in tort law, "avoidable consequences," requires that a person to whom a wrong has been done take reasonable steps to minimize the harm, on pain of having her award of damages reduced if she does not.[161] A discharged employee has a duty to mitigate her damages to receive back pay. Failure on the part of the employee to use reasonable care and diligence in reducing

---

154. 42 U.S.C. § 1981a (2000).

155. 42 U.S.C. § 1981a(b)(2) (2000).

156. *See* Pedersen v. Casey's Gen. Stores, Inc., 978 F. Supp. 926, 928 n.1 (D. Neb. 1997).

157. *Cf. Newhouse*, 110 F.3d at 643 (amount of front pay is for the court because of the factual overlap between it and the decision to award front pay in the first place); *Dominic*, 822 F.2d at 1257.

158. 990 F.2d 1051, 1061 (8th Cir. 1993).

159. *Id.* at 1056.

160. *Id.* at 1061. *See also* Williams v. Pharmacia, Inc., 137 F.3d 944, 953–54 (distinguishing between the equitable remedy of front pay, which compensates for the immediate effects of the improper termination of plaintiff's employment, and the compensatory remedy of lost future earnings, which compensate plaintiff for diminished earnings resulting from reputational harms suffered as a result of the discrimination).

161. *See* Hunter v. Allis Chalmers Corp., 797 F.2d 1417 (7th Cir. 1986).

damages constitutes a willful loss of earnings. This willful loss means that the employer is not liable for back pay. After termination, all wages earned, including those that could have been earned through the exercise of reasonable diligence, must be used to offset the plaintiff's back pay claim.[162]

The plaintiff must use reasonable care and diligence in seeking and retaining reemployment in order to mitigate damages.[163] However, there are some judicially constructed limitations to the plaintiff's duty to mitigate, which are discussed in detail in the sections that follow.

Mitigation is a question of fact. In *Ortiz v. Bank of America*,[164] the appeals court supported the district court's ruling that the mitigation question is one of fact. There was substantial evidence to support Ortiz's poor mental condition, which prevented her accepting an offer of reinstatement. Based on the evidence, the jury did not err in finding reinstatement was not a reasonable way for her to mitigate damages.[165]

If the plaintiff makes little or no effort, the court need not consider whether a suitable position would have been offered to the plaintiff if he had made the necessary effort.[166] Presumably, then, plaintiffs must be concerned that a showing of futility by the plaintiff would not be sufficient to explain an absolute failure to mitigate.[167]

1. Defendant's Burden of Proof

Once a plaintiff establishes a prima facie case of illegal discharge and presents evidence on the issue of damages, the burden of producing sufficient evidence to establish lack of diligence to mitigate damages shifts to the defendant.[168] The defendant has both the burden of production and the burden of persuasion in proving a failure to mitigate.[169] The defendant's burden of showing a failure to mitigate damages is heavy.[170] On the other hand, plaintiffs are "required to make only reasonable exertions . . . It requires only an honest good faith effort."[171]

---

162. *See* Ford Motor Co. v. EEOC, 458 U.S. 219 (1982).

163. *See* Casino v. Reichhold Chems. Inc., 817 F.2d 1338, 1345 (9th Cir. 1987); EEOC v. Cmty. Unit Sch. Dist. No. 9, 642 F. Supp. 902, 907 (S.D. Ill. 1986); Jordan v. City of Cleveland, 2006 U.S. Dist. LEXIS 76400 (N.D. Ohio 2006). *See also* Ford Motor Co. v. EEOC, 458 U.S. 219 (1982) (claimant has a statutory duty to minimize damages by using reasonable diligence to find other suitable employment); Smith v. Am. Serv. Co., 796 F.2d 1430, 1432 (11th Cir. 1986).

164. 852 F.2d 383 (9th Cir. 1987).

165. *See also* Rasimas v. Mich. Dep't of Mental Health, 714 F.2d 614 (6th Cir. 1983).

166. Logan v. Pena, 1993 U.S. Dist. LEXIS 2916 (D. Kan. 1993) (collecting cases).

167. *See id.*

168. *See, e.g.,* Reithmiller v. Blue Cross/Blue Shield, 390 N.W.2d 227, 230 (Mich. Ct. App. 1986).

169. *See* Marks v. Pratt Co., 633 F.2d 1122, 1125 (5th Cir. 1981); Glass v. Petro-Tex Chem. Corp., 757 F.2d 1554, 1559 (5th Cir. 1985); Nord v. U.S. Steel Corp., 758 F.2d 1462, 1470 (11th Cir. 1985); Brady v. Thurston Motor Lines, 753 F.2d 1269, 1274 (4th Cir. 1985).

170. *See, e.g.,* Blumstron v. Bethlehem Steel Corp., 1987 U.S. Dist. LEXIS 10871, 1263 (E.D. Pa. 1987) (collects cases).

171. EEOC v. Sandia Corp., 639 F.2d 600, 627 (10th Cir. 1980) (quoting United States v. Lee Wav Motor Freight, Inc., 625 F.2d 918, 937 (10th Cir. 1979)).

To satisfy the burden of proof, the defendant must establish (1) that the plaintiff's injuries were avoidable because the plaintiff was qualified for existing, suitable positions that furthermore were discoverable by the plaintiff; and (2) failure to use reasonable care and diligence in seeking such positions.[172]

2. Plaintiff's Duty to Exercise Diligence in Mitigating

The discharged employee must demonstrate due diligence in efforts to mitigate damages.[173] For example, in a case under the National Labor Relations Act, the Ninth Circuit reiterated what it had said in an earlier case regarding the lengths to which a plaintiff must go in mitigating damages:

> A wrongfully discharged employee is required to make only a reasonable effort to obtain interim employment, and is not held to the highest standard of diligence. Success or failure in securing interim employment is not a measure of the sufficiency of the employee's search; the law requires only an "honest good faith effort."[174]

Courts have held that activities such as sending out resumes, filing applications, using a university's career placement services, reviewing classified advertisements, and discussing employment opportunities with friends fulfill the diligence requirement.[175]

---

172. Dep't of Civil Rights v. Horizon Tube, 385 N.W.2d 685 (Mich. Ct. App. 1986); *see also* Clark v. Frank, 960 F.2d 1146, 1152 (2d Cir. 1992); Dailey v. Societe Generale, 108 F.3d 451, 456 (2d Cir. 1997); Wehr v. Burroughs Corp., 619 F.2d 276, 278 n.3 (3d Cir. 1980); Gaddy v. Abex Corp., 884 F.2d 312, 318 (7th Cir. 1989); Sias v. City Demonstration Agency, 588 F.2d 692, 696 (9th Cir. 1978); EEOC v. Kallir, Philips, Ross, Inc., 420 F. Supp. 919, 925 (S.D.N.Y.), *aff'd*, 559 F.2d 1203 (2d Cir. 1976); Spulak v. K-Mart Corp., 94 F.2d 1150, 1158 (10th Cir. 1990).

The court held in *Sellers v. Delgado Cmty. Coll.*, 839 F.2d 1132 (5th Cir. 1988), that the burden of proof was on the employer to demonstrate that comparable work was available and that the claimant did not pursue it; however, if the employer proves that the claimant did not use reasonable efforts to look for employment, the employer does not have to establish the availability of comparable employment. *See also* West v. Nabors Drilling USA, Inc., 330 F.3d 379, 393 (5th Cir. 2003) (quoting *Sellers*); Hudson v. Chertoff, 473 F. Supp. 2d 1292, 1297 (D. Fla. 2007) (applying the same rule in the 11th Circuit).

In Jordan v. City of Cleveland, 2006 U.S. Dist. LEXIS 76400, at *5–6 (N.D. Ohio 2006), the court commented on the ability of a defendant to work, but not as a fireman, the position from which he was discriminatorily terminated, stating, "[D]efendant cannot stand on the principle that plaintiff can perform other work, because this would ignore defendant's burden to show that the work was 'substantially equivalent.'"

173. *See, e.g.*, Blockel v. J.C. Penney Co., Inc., 337 F.3d 17, 27 (1st Cir. 2003); Tobin v. Liberty Mut. Ins. Co., 2007 U.S. Dist. LEXIS 23680 (D. Mass. 2007).

174. NLRB v. IBEW. Local Union 112. AFL-CIO, 992 F.2d 990 (9th Cir. 1993); *see also* Spulak v. K-Mart Corp., 894 F.2d 1150, 1158 (10th Cir. 1990); Ford v. Nicks, 866 F.2d 865, 873 (6th Cir. 1989) (holding that the plaintiff "is not required to go to heroic lengths in attempting to mitigate his damages, but only to take reasonable steps to do so"); *accord* Lathem v. Dep't of Children & Youth Servs., 172 F.3d 786, 794 (11th Cir. 1999) (suit arising under Title VII); NLRB v. Madison Courier, Inc., 472 F.2d 1307, 1318 (D.C. Cir. 1972) (NLRA suit).

175. *See* Dailey v. Societe Generale, 108 F.3d 451, 456 (2d Cir. 1997); Odima v. Westin Tucson Hotel, 53 F.3d 1484, 1497 (9th Cir. 1995); Hanna v. Am. Motors Corp., 724 F.2d 1300, 1309 (7th Cir. 1984).

The burden to find equivalent employment was also discussed by the court in *NLRB v. Westin Hotel*:

> [A] wrongfully discharged employee is only required to make a reasonable effort to mitigate damages, and is not held to the highest standard of diligence. This burden is not onerous and does not mandate that the plaintiff be successful in mitigating the damage. . . . The reasonableness of the effort to find substantially equivalent employment should be evaluated in light of the individual's background and experience and the relevant job market.[176]

3. "Substantially Equivalent Employment"

An unlawfully discharged employee is not required to accept employment that is not the same or similar to the position previously held.[177] Although an unemployed or underemployed claimant need not go into another line of work, accept a demotion, or take a demeaning position, she forfeits her right to back pay if she refuses a job substantially equivalent to the one she was denied.[178] Substantially equivalent employment has been defined as employment that affords virtually identical promotional opportunities, compensation, job responsibilities, working conditions, and status as the position from which the plaintiff has been discharged.[179]

---

176. 758 F.2d 1126 (6th Cir. 1985); *see also* Jordan v. City of Cleveland, 2006 U.S. Dist. LEXIS 76400 (N.D. Ohio 2006); Logan v. Pena, 1993 U.S. Dist. LEXIS 2916 (D. Kan. 1993) (holding that a plaintiff failed to properly mitigate when he pursued a retired lifestyle, merely looked at a few newspaper advertisements, made a few telephone calls in response to them, and informally discussed one possible job); Hunter v. Allis-Chalmers Corp., 797 F.2d 1417 (7th Cir. 1986) ("[One] cannot just leave the labor force after being wrongfully discharged in the hopes of being made whole by a judgment at law."); Haves v. Shelby Mem'l Hosp., 546 F. Supp. 259, 266 (N.D. Ala. 1982), *aff'd*, 726 F.2d 1543 (11th Cir. 1984) (holding that while the plaintiff's assumption may have proved correct, absent any efforts on her part to verify her employment opportunities, such as checking want ads and registering with employment agencies, she failed to satisfy her duty to use reasonable diligence in mitigating damages under the statute); NLRB v. Seligman Assocs. Inc., 808 F.2d 1155 (6th Cir. 1986) (although the court did not charge the plaintiffs with failure to mitigate because they refused alternative employment with the defendant, it found no excuse for the employees' refusal to seek other comparable employment in the vicinity when there was undisputed proof that such employment existed); Bossalina v. Lever Bros., 1986 U.S. Dist. LEXIS 24333 (D. Md. 1986) (following the plaintiffs' claim that emotional distress resulting from their terminations left them unable to look for work, the court ruled this assertion legally insufficient, and held that the plaintiffs failed to mitigate damages); Cole v. Consol. Rail Corp., 561 F. Supp. 645 (E.D. Mich. 1982) (finding that a female victim of sexual harassment could not claim aversion to reentering the workforce and possibly working for another male superior as a sufficient excuse for failure to mitigate).

177. *See, e.g.*, Rimedo v. Revlon. Inc., 528 F. Supp. 1380 (S.D. Ohio 1982); Glass v. I.D.S. Fin. Servs., Inc., 778 F. Supp. 1029, 105 (D. Minn. 1991).

178. Ford Motor Co. v. EEOC, 458 U.S. 219 (1982).

179. *See, e.g.*, Rasimas v. Mich. Dep't of Mental Health, 714 F.2d 614, 624 (6th Cir. 1983); Jordan v. City of Cleveland, 2006 U.S. Dist. LEXIS 76400 (N.D. Ohio 2006); *see also* Sellers v. Delgado Coll., 781 F.2d 503 (5th Cir. 1986) (finding that the new position should provide comparable hours to the previous position).

In *Brady v. Thurston Motor Lines,* the court listed criteria for determining if a position is sufficiently equivalent:

> It is well established that a plaintiff must make every reasonable effort to mitigate damages. Such a defense, however, is an affirmative one, and proof of plaintiff's failure to mitigate rests upon the defendant. . . . [A] wrongfully discharged employee is obliged to mitigate damages by accepting employment of a like nature. . . . [T]he criteria for determining like nature include the type of work, the hours of labor, the wages, tenure, working conditions, etc. Whether or not an employee is reasonable in not seeking or accepting particular employment is a question for the trier of fact.[180]

Courts recognize that practical considerations such as hours and salary are not the only factors that determine the actual comparability of a position.[181] Courts are divided regarding the responsibility of the plaintiff to accept a position geographically farther away than the original position; however, most courts have held that a plaintiff has no duty to accept a substitute job that would require moving to another location to satisfy the duty to mitigate damages.[182]

---

180. 753 F.2d 1269 (4th Cir. 1985).

181. *See, e.g.,* Williams v. Albemarle City Bd. of Educ., 508 F.2d 1242, 1243 (4th Cir. 1974) ("Comparability in status is often of far more importance—especially as it relates to opportunities for advancement or for other employment—than comparability in salary."); Logan v. Pena, 1993 U.S. Dist. LEXIS 2916 (D. Kan. 1993); *Glass,* 778 F. Supp. at 1075 (the plaintiff's claim that she felt humiliated by the new position was not sufficient to establish that it was not substantially equivalent to the original one); EEOC v. Exxon Shipping Co., 745 F.2d 967 (5th Cir. 1984) (the plaintiff—who refused a position that required her to work every weekend, unlike the position that she had sought and that had been discriminatorily denied to her—acted reasonably in refusing the position, even though both positions paid the same salary); Walters v. City of Atlanta, 803 F.2d 1135 (11th Cir. 1986) (finding that the claimant has a duty to seek alternative employment after deciding that there is no other job in his field that is acceptable).

In Sellers v. Delgado Cmty. College, 839 F.2d 1132, 1138 (5th Cir. 1988), the lower court had found that a substitute position the plaintiff obtained as a secretary at Gulf Oil was comparable to her prior position in public relations with the defendant, based purely on the level of pay received by the plaintiff. The Fifth Circuit emphasized the differences in job status, educational requirements, and promotional opportunities in finding that the plaintiff's substitute employment was not "substantially comparable" with her prior position. The *Sellers* court also held that since a Title VII claimant is not required to accept noncomparable employment, a claimant who accepts a noncomparable position is not required to remain in that position throughout the life of the claim in order to fulfill the duty to mitigate damages. *Sellers,* 839 F.2d at 1137–38. Similarly, in *EEOC v. Guardian Pools Inc.,* 828 F.2d 1507 (11th Cir. 1987), the court held that a claimant who resigned from several noncomparable positions during the back pay period because of dissatisfaction with the job had not failed to mitigate her damages.

182. *See, e.g.,* Heeler v. Bd. of Educ., 47 F.2d 1078, 1081 (8th Cir. 1971); EEOC v. Pennsylvania, 772 F. Supp. 217, 222 (M.D. Pa 1991), *aff'd on other grounds sub nom.* Binker v. Pennsylvania, 997 F.2d 738 (3d Cir. 1992); Spagnuolo v. Whirlpool Corp., 717 F.2d 114, 119 (4th Cir. 1983); Coleman v. City of Omaha, 714 F.2d 804, 808 (8th Cir. 1983).

4. The "Lowered Sights" Doctrine

The court in *Berger v. Iron Workers Reinforced Rodmen, Local 201,* discussed the "lowered sights doctrine," wherein the court may require the plaintiff to seek a nonequivalent position after a period of unsuccessful searching:

> A claimant "forfeits his right to back pay if he refuses a job substantially equivalent to the one he was denied." Ford Motor, 458 U.S. at 232. But "the unemployed or underemployed claimant need not go into another line of work, accept a demotion or take a demeaning position." *Id.* at 231. Nor is he "required to accept employment at a great distance from his home." Oil, Chem. & Atomic Workers, 547 F.2d 598 at 604. On the other hand, a claimant may reasonably conclude that he should lower his sights and seek other work, including work outside the industry. NLRB v. Madison Courier, Inc., 505 F.2d 391, 396 (D.C. Cir. 1974) (Madison Courier II). "The claimant," after all, "cannot afford to stand aside while the wheels of justice grind slowly toward the ultimate resolution of the lawsuit. The claimant needs work that will feed a family and restore self-respect." Ford Motor, 458 U.S. at 221. Indeed, a claimant "may be required ... to 'lower his sights' by seeking less remunerative work after he has unsuccessfully attempted for a reasonable period of time to locate interim employment comparable with his improperly denied position." Madison Courier I, 472 F.2d at 1321....

As we said in Madison Courier I, if the discriminatee accepts significantly lower paying work too soon after the discrimination in question, he may be subject to a reduction in back pay on the ground that he willfully incurred a loss by accepting an unsuitably low-paying position. On the other hand ... if he fails to "lower his sights" after the passage of a reasonable period of unsuccessful employment searching, he may be held to have forfeited his right to reimbursement on the ground that he failed to make the requisite effort to mitigate his losses.[183]

Although the plaintiff may need to lower her sights after a time, the court should resolve any reasonable doubt about the length of that time in favor of the innocent employee.[184]

IV. COMPENSATORY DAMAGES

A. Availability of Compensatory Damages Generally

Compensatory damages are defined under the Civil Rights Act of 1991 to include "future pecuniary losses, emotional pain, suffering, inconvenience, mental anguish, loss of enjoyment of life, and other non-pecuniary losses...."[185] Compensatory damages

---

183. 170 F.3d 1111 (D.C. Cir. 1999).

184. Nordstrom v. NLRB, 984 F.2d 479, 482 (D.C. Cir. 1993); *see also* Logan v. Pena, 1993 U.S. Dist. LEXIS 2916, 567 (D. Kan. 1993).

185. 42 U.S.C. § 1981a(b)(3) (2000).

under the Civil Rights Act are available only against employers who have engaged in intentional discrimination, and the amount of compensatory damages recoverable depends on the size of the employer.[186] Compensatory damages are in addition to the equitable relief (including back pay and front pay) awarded by the court.

A good introduction to the subject of both the compensatory and punitive damages available under the Civil Rights Act may be found in the Equal Employment Opportunity Commission (EEOC) Policy Guide on Compensatory and Punitive Damages Under 1991 Civil Rights Act (dated July 7, 1992). The policy guide illustrates the EEOC's views on compensatory damages issues. It also surveys damages issues as developed under 42 U.S.C. § 1981.[187] The policy guide provides numerous instructive illustrations from case law developed under § 1981 through 1992.[188]

The policy guide establishes that plaintiffs may seek certain pecuniary losses such as moving expenses, job search expenses, medical expenses, psychiatric expenses, physical therapy expenses, and other quantifiable out-of-pocket expenses reasonably incurred as a result of the discriminatory conduct. As a practical matter, plaintiffs have to be able to document these expenses. Plaintiffs may also seek nonpecuniary losses, such as emotional pain, suffering, inconvenience, mental anguish, loss of enjoyment, and injury to reputation. Medical records will be highly relevant and subject to discovery on such claims. Emotional harm may include sleeplessness, anxiety, depression, humiliation, stress, or loss of self-esteem. Physical manifestations of emotional harm may include ulcers, hair loss, headaches, or gastrointestinal disorders.

B. Expert Versus Nonexpert Testimony

1. Expert Testimony on Psychological Harm Is Admissible and Can Be Important for Severely Harmed Plaintiffs

The scope of harm for which recovery is permitted is very broad and can include not only emotional pain and mental anguish but damage to reputation and career, loss

---

186. The Civil Rights Act of 1991 imposes damage caps on compensatory and punitive damages for claims brought under Title VII of the Civil Rights Act of 1964 and the Americans with Disabilities Act of 1990. 42 U.S.C. § 1981a(1), (2). The caps (for combined compensatory and punitive damage awards) are as follows:

Number of Employees	Recovery Limit
15–100	$50,000
101–200	$100,000
201–500	$200,000
501+	$300,000

The damage caps do not apply to antidiscrimination claims brought under § 1981 or § 1983.

187. *See* n. 13 to *EEOC Policy Guide*, which states that § 1981 cases will be considered precedential for analysis of damage claims under the Civil Rights Act.

188. *See also* Jenson v. Eveleth Taconite Co., 130 F.3d 1287 (8th Cir. 1997) (discussing standards for proving cases alleging psychological damages); Shepherd v. ABC, 862 F. Supp. 486, 501–02 (D.D.C. 1994), *rev'd on other grounds*, 62 F.3d 1469 (D.C. Cir. 1995) (surveying emotional distress awards); Hadley v. VAMPTS, 44 F.3d 372, 375 (5th Cir. 1995) (no requirement that emotional harm be "severe" to be compensable under Civil Rights Act).

of pride or self-respect, loss of enjoyment in life or career, impact on family or close friends, and loss of community of social standing. If a plaintiff has suffered harm in any of these areas, evidence must be fully developed and introduced and will often require expert testimony.[189]

Expert psychological testimony on the extent of injuries is admissible and can be critical to maximizing compensatory damages for certain highly damaged plaintiffs. For example, in *Busby v. City of Orlando,*[190] the court held that expert testimony on the "psychological impact" of discrimination was directly relevant to the issue of causation of mental harm and was wrongly excluded. Courts have recognized that "[s]uch expert opinion is the prime—indeed usually the only—way to prove medical causation."[191] Such evidence has also been generally admitted in tort cases where mental harm is claimed as a component of damages.[192]

Courts have continued to receive expert proof of mental damages since the Daubert decision gave courts guidance on the admissibility of expert testimony.[193] In *Jenson v. Eveleth Taconite Co.,* the Court of Appeals for the Eighth Circuit reversed the exclusion of expert testimony on psychological damages where the experts were well qualified and their methodology fully explained.[194] Physicians can

---

189. Note that the Civil Rights Act explicitly authorizes recovery of expert fees under Title VII and §§ 1981 and 1981(a). *See* 42 U.S.C. § 20003-5(k). The Civil Rights Act effectively reversed *West Virginia University Hospital v. Casey,* 499 U.S. 83 (1991).

190. 931 F.2d 764, 782 (11th Cir. 1991).

191. Crinkley v. Holiday Inns, Inc., 844 F.2d 156, 164 n.4 (4th Cir. 1988). *See also* Brady v. Gebbie, 859 F.2d 1543, 1558 (9th Cir. 1988) (psychiatric testimony amply demonstrated nexus between denial of due process and emotional distress); Rowlett v. Anheuser-Busch, Inc., 832 F.2d 194 (1st Cir. 1987) (psychiatric testimony supported damage award for emotional distress); Shrout v. Black Clawson Co., 689 F. Supp. 774, 776 n.3 (S.D. Ohio 1988) (expert psychiatric opinion that harassment caused plaintiff's emotional distress); Spencer v. Gen. Elec. Co., 688 F. Supp. 1072, 1074 n.7 (E.D. Va. 1988) (posttraumatic stress disorder testimony admissible to prove damages); Moffett v. Gene B. Glick Co., Inc., 621 F. Supp. 244, 265 (N.D. Ind. 1985) (psychological expert traced anxiety symptoms such as intrusive imagery, sleep disorders, and intense fear to discrimination and testified regarding need for prolonged psychotherapy), *overruled on other grounds by* Reeder-Baker v. Lincoln Nat'l Corp., 644 F. Supp. 983 (N.D. Ind. 1986); Valdez v. Church's Fried Chicken, Inc., 683 F. Supp. 596, 613–14 (W.D. Tex. 1988) (expert witness testified that plaintiff's anguish was caused by harassment and attempted rape and that plaintiff would require lifelong therapy).

192. *See, e.g.,* Whalley v. Sakura, 804 F.2d 580, 585 (10th Cir. 1986) (citing decisions from several states upholding admission of expert proof pertaining to causation of mental harm); Kravinsky v. Glover, 396 A.2d 1349, 1354 (Pa. Super. Ct. 1979) (discussing admissibility of expert proof of causation of mental harm).

193. Daubert v. Merrell Dow Pharms., Inc., 509 U.S. 579 (1993).

194. 130 F.3d 1287 (8th Cir. 1997), *cert. denied,* 524 U.S. 953 (1998); *see also* Webb v. Hyman, 861 F. Supp. 1094, 1114 (D.D.C. 1994) (psychologist testified that harassment caused plaintiff's mental harm by bringing out deeply repressed emotions relating to her childhood abuse); Alberts v. Wickes Lumber Co., No. 93 C 4397, 1995 W.L 557473 (N.D. Ill. Sept. 15, 1995) (contemplates admission of expert proof that harassment caused plaintiff's panic disorder and of countervailing proof from defendant); Hurley v. Atl. City Police Dep't, 993 F. Supp. 396, 424 (D.N.J 1996) (expert proof showed mental harm including adjustment disorder caused by sexual harassment).

also be important to explain how medical conditions can be caused or aggravated by discrimination.[195]

Many cases require forensic testimony in addition to, or in the absence of, treating expert testimony. A treating professional may have weak credentials. His or her opinions could be considerably strengthened by the addition of a more qualified forensic expert. Specific issues relating to the nature of the harm suffered may be beyond the realm of most treating doctors and may require the specialized expertise of a forensic expert. For instance, the scope of harm suffered by victims of Title VII violations, and the causal relationship of a diagnosis such as posttraumatic stress disorder to workplace conduct, are cutting edge issues in the mental health field. An expert qualified in this narrow area may be necessary to fully develop and explain the extent of the injury and any diagnosable mental disorders or conditions.[196]

Psychiatric experts can also explain the harm Title VII violations cause to plaintiffs who are unusually susceptible or vulnerable or if the unlawful behavior has aggravated preexisting conditions.[197] Expert testimony is often critical to establish causation and the extent of injury under these circumstances.[198]

---

195. *See, e.g.*, Lindsey v. Comm'r, 422 F.3d 684, 686–88 (8th Cir. 2005) (holding that damages such as hypertension, insomnia, impotence, indigestion, and fatigue are encompassed within Congress's definition of emotional distress); Bartlett v. United States, 835 F. Supp. 1246, 1265 (E.D. Wash. 1993) (court relies upon "serious physical impairments," including severe stomach pains and sleep and appetite disturbances, in awarding $25,000 in mental anguish damages); Gleason v. Callanan Indus., 610 N.Y.S.2d 671, 673, 203 A.D.2d 750, 752 (N.Y. App. Div. 1994) (court upholds jury award of $54,000 by noting, inter alia, that harassment victim suffered from irritable bowel syndrome, migraines, and insomnia); SUNY Coll. of Envtl. Sci. & Forestry v. State Div. of Human Rights, 534 N.Y.S. 2d 270, 271, 144 A.D. 2d 962, 963 (N.Y.A.D. 1988) (court cites lack of physical manifestations of mental anguish in reducing emotional distress damage award to $100,000).

196. *See* D.A. Chaney & R.C. Russell, *An Overview of Sexual Harassment*, 151 AM. J. PSYCHIATRY 1994 at 10–17 (summarizing new studies linking sexual harassment experience to severe reactions and explaining the important role expertise in psychiatry can play in explaining this causal connection); *see also* PAUL T. GUILLORY, PH.D., OVERVIEW OF FORENSIC PSYCHOLOGICAL EXPERTISE (1997). Dr. Guillory, a psychologist, served as plaintiff's expert witness as to emotional distress damages in *Adams v. Pinole Point Steel Co.*, a race harassment class action in federal court in San Francisco.

197. *See* Jenson v. Eveleth Taconite Co., 130 F.3d at 1294 (eggshell-plaintiff doctrine applies to emotional injuries; defendant does not have to foresee the type of injury caused); Avita v. Metro. Club of Chicago, Inc. 49 F.3d 1219, 1228 (7th Cir. 1995) ("eggshell skull" doctrine applies in "statutory tort case as in a common-law tort case"); *Crinkley*, 844 F.2d at 163 ("thin-skulled plaintiff" rule establishes that wrongdoer is liable for all damages notwithstanding plaintiff's susceptibility); Williamson v. Handy Button Mach. Co., 817 F.2d 1290 at 1294 (7th Cir. 1987) (in upholding damage award for discrimination victim, court notes "perhaps she was unusually sensitive, but a tortfeasor takes its victims as she finds them"); *Webb*, 861 F. Supp. at 1114–15; Tobin v. Liberty Mut. Ins. Co., 2007 U.S. Dist. LEXIS 23680 (D. Mass. 2007) (reiterating the "eggshell plaintiff" rule and noting that aggravating a preexisting emotional condition may expose defendant to liability); Stockett v. Tolin, 791 F. Supp. 1536, 1556–57 (S.D. Fla. 1992) (the defendants must take plaintiff as they find her; preexisting vulnerability to defendants' conduct cannot reduce damage award). *Hurley*, 933 F. Supp. at 425 (defendants must take victim as they find her even though harassment might not have caused "average woman" so much harm).

198. Shimman v. Frank, 625 F.2d 80, 100 (6th Cir. 1980) ("personality structure" of victim of intentional beating rendered him vulnerable to unanticipated psychic harms), *overruled on other grounds*, Shimman v. Int'l Union of Operating Eng'rs, 744 F.2d 1226 (6th Cir. 1984); Wakefield v. NLRB, 779 F.2d 1437, 1438

2. Expert Testimony Invites Rule 35 Examinations

If a Title VII plaintiff uses expert testimony to establish damages, he or she will almost certainly have to undergo an adverse psychological examination. A trial court has broad discretion in dictating the manner and conditions of adverse medical examinations.[199] Some cases suggest that legal counsel can be present during such an exam.[200] Expert testimony can be excluded if the technique employed by the expert during an examination is not proper.[201]

Although adverse psychological examinations are largely unavoidable, plaintiffs need not simply accept broad, unlimited discovery into any aspect of their personal life. Limits can and will be imposed by responsible judges. For example, in *Jenson v. Eveleth Taconite Co.*,[202] a sexual harassment case, the Court of Appeals for the Eighth Circuit stated:

> Before trial, the defendants sought discovery of the personal background of each of the plaintiffs relating to events that allegedly affected plaintiff's emotional well being. Personal events defendants sought to discover included detailed medical histories, childhood experiences, domestic abuse, abortions, and sexual relationships, etc. The plaintiff class describes this as the "scorched earth" defense. . . . We would agree that much of this discovery (e.g., domestic abuse, earlier illness, and personal relationships, etc.) was not relevant or was so remote in time that it should not have been allowed.[203]

3. Nonexpert Testimony Can Establish Compensatory Damages

a. Recovery for Emotional Harm Does Not Require Expert Testimony

Most courts recognize that compensation for emotional distress/mental anguish does not have to be supported by expert testimony.[204] Court decisions in this area are replete with statements about the harm necessarily caused by discrimination and a court's

---

(9th Cir. 1986) (ignoring employee's psychological vulnerability overlooked "time-honored legal principle that a wrongdoer takes his victim as he finds him"); Freyermuth v. Lofty, 376 Mass. 612, 382 N.E.2d 1059, 1064 (1978) (tortious conduct reactivated dormant mental illness resulting in victim's suicide); Tate v. Canomica, 5 Cal. Rptr. 28 (Cal. Ct. App. 1960); Cauverien v. De Metz, 188 N.Y.S.2d 627 (N.Y. 1959).

199. *See* Sanden v. Mayo Clinic, 495 F.2d 221 (8th Cir. 1974).

200. *See* Acosta v. Tenneco Oil Co., 913 F.2d 205 (5th Cir. 1990); Di Bari v. Incaica Armadora, S.A., 126 F.R.D. 12 (E.D.N.Y. 1989).

201. *See* Tomlin v. Holecek, 150 F.R.D. 628, 630 (D. Minn. 1993).

202. Jenson v. Eveleth Taconite Co., 130 F.3d 1287 (8th Cir. 1997).

203. *Jenson*, 130 F.3d at 1292–93; *see also* Bottomly v. Leucadia Nat'l, 163 F.R.D. 617, 620–21 (D. Utah 1995) (limiting scope of discovery into plaintiff's personal life based in part on *Daubert* factor that testimony must be based on relevant facts and fit the issue of the case).

204. *See* Meritor Sav. Bank v. Vinson, 477 U.S. 57, 66 (1986) (a work environment may be so polluted with discrimination in the form of sexual harassment "as to destroy completely the emotional and psychological stability of minority group workers" (quoting Rogers v. EEOC, 454 F.2d 234, 238 (5th Cir. 1971)); Harris v. Forklift Sys., Inc., 510 U.S. 17, 22 (1993) (sexual harassment may "seriously affect employees'

need to properly assess the full scope of this harm. In *Mandell v. Harleysville Life Insurance,* the court stated: "A victim of discrimination suffers a dehumanizing injury as real as, and often far more severe and lasting than, a blow to the jaw."[205] The court in *United States v. Balistieri*[206] recognized that the effect of discrimination accumulates over time:

> [D]iscrimination is not always immediately apparent, and a victim must often see the full picture before he realizes he has been discriminated against. The fact that a victim does not suffer the full effects of the discrimination until he discovers the big picture does not change the fact that the defendant's discrimination was the primary cause of his harm.[207]

In weighing the plaintiff's testimony regarding emotional distress and calculating the appropriate damage award, the totality of the workplace conduct, not simply isolated instances of discriminatory conduct, must therefore be reviewed.[208] Moreover, the circumstances of all acts giving rise to the distress must be considered together:

> [I]n determining whether the evidence of emotional distress is sufficient to support an award of damages, we must look at both the direct evidence of emotional distress and the circumstances of the act that allegedly caused the distress. Cf. Carey, 435 U.S. at 263–64, 98 S. Ct. at 1052 ("Distress . . . is customarily proved by showing the nature and circumstances of the wrong and its effect upon the plaintiff.") The more inherently degrading or humiliating the defendant's action is, the more reasonable it is to infer that a person would suffer humiliation or distress from that action; consequently, somewhat more conclusory evidence of emotional distress will be accepted to support an award for emotional distress.[209]

However, where courts do allow plaintiffs to recover emotional distress damages, they will often reduce the amount drastically, particularly in these "garden variety" cases, where the plaintiff required no medical treatment.[210]

---

psychological well being"); Block v. H.R. Macy & Co., Inc., 712 F.2d 1241, 1245 (8th Cir. 1983) ("Courts do not demand precise proof to support a reasonable award of damages for such injuries.").

205. Mardell v. Harleysville Life Ins. Co., 31 F.3d 1221, 1232 (3d Cir. 1994), *vacated,* 514 U.S. 1034, *reinstated,* 65 F.3d 1074 (3d Cir. 1995).

206. 981 F.2d 916 (7th Cir. 1992).

207. *Id.* at 933; *see also* Townsend v. Ind. Univ., 995 F.2d 691, 693 (7th Cir. 1993) (delay in time of several years between alleged harassment and constructive discharge does not defeat causation).

208. *See* Harris v. Forklift Sys., 510 U.S. 17, 23 (1993); Robinson v. Jacksonville Shipyards, Inc., 760 F. Supp. 1486, 1524 (M.D. Fla. 1991) (each episode has predecessors, impact may accumulate and "work environment created may thereby exceed the sum of individual episodes").

209. *Balistieri,* 981 F.2d at 932.

210. *See* Binder v. LILCO, 847 F. Supp. 1007, 1028 (E.D.N.Y. 1994) (reducing jury award of nearly $500,000 to $5,000 in ADEA and NYSHRL case), *aff'd in part,* 57 F.3d 193, 202 (2d Cir. 1995); *In re* Quality Care, Inc. v. Rosa, 194 A.D.2d 610, 611, 599 N.Y.S.2d 65, 66 (2d Dep't 1993) (reducing $10,000 mental anguish and humiliation award to $5,000 under NYSHRL); Pioneer Group v. State Div. of Human Rights, 174

b. Effective Lay Testimony Is Also Key to Establishing Emotional Distress Damages

To be effective, a plaintiff's testimony must fully explain the emotional impact of each allegedly discriminatory act and the cumulative effect of the discrimination. A spouse, friend, or supporting witness can be critical in establishing the gravity of the harm and affirming the credibility of the victim's testimony.[211]

C. Constructive Discharge and Its Role in Proving Certain Title VII Claims

The general rule is that voluntary termination of employment after a discriminatory denial of promotion or transfer cuts off the right to damages.[212] However, when the employee is constructively discharged, her termination will not cut off back pay liability.[213] Instead, the defendant's back pay liability will begin as of the date the plaintiff left the defendant's employ.[214]

Under the doctrine of constructive discharge, a plaintiff alleges that the defendant's unlawful conduct made the plaintiff's "working conditions . . . so difficult or unpleasant that a reasonable person in the employee's shoes would have felt compelled to resign."[215] The courts have developed two standards for determining constructive discharge: the subjective test and the objective test. The subjective test requires a finding that the

---

A.D.2d 1041, 572 N.Y.S. 2d 207, 208 (4th Dep't 1991) (reducing $10,000 award to $5,000 under New York law, calling $10,000 excessive as a matter of law); *In re* N.Y.C. Transit Auth. v. State Div. of Human Rights, 160 A.D.2d 874, 875, 554 N.Y.S.2d 308, 309 (2d Dep't 1990) (reducing a $75,000 compensatory damages award to $5,000), *amended on other grounds*, 560 N.Y.S.2d 880 (2d Dep't 1990); Cosmos Forms, Ltd. v. State Div. of Human Rights, 150 A.D.2d 442, 541 N.Y.S.2d 50, 51 (2d Dep't 1989) (reducing a $35,000 mental anguish award to $5,000); *In re* Trans World Airlines, Inc. v. N.Y. Exec. Dep't, 147 A.D. 2d 575, 576, 537 N.Y.S.2d 868, 870 (2d Dep't 1989) (vacating a mental anguish award of $ 5,000 that was based solely on depression); Bd. of Ed. v. State Div. of Human Rights, 109 A.D.2d 988, 990–91, 486 N.Y.S.2d 469, 472 (3d Dep't 1985) (reducing a $10,000 mental anguish award to $5,000, the amount the plaintiff had requested); Kuper v. Empire Blue Cross & Blue Shield, 2003 U.S. Dist LEXS 2362, No. 99 Civ. 1190 (S.D.N.Y. Feb. 18, 2003). *But see* Whitford v. Frederick Goldman, Inc., 1995 WL 511134 (S.D.N.Y. 1995) (sustaining an award of $100,000); Hamilton v. N.Y.C. Comm'n on Human Rights, 199 A.D.2d 223, 224 (1st Dep't 1993) (sustaining an award of $20,000); Luciano v. Olsten Corp., 912 F. Supp. 663, 674 (D.N.Y. 1996) (sustaining an award of $11,400).

211. *See, e.g.*, Lilley v. BTM Corp., 958 F.2d 746 (6th Cir. 1992), *reh'g denied* (Apr. 20, 1992), *cert. denied*, 506 U.S. 940 (Oct. 19, 1992) (court upheld a $350,000 award of mental anguish damages in part because plaintiff's testimony regarding feelings of anguish and embarrassment following his discharge was corroborated by his wife's testimony).

212. *See, e.g.*, Satterwhite v. Smith, 744 F.2d 1380, 1381 n.1 (9th Cir. 1984); Derr v. Gulf Oil Corp., 796 F.2d 340, 342–43 (10th Cir. 1986).

213. *See, e.g.*, Bourque v. Powell Elec. Mfg Co., 617 F.2d 61, 66 & n.8 (5th Cir. 1980); Garner v. Wal-Mart Stores, Inc., 807 F.2d 1536, 1539 (11th Cir. 1987).

214. Easter v. Jeep Corp., 538 F. Supp. 515, 522 (N.D. Ohio 1982), *aff'd in part, rev'd in part on other grounds*, 750 F.2d 520 (6th Cir. 1984).

215. Held v. Gulf Oil Co., 684 F.2d 427, 432 (6th Cir. 1982) (quoting Bourgue v. Powell Elec. Mfg Co., 617 F.2d 61, 65 (5th Cir. 1980)); *see also* EEOC v. Barton Protective Servs., Inc., 47 F. Supp. 2d 57, 59 (D.D.C. 1999) (citing Katradis v. Dav-El of Wash., D.C., F.2d 1482, 1485 (D.C. Cir. 1988)).

discrimination complained of amounts to an intentional course of conduct calculated to force the employee's resignation.[216] The objective test requires a finding that the conduct complained of would have the foreseeable result of creating working conditions that would be so unpleasant or difficult that a reasonable person in the employee's position would resign.[217]

Although some courts have required a showing that the employer specifically intended the plaintiff to quit,[218] the majority view is that the employer need only engage in activities whose reasonably foreseeable consequence is the plaintiff's resignation.[219] A claim of constructive discharge will not be precluded simply because the defendant encouraged the plaintiff not to quit.[220]

Several courts have held that a voluntary resignation will not cut off back pay liability when the position that the plaintiff was discriminatorily denied was so dissimilar to the prior position held by the plaintiff with the employer that the denial of the new position was in effect a refusal to hire. For instance, in *Thome v. City of El Segundo*,[221] a clerk-typist for a police department was found to have been discriminatorily denied a job as a police officer. The Ninth Circuit stated that had the plaintiff remained a clerk-typist, she "would not have been in any better position to attack discrimination in police officer hiring than any other applicant" and therefore, her resignation from the clerk-typist position did not cut off her back pay claim.

The need to prove constructive discharge is especially prevalent in "hostile work environment" sexual harassment claims. For instance, in *Bennett v. Corroon & Black Corp.*,[222] the court found that no compensatory damages could be awarded to a female employee who quit her job because of sexual harassment when the employer paid all of her medical and psychiatric treatment expenses and paid her salary until she found alternative employment. But *Shrout v. Black Clawson Co.*[223] held that an employee denied good performance evaluations and salary reviews as part of a campaign of sexual harassment against her was entitled to have her salary increased to the level it would have been but for the harassment. Constructive discharge was adequately shown

---

216. Bristow v. Daily Press, Inc., 770 F.2d 1251, 1255 (4th Cir. 1985); Coe v. Yellow Freight Sys., Inc., 646 F.2d 444, 454 (10th Cir. 1981).

217. Brooms v. Regal Tube Co., 881 F.2d 412, 423 (7th Cir. 1989); Watson v. Nationwide Ins. Co., 823 F.2d 360, 361 (9th Cir. 1987); Williams v. Caterpillar Tractor Co., 770 F.2d 47, 50 (6th Cir. 1985); Goss v. Exxon Office Sys. Co., 747 F.2d 885, 888 (3d Cir. 1984).

218. EEOC v. Fed. Reserve Bank of Richmond, 698 F.2d 633 (4th Cir. 1983).

219. Wheeler v. Southland Corp., 875 F.2d 1246 (1989) (constructive discharge established by defendant's failure to advise plaintiff when and if supervisor who had harassed her would be replaced); Hunter v. Countryside Ass'n for the Handicapped, Inc., 710 F. Supp. 233 (N.D. 111. 1989) (plaintiff's allegation that she was raped by supervisor at purported business meeting at his apartment required denial of motion to dismiss constructive discharge claim).

220. Paroline v. Unisys Corp., 879 F.2d 100 (4th Cir. 1989).

221. 802 F.2d 1131, 1133–34 (9th Cir. 1986).

222. 845 F.2d 104 (5th Cir. 1988).

223. 689 F. Supp. 774 (S.D. Ohio 1988).

in *Arnold v. City of Seminole*,[224] which found that damages were recoverable for the claimant's lost salary caused when she was unable to return to work because of sexual harassment at the workplace. In this regard, it is also important to link the discharge to the harassment suffered. For example, in *Mitchell v. USAir, Inc.*,[225] a hostile work environment was found, but because termination was unrelated to the sexual harassment suffered, the plaintiff, who no longer worked for the defendant and would not be reinstated, was entitled only to declaratory relief and attorney's fees, not to injunctive relief, back pay, front pay, or reinstatement.

By contrast, one does not necessarily have to show constructive discharge to be entitled to compensatory damages for quid pro quo sexual harassment. For example, in *Trustees of Columbia University v. Karibian*,[226] the court held that an employee complaining of sexual harassment by a supervisor does not have to show actual economic loss to prevail on a claim of quid pro quo harassment under Title VII of the Civil Rights Act of 1964 (Title VII).

V. PUNITIVE DAMAGES

From the plaintiff's perspective, the best advice for any practitioner seeking to maximize punitive damages is to avoid Title VII's damage caps by including parallel state or local antidiscrimination and/or tort claims. Often an egregious discrimination case can also give rise to tort claims like defamation, intentional infliction of emotional distress, assault, and battery. These tort claims are not subject to any punitive damage caps. Moreover, unlimited punitive damages are available in § 1981 and § 1983 claims.[227]

A. General Standard and Preserving the Right to Recovery

Punitive damages are available against the defendant (other than a government, government agency, or political subdivision) "if the [plaintiff] demonstrates that the [defendant] engaged in a discriminatory practice with malice or with reckless indifference to the federally protected rights of an aggrieved individual."[228] The standard of proof required to sustain awards of punitive damages under the Civil Rights Act is the same as that required under 42 U.S.C. §§ 1981 and 1983.[229] The evidence that establishes intentional discrimination is sufficient to permit a jury to award punitive damages.[230] Whether to award plaintiff punitive damages, as well as the amounts of any such damages awarded, is within the jury's sound discretion.

---

224. 614 F. Supp. 853 (E.D. Okla. 1985).

225. 629 F. Supp. 636, 643 (N.D. Ohio 1986), *appeal dismissed*, 816 F.2d 681 (6th Cir. 1987).

226. 62 U.S.L.W. 2477 (2d Cir. 1994), *cert. denied*, 62 U.S.L.W. 3822 (1994).

227. *See* Patterson v. McClean Credit Union, 491 U.S. 164, 182 n.4 (1989) (§ 1981 action).

228. 42 U.S.C. § 1981a (2000).

229. Kolstad v. Am. Dental Ass'n, 108 F.3d 1431 (D.C. Cir. 1997). 42 U.S.C. § 1981a(b)(1).

230. *Id.*; *see also* Adams v. Pinole Point Steel Co., 1995 U.S. Dist. LEXIS 2036 (N.D. Cal. Feb. 10, 1995); Stender v. Lucky Stores, Inc., 803 F. Supp. 259, 324 (N.D. Cal. 1993).

Even where the employer's unlawful is egregious, some courts have suggested that punitive damages are unavailable where the employer promptly and effectively takes action to end the unlawful conduct. For example, in *Dominic v. DeVilbiss Air Power Co.,* the Eighth Circuit held that "[w]hen an employer promptly and conscientiously responds to complaints of harassment or discrimination with good faith efforts punitive damages are not warranted."[231]

The following factors should be considered in fixing the appropriate punitive damage award:

1. The severity of the misconduct
2. The amount needed to prevent repetition in light of defendant's financial condition or to deter others from similar discriminatory conduct in the future
3. The nature, extent, and severity of the harm caused by the misconduct
4. The existence and frequency of post-discriminatory conduct
5. Whether the employer has lied or attempted to conceal discriminatory conduct
6. Whether the employer has made threats or engaged in retaliatory conduct[232]

Some jurisdictions require a party to move to amend the complaint to add a claim for punitive damages, and subject this motion and the ultimate recovery to a "clear and convincing" evidence standard.

B. The Role of Expert Testimony

The factors that govern awarding punitive damages suggest strongly that expert testimony is necessary, or at least helpful, in maximizing recovery. Evidence of the defendant's financial condition is often introduced through an expert economist, who can interpret the data and explain to the jury why a punitive damage award is needed and the potential impact of such an award on the defendant. Failure to offer evidence of the defendant's financial condition can justify reversal of a punitive damage award.[233]

The importance of bringing claims under state law is illustrated by *EEOC v. Farmers Brothers Co.*[234] In *Farmers Brothers*, the Ninth Circuit upheld an award of more than $800,000 in punitive damages under both the Civil Rights Act and the California Fair Employment and Housing Act. Although cases under the Title VII damages cap do not compel plaintiffs to be concerned with proportionality, *Farmers Brothers* also illustrates

---

231. 493 F.3d 968, 974 (8th Cir. 2007).

232. *See* EEOC POLICY GUIDE ON COMPENSATORY AND PUNITIVE DAMAGES (July 7, 1992); DEVITT, BLACKMAR, & O'MALLEY, FEDERAL JURY PRACTICE AND INSTRUCTIONS, 1994 Supp. § 104.07 (modified); 42 U.S.C. § 1981(a)(b)(1); Smith v. Wade, 461 U.S. 30 (1983); Block v. R.H. Macy & Co., 712 F.2d 1241 (8th Cir. 1983).

233. *See* Adams v. Murakami, 813 P.2d 1348 (Cal. 1991); Carr v. Barnabey's Hotel Corp., 1994 Cal. LEXIS 2895 (Cal. Ct. App. 1994).

234. 31 F.3d 891 (9th Cir. 1994).

that when the caps are exceeded, plaintiffs will need to defend the ratio of punitive damages against back wages and/or compensatory damages.[235]

C. Punitive Damages in the Absence of Compensatory Damages

In Title VII cases where the plaintiff adequately shows entitlement to punitive damages, courts appear to be split on whether such damages may be granted even in the absence of a compensatory damage award. Some courts have allowed such awards in these circumstances. For example, in *Abner v. Kansas City Southern Railroad Co.,* a case of egregious racial harassment, the Fifth Circuit upheld an award of $125,000 in punitive damages to each of the eight plaintiffs, notwithstanding the fact that the plaintiffs had only been awarded nominal compensatory damages in the amount of $1 each.[236]

The court reasoned that Title VII's plain language points to congressional acceptance of independent awards of punitive damages in Title VII cases. It contains a clause ("Determination of punitive damages") providing, "A complaining party may recover punitive damages under this section against a respondent" if that party proves certain conditions—namely discrimination with "malice or with reckless indifference to federal rights." [N]othing in the text of the statute limits an award of punitive damages to cases in which the plaintiff also receives compensatory damages . . . [P]reventing juries from awarding punitive damages when an employer engaged in reprehensible discrimination without inflicting easily quantifiable physical and monetary harm would quell the deterrence that Congress intended in the most egregious discrimination cases under Title VII.[237]

In addition to the fact that the plaintiffs had established the requisite level of culpability on the part of their employer to be entitled to punitive damages, the court also justified its holding on the facts that the total award still fell below Title VII's damages cap, and there was no indication of jury bias.[238] In rejecting the defendant's argument that the punitive damages award violated the US Supreme Court's holding in *BMW of North America v. Gore*[239] that punitive damage awards must be proportional to compensatory damage awards, the Fifth Circuit reasoned that the combination of Title VII's damages cap and high threshold of culpability for any punitive damages award made a ratio-based proportionality inquiry irrelevant, particularly when only nominal compensatory damages have been awarded.[240] In this regard, the court seems to have suggested that it would always consider punitive damage awards "proportional" for the purposes of the BMW case so long as the total damages awarded still fell below Title VII's damages cap.

---

235. *Id.; see also* BMW of N. Am., Inc. v. Gore, 517 U.S. 559 (1996); Hennessy v. Penril Datacomm Networks, 69 F.3d 1344 (7th Cir. 1995).

236. 513 F.3d 154 (5th Cir. 2008).

237. *Id.* at 161–63.

238. *Id.*

239. 517 U.S. 559 (1996).

240. 513 F.3d at 161–63.

Similarly, in *Cush-Crawford v. Adchem Corp.*,[241] a sexual harassment case, the Second Circuit held that where a plaintiff establishes entitlement to punitive damages under Title VII, punitive damages may be awarded within the limits of the statutory caps, regardless of whether the plaintiff also receives an award of compensatory or nominal damages. The court reasoned that "there is some unseemliness for a defendant who engages in malicious or reckless violations of legal duty to escape either the punitive or deterrent goal of punitive damages merely because either good fortune or a plaintiff's unusual strength or resilience protected the plaintiff from suffering harm."[242] It appears that the Third, Seventh, and Eighth Circuits have adopted this rule as well.[243]

Other circuits appear to have adopted the opposite view on this issue. For example, the First Circuit has held in a Title VII case that "punitive damages award[s] must be vacated absent either a compensatory damages award, or a timely request for nominal damages."[244] Similarly, in a case dealing with an analogous provision of the Fair Housing Act (FHA), the Fourth Circuit has held that punitive damages are not available absent a compensatory damages award.[245] However, the applicability of this Fourth Circuit FHA ruling to the context of Title VII cases is questionable—especially in light of the fact that the Fifth Circuit similarly disallowed punitive damages without compensatory damages in an FHA case[246] but, as noted already, allowed such an award in the context of Title VII violations in Abner.

VI. ATTORNEY'S FEES AWARDS

A. Availability of Attorney's Fees Awards Generally

A plaintiff who proves that the employer is liable for Title VII violations can be awarded reasonable attorney's fees.[247] Specifically, § 706(k) of Title VII provides: "In any action or proceeding under this title the court, in its discretion, may allow the prevailing party, other than the Commission or the United States, a reasonable attorney's fee as

---

241. 271 F.3d 352 (2d Cir. 2001).

242. *Id.* at 359.

243. *See* Timm v. Progressive Steel Treating, Inc., 137 F.3d 1008, 1010–11 (7th Cir. 1998) (affirming a jury award of punitive damages in a Title VII case without actual damages and apparently without nominal damages); Alexander v. Riga, 208 F.3d 419, 430–34 (3d Cir. 2000), *cert. denied*, 531 U.S. 1069 (2001) (upholding a punitive damage award under an analogous provision of the Fair Housing Act despite the absence of actual or nominal damage awards); Hicks v. Brown Group, Inc., 902 F.2d 630, 652–54 (8th Cir. 1990), *vacated on other grounds*, 499 U.S. 914 (1991) (upholding a punitive damage award in a case brought under 42 U.S.C. § 1981 notwithstanding the absence of compensatory damages and only a $1 award of nominal damages).

244. Kerr-Selgas v. Am. Airlines, Inc., 69 F.3d 1205, 1215 (1st Cir. 1995).

245. People Helpers Found., Inc. v. City of Richmond, 12 F.3d 1321, 1327 (4th Cir. 1993).

246. La. ACORN Fair Hous. v. LeBlanc, 211 F.3d 298, 303 (5th Cir. 2000).

247. 42 U.S.C. § 2000e-5(g) (2000). *See also* N.Y. Gaslight Club, Inc. v. Carey, 447 U.S. 54 (1980) (holding that in a Title VII suit, when the plaintiff was required to exhaust state employment discrimination procedures before filing a Title VII claim in federal court, attorney's fees could be recovered for the state proceedings).

part of the costs, and the Commission and the United States shall be liable for costs the same as a private person."[248] Provision for attorney's fees is common in civil rights statutes. Congress has indicated that it considers such provisions integral to civil rights enforcement—that is, the provisions were enacted in an effort to "mak[e] it easier for victims of civil rights violations to find lawyers willing to take their cases."[249] For that reason, the US Supreme Court has held that Title VII creates a presumption in favor of awarding attorney's fees to successful Title VII plaintiffs.[250]

Defendants are also sometimes entitled to attorney's fees in very limited circumstances. The US Supreme Court has held that the prevailing defendant may recover attorney's fees from the plaintiff only if the plaintiff brought suit in bad faith, the lawsuit was clearly frivolous, vexatious, or brought to harass the defendant, or was unreasonable or groundless.[251]

B. Calculating Reasonable Attorney's Fees Awards

In an article for the Temple Law Review, Thomas H. McDonough summarizes the competing processes of calculating reasonable attorney's fees awards in civil rights cases:

> There are two general methodologies for calculating reasonable attorneys' fees in statutory fee shifting [civil rights] cases: 1) the "lodestar" analysis, which calculates a fee award on the basis of compensating counsel for the time reasonably spent in representing the prevailing party; and 2) the "proportionality" analysis, which calculates a fee award as a proportion of the monetary damages won by the prevailing plaintiff. Generally, fee awards calculated using proportionality analysis are smaller than those calculated using the lodestar analysis. Predictably, the controversy over which is the preferred methodology has pitted plaintiff, arguing for the lodestar approach, against defendant, advocating the proportionality approach.[252]

However, while the lodestar approach is generally accepted and used by the federal courts in determining attorney's fees awards, the propriety of applying a

---

248. 42 U.S.C. § 2000e-5(k) (2000).

249. Evans v. Jeff D., 475 U.S. 717, 745 (1986) (Brennan, J., dissenting) ("Congress provided fee awards to ensure that there would be lawyers available to plaintiffs who could not otherwise afford counsel, so that these plaintiffs could fulfill their role in the federal enforcement scheme as 'private attorneys general,' vindicating the public interest."); *see also id.* at 732 n. 22 (noting the importance of fee-shifting provisions in "enlisting the aid of 'private attorneys general'"); Grace v. Ludwig, 484 F.2d 1262, 1267 (2d Cir. 1973), *cert. denied*, 416 U.S. 905 (1974).

250. Christiansburg Garment Co. v. EEOC, 434 U.S. 412, 417 (1978).

251. *Id.*

252. Thomas H. McDonough, *Civil Rights—Third Circuit Disallows Use of Proportionality Analysis in Awarding Attorney's Fees Pursuant to the Federal Civil Rights Attorney's Fees Awards Act of 1976—Washington v. Philadelphia County Court of Common Pleas, 89 F.3d 1031 (3d Cir. 1996)*, 71 TEMP. L. REV. 449, 450 (Summer 1998).

proportionality analysis to attorney's fees awards in civil rights cases is controversial.[253] In *Washington v. Philadelphia County Court of Common Pleas,* the Third Circuit discussed the tension between these competing rules in a case brought under 42 U.S.C. § 1988—a civil rights statute. The court began by describing the general acceptance of the lodestar approach.

The US Supreme Court has held that "[t]he most useful starting point for determining the amount of a reasonable fee is the number of hours reasonably expended on the litigation multiplied by a reasonable hourly rate."[254] The result of this computation is called the lodestar. The lodestar is strongly presumed to yield a reasonable fee.[255] . . . The general rule is that a reasonable hourly rate is calculated according to the prevailing market rates in the community.[256] The prevailing party bears the burden of establishing by way of satisfactory evidence, "in addition to [the] attorney's own affidavits,"[257] that the requested hourly rates meet this standard. The court then went on to hold that the district court's consideration of proportionality of damages to attorney's fee awards in this civil rights action was reversible legal error.

[T]his Court has expressed serious concerns with the practice of limiting an award of attorney's fees to maintain proportionality between the fees and the amount of damages awarded.[258] . . . "[U]nlike most private tort litigants, a civil rights plaintiff seeks to vindicate important civil and constitutional rights that cannot be valued solely in monetary terms. . . . Regardless of the form of relief he actually obtains, a successful civil rights plaintiff often secures important social benefits that are not reflected in nominal or relatively small damages awards."[259] [Therefore, in civil rights cases], the monetary amount awarded to the plaintiff would not be an accurate measure of the success achieved by the attorneys in the case, and therefore attorney's fees assessed in proportion to the damage award would not adequately compensate the attorneys for their labor, which [the plurality in the Supreme Court decision in Riverside] compared to that of a "private attorney general."[260] The plurality concluded that "[a] rule of

---

253. *See, e.g.,* City of Riverside v. Rivera, 477 U.S. 561 (1986); Washington v. Philadelphia County Court of Common Pleas, 89 F.3d 1031 (3d Cir. 1996).

254. Hensley v. Eckerhart, 461 U.S. 424, 433, 103 S.Ct. 1933, 1939, 76 L.Ed.2d 40 (1983); *see also* Rode, 892 F.2d at 1183 (same).

255. City of Burlington v. Dague, 505 U.S. 557, 112 S.Ct. 2638, 120 L.Ed.2d 449 (1992).

256. Blum v. Stenson, 465 U.S. 886, 895–96 n. 11, 104 S.Ct. 1541, 1547 n. 11, 79 L.Ed.2d 891 (1984); Student Public Interest Research Group, Inc., 842 F.2d at 1448 (adopting the community market rule).

257. Blum, 465 U.S. at 895 n. 11, 104 S.Ct. at 1547 n. 11.

258. *See, e.g.,* Cunningham v. City of McKeesport, 807 F.2d 49, 52–54 (3d Cir. 1986), *cert. denied,* 481 U.S. 1049, 107 S.Ct. 2179, 95 L.Ed.2d 836 (1987); Northeast Women's Center v. McMonagle, 889 F.2d 466, 474–75 (3d Cir. 1989), *cert. denied,* 494 U.S. 1068, 110 S.Ct. 1788, 108 L.Ed.2d 790 (1990).

259. City of Riverside v. Rivera, 106 S.Ct. 2686, 2694 (1986).

260. *Id.* at 575, 106 S.Ct. at 2694 (citation omitted).

proportionality would make it difficult, if not impossible, for individuals with meritorious civil rights claims but relatively small potential damages to obtain redress from the courts,"[261] and for this reason rejected such a rule.[262]

Therefore, plaintiffs' counsel can rest relatively certain that federal courts will apply the lodestar approach to the calculation of attorney's fees. Similarly, while the proportionality approach has not been discontinued or abolished by the courts per se in every context, defense counsel should at least be aware of the relative disfavor in which the approach is viewed by federal courts in civil rights cases.

Occasionally, questions will arise as to whether enhancement of lodestar attorney's fees is appropriate in a given case. For example, in *Pennsylvania v. Delaware Valley Citizens' Council for Clean Air (Delaware I)*,[263] the US Supreme Court discussed the appropriateness of increasing the lodestar amount by a contingent risk factor, and stated that "no enhancement for risk is appropriate unless the applicant can establish that without an adjustment for risk the prevailing party 'would have faced substantial difficulties in finding counsel in the local or other relevant market.'" Later, in *Pennsylvania v. Delaware Valley Citizens' Council for Clean Air (Delaware II)*,[264] the court stated in a plurality decision that the novelty and difficulty of issues cannot be the basis for a contingency multiplier, and that specific findings must be made by the district court to support any such award. In *Blum v. Stenson*,[265] the court held that enhancement of fees is limited to cases of "exceptional success." Later, in *City of Burlington v. Dague*,[266] the court rejected contingency enhancement of an attorney's fee award, suggesting that such enhancement is rarely appropriate.[267]

VII. INTEREST AWARDS

A. Availability of Interest Awards Generally

The courts have discretion to award prejudgment interest to a plaintiff. An interest award can significantly increase an employer's liability, especially if the case has been pending for several years. Because an interest award can be substantial, both the defendant and the plaintiff should vigorously litigate the issue.

---

261. *Id.* at 578, 106 S.Ct. at 2696,

262. *Id.* at 1039–41. *See also* City of Riverside v. Rivera, 477 U.S. 561 (1986) (A plurality in the Supreme Court upheld an award of $250,000 in attorney's fees, even though the plaintiff recovered only $33,000 in damages and insignificant injunctive relief.).

263. 478 U.S. 546 (1986).

264. 483 U.S. 711 (1987).

265. 465 U.S. 886 (1984).

266. 505 U.S. 504 (1992).

267. *See also* King v. Palmer, 950 F.2d 771 (D.C. Cir. 1991) (*en banc*) (court rejected enhancement of fees in employment discrimination cases so as not to compensate attorneys for the risk of losing the case).

Title VII authorizes a district court to grant prejudgment interest on a back pay award.[268] Prejudgment interest discourages an employer from attempting to "enjoy an interest-free loan for as long as [it can] delay paying out back wages."[269] Thus, the courts have held that "it is ordinarily an abuse of discretion not to include prejudgment interest in a back-pay award."[270] A number of courts of appeals have held that the district court has discretion to award or refuse to award prejudgment interest.[271] At least one circuit has suggested that recovery of prejudgment interest should be awarded as a matter of course.[272] In circuits where an award of prejudgment interest is discretionary, courts have articulated some factors to be considered in determining whether to make such an award.[273]

Some courts grant postjudgment interest awards in addition to prejudgment awards. "Post-judgment interest is designed to compensate the plaintiff for the delay it suffers from the time damages are reduced to an enforceable judgment to the time the defendant pays the judgment."[274]

B. Rates Chosen and Calculation of Interest Awards

Once the court has decided to award prejudgment interest, "the more difficult questions are what rate should apply and how the prejudgment interest should be calculated."[275] In setting the interest rate and calculating interest, the court should do so with the interests of making the plaintiff whole. However, the district court is given wide discretion in how to go about doing so. The prejudgment interest rate to be applied is usually left

---

268. 42 U.S.C. § 2000e-5(g). *See also* Loffler v. Frank, 486 U.S. 549, 557 & n. 5 (1988) (citing cases); Shorter v. Hartford Fin. Servs. Group, Inc., 2005 U.S. Dist. LEXIS 19902 (D. Conn. 2005).

269. Donovan v. Sovereign Sec. Ltd., 726 F.2d 55, 58 (2d Cir. 1984).

270. *Id. See also* EEOC v. County of Erie, 751 F.2d 79, 81 (2d Cir. 1984); Sands v. Runyon, 28 F.3d 1323, 1327 (2d Cir. 1994); Miner v. City of Glens Falls, 999 F.2d 655, 661 (2d Cir. 1993) (upholding prejudgment interest award in a § 1983 case); EEOC v. County of Erie, 751 F.2d 79, 81 (2d Cir. 1984) (same under Equal Pay Act); Donovan v. Sovereign Sec., Ltd., 726 F.2d 55, 58 (2d Cir. 1984) (same under Fair Labor Standards Act).

271. *See, e.g.,* Earnhardt v. Commonwealth of P.R., 744 F.2d 1 (1st Cir. 1984); EEOC v. Wooster Brush Co. Employees Relief Ass'n, 727 F.2d 566, 578–79 (6th Cir. 1984); Hunter v. Allis-Chalmers Corp., 797 F.2d 1417 (7th Cir. 1986) (suggesting that federal courts should follow the common-law rule that allows recovery of prejudgment interest on back wages).

272. Smith v. Am. Serv. Co., 796 F.2d 1430, 1432–33 (11th Cir. 1986) (courts should look to the practice of the NLRB, which has consistently awarded prejudgment interest); *see also* EEOC v. U.S. Steel Corp., 51 FEP Cases (BNA) 739, 741 (W.D. Pa. 1989) ("pre-judgment interest should be presumed in back pay awards under the ADEA.").

273. *See* Domingo v. New England Fish Co., 727 F.2d 1429 (9th Cir. 1984) (fact that amount of back pay was not easily ascertainable mitigated against an award of prejudgment interest). *Glenn v. Gen. Motors,* 658 F. Supp. 918 (N.D. Ala. 1987), *aff'd in part, rev'd in part,* 814 F.2d 1567 (11th Cir. 1988), appears to hold that no prejudgment interest may be recovered under the Equal Pay Act.

274. Andrulonis v. United States, 26 F. 3d 1224, 1230 (2d Cir. 1994); *see also Shorter,* 2005 U.S. Dist. LEXIS 19902, at *28–29 (D. Conn. 2005).

275. *Shorter,* 2005 U.S. Dist. LEXIS 19902.

to the discretion of the court.[276] The rate of interest could be determined from a variety of sources, such as the postjudgment interest rate provided in 28 U.S.C. § 1961, state statutory interest rates, market rates, or numerous other sources.[277]

The court in Shorter concluded that 28 U.S.C. § 1961 should be used to find the correct rate, and noted the following:

> Although the courts have applied different interest rates in employment discrimination cases, the majority of courts appear to favor the post-judgment statutory rate of 28 U.S.C. § 1961, "because it takes into account the effects of inflation, but does not overly compensate the plaintiff." Worthington, 1999 U.S. Dist. LEXIS 16104, 1999 WL 958627, at 17, (citing cases); Fisher v. Town of Windsor, 1997 U.S. Dist. LEXIS 23542, No. 3:94CV02050, 1997 WL 76669, at 6 (D. Conn. Feb. 7, 1997) (using the rates set forth in § 1961(a), compounded monthly, to calculate prejudgment interest in an employment discrimination case); Association against Discrimination in Employment, Inc. v. Bridgeport, 572 F. Supp. 494, 495 (D. Conn. 1983) (same).[278]

However, some courts rationalize that the rate should not be calculated according to 28 U.S.C. § 1961, as it applies to postjudgment interest.[279] Numerous other courts have used, as does the NLRB, the IRS rates for underpayment of taxes in employment cases.[280] Rates not appearing in 28 U.S.C. § 1981 are available online at http://www.federalreserve.gov at their most recent levels.

Further, once the interest rate is chosen, there are several ways in which courts may calculate prejudgment interest. Even within the same court, interest is sometimes calculated differently for different cases. For example, in three decisions decided by the

---

276. *See, e.g.*, Anderson v. CONRAIL, 2000 U.S. Dist. LEXIS 15987, at *12–13 (D. Pa. 2000); Sun Ship, Inc. v. Matson Navigation Co., 785 F.2d 59, 63 (3d Cir. 1986).

277. Chandler v. Bombardier Capital Inc., 44 F.3d 80, 84 (1994) (approving the trial court's use of the federal postjudgment rate of interest, 28 U.S.C. § 1961); EEOC v. County of Erie, 751 F.2d at 82 (applying the adjusted prime rate of interest as established by the Secretary of the Treasury in an employment discrimination case); Shaw v. Greenwich Anesthesiology Assoc. 200 F. Supp. 110, 119 (applying a prejudgment interest rate of 7.5 percent, compounded semimonthly, in an employment discrimination case); Malarkey v. Texaco, Inc., 794 F. Supp. 1237, 1243 (S.D.N.Y. 1992) (applying the New York statutory rate to an employment discrimination case), *aff'd*, 983 F.2d 1204 (2d Cir. 1993); EEOC v. O'Grady, 857 F.2d 383 (7th Cir. 1988) (court used the Internal Revenue Service adjusted prime rate); Partington v. Brovhill Furniture, 999 F.2d 269 (7th Cir. 1993), 62 FEP Cases (BNA) 534, 538 (holding that it was error to use the Treasury bill rate and the prime rate must be used instead); Gelof v. Papineau, 648 F. Supp. 912, 930 (D. Del. 1986) (using a state statute setting interest); Metz v. Transit Mix, Inc., 692 F. Supp. 987 (N.D. Ind. 1988) (using the prejudgment interest rate under 28 U.S.C. § 1961).

278. 2005 U.S. Dist. LEXIS 19902, at *25–26; *see also* Sun Ship, Inc. v. Matson Navigation Co., 785 F.2d 59, 63 (3d Cir. 1986) (stating that "the court may be guided by the rate set out in 28 U.S.C. § 1961"); Becker v. ARCO Chem. Co., 15 F. Supp. 2d 621, 638 (E.D. Pa. 1998); Corbett v. Nat'l Prods. Co., 1995 U.S. Dist. LEXIS 6425 (E.D. Pa. May 9, 1995); Young v. Lukens Steel, 881 F. Supp. 962, 977–78 (E.D. Pa. 1994).

279. *See, e.g.*, Newfield v. Searle Lab., 46 FEP Cases (BNA) 5, 6 (W.D. Mo. 1988).

280. *See supra* note 37.

Eastern District of Pennsylvania within less than a decade, interest in one case was calculated using simple interest on the lump sum damage award;[281] another was calculated using annual compound interest;[282] and the third was calculated using compound annual interest with a separate rate for each year.[283] Some courts compound interest quarterly,[284] while others compound it annually.[285]

Thus, when trying to predict the amount of interest that a court may award, or in arguing that a particular amount should be granted, the practitioner would be wise to research how the court in the case at hand tends to determine interest rates and calculate interest in the particular kind of case at hand, as these issues may vary by court and by type of case.

VIII. INJUNCTIVE RELIEF AND OTHER EQUITABLE REMEDIES

Upon finding a violation of Title VII, a court has a "'duty to render a decree which will so far as possible eliminate the discriminatory effects of the past as well as bar like discrimination in the future.'"[286] Such relief is often granted in the form of an injunction of the employer's future unlawful behavior. Furthermore, such an injunction may be issued even when the unlawful behavior complained of has ceased. "A suit for injunctive relief does not become moot simply because the offending party has ceased the offending conduct, since the offending party might be free otherwise to renew that conduct once the court denied the relief."[287] Similarly, in *EEOC v. Hacienda Hotel,*[288] the court found that the plaintiff was entitled to a permanent injunction against the defendant, even though the particular victims of harassment would not likely suffer again from the defendant's unlawful conduct. Under a ruling in *EEOC v. FLC & Brothers Rebel Inc.,*[289] the court enjoined the defendant from further engaging in practices that discriminate against persons because of their sex, and required the defendant to post notices informing employees of their rights under Title VII. The plaintiff's failure to allege a pattern of discriminatory activity did not prevent the issuance of an injunction.

In some instances courts will require employers to take affirmative action to eradicate unlawful conduct in the workplace. For example, in *Boyd v. Havens Living Health*

---

281. *See, e.g.,* Becker v. ARCO Chem. Co., 15 F. Supp. 2d 621, 638 (E.D. Pa. 1998).

282. *See, e.g.,* Young v. Lukens Steel Co., 881 F. Supp. 962, 978 (E.D. Pa. 1994).

283. *See, e.g.,* O'Neill v. Sears, Roebuck & Co., 108 F. Supp. 2d 443, 445–46 (E.D. Pa. 2000).

284. *See, e.g., Shorter,* 2005 U.S. Dist. LEXIS 19902.

285. *See, e.g.,* Young v. Lukens Steel Co., 881 F. Supp. 962, 978 (E.D. Pa. 1994).

286. Albemarle Paper Co. v. Moody, 422 U.S. 405, 418 (quoting Louisiana v. United States, 380 U.S. 145, 154 (1965)).

287. Bundy v. Jackson, 641 F.2d 934, 946 n.13 (D.C. Cir. 1981). *See also id.* at 948 n. 15 for an example of an injunction that the circuit court suggested to the lower court upon remand.

288. 881 F.2d 1504 (9th Cir. 1989).

289. 663 F. Supp. 864, 871 (S.D.N.Y. 1987).

Care Agency,[290] an employer was required to submit a plan outlining steps it would take to prevent future sexual harassment. Similarly, in *EEOC v. Gurnee Inn Corp.,*[291] the employer was required to institute a company-wide policy concerning sex discrimination, give written notice of that policy to employees and job applicants, implement a training program for supervisory employees, and prohibit the violator's reemployment there.[292]

---

290. 671 F. Supp. 1155, 1169 (W.D. Tenn. 1987).

291. 46 FEP Cases (BNA) 871 (N.D. Ill. 1988).

292. Washington v. Philadelphia County Court of Common Pleas, 89 F.3d 1031, 1035 (3d Cir. 1996).

CHAPTER 21

Damage Issues and Mitigation

Amy S. Wilson

I. MITIGATION PRINCIPLES GENERALLY

Certain set-offs must or may be made from the base back pay award in determining the plaintiff's net back pay entitlement. Title VII of the Civil Rights Act of 1964 (Title VII) expressly includes a mitigation requirement: Interim earnings or amounts earnable with reasonable diligence by the person or persons discriminated against shall operate to reduce the back pay otherwise allowable.[1]

Mitigation is required under other federal harassment statutes as well.[2] A failure to mitigate damages does not completely cut off the right to a back pay award in harassment (or discrimination) cases; such a conclusion would frustrate the statutes' "make-whole" objective.[3]

---

1. 42 U.S.C. § 2000e-5(g) (1) (2012).

2. *See, e.g.*, Deffenbaugh-Williams v. Wal-Mart, Inc., 156 F.3d 581 (5th Cir. 1998) (§ 1981 and Title VII decision); Denesha v. Farmers Ins. Exch., 161 F.3d 491 (8th Cir. 1998) (ADEA decision); Greenway v. Buffalo Hilton Hotel, 143 F.3d 47 (2d Cir. 1998) (ADA decision); Arneson v. Callahan, 128 F.3d 1243 (8th Cir. 1997) (Rehabilitation Act); Carter v. DecisionOne Corp., 122 F.3d 997 (11th Cir. 1997) (ADEA and Title VII decision); Doane v. City of Omaha, 115 F.3d 624 (8th Cir. 1997) (ADA decision); EEOC v. Massey Yardley Chrysler Plymouth, Inc., 117 F.3d 1244 (11th Cir. 1997) (ADEA decision); Barbour v. Merrill, 48 F.3d 1270 (per curiam) (D.C. Cir.), *cert. granted in part,* 516 U.S. 1086, *cert. dismissed,* 516 U.S. 1155 (1996) (§ 1981 decision); Marcing v. Fluor Daniel, Inc., No. 93-3098, 36 F.3d 1099 (7th Cir. 1994) (unpublished decision) (Equal Pay Act decision); Hunter v. Allis-Chalmers Corp., 797 F.2d 1417 (7th Cir. 1986) (§ 1981 and Title VII decision); Coleman v. Lane, 949 F. Supp. 604 (N.D. Ill. 1996) (§ 1983 decision). *See also* 42 U.S.C. § 12117(a) (2012) (incorporating Title VII mitigation principles into the ADA); 29 U.S.C. § 794a(a) (1) (2012) (incorporating same into the Rehabilitation Act).

3. Booker v. Taylor Milk Co., Inc., 64 F.3d 860, 867 (3d Cir. 1995); Barbour v. Merrill, 48 F.3d 1270 (per curiam) (D.C. Cir.), *cert. granted in part,* 516 U.S. 1086, *cert. dismissed,* 516 U.S. 1155 (1996) (§ 1981 decision).

A. The Parties' Burdens

1. The Plaintiff

It is the plaintiff's burden to show that she used "reasonable diligence in finding other suitable employment."[4] Her job search effort need not be successful to show that she was reasonably diligent.[5] "The plaintiff might elect to allege facts relevant to mitigation in her pleading or to present those facts in her case in chief, but she would do so in anticipation of the employer's affirmative defense, not as a legal requirement."[6] Failure to respond to reasonable discovery requests related to mitigation may result in sanctions[7] or a reduced back pay award, or both.

It is in the plaintiff's attorney's best interest to ensure that his client is doing a reasonably diligent job to mitigate her damages. The inquiry at time of trial or summary judgment will be fact-specific, not only to the plaintiff, but to the plaintiff's typical line of work, and possibly to her geographical location.[8] It is not enough that the plaintiff's counsel ensures that his client is looking for work and keeping notes and other documentation of that effort. It is important to research and understand how individuals with the plaintiff's level of education and occupation generally look for work; how workers in the geographical area generally look for work; and whether the client's efforts at mitigation fall in line with the court's expectations.[9]

A plaintiff who deliberately removes herself from the job market will not recover back pay.[10] In *Holocheck v. Luzerne County Head Start, Inc.*, the court held that the "willful loss of earnings" concept applied where the plaintiff made no effort to find substitute employment either in or outside of her field.[11] A willful loss of earnings exists where the plaintiff fails to stay in the labor market, refuses to accept comparable employment, fails to search diligently for other work, or voluntarily quits alternative employment without cause.[12] Here, the plaintiff did not look for work because she thought the employer would provide a negative reference to prospective employers.[13] However, she never applied for any positions and therefore had no basis for her

---

4. Ford Motor Co. v. EEOC, 458 U.S. 219, 231 (1982).

5. Dailey v. Societe Generale, 108 F.3d 451, 456 (2d Cir. 1997) (quoting Rasimas v. Mich. Dep't of Mental Health, 714 F.2d 614, 624 (6th Cir. 1983)); United States v. Lee Way Motor Freight, Inc., 625 F.2d 918, 938 (10th Cir. 1979).

6. Pa. State Police v. Suders, 542 U.S. 129, 152 (2004).

7. *See, e.g.*, Chodkowski v. Cuno Inc., No. 3:05CV997, 2006 WL 1062115 (D. Conn. Mar. 30, 2006).

8. *See* EEOC v. Serv. News Co., 898 F.2d 958, 963 (4th Cir. 1990).

9. *See id.* (holding that where plaintiff was an eighteen-year-old unskilled employee, merely looking through want ads for unskilled positions is insufficient).

10. *See* Crawford v. George & Lynch, Inc., No. 10-949–GMS–SRF, 2013 WL 6504635 at *15–16 (D. Del. 2013); Holocheck v. Luzerne County Head Start, Inc., No. 3:CV-04-2082, 2007 WL 954308 at *15–17 (M.D. Penn. March 28, 2007).

11. *Holocheck*, 2007 WL 954308 at *15.

12. *Id.* at *14.

13. *Id.* at *16.

assumption.[14] The court concluded that the plaintiff completely withdrew from the labor market; summary judgment was entered against her on her claim for back pay for failing to mitigate.[15]

In *EEOC v. Pape Lift, Inc.*, the court determined that it was not per se unreasonable for the plaintiff to have searched for available jobs solely in the newspaper want ads.[16] The court "[thought] it more appropriate to tailor the reasonableness inquiry to the particular characteristics of the injured plaintiff."[17]

2. The Defendant

Defense counsel should include the failure to mitigate damages as an affirmative defense in the answer, although failure to do so may not prove fatal.[18] In practice, defendants typically plead this affirmative defense in any answer to an employment-related complaint, no matter what the circumstances. It is the defendant-employer's burden to prove that the plaintiff failed to mitigate her damages.[19] The circuits are split as to how this must be accomplished. The First,[20] Third,[21] Sixth,[22] Seventh,[23] Ninth,[24] and Tenth[25] Circuits suggest a two-step analysis, where the defendant must prove that

1. the plaintiff did not exercise reasonable diligence in mitigating her damages; and
2. there was a reasonable likelihood that she might have found substantially equivalent work if she had exercised reasonable diligence in her job search efforts.[26]

---

14. *Id.*

15. *Id.* at *17.

16. 115 F.3d 676, 684–85 (9th Cir. 1997).

17. *Id.* at 684.

18. *See* Fox v. Dist. of Columbia, 990 F. Supp. 13, 24–25 (D.C. 1997) (and cases cited therein); Garon v. Miller Container of Ind., Inc., No. 05-4088, 2007 WL 158726 (C.D. Ill. Jan. 18, 2007).

19. Fogg v. Gonzales, 492 F.3d 447, 455 (D.C. Cir. 2007); Gaffney v. Riverboat Servs. of Ind., 451 F.3d 424, 460 (7th Cir. 2006); Sarkis' Café, Inc. v. Sarks in the Park, LLC, 55 F. Supp. 1034, 1040–41 (N.D. Ill. 2014).

20. *See, e.g.,* Conetta v. Nation Hair Care Ctrs., 236 F.3d 67 (1st Cir. 2001) (defendant met burden of proof showing plaintiff's failure to mitigate by showing less than diligent job search and the availability of substantially equivalent positions; pursuing one job application and reviewing newspaper ads daily inadequate; back pay award discounted); Quint v. A.E. Staley Mfg. Co., 172 F.3d 1, 16 (1st Cir. 1999) ("the defendant-employer [should be relieved] of the burden to prove the availability of substantially equivalent jobs in the relevant geographic area once it has been shown that the former employee made no effort to secure suitable employment"); Carey v. Mount Desert Island Hosp., 156 F.3d 31, 41 (1st Cir. 1998).

21. *See* Le v. Univ. of Pa., 321 F.3d 403, 407 (3d Cir. 2003); Booker v. Taylor Milk Co., 64 F.3d 860, 864 (3d Cir. 1995).

22. Killian v. Yorozu Auto. Tenn., Inc., 454 F.3d 549, 557 (6th Cir. 2006).

23. Wheeler v. Snyder Buick, Inc., 794 F.2d 1228, 1234 (7th Cir. 1986).

24. EEOC v. Farmer Bros. Co., 31 F.3d 891, 906 (9th Cir. 1994) (to prevail on summary judgment motion, defendant had to prove that during time in question there were substantially equivalent jobs available and that plaintiff failed to use reasonable diligence in pursuing them).

25. Ziegler v. K-Mart Corp., No. 95-3019, 1996 WL 8021. at *7 (10th Cir. Jan. 10, 1996).

26. *Booker*, 64 F.3d at 864.

The Second,[27] Fourth,[28] Fifth,[29] Eighth,[30] and Eleventh[31] Circuits only require that the employer to show that the plaintiff failed to make reasonable efforts to obtain other work.

It is not unusual for a defendant to attack a plaintiff's mitigation efforts in intervals, that is, (1) the period between discharge and reemployment, (2) the period between reemployment and separation from reemployment, and (3) the period following the separation from reemployment.[32]

Consequently, it is important that the plaintiff maintain specific information concerning dates, times, and places in an attempt to frustrate the defendant's efforts.

B. The Types of Damages to Which Mitigation Applies

1. Back Pay

Lost wages and benefits generally compose a back pay award.[33] This could include, among other items, bonus pay,[34] overtime pay,[35] and lost 401(k) contributions.[36] It is the plaintiff's burden to show what she would have received from the defendant had she remained in its employ.[37]

2. Front Pay

Although reinstatement is a strongly preferred remedy in cases of discriminatory discharge, it will not be ordered when it is truly unworkable for the plaintiff, or for the employer.[38] When reinstatement is impossible or futile, the judge may consider an

---

27. Greenway v. Buffalo Hilton Hotel, 143 F.3d 47, 54 (2d Cir. 1988) ("[A]n employer should not be saddled by a requirement that *it* show other suitable employment in fact existed—the threat being that if it does not, the employee will be found to have mitigated his damages—when the employee who is capable of finding replacement work, failed to pursue employment at all.").

28. Miller v. AT&T Corp., 250 F.3d 820, 838 (4th Cir. 2001).

29. West v. Nabors Drilling U.S.A., Inc., 330 F.3d 379, 393 (5th Cir. 2003).

30. Hartley v. Dillard's, 310 F.3d 1054, 1061–62 (8th Cir. 2002).

31. Weaver v. Casa Gallardo, Inc., 922 F.2d 1515, 1527 (11th Cir. 1991).

32. *See, e.g.,* Brady v. Thurston Motor Lines, Inc., 753 F.2d 1269, 1277–78 (4th Cir. 1985); Richardson v. Tricom Pictures & Productions, Inc., 334 F. Supp. 2d 1303, 1313–14 (S.D. Fla. 2004).

33. *See, e.g.,* Taylor v. Cent. Pa. Drug & Alcohol Servs. Corp., 890 F. Supp. 360, 368 (M.D. Pa. 1995).

34. *See, e.g., id.* at 370–72.

35. *See, e.g.,* United States v. City of Warren,, 138 F.3d 1083, 1097 (6th Cir. 1998).

36. *See, e.g.,* Gaworski v. ITT Commercial Fin. Corp., 17 F.3d 1104, 1111 (8th Cir. 1994).

37. Barbour v. Merrill, 48 F.3d 1270, 1278 (D.C. Cir.) (per curiam), *cert. granted in part,* 516 U.S. 1086, *cert. dismissed,* 516 U.S. 1155 (1996) (no entitlement to recover lost car allowance received by another employee where no evidence received about why court should award it to plaintiff).

38. *See, e.g.,* Farley v. Nationwide Mut. Ins. Co., 197 F.3d 1322, 1338 (11th Cir. 1999) (request for reinstatement denied when the "obvious animosity" between plaintiff and his former supervisors made his return to work "unfeasible").

award of front pay instead.[39] Awards of front pay are generally entrusted to the district court judge's discretion and are available in a more limited set of circumstances than back pay,[40] partly because they necessarily involve predictions of events yet to come.[41] Front pay is considered a substitute for reinstatement, and thus is an equitable remedy.[42] Front pay awards are likewise subject to mitigation principles.[43] For these reasons, district court decisions as to front pay are generally afforded more appellate deference than decisions as to back pay.[44]

C. Types of Damages to Which Mitigation Does Not Apply

1. Compensatory and Punitive Damages

The mitigation principles do not apply to compensatory and punitive damage awards.[45] A motion for remittitur is the appropriate way to challenge an award's excessiveness.[46]

2. Attorney's Fees and Costs

The mitigation principles discussed in this chapter do not apply to the recovery of attorney fees and costs.[47] Practitioners should look to the laws of their respective circuits with respect to fee petitions and to their local rules with respect to the awarding of costs.

D. The Role of Prejudgment Interest

Prejudgment interest is generally awarded to make a plaintiff whole. "An award of prejudgment interest adjusts the back pay award for inflation and reflects the present-day value of income that should have been paid to the claimant in the past."[48] A second

---

39. Williams v. Pharmacia, Inc., 137 F.3d 944, 951–52 (7th Cir. 1998); Wildman v. Lerner Stores Corp., 771 F.2d 605, 616 (1st Cir. 1985).

40. Johnson v. Spencer Press of Me., Inc., 364 F.3d 368, 380 (1st Cir. 2004); Lussier v. Runyon, 50 F.3d 1103, 1108–09 (1st Cir. 1995).

41. *Lussier*, 50 F.3d at 1109.

42. *See Farley*, 197 F.3d at 1338.

43. *See, e.g.*, Excel Corp. v. Bosley, 165 F.3d 635, 640 (8th Cir. 1999); Denesha v. Farmers Ins. Exch., 161 F.3d 491, 501 (8th Cir. 1998); Barbour v. Merrill, 48 F.3d 1270, 1281 (D.C. Cir.) (per curiam), *cert. granted in part,* 516 U.S. 1086, *cert. dismissed,* 516 U.S. 1155 (1996).

44. *Johnson*, 364 F.3d at 380.

45. *See* Zerilli v. N.Y.C. Transit Auth., 973 F. Supp. 311, 323 (E.D.N.Y. 1997) (defendant unsuccessfully asserted, without authority, that court erred in rejecting proposed jury instruction that plaintiff failed to mitigate compensatory damages because she declined to enter a psychological counseling program).

46. FED. R. CIV. P. 59(a). *See, e.g.*, Blakey v. Cont'l Airlines, Inc., 992 F. Supp. 731, 738 (D.N.J. 1998); Neal v. Honeywell, Inc., 995 F. Supp. 889, 895 (N.D. Ill. 1998).

47. *See* Clarke v. Frank, 960 F.2d 1146, 1154 (2d Cir. 1992).

48. EEOC v. Joe's Stone Crab, Inc., 15 F. Supp. 2d 1364, 1379 (S.D. Fla. 1998), *aff'd in part,* 220 F.3d 1263 (11th Cir. 2000); *see also* Reed v. A.W. Lawrence & Co., 95 F.3d 1170, 1182–83 (2d Cir. 1996) (plaintiff awarded prejudgment interest for ten-month period between the jury verdict and entry of judgment after resolution of posttrial motions).

purpose is to prevent the defendant from "enjoy[ing the benefits of] an interest-free loan for as long as it can delay paying out back wages."[49] Although an award of prejudgment interest is ordinarily committed to the trial court's discretion,[50] a judge cannot deny prejudgment interest where the case has been tried to a jury based on his feeling that the plaintiff failed to mitigate her damages, assuming he has instructed the jury on mitigation.[51]

II. SATISFYING THE PARTIES' RESPECTIVE BURDENS

Attempts to maximize or reduce the back pay to which the plaintiff claims entitlement should focus on the following areas:

- Amount paid by the defendant to the plaintiff
- Amount paid to the plaintiff by nonemployer third parties, except third-party insurance(s) or other "collateral sources"
- Amount earned in interim employment with another employer
- Amount the plaintiff should have earned but for her failure to mitigate her damages

In *Griffin v. Four Season Resorts & Hotels, Ltd.*,[52] "the plaintiff offered evidence at trial that she was obliged to reject an employment offer so she could relocate to Australia to tend to her terminally ill mother." The court held "that a decision to forgo comparable employment for personal reasons, however understandable, constitute[d] a failure to mitigate damages as a matter of law."[53]

A. Amounts Paid by the Defendant to the Plaintiff

Severance pay from the employer to the plaintiff is properly deducted because, but for the firing, the plaintiff would never have received the payment.[54]

---

49. Gierlinger v. Gleason, 160 F.3d 858, 874 (2d Cir. 1998) (quoting Saulpaugh v. Monroe Cmty. Hosp., 4 F.3d 134, 145 (2d Cir. 1993)).

50. *See* Criado v. IBM Corp., 145 F.3d 437, 445 (1st Cir. 1998) (no abuse of discretion for district court to determine that prejudgment interest was inappropriate where large award of damages made her whole and was sufficient to deter employer from future wrongdoing); Greenway v. Buffalo Hilton Hotel, 143 F.3d 47, 56 (2d Cir. 1998) ("it is within the trial court's broad discretion to elect whether and how to compute prejudgment interest"); Hunter v. Allis-Chalmers Corp., 797 F.2d 1417, 1425–27 (7th Cir. 1986) (discussion of whether entitlement is automatic or committed to court's discretion).

51. *Gierlinger*, 160 F.3d at 875.

52. Griffin v. Four Seasons Resorts & Hotels, Ltd., No. 96 CIV. 4759 JSR, 1999 WL 212679, at *1 (S.D.N.Y. Apr. 12, 1999).

53. *Id.*

54. Laugesen v. Anaconda Co., 510 F.2d 307, 317 (6th Cir. 1975).

B. Amounts Paid to the Plaintiff by Nonemployer Third Parties

The collateral source rule is applicable in harassment actions.[55] The general rule is that an employer cannot set off from a back pay award any funds the employee receives from a collateral source, such as unemployment compensation or social security benefits. [56]

1. Unemployment Insurance Compensation

No court has held that a plaintiff must file for unemployment compensation benefits (despite whether she actually receives them) as a condition of mitigation. There is a split in the circuits concerning whether the amounts earned from unemployment insurance programs should be deducted from back pay awards:

- Not set off: First, Third, Sixth, Eighth, Ninth, and Eleventh Circuits[57]
- Left to court's discretion: Second, Fourth, Fifth, Seventh, and Tenth Circuits[58]

A review of the case law shows that intracircuit, courts are at times unsure which approach is mandated: no set-off or court's discretion. What is clear, however, is that no court has held that unemployment compensation benefits must be set off.

2. Disability Insurance and Related Benefits

Few courts have a firm rule concerning the offset of disability insurance-type benefits:

- Left to court's discretion: Second Circuit[59]

3. Social Security Benefits

Similarly, few courts have a firm rule concerning the offset of social security benefits:

- Not set off: Third, Eleventh Circuits[60]

---

55. Gaworski v. ITT Commercial Fin. Corp., 17 F.3d 1104, 1111 (8th Cir. 1994).

56. *Id.*

57. Thurman v. Yellow Freight Sys., Inc., 90 F.3d 1160, 1170–71 (6th Cir. 1996); Brown v. A. J. Gerrard Mfg. Co., 715 F.2d 1549, 1550–51 (11th Cir. 1983); Craig v. Y&Y Snacks, Inc., 721 F.2d 77, 84 (3d Cir. 1983); *Gaworski*, 17 F.3d at 1113–14; Kauffman v. Sidereal Corp., 695 F.2d 343, 346–47 (9th Cir. 1983); Toro v. Sanchez, 141 F. Supp. 2d 195 (D.P.R. 2001).

58. Dailey v. Societe Generale, 108 F.3d 451, 459–61 (2d Cir. 1997) (upholding lower court's back pay award that had not been reduced by unemployment benefits received by plaintiff in sex discrimination action); Cooper v. Asplundh Tree Expert Co., 836 F.2d 1544, 1555 (10th Cir. 1988); Hunter v. Allis-Chalmers Corp., Engine Div., 797 F.2d 1417, 1429 (7th Cir. 1986); Ford Motor Co. v. EEOC, 645 F.2d 183, 195 (4th Cir. 1981), *rev'd and remanded on other grounds*, 458 U.S. 219 (1982); Grant v. Bethlehem Steel Corp., 622 F.2d 43, 47 (2d Cir. 1980); Marshall v. Goodyear Tire & Rubber Co., 554 F.2d 730, 736 (5th Cir. 1977).

59. Meling v. St. Francis Coll., 3 F. Supp. 2d 267, 275–76 (E.D.N.Y. 1998) (court preferred that plaintiff gain the unavoidable windfall).

60. Dominguez v. Tom James Co., 113 F.3d 1188, 1190–91 (11th Cir. 1997); Maxfield v. Sinclair Int'l, 766 F.2d 788, 793–95 (3d Cir. 1985).

- Left to court's discretion: Fifth, Seventh, and Tenth Circuits[61]

When social security benefits may be relevant to the issue of mitigation, a plaintiff must produce documents relating to his application for, and receipt of, the same.[62]

4. Workers' Compensation Benefits

More courts permit a set-off where the plaintiff has received compensation under workers' compensation laws:

- Set off: Second, Third, Fourth, Ninth, and Eleventh Circuits[63]
- Not set off: Sixth Circuit[64]

5. Other Welfare Benefits

- Not set off: Third Circuit[65]
- Left to court's discretion: Seventh Circuit[66]

C. Interim Earnings

The wages that the plaintiff receives from a subsequent employer following her employment with the defendant are subtracted from the gross back pay award.[67] The interim earnings include straight time and overtime pay.[68]

1. Separation from Subsequent Employment

To be entitled to back pay, a successful plaintiff must remain involved in the job market or labor force. [69] If she does not, her back pay may be tolled.[70] Awards of back pay are

---

61. Flowers v. Komatsu Mining Sys., Inc., 165 F.3d 554, 557–58 (7th Cir. 1999); Guthrie v. J.C. Penney Co., Inc., 803 F.2d 202, 209 (5th Cir. 1986); EEOC v. Wyo. Ret. Sys., 771 F.2d 1425, 1431 (10th Cir. 1985).

62. Noble v. Ruby Tuesdays Rests., Inc., No. 2:06-CV-259, 2007 WL 3125131 at *2 (S.D. Ohio Oct. 23, 2007).

63. Creswell v. HCAL Corp., No. 04cv388 BTM, 2007 WL 628036 (S.D. Cal. Feb. 12, 2007); Muller v. Costello, 997 F. Supp. 299, 305 (N.D.N.Y. 1998); Mason v. Ass'n for Indep. Growth, 817 F. Supp. 550, 557–58 (E.D. Pa. 1993); Austen v. Hawaii, 759 F. Supp. 612, 619–21 (D. Haw. 1991), aff'd, 967 F.2d 583 (11th Cir. 1992); Nichols v. Frank, 771 F. Supp. 1075, 1079 (D. Or. 1991).

64. Knafel v. Pepsi-Cola Bottlers of Akron, 899 F.2d 1473, 1480 (6th Cir. 1990); Thurman v. Yellow Freight Systems, Inc., 90 F.3d 1160, 1171 (6th Cir.1996).

65. McDowell v. Avtex Fibers, Inc., 740 F.2d 214, 217 (3d Cir. 1984), vacated and remanded on other grounds, 469 U.S. 1202 (1985).

66. Hunter v. Allis-Chalmers Corp., 797 F.2d 1417, 1429–30 (7th Cir. 1986) (benefits should be returned to government agency, not to employer).

67. 42 U.S.C. § 2000e-5(g) (2012); Nord v. U.S. Steel Corp., 758 F.2d 1462, 1472 (11th Cir. 1985); Meadows v. Ford Motor Co., 510 F.2d 939, 942 (6th Cir. 1975).

68. Meadows, 510 F.2d at 947.

69. See Quinones Candelario v. Postmaster Gen. of the U.S., 906 F.2d 798, 800 (1st Cir. 1990).

70. See id. at 799–802.

offset by any wages that could have been earned with reasonable diligence after the illegal discharge, regardless of whether they were actually earned.[71]

a. Involuntary Separation

The back pay entitlement period is tolled where the new employer fires the plaintiff for intentional misconduct, including excessive absenteeism.[72] However, if the new employer discharges the plaintiff for wrongdoing that was not his fault, there is no tolling.[73]

b. Voluntary Separation

A plaintiff who resigns from her employment generally ends the period of back pay entitlement.[74] However, if the plaintiff's departure is due to unreasonable working conditions or her search for more suitable employment, the period may not be tolled.[75] For example, in *Brooks v. Fonda-Fultonville Central School District*,[76] the plaintiff voluntarily left her new job in anticipation of caring for a patient in her home, at a higher wage. Sadly, the patient died before the home care began.[77] The court found no reason to toll the back pay period.[78]

2. "Moonlighting"

What if the plaintiff was working for someone else while employed by the defendant? How do those "moonlighting" earnings fit into the mitigation scheme? It is the defendant's burden to prove that the plaintiff would not have earned the income had she not been discharged for there to be a reduction:[79]

If the supplemental or "moonlighting" job is one that the discriminatee cannot perform when he wins his new position, the supplemental job "is necessarily temporary, provisional or 'interim.' By contrast, if one can hold his supplemental job and his desired full time job simultaneously and there is reason to believe he will do so, the supplemental job assumes a permanent rather than interim nature."[80]

---

71. *See* 42 U.S.C. § 2000e-5(g) (1) (2012); *Quinones Candelario*, 906 F.2d at 799–802.

72. *See* NLRB v. Pessoa Const. Co., 632 F. App'x 760, 763–64 (4th Cir. 2015), NLRB v. Pepsi Cola Bottling Co., 258 F.3d 305, 311 (4th Cir.2001).

73. *See, e.g.*, Thurman v. Yellow Freight Sys., Inc., 90 F.3d 1160 (6th Cir. 1996) (no tolling where truck driver fired from subsequent employer after unintentionally driving truck under overpass that was too low).

74. Purvis v. Taber Extrusions, L.P., No. 1:06CV863-LG-JMR, 2008 WL 2389749, at *8 (S.D. Miss. June 10, 2008); EEOC v. Domino's Pizza, Inc., No. 81-74381, 1983 WL 477, at *3(E.D. Mich. 1983).

75. EEOC v. Delight Wholesale Co., 973 F.2d 664, 670 (8th Cir. 1992); Brady v. Thurston, 753 F.2d 1269, 1278 (4th Cir. 1985).

76. 938 F. Supp. 1094, 1099 (N.D.N.Y. 1996).

77. *Id.*

78. *Id.*

79. Gaworski v. ITT Commercial Fin. Corp., 17 F.3d 1104, 1112 (8th Cir. 1994); Willis v. Watson Chapel Sch. Dist., 749 F. Supp. 923, 925 (E.D. Ark. 1990). *See also* Selgas v. Am. Airlines, Inc., 858 F. Supp. 316, 323 (D.P.R. 1994), *aff'd in part and vacated in part*, 69 F.3d 1205 (1st Cir. 1995).

80. *Willis*, 749 F. Supp. at 925 (quoting Bing v. Roadway Express, 485 F.2d 441, 454 (1973)).

Where the plaintiff worked part time as a cashier before and after her discharge, her back pay was not reduced by her part-time earnings.[81] Yet where a plaintiff's self-employed earnings from his engraving business tripled following his discharge, they were properly deducted.[82] Consider also where an individual had been discriminatorily demoted from a job where he had worked long hours.[83] The court found that the plaintiff worked long hours in the original position, and that he would have done so if he remained in that job; as a result, he would have been unable to "moonlight."[84] His "moonlighting" wages were offset.[85]

3. When Interim Earnings Exceed Back Pay

There are occasions when the plaintiff's interim earnings exceed her entitlement to back pay. Courts, even in the same circuit, have taken different approaches to this issue.

- **Aggregate approach.** Under this approach, if the total amount of interim income earned by the plaintiff for all relevant periods exceeds the award of possible back pay, the plaintiff will not recover back pay.[86] Courts using this approach include the Sixth Circuit.[87]
- **Pay period approach.** Other courts compare each pay period's actual earnings with what the employee would have earned but for the violation during the entire back pay period.[88] Courts using this approach include the Eighth Circuit.[89]
- **Quarterly approach.** The Eleventh Circuit uses a quarterly comparison, rather than a pay period comparison.[90]
- **Yearly approach.** The First, Fifth, and Eighth Circuits use an annual comparison.[91]
- **Periodic approach.** The Tenth Circuit permits its courts to choose whatever period they deem appropriate, that is, monthly, quarterly, or yearly.[92]

---

81. Somers v. Aldine Indep. Sch. Dist., 464 F. Supp. 900, 903 (S.D. Tex. 1979), aff'd, 620 F.2d 298 (5th Cir. 1980) (table).

82. Herman v. City of Allentown, 985 F. Supp. 569, 581 (E.D. Pa. 1997).

83. Whatley v. Skaggs Cos., Inc., 508 F. Supp. 302, 303–04 (D. Co. 1981), aff'd, 707 F.2d 1129 (10th Cir. 1983).

84. Id.

85. Id.

86. See EEOC v. N.Y. Times Broad. Serv., Inc., 542 F.2d 356, 359 (6th Cir. 1976).

87. See, e.g., id.

88. See Dyer v. Hinky Dinky, Inc., 710 F.2d 1348, 1351–52 (8th Cir. 1983) (NLRA action).

89. See, e.g., id. at 1352.

90. See, e.g., Darnell v. City of Jasper, 730 F.2d 653, 656–57 (11th Cir. 1984).

91. See, e.g., Leftwich v. Harris-Stowe State Coll., 702 F.2d 686, 693–94 (8th Cir. 1983); Butta v. Anne Arundel County, 473 F. Supp. 83, 89 (D. Md. 1979); Harkless v. Sweeney Indep. Sch. Dist., 466 F. Supp. 457, 469 (S.D. Tex.), aff'd, 427 F.2d 319 (5th Cir. 1970).

92. Leidel v. Ameripride Servs., Inc., 276 F. Supp. 2d 1138, 1142 n.8 (D. Kan. 2003).

D. Amounts the Plaintiff Should Have Earned but for a Failure to Mitigate Damages

A successful plaintiff must have used reasonable diligence to find comparable or substantially equivalent employment to the position she once held with the defendant to recover back pay.[93] There is no defined duration or scope that a search for work must fulfill to be reasonably diligent.[94] There is no magic number of applications that need to be submitted, interviews that have to be conducted, phone calls that have to be made, or internet searches that have to be done. Reasonable diligence depends on factors such as geographic location, type of job for which the plaintiff is qualified, and other facts of the case.[95]

Although the duty to mitigate may require that an unemployed plaintiff search employment listings, register with employment agencies, and pursue reasonable leads for employment,[96] Title VII does not require that the plaintiff be hired,[97] or that she accept a job that is not substantially equivalent.[98] "Comparable" or "substantially equivalent" employment gives the plaintiff nearly identical compensation, status, promotional opportunities, and job responsibilities.[99] The number of hours that are required may also be considered.[100]

The fact finder will consider, among other things, the availability of comparable jobs advertised in the media,[101] how many potential employers the plaintiff

---

93. Dailey v. Societe Generale, 108 F.3d 451, 456 (2d Cir. 1997).

94. *Id.*

95. *E.g.*, Mathieu v. Gopher News Co., 273 F.3d 769, 784 (8th Cir. 2001) (a terminated manager applying to eight to ten employers for the first three months, then spending six to eight hours attempting to obtain work was found to have exercised reasonable diligence); Hawkins v. 1115 Legal Serv. Care, 163 F.3d 684, 696 (2d Cir. 1998) (reasonable for plaintiff to postpone start date due to mother's death); Newhouse v. McCormick & Co., 110 F.3d 635, 641 (8th Cir. 1997) (plaintiff used reasonable diligence where he took the only position offered to him in his industry, a part-time job, and applied later for only other comparable job); EEOC v. Farmers Bros. Co., 31 F.3d 891, 906 (9th Cir. 1994) (decision to stop job search unreasonable where evidence showed plaintiff would have secured comparable employment); Coleman v. Lane, 949 F. Supp. 604, 611–12 (N.D. Ill. 1996) (plaintiff neither checked want ads nor registered with employment agencies); Proulx v. Citibank, N.A., 681 F. Supp. 199, 204–05 (S.D.N.Y. 1988) (plaintiff avoided employment agencies because he could not afford them; fact finder included in back pay award funds he would have used to do so).

96. Wheeler v. Snyder Buick, Inc., 794 F.2d 1228, 1234 (7th Cir. 1986).

97. *See, e.g.*, Killian v. Yoruzu Auto. Tenn., Inc., 454 F.3d 549, 557 (6th Cir. 2006).

98. Ford Motor Co. v. EEOC, 458 U.S. 219, 248–49 (1982).

99. Hutchinson v. Amateur Elec. Supply, Inc., 42 F.3d 1037, 1044 (7th Cir 1994); Rasimas v. Michigan Dept. of Mental Health, 714 F.2d 614, 624 (6th Cir.1983); Ward v. Tipton County Sheriff Dep't, 937 F. Supp. 791, 797 (S.D. Ind. 1996).

100. *See, e.g.*, Sellers v. Delgado Cmty. Coll., 839 F.2d 1132, 1138 (5th Cir. 1988); McCann Steel Co. v. NLRB, 570 F.2d 652, 655 (6th Cir.1978); Meyer v. United Air Lines, Inc., 950 F. Supp. 874, 876 (N.D. Ill. 1997).

101. *See, e.g.*, Williams v. Imperial Eastman Acquisition Corp., 994 F. Supp. 926, 931 (N.D. Ill. 1998); Huffman v. Ace Elec. Co., 883 F. Supp. 1469, 1477 (D. Kan. 1995).

contacted,[102] whether the plaintiff used employment agencies,[103] and whether the plaintiff followed through on job opportunities suggested by friends and relatives.[104] With respect to the latter, it is a good practice to suggest to the plaintiff that she have personal "calling cards" printed so that she has them ready should a job prospect come to her attention. Furthermore, the plaintiff's lawyer should insist that the plaintiff maintain a notebook of all the attempts that she made to find comparable employment, including as much information as possible.[105] The plaintiff should record the name of the potential employer, name of the contact person, date of contact or application, job title, method by which the plaintiff contacted the employer (email, phone, filling out an application, etc.), copies of all materials that were provided to the employer, and details about the available position (salary, hours, job responsibilities, etc.). This will help the plaintiff counter any attacks that the defendant may make on the sufficiency of her mitigation efforts, and aid in her effort to find a substantially equivalent position.

In *Carey v. Mt. Desert Island Hospital*,[106] the male plaintiff alleged sex discrimination concerning his discharge as vice president of finance.[107] A jury found in his favor.[108] The hospital showed through expert testimony that the plaintiff did not exercise reasonable diligence in seeking comparable employment.[109] The expert compared the number of applications the plaintiff made with the number of comparable positions available.[110] Similarly, in *Sellers v. Delgado College*, the plaintiff was separated from her employment in February 1978.[111] She submitted her first job application in October, and two more during the balance of 1978.[112] In 1979, she submitted only nine job applications, two for positions for which she was unqualified.[113] She did work as a substitute teacher and as a temporary clerical worker.[114] In 1980, she submitted fifteen job applications, some (yet again) for positions for which she was unqualified.[115] The magistrate found that she failed to mitigate during this nearly three-year period.[116]

---

102. *See, e.g.,* Gaddy v. Abex Corp., 884 F.2d 312, 318–19 (7th Cir. 1989); Sellers v. Delgado Coll., 902 F.2d 1189, 1192, 1195 (5th Cir.), *cert. denied*, 498 U.S. 987 (1990).

103. *See, e.g., Sellers,* 902 F.2d at 1195.

104. *See, e.g., Gaddy,* 884 F.2d at 318–19; Coleman v. Lane, 949 F. Supp. at 604, 611–12 (N.D. Ill. 1996).

105. *See, e.g., Williams,* 994 F. Supp. at 932 (plaintiff had no records of his search).

106. 156 F.3d 31 (1st Cir. 1998).

107. *Id.* at 34.

108. *Id.* at 33.

109. *Id.* at 41.

110. *Id.*

111. 902 F.2d at 1194–95.

112. *Id.* at 1194.

113. *Id.*

114. *Id.* at 1195.

115. *Id.*

116. *Id.*

1. School Attendance

Whether a return-to-student status ends or otherwise affects the back pay period depends on the circumstances of each particular case.[117] In *Dailey v. Societe Generale*,[118] the female plaintiff alleged, and a jury found, that the defendant fired her from her New York City bank employment due to her sex.[119] The plaintiff searched and interviewed for comparable bank positions in New York City for six months, without receiving one offer.[120] She used the bank's outplacement services until it cut off her access to them; she also contacted executive recruiters on her own.[121] Unable to support herself financially in New York City, the plaintiff moved to Pennsylvania and enrolled full time in a physician's assistant program, her education being funded by student loans, and later, by a federal grant.[122] In a posttrial motion, the bank argued that the plaintiff had not met her mitigation burden because she stopped her job search after six months and enrolled in school full time.[123] The district court, later affirmed by the appellate court, disagreed.[124]

In *Martini v. Federal National Mortgage Association*, the plaintiff was a high-ranking bank director when she was fired.[125] Given the challenges of her position, there were no comparable positions available to her.[126] After an unsuccessful search, she returned to school to become a certified financial planner, in an effort to become qualified to make a salary similar to that which she lost.[127] The jury found this mitigation effort

---

117. *See, e.g.*, Dailey v. Societe Generale, 108 F.3d 451, 457 (2d Cir. 1997) (decision to return to school, financed by student loans and grants, reasonable due to job market and plaintiff's lack of financial resources); Gaddy v. Abex Corp., 884 F.2d 312, 318 (7th Cir. 1989) (defendant failed to produce evidence that plaintiff suspended her job search efforts when she attended school part-time and was no longer "ready, willing, and able to accept employment"); Miller v. Marsh, 766 F.2d 490, 492 (11th Cir. 1985) (plaintiff submitted law school application before unlawfully denied position, and therefore back pay tolled); Cloud v. G.C.A. Int'l, Inc., 2006 U.S. Dist. LEXIS 53201 at *1 (D. Md. July 31, 2006) (decision to return to school on a full-time basis, when had attended only part-time before, interfered with job search efforts and reduction appropriate); Dollar Gen. Partners v. Upchurch, 214 S.W.3d 910, 919 (Ky. Ct. App. 2006) (return to full-time-student status ended job search efforts); Cooper v. Paychex, Inc., 960 F. Supp. 966, 976 (E.D. Va. 1997) (decision to attend law school did not completely toll back pay period as plaintiff continued search during this period); Overman v. City of East Baton Rouge, 656 F. App'x 664, 670 (remanded to determine whether applicant's decision to attend graduate school resulted after a diligent but unsuccessful job search or was in replace of job search).

118. 108 F.3d 451 (2d Cir. 1997).

119. *Id.* at 453.

120. *Id.* at 455.

121. *Id.*

122. *Id.*

123. *Id.*

124. *Id.* at 453.

125. 977 F. Supp. 464, 475 (D.D.C. 1997), *vacated and remanded on other grounds*, 178 F.3d 1336 (D.C. Cir. 1999).

126. *Id.*

127. *Id.*

successful.[128] Similarly, a welder's attendance at cosmetology school after eight months of searching for work did not frustrate her mitigation efforts.[129]

2. Part-Time Employment

Acceptance of a part-time job without making reasonable attempts to find a comparable full-time position may toll the right to relief.[130] Where the part-time work does not interfere with the plaintiff's efforts to find comparable full-time work (as where an individual attempted to help a friend start up a gymnastics equipment business after his termination but continued to search for work in his field), tolling will not occur.[131] Where the part-time worker completely gives up searching for other work, tolling is appropriate.[132] In *Denesha v. Farmers Insurance Exchange*,[133] the plaintiff looked for comparable employment in the insurance industry following his separation.[134] Unsuccessful, he worked part-time at a toy store and as a substitute teacher.[135] During the next thirty-three months, he applied for only one job in the insurance industry.[136] The appellate court concluded that it was proper to deduct the amounts that the plaintiff could have earned during that period from a front pay award.[137]

If the job from which the plaintiff was unlawfully fired or constructively discharged was part time, mitigation principles apply in a pro rata fashion.[138] For example, in *EEOC v. Lutheran Family Services*, the plaintiff, a full-time teacher, was fired from her part-time job as a residential counselor.[139] She unsuccessfully applied for comparable part-time employment.[140] She also tried to find alternative full-time employment at a salary that would make up for the loss of her part-time earnings.[141] Her unsuccessful job search efforts were, nonetheless, successful mitigation efforts.[142]

---

128. *Id.* at 474–75.

129. Killian v. Yorozu Auto. Tenn., Inc., 454 F.3d 549, 556 (6th Cir. 2006) (applying Title VII mitigation of damages framework to The Family and Medical Leave Act).

130. Meyer v. United Air Lines, Inc., 950 F. Supp. 874, 876 (N.D. Ill. 1997).

131. *See* Davis v. Rutgers Cas. Ins. Co., 964 F. Supp. 874, 876 (N.D. Ill. 1997).

132. *See* Callow v. Riverview Marina, Inc., No. CIV 03-129-S-BLW, 2006 WL 1075454, at *3(D. Idaho Apr. 20, 2006).

133. 161 F.3d 491 (8th Cir. 1998).

134. *Id.* at 502.

135. *Id.*

136. *Id.*

137. *Id. See also Meyer*, 950 F. Supp. at 876 ("A substantially equivalent position is one which affords the 'claimant virtually identical promotional opportunities, compensation, job responsibilities, working conditions, and status.'") (quoting Rasimas v. Michigan Dept. of Mental Health, 714 F.2d 614, 624 (6th Cir.1983)).

138. *See* EEOC v. Lutheran Family Servs. in the Carolinas, 884 F. Supp. 1033 (E.D.N.C. 1994).

139. *Id.* at 1035.

140. *Id.* at 1041.

141. *Id.*

142. *Id.*

3. Self-Employment

There is no fixed amount of time that a plaintiff must continue her job search efforts.[143] Reasonable self-employment will satisfy a plaintiff's mitigation obligation.[144] It is a factual issue as to whether the decision to be self-employed is reasonable where the plaintiff says the defendant's harassment drove her to be self-employed.[145] If the plaintiff lacks entrepreneurial experience, pursuing self-employment may be considered unreasonable.[146] So may remaining unavailable for work during periods of self-employment.[147]

A nonexhaustive list of questions in considering whether it is reasonable to mitigate with self-employment includes the following:

- Has the plaintiff drawn a salary that has reduced, if not eliminated, the year-end profit?
- Have personal expenses, normally paid by a wage earner from a salary, been absorbed by the business, for example, personal car expenses, insurance, vacations, and other personal expenses?
- Have dividends been paid?
- Have profits been earned?
- Have particular expenses been appropriately offset against revenues?
- Have profits been reinvested in capital assets and have reserves been established? If so, how should they be treated in a mitigation context?
- Has the plaintiff benefited by an increase in value of the business?[148]

Evidence that the plaintiff's business venture ultimately failed does not mandate a per se conclusion that the fact finder must toll the back pay period.[149]

The plaintiff's self-employment effort was insufficient in *Clarke v. Whitney*.[150] He had been employed as a salesman for a corrugated products distributor.[151] During the first three months after his discharge, he unsuccessfully contacted ten to fifteen companies

---

143. Dailey v. Societe Generale, 108 F.3d 451, 456 (2d Cir. 1997).

144. *See* Brown v. Smith, 827 F.3d 609, 616 (7th Cir. 2016); Smith v. Great Am. Rests., Inc., 969 F.2d 430, 437–39 (7th Cir. 1992); Carden v. Westinghouse Elec. Corp., 850 F.2d 996, 1005 (3d Cir.1988); Brooks v. Woodline Motor Freight, Inc., 852 F.2d 1061, 1065 (8th Cir.1988).

145. McHugh v. Papillon Airways, Inc., No. 2:05-cv-00976-RLH-PAL, 2008 WL 182259 at *5(D. Nev. Jan. 16, 2008).

146. Coleman v. Lane, 949 F. Supp. 604, 612 (N.D. Ill. 1998).

147. *See, e.g.*, Hansard v. Pepsi-Cola Metro. Bottling, Co., 865 F.2d 1461, 1468 (5th Cir. 1989).

148. Carden v. Westinghouse Elec. Corp., 850 F.2d 996, 1006 (3d Cir. 1988). *See also* Raya & Haig Hair Salon v. Pa. Human Relations Comm'n, 915 A.2d 728, 736–37 (Pa. Commw. Ct. 2007) (remanded for consideration of *Carden*).

149. EEOC v. Joe's Stone Crab, Inc., 15 F. Supp. 2d 1364, 1379 (S.D. Fla. 1998) (defendant failed to demonstrate that plaintiff's self-employment was unreasonable, as opposed to unsuccessful).

150. 975 F. Supp. 754, 759 (E.D. Pa. 1997) (Pennsylvania Human Relations Act).

151. *Id.* at 760.

for employment, most within his industry.[152] He then decided to start his own packaging company and quit his job search.[153] The plaintiff had no written business plan for his new company, nor did he capitalize the company.[154] The company did not fare well financially in the first year, but then realized some profit.[155] The court found that self-employment here was not reasonable, relying heavily on the fact that the plaintiff invested no capital in the business.[156]

Elsewhere, failing to find comparable employment, a plaintiff tried twice to start her own business.[157] First, she opened a gift shop with money borrowed from relatives.[158] This venture failed.[159] Next, she opened a card shop with money borrowed from her son; this too failed.[160] She did, however, remain available for other work while operating the shops.[161] Her right to back pay was not tolled for the periods of self-employment: to do so "would serve as a disincentive to Title VII plaintiffs unable to secure employment."[162]

This effort is thus distinguishable from that in *Hansard v. Pepsi-Cola Metropolitan Bottling Co., Inc.*[163] There, the plaintiff abandoned his job search after several years to operate a flea market booth on weekends.[164] He never made a profit.[165] The court found that this effort at self-employment, as well as part-time employment, insufficient as he should have continued his job search efforts.[166]

4. Locale of Potential Employment

It is reasonable for a plaintiff to move elsewhere to seek employment after sufficiently exhausting her job search efforts in her home community.[167] On the other hand, a plaintiff is not required to do so.[168] For example, in *Coleman v. City of Omaha*, the former Omaha deputy police chief had lived in Omaha nearly his entire life.[169] He was not required to leave Omaha to assume a position in either of two small towns outside of

---

152. *Id.* at 757.

153. *Id.*

154. *Id.*

155. *Id.*

156. *Id.* at 759–60.

157. Taylor v. Cent. Pa. Drug & Alcohol Servs. Corp., 890 F. Supp. 360, 367 (M.D. Pa. 1995).

158. *Id.*

159. *Id.*

160. *Id.*

161. *Id.*

162. *Id.* at 372–73.

163. 865 F.2d 1461, 1468 (5th Cir. 1989).

164. *Id.*

165. *Id.*

166. *Id.*

167. *See, e.g.,* EEOC v. Massey Yardley Chrysler Plymouth, Inc., 117 F.3d 1244, 1252 (11th Cir. 1997).

168. Coleman v. City of Omaha, 714 F.2d 804, 808 (8th Cir. 1983).

169. *Id.*

Omaha to successfully mitigate.[170] Similarly, in *Gaddy v. Abex Corp.*,[171] the defendant's position that the plaintiff failed to follow up on a possible job opportunity, which would have required relocating her family, was untenable because there was no evidence that the opportunity was viable.[172] In Washington State, summary judgment was denied concerning the tolling of back pay given the plaintiff's evidence that the commute to a particular job opportunity was too difficult.[173]

5. Employment in a Different Field

A plaintiff is not required to seek work in the same field.[174] Nor is a plaintiff required to seek work in a different field; however, if she decides that there are no suitable jobs in her area, she is obligated to do so.[175] However, a plaintiff may also be obligated to end his new career if it does not generate sufficient income and seek alternative employment.[176]

In *McCall v. Myrtle Beach Hospital, Inc.*,[177] it took the plaintiff, an obstetric nurse, eight months to find a new job; she rejected four other job offers during the first two months because none of the jobs was in obstetrics.[178] The court found that she failed to use reasonable diligence to mitigate her damages and that her damages must be reduced by the amount that she could have obtained from the most remunerative of the employment offers she received but rejected.[179]

In *Fogg v. Gonzalez*,[180] a deputy US marshal alleged racial discrimination against the US Marshals Service following his dismissal for insubordination.[181] A jury found in his favor.[182] The government argued that the plaintiff had failed to mitigate his damages because he failed to look for police work or other similar work.[183] The government ignored the fact that it had fired the plaintiff for insubordination, a fact that would have made it unreasonable for the plaintiff to stay in his former line of work.[184] To find that the plaintiff failed to mitigate under these circumstances would have

---

170. *Id.*

171. 884 F.2d 312 (7th Cir. 1989).

172. *Id.* at 318–19.

173. England v. Mack Trucks, Inc., No. C07-5169-RBL, 2008 WL 168689 at *4 D. Wash. Jan. 16, 2008) (applying Washington law).

174. *See* NLRB v. Ryder Sys., Inc., 983 F.2d 705, 715 (6th Cir. 1993) (back pay allowed to truck driver who took work as a painter).

175. *See* Walters v. City of Atlanta, 803 F.2d 1135, 1145–46 (11th Cir. 1986).

176. Tuszynski v. Innovative Servs., Inc., No. 01-CV-6302, 2005 WL 221234 (W.D.N.Y. Jan. 29, 2005).

177. No. 96-1201, 1997 WL 560015 (4th Cir. Sept. 10, 1997).

178. *Id.* at *7.

179. *Id.*

180. 492 F.3d 447 (D.C. Cir. 2007).

181. *Id.* at 450.

182. *Id.*

183. *Id.* at 455.

184. *Id.*

amounted to allowing the government to benefit from its own wrongful conduct, an unjust result.[185]

6. Effect of a Noncompetition Covenant

It may be reasonable for an employee not to seek comparable employment if she is bound by a restrictive covenant. For example, in *New Boston Select Group, Inc. v. DeMichele*, the judge did not instruct the jury concerning mitigation of damages because of the unchallenged evidence that the plaintiff, who had worked for the defendant's staffing agency, did not seek comparable employment due to a restrictive covenant.[186] The court in *Miller v. Perry Corporation* held that the plaintiff could not rely on a restrictive covenant with respect to his mitigation burden because he did not seek an injunction to preclude its enforcement.[187]

7. Offer of Reemployment by the Defendant

The US Supreme Court, in *Ford Motor Co. v. EEOC*,[188] determined that if a defendant offers unconditional reinstatement to the plaintiff, the back pay period is tolled.[189] If the plaintiff accepts, he can continue with his lawsuit and seek the back pay and benefits of which the defendant deprived him during his period of unemployment.[190]

A defendant may want to consider whether to file a motion for summary judgment or a motion *in limine* with respect to damages when an unconditional offer of reinstatement has been made. The courts disagree as to the parameters governing whether a plaintiff's refusal of reinstatement will toll the back pay period.[191] They do agree, however, that refusing an unconditional offer of reinstatement that returns the plaintiff to comparable employment and does not require the plaintiff to waive any legal rights or dismiss his claim is a failure to mitigate damages.[192]

If a defendant wants to toll the back pay period by offering to reinstate the plaintiff, the following principles apply:

- The offer need not include back pay.[193]
- The offer should not be conditioned on the plaintiff settling or dismissing the lawsuit (or charge of discrimination, as may be).[194]

---

185. *Id.*

186. 458 U.S. 219 (1982). *See* Geiger v. Kraft Foods Global, Inc., No. 1:06-CV-874, 2008 WL 648192 (S.D. Ohio Mar. 34 2008) for a more recent and comprehensive discussion of this issue.

187. No. 3:05CV7454, 2007 WL 1139235 at *5 (N.D. Ohio Apr. 17, 2007).

188. 458 U.S. 219 (1982). *See* Geiger v. Kraft Foods Global, Inc., No. 1:06-CV-874, 2008 WL 648192 (S.D. Ohio Mar. 34 2008) for a more recent and comprehensive discussion of this issue.

189. *Id.* at 232–33.

190. *Id.*

191. *Compare* Aston v. Tapco Intern. Corp., 631 F. App'x 292, 298 (6th Cir. 2016), *with* Clarke v. Frank, 960 F.2d 1146, 1151 (2d Cir. 1992).

192. *See, e.g.*, EEOC v. Massey Yardley Chrysler Plymouth, Inc., 117 F.3d 1244, 1252 (11th Cir. 1997).

193. *See* Ford Motor Co. v. EEOC, 458 U.S. 219, 231–32 (1982).

194. Odima v. Westin Tucson Hotel, 53 F.3d 1484, 1496–97 (9th Cir. 1995).

- The defendant should not offer a position that would be considered a demotion, either in compensation or prestige.[195]
- The defendant need not offer the plaintiff retroactive seniority to the date of separation.[196]
- The defendant can require the plaintiff to comply with the terms of a valid collective bargaining agreement as a condition of reinstatement.[197]

An offer of reinstatement to a blind man that required him to find his own transportation, relocate, and accept wage concessions was not considered unconditional.[198] Whether a plaintiff's refusal of reinstatement is reasonable is measured by an objective standard: Would a reasonable person in the plaintiff's shoes refuse reinstatement?[199] Of course, what is reasonable is, for all intents and purposes, subjective. For example, in *EEOC v. Massey Yardley Chrysler Plymouth, Inc.*, the plaintiff rejected an unconditional offer of reinstatement because she believed that she would continue to suffer harassment due to her age and because she did not want to return to work with certain supervisors.[200] The court tolled the back pay period. However, in *Martini v. Federal National Mortgage Association*, a jury found a plaintiff's refusal of reinstatement reasonable where she would have had to work closely with her alleged harassers.[201]

In *Lightfoot v. Union Carbide Corp.*,[202] the defendant offered the plaintiff a similar position on the same terms and conditions as when he was terminated "and with no loss of service credit."[203] The plaintiff ignored the request, arguing to the court that a return to the same terms and conditions that existed at the time he was fired did not toll the back pay period because had he not been a victim of discrimination, he would have been receiving a higher salary at the time of his separation.[204] The court disagreed:

> To toll the accrual of back-pay liability, an employer need only offer reinstatement to a "job substantially equivalent to the one he was denied," not a job equivalent to the one to which the employee must prove he was entitled if he

---

195. *See, e.g.*, Boehms v. Crowell, 139 F.3d 452, 459–61 (5th Cir. 1998); Artis v. Hitachi Zosen Clearing, Inc., 967 F.2d 1132, 1143 (7th Cir. 1992); Woodline Motor Freight, Inc., v. NLRB., 972 F.2d 222, 227 (8th Cir. 1992); Thomas v. St. Joseph Hospice of Southern Miss., LLC, NO. 2:16-CV-57-KS-MTP, 2016 WL 4148405 (S.D. Miss. Aug. 4, 2016).

196. Morris v. Am. Nat'l Can Corp., 941 F.2d 710, 713 (8th Cir.1991) (quoting *Ford Motor Co.*, 458 U.S. at 232).

197. *Id.* (requirement to transmit medical records and submit to physical examination appropriate).

198. Canny v. Dr. Pepper/Seven-Up Bottling Group, Inc., 439 F.3d 894, 905 (8th Cir. 2006).

199. *Morris*, 941 F.2d at 714 (quoting Fiedler v. Indianhead Truckline, Inc., 670 F.2d 806, 808 (8th Cir. 1982)). *See, e.g.*, McCall v. Myrtle Beach Hosp., Inc., No. 96-1201, 1997 WL 560015 at *7 (4th Cir. Sept. 10, 1997) (not unreasonable to refuse to return to hostile environment).

200. 110 F.3d 898 (2d Cir. 1997).

201. 977 F. Supp. 464, 475 (D.D.C. 1997).

202. *Id.* at 904.

203. *Id.*

204. *Id.* at 907.

is to prevail in his suit. In short, an employer is not required to "insure the claimant against the risk that the employer might win at trial."[205]

In another case, the employee, a resort housekeeper, was terminated after she had filed an age claim.[206] Thereafter she also claimed her supervisor disrespected her.[207] The employer subsequently rescinded the termination via a letter from counsel, to plaintiff's counsel, containing an unconditional offer of reinstatement with the assurance that she would be protected from retaliation and any additional potentially harassing conduct from her supervisor.[208] She rejected the employer's unconditional offer of reinstatement because it would require her to return to a stressful, allegedly harassing work environment that would necessitate "medical treatment."[209] The court held the plaintiff's rejection of the offer tolled the calculation of back pay as it was unreasonable since plaintiff presented absolutely no evidence that she was receiving medical treatment for her alleged condition, her supervisor's harassing comments were unrelated to her age claims and were not otherwise illegal, and the employer provided its assurances that she would be protected from any potentially harassing conduct.[210]

8. Mitigation Obligation in Absence of Discriminatory Discharge

Not all discriminatory actions involve discharge.[211] In those cases, what is the plaintiff's mitigation obligation? The court in *Tse v. UBS Financial Services, Inc.*[212] phrased the issue as whether (and if so under what circumstances) "a plaintiff who has been subjected to discriminatory conditions on the job, and thereafter is terminated for lawful reasons or resigns her employment, may nevertheless receive post-employment economic damages."[213]

In *Tse*, a jury found discrimination only for the period that the plaintiff was on a business development plan.[214] She was terminated for job abandonment, alleged constructive discharge, but the jury found that the discharge was not discriminatory.[215]

The *Tse* court reviewed the appellate circuit decisions on this issue (the Second Circuit, where the case arose, had yet to address it, although several districts within the Second Circuit had).[216] The Fifth Circuit has held that at least in cases involving a failure to promote, an employee's mitigation duty includes remaining in the

---

205. *Id.* (quoting Ford Motor Co. v. EEOC, 458 U.S. 219, 232 (1982) (internal citations omitted)).

206. Bragalone v. Kona Coast Resort Joint Venture, 866 F. Supp. 1285. 1289 (D. Haw. 1994).

207. *Id.* at 1296.

208. *Id.* at 1296–97.

209. *Id.* at 1296.

210. *Id.* at 1296–97.

211. *See, e.g.,* Tse v. UBS Financial Services, Inc., 568 F. Supp. 2d 274 (S.D.N.Y. 2008).

212. *Id.*

213. *Id.* at 300.

214. *Id.* at 282–83.

215. *Id.* at 284–86.

216. *Id.* at 300.

defendant's employ.[217] The court found that there was no way to determine how the plaintiff could have mitigated had she remained employed given her job abandonment, and thus limited her damages to those incurred while she was on the business development plan.[218]

9. Effect of Depression or Mental Suffering Caused by Defendant

If depression caused by the employer's conduct affects the plaintiff's ability to search for and maintain employment, her back pay period should not be tolled.[219] But tolling is appropriate based on the plaintiff's failure to look for work based on her embarrassment to admit to prospective employers that she was fired.[220]

In *Doane v. City of Omaha*,[221] the plaintiff had been a police officer for nearly two years when glaucoma blinded him in one eye.[222] Nonetheless, he continued to work as a police officer for nearly a decade, when the department forced him to retire or accept a 911 communications position.[223] He eventually took a higher paying position as a dispatcher, which required him to work closely with police officers.[224] He left that job to return to the 911 communications position because he found it distressing to work so closely with other police officers when he no longer served in that capacity.[225] Although the defendant failed to timely raise this circumstance as a reason to toll the back pay period, the court said that it would not have mattered as the record supported a finding that the plaintiff successfully mitigated.[226]

10. Effect of Disability on Mitigation Efforts

An individual is generally not allowed to recover back pay for periods he is disabled.[227] For example, in *Rush v. Speedway Buick Pontiac GMC, Inc.*,[228] the employer was not liable for back pay on the plaintiff's Title VII claim for the period when she did not actively seek employment due to pregnancy complications and childbirth.[229] However, an individual who tries to find work that satisfies the restrictions caused by his disability has satisfied his mitigation obligation, even if his efforts are unsuccessful.[230]

---

217. Jurgens v. EEOC, 903 F.2d 386, 389 (5th Cir. 1990).

218. *Id.*

219. Ward v. Tipton County Sheriff, 937 F.Supp. 791, 798–99 (S.D. Ind. 1996).

220. *Huffman v. Ace Elec. Co., Inc.*, 883 F.Supp. 1469, 1477 (D. Kan. 1995).

221. 115 F.3d 624 (8th Cir. 1997).

222. *Id.* at 625.

223. *Id.* at 625–26.

224. *Id.* at 630.

225. *Id.*

226. *Id.*

227. Stephenson v. Nokia, No. 3:06–CV–2204–B, 2008 WL 2669492 at *8 n.8 (N.D. Tex. May 1, 2008).

228. 525 F. Supp. 2d 1265 (D. Kan. 2007).

229. *Id.* at 1278.

230. *See* Hughes v. U.S. Food Serv., Inc., 168 Fed. Appx. 807, 809 (9th Cir. 2006).

III. THE AFTER-ACQUIRED EVIDENCE DOCTRINE

The courts recognize the "after-acquired evidence" defense as a separate defense from the failure to mitigate damages.[231] However, since the application of this doctrine affects damages (and not liability at all),[232] it is properly discussed in this chapter.

In *McKennon v. Nashville Banner Publishing Co.*,[233] the US Supreme Court considered the effect of an employee's pretermination misconduct on her entitlement to relief.[234] There, the defendant discharged the plaintiff, the secretary to the defendant's comptroller, ostensibly as part of a reduction in force.[235] She sued, claiming that her discharge violated the Age Discrimination in Employment Act of 1967.[236] During her deposition, the plaintiff testified that she had copied the employer's confidential financial documents, removed them from the workplace, and showed them to her husband.[237] She claimed to have copied them to protect herself in case she was terminated due to her age.[238] Shortly after the deposition, the employer sent her a second letter of termination, firing her for copying and removing the documents.[239] The letter further advised the plaintiff that had the company known of her actions, she would have been discharged immediately.[240]

The employer conceded for summary judgment purposes that it had discriminated against the plaintiff.[241] It argued that her actions were grounds for termination and, thus, she was not entitled to relief under the ADEA.[242] Agreeing, the district court entered summary judgment for the employer.[243] The Sixth Circuit agreed that a plaintiff's malfeasance was a complete bar to recovery.[244]

The Supreme Court, however, reversed and remanded the case.[245] Justice Kennedy, writing for a unanimous Court, said that discovery of prediscrimination malfeasance had bearing on the plaintiff's entitlement to relief, but should not be an absolute bar to recovery.[246] Neither reinstatement nor front pay would be available to the plaintiff, but the fact finder could award back pay for the time accrued prior to the discovery

---

231. *See* Roalson v. Wal-Mart Stores, Inc., 10 F. Supp. 2d 1234, 1235–37 (D. Kan. 1998).

232. *See, e.g., id.*; Coleman v. Keebler Co., 997 F. Supp. 1102, 1123 (N.D. Ill. 1998).

233. McKennon v. Nashville Banner Publishing Co., 513 U.S. 352 (1995).

234. *Id.* at 360–61.

235. *Id.* at 355.

236. *Id.*

237. *Id.*

238. *Id.*

239. *Id.*

240. *Id.*

241. *Id.*

242. *Id.* at 355–56.

243. *Id.* at 355.

244. *Id.* at 359.

245. *Id.* at 363.

246. *Id.* at 359–60.

of the misdeed.[247] The employer had the burden of proof.[248] The Court did not address whether the plaintiff's wrongful act had to be an intentional one or not, but emphasized that an employer has the right to make and enforce appropriate rules to regulate its workplace.[249]

From a procedural standpoint, to use the after-acquired evidence defense, the employer must show that the malfeasance was so severe that the employee would have in fact been fired if the defendant had discovered the malfeasance during her employment.[250] The Court stated that employer campaigns to "dig up dirt" on plaintiffs would be deterred by the availability of attorney's fees and sanctions against defendants and their lawyers.[251]

Justice Kennedy's opinion does not set forth precise parameters concerning the use of this defense.[252] It merely gives the district courts general guidance to fashion appropriate remedies.[253]

After the Supreme Court decided *McKennon*, the Equal Employment Opportunity Commission (EEOC) issued after-acquired evidence guidance analyzing the impact of the decision on EEOC charge processing:

> Even where the employer proves that it would have taken the same or more harsh adverse action had it known of employee misconduct, a Charging Party will still be entitled to relief under the laws enforced by the EEOC, but that relief may be subject to some limitations. If an employer fails to prove that it would have taken a similar action on the basis of subsequently discovered misconduct, the Charging Party's relief may not be limited by the after-acquired evidence. *See* Ricky v. Mapco, Inc., 50 F.3d 874, 876 (10th Cir. 1995) (employer "must demonstrate . . . that the misconduct . . . alleged was serious enough to justify discharge and that [the employer] would have discharged [the employee] if it had known about the [alleged misconduct]"). To resolve the issue, the investigator should consider whether there have been incidents of like misconduct by other employees. Specifically, the investigator should analyze whether other applicants were rejected or other employees were dismissed, reprimanded, suspended, or forgiven for similar behavior.
>
> If no comparable past incidents are discovered, other criteria may be used in ascertaining whether the misconduct would have prompted the employer to take the adverse action. Such inquiries may include whether: 1) the misconduct is criminal in nature (e.g., embezzlement, fraud, assault, or theft); 2) the employee's behavior compromised the integrity of the employer's business (divulgence

---

247. *Id.* at 361–62.

248. *Id.* at 362–63.

249. *Id.* at 361.

250. *Id.* at 359.

251. *Id.* at 363.

252. *See generally id*

253. *See generally id.*

of trade secrets, security, or confidential information); or 3) the nature of the employee's misconduct was such that the adverse action appears reasonable and justifiable.

Where an employee's misconduct is so severe that an employer would have taken the same or harsher adverse action even absent the discrimination, back pay may generally be limited to the period from the date of the unlawful employment action to the date that the misconduct was discovered. Therefore, when processing charges or complaints where after-acquired evidence is presented by an employer, investigators should evaluate the severity of the misconduct and the employer's response to similar misconduct.[254]

A. Expansion of the Doctrine

There are other avenues that an employer may consider in attempting to reduce the back pay period further, assuming the offense would have warranted termination. For example, learn whether the employee misrepresented his education, experience, or prior wages and benefits on her application, resume, or during the interview process, thus raising an argument that the defendant would never have hired the employee.[255] Also, discover whether the employee breached a fiduciary duty she owed to the employer, thus raising an argument that any wages earned during the period of breach must be returned to the employer.

B. Considerations for the Plaintiff's Lawyer

- Request a copy of the plaintiff's personnel file as soon as possible to review the file for possibly damaging or helpful materials. If it includes potentially damaging documents, determine their relevance to the position for which the defendant hired the plaintiff.
- Discuss the issue with your client. There may or may not be a reasonable explanation. Help your client understand the gravity of the issue. For example, the plaintiff may have to adjust her expectations based on any newly discovered evidence. Counsel may also have to adjust her expectations, if the case is being handled on a contingency fee basis.
- Issue early written discovery requests seeking information relating to all bases used by the employer to support termination decisions.

---

254. EEOC Notice No. 915.002, http://www.eeoc.gov/policy/docs/mckennon.html (Dec. 14, 1995).

255. *See, e.g.,* Patterson v. P.H.P. Healthcare Corp., 90 F.3d 927, 934–35 (5th Cir. 1996) (no clear error in district court's decision to award back pay and reinstatement despite plaintiff failing to include conviction that he had believed to be expunged on his employment application); Thurman v. Yellow Freight Sys., Inc., 90 F.3d 1160, 1169 (6th Cir. 1996) (no tolling where applicant misstated dates of prior employment since he still met the employer's qualifications); Coleman v. Keebler Co., 997 F. Supp. 1102, 1120–23 (N.D. Ind. 1998) (admission of affidavit on motion for summary judgment, establishing that plaintiff would have been fired if defendant knew the plaintiff lied on employment application).

- If the employer has policies related to termination, may the employer fire for certain infractions or shall the employer fire for certain infractions?
- If the defendant raises the after-acquired defense, issue discovery requests seeking information relating to all individuals whom it did not hire under similar circumstances and those who were fired after similar circumstances were discovered, such as "resume fraud."
- Discover whether others who engaged in conduct similar to the plaintiff were fired.
- Seek information tending to show that the employer knew of the plaintiff's misconduct prior to the time it fired her, yet did not act on the information it had.
- Understand the nature of your client's former job. Did she have any fiduciary duties that could have been breached? Did she have a noncompete agreement? Address these issues early and ensure that your client understands any lingering duties that she has to her former employer postemployment.

As an aside, but an important one, discuss with your client her responsibility to not create a new cause of action against her, such as defamation or improper use of confidential information.

C. Considerations for the Defendant's Lawyer

- If it does not have one already, add to the employer's job application a statement that any fraudulent representation is grounds for immediate termination.
- If appropriate, revise the employer's personnel policies to include mandatory termination for misrepresentations.
- Train the employer's hiring personnel to interview properly and thoroughly.
- Know what conduct the employer considers grounds for termination and the manner in which it has treated similar offenses in the past.
- Issue thorough written discovery requests early in the lawsuit and take the plaintiff's deposition as soon as conceivable. In the event the plaintiff's lawyer requests a continuance, consider asking the plaintiff's lawyer to stipulate that any after-acquired evidence will date back to the day on which the defendant's lawyer originally scheduled the deposition.
- As soon as the defendant has enough evidence to support the position that a discharge for the misconduct would have occurred (and not before), document the date of discovery.
- Move for partial summary judgment on the issue of damages, arguing that the relief should be limited to back pay and the limitations on that award, if any.

It is not enough to posit that the employee would have been fired if the employer had knowledge of the prior bad act; the employer must prove that hypothetical.[256]

---

256. EEOC v. Custom Cos., Inc., Nos. 02 C 3768, 03 C 2293, 2007 WL 734395 at *15 (N.D. Ill. Mar. 8, 2007).

IV. DEDUCTIONS FOR OTHER EVENTS

A. Change in Defendant's Status

The anti-harassment laws do not envision that companies will operate forever and ever, at full efficiency, and with a full work force. Consequently, the laws recognize that back pay may be tolled if the defendant can show that due to a particular circumstance, the plaintiff would not have remained in its employ beyond a particular date.[257] For example, the fact finder may reduce pay to reflect periodic plant closings during which the plaintiff would not have worked.[258] Or, if there is sufficient evidence to prove that the defendant would have laid off the plaintiff if she remained in the defendant's employ, the back pay period is tolled.[259] Similarly, if the plaintiff would have been fired when the employer ceased operations, the back pay period is tolled.[260] Furthermore, back pay may be tolled if the defendant sells its business. However, the employer must show that it would not have retained the plaintiff.[261]

B. Change in Plaintiff's Status

A change in the employee's status may also affect the back pay period. Tolling of the back pay period was found proper for the two periods during which an airline stewardess was pregnant.[262] The pregnancies were planned, and she would have been unavailable for work during those periods.[263] Periods during which a plaintiff could not have worked for other reasons are also properly excluded.[264]

V. MITIGATION-RELATED DISCOVERY AND EVIDENTIARY ISSUES

A. Plaintiff's Obligations

Plaintiffs are required to produce evidence related to their mitigation efforts. This includes responding to discovery related to the loss of any job held after the allegedly wrongful discharge.[265] A plaintiff is also required, when asked, to provide information

---

257. Taylor v. Cent. Pa. Drug & Alcohol Servs. Corp., 890 F. Supp. 360, 371 (M.D. Pa. 1995).

258. Gaddy v. Abex Corp., 884 F.2d 312, 319–20 (7th Cir. 1989).

259. *See, e.g.*, Blackburn v. Martin, 982 F.2d 125, 129 (4th Cir. 1992); Bhaya v. Westinghouse Elec. Corp., 709 F. Supp. 600, 604 (E.D. Pa. 1989).

260. *See, e.g.*, Darlington Mfg. Co. v. NLRB, 397 F.2d 760, 773 (4th Cir. 1968).

261. *See, e.g.*, Coronet Foods v. NLRB., 158 F.3d 782, 798 (4th Cir. 1998); Mennen v. Easter Stores, 951 F. Supp. 838, 861–62 (N.D. Iowa 1997).

262. Inda v. United Airlines, Inc., 405 F. Supp. 426, 434 (N.D. Cal. 1975), *aff'd in relevant part*, 565 F.2d 554, 562 (9th Cir. 1977), *cert. denied*, 435 U.S. 1007 (1978).

263. *Id.*

264. Taylor v. Cent. Pa. Drug & Alcohol Servs. Corp., 890 F. Supp. 360, 371 (M.D. Pa. 1995), *relying on Inda*.

265. Kinnee v. Shack, Inc., No. 07-1463-AC, 2008 WL 1995458 at *1–2 (D. Or. May 6, 2008).

concerning a witness who has mitigation-related evidence.[266] A plaintiff's failure to provide this information, including current contact information if the plaintiff has it, need not be intentional to be sanctionable; negligent conduct will suffice to warrant sanctions.[267] One court dismissed a pro se plaintiff's case as a sanction for discovery abuses, including his failure to produce, as ordered by the court, a calendar that he had with him at his deposition, which showed his employment interviews and other mitigation-related information.[268]

B. Subpoenas Served on New Employers

It is not unusual for the defendant to seek third-party discovery from the plaintiff's subsequent employers.[269] In the absence of a showing of potential harm if the discovery is permitted, it will be allowed.[270] However, such discovery requests may not be overbroad.[271] They must be limited to information regarding the plaintiff's dates of employment with the subsequent employers.[272] In *Richards v. Convergys Corp.*,[273] a subpoena was found overbroad because it contained a blanket request for all documents related to the plaintiff's employment; the defendant was allowed to redraft it in a narrower fashion.[274]

C. Disclosure of Immigration Status

Mitigation is not an issue in cases brought under the Fair Labor Standards Act (FLSA), as there appears to be universal agreement that even an undocumented worker is entitled to be compensated for work already performed.[275] In *Hoffman Plastics Compounds v. NLRB*,[276] the US Supreme Court stated, inter alia, that an undocumented worker could not mitigate his damages without incurring violations of immigration law, and thus an award of back pay under the National Labor Relations Act would be

---

266. *See, e.g.*, Tse v. UBS Financial Services, Inc., 568 F. Supp. 2d 274, 319 (S.D.N.Y. 2008); Drake v. Laurel Highlands Found., Inc., No. 07-252, 2007 WL 4205820 at *10 (W.D. Pa. Nov. 27, 2007).

267. *See, e.g.*, *Tse*, 568 F. Supp. 2d at 319; *Drake.*, 2007 WL at *100 (W.D. Pa. Nov. 27, 2007).

268. Medlock v. Otsuka Pharm., Inc., No. 07–2013–JPO, 2008 WL 243674 at *12–14 (D. Kan. Jan. 29, 2008).

269. *See, e.g.*, Walker v. JPMorgan Chase Bank, N.A., No. 3:13–cv–356, 2014 WL 10156622 at *1 (S.D. Ohio Nov. 14, 2014); Shaw v. Mgmt. & Training Corp., No. 04–2394–KHV–DJW, 2005 WL 375666 at *1–2 (D. Kan. Feb. 9, 2005).

270. *Shaw*, 2005 WL 375666 at *1–2.

271. *See* Anderson v. Abercrombie & Fitch Stores, Inc., No. 06cv991-WQH, 2007 WL 1994059 at *7 (S.D. Cal. July 2, 2007).

272. *Id.*

273. Nos. 2:05–CV–00790–DAK, 2:05–CV–00812 DAK, 2007 WL 474012 (D. Utah Feb. 7, 2007).

274. *Id.* at *4.

275. Flores v. Amigon, 233 F. Supp. 2d 462, 463–64 (E.D.N.Y. 2002) (cases cited therein).

276. 535 U.S. 137 (2002).

inappropriate.[277] *Hoffman Plastics*'s holding is limited to cases where the work for which pay is sought has not been performed, meaning it is inapplicable in FLSA actions where, for example, overtime pay is sought.[278] Therefore, employers are not entitled to discovery of a plaintiff's immigration status.

The lower courts, however, have been hesitant to apply *Hoffman Plastics* when addressing undocumented workers' claims to back pay under the federal antidiscrimination statutes.[279] Therefore, immigration status does become an issue in those cases, at least in the damages phase.[280] *Rivera v. NIBCO, Inc.*[281] is instructive on how to handle this issue. This Title VII national origin discrimination case involved twenty-three plaintiffs.[282] Early in the case, the court issued a protective order, affirmed on appeal, prohibiting the defendant from inquiring into the plaintiff's place of birth and immigration status.[283] The plaintiffs sought back pay, in a bifurcated proceeding.[284] The plaintiffs agreed that any plaintiffs who were not legally entitled to work during the relevant period would not seek back pay.[285] The district court agreed to bifurcation of all damages issues.[286] The jury would hear all evidence regarding damages, except that relating to immigration status, and determine a back pay award.[287] The court would then conduct an in-camera review of letters from the Social Security Administration to determine who was entitled to back pay and who was not, and the judge would then make the appropriate reductions.[288]

---

277. *Id.* at 150–51.

278. *See, e.g.,* Montoya v. S.C.C.P. Painting Contractors, Inc. 589 F. Supp. 2d 569, 577 n. 3 (D. Md. 2008); Liu v. Donna Karan Int'l, Inc., 207 F. Supp. 2d 191, 192 (S.D.N.Y. 2002); Flores v. Albertsons, Inc., No. CV0100515AHM, 2002 WL 1163623 at *5 (C.D. Cal. Apr. 9, 2002); Flores v. Amigon, 233 F. Supp. 2d 462, 463 (E.D.N.Y. 2002).

279. *But see* Crespo v. Evergo Corp., 841 A.2d 471, 475–76 (N.J. Super. 2004) (applying N.J. law).

280. *See, e.g.,* Avila-Blum v. Casa De Cambio Delgado, Inc., 236 F.R.D. 190, 192 (S.D.N.Y. 2006); Urrea v. New England Tea & Coffee Co., No. CIV. A. 98-6030, 2000 WL 33674441 at *3 (Superior Ct. Sept. 1, 2000) (applying Mass. law).

281. No. CIV-F-99-6443 AWISMS, 2006 WL 845925 (E.D. Cal. Mar. 31, 2006).

282. *Id.* at *1.

283. *Id.*

284. *Id.*

285. *Id.*

286. *Id.* at *7.

287. *Id.* at *4.

288. *Id.*

CHAPTER 22

Using Psychiatric and Psychological Experts at Trial: Defense Perspective

Holly M. Robbins, Susie P. Wine, and Cecilia B. Wagner

I. INTRODUCTION

In an unlawful harassment or discrimination case, the plaintiff may seek damages for mental anguish and emotional distress arising from the alleged harassment. Plaintiffs in harassment and discrimination cases brought under employment law statutes, including Title VII, the Americans with Disabilities Act of 1990 (ADA), and state employment law statutes, may seek such damages. Emotional distress damages can be a significant portion of a plaintiff's claim. Such damages claims, by their very nature, are neither easily verifiable nor quantifiable. Moreover, no one can enter the plaintiff's mind to examine and verify the plaintiff's complaints about the alleged symptoms he or she is experiencing or about the symptoms' effects on the plaintiff's daily activities.

In harassment and discrimination lawsuits, plaintiffs regularly offer the testimony of psychiatric and psychological experts in an attempt to prove that (1) the claimed mental anguish or emotional distress actually exists; (2) the employer-defendant's conduct caused those injuries; and (3) the mental injuries are severe in their nature and effect. Consequently, legal counsel for employer-defendants must educate themselves about the proper role of psychiatric and psychological experts in harassment and discrimination litigation. Defense counsel must be able to understand and analyze the opinions of the plaintiff's psychiatric and psychological experts, as well as the bases for those opinions. Defense counsel also must make informed decisions regarding experts, including decisions on the following issues:

- Whether the defendant should offer its own expert psychiatric or psychological testimony concerning the existence, extent, and cause of the plaintiff's alleged mental anguish
- What type of expert is best suited to analyzing the issues particular to the lawsuit

- Whether the defendant should seek to have the plaintiff undergo an independent medical examination
- Whether to challenge the admissibility of the opinions of the plaintiff's psychiatric or psychological expert to the extent the opinions do not meet legal standards for admissibility
- How to ensure that opinions offered by the defendant's own expert meet the legal standards for admissibility

This chapter provides guidance on these points, including practical tips on how to work with and question psychiatric and psychological expert witnesses during the discovery and trial phases of a harassment or discrimination lawsuit.

II. THE DIFFERENCES BETWEEN PSYCHOLOGISTS AND PSYCHIATRISTS

The two types of mental health experts used most often in harassment and discrimination litigation are psychiatrists and psychologists. To assess whether a psychologist or psychiatrist is qualified to offer expert opinions at trial, legal counsel must discover and evaluate that particular individual's educational background and training. Legal counsel must also understand the different functions that psychiatrists and psychologists are qualified to perform in the diagnosis and treatment of mental conditions.

A. Psychiatrists

To be a psychiatrist, an individual must be a licensed medical doctor and must have taken specialty training in psychiatry. As a medical doctor, a psychiatrist can make medical diagnoses and prescribe medication. A psychiatrist can analyze whether a particular physical health problem may be causing the symptoms that a plaintiff attributes to the alleged workplace harassment or discrimination. A psychiatrist also can analyze whether, and in what way, medication or combinations of medications affect the plaintiff's mental condition. For example, some medications actually may cause some or all of the symptoms that the plaintiff seeks to attribute to workplace events. Additionally, a psychiatrist can perform an independent medical examination to determine the plaintiff's current mental status, including whether the plaintiff has a mental disorder, and to determine what treatment, if any, is appropriate.

B. Psychologists

Each state establishes its own criteria for licensing professionals as psychologists. Because these criteria differ from state to state, the educational and training backgrounds of psychologists can vary. Thus, to determine whether a psychologist is qualified to offer expert opinions on the issues within a particular harassment lawsuit, legal counsel must discover and evaluate the credentials of the psychologist rather than simply relying on that person's title.

State licensing criteria typically require that a psychologist must have earned a college degree, completed a certain number of hours of supervised clinical experience, and passed a state certification examination. Some psychologists will have earned a Ph.D. (Doctor of Philosophy in Psychology, which is a research-based academic degree) or a Psy.D. (Doctor of Psychology, which is a more practice-based, applied degree). Some psychologists, however, have only an undergraduate or master's degree in psychology. Moreover, some psychologists may have been grandfathered in under a particular state's licensing procedures and, therefore, may have even less education and training than is currently required to meet state licensing requirements.

A psychologist may have more training and experience in the administration and scoring of various psychological tests than a psychiatrist. Unlike a psychiatrist, however, a psychologist cannot make medical diagnoses and cannot prescribe medication. As a result, a patient may have been treated by a psychiatrist for drug therapy and by either a psychiatrist or psychologist for psychotherapy. Likewise, for purposes of litigation, a psychologist and a psychiatrist may need to work together to conduct tests and fully analyze the plaintiff's mental distress claims.

III. UNDERSTANDING THE DIFFERENCES BETWEEN CLINICAL AND FORENSIC EVALUATIONS

Psychologists and psychiatrists who perform clinical evaluations for the purpose of treating patients differ in many important respects from psychologists and psychiatrists who perform forensic evaluations for the specific purpose of offering expert opinions in harassment litigation. Frequently, plaintiffs in harassment or discrimination lawsuits will use their treating psychiatrists or psychologists as their expert witnesses. Such a choice may make the experts vulnerable to attack by the defense. A clinical evaluation is less likely to meet legal standards for admissibility of expert testimony. Moreover, changing from a treating role to a forensic role can destroy the special patient-psychologist/psychiatrist relationship and may raise ethical issues.

A. Clinical Evaluation

In a clinical setting, a psychiatrist's or psychologist's goal is to relieve the patient's acute symptoms and ultimately to modify any maladaptive behaviors (that is, behaviors exceeding a normal range). To accomplish this goal, the psychiatrist or psychologist listens uncritically to the patient's symptoms and perceptions, even if they are not plausible, to gain insight about the patient. The clinician makes no attempt to verify if what the patient says is true. The clinician's role is as a healer. The clinician seeks to do no harm.

In a clinical setting, emphasis is placed on addressing acute symptoms and determining what, if any, additional treatment may be necessary. As the patient's treatment progresses, the clinician continually receives new information about the patient and may alter the initial diagnosis.

Because the purpose of a clinical evaluation is treatment, the clinician need not address many of the issues that a forensic psychiatrist must address in a legal setting. For example, the clinician may not need to make a complete multiaxial diagnosis (that is, an assessment on several axes, each of which refers to a different domain of information that may help the clinician plan treatment and predict outcome), may not need to identify a cause of the symptoms, and may not need to diagnose personality disorders.

B. Forensic Evaluation

A psychologist or psychiatrist performs a forensic evaluation of the plaintiff in the context of litigation to obtain information needed to assist the judge or jury in answering specific legal questions. The forensic evaluator must consider that the person being evaluated is submitting to the evaluation for purposes of building testimony in court, not for treatment. This requires that the forensic evaluator consider the possibility that the plaintiff is malingering for economic gain in the litigation, withholding information, or otherwise tailoring his or her responses for litigation purposes, something that a treating evaluator does not have to consider.

A proper forensic evaluation includes the following elements:

- Obtaining and analyzing collateral information (such as the plaintiff's counseling, hospital, medical, chemical dependency, legal, and even employment records) before the psychiatric or psychological evaluation
- Obtaining and analyzing complete psychological testing results regarding the plaintiff as part of the psychiatric or psychological evaluation
- Conducting a thorough and complete psychiatric or psychological evaluation, including a mental status exam, in light of information already gathered from other sources such as the plaintiff's medical, psychiatric, occupational, social, chemical dependency, family, and family medical histories

The forensic evaluator has only one opportunity to interview the plaintiff. Because of this limited time and the need to obtain the information relevant to the legal questions at issue in the lawsuit, the forensic evaluator's interview with the plaintiff may begin with open-ended questions but ultimately must move to more structured, pointed questions. Because the forensic evaluator is trying to form specific opinions relevant to the lawsuit's legal questions, the forensic evaluator seeks as little ambiguity as possible with respect to the information obtained from and about the plaintiff. In addition, the forensic evaluator must be cautious in conducting the mental status exam because the interview technique can affect the symptoms identified and therefore the diagnosis.

C. Ethical Issues When the Plaintiff's Treating Psychologist or Psychiatrist Testifies at Trial

A forensic evaluator's purpose in evaluating the plaintiff is not to treat the plaintiff, but rather to assist in answering specific legal questions in the harassment or discrimination lawsuit. Moreover, the forensic evaluator cannot keep confidential the information learned in the mental status exam of the plaintiff. If the plaintiff's treating psychiatrist or psychologist becomes involved in the litigation, the special relationship between the psychiatrist or psychologist and the patient-plaintiff that has developed during treatment may be damaged. The treating psychiatrist may disclose confidences during a deposition or at trial and may have to make statements about the plaintiff that may affect the plaintiff's treatment. For these reasons, having a treating psychiatrist or psychologist switch from a clinical role to the role of a forensic or expert witness raises ethical issues. The treating psychiatrist or psychologist may be forced to withdraw from the treatment role.

D. Legal Bases for Challenging the Trial Testimony of Plaintiff's Treating Psychologist or Psychiatrist

A forensic evaluator is more like a neutral investigator trying to make a truthful and accurate evaluation of the plaintiff's condition than is the plaintiff's own treating psychologist or psychiatrist. Consequently, a forensic evaluator must develop methods for testing the plaintiff's ability to perceive and report events. A forensic evaluator must confront the plaintiff with inconsistent information and determine if the plaintiff is unwittingly attributing all of his or her mental health issues to the events at issue in the lawsuit, as well as whether the plaintiff is exaggerating or even faking his or her condition.

In short, the goals for and methodology used in a forensic evaluation differ from the treatment setting. Accordingly, the education, training, and skills necessary to conduct forensic evaluations are different from those for treatment. A treating psychiatrist or psychologist who lacks the necessary forensic expertise may, therefore, be vulnerable to attack at trial as unqualified to render opinions regarding the psychiatric issues relevant in harassment or discrimination litigation.

IV. THE FRAMEWORK USED BY CLINICIANS AND FORENSIC EVALUATORS

The *Diagnostic and Statistical Manual of Mental Disorders* (DSM-V) is used in the fields of psychiatry and psychology to diagnose mental disorders in clinical, educational, and research settings. The DSM-V was published in 2013, replacing the DSM-IV, which was published in 1994. The DSM-V is not intended for purposes of litigation. In fact, the DSM-V expressly warns that the clinical and scientific considerations involved in categorizing mental disorders may not be relevant to legal judgments.[1] There is a

---

1. Am. Psychiatric Ass'n, Diagnostic and Statistical Manual of Mental Disorders, at 25 (5th ed. 2013) [hereinafter DSM-V].

significant risk that the DSM-V diagnosis will be misused or misunderstood because of the imperfect fit between questions of law and the information contained in a clinical diagnosis.[2]

For example, we all experience emotional responses to ongoing events in our lives. A person who loses his or her job may experience a wide range of typical and expected responses such as sadness, anger, tearfulness, or depression for a varied period of time following the event. However, the mere existence of these symptoms or responses does not mean that the person has a mental disorder.[3] Only when the symptoms' duration or effect exceeds an expected level may that person be diagnosed as having a mental disorder. To prove that someone has a mental disorder caused by unlawful harassment or discrimination in the workplace, the plaintiff must prove that he or she experienced symptoms, that the symptoms were beyond a normal response, and that the harassment or discrimination caused those symptoms.

Moreover, a DSM-V diagnosis of a specific mental disorder does not imply that a plaintiff suffers from any specific level of impairment or disability. Therefore, the diagnosis does not answer the question of the severity of the mental or emotional distress that the plaintiff has experienced as a result of the events alleged in the lawsuit

Perhaps most importantly, in most cases, a DSM-V diagnosis does not mean that the cause of the disorder also has been identified. Although some mental disorder classifications do require an etiology determination (a study of the cause or origin of the disorder), many diagnoses relevant to harassment and discrimination cases either have no known cause or may have multiple potential causes with no methodology for determining exactly which one actually is the cause of the condition. For example, depression may be caused by childhood events, a medical problem, a current social situation, a genetic predisposition, or a combination of causes.

V. THE LEGAL FRAMEWORK FOR ADMITTING AND EXCLUDING PSYCHIATRIC/PSYCHOLOGICAL EXPERT TESTIMONY

Federal Rule of Evidence (FRE) 104 provides that the trial court must determine questions concerning whether "evidence is admissible." FRE 702 governs admissibility of expert testimony at trial and provides, "A witness who is qualified as an expert by knowledge, skill, experience, training, or education may testify in the form of

---

2. *Id.*

3. The DSM-V defines "mental disorder" as "a syndrome characterized by clinically significant disturbance in an individual's cognition, emotion regulation, or behavior that reflects a dysfunction in the psychological, biological, or developmental processes underlying mental functioning. Mental disorders are usually associated with significant distress or disability in social, occupational, or other important activities. An expectable or culturally approved response to a common stressor or loss, such as the death of a loved one, is not a mental disorder. Socially deviant behavior (e.g., political, religious, or sexual) and conflicts that are primarily between the individual and society are not mental disorders unless the deviance or conflict results from a dysfunction in the individual, as described above." DSM-V at 20.

an opinion or otherwise if: (a) the expert's scientific, technical, or other specialized knowledge will help the trier of fact to understand the evidence or to determine a fact in issue; (b) the testimony is based on sufficient facts or data; (c) the testimony is the product of reliable principles and methods; and (d) the expert has reliably applied the principles and methods to the facts of the case." Defendants should carefully explore whether the plaintiff's psychiatric/psychological expert satisfies FRE 702's rigorous standards. Defendants must also ensure that their own experts' testimony will be admitted.

A. Procedural Issues Regarding Admissibility of Expert Testimony

A party's failure to object in a timely manner to expert testimony precludes that party from later seeking its exclusion. For instance, in *Christopher v. Cutter Laboratories*,[4] although an expert epidemiologist's testimony regarding how the plaintiff contracted human immunodeficiency virus was based on statistically invalid research, the court allowed the testimony to stand because the defendant failed to object at trial. Similarly, in *McKnight v. Johnson Controls, Inc.*,[5] the court indicated that without an objection and a proper request for relief, the issue of the admissibility of an expert's testimony is waived and will receive no consideration absent plain error.

In general, the trial court should determine whether expert testimony is admissible before trial begins. If necessary, the trial court may hold a special hearing on admissibility issues.[6] The proponent of expert testimony bears the burden of establishing its admissibility by a preponderance of the evidence.[7]

B. *Daubert v. Merrell Dow Pharmaceuticals*

In *Daubert v. Merrell Dow Pharmaceuticals*,[8] the US Supreme Court established the standards for admissibility of expert evidence under FRE 702.[9] The Supreme Court stated that the term "scientific . . . knowledge," as used in FRE 702, suggests that an

---

4. 53 F.3d 1184 (11th Cir. 1995).

5. 36 F.3d 1396, 1406–07 (8th Cir. 1994) (citing *Owen v. Patton*, 925 F.2d 1111, 1115 (8th Cir. 1991)).

6. Parties should check the court rules to determine how the judge prefers to address expert motions. Some courts may handle such motions as dispositive motions, while others handle them as nondispositive motions.

7. *Daubert v. Merrell Dow Pharms.*, 509 U.S. 579, 592 n. 10 (1993).

8. 509 U.S. 579.

9. *Daubert* was a lawsuit brought by two children who were born with birth defects. The children sued Merrell Dow Pharmaceuticals, alleging that the birth defects had been caused by their mothers' ingestion of Bendectin, a prescription antinausea drug marketed by Merrell Dow Pharmaceuticals. After extensive discovery, Merrell Dow Pharmaceuticals moved for summary judgment on the grounds that Bendectin does not cause birth defects in humans and that the plaintiffs would be unable to come forward with any admissible evidence to the contrary. In support of its motion, Merrell Dow Pharmaceuticals submitted an affidavit of a well-credentialed expert who stated that he had reviewed all of the literature on Bendectin and human birth defects (more than thirty studies) and that no study had found Bendectin

expert's assertion must be derived from the scientific method and be validated, which establishes a standard of evidentiary reliability.[10] The Supreme Court also found that to "assist the trier of fact," the expert witness testimony and opinions must be relevant to the facts at issue in the case.[11] The Supreme Court stated that the trial judge has the responsibility to ensure that expert witness testimony admitted at trial is both relevant and reliable: "This entails a preliminary assessment of whether the reasoning or methodology underlying the testimony is scientifically valid and of whether that reasoning or methodology properly can be applied to the facts in issue."[12] The Supreme Court then identified the following nonexclusive list of factors that should be considered in determining whether a proffered theory or technique derives from scientific knowledge:

- Can the proffered theory or technique be (and has it been) tested?
- Has it been subjected to peer review and publication?
- What is its known (or potential) rate of error?
- Is it generally accepted within the scientific community?[13]

Applying *Daubert*, courts have excluded expert testimony when the testimony does not satisfy the four factors listed. In other words, courts have excluded expert testimony when the theory espoused cannot be, or has not been, tested;[14] has not been subject

---

to be capable of causing malformations in fetuses. The plaintiffs responded with testimony from eight well-credentialed experts who concluded that Bendectin can cause birth defects, based on test-tube and live-animal studies, studies comparing the chemical structure of Bendectin and other substances known to cause birth defects, and the reanalysis of previously published studies. The trial court excluded the plaintiffs' expert evidence on the grounds that the methods by which these experts reached their conclusions were not sufficiently established in the scientific field. The court granted summary judgment in favor of Merrell Dow Pharmaceuticals, and the Ninth Circuit affirmed. The Supreme Court vacated the court of appeals' judgment and remanded the case for further proceedings consistent with the Supreme Court's opinion.

10. 509 U.S. at 590.

11. 509 U.S. at 591.

12. 509 U.S. at 592–93.

13. 509 U.S. at 593–94.

14. *See, e.g.*, Peitzmeier v. Hennessy Indus., 97 F.3d 293, 297–98 (8th Cir. 1996) (excluding expert engineer's testimony that tire changer was defectively designed and that simple design changes could reduce potential for injuries; expert had not designed or tested for safety or utility any of the proposed safety devices that he claimed to be missing from the allegedly defective tire changer), *cert. denied*, 520 U.S. 1196 (1997); Am. & Foreign Ins. Co. v. Gen. Elec. Co., 45 F.3d 135, 139 (6th Cir. 1995) (excluding expert electrical engineer's testimony regarding the cause of a fire where testing of expert's theory appeared inadequate and expert could not produce records of tests to show that they were reliable and supported by raw data); EEOC v. Dial Corp., No. Civ. A 99-C-3356, 2002 WL 31061088 (N.D. Ill. Sept. 17, 2002) (excluding expert testimony based on psychologist's workplace survey about sexual harassment in which questions were poorly worded and biased, and sample size was too small to provide statistically significant results); Schmaltz v. Norfolk & W. Ry., 878 F. Supp. 1119, 1122–23 (N.D. Ill. 1995) (excluding expert's testimony that exposure to herbicides in workplace caused plaintiff's airway dysfunction syndrome where expert

to peer review and publication;[15] has no known or potential rate of error, or the rate of error is unacceptable;[16] when the theory espoused is not generally accepted within the scientific community; or all of the aforementioned.[17] Courts also have excluded expert testimony under *Daubert* when the testimony is irrelevant and, therefore, does

---

(1) had not performed or identified any study supporting his theory that indirect exposure to herbicide causes syndrome in humans; (2) never tested plaintiff to determine whether and to what degree he was exposed to herbicide; and (3) could not demonstrate adequately how studies of effects of herbicide in animals supported his theory of causation in humans).

15. *See, e.g.,* United States v. Walton, 1997 WL 525179 (9th Cir. Aug. 20, 1997) (excluding expert psychologist's testimony regarding eyewitness identification because no evidence had been submitted to show that the expert's studies had been subjected to peer review; fact that psychologist had published studies was insufficient without evidence that studies had been reviewed by other psychologists); Lust v. Merrell Dow Pharms., Inc., 89 F.3d 594, 597–98 (9th Cir. 1996) (excluding expert's testimony regarding alleged association between drug and birth defects where expert did not subject any of his research to peer review and admitted that no peer-reviewed article advanced the theory he raised at trial; finding that fact that expert raised his theory in an article was not probative because article (1) was not peer-reviewed and (2) was written after he had become an expert witness in the area); Tuli v. Brigham & Women's Hosp., Inc., 592 F. Supp. 2d 208, 213 (D. Mass. 2009) (excluding proposed expert testimony of a neurologist on the subject of "sham peer review" because, among other issues, the "sham process" was based on the expert's own value judgments that could not be reviewed or validated, and in fact the expert had created the field of "sham review" based on his own experiences); Valentine v. Pioneer Chlor Alkali Co., 921 F. Supp. 666, 672–73 (D. Nev. 1996) (excluding expert psychiatrist's testimony that plaintiff's neurological complaints were due to exposure to chlorine because expert did not publish conclusions regarding such causation in any recognized journal, did not conduct any prelitigation research into the area, and could not point to some objective source (a treatise, a policy statement of a professional organization, or a published article) to show that he followed a scientific method practiced by at least a recognized minority of scientists in his field); Pennington v. State, 913 P.2d 1356, 1376 (Okla. Crim. App. 1995) (precluding introduction of expert forensic psychologist's testimony regarding "steroid rage syndrome" where evidence suggested that the study of that syndrome was in its infancy and that only twelve published articles on the subject existed, several of which disclaim the fact that the syndrome even exists), *cert. denied*, 519 U.S. 841 (1996).

16. *Compare* Hein v. Merck & Co., 868 F. Supp. 230, 233 (M.D. Tenn. 1994) (excluding expert economist's testimony regarding plaintiff's hedonic damages because of magnitude of spread in values for an anonymous life in various studies, which "not only admits the possibility of error, [but also] casts serious doubt on the validity and usefulness of the exercise"), *with* O'Loughlin v. USTA Player Dev. Inc., No. 14 CV 2194 (VB), 2016 WL 5416513 (S.D.N.Y. Sept. 28, 2016) (admitting expert psychiatrist's opinion evidence on the cause of plaintiff's eating disorder and its relationship with participation in a residential tennis training program despite acknowledging that no scientific tools or analysis can be used in the field of psychiatry to quantify or isolate the cause of an eating disorder such as differential diagnoses, reasoning that the focus of the court's inquiry is on the methodology the expert uses in reaching opinions, rather than on the ultimate opinions themselves).

17. *See, e.g.,* Smith v. DeBeers, No. 03-C-0103, 2006 WL 2253073 (E.D. Wis. Aug. 4, 2006) (excluding expert testimony from admittedly qualified expert anesthesiologist where his opinion that plaintiff could not have consented to sexual encounter and could have been easily influenced due to the effect of general anesthesia was based on unsupported speculation and no scientific data or information); *In re* Aluminum Phosphide Antitrust Litig., 893 F. Supp. 1497, 1506–07 (D. Kan. 1995) (excluding expert economist's testimony where expert did not follow any recognized economic methodology in selecting normative period that served as a basis for his ultimate conclusion).

not "assist the trier of fact"[18] or when the expert's qualifications do not relate to the subject matter of the testimony.[19] All of these areas offer potential grounds for seeking to exclude the opinions of plaintiff's psychiatric/psychological expert.

---

18. *See, e.g.*, Chin v. Port Auth. of N.Y. & N.J., 685 F.3d 135, 160–61 (2d Cir. 2012) (affirming district court decision to exclude testimony of industrial psychologist that the promotion process was not effective by comparing qualifications of white officers who were promoted instead of the Asian-American plaintiff because in relying on comparing the officers' years of experience, commendations, and discipline history, the expert proposed to make same points as plaintiff's attorneys made in argument, which was not helpful to the jury); Raskin v. Wyatt Co., 125 F.3d 55, 67 (2d Cir. 1997) (excluding as irrelevant a statistical expert's report in age discrimination case where report artificially inflated the average retirement age in the general population, contained statistical errors, and made no attempt to rule out other possible causes for statistical anomalies); Schudel v. Gen. Elec. Co., 120 F.3d 991, 996 (9th Cir. 1997), (reversing district court for admitting expert's testimony on the grounds that the testimony was irrelevant to causation given that the expert could testify only that the drug at issue "could possibly have caused" plaintiff's injuries), *abrogated on other grounds by* Weisgram v. Marley Co., 528 U.S. 440 (2000); People Who Care v. Rockford Bd. of Educ., 111 F.3d 528, 537–38 (7th Cir. 1997) (excluding expert's study regarding the achievement gap in a school district as having "no value as causal explanation" when the study failed to correct for explanatory variables and failed to make elementary comparisons); Gardner v. Chrysler Corp., 89 F.3d 729, 737 (10th Cir. 1996) (excluding as irrelevant expert testimony regarding whether defendant improperly designed car seat where expert had no personal knowledge of seat design or performance, had not reviewed seat assembly information regarding the relevant time period, had never witnessed a rear-end crash, and was unable to elaborate on proffered conclusions); Wilson v. City of Chicago, 6 F.3d 1233, 1239 (7th Cir. 1993) (excluding expert pathologist's testimony regarding effects of electroshock treatments on humans where expert's study of that subject was nothing more than an avocation and expert failed to show that he had the requisite medical or scientific knowledge on the subject), *cert. denied*, 511 U.S. 1088 (1994); Pickens v. Wal-Mart Stores, East LP, No. 3:14–cv–318–CAN, 2015 WL 4997064, at *2–3 (N.D. Ind. Aug. 20, 2015) (excluding proposed expert testimony regarding considerations a person makes in navigating a retail store, as it is expected jurors are already familiar with the "realities and circumstances of shopping at a large retail store" and are prepared to make judgments about the circumstances surrounding the plaintiff shopper's slip and fall; thus, the expert's testimony would be superfluous and unnecessarily confusing); *Tuli.*, 592 F. Supp. 2d at 212–13 (excluding proposed expert testimony by a surgeon who reviewed documents about the plaintiff, also a surgeon, and was prepared to "opine" that the surgeon was not subject to disparate treatment or gender discrimination where testimony would be prejudicial under Federal Rule of Civil Procedure 403, as supplanting rather than assisting the fact-trier); Zhao v. Kaleida Health, No. 04-CV-467-JTC(JJM), 2008 WL 346205, at *8 (W.D.N.Y. Feb. 7, 2008) (excluding expert testimony by forensic psychologist as to plaintiff's possible reasons for not complaining about sexual harassment as irrelevant where "task at hand" on motion was to determine whether a jury could rationally conclude that defendant's conduct was "unwelcome"); EEOC v. GLC Rests., Inc., No. CV05-618-PCT-DGC, 2007 WL 30269 (D. Ariz. Jan. 4, 2007) (excluding testimony by psychologist as irrelevant where expert was to testify about behavior of sexual predators in general and court considered it likely jury would misunderstand him to be testifying about the specific behavior of the alleged sexual harasser in this case).

19. *Tuli*, 592 F. Supp. 2d at 212–13 (excluding defendant's proposed expert physician testimony regarding disparate treatment gender discrimination because the expert was a neurosurgeon with no expertise in the matter of gender discrimination, which has a specialized meaning in the law, even though the plaintiff was also a physician); Summers v. Mo. Pac. R.R., 897 F. Supp. 533, 540 (E.D. Okla. 1995) (excluding expert psychologist's testimony that neuropsychological evaluation revealed that plaintiff suffered a toxic exposure that caused brain damage; question of causation was a medical issue, and expert psychologist was not an expert in the fields of medicine or toxicology), *aff'd in part, rev'd in part*, 132 F.3d 599 (10th Cir. 1997); McLendon v. Ga. Kaolin Co., 841 F. Supp. 415, 417–19 (M.D. Ga. 1994) (excluding expert economic geologist's testimony regarding the value of a particular mineral deposit where expert had never studied the mineral in any depth, had minimal work experience with valuation of the mineral, and was unaware of various processes involving and uses for the mineral).

C. *Kumho Tire Co., Ltd. v. Carmichael*

In *Kumho Tire Co., Ltd. v. Carmichael*,[20] the Supreme Court addressed the applicability of *Daubert* standards to nonscientific expert testimony. The Supreme Court held that "*Daubert*'s general holding—setting forth the trial judge's general 'gatekeeping' obligation—applies not only to testimony based on 'scientific' knowledge, but also to testimony based on 'technical' and 'other specialized' knowledge."[21] Thus, whether psychological expert testimony is considered to be scientific knowledge, technical knowledge, or specialized knowledge, *Kumho Tire* makes clear that a court must apply the *Daubert* standard to determine the admissibility of psychiatric or psychological opinions.

D. Applying *Daubert* to Determine What Opinions Can Be Offered at Trial by a Psychiatric or Psychological Expert

Before they began appearing in employment law litigation, psychiatric and psychological experts testified in personal injury cases, child welfare proceedings, juvenile proceedings, and criminal proceedings, to name a few. Judges and attorneys have become accustomed to having psychiatric and psychological experts qualified and admitted to testify at trial. However, although psychiatric and psychological expert testimony has been generally admitted in the past, opposing lawyers in discrimination and harassment litigation should not be complacent about challenging the expert's qualifications or opinions. *Daubert* offers defense counsel a basis for challenging psychiatric and psychological expert testimony that is offered in employment cases by bringing a *Daubert* motion prior to trial.[22]

In employment cases, psychiatric and psychological experts are often asked to render opinions about areas such as the following:

- Whether the expert believes the plaintiff is telling the truth about what happened in the workplace
- Whether the plaintiff experienced harassment or discrimination
- Whether the harassment or discrimination caused a particular disorder such as posttraumatic stress disorder

---

20. 526 U.S. 137 (1999).

21. *526 U.S.* at 141.

22. *See, e.g.,* United States v. Scholl, 166 F.3d 964, 970–71 (9th Cir. 1999), *cert. denied,* 528 U.S. 873 (1999) (affirming district court's limitation of psychological expert's testimony regarding distortions in thinking and denial because they are not recognized as diagnostic criteria under DSM-IV); Corneveaux v. CUNA Mut. Ins. Group, 76 F.3d 1498, 1505 (10th Cir. 1996) (affirming district court's exclusion of psychological expert's testimony, offered to interpret manager's actions as age bias, when manager had already testified about the meaning of his actions and additional testimony on this point would not be helpful to the jury); Gier v. Educ. Serv. Unit No. 16, 66 F.3d 940, 943–44 (8th Cir. 1995) (analyzing admissibility of expert psychologists' testimony under *Daubert* factors and finding their methodology not reliable enough to make factual or investigative conclusions in legal proceedings).

- Whether the plaintiff is disabled
- How long the plaintiff will be disabled

Most opinions in these categories are outside the expertise and training of psychiatric and psychological experts and are not based upon methodology or procedures in the fields of psychiatry or psychology. In addition, neither psychiatrists nor psychologists have the expertise to render legal opinions about issues such as whether a plaintiff suffered from harassment or discrimination.

Defense counsel should identify each opinion that the plaintiff's expert intends to offer at trial and carefully analyze whether each opinion meets the *Daubert* standards. Defense counsel should consider the following questions:

- Does this opinion involve subject matter in the field of psychiatry or psychology?
- Does this witness have the training, education, and experience to offer this opinion?
  - Is the witness a clinician and not trained as a forensic evaluator?
  - Is the witness a psychologist and, therefore, unable to rule out medical causes, substance abuse issues, reactions to medications, and other issues requiring medical expertise?
  - Does the witness have the qualifications necessary to assess the existence of personality disorder?
- Did the witness conduct a proper forensic evaluation?
  - Did the witness make a multiaxial assessment?
- Are there methodologies or procedures generally accepted in the field of psychiatry or psychology for developing the opinion so that it has a scientific basis?
  - Opinions for which there is no scientific basis, methodology, or procedure generally accepted in the field of psychiatry or psychology may include opinions regarding
    - the cause of a disorder;
    - the plaintiff's prognosis;
    - the plaintiff's ability to work now or in the future;
    - whether the plaintiff is telling the truth;
    - whether the events alleged by the plaintiff constitute unlawful harassment or discrimination;
    - whether the plaintiff has a legal disability;
    - whether a series of incidents in the workplace caused posttraumatic stress disorder.
- Has the witness performed an adequate differential diagnosis to rule out other explanations for diagnosis of plaintiff's mental disorder, such as malingering, a substance or chemical use issue, a medical health issue, an adjustment disorder, or an inappropriate judgment about the boundary between mental disorder and no mental disorder?

- Did the witness follow a scientifically valid methodology when applying the differential diagnosis?
- Has the witness investigated preexisting mental disorders?
- Did the witness follow a scientifically valid methodology in ruling out preexisting mental disorders as a possible cause, or a forerunner, of the current diagnosis of a mental disorder?
- Did the witness follow a scientifically valid methodology in ruling out alternative stressors that may have caused the mental disorder?
- Did the witness follow a scientifically valid methodology in ruling out a personality disorder?
- Does the witness have a scientifically valid methodology or procedure for arriving at his or her opinion regarding causation?
- Did the witness follow the generally accepted methodologies or procedures in reaching an opinion in the case?
- Are there treatises or research generally accepted in the field of psychiatry or psychology supporting the opinion?
- If the witness offers opinions arising out of research that the witness conducted, has the research been subjected to peer review to determine its reliability and validity?
- Can the plaintiff's psychological witness identify a mental disorder with the scientific validity required by *Daubert*?
- Does the DSM-V demonstrate soundly established scientific principles sufficient to satisfy *Daubert*?
- Does the DSM-V effectively establish the boundary between an individual who has a mental disorder and someone who does not but who is exhibiting a period of anxiety, depression, sleeplessness, or a similar condition normally experienced during a lifetime?

If an opinion is subject to challenge, then defense counsel must decide whether to challenge the opinion in a *Daubert* hearing or whether there is some strategic reason to allow the witness to offer the opinion as an expert unchallenged at trial. Defense counsel may believe that cross-examination will show that the proffered expert's opinions are not reliable because they are based upon inaccurate facts or exceed the capabilities of the field of psychiatry or psychology. Defense counsel also may believe that cross-examination will demonstrate that the proffered expert is biased as a prior treating psychologist or psychiatrist and, therefore, lacks credibility.

Every challenge to a psychological or psychiatric expert must, inevitably, be based on the facts and circumstances of the particular case. Counsel for the defendant will need to become knowledgeable about psychiatric or psychological methodology to formulate a strong challenge to psychiatric or psychological expert testimony. Even if the defense chooses not to proffer a psychological or psychiatric expert of its own, having a consulting expert may prove helpful. Defense counsel also should be prepared to educate the court of the need to seriously analyze psychiatric or psychological expert testimony under the *Daubert* framework. Because the fields of psychiatry and psychology have a long history in the social sciences, some courts may start from the assumption that psychiatric or psychological expert testimony is based on scientifically valid methodology, particularly those courts that have not addressed previously the validity of psychiatric or psychological expert testimony under *Daubert*.

VI. ESTABLISHING THE GROUNDWORK FOR A CHALLENGE TO THE PLAINTIFF'S PSYCHIATRIC OR PSYCHOLOGICAL EXPERT

The basis for the defendant's challenge to the plaintiff's psychiatric or psychological expert witness should be established during discovery. Only if defense counsel obtains the right documents and asks the right questions during discovery will he or she be able to marshal a successful challenge to psychiatric or psychological expert witness testimony at trial. It is imperative to understand the nature of psychological and psychiatric evidence and the framework for challenge under the federal rules before formulating the defendant's discovery plan. The following categories describe the types of information that the defendant will need about plaintiff's expert witness in virtually every circumstance. These categories should be supplemented by specific questions relevant to the particular case and the specific expert witness.

A. Qualifications

Defense counsel should obtain at least the following information about the qualifications of the plaintiff's psychiatric or psychological expert witness:

- Education
- Training
- Licenses
- Board certifications (including whether the certification is current, and whether the certification is in a subject area relevant to the lawsuit)
- Employment history
- Research
- Publications
- Patents
- Membership in professional organizations
- Type of practice (research, clinical, forensic)
- Malpractice suits

In addition, defense counsel should find out the following information about the expert's forensics work and testimony:

- How many forensic evaluations has the expert performed?
- How many times has the expert testified and under what circumstances?

- Did the expert follow the same procedures in the forensic evaluation of the plaintiff that the expert followed in the forensic evaluations of other individuals? If not, why not?
- What types of opinions and diagnoses has the expert rendered as a result of other forensic evaluations?
- Has the expert's testimony ever been excluded, in whole or in part, by a court in any other case?
- Has the expert's testimony ever been admitted, in whole or in part, by a court in any other case?

B. Methodology

Defense counsel also should obtain information about the methodology of the plaintiff's psychiatric/psychological expert. Did the expert use or rely upon

- procedures generally accepted in the field of psychiatry or psychology for determining a diagnosis?
- treatises or research generally accepted in the field of psychiatry or psychology for determining a diagnosis?
- procedures generally accepted in the field of psychiatry or psychology for determining type and length of treatment?
- treatises or research generally accepted in the field of psychiatry or psychology for determining type and length of treatment?
- procedures generally accepted in the field of psychiatry or psychology for determining the cause of a particular diagnosis?
- treatises or research recognized in field of psychiatry or psychology for determining the cause of a particular diagnosis?

C. Expert's Role in the Plaintiff's Case

Defense counsel should determine the role the expert is performing with respect to the plaintiff. In other words, what was the expert asked to do in the case? Is the expert a treating psychiatrist or psychologist? A forensic evaluator? Both?

D. Expert's Knowledge of Facts About the Plaintiff

Defense counsel should determine the following:

- What information the expert had about the plaintiff before the expert made a diagnosis or developed other opinions
- Where the expert obtained this information
- Which information the expert used in reaching his or her opinions
- What specific ways the expert used the information in reaching his or her opinions

Pertinent questions include the following:

- Did the expert review prior medical records, including prior treatment?
- Did the expert review litigation materials?
- Did the expert interview the plaintiff, the plaintiff's family members, or the plaintiff's friends?
- Did the expert maintain accurate records of the forensic evaluation?
- Did the expert refer the plaintiff to other professionals?
- Did the expert rely on conversations with the plaintiff's lawyer?
- Did the expert choose not to review certain records or information that were available?

E. Expert's Diagnosis and Treatment of Plaintiff

It is important to find out in detail the exact information the expert had available prior to making the diagnosis and the exact procedure followed to reach the diagnosis.

- What type of examination did the expert conduct?
- What testing did the expert or someone else conduct?
- What expertise does the expert have in administering, scoring, and interpreting psychiatric or psychological tests?
- What procedures were followed in psychological testing?
- What information did the expert use from tests?
- Upon what other professionals did the expert rely in reaching the opinions?
- What information did the expert have about medical, social, educational, family, and chemical dependency history for the plaintiff?
  - Which information did the expert deem important in developing a diagnosis?
  - How, specifically, did the expert use that information in developing a diagnosis?
- What facts did the expert assume to be true and on what basis?
  - Specifically what facts did the expert assume to be true concerning the plaintiff's symptoms?
- What procedure did the expert follow to reach a diagnosis?
- What, if any, mental disorder exists?
- What procedure did the expert follow to determine the cause of the mental disorder?
- What is the expert's opinion as to the cause of the mental disorder?
  - What methodology was used to determine cause?
- What are all of the opinions that the expert has about the plaintiff at this point?
- What procedure, methodology, treatises, or research did the expert use or rely on in reaching the opinion?
- Has the expert been asked to provide any other opinions regarding the plaintiff for whom the work has not been completed?

F. Deposition of the Plaintiff's Expert Witness

Federal Rules of Civil Procedure (FRCP) 26(b)(4) and 35(b) authorize expert witness depositions. In most cases, to determine the necessary information about the qualifications, opinions, and factual bases for the opinions of the plaintiff's expert, defense counsel will need to take the expert's deposition. Some state rules of civil procedure do not provide the same access to expert information during discovery as the federal rules. A thorough deposition of the expert witness covering the areas set out already provides important information for any motion *in limine* prior to trial to exclude certain opinions. The deposition also will provide information needed to develop an effective voir dire and cross-examination of the plaintiff's expert at trial.

VII. COPING WITH PLAINTIFF'S PSYCHIATRIC OR PSYCHOLOGICAL EXPERT AT TRIAL

If, after a *Daubert* hearing, the defendant is unsuccessful in keeping out all of the testimony of plaintiff's psychiatric or psychological expert, defense counsel must decide what can be accomplished during the cross-examination at trial. Defense counsel may use the cross-examination to

- have the plaintiff's expert confirm areas in which there is agreement with the position of the defendant's expert;
- attack the expert's qualifications;
- attack the expert's methodology or procedures in this case;
- attack the expert's knowledge of the facts in the case;
- impeach the expert with his or her own prior deposition testimony, in this case or in other cases;
- impeach the expert with a treatise; or
- show that the expert is biased.

To determine in what areas the expert may be vulnerable on cross-examination, defense counsel must obtain during discovery all of the same information that was necessary to determine if there were grounds for a *Daubert* hearing.

To effectively cross-examine the plaintiff's expert witness, defense counsel must carefully plan the questions, including leading questions. Frequently, an expert witness has a great deal of experience providing testimony, and the expert may try to control the cross-examination. If the expert witness gives a different answer at trial than was given in his or her deposition testimony, defense counsel may impeach the expert immediately with the prior inconsistent testimony.

In preparing for trial, the defense's expert witness can assist defense counsel in determining the strengths and weaknesses of the opinions offered by the plaintiff's expert witness and may help identify particular questions. This assistance is important in developing cross-examination of the plaintiff's expert witness. At deposition or trial, it may be helpful for the defense's expert witness to be present during the testimony of the plaintiff's expert, particularly if he or she will be rendering opinions about that testimony.

The key to an effective cross-examination is limiting its purpose and controlling the examination. If after cross-examination, the defense did not bolster the plaintiff's case and was able to gain admissions or even impeach the plaintiff's expert, the defense strategy was probably successful.

VIII. RETAINING A PSYCHIATRIC/PSYCHOLOGICAL EXPERT FOR THE DEFENSE

A. When the Defense Needs Its Own Psychiatric or Psychological Expert

The defendant in a harassment or discrimination lawsuit might want to retain its own psychiatric or psychological expert witness, either a consultant or testifying expert or both. There are several roles that this expert can play, including

- to advise defense counsel regarding the methodology, testing, report, and opinions of the plaintiff's expert for purposes of determining whether there are grounds to challenge the expert's opinions;
- to offer opinions about whether either the methodologies or the opinions offered by the plaintiff's expert are outside the field of psychiatry or psychology;
- to determine whether the plaintiff has a diagnosis;
- to identify possible multiple causes of a diagnosis;
- to testify about the effects that a particular personality disorder may have on the plaintiff and the plaintiff's ability to perceive and report events; and
- to address specific problems that the plaintiff may have now or in the past (for example, a medical problem that may cause psychiatric symptoms, or a chemical dependency problem and the impact that it may have on plaintiff's ability to function socially and in a job).

It may be difficult to determine at the beginning of a harassment lawsuit whether the defendant will need its own psychiatric or psychological expert and for what purpose. Factors to consider include the following:

- The severity of the plaintiff's damage claims. A claim that the plaintiff was embarrassed or angry will be handled differently from a claim that the plaintiff suffers from posttraumatic stress syndrome and can never work again.
- Whether the case will be heard by a judge or a jury. Many judges, jury consultants, and trial lawyers believe that in jury cases, expert witness testimony offered by the plaintiff's and the defendant's experts tend to cancel each other out. If this perception is accurate, then the defense needs its own

expert witness at a minimum to cancel the effect of the testimony of the plaintiff's expert.

- The presence of facts regarding the plaintiff that the plaintiff's expert has not considered, such as physical health problems, traumatic events unrelated to the workplace, substance abuse, or reactions to prescribed medication. Cross-examination alone cannot establish that the plaintiff's expert has rendered a faulty opinion because he or she has failed to consider these facts in forming that opinion.
- The failure of the plaintiff's expert to conduct a proper forensic evaluation. In this instance, the defendant needs its own expert to establish the generally accepted standards or procedures in the field of psychiatry or psychology and to render an opinion on whether the plaintiff's expert met those standards.
- An attempt by the plaintiff's expert to offer opinions beyond his or her expertise. The defendant may want to retain a psychiatric/psychological expert witness to testify about the limitations of psychiatry's ability to establish that a particular mental condition was caused by a particular event or events in the workplace.

The tougher question is whether the defense should offer expert testimony at trial if the plaintiff does not do the same. The answer depends upon the specific factual and legal issues in the case. If it appears that, by having the only psychological/psychiatric expert witness at trial, the defendant is being heavy-handed or is making more of the mental anguish claims than the plaintiff is, the defense may decide not to call an expert.

Even if the defense decides not to hire a testifying expert, it may be useful to hire a consulting expert. A consulting expert can help formulate questions for the plaintiff and the plaintiff's expert, interpret medical records, formulate questions for fact witnesses (including medical providers), and otherwise negotiate medical issues in the case.

At trial, defense counsel's job will be to establish the qualifications of its expert and the scientific basis for all of its expert's opinions as required by *Daubert*. Defense counsel must look at its expert and the expert's testimony from the plaintiff's perspective to determine in what areas the expert may be vulnerable on cross-examination. It is also important that the defendant's expert witness present the facts and opinions in a clear, understandable manner so that a judge or jury is likely to consider and use the information.

B. Selecting an Expert

After the defense concludes that a psychiatric or psychological expert witness would be advantageous, the next step is finding the right expert for the case. In choosing an expert witness, defense counsel should obtain much of the same information that it seeks about the plaintiff's expert witness. The defense should identify an expert witness who is qualified to render opinions on each issue raised by the plaintiff's expert witness. In addition, the defense will want an expert who can provide opinions least subject to attack by the plaintiff's lawyer. Finally, the defense will want an expert witness who can provide clear, credible testimony to either a judge or jury. Defense counsel should consider the expert's past history: Does the expert always testify for the defense or the plaintiff? Has the expert been qualified as an expert in the past? Has the expert's testimony ever been excluded and why? Has the expert testified in the past in ways that may impeach him or her in this case? Has the expert been subject to malpractice claims? What is the expert's educational and work background?

An important decision is whether to retain a psychiatrist or a psychologist. Knowledge of the plaintiff's family, social, work, medical, psychiatric, and chemical dependency history is essential in determining what type of expert to retain. For example, the more medical issues that the plaintiff currently has or had in the past, the greater the need for a psychiatrist, who can analyze the medical as well as the psychological issues. If the plaintiff's medical records show chemical dependency issues or a prior diagnosis of a specific mental disorder, the defense may want an expert who has specialized expertise in these areas.

Psychiatric or psychological expert witnesses may be found by reviewing court files involving similar claims, talking to other employment lawyers, reviewing professional periodicals written about harassment or discrimination emotional distress damage claims, contacting universities that have graduate-level psychology programs or medical schools, and contacting organizations that gather information about expert witnesses.

It is important to discover an expert's background and examine it in detail to determine if he or she is qualified to render opinions as a forensic evaluator. Lack of a forensic background may be an area of vulnerability and a basis to challenge the defense's expert witness. Defense counsel should review the expert's curriculum vitae, interview the expert, talk to lawyers who have had prior experience with that particular expert, and review past testimony or case law involving cases in which the expert has testified.

C. Providing Defendant's Expert with All the Necessary Information

Once the defense has retained a psychiatric or psychological expert, defense counsel must provide the expert with the tools to best analyze the plaintiff's mental health and how it pertains to the plaintiff's harassment allegations. Defense counsel should provide as much information about the plaintiff as possible and should keep a record of all materials provided. At a minimum the defendant's expert should have the following:

- The plaintiff's medical records
- The plaintiff's complaint and the defendant's answer
- The plaintiff's interrogatory answers
- The plaintiff's personnel file
- The plaintiff's deposition transcript
- The plaintiff's psychiatric or psychological expert's report
- Information about the plaintiff's current employer and the job duties he or she is performing

If a protective order is in place, defense counsel should be mindful of provisions for providing confidential information to experts.

Defense counsel should also ask whether there is other information the expert would like to review or suggests seeking in discovery. FRCP 26 offers some protection for attorney-expert communications. In 2010, FRCP 26(a)(2)(B) was amended to narrow the required expert disclosures to include "facts or data considered by the witness forming them" versus the previous "data and other information" under the 1993 rule. According to the Committee Notes, this amendment was intended to exclude theories or mental impressions of counsel and to focus the requirement on facts and data the expert both relied on and considered in forming his or her opinion. Additionally, the 2010 addition of FRCP 26(b)(4)(B) and 26(b)(4)(C) extended work production protection to include all draft expert reports and disclosures, whether written, electronic, or in any other form.[23] Counsel should remain aware, however, that the Advisory Committee Notes to the 2010 amendments to Federal Rule 26 caution: "The addition of Rule 26(b)(4)(C) is designed to protect counsel's work product and ensure that lawyers may interact with retained experts without fear of exposing those communications to searching discovery. The protection is limited to communications between an expert witness required to provide a report under Rule 26(a)(2)(B) and the attorney for the party on whose behalf the witness will be testifying, including any "preliminary" expert opinions. Protected "communications" include those between the party's attorney and assistants of the expert witness. The rule does not itself protect communications between counsel and other expert witnesses, such as those for whom disclosure is required under Rule 26(a)(2)(C). The rule does not exclude protection under other doctrines, such as privilege or independent development of the work-product doctrine."

D. Performing a Rule 35 Independent Medical Examination

If the defendant's expert witness will be testifying about the plaintiff's mental condition, the expert should have the opportunity to examine and perform appropriate testing to provide credible opinions. An independent medical examination (IME) of the plaintiff pursuant to FRCP 35 will provide the defendant a means to challenge the plaintiff's allegations of mental injury, including whether a psychiatric diagnosis is correct, whether it is possible to establish whether the alleged injury was caused by a particular event, and whether the mental injury will continue into the future. In addition, ethical constraints may limit a psychiatrist's or psychologist's ability to render opinions without actually having personally examined the plaintiff.

---

23. The Advisory Committee Notes to the 2010 amendments to Federal Rule 26 discuss the three exceptions to the Rule 26(b)(4)(C) exceptions: (1) Attorney-expert communications about compensation for the expert's study or testimony may be discoverable; (2) Facts or data that the party's attorney provided to the expert and that the expert considered in forming his or her opinions is also discoverable; and, (3) Assumptions that counsel provided to the expert and the expert relied upon in forming opinions may be subject to discovery, although "[t]his exception is limited to those assumptions that the expert actually did rely on in forming the opinions to be expressed. More general attorney-expert discussions about hypotheticals, or exploring possibilities based on hypothetical facts, are outside this exception.

The IME usually will include testing and one or more interview sessions with the plaintiff. Preferably the expert will have and be familiar with all the information defense counsel has provided about the plaintiff prior to conducting the independent medical examination. Depending upon the case, defense counsel may want the expert witness to prepare a written report. The expert may want to consider videotaping the IME.

1. Rule 35 of the Federal Rules of Civil Procedure, Generally

FRCP 35 creates a means through which a party can order another party to submit to an independent physical or mental examination by a "suitably licensed or certified examiner."[24] However, FRCP 35 does not provide blanket permission for a party to make such a demand of another. Instead, the rule lays out certain conditions that must be met before a court will order a party to submit to an IME. First, only a party whose mental or physical condition is "in controversy" can be ordered to submit to an examination.[25] Second, the order may be made "only on motion for good cause," and on notice to all parties and the person to be examined.[26] Finally, the order must specify the time, place, manner, conditions, and scope of the examination, as well as the person(s) who will perform it. Among the conditions specified in FRCP 35, the first ("in controversy") and second ("on motion for good cause") conditions are sometimes the subjects of motion practice.

The US Supreme Court addressed the requirements of FRCP 35 mental and physical examinations in *Schlagenhauf v. Holder*.[27] *Schlagenhauf* involved personal injury claims of bus passengers injured when the bus in which they were riding rear-ended a tractor-trailer. Amid allegations that the bus driver was not mentally or physically capable of driving the bus at the time of the accident, the plaintiffs requested that the bus driver submit to mental and physical examinations by a specialist in internal medicine, an ophthalmologist, a neurologist, and a psychiatrist. The trial court ordered the examinations, and the bus driver appealed. The court of appeals declined a writ of mandamus.

The Supreme Court granted certiorari and, finding that the plaintiffs had not satisfied the requirements of Rule 35, vacated and remanded.[28] The Supreme Court stated that the "in controversy" and "good cause" requirements of FRCP 35 "are not met by mere conclusory allegations of the pleadings, nor by mere relevance to the case, but require an affirmative showing by the movant that each condition as to which the examination is sought is really and genuinely in controversy and that good cause exists for ordering each particular examination."[29] The Supreme Court further stated that in some situations, the pleadings alone can satisfy FRCP 35, such as when a plaintiff asserts a mental or physical injury. The Supreme Court found that FRCP 35 was not

---

24. FED. R. CIV. P. 35(a).

25. *Id.* at 35(a)(1).

26. *Id.* at 35(a)(2).

27. 379 U.S. 104 (1964).

28. *Id.* at 121–22.

29. *Id.* at 118.

satisfied by the record in that case, however, because the bus driver did not assert his mental or physical condition either in support of or in defense of a claim, and the plaintiffs made no affirmative showing that the bus driver's mental or physical condition was in controversy or that an examination was needed for good cause. *Schlagenhauf v. Holder* remains the seminal Supreme Court case on the requirements of FRCP 35 examinations.

2. FRCP 35 Requirements: Mental State "In Controversy" and "Good Cause" for Examination

In general, courts have found the "in controversy" requirement satisfied (1) where a plaintiff asserts a specific psychiatric injury or disorder or severe emotional distress;[30] (2) where a plaintiff states a separate tort claim for emotional distress, such as intentional or negligent infliction of emotional distress;[31] (3) where a plaintiff plans to offer

---

30. *See, e.g.*, Gurshin v. Bank of America, National Association, No. 2:15–cv–323–GMN–VCF, 2016 WL 384929 (D. Nev. Jan. 27, 2016) (finding that plaintiff's mental condition was in controversy "because her emotional distress is unusually severe" even where she did not separately plead a claim for emotional distress); Ortiz v. Potter, No. 2:08-cv-01326 LKK KJN, 2010 WL 796960 (E.D. Cal. Mar. 5, 2010) (finding that harassment plaintiff placed her mental condition "in controversy" where she alleged "unusually severe emotional distress," among other things); Wilson v. Dalton, 24 F. App'x 777, 778 (9th Cir. 2001) (in disability discrimination case where plaintiff alleged severe emotional distress and mental anguish and testified about significant emotional injury, "in controversy" requirement sufficiently satisfied); Cauley v. Ingram Micro, Inc., 216 F.R.D. 245, 247 (W.D.N.Y. 2003) (finding no error in an order for an IME in discrimination suit where plaintiff alleged that she suffered severe emotional harm as a result of defendant's misconduct, and that the degree of emotional harm suffered was so severe as to warrant various forms of medical attention, including treatment in a hospital); Cabana v. Forcier, 200 F.R.D. 9, 11–12 (D. Mass. 2001) (finding that in a suit alleging damages for injuries caused by exposure to hazardous waste, plaintiff had put his medical condition in controversy and would be required to submit to an IME where plaintiff's clinical neuropsychologist submitted a report diagnosing plaintiff with multiple chemical sensitivity and cognitive deficits and depression); Womack v. Stevens Transp., Inc., 205 F.R.D. 445, 446–47 (E.D. Pa. 2001) (holding that plaintiff's mental condition was "in controversy," satisfying requirement for order compelling an IME, where plaintiff alleged he had suffered "excruciating and agonizing aches, pains, mental anguish, suffering, emotional distress, [and] humiliation" as a result of the accident that gave rise to the suit); Large v. Our Lady of Mercy Med. Ctr., 94 Civ. 5986, 1998 U.S. Dist. LEXIS 1702, at *18–19 (S.D.N.Y. Feb. 17, 1998) (holding that plaintiff's mental condition was sufficiently in controversy when diagnosed as suffering from paranoia); Chrissafis v. Cont'l Airlines, Inc., No. 95-C 5080, 1997 WL 534874 (N.D. Ill. Aug. 21, 1997) (holding that plaintiff's mental condition was in controversy for purposes of Rule 35 examination where she specifically alleged that she suffered from posttraumatic stress disorder caused by defendant's wrongs and refused to declare that there would be no testimony regarding future effects or relapses at trial); Hlinko v. Virgin Atl. Airways, No. 96 Civ. 2873, 1997 WL 68560, at *1–2 (S.D.N.Y. Feb. 19, 1997) (finding plaintiff's mental condition in controversy in gender discrimination case where plaintiff allegedly had ongoing posttraumatic symptoms, "including phobic avoidance of working with and being alone with men").

31. *See, e.g.*, Alexis v. Rogers, No. 15cv691-CAB (BLM), 2017 WL 1073404 (S.D. Cal. 2017) (IME warranted where, among other reasons, plaintiff alleged claims for both negligent and intentional infliction of emotional distress, describing her distress as "severe"); Herrera v. Lufkin Indus., Inc., 474 F.3d 675 (10th Cir. 2007) (in race discrimination suit, plaintiff's separate claim for intentional infliction of emotional distress is sufficient to place the plaintiff's mental state in controversy); *See also* Geremia v. Colo. Bell Corp., 54 F. App'x 646, 647 (9th Cir. 2003) (holding that "[t]he district court did not abuse its discretion by requiring [plaintiff] to appear for an independent medical examination regarding her intentional

expert testimony to support a claim of emotional distress;[32] or (4) where the plaintiff concedes that his or her mental condition is "in controversy" within the meaning of FRCP 35.[33]

Courts have found the "good cause" requirement satisfied when the information is necessary and cannot be otherwise obtained.[34] Courts may also find the good cause

---

inflication of emotional distress claim"); Gattegno v. PricewaterhouseCoopers, 204 F.R.D. 228, 232–33 (D. Conn. 2001) (holding that by alleging negligent infliction of emotional distress as a separate cause of action, employee in age and gender discrimination and retaliation suit had sufficiently put her mental condition in controversy to warrant order of IME); *Stevenson v. Stanley Bostitch, Inc.*, 201 F.R.D. 551, 557 (N.D. Ga. Atlanta Div. 2001) (finding that plaintiff in Title VII sexual harassment suit put her mental condition in controversy by separately alleging a tort cause of action of intentional infliction of emotional distress under Georgia law); *Lahr v. Fulbright & Jaworski, L.L.P.*, 164 F.R.D. 204 (N.D. Tex. 1996) (noting that plaintiff put her mental condition in controversy through her intentional infliction of emotional distress claim; claim for compensatory damages, including mental anguish, under Title VII did not put plaintiff's mental condition in controversy).

32. *See, e.g.*, Conforto v. Mabus, No. 12cv1316–W (BLM), 2014 WL 3407053 (S.D. Cal. July 10, 2014) (determining good cause existed where plaintiff designated three non-retained experts to "testify as to her mental state," among other things); Simpson v. Univ. of Colo., 220 F.R.D. 354, 362 (D. Colo. 2004), *rev'd on other grounds*, 500 F.3d 1170 (10th Cir. 2007) (ordering a pretrial mental examination of female student in her action against university alleging indifference to sexual harassment within athletic department in violation of Title IX, allegedly leading to sexual assaults against student; student alleged specific psychiatric injury, i.e. posttraumatic stress disorder, and intended to offer expert testimony to that effect); Smith v. Koplan, 215 F.R.D. 11, 13 (D.D.C. 2003) (holding that Title VII plaintiff would be required to submit to an IME where, among other factors putting her mental condition in controversy, she had also asserted that she was in the process of finding an expert to substantiate her damages for physical, emotional and economic harm she suffered as a result of discrimination); Stoner v. N.Y.C. Ballet Co., No. 99Civ.0196 (BSJ) (MHD), 2002 WL 31875404, at *5 (S.D.N.Y. Dec. 24, 2002) (finding that there was no basis for precluding any examination of plaintiff because he "most assuredly put his emotional and psychiatric status into issue by seeking damages for serious emotional distress and proffering Dr. Goldstein as a witness to testify about his alleged psychological problems"); Jansen v. Packaging Corp. of Am., 158 F.R.D. 409 (N.D. Ill. 1994) (finding that plaintiff's mental condition was in controversy when she claimed that she had suffered and continued to suffer ongoing emotional distress caused by alleged sexual harassment and retaliation).

33. *See, e.g.*, Letcher v. Rapid City Regional Hosp., Inc., No. CIV. 09–5008–JLV, 2010 WL 1930113 (D. S.D. May 12, 2010) (plaintiff conceded that her mental status was in controversy and IME ordered); Shirsat v. Mut. Pharm. Co., 169 F.R.D. 68 (E.D. Pa. 1996) (ordering IME in wrongful discharge case where both parties conceded the plaintiff's mental condition was in controversy); Simpson v. Univ. of Colo., 220 F.R.D. 354 (D. Co. 2004), *rev'd on other grounds*, 500 F.3d 1170 (10th Cir. 2007) (same in Title IX action).

34. *See, e.g.*, Gavin v. Hilton Worldwide, Inc., 291 F.R.D. 161 (N.D. Cal. 2013) (good cause found when plaintiff had not sought in-person medical treatment for some time, therefore employer could not depose any of plaintiff's treaters to determine her continuing emotional distress); O'Sullivan v. Rivera, 229 F.R.D. 184, 186 (D.N.M. 2004) (finding that there was good cause for conducting physical examination of plaintiff in personal injury action, even though defendants had access to plaintiff's medical records, where plaintiff's left knee, right shoulder, and back injuries were at issue, and it was unclear whether plaintiff's former treating physician was able to determine extent to which accident had aggravated plaintiff's prior medical condition); Womack v. Stevens Transp., Inc., 205 F.R.D. 445, 447 (E.D. Pa. 2001) (finding good cause existed in ordering IME where examination was relevant in determining whether plaintiff was unable to work due to injuries sustained in accident that gave rise to the suit, and where there were no other means of determining plaintiff's present psychological state); McKitis v. Defazio, 187 F.R.D. 225, 227 (D. Md. 1999) (holding that defendant had made an adequate showing of "good cause" to warrant medical

requirement met when one of the factors supporting the "in controversy" requirement is present or when the plaintiff seeks substantial emotional distress damages.[35] Plaintiffs sometimes argue that good cause does not exist for an IME, even though the plaintiff's mental condition may be in controversy, because the information the defendant is seeking is available from other sources.[36]

---

examination where additional examinations were necessary and not duplicative because plaintiff sought recovery for injuries to which orthopedist was not qualified to testify); Chrissafis v. Cont'l Airlines, Inc., No. 95 C 5080, 1997 WL 534874, at *3 (N.D. Ill. Aug. 21, 1997) (stating that "good cause" requirement satisfied if defendant can show "that the mental examination is necessary and that the desired information cannot be otherwise obtained;" finding "good cause" based on expert's affidavit that examination would help him determine other causes of plaintiff's symptoms, whether plaintiff is predisposed to posttraumatic stress disorder, and the state of plaintiff's current mental condition). *But see* Acosta v. Tenneco Oil Co., 913 F.2d 205, 209 (5th Cir. 1990) (finding lack of "good cause" for plaintiff to undergo a vocational rehabilitation examination pursuant to Rule 35 on grounds that it would be "repetitive" when defendant had a copy of test results conducted by plaintiff's expert and defendant had opportunity to depose plaintiff's expert and plaintiff), *superseded by statute on other grounds*, FED. R. CIV. P. 35(a); *Hill ex rel.* Hill v. McNairy County Bd. of Educ., 229 F.R.D. 563, 568 (W.D. Tenn. E.D. 2004) (holding that "good cause" requires a showing of specific facts that demonstrate the need for the information sought, and lack of means for obtaining it elsewhere); Plaisted v. Geisinger Med. Ctr., 210 F.R.D. 539, 542 (M.D. Pa. 2002) (finding in medical malpractice action that defendants failed to meet good cause requirement for taking additional tissue samples from deceased minor patient's brain where original samples were sufficient to complete the neuropathological evaluation of patient's brain); *Caban ex rel.* Crespo v. 600 E. 21st St. Co., 200 F.R.D. 176, 182 n.17 (E.D.N.Y. 2001) (finding that in negligence action instituted against landlords by mother of child suffering from low IQ due to exposure to lead paint, good cause did not exist to order mother of child to submit to psychological examination where other evidence of mother's academic performance was available).

35. *See, e.g.*, Kaytor v. Electric Boat Corp., No. 3:06CV01953(DJS), 2007 WL 4322546 (D. Conn. Dec. 11, 2007) (good cause found due to the severity of the emotional distress alleged by the plaintiff and the amount of damages sought for that distress, $10,000,000); Ali v. Wang Lab., 162 F.R.D. 165, 168 (M.D. Fla. 1995) (finding good cause shown where plaintiff was seeking substantial damages). *But see* Kunstler v. City of N.Y., 242 F.R.D. 261 (S.D.N.Y. 2007) (in case where plaintiffs alleged false arrest, malicious prosecution, and excessive force arising out of arrests made in the course of a demonstration, finding that emotional distress claims did not warrant IMEs because injuries were temporary and no evidence that they were claiming any "ongoing, serious psychological maladies").

36. *See, e.g.*, Gurshin v. Bank of America, National Association, Case No. 2:15–cv–323–GMN–VCF, 2016 WL 384929 (D. Nev. Jan. 27, 2016) (finding good cause for an IME even where plaintiff alleged that any information employer could obtain from a mental exam could also be obtained from her medical records because a mental exam would allow employer to "adduce relevant information about [plaintiff's] mental condition" that it would be unable to obtain from medical records); Roberson v. Blair, 242 F.R.D. 130, 132 (D.D.C. 2007) (in sex and age discrimination case, rejecting plaintiff's argument that the defendant's motion for IME should be denied because the information could be obtained through less intrusive means, that is, through a deposition of her treating physician, because a deposition of the plaintiff's treating physician could not provide the defendant with all the information it needed to rebut and challenge the plaintiff's claim); Doe v. Dist. of Columbia, 229 F.R.D. 24, 26 (D.D.C. 2005) (although plaintiff objected to IME on the grounds that the defendant failed to show good cause because the information was available from other sources, holding that the defendant had demonstrated good cause to obtain an IME because the several medical examinations that had already been performed on the plaintiff, including some while the plaintiff was in defendant's custody, were only an "incomplete snapshot" of the plaintiff's mental condition); *cf.* Acosta v. Tenneco Oil Co., 913 F.2d 205 (5th Cir. 1990) (finding good cause not shown for IME in ADEA case where defendant sought to compel examination

3. Prohibition of the Use of IMEs for "Garden Variety" Emotional Distress Claims

Increasingly, plaintiffs rely on arguments that they suffer from only "garden variety" emotional distress in opposing defendants' efforts to obtain Rule 35 independent medical examinations in harassment cases. The question is, what constitutes "garden variety"?

Many courts have refused to order FRCP 35 mental examinations on the basis of boilerplate allegations of emotional distress in the complaint alone or when the plaintiff claims to suffer only from the type of stress naturally resulting from the loss of a job or unlawful discrimination, harassment, or retaliation.[37] However, some courts continue

---

by vocational rehabilitation expert to support its failure to mitigate affirmative defense; plaintiff had not placed medical condition in controversy, expert was not a suitable medical examiner per Rule 35, and the defendant already had "the information it [sought] to pursue [] without [the need for] a repetitive examination of its own").

37. *See, e.g.*, Winstead v. Lafayette Cty. Bd. of Cty. Comm'rs, 315 F.R.D. 612, 615 (N.D. Fla. 2016) (finding a garden variety claim where plaintiff's anxiety was the "type of anguish that normally accompanies workplace discrimination, or perhaps something only slightly more serious than that"); Montez v. Stericycle, Inc., No. 1:12–cv–0502–AWI–BAM, 2013 WL 2150025 (E.D. Cal. May 16, 2013) (IME not ordered where plaintiff did not undergo mental health treatment, make a claim for an ongoing mental injury, claim serious psychological injury, and did not indicate that he would offer medical evidence to support his emotional distress damages); Acosta v. Tenneco Oil Co., 913 F.2d 205 (5th Cir. 1990) (finding the requirements of a Rule 35 examination not satisfied when the plaintiff in an age discrimination suit did not seek or allege emotional or mental damages); Kunstler v. City of N.Y., 242 F.R.D. at 264 (adopting the majority view and noting that there was "a distinction between a serious psychological injury and an emotional injury that a well-adjusted person could be expected to suffer in like circumstances, a so-called 'garden variety' distress claim"); Bowen v. Parking Auth. of City of Camden, 2114 F.R.D. 188, 194–95 (D.N.J. 2003) (holding that the former employee did not place his mental condition "in controversy" in suit against employer for discrimination and retaliation so as to warrant a psychiatric examination, where he alleged that he suffered emotional stress because of the work environment, but did not assert an ongoing mental injury, or a psychiatric disorder, or an independent cause of action for intentional or negligent infliction of emotional distress); Ricks v. Abbott Labs., 198 F.R.D. 647, 648–49 (D. Md. 2001) (holding plaintiff's mental condition was not in controversy merely because plaintiff pleaded emotional distress damages in complaint); Nolan v. Int'l Bhd. of Teamsters Health & Welfare Funds, Local 705, 199 F.R.D. 272, 273, 276 (N.D. Ill. 2001) (finding that plaintiff in sexual harassment and gender bias suit had not put her mental condition in controversy by claiming damages for "emotional pain, suffering, inconvenience, and mental anguish," which fell under the category of "humiliation and embarrassment" because such claims were "garden variety" emotional distress claims); Ford v. Contra Costa County, 179 F.R.D. 579, 579–80 (N.D. Cal. 1998) (holding that claim for emotional distress, alone, does not place plaintiff's mental condition in controversy); Fox v. Gates Corp., 179 F.R.D. 303, 308 (D. Colo. 1998) (holding that no Rule 35 exam was allowed even though large emotional distress damages were claimed); O'Sullivan v. Minnesota, 176 F.R.D. 325, 327 (D. Minn. 1997) (holding boilerplate allegations of "mental anguish," "emotional distress," and "embarrassment and humiliation" insufficient to put plaintiff's mental condition in controversy); O'Quinn v. N.Y. Univ. Med. Ctr., 163 F.R.D. 226, 228 (S.D.N.Y. 1995) (denying defendant's request for a Rule 35 examination because plaintiff represented that she would not be offering evidence of ongoing emotional harm at trial); Turner v. Imperial Stores, 161 F.R.D. 89, 97 (S.D. Cal. 1995) (holding that plaintiff's mental condition not "in controversy" on basis of claim for emotional distress damages in an amount in excess of $1 million; and that amount of claim for damages does not turn "garden variety" claim for emotional distress damages into claim where mental condition is in controversy); Bridges v. Eastman Kodak Co., 850 F. Supp. 216, 222 (S.D.N.Y. 1994) (denying defendant's request for Rule 35 examination of plaintiff in sexual harassment case in the absence of either a separate tort claim for emotional distress or allegations of severe ongoing mental injury).

to espouse the view that an FRCP 35 examination is appropriate whenever emotional distress is alleged.[38]

Of course, courts reject plaintiffs' claims of mere garden variety emotional distress when one of the "in controversy" factors discussed already—(1) plaintiff has asserted a specific cause of action for intentional or negligent infliction of emotional distress; (2) plaintiff has alleged a specific mental or psychiatric injury or disorder; (3) plaintiff has claimed unusually severe emotional distress; (4) plaintiff has offered expert testimony in support of her claim for emotional distress damages; or (5) plaintiff concedes that her mental condition is in controversy within the meaning of Rule 35(a)—is present in the case.[39] Frequently, a dispute arises regarding whether the plaintiff has asserted a specific psychiatric injury or disorder or unusually severe emotional distress. If a plaintiff claims to suffer from posttraumatic stress disorder, depression, or some other mental condition, those allegations go well beyond boilerplate allegations of mental anguish and emotional distress. Furthermore, when a plaintiff identifies specific injuries resulting from a defendant's alleged misconduct and links these symptoms to the defendant's actions, the "in controversy" and "good cause" requirements of FRCP 35(a)

---

38. Nuskey v. Lambright, 251 F.R.D. 3, 7–8 (D.D.C. 2008) (finding that while it is not the majority view, an IME is warranted when "a defendant seeks compensatory damages for the emotional pain she claims to have suffered as a result of a defendant's actions"); Boling v. First Util. Dist. of Knox County, No. 3:97-CV-832, 1998 U.S. Dist. LEXIS 21132, at *2–6 (E.D. Tenn. June 5, 1998) (granting motion for Rule 35 exam when plaintiff alleged emotional distress, humiliation, fear and embarrassment arising out of alleged hostile work environment); Haensel v. Chrysler Corp., No. CIV. A 96-1103, 1997 WL 537995 (E.D. La. Aug. 25, 1997) (holding that boilerplate allegations of emotional distress satisfy Rule 35 requirements); Jansen v. Packaging Corp. of Am., 158 F.R.D. 409, 410 (N.D. Ill. 1994) (finding that plaintiff's mental condition was in controversy when she claimed that she had suffered and continued to suffer ongoing emotional distress caused by alleged sexual harassment and retaliation).

39. Nguyen v. Qualcomm Inc., No. 09–1925–MMA (WVG), 2013 WL 3353840 (S.D. Cal. July 3, 2013) (IME ordered where terminated plaintiff's allegation that she suffers from conversion disorder distinguishes her from garden-variety emotional distress cases); Robinson v. HD Supply, Inc., No. 2:12–cv–604 GEB AC, 2013 WL 3815987 (E.D. Cal. July 19, 2013) (plaintiff's emotional distress was not garden variety where he alleged the following symptoms: "anxiety, sleepness, nightmares, nervousness, depression, worry, loss of appetite, loss of libido, rapid weight gain, hair loss, headaches, nervous twitching, stress, anger, feelings of hopelessness, feelings of isolation, embarrassment, mental anguish, indignation, apprehension, and feelings of betrayal"); Greenhorn v. Marriot Int'l. Inc., 216 F.R.D. 649, 650 (D.N.J. 2003) (in sexual harassment suit, rejecting plaintiff's argument of only "garden variety" emotional distress in response to request for independent medical examination (IME) because plaintiff alleged a separate cause of action for intentional infliction of emotional distress and alleged that the defendants' conduct caused her to sustain "lasting and permanent emotional . . . injury in the form of . . . emotional trauma causing insomnia, severe depression, avoidance, withdrawal, suicidal ideation, suspiciousness, social discomfort, low self-esteem, [and] resentfulness"); Javeed v. Covenant Med. Ctr., Inc., 218 F.R.D. 178, 179 (N.D. Iowa 2001) (allowing IME in sexual harassment suit, where allegations of damages for emotional distress associated with working in a hostile work environment did not themselves warrant a Rule 35 medical examination, but in addition to a claim for emotional distress damages, one of the factors discussed above also was present); Ricks v. Abbott Labs., 198 F.R.D. 647, 648–49 (D. Md. 2001) (adopting the majority view as described in *Javeed*); Houghton v. M & F Fishing, Inc., 198 F.R.D. 666, 668 (S.D. Cal. 2001) (denying IME because the emotional distress claims asserted by plaintiff were "garden variety," and noting that emotional distress claims give rise to order for IME only where, in addition to emotional distress claim, one of the factors discussed already is present).

are generally met even if the plaintiff alleges only garden variety emotional distress.[40] In addition, defendants may overcome plaintiff's argument of garden variety emotional distress by showing that the record suggests that the plaintiff's alleged emotional injuries may have been caused by other experiences.[41]

4. Other Considerations in Seeking an IME

The standards for admissible expert evidence articulated by the Supreme Court in *Daubert v. Merrell Dow Pharmaceuticals* also provide parameters for the scope of discovery, thus affecting FRCP 35 examinations. For instance, a party may object to a Rule 35 examination on the grounds that the evidence obtained would be inadmissible in court under *Daubert*. In *Chrissafis v. Continental Airlines, Inc.*,[42] the plaintiff resisted a Rule 35 examination on the grounds that the psychological test proposed by the defendant, the Minnesota Multiphasic Personality Inventory-2 (MMPI-2), was unreliable, of suspect validity, subject to error, and considered controversial among mental health professionals. After considering the MMPI-2, the court found that it satisfied *Daubert*'s requirements and ordered the plaintiff to submit to the test. Similarly, in *Favale v. Roman Catholic Diocese of Bridgeport*,[43] the plaintiff sought a protective order prohibiting the defendant's examiner from administering the Millon Behavioral Medicine Diagnostic (MBMD) test during an IME, arguing that the test was not designed to be used on a person such as the plaintiff, whose injury was purely psychological and

---

40. *See* Barry v. Shell Oil Co., No. 2:15-CV-00004 JWS, 2017 WL 1227910 (D. Alaska April 3, 2017) (plaintiff's claims were not garden variety when he claimed to be suffering from Major Depressive Disorder, for which he requested future mental health treatment); Thiessen v. Gen. Elec. Capital Corp., 178 F.R.D. 568, 570 (D. Kan. 1998) (citing specific symptoms identified by plaintiff in granting motion to compel examination); Phalp v. City of Overland Park, No. 00-2354, 2002 U.S. Dist. LEXIS 999, at *4–8 (D. Kan. Jan. 21, 2002) (granting motion for IME where plaintiff claimed to suffer from depression).

41. Nguyen v. Qualcomm Inc., No. 09–1925–MMA (WVG), 2013 WL 3353840 (S.D. Cal. July 3, 2013) (finding good cause exists and IME is necessary to enable employer to determine the existence of possible pre-existing causes to plaintiff's injuries, which would "have a direct, mitigating effect on Plaintiff's claimed damages"); EEOC v. 704 HTL Operating, LLC, No. 11-845 BB/LFG, 2012 WL 12870350 (D. N.M. July 25, 2012) (noting, while ordering an IME, that plaintiff's emotional condition may be related to the life stressors she suffered as a result of her refugee status rather than exclusively the defendants' alleged refusal to accommodate her religious dress); Dahdal v. Thorn Ams., Civ. A. 97-2119-GTV, 1997 WL 599614 (D. Kan. Sept. 15, 1997) (despite plaintiff's allegation that she only suffered "garden variety" emotional distress, finding that plaintiff could not avoid submission to a Rule 35 examination where the record suggested that her emotional injuries could have resulted from earlier experiences); Moore v. Epperson Underwriting Co., 06-cv-02563 (D. Minn. May 17, 2007) (granting motion to compel IME where plaintiff put mental condition in controversy because emotional distress may have been caused by employment-related circumstances, posttraumatic stress disorder, or any other factor or combination of circumstances).

42. No. 95 C 5080, 1997 WL 534874 (N.D. Ill. Aug. 21, 1997).

43. 235 F.R.D. 553 (D. Conn. 2006); *see also* Gadson v. Verizon Fla., Inc., No. 8:04-cv-1522-T-27TBM, 2005 WL 5918730 (M.D. Fla. July 25, 2005) (overruling plaintiff's objection that the MMPI/MMPI-s, the Rorschach Inkblot Test, the Thematic Apperception Test, the Shipley Institute for Living Scale (IQ), and Sixteen Personality Factors Inventory are of undocumented scientific validity and ordering that examining psychiatrist could "utilize diagnostic methods and tests that he determines, in his medical judgment, appropriate to evaluate the plaintiff's conditions" within the scope of the order).

who had no chronic medical illness. The court found the plaintiff had not shown that the MBMD test was unorthodox, harmful, burdensome, or prejudicial and that the test could lead to relevant evidence and ordered the plaintiff to submit to the test. On the other hand, in *Usher v. Lakewood Engineering & Manufacturing Co.*,[44] the court granted the plaintiff a protective order protecting the plaintiff from submitting to the Minnesota Multiphasic Personality Inventory, the Rorschach test, and the Thematic Apperception Test, on the grounds that the tests' reliability was in question.

Of course, a plaintiff challenging the admissibility of psychiatric or psychological evidence under *Daubert* at the discovery stage could not, with credibility, later rely on such psychiatric or psychological evidence in support of his or her claim.

IX. CONCLUSION

Defending against psychiatric or psychological testimony offered at trial, as well as affirmatively offering expert testimony in support of the defense, requires specialized knowledge and expertise both by the defense counsel and the defense's psychiatric or psychological expert witness. Defense counsel must develop a general understanding of the DSM-V; psychiatric and psychological testing; the education, training, and experience that psychiatrists and psychologists must have to act as expert witnesses; the generally accepted methodologies and procedures in the field of psychiatry and psychology; and the subject matter and opinions that lie within, and those that lie outside, the fields of psychiatry or psychology. In each case, defense counsel also must carefully analyze whether the psychiatric/psychological testimony meets the *Daubert* standards and whether that testimony should be challenged. Finally, knowing how to conduct a well-planned and carefully controlled cross-examination of the plaintiff's expert witness is essential to the successful handling of psychiatric or psychological testimony in a harassment or discrimination trial.

---

44. 158 F.R.D. 411 (N.D. Ill. 1994).

Bibliography

American Psychiatric Association, *Diagnostic and Statistical Manual of Mental Disorders, 5th ed.* (2013). American Psychiatric Publishing: Arlington, VA.

James J., McDonald, Jr., and Francine B. Kulick (eds), *Mental and Emotional Injuries in Employment Litigation* (The Bureau of National Affairs, Inc., 1994 & 1998 Supp.). The Bureau of National Affairs, Inc.: Washington, DC.

Jay Ziskin, *Coping with Psychiatric and Psychological Testimony, 5th ed.* (Law and Psychology Press, 1995). Oxford University Press: New York, NY.

CHAPTER 23

Closing Argument and Jury Instructions: Plaintiff's Perspective

Lynne Bernabei, Alan R. Kabat, and Devin Wrigley[1]

I. INTRODUCTION

Closing arguments and jury instructions are critical phases of trial proceedings. A successful plaintiff's advocate should know how best to draft instructions that will clearly explain the law to the jury, and how to craft a closing argument that will persuade the jury to reach a verdict for her client. Moreover, a plaintiff's advocate should know how to use the jury instructions to guide her closing argument, so that the jurors will understand why her client should prevail under the law as instructed. This chapter will offer a plaintiff's perspective on how to draft jury instructions and closing arguments, and on potential objections that may be raised by either side during those phases of trial.

II. JURY INSTRUCTIONS

Jury instructions direct the jurors to reach a verdict by applying the law of that jurisdiction to the facts proven at trial. In addition to outlining the controlling law, jury instructions generally explain what constitutes "evidence," how to evaluate a witness's credibility, and how to calculate or determine damages. As a practical matter, the plaintiff should draft the instructions in a manner that the average juror understands.[2] The instructions "should be concise, concrete, and simple, be in the active voice, avoid negatives and double-negatives, and be organized in logical sequence."[3] In other words, the jury instructions should offer a clear and compact "roadmap" to the jurors of what must be proven at trial for the plaintiff to prevail.

---

1. Lynne Bernabei, Alan R. Kabat, and Devin Wrigley are with Bernabei & Kabat, PLLC (Washington, D.C.).

2. *See* Fed. Judicial Ctr., Manual for Complex Litigation, Fourth, § 12.431 (2004).

3. *Id.*

Rule 51 of the Federal Rules of Civil Procedure (FRCP) governs when counsel must submit proposed jury instructions,[4] how the court must decide on jury instructions,[5] how and when counsel must object to the instructions to preserve the objection,[6] and how a party may assign error based either on an instruction given over a timely objection[7] or on an instruction not given despite a timely request.[8] If a party does not preserve an objection, a court may still consider "plain error" in the instructions if the error affects "substantial rights."[9] Moreover, many federal courts and individual judges publish local rules on jury instructions and objections.

A. Timing

1. Preliminary Instructions

FRCP Rule 51 authorizes the court to give preliminary instructions at the outset of the case, so long as the jury is again instructed at the end.[10] Preliminary instructions can be both substantive and procedural.[11] They generally include a concise statement of the legal principles and key factual issues relevant to the case; an explanation of courtroom procedures; an outline of the trial schedule; warnings to the jurors to avoid a mistrial, such as an instruction not to communicate with the parties involved and not to conduct Internet searches related to the case; a summary of pretrial procedures and of how evidence obtained through discovery may be utilized during trial; and an explanation of the jury's role at trial.[12]

Preliminary instructions offer several advantages to a plaintiff. They provide the jury with "ground rules" for understanding the case and the court's procedures, and are usually issued before the plaintiff's counsel gives her opening statement, which allows her to situate her opening arguments into the framework of the preliminary instructions. Justice Sandra Day O'Connor has commented on the additional benefits of preliminary instructions:

> [J]urors should be given general instructions on the applicable law before the case begins. How are they to make sense of the evidence and the mass of

---

4. FED. R. CIV. P. 51(a).

5. FED. R. CIV. P. 51(b).

6. FED. R. CIV. P. 51(c).

7. FED. R. CIV. P. 51(d)(1)(A).

8. FED. R. CIV. P. 51(d)(1)(B).

9. FED. R. CIV. P. 51(d)(2).

10. FED. R. CIV. P. 51.; *see also* Elecs. Corp. v. Westcoast Broad. Co., 341 F.2d 653, 665 (9th Cir. 1965).

11. *See* William W. Schwarzer, *Reforming Jury Trials*, 132 F.R.D. 575, 584 (1991) ("[S]ubstantive instructions provide a framework which will help the jury understand the issues in the case and organize and recall the evidence; procedural instructions will help jurors deal with questions of credibility and inference as they come up, rather than retrospectively.").

12. FED. JUDICIAL CTR., MANUAL FOR COMPLEX LITIGATION, FOURTH, § 12.432 (2004).

information that the parties will put before them, unless they know in advance what they are looking for? Jurors are not mere receptacles in which information can be stored, to be retrieved intact when the jurors finally are told what to do with it. Jurors are people, and people organize information as they receive it, according to their existing frames of reference. Unless they are given proper frames of reference at the beginning of a case, jurors are likely either to be overwhelmed by a mass of information they are incapable of organizing, or to devise their own frames of reference, which may well be inconsistent with those that the law requires.[13]

As William W. Schwarzer, former district judge for the Northern District of California, explained in more colloquial terms: "[N]ot giving preinstructions is like telling jurors to watch a baseball game and decide who won without telling them the rules until the end of the game."[14]

2. Final Instructions

Rule 51 also gives the court discretion to issue final instructions before or after closing argument, or at both times.[15] As a strategic matter, there are several advantages to instructing the jury prior to closing arguments. Importantly, instructions on the applicable law help jurors to better understand the legal arguments made by counsel and to provide context for understanding the evidence in the record. Moreover, they allow counsel to refer to the instructions in their closing arguments, and to explain to the jury how to apply the facts to the law as instructed. However, final instructions should always be reserved for after closing arguments, to "remind[ ] the jury of the instructions previously given and instruct[ ] them about the procedures to follow in deliberations."[16]

B. Pattern Instructions

The use of "pattern" (or "standard") jury instructions is becoming increasingly common, and offers a number of practical advantages for both the court and the parties. Of primary importance, pattern instructions provide a clear and concise statement of the law for the layperson, which avoids confusing the jury with instructions that include difficult legal terminology and complex syntax.[17] Pattern instructions are also,

---

13. Justice Sandra Day O'Connor, The Majesty of the Law: Reflections of a Supreme Court Justice 221 (2003).

14. Schwarzer, *supra* note 11, at 583.

15. Fed. R. Civ. P. 51.

16. Fed. Judicial Ctr., Manual for Complex Litigation, Fourth, § 12.434 (2004).

17. *See* Bethany K. Dumas, *Jury Trials: Lay Jurors, Pattern Jury Instructions, and Comprehension Issues,* 67 Tenn. L. Rev. 701, 701–05 (2000) ("The exact syntactic and semantic bars to juror comprehension of instructions are now well-documented by linguists and psycholinguists.").

theoretically, crafted to be neutral and nonslanted, so as not to favor either party.[18] For the courts, pattern instructions are often preferred because of their uniformity, which provides for an easier review on appeal.[19]

A majority of federal circuits have pattern instructions for employment cases on their websites, including the First,[20] Third,[21] Fifth,[22] Seventh,[23] Eighth,[24] Ninth,[25] and Eleventh Circuits.[26] Many state courts and bar associations also publish pattern jury instructions on their websites.[27] Additionally, the American Bar Association's (ABA's) Litigation Committee has published model jury instructions for employment cases.[28] However, plaintiffs' advocates should tread carefully when using the ABA's instructions, for two reasons: (1) jury instructions produced by the ABA's Litigation Committee tend to be slanted in favor of employers; and (2) these instructions have not been updated since 2005, and are therefore outdated. Federal courts have also reached different holdings as to whether the ABA's model instructions are appropriate for specific claims or defenses in employment cases.[29]

---

18. *See* William R. Amlong, American Law Institute, *Closing Arguments and Jury Instructions for Sexual Harassment Cases: The Plaintiff's Perspective (With Forms)*, 21:2 PRAC. LITIGATOR 43, 44 (2010) ("There are specific benefits to using court-approved pattern instructions. For the advocate, they provide an accurate explanation of the law that is as brief and concise as possible, understandable to the average jury, and completely neutral, unslanted, and free of argument.").

19. *See id.* ("For appellate courts, [pattern instructions] provide a measure of uniformity that makes appellate review easier and quicker.").

20. PATTERN JURY INSTRUCTIONS FOR CASES OF EMPLOYMENT DISCRIMINATION (DISPARATE TREAT-MENT) FOR THE DISTRICT COURTS OF THE UNITED STATES COURT OF APPEALS FOR THE FIRST CIRCUIT, http://www.med.uscourts.gov/pdf/empl_discr_pi.pdf (last visited Nov. 5, 2018).

21. MODEL CIVIL JURY TABLE OF CONTENTS AND INSTRUCTIONS, http://www.ca3.uscourts.gov/model-civil-jury-table-contents-and-instructions (last visited Nov. 5, 2018).

22. PATTERN JURY INSTRUCTIONS (CIVIL CASES), http://www.lb5.uscourts.gov/juryinstructions/Fifth/2014civil.pdf (last visited Nov. 5, 2018).

23. FEDERAL CIVIL JURY INSTRUCTIONS OF THE SEVENTH CIRCUIT, http://www.ca7.uscourts.gov/pattern-jury-instructions/7th_cir_civil_instructions.pdf (last visited Nov. 5, 2018).

24. MANUAL OF MODEL CIVIL JURY INSTRUCTIONS FOR THE DISTRICT COURTS OF THE EIGHTH CIRCUIT, http://www.juryinstructions.ca8.uscourts.gov/2018-REV_3.0_Jury_Instructions.pdf (last visited Nov. 5, 2018).

25. MANUAL OF MODEL CIVIL JURY INSTRUCTIONS FOR THE DISTRICT COURTS OF THE NINTH CIRCUIT, http://www3.ce9.uscourts.gov/jury-instructions/model-civil (last visited Nov. 5, 2018).

26. ELEVENTH CIRCUIT PATTERN JURY INSTRUCTIONS (CIVIL CASES), http://www.ca11.uscourts.gov/sites/default/files/courtdocs/clk/FormCivilPatternJuryInstruction.pdf (last visited Nov. 5, 2018).

27. *See, e.g.*, JUDICIAL COUNCIL OF CALIFORNIA CIVIL JURY INSTRUCTIONS, http://www.courts.ca.gov/partners/317.htm (last visited, Nov. 5, 2018); WASHINGTON CIVIL JURY INSTRUCTIONS, https://govt.west-law.com/wciji/Index?transitionType=Default&contextData=(sc.Default) (last visited Sept. 24, 2018); ILLINOIS PATTERN JURY INSTRUCTIONS-CIVIL, http://www.illinoiscourts.gov/CircuitCourt/CivilJuryIn-structions/default.asp (last visited Nov. 5, 2018).

28. AMERICAN BAR ASSOCIATION, EMPLOYMENT LITIGATION: MODEL JURY INSTRUCTIONS (2d ed. 2005).

29. *Compare* Woodson v. Scott Paper Co., 109 F.3d 913, 935 n. 29 (3d. Cir. 1997) (citing ABA instructions as informative to the issue of whether § 107(a) of the Civil Rights Act of 1991 is limited to mixed motive cases), *with* McClurg v. Santa Rosa Golf & Beach Club, Inc., 46 F. Supp. 2d 1244, 1246 (N.D. Fla. 1999) ("This difficulty in instructing the jury is evident in the American Bar Association Litigation Section's

Although pattern instructions provide clear, uniform statements of the law, advocates who consider borrowing pattern instructions from other states or circuits should be mindful of whether those jurisdictions have ruled differently on any legal issues involved. Moreover, since "[p]attern jury instructions are crafted to address the most-typical factual scenario," they "might not be suitable for all cases."[30] Therefore, while appellate courts generally prefer the use of pattern instructions, district courts maintain discretion to modify them where appropriate,[31] and counsel should carefully consider whether pattern instructions are suitable for the case at bar. For example, if a plaintiff is seeking a change in the law, such as by bringing a Title VII claim for discrimination on the basis of sexual orientation in a circuit that has not held that sexual orientation falls under Title VII's protected classes, the plaintiff's counsel should request an instruction in accordance with that new legal theory. Otherwise, any change in the law could be held to apply only prospectively.[32]

Advocates often face an uphill battle in objecting to pattern jury instructions.[33] To strengthen such an objection, counsel should be prepared to cite case law from other jurisdictions, treatises, or other authority to support their theory.[34] Counsel should also check the date of the last update to the instructions, for, as noted above, they may be outdated and not reflective of recent changes in the law. Moreover, counsel should always check the notes to the pattern instructions, which may raise red flags or provide further information about additional instructions that should be given to the jury for context.[35]

C. Nonstandard Instructions

As discussed *supra*, it is best practice to consider modifying any applicable pattern instructions to accommodate unique fact patterns in one's case. Modified instructions may also be helpful in cases involving developing areas of law. For example, in *Bruno*

Model Jury Instructions—Employment Litigation (ABA 1994) . . . The multiple instructions on the use of indirect evidence require the jury to perform a *McDonnell Douglas–Burdine* analysis, which also seems inappropriate. For reasons discussed below, I do not believe these forms of instruction are desirable or necessary.") (citations omitted).

30. Burzlaff v. Thoroughbred Motorsports, Inc., No. 12-CV-92, 2013 WL 3148413, at *3–5 (E.D. Wis. June 19, 2013) ("It is clear that this was not a pattern case and the pattern jury instructions were not wholly appropriate.").

31. *See* Aliotta v. Nat'l R.R. Passenger Corp., 315 F.3d 756, 765 (7th Cir. 2003) (noting that state pattern instructions "are not law," and that "there are many circumstances which justify modifying" them); *see also* Keltner v. Ford Motor Co., 748 F.2d 1265, 1267 (8th Cir. 1984) ("In states with pattern instructions, the district court may, but need not, use such instructions.").

32. *See* Maiz v. Virani, 253 F.3d 641, 677 (11th Cir. 2001).

33. *See* Sylvia Walbot & Cristina Alonso, *Jury Instructions: A Road Map for Trial Counsel*, 30:2 LITIGATION 31, 32 (2004).

34. *See id.*

35. *See id.*

v. Monroe County, involving a Title VII of the Civil Rights Act of 1964 (Title VII) sexual harassment claim,[36] the district court modified the Eleventh Circuit's pattern instructions to incorporate the subsequent holding of *Miller v. Kenworth of Dothan, Inc.*, that an "on paper" policy against sexual harassment "must be found ineffective when company practice indicates a tolerance towards harassment or discrimination."[37] Accordingly, the court in *Bruno* instructed the jury as follows:

> In determining whether the employer exercised reasonable care, you should also consider the level of the employer's demonstrated commitment to adhere to its policy. For example, an employer does not exercise reasonable care when its practice indicates tolerance towards harassment or discrimination, despite the fact that the policy itself states otherwise.[38]

Additionally, in employment cases, the plaintiff's counsel should consider requesting other nonstandard instructions such as instructions on the law of the case doctrine and instructions on implicit bias. Under the law of the case doctrine, "when a court rules on an issue of law, the ruling 'should continue to govern the same issues in subsequent stages in the same case.'"[39] Consequently, counsel may request jury instructions on issues of law already decided by the court during earlier stages of litigation, such as on summary judgment, and a district court's failure to give such instructions may constitute an abuse of discretion.[40]

Moreover, although pattern instructions often generally instruct the jury to "not let 'bias, sympathy, prejudice, or public opinion influence [their] decision,'"[41] where appropriate, plaintiff's counsel should consider requesting more specific instructions on implicit jury bias. For example, in *State v. Plain*, the Supreme Court of Iowa reversed the conviction of a black man, Plain, by an all-white jury for harassment in the first degree.[42] At the trial level, the district court refused to give to the jury the following cautionary instruction requested by Plain:

> Reach your verdict without discrimination. In reaching your verdict, you must not consider the defendant's race, color, religious beliefs, national origin, or

---

36. Bruno v. Monroe Cty., 383 Fed. App'x 845, 846 (11th Cir. 2010).

37. Miller v. Kenworth of Dothan, Inc., 277 F.3d 1269, 1280 (11th Cir. 2002).

38. Bruno v. Monroe Cty., Case No. 07-10117-Civ-Moore (S.D. Fla. 2008), Instructions to the Jury, Dkt. Entry 58, at 9, inserting into 11th Circuit Pattern Jury Instruction § 1.2.2 language to reflect the holding in *Miller*.

39. Vehicle Mkt. Research, Inc. v. Mitchell Int'l, Inc., 839 F.3d 1251, 1256 (10th Cir. 2016) (citations omitted).

40. *See* Gulliford v. Thrash, 8 Fed. App'x 766, 767–68 (9th Cir. 2001) ("We therefore find that the district judge in the second trial abused his discretion by formulating jury instructions in violation of the law of the case.").

41. Jennifer K. Elek & Paula Hannaford-Agor, *Implicit Bias and the American Juror*, 51 Ct. Rev. 116, 117 (2015).

42. State v. Plain, 898 N.W.2d 801, 809–11 (Iowa 2017).

sex. You are not to return a verdict for or against the defendant unless you would return the same verdict without regard to his race, color, religious belief, national origin, or sex.[43]

In holding that the district court abused its discretion in refusing to give that instruction, the Supreme Court of Iowa stated:

> While there is general agreement that courts should address the problem of implicit bias in the courtroom, courts have broad discretion about how to do so. One of the ways courts have addressed implicit bias is by giving jury instructions similar to the one proposed by Plain in this case. We strongly encourage district courts to be proactive about addressing implicit bias; however, we do not mandate a singular method of doing so.[44]

Counsel should be creative in crafting their suggested implicit-bias instructions; however, it is recommended that such instructions "be couched in accurate, evidence-based, and scientific terms," to avoid putting jurors "on the defensive."[45] For example, Judge Mark Bennett, of the US District Court for the Northern District of Iowa, generally issues the following implicit-bias instruction before opening statements:

> Do not decide the case based on "implicit biases." As we discussed in jury selection, everyone, including me, has feelings, assumptions, perceptions, fears, and stereotypes, that is, "implicit biases," that we may not be aware of. These hidden thoughts can impact what we see and hear, how we remember what we see and hear, and how we make important decisions. Because you are making very important decisions in this case, I strongly encourage you to evaluate the evidence carefully and to resist jumping to conclusions based on personal likes or dislikes, generalizations, gut feelings, prejudices, sympathies, stereotypes, or biases. The law demands that you return a just verdict, based solely on the evidence, your individual evaluation of that evidence, your reason and common sense, and these instructions. Our system of justice is counting on you to render a fair decision based on the evidence, not on biases.[46]

---

43. *Id.* at 816.

44. *Id.* at 817. However, the Supreme Court of Kansas recently rejected an attempt to use *Plain* to argue for a similar jury instruction that would have highlighted potential racial prejudice. State v. Nesbitt, 417 P.3d 1258, 1068–69 (Kan. 2018).

45. Jerry Kang et al., *Implicit Bias in the Courtroom*, 59 UCLA L. Rev. 1124, 1183 (2012).

46. Jury Instructions from Judge Mark Bennett (N.D. Iowa), https://www.americanbar.org/content/dam/aba/administrative/litigation/materials/2017_sac/written_materials/2_instruction.authcheckdam.pdf (last visited Nov. 5, 2018).

D. Objections to Jury Instructions

The US Supreme Court has recognized "the almost invariable assumption of the law that jurors follow their instructions."[47] Across the board, federal courts adhere to this presumption.[48] Therefore, it is paramount that counsel raise any and all objections to the jury instructions before the judge instructs the jury. Otherwise, the objection will be waived.[49]

A jury instruction may be found erroneous "if it misleads the jury as to the correct legal standard or does not adequately inform the jury on the law."[50] FRCP Rule 51(d) governs objections to jury instructions:

> (d) ASSIGNING ERROR; PLAIN ERROR.
> > (1) Assigning Error. A party may assign as error:
> > > (A) an error in an instruction actually given, if that party properly objected; or
> > > (B) a failure to give an instruction, if that party properly requested it and—unless the court rejected the request in a definitive ruling on the record—also properly objected.
> > (2) Plain Error. A court may consider a plain error in the instructions that has not been preserved as required by Rule 51(d)(1) if the error affects substantial rights.[51]

Under Rule 51, appellate courts review timely objections to jury instructions de novo.[52] However, absent a timely objection, appellate courts may only conduct plain error review, an "extremely stringent" form of review that will be met only in "rare cases":

> [R]eversal for plain error in the jury instructions or verdict form will occur only in exceptional cases where the error is so fundamental as to result in a

---

47. Richardson v. Marsh, 481 U.S. 200, 206 (1987) (citing Francis v. Franklin, 471 U.S. 307, 325 n. 9 (1985)); *see also* Weeks v. Angelone, 528 U.S. 225, 234 (2000).

48. *See, e.g.,* Rinehimer v. Cemcolift, Inc., 292 F.3d 375, 383 (3d Cir. 2002); Conwood Co. v. U.S. Tobacco Co., 290 F.3d 768, 794 (6th Cir. 2002); Johnson v. Breeden, 280 F.3d 1308, 1319–20 (11th Cir. 2002); Nichols v. Ashland Hosp. Corp., 251 F.3d 496, 501 (4th Cir. 2001); Loehr v. Walton, 242 F.3d 834, 836 (8th Cir. 2001); Ramos v. Davis & Geck, Inc., 224 F.3d 30, 32 (1st Cir. 2000); Caudle v. Bristow Optical Co., 224 F.3d 1014, 1023 (9th Cir. 2000); Jones v. Lincoln Elec. Co., 188 F.3d 709, 732 (7th Cir. 1999); Townsend v. Daniel, Mann, Johnson & Mendenhall, 196 F.3d 1140, 1150 (10th Cir. 1999); Gierlinger v. Gleason, 160 F.3d 858, 874 (2d Cir. 1998); Russell v. Piano Bank & Trust, 130 F.3d 715, 721 (5th Cir. 1997); Williams v. U.S. Elevator Corp., 920 F.2d 1019, 1024 (D.C. Cir. 1990).

49. *See* Lewis v. City of Chicago, 563 F. Supp. 2d 905, 911–12 (N.D. Ill. 2008) ("Failure to object to a jury instruction at trial results in a waiver . . . In the absence of a proper objection, the Court can consider whether there was plain error in the instruction that affected the plaintiff's substantial rights.").

50. Anderson v. Branen, 17 F.3d 552, 556 (2d Cir. 1994).

51. FED. R. CIV. P. 51(d).

52. Stanczyk v. City of New York, 752 F.3d 273, 278 n. 3 (2d Cir. 2014) ("We review jury instructions de novo and will grant a new trial if, viewing the charge as a whole, we find that it was erroneous and prejudicial.").

miscarriage of justice. To meet this stringent standard, a party must prove that the "challenged instruction was an incorrect statement of the law and [that] it was probably responsible for an incorrect verdict, leading to substantial injustice." This element is satisfied if a party proves that the instruction will "mislead the jury or leave the jury to speculate as to an *essential* point of law."[53]

In other words, to prevail under plain error review, the appellant must prove: "(1) that there was an error; (2) that the error was clear or obvious; (3) that it affected the appellant's substantial rights; and (4) that it seriously affected the fairness, integrity, or public reputation of the judicial proceedings."[54] To avoid this strict standard of review, counsel must raise any objections to the jury instructions before they are given. It is especially important for the plaintiff's counsel to preserve these objections at the trial level, as verdicts against plaintiffs are rarely overturned on appeal.[55]

Further, failure to object to jury instructions may preclude the losing party from seeking post-trial relief (or relief on appeal). The Second Circuit has held that the losing party could not use FRCP Rule 59(e) (a posttrial motion to alter or amend a judgment) where the party "fail[ed] to comply with the carefully crafted structure and standards of Rules 50 and 51."[56] The rationale is that "Rule 51 requires parties to articulate and lodge their objections to jury charges before they are delivered so that 'the trial court will have an opportunity to cure any defects in the instructions before sending the jurors to deliberate.'"[57] Thus, it is necessary for a party to object to the jury instructions in a timely manner, or to renew the objection in a Rule 50(b) motion for judgment as a matter of law. The Sixth Circuit, in an insurance fraud case, noted that, although the parties disputed whether the insurance company had objected to a jury instruction, "Rule 51 does not prevent normal appellate review, since Zurich made all necessary arguments to preserve the issues raised in its appeal in its Rule 56 motion for summary judgment and in its Rule 50(b) motion for judgment as a matter of law or alternatively for a new trial."[58] As the Supreme Court has remarked, "the failure to object to an instruction does not render the instruction the 'law of the case' for purposes of appellate review of the denial of a directed verdict or judgment notwithstanding the verdict."[59] Nonetheless, the safer course is to object to a jury instruction in a timely manner at least once if not twice—first through a Rule 51 objection, and second through a Rule 50 posttrial motion.

---

53. Farley v. Nationwide Mut. Ins. Co., 197 F.3d 1322, 1329–30 (11th Cir. 1999) (emphasis in original) (citations omitted).

54. Coleman-Lee v. Govt. of the Dist. of Columbia, 788 F.3d 296, 299 (D.C. Cir. 2015) (citations omitted).

55. *See* Theodore Eisenberg & Henry S. Farber, *Why do Plaintiffs Lose Appeals? Biased Trial Courts, Litigious Losers, or Low Trial Win Rates?*, 15:1 AM. LAW & ECON. REV. 73, 73 (2013).

56. ING Global v. United Parcel Service Oasis Supply Corp., 757 F.3d 92, 96 (2d Cir. 2014).

57. *Id.* at 97.

58. K&T Enterprises, Inc. v. Zurich Ins. Co., 97 F.3d 171, 174–75 (6th Cir. 1996).

59. City of St. Louis v. Praprotnik, 485 U.S. 112, 120 (1988).

Even if counsel succeeds in demonstrating that the erroneous instruction created a "substantial and eradicable doubt about whether the jury has been properly guided in its deliberations,"[60] appellate courts will order a new trial only if they determine that the challenged instruction could have affected the outcome of the case.[61] One such example is *Woods v. START Treatment & Recovery Centers, Inc.*, in which the Second Circuit vacated and remanded the decision of the district court below based on reversible error in the jury instructions.[62] The plaintiff, Cassandra Woods, sued her former employer for retaliation and interference under the Family and Medical Leave Act (FMLA).[63] In her deposition taken during discovery, Ms. Woods invoked the Fifth Amendment and refused to answer questions from her employer about her alleged prior criminal conduct, which the employer argued evidenced performance issues.[64] Before trial, the district court granted the employer's motion *in limine*, which sought an adverse inference instruction that the jurors should "presume that Woods would have answered the deposition questions in the affirmative."[65] Moreover, on Ms. Woods's retaliation claim, the district court instructed the jury on the "but for" standard of causation, rather than on the "motivating factor" standard.[66] On appeal, the Second Circuit found that the district court committed reversible error by giving the adverse inference instruction,[67] as well as by instructing the jury on a higher standard of causation than Ms. Woods was actually required to prove under her retaliation claim.[68]

Potential objections to jury instructions may be more easily resolved in advance of trial through rulings on motions *in limine*. For example, in *U.S. ex rel. Scutellaro v. Capitol Supply, Inc.*, brought under the False Claims Act (FCA), the plaintiff filed a motion in limine to prevent the defendant from telling the jury that the plaintiff could be awarded treble damages by the judge under the FCA.[69] In granting the plaintiff's

---

60. Jowers v. Lincoln Elec. Co., 617 F.3d 346, 352 (5th Cir. 2010) (citations omitted).

61. *See* Bender v. Brumley, 1 F.3d 271, 276–77 (5th Cir. 1993) ("Assessing whether the jury was properly guided, however, is only one-half of the inquiry. Even though error may have occurred, we will not reverse if we find, based upon the record, that the challenged instruction could not have affected the outcome of the case.") (citations and internal quotation marks omitted).

62. Woods v. START Treatment & Recovery Ctrs., Inc., 864 F.3d 158, 162, 171 (2d Cir. 2017) ("If a jury finds against Woods, but it was wrongly instructed on the law, can its verdict still stand? In this case, our answer is no.").

63. *Id.* at 164.

64. *Id.*

65. *Id.*

66. *Id.*

67. *Id.* at 170–71 ("Such adverse inferences are appropriately admitted . . . only if they are relevant, reliable, and not unduly prejudicial. We conclude that the district court exceeded the bounds of its discretion in admitting and permitting the adverse inferences to be drawn here.") (citations omitted).

68. *Id.* at 170 ("Although there is evidence from which a reasonable jury could conclude that Woods's deficient performance served as the sole basis for her termination, we are unable to conclude that that evidence is so overwhelming as to render the erroneous instruction harmless. That error, coupled with the erroneous admission of the adverse inferences . . . resulted in impermissible prejudice.").

69. Scutellaro v. Capitol Supply, Inc., C.A. No. 10-1094 (BAH), 2017 WL 9889370 (D.D.C. Sept. 20, 2017) (Howell, J.).

motion, the district court stated that "there is a risk that a jury could use knowledge of the trebling of damages and statutory penalties 'as an intimation to keep the damages at a low level, in view of the fact that the amount allowed by the jury would be multiplied by three.'"[70] The district court also broadened its holding by noting that "the weight of authority in other contexts strongly establishes a general rule that a jury should not be instructed as to trebling of damages, attorneys' fees, or other court-determined awards that might alter a jury's damages finding."[71] Therefore, plaintiffs' attorneys should consider filing similar motions *in limine* when bringing to trial statutory claims involving the trebling of damages, such as claims under state wage and hour statutes.

E. Interim and Limiting Instructions

The need for "interim" or "limiting" instructions may arise during the course of trial proceedings. For example, under Rule 105 of the Federal Rules of Evidence:

> If the court admits evidence that is admissible against a party or for a purpose—but not against another party or for another purpose—the court, on timely request, must restrict the evidence to its proper scope and instruct the jury accordingly.[72]

The trial judge may issue interim or limiting instructions at any time during trial when they could be helpful to the jury, as "[a]n explanation of applicable legal principles may be more helpful when the issue arises than if deferred until the close of trial."[73] However, when the need for interim instructions arises, "counsel should be permitted to comment or object before an instruction is given," and "the judge should caution the jury that these are only interim explanations, and that the final, complete instructions on which they will base their verdict will come at the close of trial."[74]

For example, in *Howard University v. Roberts-Williams*, a common-law breach of contract case brought by a professor denied tenure by Howard University, the trial judge issued an interim instruction regarding the biennial evaluations that the university was contractually obligated to provide to the professor.[75] During cross-examination of the plaintiff, defense counsel asked a question that implied that the plaintiff received the required evaluations during her application process for promotion to assistant professor, and her counsel objected "on the ground that Howard's counsel was 'equating' the promotion application evaluation with the required handbook evaluations; that 'the

---

70. *Id.* at *1.

71. *Id.* at *2.

72. Fed. R. Evid. 105.

73. Fed. Judicial Ctr., Manual for Complex Litigation, Fourth, § 12.431 (2004).

74. *Id.* at § 12.433.

75. Howard Univ. v. Roberts-Williams, 37 A.3d 896, 903–04 (D.C. 2012).

question implies they're the same thing, and they're not."[76] To remedy this confusing line of questioning, the trial judge gave the following interim instruction at the close of her testimony:

> [T]he gist [of the faculty handbook provision] is that the university undertakes to give biennial evaluations, to evaluate the faculty member every two years, and it explicitly mentions tenure being benefitted by the biennial evaluations for those on the tenure track, as was the plaintiff . . . That is part of the contract that the plaintiff had with the defendant . . .
>
> Now, you're further instructed . . . that although a candidate for tenure may have available[ ] colleagues to reach out [to] for advice and counsel with respect to tenure and the applications for tenure, that doesn't relieve the university of its contractual duty to biennially evaluate the candidate . . .[77]

Prior to issuing this instruction, the trial judge allowed defense counsel to explain his objection to the instruction, in that "it would 'unduly influence the jury,'" who "would 'begin to believe that the [c]ourt is favoring the plaintiff.'"[78] On appeal, the D.C. Court of Appeals held that the interim instruction was not prejudicial because it "accurately reflected the fact that Howard's faculty handbook's provisions regarding tenure constituted part of an employee's contract," and the trial court "properly informed the jury as to their meaning."[79] As in *Roberts-Williams*, plaintiffs' advocates should consider requesting interim or limiting instructions where such instructions might aid the jury in understanding legal issues as they arise during trial proceedings.

F. Curative Instructions

A curative jury instruction "is one that is designed to correct a trial error," and "is usually given at a party's request after there has been a sustained objection, although a trial judge may give such an instruction *sua sponte* to protect the record on appeal."[80] Curative instructions may be given at any stage during trial, and, most commonly, instruct the jurors to ignore an inadmissible exhibit or an erroneous or prejudicial remark, "and not allow such statement or exhibit to influence their verdict."[81] Although curative instructions are generally given immediately following a timely objection, they may be reserved for the end of trial, to be given with the final instructions.[82] However, it is good practice to ask for the curative instruction immediately following the objection,

---

76. *Id.* at 903.
77. *Id.* at 904.
78. *Id.*
79. *Id.* at 907.
80. ROBERT E. LARSEN, NAVIGATING THE FEDERAL TRIAL, 2017 ED. § 2:30 (2017).
81. *Id.*
82. *See id.*

so as to promptly cure any error as it arises.[83] A trial judge's refusal to give a curative instruction may constitute an abuse of discretion and result in a mistrial.[84]

G. Readbacks, Jury Questions, and Supplemental Instructions

Often, juries will request readbacks of testimony during their deliberations.[85] The Federal Judicial Center (FJC) advises that "[r]eadbacks should never be authorized absent counsel's consent, or, at least, absent an opportunity to be heard," as "[r]eadbacks should not unduly emphasize any part of the evidence."[86] The FJC also advises that "[t]he court should instruct the jury to make requests as specific and narrow as possible to avoid excessively long readbacks, then should confer with the attorneys to seek agreement on the portions of the testimony to be read. Counsel should state any objections on the record."[87] The Second Circuit has explained the rationale for such advisements:

> [A] court's response to a jury request for a readback should balance the jurors' need to review the evidence before reaching their verdict against the difficulty involved in locating the testimony to be read back, the possibility of undue emphasis on a particular portion of testimony read out of context, and the possibility of undue delay in the trial.[88]

Additionally, during the course of their deliberations, juries will often ask follow-up questions to the court about particular instructions. Although trial judges maintain discretion over whether to reinstruct the jury to address their question(s), the US Supreme Court has stated that, "[w]hen a jury makes explicit its difficulties, a trial judge should clear them away with concrete accuracy."[89] If a reinstruction is given, counsel should ask the court to read back all of the instructions on that particular legal issue to provide jurors with the appropriate context.[90] As the Seventh Circuit has noted: "Instructions must be read as a whole with due regard for the artificiality of assuming that isolated passages in a lengthy set of instructions are apt to spell the difference between victory and defeat."[91] Additionally, in some cases:

> Referral to the original instruction cannot be adopted as a reflexive response (even if the original instruction was proper) because a jury's question that comes after instruction suggests that—at least in the jurors' estimation—the

---

83. *See id.*

84. *See* Wilson v. NHB Indus., Inc., 219 Fed. App'x 851, 852–54 (11th Cir. 2007).

85. FED. JUDICIAL CTR., MANUAL FOR COMPLEX LITIGATION, FOURTH, § 12.436 (2004).

86. *Id.* (citations omitted).

87. *Id.*

88. U.S. v. Criollo, 962 F.2d 241, 243 (2d Cir. 1992).

89. Bollenbach v. U.S., 326 U.S. 607, 612–13 (1946).

90. *See* Walbot & Alonso, *supra* note 33, at 37.

91. W.T. Rogers Co. v. Keene, 778 F.2d 334, 342 (7th Cir. 1985).

original instructions have not provided sufficient guidance on the law the jury is to apply to the evidence presented at trial.[92]

If the judge elects to provide supplemental instructions to the jury, counsel should timely raise any appropriate objections, as such additional instructions or responses to questions from the jury could result in a reversal on appeal.[93] The Second Circuit suggests the following four-step response to jury questions:

> (1) The jury's question should be submitted in writing, (2) the question should be marked as a court exhibit and read into the record, (3) counsel should be afforded an opportunity to suggest appropriate responses, and (4) once the jurors are recalled, the question, if substantive, should be read into the record in their presence.[94]

H. Verdict Forms

Similar to jury instructions, verdict forms must be clear and understandable to the average juror. Logically, "[t]he verdict form should conform to the [jury] instructions or it may be deemed a waiver of an issue."[95] Verdict forms should be "reasonably capable of an interpretation that would allow the jury to address all factual issues essential to judgment."[96] If the verdict form "creates an erroneous impression of the law in the minds of the jurors that affects the outcome of a case," its usage could be held reversible error.[97] For example, in *McNely v. Ocala Star-Banner Corp.*, involving claims of retaliation under the Americans with Disabilities Act (ADA), the special interrogatory verdict form stated *inter alia* the following questions:

> 5. Do you find, by a preponderance of the evidence, that Plaintiff has proved that he was terminated solely because of his alleged disability?
>
> . . .
>
> 6. Do you find, by a preponderance of the evidence, that Plaintiff has proved that he was terminated solely because he engaged in a statutorily protected expression?[98]

---

92. Ivey v. Dist. of Columbia, 46 A.3d 1101, 1108 (D.C. 2012).

93. *See* Chu v. Am. Airlines, 285 F.3d 756, 758 (8th Cir. 2002); *see also Hoard v. Hartman*, 904 F.3d 780, 786 n.7 (9th Cir. 2018) ("The standard of review is identical for jury instructions and supplemental jury instructions given in response to a jury's questions.") (citations omitted).

94. U.S. v. Ulloa, 882 F.3d 41, 45 (2d Cir. 1989).

95. *See* Walbot & Alonso, *supra* note 33, at 36.

96. Rooney v. Sprague Energy Corp., 554 F. Supp. 2d 39, 43 (D. Me. 2008) (citations omitted).

97. FRANCIS C. AMENDOLA ET AL., CORPUS JURIS SECUNDUM, 89 C.J.S. TRIAL § 1012 (Sept. 2017).

98. McNely v. Ocala Star-Banner Corp., 99 F.3d 1068, 1071 (11th Cir. 1996).

The jury found that the plaintiff, McNely, proved that he was "an individual with a disability" under the ADA; he was able to perform the essential functions of his position; his employer failed to prove that it reasonably accommodated his condition; and that McNely's proposed reasonable accommodation would not impose an undue hardship on his employer.[99] Despite these findings, the jury returned a verdict for the employer, answering "yes" to Question 6, but "no" to Question 5.[100] On appeal, McNely's counsel argued that the verdict form was "fatally flawed," in that (1) "inclusion of the term 'solely' in questions five and six erroneously prevented the jury from returning a verdict for the plaintiff if the jury found that impermissible discrimination or retaliation had a determinative effect on the defendants' decisionmaking process, but was not the sole reason for the employment decision," and (2) "questions five and six erroneously narrowed the jury's inquiry to whether McNely was 'terminated' because of discrimination or retaliation, even though the ADA authorizes recovery for adverse employment actions that fall short of termination and even though McNely had put on evidence of such actions in this case."[101] The Eleventh Circuit agreed with McNely's counsel that these errors merited reversal:

> The verdict form submitted to the jury in this case did not accurately reflect the law or the evidence presented at trial. First, the verdict form required a finding of sole causation in order for [Plaintiff] to recover, while the ADA requires only a finding of "but-for" causation. Second, the verdict form barred recovery for adverse employment actions short of termination, when the ADA permits recovery for those less drastic forms of discrimination and when evidence of such lesser discrimination was presented at trial. Under these circumstances, we cannot conclude that the jurors understood the issues and were not misled by the verdict form.[102]

III. CLOSING ARGUMENT

Closing argument is the advocate's last opportunity to persuade the jury that his or her client should prevail. The purpose of closing arguments is to "assist the jury in analyzing the evidence" presented at trial.[103] However, as discussed *infra*, there are limits to what counsel may discuss during closing. Specifically, closing argument must involve "a fair presentation of a party's case and claims from [that party's] point of view; it must be confined to the evidence and must not appeal to passion or prejudice or sympathy in an unfair way."[104]

---

99. *See id.*

100. *Id.*

101. *Id.*

102. *Id.* at 1078.

103. U.S. v. Iglesias, 915 F.2d 1524, 1529 (11th Cir. 1990) (citations omitted).

104. Tashjian v. Boston & M.R.R., 80 F.2d 320, 322 (1st Cir. 1935).

A. Scope and Strategy

An advocate's main objective during closing argument is "to provide jurors sympathetic to [her] side with points that will enable them to persuade other, undecided or doubting jurors" by explaining how the promises she made during the opening statement were met during trial, and, conversely, how the promises made by opposing counsel were not fulfilled by the evidence presented at trial.[105] To accomplish this objective, it is helpful to use the jury instructions as a roadmap for the jury, by clearly demonstrating during closing how each piece of evidence proven at trial, collectively, satisfies the burden of proof required for the jury to issue the desired verdict.[106] For this reason, as discussed *supra*, it is often helpful for the plaintiff's counsel to request that final jury instructions be issued prior to closing arguments. If so, counsel may use the instructions as a demonstrative aid for the jury, to illustrate how the evidence presented by the plaintiff satisfies each element of her claim.

Also during closing, the plaintiff's counsel should carefully highlight the weaknesses of the defendant's case, but only based on the evidence presented at trial, as the "cardinal rule of closing argument" is "that counsel must confine comments to evidence in the record and to reasonable inferences from that evidence."[107] The Seventh Circuit has explained that:

> Closing arguments are the time in the trial process when counsel is given the opportunity to discuss more freely the weaknesses in his opponent's case and to highlight the strength of his own. Indeed . . . a significant part of the lawyer's role during closing arguments is to bolster the strength of his case by calling the jury's attention to certain facts or inferences that might otherwise escape the jury's attention. It is perfectly reasonable for defense counsel to discuss the weaknesses of an opponent's case during closing argument so long as counsel's argument is based on evidence admitted at trial.[108]

Moreover, closing arguments are an opportunity for counsel to use visual aids and demonstratives based on record evidence to appeal to the jurors through multiple senses. Such aids are critical persuasive tools, "since communicating through multiple channels and repeating key information enhances retention—to as much as 60 per cent over three days, as opposed to only 10 per cent if merely heard or 20 per cent if only seen."[109] To enhance juror retention of the information presented during closing argument, advocates can enlarge important trial exhibits, summarize critical testimony, and use charts, graphs, or other visual aids to emphasize their point, if such aids are

---

105. Tucker Ronzetti & Janet L. Humphreys, *Avoiding Pitfalls in Closing Arguments*, 74 THE FLORIDA BAR. J. 36, 36 (2003).

106. *See* Amlong, *supra* note 18, at 54.

107. Whittenburg v. Werner Enters. Inc., 561 F.3d 1122, 1128–29 (10th Cir. 2009).

108. Jones v. Lincoln Elec. Co., 188 F.3d 709, 731 (7th Cir. 1999) (citations omitted).

109. THOMAS A. MAUET, TRIALS: STRATEGY, SKILLS, AND THE NEW POWER OF PERSUASION 4 (2005).

created based on the evidence presented at trial.[110] Additionally, counsel can enlarge the verdict form for use as a demonstrative aid and explain how to complete it to reach a verdict in favor of the plaintiff.[111]

Though counsel should be careful not to make inflammatory statements that will invite objections, "closing argument need not, nor should, be a sterile exercise devoid of passion,"[112] as "some degree of emotionally charged language during closing argument in a civil case is a well-accepted tactic in American courtrooms."[113] Unlike the dramatic closing arguments often depicted in television dramas, counsel should maintain professionalism and make logical arguments based upon the record. The key for a plaintiff's advocate, therefore, is to present a compelling argument by persuading the jury to view the facts presented at trial in the light most favorable to the plaintiff, without inviting objections from the opponent.

B. Objections to Closing Arguments

There are numerous bases on which to object to closing arguments. Such objections are grounded in precedent, as well as in Rule 3.4(e) of the Model Rules of Professional Conduct:

> A lawyer shall not: . . . in trial, allude to any matter that the lawyer does not reasonably believe is relevant or that will not be supported by admissible evidence, assert personal knowledge of facts in issue except when testifying as a witness, or state a personal opinion in issue except when testifying as a witness, or state a personal opinion as to the justness of a cause, the credibility of a witness, the culpability of a civil litigant or the guilt or innocence of an accused.[114]

FRCP Rule 51 governs objections to closing arguments.[115] Similar to jury instructions, objections to closing arguments will be waived if not timely made on the record,[116] and, if not preserved, may only be reviewed on appeal for plain error.[117] However, as a strategic matter, it is not always wise to object during closing argument, as juries tend to look negatively on such objections:

> [O]bjecting is risky because of its effect on jurors' perceptions. The jury may consider the objection an effort by counsel to obfuscate, and the objection itself

---

110. *See* Jacob A. Stein, Closing Arguments §1:66 (2016).

111. *See* Amlong, *supra* note 18, at 54.

112. Whittenburg, 561 F.3d at 1133.

113. Settlegoode v. Portland Pub. Schs., 371 F.3d 503, 518 (9th Cir. 2004).

114. Model Rules of Prof'l Conduct R. 3.4(e) (Am. Bar Ass'n 1983).

115. Fed. R. Civ. P 51.

116. Fed. R. Civ. P 51(d)(1).

117. Fed. R. Civ. P 51(d)(2).

is likely to highlight the point at issue, especially if the objection is overruled. In lieu of an objection, counsel can point out the misstating of evidence in the defendant's closing or the plaintiff's rebuttal. In doing so, counsel should carefully provide a clear and correct recitation of the evidence, and remind the jurors that their own collective memory is controlling.[118]

Moreover, "improper comments made during closing argument rarely rise to the level of reversible error,"[119] and "warrant reversal only if they 'influenced the jury in such a way that substantial prejudice resulted to' the opposing party."[120] Therefore, counsel should carefully weigh the pros and cons of objecting during closing argument prior to doing so.

The following is a list of common instructions to arguments made during closing, with examples of cases in which such objections were raised.

1. Improper Statements of Law

A misstatement of law made during closing argument could be grounds for a new trial, as counsel should refer only to the law as instructed by the court in the case at bar.[121] For example, in *Wilson v. NHB Industries, Inc.*, involving alleged FMLA violations, one of the central issues at trial concerned whether the plaintiff's employer was put on notice of his health condition.[122] During closing argument, defense counsel stated that the plaintiff "failed to establish that he had a serious health condition because he failed to put on testimony from any medical provider . . . or any emergency room employee who could corroborate [Plaintiff's] own testimony regarding his condition."[123] In response, the plaintiff's counsel suggested during closing argument that the employer should have contacted the plaintiff's doctor directly to learn about his health condition: "Ask yourself, what did [the employer] do to find out what was going on with his condition? . . . [The employer] never tried to call Dr. Hakim to see what was going on to see what they could do."[124] Defense counsel timely objected, noting, correctly, that such action would have violated the FMLA.[125] On appeal, the Eleventh Circuit vacated and remanded the case for new trial, holding:

> Given that the jury heard the parties' closing arguments after they had already been instructed on the law, and where the improper comments

---

118. Ronzetti & Humphreys, *supra* note 105, at 39.

119. Probus v. K-Mart, 794 F.2d 1207, 1210 (7th Cir. 1986).

120. Arcor, Inc. v. Textron, Inc., 960 F.2d 710, 713 (7th Cir. 1992); *see also Smith v. Rosebud Farm, Inc.*, 898 F.3d 747, 753 (7th Cir. 2018) ("Improper statements made during closing arguments seldom warrant a new trial...") (citations omitted).

121. Ronzetti & Humphreys, *supra* note 105, at 36.

122. Wilson v. NHB Indus., Inc., 219 Fed. App'x 851, 852 (11th Cir. 2007).

123. *Id.*

124. *Id.* at 853.

125. *Id.*

occurred during [Plaintiff's] counsel's rebuttal when [Defendant] had no further opportunity to speak to the jury, and where the comments constituted a misstatement of the law which went directly to the very issues contested in the case, the Court finds that counsel's improper comments, especially without a curative instruction, cast an impermissible taint over the jury's verdict.[126]

2. Evidence Not in the Record

In addition to misstatements of law, misstatements of fact are also grounds for objecting. Although asking the jury to draw inferences based on record evidence is proper, creating evidence without factual support is not, and counsel must tread this line carefully.[127] In *Schandelmeier-Bartels v. Chicago Park District*, a discriminatory termination case, the plaintiff's counsel improperly suggested during closing that the defendant employer fabricated an email allegedly sent prior to terminating the plaintiff, which discussed her performance issues.[128] Specifically, the plaintiff's counsel stated:

> I would suggest to you that they put that e-mail up there that supposedly got written by Rowland. And I would suggest to you that you should think about, not conclude but think about the possibility that that document didn't get created till after Cathleen Schandelmeier got fired . . . Even if it is a legit document, which I strongly suggest to you that it's not, they didn't do anything about it.[129]

On appeal, the Seventh Circuit held that these comments were improper:

> No evidence put before the jury supported that inference. A suggestion that an opposing party—and, by extension, its counsel—has put forth falsified evidence is very different from (and much more serious than) a contention that one witness's version of events has a better factual foundation and thus is more likely to be true than another witness's version of the same events, or that one document is inconsistent with another.[130]

However, the court declined to order a new trial, holding that a curative instruction issued to the jury that "[t]he lawyers' opening statements and closing arguments to you are not evidence" properly mitigated the prejudice caused by the comments.[131]

---

126. *Id.* at 854.

127. Ronzetti & Humphreys, *supra* note 105, at 36.

128. Schandelmeier-Bartels v. Chicago Park Dist., 634 F.3d 372, 387–88 (7th Cir. 2011).

129. *Id.* at 387.

130. *Id.* at 388.

131. *Id.* ("We presume that curative instructions to the jury mitigate harm that may otherwise result from improper comments during sometimes heated closing argument.").

3. "Golden Rule" Arguments

"Golden Rule" arguments ask the jurors to "do unto others as you would have them do unto you,"[132] to "place themselves in the position of a party,"[133] or "to grant a party the recovery they would wish themselves if they were in the same position."[134] Such arguments are "universally condemned because [they] encourage[ ] the jury to depart from neutrality and to decide the case on the basis of personal interest and bias rather than on evidence."[135]

In *Caudle v. District of Columbia*, involving Title VII claims of retaliation brought by African-American police officers against the District of Columbia, the D.C. Circuit held that the following statements were impermissible "Golden Rule" arguments: (1) "would *you* hesitate to speak up if *you* knew that speaking up would mean that *your* boss would call a meeting with *your* entire office . . . ;" (2) "[w]ouldn't *you* think twice about complaining about workplace discrimination . . . ;" and (3) "we ask yourselves [sic] to *put yourselves in the plaintiffs' shoes*. What would it do to *you* to have *your* complaint broadcast to *your* entire office, to be the only one excluded . . ."[136] In so holding, the court noted that the third statement was a "quintessential invocation of the golden rule," and that the first two, while "closer question[s]," also constituted improper "Golden Rule" arguments.[137] The D.C. Circuit granted a new trial, holding that, given the closeness of the case, these improper arguments were not harmless error, and that the district court's curative instruction to the jury "to decide the case without prejudice, sympathy, fear, favor or public opinion" did not eliminate the prejudice caused by the improper arguments.[138]

4. "Send a Message" Statements

"Send a message" statements ask the jury to "punish the defendant rather than compensate the plaintiff," and are improper in cases where punitive damages are unavailable.[139] For example, in *Caudle*, in addition to the three improper "Golden Rule" arguments, plaintiffs' counsel made the following "send a message" statement during closing:

> By protecting plaintiffs' right to complain about unlawful conduct without reprisal, you preserve the rights *not just of plaintiffs but of everyone*. By ensuring that plaintiffs are made whole for what they have endured, you ensure that *others will*

---

132. Klotz v. Sears, Roebuck & Co., 267 F.2d 53, 54 (7th Cir. 1959).

133. Ins. Co. of N. Am. v. U.S. Gypsum Co., 870 F.2d 148, 154 (4th Cir. 1989).

134. Stein, *supra* note 110, at §1:80.

135. Granfield v. CSX Transp., Inc., 597 F.3d 474, 491 (1st Cir. 2010); *see also* Har-Pen Truck Lines, Inc. v. Mills, 378 F.2d 705, 714 (5th Cir. 1967) ("The real danger is that the sympathy and the feelings of the jury will be encouraged and aroused so that the jury will decide the case and award damages out of relation to actual fault and actual damage.").

136. Caudle v. Dist. of Columbia, 707 F.3d 354, 358–61 (D.C. Cir. 2013) (emphasis in original).

137. *Id.* at 360.

138. *Id.* at 361–63. On remand, the jury again returned verdicts in favor of Plaintiffs. *See* Caudle v. Dist. of Columbia, C.A. No. 08-205 (BJR) (ECF No. 426) (D.D.C. Dec. 19, 2013) (Rothstein, J.).

139. Ronzetti & Humphreys, *supra* note 105, at 37.

be free to exercise their rights without fear. Yours is an important job and we trust that you will *[do what] is right and ensure that justice is done.*[140]

On appeal, the D.C. Circuit noted that, while this "send a message" statement might not be grounds for reversal on its own:

> [G]iven the fact that [Plaintiffs'] counsel made this argument after the district court had sustained *three* objections to golden rule arguments—her send a message argument was also inappropriate because, like the golden rule arguments, it diverted the jury's attention from its duty to decide the case based on the facts and the law instead of emotion, personal interest or bias.[141]

5. "Conscience of the Community" Statements

"Conscience of the community" statements ask the jury to act as the "conscience of the community" when reaching a verdict.[142] Such statements are not error per se: "Unless calculated to inflame, an appeal to the jury to act as the conscience of the community is not impermissible."[143] However, "conscience of the community" statements are problematic when they ask the jury to "abandon its traditional role as the fact finder in the case and, instead, use its verdict to correct some larger societal problem."[144] Such statements are most commonly made during criminal cases, although similar statements in civil cases may be objectionable. For example, in *Gilster v. Primebank*, involving Title VII claims of sexual harassment and retaliation, the plaintiff's counsel made a number of improper statements during closing argument, and ended her argument "by 'giving' to the jury 'the power and responsibility for correcting injustice.'"[145] On appeal, the Eighth Circuit stated that "[t]his was no different than a prosecutor urging the jury at the end of a criminal case 'to be the conscience of the community,' an improper argument that, in a close case, may warrant a new trial."[146] The court held that this statement, in combination with the "timing and emotional nature of counsel's improper and repeated personal vouching for her client [and] using direct references to facts not in evidence," warranted a new trial.[147]

6. Appeals to Sympathy

Appeals to sympathy are also not necessarily improper, if firmly grounded in the facts of the case.[148] On the other hand, appeals to sympathy based on matters not in evidence

---

140. Caudle, 707 F.3d at 358 (emphasis in original).

141. *Id.* at 361.

142. Ronzetti & Humphreys, *supra* note 105, at 38.

143. U.S. v. Lewis, 547 F.2d 1030, 1037 (8th Cir. 1976).

144. Larsen, *supra* note 80, at § 14:47.

145. Gilster v. Primebank, 747 F.3d 1007, 1011 (8th Cir. 2014).

146. *Id.*

147. *Id.* at 1013.

148. *See* Amendola et al., *supra* note 97, at § 321.

and that cannot, in any legitimate way, be brought to the attention of the jury are highly improper."[149] For example, contrasting a defendant's wealth with a plaintiff's poverty is an impermissible appeal to sympathy, as it would have no bearing on the facts or legal claims at issue.[150] In *Gilster*, discussed *supra*, the Eighth Circuit found that, in addition to making improper "conscience of the community" statements, the plaintiff's counsel also made improper appeals to sympathy by discussing her personal experiences with sexual harassment:

> Mindy Gilster had the strength to make that complaint back on July 2, 2009. I sure didn't. Back in 2006 I was sexually harassed by a professor at Drake, but I was on my way out. I was a third-year law student, and I had been a student bar association president for the last year, and I was well respected and liked by my peers. I had a great relationship with the dean of the law school because of my role as president . . . And I refused to stand up for myself. It takes great strength and fearlessness to make a complaint against your supervisor.[151]

In granting a new trial, the Eighth Circuit stated:

> Counsel made a deliberate strategic choice to make emotionally-charged comments at the end of rebuttal closing argument, when they would have the greatest emotional impact on the jury, and when opposing counsel would have no opportunity to respond. Referring to an experience in her own life was "plainly calculated to arouse [the jury's] sympathy."[152]

Therefore, while appeals to sympathy can be useful rhetorical tools for an advocate, counsel should exercise caution when injecting pathos into a closing argument.

7. Appeals to Bias

Arguments made during closing that are "designed to tap into jurors' biases or prejudices" are improper.[153] Such arguments present concerns similar to those posed by improper appeals to sympathy: "Fairness to the parties and our system of justice dictates that 'there must be limits to pleas of pure passion and there must be restraints against blatant appeals to bias and prejudice.'"[154] Common examples of appeals to

---

149. *Id.*

150. *See* Koufakis v. Carvel, 425 F.2d 892, 902 (2d Cir. 1970) ("Remarks such as these, which can be taken as suggesting that the defendant should respond in damages because he is rich and the plaintiff is poor, are grounds for a new trial.").

151. Gilster, 747 F.3d at 1010.

152. *Id.* at 1011.

153. Larsen, *supra* note 80, at. § 14:38.

154. Whittenburg, 561 F.3d at 1128 (citations omitted).

jurors' biases include appeals to regional bias,[155] racial bias,[156] and religious beliefs.[157] In *Pappas v. Middle Earth Condominium Ass'n*, a "slip and fall" case brought by New Jersey natives who were injured during a ski trip in Vermont, the plaintiffs appealed a judgment in favor of the defendants, arguing that defense counsel improperly appealed to the jurors' regional biases.[158] During closing, defense counsel stated the following:

> But isn't what they're really asking is that they can come up from New Jersey—[objection overruled]—if they can come up here from New Jersey to Vermont to enjoy what we experience every year, for those of us who are here originally for most of our lives, for most of us who come here for our own reasons, for the rest of the time that we're here, and without a care in the world for their own safety when they encounter what we, ourselves do not take for granted, and they can injure themselves, and they can sit back and say, "Well, yes. I'm on long-term disability, and I sit around and I watch golf on TV, but I'd like you to retire me. Retire me now. Pay me now what I would get or what I claim I would get until I work for age 65," . . .
>
> Would we go to New Jersey and walk on a tugboat without looking where we were going?[159]

On appeal, the Second Circuit ruled that these statements constituted improper appeals to the jury's regional bias:

> What counsel appears to be suggesting in this argument is that plaintiff and his party were in Vermont to enjoy the snow that people in Vermont are forced to "experience" every year. Counsel continues in like vein later, when he asks would "we"—apparently including himself and the Vermont-resident members of the jury as one group—"go to New Jersey and walk on a tugboat without looking where we were going?" In that way defense counsel made a blatant "us-against-them" appeal to the jury . . .[160]

Accordingly, the Second Circuit ordered a new trial, holding that:

> There is no doubt whatever that appeals to the regional bias of a jury are completely out of place in a federal courtroom. Appeals tending to create feelings of hostility against out-of-state parties are so plainly repugnant that the Supreme

---

155. *See* Whitehead v. Food Max of Mississippi, 163 F.3d 265, 276–78 (4th Cir. 1998); Pappas v. Middle Earth Condo. Ass'n, 963 F.2d 534, 541 (2d Cir. 1992).

156. *See* Bird v. Glacier Elec. Coop., Inc., 255 F.3d 1136, 1150–51 (9th Cir. 2001).

157. *See* Cunningham v. Zant, 928 F.2d 1006, 1020 (11th Cir. 1991).

158. *See* Pappas, 963 F.2d at 535–36.

159. *Id.* at 536–37.

160. *Id.* at 539.

Court long ago stated their condemnation "require[d] no comment." This sort of argument improperly distracts the jury from its sworn duty to hand down a just verdict based on the evidence presented to it.[161]

8. Counsel's Personal Opinion

It is also improper for attorneys to state their personal opinions or beliefs during closing argument, as "[c]ourts have long recognized that statements of counsel's opinions or personal beliefs have no place in a closing argument of a criminal or civil trial."[162] The rationale underlying this rule is to "prevent putting relative credibility of counsel at issue or allowing counsel to imply that he possesses knowledge not shared with the jury."[163] In *Polansky v. CNA Insurance Co.*, the plaintiff brought suit for breach of contract against his insurance company for its failure to reimburse him for damage caused by an apartment building fire.[164] On appeal, the First Circuit vacated and remanded a verdict for the plaintiff, holding that it was error for the district court to fail to cure objections to statements made during closing argument by the plaintiff's counsel, including, "[w]ell, it wasn't convincing to me. I hope it wasn't convincing to you," referring to the credibility of the defendant's testimony regarding a key piece of evidence, and, "I say to you there is absolutely no way, in my opinion, that they would have agreed," referring to the possibility that the plaintiff could have used insurance money to repair the apartment building.[165] To avoid this outcome, it is recommended that counsel carefully scrutinize their language, and avoid using personal references such as "I think" or "I believe."[166]

9. Vouching for Witnesses

Counsel should also take care to avoid vouching for witnesses, as "[i]t is unprofessional conduct, meriting discipline by the court, for counsel either to vouch for his own witnesses or to categorize opposing witnesses as 'liars;' that issue is for the jury."[167] Generally, "comments that a witness was honest, truthful, or worthy of belief" invite objections on grounds of improper vouching,[168] because, "[b]y presenting purported first-hand knowledge of a witness's character, a lawyer would effectively become a witness who has never been subjected to cross examination," which is improper.[169]

---

161. *Id.* (citations omitted).

162. Polansky v. CNA Ins. Co., 852 F.2d 626, 628 (1st Cir. 1988) (citations omitted).

163. *Id.*

164. *Id.* at 627.

165. *Id.* at 627–28.

166. Ronzetti & Humphreys, *supra* note 105, at 37.

167. Olenin v. Curtin & Johnson, Inc., 424 F.2d 769, 769 (D.C. Cir. 1968); *see also Morris v. Pruitt*, 308 F. Supp. 3d 153, 166–67 (D.D.C. 2018) (finding plaintiff's counsel's statement that a witness "seemed to me to be very believable" to constitute error because "'it is for the jury, and not the lawyers, to say which witnesses are telling the truth.'") (citations omitted).

168. William B. Johnson, *Proprietary and Prejudicial Effect of Comments by Counsel Vouching for Credibility of Witnesses – Federal Cases §2[a]*, 78 A.L.R. 23 (1986).

169. Ronzetti & Humphreys, *supra* note 105, at 37.

However, there is a difference between asking the jury to find a witness credible based on record evidence, which is proper, and personally opining on the witness's character, which is improper.[170] When discussing a witness's credibility, therefore, counsel should refer only to evidence on the record.

Additionally, it is improper for counsel to "express his belief regarding *opposing counsel's* opinion of honesty."[171] In *Spicer v. Rossetti*, a civil rights action based on an injury suffered by an inmate, the Seventh Circuit found that "defense counsel's closing argument went beyond the range of acceptable advocacy" by "improperly comment[ing] . . . that plaintiff's counsel did not believe his client."[172] Specifically, defense counsel stated:

> His own lawyer tells you we will never know. What does that tell you about the case. It tells you his own lawyer doesn't believe his client . . .
>
> Ladies and gentlemen, he just stood up here and said we will never know how Mr. Spicer got injured. He's had conversations with his client and he's not even sure. He's not even convinced.[173]

These comments were held to be reversible error.[174]

10. Attacking Opposing Counsel

Likewise, it is improper for counsel to make personal attacks on opposing counsel, or to accuse opposing counsel of committing fraud on the court.[175] In general, "[c]ourts find it objectionable for counsel to refer to the personal peculiarities and idiosyncrasies of opposing counsel during closing argument."[176]

As the Fifth Circuit explained in *Bufford v. Rowan Cos., Inc.*,:

> What is not permitted is an unsupported, irresponsible attack on the integrity of opposing counsel. When such unprofessional conduct rears its unethical head in a courtroom, it is the duty of the trial court to suppress same, quickly and unqualifiedly, and to instruct the offending counsel to cease and desist. The court must take great care not to exacerbate the situation or to give the impression to the jury that it approves or condones any unjustified impugning of the ethical standards or integrity of an officer of the court practicing before it.[177]

---

170. *Id.* at 36–37.

171. Spicer v. Rossetti, 150 F.3d 642, 644 (7th Cir. 1998) (emphasis added).

172. *Id.* at 643.

173. *Id.* at 644.

174. *Id.*

175. *See* United States v. Young, 470 U.S. 1, 9 (1985) ("Defense counsel, like his adversary, must not be permitted to make unfounded and inflammatory attacks on the opposing advocate.").

176. Craig Lee Montz, *Trial Objections from Beginning to End: The Handbook for Civil and Criminal Trials*, 29:2 Pepperdine L. Rev. 243, 304–05 (2002) (citations omitted).

177. Bufford v. Rowan Cos., Inc., 994 F.2d 155, 157–58 (5th Cir. 1993).

Throughout the trial proceedings in *Bufford*, a personal injury case, defense counsel had remarked that plaintiff's counsel was bringing a baseless case, as a "copycat" to *Pearson v. Rowman Cos., Inc.*,[178] which the plaintiff's counsel previously litigated:

> Defendants' theory was that the Bufford case was a "copycat" lawsuit. Specifically, defendants contended that the Buffords got the idea of staging an accident, or exaggerating a minor mishap, from a former co-worker, Ray Pearson. Pearson previously had settled a suit against Rowan for on-the-job injuries. One of the ways in which Bufford purportedly "copied" Pearson was by using the same lawyers. Defendants repeatedly referred to this fact.[179]

In reversing a verdict in favor of the defendants, the Fifth Circuit held that "[r]elying on the identity of counsel as the basis for contending that the Buffords' claim was fraudulent . . . went beyond the pale of appropriate trial advocacy," and that such an "unwarranted inference may not be drawn."[180]

11. Mentioning Statutory Caps to Damages

Mentioning statutory caps to damages is also improper during closing argument, as it could encourage the jury to award up to the statutory limit, or, conversely, to award higher amounts on other claims not subject to statutory caps.[181] In *Sasaki v. Class*, involving sexual harassment claims under the Civil Rights Act of 1991 and common law claims of assault and battery, the jury returned a verdict in favor of the plaintiff, awarding $50,000 for pain and suffering caused by the sexual harassment and $150,000 for pain and suffering caused by the assaults and batteries.[182] Prior to this decision, during closing, the plaintiff's counsel explicitly mentioned the $50,000 statutory cap imposed by the Civil Rights Act of 1991 based upon the employer's size, and defense counsel timely objected.[183] On appeal, the Fourth Circuit explained that:

> The § 1981a caps were enacted in apparent response to a concern about runaway verdicts, in which juries purportedly awarded plaintiffs excessive damages. As previously noted, the statute prohibits the court from informing the jury of the caps to ensure that the jury does not feel pressure to structure or adjust verdicts "upward or downward" to account for the caps. Restrictions on informing the jury of caps are enacted because "[l]egislators likely fear that juries would award the maximum or would otherwise adjust their awards if told of the statutory limit."[184]

---

178. 674 F. Supp. 558 (E.D. La. 1987).

179. Bufford, 994 F.2d at 157–58.

180. *Id.* at 158.

181. *See* Sasaki v. Class, 92 F.3d 232, 236–38 (4th Cir. 1996).

182. *Id.* at 237.

183. *Id.* at 235–36.

184. *Id.* at 236–38 (citations omitted).

Accordingly, in remanding the case for a new trial on the issue of damages, the Fourth Circuit held:

> The jury . . . appears to have faithfully followed Sasaki's counsel's directions with regard to the award. In awarding a significantly larger amount of damages for the "lesser included" state conduct and injury, the jury almost undoubtedly adjusted its award to account for the federal cap. Although the basis for the jury's decision can, of course, never be known to a certainty, when a jury's damages award itself indicates so strongly that the error substantially influenced the jury's verdict, the error cannot be dismissed as harmless.[185]

To avoid similar outcomes, the better strategy for a plaintiff's counsel is to ask the jury to award the plaintiff an amount that will fully compensate her for her losses and correct the injustice she suffered, without actually providing a dollar amount or range of amounts for compensatory and punitive damages.

12. Mentioning Prior Litigation Involving Either Party or Opposing Counsel

Counsel should also refrain from mentioning prior litigation involving either party or opposing counsel. For example, in *Hemmings v. Tidyman's, Inc.*, a Title VII sex discrimination case, the plaintiffs' counsel made the following comments during closing:

> [Tidyman's has] not corrected any of these [discriminatory] policies and they knew that they should because this is not the first time they have been sued. *I have sued them before in 1994,* so they had subjective policies which had disparate impact on all women, including plaintiffs, and that proves our case because they did not have a business necessity for doing it, and there were ways to fix it.[186]

Although defense counsel failed to timely object to this comment, the defendant cited it, among other grounds, in its motion for a new trial, which was denied by the district court.[187] On appeal, the Ninth Circuit "readily conclude[d]" that this statement constituted plain error because counsel "inappropriately referred to other cases that she herself had litigated," which "had no relevance to the lawsuit."[188] However, the Court declined to order a new trial based on the strength of the plaintiffs' case, and "[t]he fact that [defense] counsel did not object before the jury," which "strongly suggests that counsel made a strategic decision to gamble on the verdict and suspected that the comments would not sway the jury."[189]

---

185. *Id.* at 237.

186. Hemmings v. Tidyman's, Inc., 285 F.3d 1174, 1192 (9th Cir. 2002) (emphasis in original).

187. *Id.* at 1192–93.

188. *Id.* at 1193.

189. *Id.* at 1193–95.

13. Attacking Other Court Rulings

It is also improper to attack other court rulings during closing argument. The rationale here is clear:

> It should be obvious that it is improper to attack any court ruling before the jury, including the court's rulings on evidence. Beyond reversible error, this is simply a strategic gaffe that pits the lawyer against the credibility of the court.[190]

14. Asking for "Comparative Verdicts"

Counsel is further prohibited from mentioning a jury's reward in a different case as a means of encouraging the jury to make a similar award.[191] Such comments are considered irrelevant to the case at bar, and can merit a new trial.[192]

15. Mentioning Judicial Remittitur

It is also improper to mention the possibility of judicial remittitur during closing argument "to persuade a jury to increase an award based on the possibility that the court may reduce it later," as this improperly shifts responsibility for the final verdict from the jury to the judge.[193] Importantly, in many employment cases brought under federal anti-discrimination statutes, the judge is ultimately responsible for awarding front pay damages where front pay is considered an equitable remedy in lieu of reinstatement.[194] However, the court may still call upon the jury to issue an advisory verdict with recommendations on equitable issues that the court may draw upon in making its ultimate decision.[195] In such cases, responsibility for instructing the jury as to their authority should fall with the judge, not with counsel, but counsel should request instructions that will adequately explain the difference between front pay, which the judge will be responsible for awarding, and compensatory damages that the jury will award.[196]

IV. CONCLUSION

Counsel should not underestimate the importance of a carefully crafted closing argument, and of clear and balanced jury instructions. Closing argument is the last opportunity for an advocate to persuade the jurors to side with her client prior to their

---

190. Ronzetti & Humphreys, *supra* note 105, at 36.

191. *Id.* at 38.

192. *Id.* at 38 (citing Wright & Ford Millworks, Inc. v. Long, 412 So. 2d 892 (Fla. 5th DCA 1982)).

193. *Id.* at 38 (citing City Provisioners, Inc. v. Anderson, 578 So. 2d 855 (Fla. 5th DCA 1990)).

194. *See* Excel Corp. v. Bosley, 165 F.3d 635, 639 (8th Cir. 1999) ("The issue of front pay [under Title VII] is not an issue for the jury to decide, rather it is a form of equitable relief which must be determined by the district court after considering all aspects of the case. Front pay may be granted in lieu of reinstatement in situations where reinstatement would be impracticable or impossible.") (citations omitted).

195. Mota v. Univ. of Tex. Houston Health Science Ctr., 261 F.3d 512, 526–27 (5th Cir. 2001).

196. *See* Russell Penzer & Maryam Franzella, *Importance of Effective Jury Instructions on Front Pay*, N.Y. Law J. (Jan. 3, 2013), http://www.larypc.com/wp-content/uploads/2014/05/jury_instructions.pdf.

deliberations, and jury instructions will guide the jurors during those deliberations. By using the guidance in this chapter, and by recognizing opportunities to object during these phases of trial, a plaintiff's advocate can make strategic decisions on how best to present her client's case to the jury.

CHAPTER 24

Closing Argument and Jury Instructions: Defense Perspective

Roxella T. Cavazos

I. THE ROLE OF THE CLOSING ARGUMENT

The closing argument at the trial of a case is many things, but ultimately for the defense attorney, it is about victory and vindication for the employer. The closing argument is the lawyer's only opportunity to tell the story of the case in its entirety, without interruption and free from the procedural rules that govern the propriety of the opening statement. The closing argument is the final opportunity to communicate with and persuade the jury. It is an act of pure oral advocacy that relies on the lawyer's ability to tell a story and organize and interpret the evidence in the light most favorable to the client.

The closing argument is the lawyer's critical opportunity to strengthen and explain the significance of the mental images created during the course of the trial. In the end, all three aspects of the trial—opening statement, witness examination, and closing argument—should merge to elicit a single conception of the events.[1] No checklist or article can guarantee success in the closing argument. A lawyer's task is to determine what will work best in a given situation, including locale, and plan the closing argument.

II. BEST PRACTICES FOR PRESENTING AN EFFECTIVE CLOSING ARGUMENT[2]

A. Plan the Closing Argument Throughout the Representation

During the discovery and investigation of the case, counsel should consider the theme of the case and points to argue at the closing. The thoughts should be committed to writing. The lawyer should place notes in a trial notebook and revise the developing closing

---

1. STEVEN LUBET, MODERN TRIAL ADVOCACY: ANALYSIS AND PRACTICE 385 (NITA 1993).
2. *See* Edwin C. Lazier, *The Elements of Good and Bad Closing Arguments*, PRAC. LITIGATOR, July 1996, at 55.

argument as the case progresses through discovery and trial. Prior to trial, counsel should determine how much time the particular court allows for closing arguments.

B. Offer a Theory of the Case

A closing argument by the defense must present the lawyer's theory of the case. The theory tells the jurors why the client is entitled to a verdict. To be successful, the theory of the case at the closing argument must be logical, believable, and legally sufficient. To be logical, the theory must focus on the facts that lead to the desired conclusion. To be believable, it must be based on facts that are likely to be accepted. To be legally sufficient, it must apply the proven facts to the legal issues.

C. Convey a Theme of the Case

A well-tried case has a clearly discernible theme that wraps up the pictures and mental images developed during voir dire, opening statement, and presentation of evidence. The theme is the best way to tell the story of the case, even when the lawyer is not a regular storyteller. A good trial theme invokes shared beliefs and common precepts. Just as a theory of the case explains why a verdict is legally necessary for the employer client, the theme explains why the verdict is morally or otherwise desirable for the employer client. The theme of the case presents the reason to enter a defense verdict.

D. Acknowledge Weaknesses

Respect the jurors' intelligence and confront the weaknesses of the case by explaining them in the most favorable light. Explain what is necessary, but refrain from being overly defensive. If there is no explanation, acknowledge the weaknesses of the case and minimize them as much as possible. The cardinal rule is to not ignore the weaknesses, for opposing counsel will surely point them out. Weaknesses pointed out by an opponent look much worse than those that are acknowledged by the defense lawyer.

E. Concentrate on the Strengths

Although it is necessary to acknowledge the weaknesses of the case, to win the case, the lawyer should also argue the strengths of the case. The lawyer should deal with the weaknesses as quickly as possible, and then focus on the strong points of the case.

F. Organize the Closing Argument Logically

A closing argument presents the theme, theory, evidence, and analysis of the case in a flowing manner that entices the jury to draw the inferences in favor of the client. The best way to convey organization to the jury is to practice the closing argument well before delivery. Again, the closing argument must be logical, believable, and legally sufficient.

G. Keep the Closing Argument Concise

By the time of the closing arguments, the jury is usually more than ready for the trial to end so that they can be discharged. The more concise and powerful the closing, the greater the effect it is likely to have. The stronger the closing argument is the more likely a lawyer can endear the client to the jurors. Conciseness is achieved through organization of the theme, theory of the case, and inferences for the jury to draw upon. Neutralize sympathy for the plaintiff.

H. Present an Argument, Not a Summation

The opening statement involves summarizing what the evidence will show. The closing argument involves the tenacious presentation of the analysis, which is needed by the jurors to decide the case for the client. An effective argument involves selecting the facts to be emphasized, urging conclusions based on the evidence, drawing inferences from the facts, explaining weaknesses, and capitalizing on strengths of the case. In other words, keep the closing argument short and simple, focusing only on what is essential to the defendant's claims and defenses.

I. Refer Back to Opening

The opening statement emphasizes the key points that a lawyer will prove through evidence at trial. A good closing argument refers back to those points as a reminder to the jurors that the lawyer delivered exactly what was promised. An effective closing argument also reminds the jurors that the opponent has failed to deliver the proof that was promised at the opening.

J. Use Good Common Sense

Jurors have common sense. A closing argument that appeals to the common sense of the jurors is likely to persuade. Jurors are likely to believe the story that most comports with their experiences. If the closing argument offends the jurors' collective sense of how things work in the real world, the verdict is affected. Common sense is achieved by presenting the theory of the case simply and logically to capture the jurors' selective attention and selective retention.

K. Ask and Answer Rhetorical Questions

A closing argument anticipates and answers questions that are likely to be raised during jury deliberations. The lawyer should pose difficult or unanswerable questions in the closing argument that challenge opposing counsel to answer at closing. If this is done effectively, the opponent will either reveal the weaknesses in his or her case or fail to respond to the challenge. Either result is favorable. Before issuing a rhetorical challenge to the opponent, however, counsel should make sure the question will not backfire with a powerful response. Rhetorical questions can be rehearsed on friends, family members, or other lawyers to ensure they are effective and safe.

L. Use Analogies

A good closing argument uses analogies to convey the theory of the case and direct the jury to draw inferences and conclusions. An analogy can explain human conduct by referencing human behavior. Analogies should be practiced on family, friends, or other lawyers. Insincere or trite analogies will damage credibility with the jury.

M. Use Selective Visual Aids

A picture is truly worth a thousand words. By the time of the closing argument, the evidence has been admitted and can be used for persuasion. During the argument, the lawyer should show the jury photographs, documents, charts, blow-ups, and graphics prepared to illustrate important points and significant trial testimony. When selecting visual aids, the lawyer should try to keep the presentation simple. Most jurors are not inclined to process more than a handful of visual aids in a twenty- or thirty-minute argument. Thus, the focus should be narrow, and only critical exhibits should be used.

N. Refer to Jury Instructions and Verdict Forms

If allowed in the jurisdiction, a lawyer should weave jury instructions into the argument to help jurors connect the facts with the law. If the rules allow, counsel should show the jurors the verdict form and explain what responses the facts require. Verdict forms are often confusing, even to lawyers. A jury left with no guidance may have trouble completing the form, which can result in a mistrial, or even worse, a verdict that was not intended.

O. Stay Within the Boundaries of Proper Argument

The lawyer should know the boundaries of proper argument within the jurisdiction. Making an improper argument hurts credibility and disrupts the ability to persuade. At best, it results only in the embarrassment of a sustained objection followed by curative instructions. At worst, it can result in a mistrial, sanctions, reduction of attorney's fees, or appellate error.[3] In most jurisdictions, a lawyer will stay within the boundaries of a proper argument if he or she follows these rules:

- Do not misstate the evidence or the law.
- Do not argue facts not in evidence.

---

3. *See* Greenbaum v. Svenska Handelsbanken, 998 F. Supp. 301, 305 (S.D.N.Y. 1998) (attorney's fees to the plaintiff were reduced because plaintiff's closing argument was rife with impermissible references and necessitated constant interruptions with appropriate objections, followed by a large number of correction instructions).

- Do not state a personal belief in the justness of the client's case.
- Do not state a personal opinion on witness credibility.
- Do not appeal to the jury's passion or prejudice.
- Do not suggest that the jury should ignore the facts or misapply the law.
- Do not ask the jury to step into the shoes of the client or opponent or argue the Golden Rule.

P. Start Strong and Finish Strong

Most communications specialists say that people tend to remember the first and last pieces of information they hear. The argument should be structured to start and end on the best points, while sandwiching weaker points in the middle. For example, in defending a tort claim where liability and credibility are disputed, consider starting on credibility, then arguing damages, and finishing on liability.

Q. Use an Authentic Style of Delivery

Every lawyer has his or her own style. It is important to be genuine and stick to a style that works naturally. Otherwise, jurors will see right through the lawyer and credibility will be damaged.

R. Do Not Rely on Notes

Relying on notes destroys tempo and keeps a lawyer from making eye contact with the jurors. Before trial, the lawyer should break the habit of using notes as a backup. The more a lawyer practices, the easier it gets. If notes must be used, they should be restricted to a one-page outline of the closing argument or a few index cards with major points to be made.

III. CHARACTERISTICS OF AN INEFFECTIVE CLOSING ARGUMENT

Generally, a closing argument will be ineffective if it exhibits one or more of the following characteristics:

- It is read from a script.
- It goes on too long, covering trivial points in excruciating detail.
- It is delivered in a stream-of-consciousness style.
- It insults the jury's intelligence.
- It is overbearing and tries to bully the jury into a conclusion.
- It starts with an apology.
- It states at the beginning, "What I'm about to say is not evidence."
- It patronizes the jury.

- It attacks witnesses the jury liked and with whom they identified.
- It attempts to mislead the jury.

IV. PRACTICE TIPS FOR EFFECTIVE CLOSING ARGUMENTS

- Know the facts thoroughly before trial and review them throughout. Knowledge of the facts is necessary to develop and argue the theme and theory of the case.
- Maintain eye contact with the jurors. Do not deliver a written speech. Outline the closing argument on a single sheet of paper. Avoid the podium if permitted by the court, as it can be a communications barrier. Be mobile and approach the jurors while respecting their space.
- Do not refer to the jurors as "jury." Call them "ladies and gentlemen." Be respectful. Treat them like individuals, not an entity.
- Do not talk in legalese. "Proximate cause" sounds like "approximate cause."
- Do not insult the intelligence of the jurors.
- Refer to the client only once as the "defendant." Thereafter, use the company name or the individual witnesses' names.
- Show the client as a person and help the jurors become familiar with the individual or corporate person(s) represented. Stress the benevolent conduct of the supervisor and company.
- Just tell a story.
- Create mental images. Relate to the jurors by using analogies and metaphors from news events, sports, pop culture, history, or other areas that the jurors have in common. Exercise good judgment to make sure that analogies and metaphors do not offend the jurors. Tell them an interesting story, remembering to stick to the theme of the case.
- Use a "hook" in the theme. Begin with the hook in the opening statement and repeat it in the closing argument. A hook is a slogan, word, or phrase meant to grab one's attention and stick in one's mind. A hook evokes a mental image that is easy to remember and arouses the juror's interest to focus them on the major theme of the case. Cite evidence that relates to the hook.[4]
- Accept that a case has one or more weaknesses in facts, law, or witnesses. Confront the weaknesses in the closing argument.
- Anticipate the opponent's closing argument and discredit his or her theme. Force the opponent to respond, thereby diverting the opponent from the closing argument that he or she planned to present to the jury.
- Argue facts, not the law. Do not refer to facts that are not in the record. The closing is confined to issues and evidence presented, as well as such inferences, deductions, and analogies reasonably and properly drawn from the record.

---

4. Robert B. Fitzpatrick, *Closing Argument in Employment Cases*, in LITIGATING THE EMPLOYMENT TORT CASE 137 (ABA Tort Trial and Ins. Prac. Sec. 1995).

- Repeat key facts, buzzwords, and phrases that are critical to the story. Redundancy helps the jurors to remember.
- Be a storyteller. The human voice is a theatrical tool. Use voice modulation, word pacing, silence, and pitch.
- Exude total confidence in the case. Never let the jurors sense fear or nervousness.
- Smile sincerely and at appropriate times. There is a difference between being intense and being tense.
- When setting up a trial notebook, include a section on "closing." Throughout discovery, jot down ideas, analogies, and metaphors. Outline the closing and revise it as necessary throughout the litigation.
- If the case's value merits it and the client can afford it, hire a focus group to "test market" the themes of the case and beliefs held on the facts of the case.[5] Practice delivering the argument before audiences of nonlawyers (that is, significant others, staff) to make sure the theme and theory of the case are understood and accepted.
- Thank the jury for their service, but be careful not to patronize them, which can communicate that the client does not have a defense.
- Remind the jurors that promises made in the opening were kept. Point out where opposing counsel failed to keep promises during the opening.
- Have one or two key documents enlarged and show them to the jury. To avoid a squabble in front of the jury, have the enlarged exhibits approved in advance by the court.
- Use demonstrative evidence to argue damages. Show flip charts or summaries of testimony. Repeat in simple terms how the damage computations are inaccurate or inappropriate.
- Discuss why punitive damages are not appropriate.
- Draw the juror's attention only to the critical exhibits.
- Relate the argument with the court's jury instructions. Consider using an enlarged exhibit to emphasize one or more critical jury instructions.
- If the opponent objects during closing, regardless of the ruling, thank the court and proceed with the argument. Remember that usually the jurors will be offended by the interruption of the argument. A lawyer interrupted during the argument might resume, "As I was saying before opposing counsel interrupted me . . . "
- Do not cross the line and invoke the Golden Rule. That is, do not ask the jury to put themselves in the client's shoes.
- Remind the jurors of their oath and the promises they made at voir dire.
- Remind the jurors of the highlights of the trial. Sometimes, a significant moment during the trial encapsulates the theme. Remind them of that moment.

---

5. *See* Chapter 13.

- If a juror seems likely to be selected as the foreperson, talk directly to that juror. If one or more jurors appear to have reservations about some portion of the case, talk directly to them.
- Treat opposing counsel with respect. Even if opposing counsel is loathsome, do not show it in front of the jury.
- Deal with the reality that a key witness may not be a likable or credible person.
- Emphasize "fairness," "the American way," and "due process," if applicable. Do not underestimate the power of patriotism.
- Avoid boring the jurors by talking too long. Do not bore the judge, whom the jurors are constantly watching. Keep in mind that one's attention span is twenty to thirty minutes.
- Read the closing argument of some of America's great trial lawyers.

V. SPECIAL CONSIDERATIONS IN HARASSMENT CASES

Defense lawyers should be politically correct and never disrespect the protected status of the plaintiff or the jurors. The caps on damages should never be mentioned in argument, or a mistrial may result. The defendant's closing argument should first overcome the sympathy and emotional appeal of the plaintiff's closing argument. This can be done by changing the jurors' moods promptly and redirecting their attention positively to the defendant's case. For example, defense counsel could say, "Now you have just heard a very emotional, impassioned presentation by Ms. Smith. Of course, that is her side of the story and what she would like you to believe. But let's look at what the facts really are." It is the defense counsel's duty to convince the jury that no matter how sympathetic the plaintiff's case may seem, sympathy is not legally sufficient to support a verdict.

In closing, the defense lawyer should point out the essential elements of each claim on which the plaintiff has the burden of proof. The jury instructions on the burden of proof may be quoted. As to matters as to which the employer has the burden of proof, the defense lawyer should point out that the employer has produced credible evidence of specific facts proving these matters. Some perspective on plaintiff's damage claims should be presented to argue what is reasonable and what is excessive. As to punitive damages, defense counsel should argue that there is no wrongful state of mind on the part of the employer, no clear and convincing evidence of malice, fraud, or oppression, no need to punish the defendant because the conduct is not likely to recur, and no reason for the plaintiff to obtain a windfall.[6]

Often, the trial of a discrimination/harassment case is a swearing match between the parties. A lawyer should refrain from calling the plaintiff a liar. A lawyer, instead, should argue the facts that will lead the jury to conclude that the defendant is more believable. Generally, jurors are more comfortable concluding that the plaintiff was

---

6. *See* GERALD E. ROSEN, BARBARA A. ROTHSTEIN & MARVIN E. ASPEN, FEDERAL EMPLOYMENT LITIGATION, Section R (Rutter Group, 2006).

mistaken about the conduct, misinterpreted what happened, or does not remember the events well enough, as opposed to concluding that the plaintiff is lying. The defense should develop a theme that persuades the jurors to rule on the defendant's behalf because the law, as applied to the facts, warrants a defense verdict.

In the battle for credibility, it is critical to remind the jurors of what constitutes harassment under the protected status in question in the particular circuit. The defense lawyer should argue the lack of pervasiveness, severity, or interference with job performance and the failure to follow procedures. A lawyer may argue that while the plaintiff may be sincere in his/her belief that harassment occurred, he/she did not make the appropriate attempt to eliminate the harassment or bring such harassment to the attention of the appropriate company official. Because facts persuade the jury, the most persuasive and significant facts should be specifically referenced throughout the closing argument, with explicit references to the issues to which they apply. The persuasive testimony of a particular witness, even a plaintiff's witness, and the significance of a particular exhibit should be cited. The focus should be on trying the defendant's case and not simply opposing arguments made by the plaintiff. In following the caveat to "be yourself" at the closing argument, counsel should avoid unnecessary drama or emotion because it may have the unintended effect of overstating the value of a claim. Any display of emotion or intensity should be reserved for a fact, issue, or policy argument that strongly favors the defendant. Defense counsel should argue that deciding the fact, issue, or policy against the defendant would create an unjust result. Argument concerning the plaintiff's sexual behavior, dress, or predisposition outside the workplace should be avoided if a motion for admissibility of such evidence under Rule 412 of the Federal Rules of Evidence has not been made or if the court has denied such a motion.

VI. JURY INSTRUCTIONS

The lawyer should submit jury instructions based on the applicable circuit's (jurisdiction's) pattern jury instructions and any US Supreme Court and applicable circuit case law that may contain particular definitions of major elements and defenses of applicable to the case. The instructions that the court will submit to the jury should relate to the evidence. The jury instructions conference usually occurs at the close of all the evidence. When presenting the closing argument, a lawyer should already know which instructions the court will give. The substantive jury instructions and questions, however, should be developed and revised though discovery and trial. Instructions commonly used in harassment and retaliation cases concern the following:

- Credibility of witnesses
- Burden of proof
- Preponderance of evidence
- Elements of the causes of action
- Elements of damages, including the duty to mitigate, and items of mitigation that should be deducted from an award

- Elements of any affirmative defenses
- Definitions of important legal terms
- Duty of the jury to find out the facts and follow the law
- Opinion evidence as to expert and other witnesses
- Impeachment
- Deposition testimony

In a retaliation case, it is important that the jury be instructed, as the Supreme Court has explained, that plaintiff must prove that the alleged retaliation was "the but for cause" for the challenged employment action and not "a but for cause."[7] Instructions in a sexual harassment case are more onerous because they need to address the elements of a hostile work environment, there needs to be some basis for imputing liability to the employer, and the availability of the *Faragher/Ellerth* affirmative defense is evidence dependent.[8] The defense requires an employer to prove first, that among other things, it exercised reasonable care to promptly correct any sexually harassing behavior, and second that the plaintiff unreasonably failed to take advantage of any preventive or corrective opportunities that the employer provided.[9]

At the jury instructions conference, the lawyer should argue the key instructions that favor the defendant and object on the record to unfavorable instructions, whether or not they depart from the circuit's applicable instructions. Also, the lawyer must pay strict attention to the judge's reading of the instructions agreed upon at the charge conference. Either way, a failure to object to any instructions waives the objection on appeal.[10] The lawyer should review the rules in the jurisdiction regarding the reading of the instructions, especially whether they must be read verbatim or can be paraphrased. Again, valuable sources for jury instructions are the pattern jury instructions in the jurisdiction and reported cases that concern jury instructions on harassment (hostile work environment) and retaliation. Do not hesitate to work in the jury instructions with the closing argument.[11]

---

7. Univ. Of Tex. Sw. Med. Ctr. v. Nassar, 570 U.S. 338, 352, 133 S.Ct. 2517 (2013); McDonald v.City of Wichita, Kansas, 735 F.Appx. 529, 531–31, 2018 WL 2459911 (10th Cir. 2018).

8. Holmesley v. Freightliner Corp., 61 F.Appx. 105, 112–13 (4th Cir. 2003).

9. Faragher v. City of Boca Raton, 524 U.S. 775, 807, 118 S.Ct. 2275 (1998).

10. FED. R. CIV. P. 51. *See* EEOC v. EMC Corp. of Mass., 205 F.3d 1339, 2000 WL191819 *9–10 (6th Cir. 2000) (employer failed to object to reading of an instruction, and although instructions were reviewed for plain error, denial of motion for new trial was affirmed).

11. *See* Appendix 24A for model jury instructions in a sexual harassment case, developed by the ABA Section of Litigation. *See* Appendix 24B for instructions on harassment from the *Manual of Model Circuit Jury Instructions for the Ninth Circuit*. The instructions in both may be adapted for harassment based on any of the protected criteria. The model jury instructions for the applicable federal circuit of the case should be consulted as well as local rules. Other instructions may be developed from case law.

Model Jury Instructions

The following instructions are excerpts from *Model Jury Instructions, Employment Litigation, Second Edition,* published by the Employment and Labor Relations Law Committee, Section of Litigation, American Bar Association in 2005. For consistency, the numbering of the instructions as follows is the same as assigned in the book.

1.04[2] SEXUAL HARASSMENT—HARASSMENT BY A SUPERVISOR WITH TANGIBLE EMPLOYMENT ACTION

The plaintiff has alleged that he/she has been the subject of sexual harassment by his/her supervisor. An employer may be held liable for sexual harassment committed by its supervisor if the sexual harassment results in a tangible employment action.

In deciding if the plaintiff has met his/her burden of proving his/her claim of sexual harassment, you must first decide whether the plaintiff has proven, by a preponderance of the evidence, that he/she has suffered a tangible employment action. A tangible employment action is a significant change in employment status, such as hiring, firing, failing to promote, reassignment with significantly different responsibilities or a decision causing a significant change in compensation or benefits. A tangible employment action also includes situations where a supervisor conditions tangible job benefits, such as promotion, pay increase and job retention, on the submission to unwelcome sexual conduct. Although not required in all circumstances, a tangible employment action in most cases inflicts direct economic harm.

If you find that the plaintiff was subjected to a tangible employment action, you should determine whether the plaintiff has proven, by a preponderance of the evidence, that:

1. the supervisor subjected him/her to the tangible employment action because of the plaintiff's refusal to submit to unwelcome sexual conduct; or,
2. the supervisor conditioned tangible job benefits on the plaintiff's submission to unwelcome sexual conduct.

In making this determination, you must determine whether the sexual conduct was unwelcome. In determining whether [the plaintiff] was subjected to hostile or abusive harassing conduct, you should consider the totality of the circumstances. Sexual conduct may include groping, fondling, unwelcome sexual advances, requests for sexual favors, verbal abuse of a sexual nature, sexually suggestive, degrading or vulgar remarks or gestures, demeaning or degrading remarks based upon the employee's gender or the display of sexual pictures, objects or other materials in the workplace. Conduct is considered unwelcome if it was not solicited or invited by the plaintiff and the plaintiff regarded it as undesirable or offensive. If the plaintiff invites, solicits or participates in the hostile or abusive conduct, you may determine that the conduct is not unwelcome.

If you determine that the plaintiff has proven each of these elements by a preponderance of the evidence, then you must find for the plaintiff on his/her sexual harassment claim. If you find that the plaintiff has failed to prove any of these elements by a preponderance of the evidence, then you must find for the defendant.

AUTHORITIES

Meritor Savings Bank v. Vinson, 477 U.S. 57, 106 S. Ct. 2399, 91 L. Ed. 2d 49 (1986); Eighth Circuit Pattern Jury Instruction 5.41 (2001).

COMMENT

The language regarding tangible employment action is taken primarily from the Supreme Court's decision in Burlington Industries, Inc. v. Ellerth, 524 U.S. 742, 118 S. Ct. 2257, 141 L. Ed. 2d 633 (1998) and, to a lesser extent, Faragher v. City of Boca Raton, 524 U.S. 775, 118 S. Ct. 2275, 141 L. Ed. 2d 662 (1998); *see also* Jin v. Metropolitan Life Insurance Co., 310 F.3d 84 (2d Cir. 2002). In addition, the Supreme Court recently held that a constructive discharge could constitute a tangible employment action where an employee resigns due to intolerable discriminatory or harassing working conditions under circumstances where a reasonable person in the employee's position would feel compelled to resign and where an "official act" by the employer underlies the constructive discharge. Pennsylvania State Police v. Suders, 542 U.S. 129, 124 S. Ct. 2342 (2004). The Suders Court further discussed examples of "official acts" in this context, mentioning such actions as a demotion, unfavorable transfer, reduction in compensation, a dangerous job assignment or a failure to promote. *Id.*

1.04[3] SEXUAL HARASSMENT—HOSTILE WORK ENVIRONMENT/HARASSMENT WITHOUT TANGIBLE EMPLOYMENT ACTION

[The plaintiff] has alleged that he/she has been subjected to sexual harassment. In particular, [the plaintiff] has alleged that he/she has been subjected to a hostile and abusive working environment.

To prevail on his/her claim of sexual harassment, [the plaintiff] must prove, by a preponderance of the evidence, each of the following elements:

1. that he/she was subjected to hostile or abusive conduct which was sufficiently severe or pervasive so as to alter the terms and conditions of [plaintiff's] employment;
2. that the hostile or abusive conduct was unwelcome;
3. that the hostile or abusive conduct was based upon [the plaintiff's] sex; and,
4. that [the plaintiff] suffered damages as a result of the harassing conduct.

In determining whether [the plaintiff] was subjected to hostile or abusive harassing conduct, you should consider the totality of the circumstances. Such conduct may include groping, fondling, unwelcome sexual advances, requests for sexual favors, verbal abuse of a sexual nature, sexually suggestive, degrading or vulgar remarks or gestures, demeaning or degrading remarks based upon the employee's gender or the display of sexual pictures, objects or other materials in the workplace.

In determining whether the conduct was sufficiently severe or pervasive so as to alter the terms and conditions of [the plaintiff's] employment, you should be aware that the sexual harassment law is not a general civility code. As such, simple isolated teasing, isolated offhand comments, ordinary horseplay, infrequent sexual flirtation, sporadic or occasional use of abusive language, and isolated incidents, unless extremely serious, are not considered sufficiently severe or pervasive so as to alter an employee's terms or conditions of employment. Although no single factor is decisive, in deciding this element you should consider the following factors in addition to any other relevant factors:

1. the frequency of the conduct;
2. the severity of the conduct;
3. whether the conduct was physically threatening or humiliating, or a mere offensive utterance; and,
4. whether the conduct interfered with the employee's work performance.

In addition, you must determine not only that the environment is one that the plaintiff himself/herself subjectively perceives to be hostile and abusive, but also that it is one that a reasonable person would likewise find hostile or abusive. This must be evaluated from the perspective of a reasonable person, not from the perspective of an overly sensitive person.

As previously noted, in deciding this claim you must determine whether the hostile or abusive conduct was unwelcome. Conduct is considered unwelcome if it was not solicited or invited by [the plaintiff] and [the plaintiff] regarded it as undesirable or offensive. If the plaintiff invites, solicits or participates in the hostile or abusive conduct, you may determine that the conduct is not unwelcome.

In addition, to recover for sexual harassment, [the plaintiff] must prove that he/she suffered damages that were proximately caused by the hostile or abusive working environment. For damages to be the proximate result of the harassment, it must be shown that, except for such harassment, the damages would not have occurred.

[For cases involving alleged harassment by a supervisor, insert the language in Instruction 1.04[3](a) regarding the defendant's Faragher Affirmative Defense, if raised].

[For cases involving alleged harassment by a non-supervisory co-worker, insert the language in Instruction 1.04[3](b) regarding the "employer liability" element of plaintiff's case].

If you determine that [the plaintiff] has proven each of the elements of unlawful sexual harassment by a preponderance of the evidence [and the defendant has not proven its affirmative defense (if appropriate)], then you must find for [the plaintiff] on his/her sexual harassment claim. If you find that [the plaintiff] has failed to prove any of the elements of unlawful sexual harassment by a preponderance of the evidence [or that the defendant has proven its affirmative defense (if appropriate)], then you must find for [the defendant].

AUTHORITIES

Faragher v. City of Boca Raton, 524 U.S. 775, 118 S. Ct. 2275, 141 L. Ed. 2d 662 (1998); Harris v. Forklift Systems, Inc., 510 U.S. 17, 114 S. Ct. 367, 126 L. Ed. 2d 295 (1993); Homesley v. Freightliner Corp., 2003 WL 1908744 (4th Cir. Apr. 22, 2003); Mendoza v. Borden, 195 F.3d 1238 (11th Cir. 1999) (en banc); Eleventh Circuit Model Jury Instructions 1.2.2 (2000); Ninth Circuit Model Jury Instruction 13.1 (2001); Eighth Circuit Pattern Jury Instruction 5.42 (2001).

COMMENT

This instruction is also applicable to racial, age, religious and disability harassment claims. *See* Instruction 1.04[4].

1.04[3](A) SEXUAL HARASSMENT—HARASSMENT WITHOUT TANGIBLE EMPLOYMENT ACTION—AFFIRMATIVE DEFENSE FOR HARASSMENT BY A SUPERVISOR

If you determine that [plaintiff] has proven, by a preponderance of the evidence, that his/her supervisor subjected him/her to sexual harassment that created a hostile working environment, you should then consider [defendant's] defense that it acted reasonably under the circumstances and that the plaintiff failed to take reasonable steps to notify his superior so that the harassment could be stopped.

In particular, to prevail on its affirmative defense, [the defendant] must prove, by a preponderance of the evidence, that:

1. it exercised reasonable care to prevent and promptly correct any sexually harassing behavior; and,

2. the plaintiff unreasonably failed to take advantage of any preventive or corrective opportunities provided by the employer or to avoid harm otherwise [or if [the plaintiff] did take advantage of preventive or corrective opportunities, the defendant responded by taking reasonable and prompt corrective action].

Although not absolutely required, proof that [the defendant] had implemented and distributed an anti-harassment policy including a complaint procedure will typically suffice to establish that [the defendant] exercised reasonable care to prevent any sexually harassing behavior. Additionally, you should consider the timeliness of [the defendant's] corrective action and whether [the defendant's] corrective actions were reasonably intended to end the harassment. Similarly, proof that [the plaintiff] failed to follow the complaint procedure provided by the defendant] will typically suffice to establish that [the plaintiff] unreasonably failed to take advantage of preventive or corrective opportunities.

If you determine that [the defendant] has proven each of these elements by a preponderance of the evidence, then you must find for [the defendant] on its affirmative defense. If you find that [the defendant] has failed to prove both of these elements by a preponderance of the evidence, then you must find for [the plaintiff] on this issue.

AUTHORITIES

Faragher v. City of Boca Raton, 524 U.S. 775, 118 S. Ct. 2275, 141 L. Ed. 2d 662 (1998); *see also* Eleventh Circuit Pattern Jury Instructions 1.2.2 (2000).

COMMENT

This instruction is only available where the plaintiff has established that he/she was subjected to sexual harassment by a supervisor that did not culminate in a tangible employment action. One issue left open by the Faragher Court is whether the affirmative defense is available where the employer has instituted a policy and complaint procedure and, after receiving a complaint from the plaintiff, the employer takes prompt corrective action. Assuming that the affirmative defense is still available, this Instruction should be modified by using the bracketed language.

In addition, as discussed in the comment to instruction 1.04[2], a constructive discharge which is not predicated upon an "official act" of the employer would not constitute tangible employment action and therefore the Faragher affirmative defense is available. Pennsylvania State Police v. Suders, 542 U.S. 129, 124 S. Ct. 2342 (2004).

1.04[3](B) SEXUAL HARASSMENT—HARASSMENT WITHOUT TANGIBLE EMPLOYMENT ACTION—HARASSMENT BY CO-WORKER—EMPLOYER LIABILITY ELEMENT

In addition to proving each of the elements of sexual harassment previously discussed, to prevail on his/her claim of sexual harassment, [the plaintiff] must also prove, by a preponderance of the evidence, that the employer should be held liable for sexual harassment committed by a co-worker who is not a supervisor. Under the law, an employer may only be held liable for sexual harassment committed by a co-worker if a supervisor knew or should have known about the harassment and failed to take prompt and appropriate action to stop it.

To establish that the employer should have known about the harassment, [the plaintiff] must prove that the hostile or abusive environment was so pervasive and so open and obvious that any reasonable person in the supervisor's position would have known that the harassment was occurring. In making this determination, you should also consider whether [the defendant] has instituted an anti-harassment policy with an effective complaint procedure and whether [the plaintiff] availed himself/herself of the procedure.

AUTHORITIES

Ocheltree v. Scollon Productions, Inc., 335 F.3d 325 (4th Cir. 2003); Crowley v. L.L. Bean, Inc., 303 F.3d 387 (1st Cir. 2002); Parkins v. Civil Constructors of Illinois, Inc., 163 F.3d 1027 (7th Cir. 1998); Eleventh Circuit Model Jury Instructions 1.2.2 (2000); Eighth Circuit Model Jury Instructions 5.43 (2001).

COMMENT

This instruction should only be used when the alleged harassment was committed by a co-worker. It may be used as a separate instruction as presented here or modified and added to Instruction 1.04[2].

1.04[4] HARASSMENT BASED UPON RACE/AGE/DISABILITY/ RELIGION WITHOUT TANGIBLE EMPLOYMENT ACTION

The plaintiff has alleged that he/she has been subjected to unlawful harassment because of his/her race/age/disability/religion. In particular, the plaintiff has alleged that he/she has been subjected to a hostile and abusive working environment because of his/her race/age/disability/religion.

To prevail on his/her claim of unlawful harassment, the plaintiff must prove, by a preponderance of the evidence, each of the following elements:

1. that he/she was subjected to hostile or abusive conduct which was sufficiently severe or pervasive so as to alter the terms and conditions of plaintiff's employment;
2. that the hostile or abusive conduct was unwelcome;
3. that the hostile or abusive conduct was based upon the plaintiff's race/age/ disability/religion; and,
4. that the plaintiff suffered damages as a result of the harassing conduct.

In determining whether the plaintiff was subjected to hostile or abusive harassing conduct, you should consider the totality of the circumstances. Such conduct may include repeated demeaning or degrading remarks or epithets based upon the employee's race/age/disability/religion, the display of derogatory pictures, objects or other materials based upon the employee's race/age/disability/religion, or subjecting the employee to more harsh treatment than other employees based upon the employee's race/age/disability/religion.

In determining whether the conduct was sufficiently severe or pervasive so as to alter the terms and conditions of the plaintiff's employment, you should be aware that the law is not a general civility code. As such, simple teasing, offhand comments, ordinary horseplay, sporadic or occasional use of inappropriate language, and isolated incidents, unless extremely serious, are not considered sufficiently severe or pervasive so as to alter an employee's terms or conditions of employment. Although no single factor is decisive, in deciding this element you should consider the following factors in addition to any other relevant factors:

1. the frequency of the conduct;
2. the severity of the conduct;
3. whether the conduct was physically threatening or humiliating, or a mere offensive utterance; and,
4. whether the conduct interfered with the employee's work performance.

In addition, you must determine not only that the environment is one that the plaintiff himself/herself subjectively perceives to be hostile and abusive, but also that it is one that a reasonable person would likewise find hostile or abusive. In other words, this must be evaluated from the perspective of a reasonable person, and not from the perspective of an overly sensitive person.

As previously noted, in deciding this claim you must determine whether the hostile or abusive conduct was unwelcome. Conduct is considered unwelcome if it was not solicited or invited by the plaintiff and the plaintiff regarded it as undesirable or offensive. If the plaintiff invites, solicits or participates in the hostile or abusive conduct, you may determine that the conduct is not unwelcome.

To recover for unlawful harassment, the plaintiff must also prove that he/she suffered damages that were proximately caused by the hostile or abusive working environment. For damages to be the proximate result of the harassment, it must be shown that, except for such harassment, the damages would not have occurred.

[For cases involving alleged harassment by a supervisor, insert the language in Instruction 1.04[3](a) regarding the defendant's Faragher Affirmative Defense, if raised (modified to reflect the type of harassment at issue)].

[For cases involving alleged harassment by a non-supervisory co-worker, insert the language in Instruction 1.04[3](b) regarding the "employer liability" element of plaintiff's case (modified to reflect the type of harassment at issue)].

If you determine that [the plaintiff] has proven each of the elements of unlawful harassment by a preponderance of the evidence [and the defendant has not proven its affirmative defense (if appropriate)], then you must find for [the plaintiff] on his/her harassment claim. If you find that [the plaintiff] has failed to prove any of the elements of unlawful harassment by a preponderance of the evidence [or that the defendant has proven its affirmative defense (if appropriate)], then you must find for [the defendant].

AUTHORITIES

Faragher v. City of Boca Raton, 524 U.S. 775, 118 S. Ct. 2275, 141 L. Ed. 2d 662 (1998); Harris v. Forklift Systems, Inc., 510 U.S. 17, 114 S. Ct. 367, 126 L. Ed. 2d 295 (1993); Parks v. City of Chattanooga, 74 Fed. App. 432, 2003 WL 21674749 (6th Cir. July 16, 2003); EEOC v. Pipefitters Ass'n Local 597, 334 F.3d 656 (7th Cir. 2003).

COMMENT

In addition to this instruction, either Instruction 1.04[2](a) or 1.04[2](b) should also be used depending upon whether the case involves a supervisor or a co-worker.

The following instructions on damages reference discrimination but may be adapted for harassment or retaliation.

1.07[1] DAMAGES—COMPENSATORY DAMAGES

[The plaintiff] has alleged that, as a result of [the defendant's] discrimination, he/she has suffered [emotional pain/suffering/inconvenience/mental anguish/loss of enjoyment of life]. These damages are referred to as compensatory damages. [The plaintiff] has the burden of proving, by a preponderance of the evidence, that he/she has suffered damages as a proximate result of [the defendant's] discrimination, and the amount of the damages, if any. If [the plaintiff] does not establish that he/she has experienced [emotional pain/suffering/inconvenience/mental anguish/loss of enjoyment of life] because of [the defendant's] conduct, then he/she cannot recover compensatory damages. However, [plaintiff] is not required to prove his/her emotional distress through expert medical testimony as long as he/she presents evidence that proves that he/she actually suffered emotional distress as a result of [defendant's] unlawful conduct.

If you determine that [the plaintiff] has proven by a preponderance of the evidence that he/she has experienced [emotional pain/suffering/inconvenience/mental anguish/ loss of enjoyment of life], you may award him/her damages for those injuries. No evidence of the monetary value of such intangible things as pain and suffering has been, or needs to be, introduced into evidence. No exact standard exists for fixing the compensation to be awarded for these elements of damages. The damages that you award must be fair compensation—no more and no less. When considering the amount of monetary damages to which [the plaintiff] may be entitled, you should consider the nature, character, and seriousness of any [pain/suffering/ inconvenience/mental anguish/loss of enjoyment of life] [plaintiff] felt. You must also consider its extent or duration, as any award you make must cover the damages endured by [the plaintiff] since the wrongdoing, to the present time, and even into the future if you find that the proof presented justifies the conclusion that [the plaintiff's] emotional stress and its consequences have continued to the present time or can reasonably be expected to continue in the future.

AUTHORITIES

42 U.S.C. § 1981(b)(3); "EEOC Policy Guidelines on Damages Provisions of the 1991 Civil Rights Act," 8 FEP Manual 405:7091; Bolden v. Southeastern Pa. Transp. Auth., 21 F.3d 29 (3d Cir. 1994); Memphis Community School Dist., v. Stachura, 477 U.S. 299, 308–309 (1986); Carey v. Piphus, 435 U.S. 247 (1978); Adams v. Doehler-Harvis (On Remand), 144 Mich. App. 764 (1985); Freeman v. Kelvinator, Inc., 569 F. Supp. 999 (E.D. Mich. 1979); Slayton v. Michigan Host, Inc., 122 Mich. App. 411, 332 N.W.2d 498 (1983); Riethmiller v. Blue Cross and Blue Shield of Michigan, 151 Mich. App. 188, 390 N.W.2d 227 (1986).

COMMENT

In Section 1983 cases, several circuits have held that legal fees incurred in prior but related legal proceedings may be compensable as part of plaintiff's claim of compensatory damages. *See* Hale v. Fish, 899 F.2d 390, 403–404 (5th Cir. 1990) (legal fees expended to defend criminal charges are compensable damages); Borunda v. Richmond, 885 F.2d 1384, 189–1390 (9th Cir. 1988) (legal fees may be compensable damages); Kerr v. City of Chicago, 424 F.2d 1134, 1141 (7th Cir. 1970), cert. den., 400 U.S. 833 (1970) (legal fees may be compensable damages).

1.07[2] DAMAGES—BACK PAY

If you determine that [the defendant] discriminated against [the plaintiff,] then you must determine the amount of damages that [the defendant] has caused [the plaintiff].

You may award as actual damages an amount that reasonably compensates [the plaintiff] for any lost wages and benefits, taking into consideration any increases in salary and benefits, including pension, that [the plaintiff] would have received had he/she not been discriminated [harassed] against. Basically, you have the ability to make [the plaintiff] whole for any wages or other benefits that he/she has lost as a result of his/her [discharge/demotion/failure to be hired/failure to be promoted].

AUTHORITIES

42 U.S.C. 2000e-5g (Title VII of the 1964 Civil Rights Act); 29 U.S.C. 626(b) (ADEA); 29 U.S.C. 216(b) (Fair Labor Standards Act); Pollard v. E.I. du Pont de Nemours & Co., 532 U.S. 843, 847–848, 121 S. Ct. 1946, 150 L. Ed. 2d 62 (2001); Lorillard v. Pons, 434 U.S. 575, 98 S. Ct. 866, 55 L. Ed. 2d 40 (1978); Albemarle Paper Co. v. Moody, 422 U.S.

405, 421–422, 45 L. Ed. 2d 280, 95 S. Ct. 2362 (1975) ("It follows that, given a finding of unlawful discrimination, back pay should be denied only for reasons which, if applied generally, would not frustrate the central statutory purposes of eradicating discrimination throughout the economy and making persons whole for injuries suffered through past discrimination."); Morrison v. Circuit City Stores, 317 F.3d 646, 671–673 (6th Cir. 2003), Faris v. Lynchburg Foundry, 769 F.2d 958 (4th Cir. 1985); Blim v. Western Electric Co., 731 F.2d 1473 (10th Cir. 1984). The United States Supreme Court has recently held that a discrimination victim who proves that he/she suffered a constructive discharge may be entitled to all equitable and legal remedies authorized by Title VII. *See* Pennsylvania State Police v. Suders, 542 U.S. 129, 124 S. Ct. 2342, 2354, 159 L. Ed. 2d 204, 220 (2004).

Additionally, lost employee benefits or consequential damages have been considered part of back pay or front pay: *see, e.g.,* Metz v. Merrill Lynch, 39 F.3d 1482 (10th Cir. 1994); Greene v. Safeway Stores, 210 F.3d 1237 (10th Cir. 2000) (stock option losses are compensable under ADEA); Gaworski v. ITT Commercial Fin. Corp., 17 F.3d 1104, 1111 (8th Cir. 1994) (award of consequential damages reimbursing plaintiff for sales commissions and closing costs on sale of house, moving expenses and motel expenses was upheld). *See* Hartley v. Dillard's, Inc., 310 F.3d 1054, 1062 (8th Cir 2002); Munoz v. Oceanside Resorts, Inc., 223 F.3d 1340, 1348 (11th Cir. 2000). *See* Kelly v. Matlack, Inc., 903 F.2d 978, 984–85 (3d Cir. 1990) for the principle that back pay can include vacation pay, sick pay, insurance and retirement benefits.

1.07[3] DAMAGES—FRONT PAY

You shall also calculate separately, as future damages, a monetary amount equal to the present value of the wages and benefits that the plaintiff would have earned had he/she not been discriminated against for that period from the date of your verdict until the date when the plaintiff would have voluntarily resigned or obtained other employment.

COMMENT

See 42 U.S.C. 2000e-5g (Title VII of the 1964 Civil Rights Act); 29 U.S.C. 626(b) (ADEA); 29 U.S.C. 216(b) (Fair Labor Standards Act). This instruction may not be appropriate in jurisdictions where front pay is considered an issue for the Court to decide. *See* e.g., Newhouse v. McCormick & Co., 110 F.3d 635, 642–43 (8th Cir. 1997) (listing positions of the circuits); Salitros v. Chrysler Corp., 306 F.3d 562 (8th Cir. 2002); Thomas v. Texas Dept. of Criminal Justice, 297 F.3d 361 (5th Cir. 2002). However, the instruction may be appropriate in jurisdictions where the issue is, at least partially, a jury question or where the Court submits the issue to the jury for an advisory opinion. *See* Arban v. West Pub. Corp., 345 F.3d 390 (6th Cir. 2003) (amount of front pay is a jury issue but entitlement is an issue for the court).

The United States Supreme Court has recently held that discrimination victims that prove an illegal constructive discharge may be entitled to front pay among other remedies authorized by Title VII. *See* Pennsylvania State Police v. Suders, 542 U.S. 129, 124 S. Ct. 2342, 2354, 159 L. Ed. 2d 204, 220 (2004).

The Seventh Circuit treats front pay differently from future lost earnings by differentiating the equitable nature of front pay, which therefore may not be decided by a jury, from the common law tort remedy of the plaintiff's diminished reputation resulting from the employer's actions, which is decided by a jury. *See* Williams v. Pharmacia Corp., 137 F.3d 944, 953 (7th Cir. 1998) ("Lost future earning capacity is a non-pecuniary injury for which plaintiffs may be compensated under Title VII.")

1.07[4] DAMAGES—AFTER-ACQUIRED EVIDENCE

In this case, [the defendant] asserts that had it known of certain information regarding [the plaintiff], it would [not have hired/have earlier discharged] [the plaintiff].

To establish that it would [not have hired/have earlier discharged] [the plaintiff], [the defendant] must prove, by a preponderance of the evidence, that it became aware of information subsequent to [the plaintiff's] discharge that, if known by [the defendant] [prior to plaintiff's hiring/during the plaintiff's employment], would have caused the defendant [not to hire/to immediately discharge] [the plaintiff].

If you determine that [the defendant] has proven the preponderance of the evidence that the after-acquired evidence would have caused [the defendant] [not to hire/to immediately discharge] [the plaintiff], you should not award any damages for lost pay [the plaintiff] would have earned after the date [the defendant] became aware of the information. In other words, even if [the plaintiff] proves that he/she is entitled to damages in this case, any award for lost pay would be cut off as of the date [the defendant] became aware of information that would have led to [the plaintiff] [not being hired/or being discharged].

AUTHORITIES

McKennon v. Nashville Banner Publishing Co., 513 U.S. 352, 357, 115 S. Ct. 879, 130 L. Ed. 2d 852 (1995); Crapp v. City of Miami Beach, 242 F.3d 1017 (11th Cir. 2001); Wallace v. Dunn Construction Co., 62 F.3d 374 (11th Cir. 1995) (en banc); Delli-Santi v. CNA Insurance Companies, 88 F.3d 192 (3rd Cir. 1996); Mardell v. Harleysville Life Insurance Company, 65 F.3d 1072, 1073–1074 (3rd. Cir. 1995).

1.07[5] DAMAGES—MITIGATION

In determining the amount of damages, if any, [that plaintiff] is entitled to recover, the law provides that [the plaintiff] must make every reasonable effort to minimize or reduce his/her damages for loss of compensation by seeking employment. This is called mitigation of damages. However, it is [the defendant's] burden to prove by a preponderance of the evidence that [the plaintiff] failed to mitigate his/her damages.

If you determine that [the plaintiff] is entitled to damages, you must reduce these damages by the amount that [the plaintiff] actually earned following his/her discharge or the amount you determine that [the plaintiff] could have earned through a reasonable effort during the period from his/her discharge until the date of trial.

If you determine that [the plaintiff] failed to seek out or take advantage of a business or employment opportunity that was reasonably available to him/her, then you should reduce the amount of damages by the amount he/she could have earned if he/she would have sought out or taken advantage of the opportunity. In determining whether [the plaintiff's] failure to seek out or take advantage of a business or employment opportunity was reasonable, you should be aware that the [plaintiff] is only required to accept employment that is "of a like nature." In determining whether employment is "of a like nature," you may consider:

1. the type of work,
2. the hours worked,
3. the compensation,
4. the job security,
5. the working conditions, and
6. other conditions of employment.

AUTHORITIES

Eighth Circuit Pattern Jury Instructions 5.02; Coleman v. City of Omaha, 714 F.2d 804, 808 (8th Cir. 1985); *see also* NLRB v. Mining Specialists, 326 F.3d 602, 605 (4th Cir. 2003) ("So long as the employee does make reasonable efforts to obtain suitable interim employment, the success of those efforts is irrelevant to the employer's back pay obligation.").

1.07[7] DAMAGES—PUNITIVE DAMAGES

If you find in favor of [the plaintiff] on his/her claim [and against [the defendant] on its affirmative defenses], you should consider whether [the plaintiff] is entitled to punitive damages in addition to any award of actual damages.

To establish entitlement to punitive damages, [the plaintiff] must prove, by a preponderance of the evidence, that:

1. the employer acted with malice or reckless indifference to [the plaintiff's] rights; and,
2. the employer should be held liable for its employee's unlawful conduct.

Malice or reckless indifference may be found where the employer is motivated by an evil motive or intent or acts with reckless or callous indifference to the rights of [the plaintiff] to be free of [discrimination or harassment]. In making this determination, you should be aware that a finding by you that the employer is liable for unlawful discrimination [or harassment] does not automatically mean that the employer is liable for punitive damages. For example, if the employer believes in good faith that its actions were not discriminatory, it could not be said that the employer was acting with malice or reckless indifference to [the plaintiff's] rights and, as such, punitive damages should not be awarded.

In determining whether the employer should be held liable for the actions or decisions of its employee in this case, the law provides that punitive damages may only be assessed against the employer when the unlawful conduct was committed by an important or high-ranking managerial employee and the employer failed to make good faith efforts to comply with the law.

You should be aware that an employee employed in a managerial capacity does not include every supervisory employee. Rather, to be employed in a managerial capacity, the employee must be an "important" member of the defendant's management. You should evaluate factors such as the type of authority and discretion given by [the defendant] to the employee in making this determination. The mere fact that an employee is given a title such as "manager" or "director" does not automatically mean that the employee is employed in a managerial capacity. Rather, an employee who acts in a managerial capacity for purposes of punitive damages is one who has the power to make independent decisions regarding personnel matters, who has the authority to determine company policy or who has the authority to approve personnel actions.

In determining whether [the defendant] has engaged in good faith efforts to comply with the law, you should consider any relevant factor demonstrating [the defendant's] efforts, or lack thereof, to comply with the law against discrimination [or harassment], including such factors as whether [the defendant] has instituted an anti-discrimination [or anti-harassment] policy, and whether [the defendant] has trained its managerial personnel with respect to equal employment opportunity laws.

If you find that [the plaintiff] has proven each of these elements, then you are permitted, but not required, to assess punitive damages against [the defendant]. Punitive damages are awarded in exceptional cases as a punishment to the defendant and a warning to others not to engage in similar unlawful conduct.

The amount of punitive damages, if appropriate, is within your discretion. Punitive damages must bear a reasonable relationship to [the plaintiff's] actual injury. However, no single numerical equation exists to easily relate punitive to compensatory damages. In determining a reasonable relationship to the actual injury, you must consider all relevant factors. These include:

1. the impact or severity of [the defendant's] conduct,
2. the amount of time [the defendant] conducted itself in this manner,
3. the amount of compensatory damages,
4. the potential profits [the defendant] may have made from this conduct,
5. the attitudes and actions of [the defendant's] top management after the misconduct was discovered,
6. the effect of the damages award on [the defendant's] financial condition, and
7. any punishment [the defendant] may receive from other sources.

AUTHORITIES

42 U.S.C. § 1981a; Kolstad v. American Dental Ass'n, 527 U.S. 526, 119 S. Ct. 2118, 144 L. Ed. 2d 494 (1999); Zimmerman v. Associates First Capital Corp., 251 F.3d 376 (2d Cir. 2001); Eighth Circuit Model Jury Instruction 5.04.

COMMENT

Punitive damages are available in intentional discrimination claims brought pursuant to Title VII and the ADA. However, they are not available in ADEA actions (where liquidated damages are available instead).

The law concerning punitive damages has evolved dramatically over the last decade. The United States Supreme Court has held that to collect punitive damages the plaintiff must prove that the unlawful conduct was committed by a high-ranking managerial employee who possesses the power to make independent decisions regarding personnel matters, the authority to determine company policy, or the authority to approve personnel actions, and that the employer failed to make good faith efforts to comply with the law. *See* Kolstad v. American Dental Association, 527 U.S. 526, 119 S. Ct. 2118, 144 L. Ed. 2d 494 (1999).

In addition, the United States Supreme Court decision in State Farm Mutual Automobile Insurance Company v. Campbell, 538 U.S. 408, 123 S. Ct. 1513 (2003), held that (1) a tortfeasor cannot be held accountable in punitive damages for conduct that occurs outside the jurisdiction unless there is an evidentiary nexus to the harm suffered by the plaintiff; (2) the constitutional evaluation of the amount of the award is to be measured by the ratio between the compensatory damage award and the punitive damage award with the ratio being no higher than single digits as the compensatory damage award becomes more and more substantial; and, (3) the financial condition of the tortfeasor is not a relevant factor in a post-verdict constitutional challenge.

In light of the State Farm decision, the editors are in agreement that the jury should be given the financial data of the employer and then appropriately charged where the defendant(s) consisted of small and/or mid-sized employers. The jury's knowledge and consideration of financial status of these defendants should act as a brake on a runaway punitive damage verdict and enable these defendants to litigate the issue post-verdict by giving them the opportunity to bond the appeal. However, the editors disagree about whether the financial condition of a large employer, such as a Fortune 500 company, should be considered by the jury; defendants' counsel among the editors believe that there is a danger of a runaway punitive damage verdict against this type of defendant if such evidence is admitted. While the State Farm case holds that the financial condition of the defendant is not relevant when evaluating the constitutionality of a punitive damages verdict, the decision is left unanswered whether the jury should be apprised of the financial condition and then be instructed to consider the information. Obviously, this is an issue that needs to be clarified further by the courts and ultimately the Supreme Court.

Ninth Circuit Model Civil Jury Instructions

10.2 CIVIL RIGHTS—TITLE VII—HOSTILE WORK ENVIRONMENT—HARASSMENT COMMENT

The Supreme Court addressed the law of harassment claims under Title VII in two companion cases, *Burlington Indus. Inc. v. Ellerth*, 524 U.S. 742 (1998), and *Faragher v. City of Boca Raton*, 524 U.S. 775 (1998) [collectively, *Ellerth/Faragher*]. Although those cases relate to sexual harassment, the committee does not discern any conceptual difference between harassment because of sex and harassment because of race or any other protected status. Accordingly, the following instructions are applicable to harassment based upon race, color, sex, religion and national origin.

Ellerth/Faragher clarified the standards governing an employer's liability for harassment. Essentially, when an employee suffers a tangible employment action resulting from a direct supervisor's harassment, the employer's liability is established by proof of the harassment and a resulting tangible employment action. *See Faragher*, 524 U.S. at 807–08. No affirmative defense is available to the employer in those cases. In cases where no tangible employment action has been taken, the employer may interpose an affirmative defense to defeat liability by proving (a) that the employer exercised reasonable care to prevent and correct promptly any discriminatory conduct, and (b) the plaintiff unreasonably failed to take advantage of any preventive or corrective opportunities provided by the employer or to otherwise avoid harm. *Id.*; *Ellerth*, 524 U.S. at 764–65; *see also Holly D. v. Cal. Inst. of Tech.*, 339 F.3d 1158, 1166–67 (9th Cir. 2003); *Swinton v. Potomac Corporation*, 270 F.3d 794, 803 (9th Cir. 2001). *See* Instruction 10.2B (Civil Rights—Title VII—Hostile Work Environment Caused by Supervisor—Claim Based upon Vicarious Liability—Tangible Employment Action—Affirmative Defense). In *Pennsylvania State Police v. Suders*, 542 U.S. 129, 137–38 (2004), the Supreme Court applied the framework of *Ellerth/Faragher* to a case of constructive discharge due to a hostile work environment. In such a case, the *Ellerth/Faragher* affirmative defense is available to the employer, unless an official act, i.e., a tangible employment action, of the employer precipitated the employee's decision to resign. *Id.* at 148.

If, however, harassment is committed by a co-worker or a non-direct supervisor of the plaintiff, the employer is liable only under a negligence theory. In this situation, the employer may not invoke the *Ellerth/Faragher* affirmative defense. *See Swinton*, 270 F.3d at 803–04 (noting that the principle embodied in the affirmative defense is contained in the requirements of a prima facie case based on negligence). (*See* Instruction 10.2C (Hostile Work Environment Caused by Non-Immediate Supervisor or by Co-Worker—Claim Based on Negligence)).

An employer may be held liable for the actionable third-party harassment of its employees where it ratifies or condones the conduct by failing to investigate and remedy it after learning of it. *See Galdamez v. Potter*, 415 F.3d 1015, 1022 (9th Cir. 2005). Title VII prohibits discrimination against any individual and makes no distinction between managers and other employees; both are entitled to its protection *See id.*

In *Holly D.*, the Ninth Circuit explained how pre-*Ellerth/Faragher* cases analyzing "quid pro quo" harassment, or "sex for jobs (or job benefits)," are consistent with the *Ellerth/Faragher* analysis. *See Holly D.*, 339 F.3d at 1168–70. Inasmuch as sexual harassment claims, including those referred to as quid pro quo claims, are now analyzed under the *Ellerth/Faragher* framework, the committee has removed former Instructions 13.6 and 13.7.

10.2A CIVIL RIGHTS—TITLE VII—HOSTILE WORK ENVIRONMENT—HARASSMENT BECAUSE OF PROTECTED CHARACTERISTICS—ELEMENTS

1. the plaintiff seeks damages against the defendant for a [[racially] [sexually] [*other Title VII protected characteristic*]] hostile work environment while employed by the defendant. In order to establish a [[racially] [sexually] [*other Title VII protected characteristic*]] hostile work environment, the plaintiff must prove each of the following elements by a preponderance of the evidence:
2. the plaintiff was subjected to [[slurs, insults, jokes or other verbal comments or physical contact or intimidation of a racial nature] [sexual advances, requests for sexual conduct, or other verbal or physical conduct of a sexual nature] [*conduct affecting other Title VII protected characteristics*]];
3. the conduct was unwelcome;
4. the conduct was sufficiently severe or pervasive to alter the conditions of the plaintiff's employment and create a [[racially] [sexually] [*other Title VII protected characteristic*]] abusive or hostile work environment;
5. the plaintiff perceived the working environment to be abusive or hostile; and
6. a reasonable [woman] [man] in the plaintiff's circumstances would consider the working environment to be abusive or hostile.

Whether the environment constituted a [[racially] [sexually] [*other Title VII protected characteristic*]] hostile work environment is determined by looking at the totality of the circumstances, including the frequency of the harassing conduct, the severity of the conduct, whether the conduct was physically threatening or humiliating or a mere offensive utterance, and whether it unreasonably interfered with an employee's work performance.

COMMENT

The elements of this instruction are derived from *Fuller v. City of Oakland, California*, 47 F.3d 1522, 1527 (9th Cir. 1995). The language in the instruction regarding the factors used to determine whether a working environment was sufficiently hostile or abusive is derived from *Harris v. Forklift Sys., Inc.*, 510 U.S. 17, 23 (1993).

This instruction should be given in conjunction with other appropriate instructions, including Instructions 10.2B (Hostile Work Environment Caused by Supervisor— Claim Based Upon Vicarious Liability—Tangible Employment Action—Affirmative Defense); 10.2C (Hostile Work Environment Caused by Non-Immediate Supervisor or by Co-Worker—Claim Based on Negligence); and, if necessary, 10.4B (Tangible Employment Action Defined).

"A plaintiff must show that the work environment was both subjectively and objectively hostile." *McGinest v. GTE Service Corp.*, 360 F.3d 1103, 1113 (9th Cir. 2004); *see also Fuller*, 47 F.3d at 1527 (citing *Harris*, 510 U.S. at 21–22). For the objective element, the Ninth Circuit has adopted the "reasonable victim" standard. *Ellison v. Brady*, 924 F.2d 872, 878–80 (9th Cir. 1991). Therefore, if the plaintiff/victim is a woman, element five of the instruction should state "reasonable woman," and if the plaintiff/victim is a man, "reasonable man." *Ellison*, 924 F.2d at 879, n.11.

10.2B CIVIL RIGHTS—TITLE VII—HOSTILE WORK ENVIRONMENT CAUSED BY SUPERVISOR—CLAIM BASED UPON VICARIOUS LIABILITY—TANGIBLE EMPLOYMENT ACTION—AFFIRMATIVE DEFENSE

An employer may be liable when a supervisor with immediate or successively higher authority over the employee creates a [[racially] [sexually] [*other Title VII protected characteristic*]] hostile work environment for that employee. The plaintiff claims that [he] [she] was subjected to a [[racially] [sexually] [*other Title VII protected characteristic*]] hostile work environment by _____, and that _____ was [his] [her] [immediate supervisor] [a person with successively higher authority over plaintiff].

The defendant denies the plaintiff's claim. The plaintiff must prove [his] [her] claim by a preponderance of the evidence.

[*If Ellerth/Faragher affirmative defense applies, add the following:*]

In addition to denying the plaintiff's claim, the defendant has asserted an affirmative defense. Before you consider this affirmative defense, you must first decide whether plaintiff has proved by a preponderance of the evidence that [he] [she] suffered a tangible employment action as a result of the harassment by the supervisor. If you find that the plaintiff has proved that [he] [she] suffered a tangible employment action as a result of harassment by the supervisor, you must not consider the affirmative defense. If the plaintiff has not proved that [he] [she] suffered a tangible employment action, then you must decide whether the defendant has proved by a preponderance of the evidence each of the following elements:

1. the defendant exercised reasonable care to prevent and promptly correct the [[racially] sexually] [*other Title VII protected characteristic*]] harassing behavior, and
2. the plaintiff unreasonably failed to take advantage of any preventive or corrective opportunities provided by the employer or unreasonably failed to otherwise avoid harm.

If the defendant proves these elements, the plaintiff is not entitled to prevail on this claim.

COMMENT

See Introductory Comment to this chapter. This instruction should be given in conjunction with Instruction 10.2A (Hostile Work Environment—Harassment Because of Protected Characteristics—Elements) and, if applicable, Instruction 10.4B (Tangible Employment Action Defined).

This instruction is based upon *Burlington Indus., Inc. v. Ellerth*, 524 U.S. 742, 764–65 (1998), *Faragher v. City of Boca Raton*, 524 U.S. 775, 807–08 (1998), and *Swinton v. Potomac Corporation*, 270 F.3d 794, 802 (9th Cir. 2001), *cert. denied*, 535 U.S. 1018 (2002).

This instruction addresses harassment by a supervisor with immediate or successively higher authority over the plaintiff. Use the first two paragraphs if no *Ellerth/Faragher* affirmative defense is applicable. Use the entire instruction if an *Ellerth/Faragher* defense is to be considered by the jury.

When harassment is by the plaintiff's immediate or successively higher supervisor, an employer is vicariously liable, subject to a potential affirmative defense. *Faragher*, 524 U.S. at 780; *Nichols v. Azteca Restaurant Enterprises, Inc.*, 256 F.3d 864, 875 (9th Cir. 2001). For vicarious liability to attach it is not sufficient that the harasser be employed in a supervisory capacity; he must have been the plaintiff's immediate or successively higher supervisor. *Swinton*, 270 F.3d at 805, citing *Faragher*, 514 U.S. at 806. An employee who contends that he or she submitted to a supervisor's threat to condition continued employment upon participation in unwanted sexual activity alleges a tangible employment action, which, if proved, deprives the employer of an *Ellerth/Faragher* defense. *Holly D. v. Cal. Inst. of Tech.*, 339 F.3d 1158, 1173 (9th Cir. 2003) (affirming summary judgment for the employer due to insufficient evidence of any such condition imposed by plaintiff's supervisor). *See Pennsylvania State Police v. Suders*, 542 U.S. 129, 137–38 (2004), for discussion of tangible employment action.

The adequacy of an employer's anti-harassment policy may depend on the scope of its dissemination and the relationship between the person designated to receive employee complaints and the alleged harasser. *See, e.g., Faragher*, 524 U.S. at 808 (policy held ineffective where (1) the policy was not widely disseminated to all branches of the municipal employer and (2) the policy did not include any mechanism by which an employee could bypass the harassing supervisor when lodging a complaint).

"While proof that an employer had promulgated an antiharassment policy with complaint procedure is not necessary in every instance as a matter of law, the need for a stated policy suitable to the employment circumstances may appropriately be addressed in any case when litigating the first element of the defense." *Ellerth*, 524 U.S. at 765; *Faragher*, 524 U.S. at 807.

Although proof that the plaintiff failed to use reasonable care in avoiding harm is not limited to showing an unreasonable failure to use any complaint procedure provided by the defendant, a demonstration of such failure will normally suffice to satisfy this prong. *See Ellerth*, 524 U.S. at 765; *Faragher*, 524 U.S. at 807–08.

If the harasser is not the plaintiff's immediate or successively higher supervisor, an employer's liability can only be based on negligence. The *Ellerth/Faragher* affirmative defense is not applicable if the claim is based on negligence. *See* Instruction 10.2C (Hostile Work Environment Caused by Non-Immediate Supervisor or by Co-Worker— Claim Based on Negligence).

10.2C CIVIL RIGHTS—TITLE VII—HOSTILE WORK ENVIRONMENT CAUSED BY NON-IMMEDIATE SUPERVISOR OR BY CO-WORKER— CLAIM BASED ON NEGLIGENCE

The plaintiff seeks damages from the defendant for a hostile work environment caused by [[sexual] [racial] [*other Title VII protected characteristic*]] harassment. The plaintiff has the burden of proving both of the following elements by a preponderance of the evidence.

1. the plaintiff was subjected to a [[sexually] [racially] [*other Title VII protected characteristic*]] hostile work environment by a [non-immediate supervisor] [co-worker]; and
2. the defendant or a member of the defendant's management knew or should have known of the harassment and failed to take prompt, effective remedial action reasonably calculated to end the harassment.

A person is a member of management if the person has substantial authority and discretion to make decisions concerning the terms of the harasser's employment or the plaintiff's employment, such as authority to counsel, investigate, suspend, or fire the accused harasser, or to change the conditions of the plaintiff's employment. A person who lacks such authority is nevertheless part of management if he or she has an official or strong duty in fact to communicate to management complaints about work conditions. You should consider all the circumstances in this case in determining whether a person has such a duty.

The defendant's remedial action must be reasonable and adequate. Whether the defendant's remedial action is reasonable and adequate depends upon the remedy's effectiveness in stopping the individual harasser from continuing to engage in such conduct and in discouraging other potential harassers from engaging in similar unlawful conduct. An effective remedy should be proportionate to the seriousness of the offense.

If you find that the plaintiff has proved both of the elements on which the plaintiff has the burden of proof, your verdict should be for the plaintiff. If, on the other hand, the plaintiff has failed to prove either of these elements, your verdict should be for the defendant.

COMMENT

See Introductory Comment to this chapter. *See also Swinton v. Potomac Corporation*, 270 F.3d 794, 803–05 (9th Cir. 2001), *cert. denied*, 535 U.S. 1018 (2002). Use this instruction when the claim against the employer is based on negligence and involves harassment by another co-worker or a supervisor who is not the plaintiff's direct (immediate or successively higher) supervisor.

Use this instruction in conjunction with Instruction 10.2A (Hostile Work Environment—Harassment Because of Protected Characteristics—Elements).

Under a negligence theory, an employer is liable if the employer (or its "management") knew or should have known of the harassing conduct and failed to take reasonably prompt corrective action to end the harassment. *Swinton*, 270 F.3d at 803–04. There are two categories of employees who constitute "management" for purposes of a negligence claim. *Id.* at 804. The first category is a member of management who possesses substantial authority and discretion to make decisions over the plaintiff's or the harasser's employment, such as "authority to counsel, investigate, suspend or fire the accused harasser, or to change the conditions of the harassee's employment." *Id.* The second category of employees who qualify as management consists of any supervisor who lacks this authority but nonetheless "has an official or strong de facto duty to act as a conduit to management for complaints about work conditions." *Id.* at 805 (citations omitted).

It should be noted, however, that neither *Swinton* nor any of the cases relied upon by *Swinton* provide a definition of a supervisor or other employee with "an official or strong de facto duty to act as a conduit to management for complaints about work conditions." *See Swinton*, 270 F.3d at 804–05. To aid jury understanding, the committee has modified the *Swinton* language of "de facto duty to act as a conduit to management . . .", *id.* at 805, to "duty in fact to communicate to management."

The two elements of this instruction are based upon *Burrell v. Star Nursery, Inc.*, 170 F.3d 951, 955 (9th Cir. 1999) and *Mockler v. Multnomah County*, 140 F.3d 808, 812 (9th Cir. 1998). The text of the instruction addressing remedial action is based upon *Mockler*, 140 F.3d at 813 (citing *Ellison v. Brady*, 924 F.2d 872, 882 (9th Cir. 1991)).

The burden is on the plaintiff to "show that the employer knew or should have known of the harassment, and took no effectual action to correct the situation." *Mockler*, 140 F.3d at 812 (citations omitted). "This showing can . . . be rebutted by the employer directly, or by pointing to prompt remedial action reasonably calculated to end the harassment." *Id.* In determining whether an employer's response to the harassment is sufficient to absolve it from liability, "the fact that [the] harassment stops is only a test for measuring the efficacy of a remedy, not a way of excusing the obligation to remedy." *Fuller v. City of Oakland*, 47 F.3d 1522, 1528 (9th Cir. 1995). "Once an employer knows or should know of harassment, a remedial obligation kicks in." *Id.* Therefore, if 1) no remedy is undertaken, or 2) the remedy attempted is ineffectual, liability will attach." *Id.* at 1528–29.

For purposes of proving that the defendant "knew or reasonably should have known of the harassment," it is appropriate to impute this knowledge to a defendant employer if a management-level employee of the employer defendant knew or reasonably should have known that harassment was occurring. *Swinton*, 270 F.3d at 804.

Case Index

Conforto v. Mabus, 2014 WL 3407053 (S.D. Cal. 2014), 502n32

Congreso de Uniones Industriales v. Bacardi Corp., 961 F. Supp. 338 (D.P.R. 1997), 40n49

Conigliaro v. Horace Mann Sch., 1997 WL 189058 (S.D.N.Y. 1997), 99n20

Contra Markham v. White, 171 F.R.D. 217 (N.D. Ill. 1997), 173n92

Cook Cty. Coll. Teachers Union v. Byrd, 456 F.2d 882 (7th Cir. 1972), 164n52

Cook v. Life Credit Union, 138 F.Supp.3d 981 (M.D. Tenn. 2015), 5n26

Cooper v. Asplundh Tree Expert Co., 836 F.2d 1544 (10th Cir. 1988), 425n149, 457n58

Cooper v. Paychex, Inc., 960 F. Supp. 966 (E.D. Va. 1997), 419n106, 420n111, 463n117

Corbett v. Nat'l Prods. Co., 1995 U.S. Dist. LEXIS 6425 (E.D. Pa. 1995), 447n278

Corley v. Jackson Police Dept., 639 F.2d 1296 n.6 (5th Cir. 1981), 17n98

Corneveaux v. CUNA Mut. Ins. Group, 76 F.3d 1498 (10th Cir. 1996), 489n22

Coronet Foods v. NLRB., 158 F.3d 782 (4th Cir. 1998), 476n261

Coser v. Moore, 739 F.2d 746 (2d Cir. 1984), 170n82

Cosmos Forms, Ltd. v. State Div. of Human Rights, 150 A.D.2d 442 (2d Dep't 1989), 437n210

Coston v. Plitt Theatres, Inc., 44 F.E.P. Cas. (BNA) 1717 (N.D. Ill. 1986), 409n47

Coston v. Plitt Theatres, Inc., 831 F.2d 1321 (7th Cir. 1987), 402, 408n43, 415n85, 422n131

Cotran v. Rollins Hudig Hall Int'l, Inc., 948 P.2d 412 (Cal. 1997), 43–44, 43n60

Countrywide Financial Corp. v. Bundy 187 Cal. App. 4th 234, 113 Cal. Rptr. 3d 705, (2010), 134n120, 134n123

Cox v. Ocean View Hotel Corp., 533 F.3d 1114 (9th Cir. 2008), 121n32

Coy v. County of Delaware, 993 F. Supp. 2d 770 (S.D. Ohio 2014), 261n14

Crabtree v. Baptist Hosp., 749 F.2d 1501 (11th Cir. 1985), 407n34, 408n40

Craig v. Y&Y Snacks, Inc., 721 F.2d 77 (3d Cir. 1983), 413n74, 457n57

Cram v. Lamson & Sessions Co., 49 F.3d 466 (8th Cir. 1995), 9, 9n54

Crawford v. Carroll, 529 F.3d 961 (11th Cir. 2008), 268n49

Crawford v. George & Lynch, Inc., 2013 WL 6504635 (D. Del. 2013), 452n10

Crawford v. Metropolitan Government of Nashville & Davidson County, 555 U.S. 271 (2009), 16, 16n87

Crespo v. Evergo Corp., 841 A.2d 471 (N.J. Super. 2004), 478n279

Creswell v. HCAL Corp., 2007 WL 628036 (S.D. Cal. 2007), 458n63

Criado v. IBM Corp., 145 F.3d 437 (1st Cir. 1998), 456n50

Crinkley v. Holiday Inns, Inc., 844 F.2d 156 (4th Cir. 1988), 433n191, 434n197

Crowley v. L.L. Bean, Inc., 303 F.3d 387 (1st Cir. 2002), 246n76

Crown, Core & Seal Co., Inc. v. Parker, 462 U.S. 345 (1983), 144n59

Cruz v. Bristol Myers Squibb Co. PR, Inc., 777 F. Supp. 2d 321 (D.P.R. 2011), 262n16

Cruz v. Cingular Wireless, LLC, 648 F.3d 1205 (11th Cir. 2011), 127n66

Cruz v. Coach Stores, Inc., 202 F.3d 560 (2d Cir. 2000), 367–368, 367n170

Cummings v. Roberts, 628 F.2d 1065 (8th Cir. 1980), 250n87

Cunningham v. City of McKeesport, 807 F.2d 49 (3d Cir. 1986), 444n258

Curwick v. Ford Motor Company, 1998 WL 887067 (N.D. Ill. 1998), 145, 145n66

Cush-Crawford v. Adchem Corp., 271 F.3d 352 (2d Cir. 2001), 442, 442n241

Dafflin v. Ford Motor Co., 458 F.3d 549 (6th Cir. 2006), 137n7

Dahdal v. Thorn Ams., 1997 WL 599614 (D. Kan. 1997), 506n41

Dailey v. Societe Generale, 108 F.3d 451 (2d Cir. 1997), 412n67, 414n77, 428n172, 428n175, 452n5, 457n58, 461n93, 463, 463n117, 463n118, 465n143

Dailey v. Societe Generale, 889 F. Supp. 108 (S.D.N.Y. 1995), 425n148

Subject Index